MW00807686

An Introduction to Agency, Partnerships, and LLCs

THIRD EDITION

by

MELVIN ARON EISENBERG
Koret Professor of Law,
University of California at Berkeley

NEW YORK, NEW YORK
FOUNDATION PRESS

2000

Foundation Press, a division of West Group has created this publication to provide you with accurate and authoritative information concerning the subject matter covered. However, this publication was not necessarily prepared by persons licensed to practice law in a particular jurisdiction. Foundation Press is not engaged in rendering legal or other professional advice, and this publication is not a substitute for the advice of an attorney. If you require legal or other expert advice, you should seek the services of a competent attorney or other professional.

COPYRIGHT © 1987, 1995 FOUNDATION PRESS

COPYRIGHT © 2000 By FOUNDATION PRESS

        11 Penn Plaza, Tenth Floor

        New York, NY 10001

        Phone Toll Free 1–877–888–1330

        Fax (212) 760–8705

        fdpress.com

All rights reserved
Printed in the United States of America

ISBN 1–56662–939–X

 TEXT IS PRINTED ON 10% POST CONSUMER RECYCLED PAPER

PREFACE

In many areas of corporate law, it is difficult to fully understand the issues and the legal rules without some background knowledge of basic accounting and financial concepts. Accordingly, this casebook includes introductory materials on such topics as financial statements, the present-value rule, diversification, valuation, the efficient capital market hypothesis, and dividend policy. These materials have been chosen and edited with an eye to ensuring that they are accessible to students who don't have an accounting and financial background. The materials are introduced gradually, at relevant points throughout the book, so that students are not faced with an onslaught of unfamiliar concepts.

Because of the importance of statutes in corporation law, students should refer to the Statutory Supplement whenever a cross-reference to that Supplement appears. When a cross-referenced statutory provision includes an Official Comment, the Comment should be read as well. Other cross-references to the Statutory Supplement (for example, references to excerpts from the Restatement (Second) of Agency) should be treated the same way.

In the preparation of this casebook, the following conventions have been used: Where a portion of the text of an original source (such as a case) has been omitted, the omission is indicated by ellipses The omission of footnotes from original sources is not indicated, but the original footnote numbers are used for those footnotes that are retained.

The American Law Institute's Principles of Corporate Governance: Analysis and Recommendations (1994) is cited simply as ALI, Principles of Corporate Governance.

I thank Uriel Procaccia for wonderful suggestions concerning the organization of the chapter on distributions to shareholders; David Ruder for valuable help on the Williams Act; Pilar Sansone for excellent work as a research assistant; Sue Smith for exceeding skill and diligence in preparing the manuscript for publication; and Elizabeth Erdinger, Marlene Harmon, Ginny Irving, Debby Kearney, Janice Kelly, Michael Levy, and Alice Youmans, Reference Librarians at the Law School at the University of California at Berkeley, and Kathleen Vanden Heuvel, the Library's Associate Director, for their thorough, accurate, fast, unflagging, and marvelous responses to the innumerable problems I sent them.

*

TABLE OF CONTENTS

TABLE OF CASES

Principal cases are in bold type. Non-principal cases are in roman type. References are to Pages.

AN INTRODUCTION TO AGENCY, PARTNERSHIPS, AND LLCS

*

CHAPTER I

AGENCY

SECTION 1. INTRODUCTION

Courses in corporations or business associations are, in large part, courses in organizational law. The most common forms of business organization in this country are sole proprietorships, corporations, general and limited partnerships, and limited liability companies. Based on tax filings, as of 1995 there were 16,424,000 sole proprietorships in the United States (exclusive of farms), 4,474,000 corporations, and 1,581,000 partnerships. U.S. Bureau of the Census, Statistical Abstract of the United States 541 (1998).

A *sole proprietorship* is a business organization that is owned by a single individual, and is not cast in a special legal form of organization, such as a corporation, that can be utilized only by filing an organic document with the state pursuant to an authorizing statute.

The term *business organization* may seem to be an inappropriate characterization of a form that involves only a single owner. That terminology can, however, be justified on at least two grounds.

First, a business enterprise that is owned by an individual is likely to have a degree of psychological and sociological identity separate from that of the individual. This separateness of a sole proprietor's enterprise is often expressed by giving the enterprise its own name, like "Acme Shoe Company." Furthermore, a sole proprietor usually will consider only a certain portion of his property and cash as invested in the business, and will keep a separate set of financial records for the enterprise, as if the enterprise's finances were separate from her own.

Thus, if Alice Adams begins a new business in 2000—say, Acme Shoe Company—she is likely to issue a balance sheet for the business that does not show all of her assets and liabilities, but only those assets dedicated to, and those liabilities arising out of, the enterprise's operations. (See Section 4, An Introduction to Financial Statements, infra.) In short, as a psychological matter Adams, and to a certain extent those who deal with her, are likely to regard Acme Shoe Company as an enterprise or firm that has a certain degree of separateness from Adams herself, and a certain amount of capital. As a matter of law, however, a sole proprietorship has no separate identity from its owner. If Adams takes no special legal step, like incorporating the enterprise, all of her wealth will be effectively committed to the enterprise, because an individual who owns a sole proprietorship has unlimited personal liability for obligations incurred in the conduct of the business.

The second reason for calling a sole proprietorship an organization is that a sole proprietor typically will not conduct the business by herself, but will engage various people—salespersons, mechanics, managers—to act on her behalf, and subject to her control, in conducting the business. The employment by one person, *P*, of another, *A*, to act on *P*'s behalf, and subject to her control, brings us to the most elementary form of organizational law, known as the law of agency. An *agent* is a person who by mutual assent acts on behalf of another and subject to the other's control. Restatement, Second, Agency § 1. The person for whom the agent acts is a *principal*. Id. Agency law governs: (1) The relationship between agents and principals. (2) The relationship between agents and third persons with whom an agent deals, or purports to deal, on a principal's behalf. (3) The relationship between principals and third persons when an agent deals, or purports to deal, with a third person on the principal's behalf.

Although agency is a consensual relationship, whether an agency relationship has been created does not turn on whether the parties *think of themselves* as or *intend* to be agent and principal. "Agency is a legal concept which depends upon the existence of required factual elements: the manifestation by the principal that the agent shall act for him, the agent's acceptance of the undertaking and the understanding of the parties that the principal is to be in control of the undertaking. The relation which the law calls agency does not depend upon the intent of the parties to create it, nor their belief that they have done so. To constitute the relation, there must be an agreement, but not necessarily a contract, between the parties; if the agreement results in the factual relation between them to which are attached the legal consequences of agency, an agency exists although the parties did not call it agency and did not intend the legal consequences of the relation to follow. Thus, when one ... asks a friend to do a slight service for him, such as to return for credit goods recently purchased from a store, [an agency relationship may be created although] neither one may have any realization that they are creating an agency relation or be aware of the legal obligations which would result from performance of the service." Restatement (Second) of Agency § 1, Comment b.

SECTION 2. AUTHORITY

Morris Oil Co. v. Rainbow Oilfield Trucking, Inc.

New Mexico Court of Appeals, 1987.
106 N.M. 237, 741 P.2d 840.

■ GARCIA, JUDGE....

Defendant Dawn appeals from the judgment rendered against it in favor of Morris Oil Company, Inc. (Morris), based upon a determination that Rainbow Oilfield Trucking, Inc. (Rainbow) was Dawn's agent when it incurred indebtedness with Morris. We affirm the trial court.

FACTS

Appellant Dawn, the holder of a certificate of public convenience and necessity, is engaged in the oilfield trucking business in the Farmington area. Rainbow was a New Mexico corporation established for the purpose of operating an oilfield trucking business in the Hobbs area. Defendant corporations entered into several contracts whereby Rainbow would be permitted to use Dawn's certificate of public convenience and necessity in operating a trucking enterprise in Hobbs. Dawn reserved the right to full and complete control over the operations of Rainbow in New Mexico. Dawn was to collect all charges due and owing for transportation conducted by Rainbow and, after deducting a $1,000 per month "clerical fee" and a percentage of the gross receipts, was to remit the balance to Rainbow. Under a subcontract entered into by defendants, Rainbow was to be responsible for payment of operating expenses, including fuel; further, the subcontract provides that all operations utilizing fuel were to be under the direct control and supervision of Dawn. All billing for services rendered by Rainbow would be made under Dawn's name, with all monies to be collected by Dawn.

Defendants also entered into a terminal management agreement which provided that Dawn was to have complete control over Rainbow's Hobbs operation. The agreement further recited that Rainbow was not to become the agent of Dawn and was not empowered to incur or create any debt or liability of Dawn "other than in the ordinary course of business relative to terminal management." The agreement recited that Rainbow was to be an independent contractor and not an employee, and that liability on the part of Rainbow for creating charges in violation of the agreement would survive the termination of the agreement. Dawn was to notify Rainbow of any claim of such charges whereby Rainbow would assume the defense, compromise or payment of such claims.

Rainbow operated the oilfield trucking enterprise under these contractual documents, during which time Rainbow established a relationship with plaintiff Morris, whereby Morris installed a bulk dispenser at the Rainbow terminal and periodically delivered diesel fuel for use in the trucking operation. The enterprise proved unprofitable, however, and Rainbow ceased its operations and ultimately declared bankruptcy, owing Morris approximately $25,000 on an open account.

When Morris began its collection efforts against Rainbow, it determined that Rainbow had ceased its operations, everyone associated with Rainbow had moved back to Texas and it did not appear likely that the account would be paid. Morris was directed by Rainbow's representative in Texas to Dawn for payment of the account.

When Rainbow ceased its operations, Dawn was holding some $73,000 in receipts from the Hobbs operation. Dawn established an escrow account through its Roswell attorneys to settle claims arising from Rainbow's

Hobbs operation. When Morris contacted Dawn with regard to the outstanding account, it was notified of the existence of the escrow account and was asked to forbear upon collection efforts, indicting that payment would be forthcoming from the escrow account. Dawn's representatives indicated that it was necessary to wait for authorization from Rainbow's parent Texas corporation before paying the account. At no time did Rainbow or Dawn question the amount or legitimacy of Morris' open account balance.

Dawn's principal [owner] further testified that the subcontract and terminal management agreement were cancelled by Dawn when he learned that Rainbow was incurring debts in Dawn's name. The charges owing to Morris, however, were incurred in the name of Rainbow and not Dawn.

Although some claims were paid from the attorneys' escrow account established by Dawn, there was no explanation at trial why the Morris claim was not paid. When Morris learned that the escrow funds had been disbursed without payment of its charges, it instituted this action and also sought to garnish the remaining $13,000 held by Dawn from the impounded funds. Rainbow did not defend, and the trial court entered a default judgment against Rainbow, from which it does not appeal.

DISCUSSION

The trial court found that Dawn retained the right to direct control and supervision of Rainbow's New Mexico operations, and that in the course of those operations, Rainbow incurred a balance of almost $25,000 on an open account with Morris for fuel used in the New Mexico operations. The trial court further found that when Rainbow defaulted on payments on Morris' account, Dawn made representations over a period of time concerning the existence of a fund held by Dawn to settle indebtedness created by Rainbow operating under the subcontract. The court determined that Morris delayed its collection efforts pending disbursement of the funds, and that Dawn was aware that Morris was relying upon Dawn's representations that payment would be made from the impounded fund. The trial court concluded that Rainbow was at all times in its dealings with Morris the agent of Dawn and, therefore, Dawn was responsible for the account balance.

Dawn urges one point of error on appeal; that the trial court erred in finding liability based on a principal-agent relationship between the defendants. Dawn relies upon the language in the terminal management agreement which states:

4. Rainbow is not appointed and shall not become the agent of Dawn and is not empowered to incur or create any debt or liability of Dawn other than in the ordinary course of business relative to terminal management. Rainbow shall not enter into or cause Dawn to become a party to any agreement without the express written consent of Dawn.

5. Rainbow shall be considered an independent contractor and not an employee of Dawn.

Dawn's reliance upon these paragraphs of the agreement is unpersuasive for two reasons. First, the agreement specifically states that Rainbow may create liabilities of Dawn in the ordinary course of business of operating the terminal. There is no question that the liability to Morris was incurred in the ordinary course of operating the trucking business. Second, the recitation of the parties in their contractual documents need not bind third parties who deal with one of them in ignorance of those instructions. See South Second Livestock Auction, Inc. v. Roberts, 69 N.M. 155, 364 P.2d 859 (1961); see also Great Northern R.R. Co. v. O'Connor, 232 U.S. 508, 34 S.Ct. 380, 58 L.Ed. 703 (1914).

While Dawn argues from cases discussing apparent authority, we view this as a case of undisclosed agency. Rainbow contracted in its own name and not in the name of Dawn Enterprises, Inc. Thus, this case involves concepts relating to undisclosed agency rather than to apparent authority, and is governed by principles of undisclosed principal-agent contracts. See, e.g., 3 Am.Jur.2d Agency § 316 (1986).

It is well established that an agent for an undisclosed principal subjects the principal to liability for acts done on his account if they are usual or necessary in such transactions. Restatement (Second) of Agency § 194 (1958). This is true even if the principal has previously forbidden the agent to incur such debts so long as the transaction is in the usual course of business engaged in by the agent. Id.

The indebtedness in the instant case is squarely governed by well-established principles of agency where an undisclosed principal entrusts the agent with the management of his business. The undisclosed principal is subject to liability to third parties with whom the agent contracts where such transactions are usual in the business conducted by the agent, even if the contract is contrary to the express directions of the principal. Restatement (Second) of Agency § 195 (1958).

Dawn's reliance upon Bloodgood v. Woman's Ben. Ass'n, 36 N.M. 228, 13 P.2d 412 (1932) is misplaced. Indeed, the case stands for the proposition that a principal may limit an agent's authority, and further, that the limitation will be binding upon a third party dealing with the agent if the third party has knowledge of the limitation of authority. Here there is no evidence that Morris had any actual knowledge of the existence of the Rainbow-Dawn agency, let alone any claimed limitations by Dawn on Rainbow's authority. It is undisputed that Morris thought it was dealing solely with Rainbow when it sold fuel.

Morris correctly observes that secret instructions or limitations placed upon the authority of an agent must be known to the party dealing with the agent, or the principal is bound as if the limitations had not been made. Chevron Oil Co. v. Sutton, 85 N.M. 679, 515 P.2d 1283 (1973)....

Moreover, assuming arguendo that Dawn was not responsible for the indebtedness to Morris for the reasons urged on appeal, it is clear that Dawn ratified the open account after learning of its existence when Morris contacted Dawn regarding payment. A principal may be held liable for the

5

unauthorized acts of his agent if the principal ratifies the transaction after acquiring knowledge of the material facts concerning the transaction. Ulibarri Landscaping Material, Inc. v. Colony Materials, Inc., 97 N.M. 266, 639 P.2d 75 (Ct.App.1981).

It was undisputed that in several telephone conversations between the principals of Dawn and Morris, the material facts of the Morris open account were disclosed to Dawn. At no time did Dawn dispute the legitimacy or amount of the open account, and indeed assured Morris that payment would be forthcoming from the funds retained from Rainbow's revenues. Despite this, Dawn used the fund to pay itself a $1,000 per month clerical fee, to pay legal fees incurred as a result of its agency with Rainbow and to settle other claims arising from the Rainbow operations. Where the principal retains the benefits or proceeds of its business relations with an agent with knowledge of the material facts, the principal is deemed to have ratified the methods employed by the agent in generating the proceeds. See id. See also 3 Am.Jur.2d Agency § 194 (1986). The diesel fuel provided by Morris was used in Rainbow's trucking operation. Dawn collected the receipts due to Rainbow. Dawn seeks to retain the benefits of the agency with Rainbow, and yet at the same time disclaims responsibility for the business of the agent by which the benefits were generated. This it cannot do. Ulibarri Landscaping Material, Inc. v. Colony Materials, Inc.

In sum, for the foregoing reasons, we affirm.

IT IS SO ORDERED....

■ BIVINS and MINZNER, JJ., concur.

NOTE ON AUTHORITY

1. *Terminology.* An *agent* is a person who acts on behalf and subject to the control of another. For some purposes, agents are classified as general or special. A *general agent* is an agent who is authorized to conduct a series of transactions involving continuity of service. A *special agent* is an agent who is authorized to conduct only a single transaction, or only a series of transactions not involving continuity of service.

A *principal* is a person on whose behalf and subject to whose control an agent acts. Principals are conventionally divided into three classes: disclosed, partially disclosed, and undisclosed.

A principal is *disclosed* if at the time of a transaction between the agent and a third person, the third person knows that the agent is acting on behalf of a principal and knows the principal's identity.

A principal is *partially disclosed* if at the time of the transaction the third person knows that the agent is acting on behalf of a principal, but does not know the principal's identity.

A principal is *undisclosed* if the agent, in dealing with the third person, purports to be acting on his own behalf. An undisclosed principal is liable for her agent's authorized activities, even though, because the agent does not disclose his agency, the third person believes the agent is acting strictly on his own behalf. One reason the undisclosed principal is liable is that she set the transaction in motion and stood to gain from it. A second reason is this: Even if the undisclosed principal was not directly liable to the third person, the agent would be. Therefore, the third person could sue the agent. If he did so, the agent could then sue the principal for indemnification of the damages he had to pay the third person. See Section 6 of this Note, infra. Accordingly, allowing the third person to sue the undisclosed principal does not materially enlarge the principal's liability, and collapses two lawsuits into one.

In the area of torts, a principal is usually referred to as a master and an agent is usually referred to as a servant. A *master* is a principal who controls or has the right to control the *physical conduct* of an agent in the performance of the agent's services. A *servant* is an agent whose physical conduct in the performance of services for the principal is subject to the control of the principal. Restatement (Second) Agency § 2. Both terms are purely technical, and "do not denote menial or manual service. Many servants perform exacting work requiring intelligence rather than muscle. Thus the officers of a corporation or a ship, [and the intern] in a hospital . . . are servants. . . ." Id., Comment c.

The liability of a master for the tort of a servant is referred to as liability in *respondeat superior*. Under the doctrine of respondeat superior, a master is liable for torts of servant if the servant's physical conduct in the performance of services for the master is subject to the master's control, and the tort is committed while the servant is acting within the scope of her employment. The rationale of this doctrine has been well-summarized by Professor Fishman:

> The adoption of enterprise liability under respondeat superior is justified on several policy grounds. First, the ability of the enterprise to spread the risk from losses is important. The enterprise is in a better position than . . . the injured third person to spread the risk of loss, either through insurance or the ability to factor the potential losses into the price for the goods produced. A second reason suggests that proper allocation of resources is promoted by requiring an enterprise to include in the price of its goods the costs of the accidents which are closely associated with the enterprise's operations. A third reason . . . is that the [principal] is in a position to control the employee and placing the risk of loss here could lead to greater safety. A fourth reason is that it is considered more equitable to place the liability on the [principal], because it provides greater assurance that the accident victim will be paid, or because there is a societal preference to make certain losses costs of doing business rather than losses to be borne by individual households.

Fishman, Inherent Agency Power—Should Enterprise Liability Apply to Agents' Unauthorized Contracts?, 19 Rutgers L.J. 1, 48–49 (1987).

A variety of problems can arise out of an actual or alleged principal-agency relationship. Perhaps the most common problem is what liabilities arise out of a certain transaction between the agent and a third person? Most of the issues implicated by that question are addressed by the legal rules governing *authority*. This Note will emphasize the liability of the principal to the third person (Section 2), but will also consider the liability of the third person to the principal (Section 3); the liability of the agent to the third person (Section 4); and the duties and liabilities of the agent and the principal to each other (Sections 5 and 6). Although the law of agency encompasses liabilities in tort as well as in contract, for the most part this Note will address only issues that relate to contractual transactions.

2. *Liability of Principal to Third Person.* Under the law of agency, a principal becomes liable to a third person as a result of an act or transaction by another, A, on the principal's behalf, if A had actual, apparent, or inherent authority, or was an agent by estoppel, or if the principal ratified the act or transaction.

a. *Actual authority.* An agent has *actual authority* to act in a given way on a principal's behalf if the principal's words or conduct would lead a reasonable person in the agent's position to believe that the principal had authorized him to so act.

> *Restatement (Second) of Agency § 26, Illustration 2:* P goes to an office where, as he knows, several brokers have desks, and leaves upon the desk of A, thinking it to be the desk of X, a note signed by him, which states: "I authorize you to contract in my name for the purchase of 100 shares of Western Union stock at today's market." A comes in, finds the note and, not knowing of the mistake, immediately makes a contract with T in P's name for the purchase of the shares. A had actual authority to make the contract.[1]

Actual authority may be either *express* or *implied:* "It is possible for a principal to specify minutely what the agent is to do. To the extent that he does this, the agent may be said to have express authority. But most authority is created by implication. Thus, in the authorization to 'sell my automobile', the only fully expressed power is to transfer title in exchange for money or a promise to give money. In fact, under some circumstances ... there may ... be power to take or give possession of the automobile or to extend credit or to accept something in partial exchange. These powers are all implied or inferred from the words used, from customs and from the relations of the parties. They are described as 'implied authority.'" Restatement (Second) of Agency § 7, Comment c.

A common type of implied actual authority is *incidental authority,* which is the authority to do incidental acts that are reasonably necessary to

---

1. Restatement (Second) of Agency uses the term "authority" to mean what is conventionally called "actual authority." The latter term is used in this Note, both because it is the term normally used by the courts and because it sets up a clear opposition between different types of authority. All quotations from the Restatement have been modified accordingly, without further indication.

accomplish an actually authorized transaction, or that usually accompany it. If the principal has authorized the agent to engage in a given transaction, and certain acts are reasonably necessary to accomplish the transaction, or usually accompany it, a reasonable person in the agent's position would believe that the authority to engage in the transaction also conferred authority to engage in those acts. Here are two examples of implied actual authority:

> *Restatement (Second) of Agency § 35, Illustration 4:* P directs A to sell goods by auction at a time and place at which, as P and A know, a statute forbids anyone but a licensed auctioneer to conduct sales by auction. Nothing to the contrary appearing, A's actual authority includes [implied] actual authority to employ a licensed auctioneer.

> *Restatement (Second) of Agency § 26, Illustration 5:* P authorizes A, a local broker, to sell and convey land. At the time and place it is the custom to make such sales with a warranty of title. A has implied actual authority to execute and deliver a proper deed to the purchaser and to insert in the deed the usual covenants as to title.

Note that if an agent has actual authority, the principal is bound even if the third person did not know that the agent had actual authority, and indeed even if the third person thought the agent was herself the principal, not merely an agent. These issues will be discussed below.

On the issues discussed in this section, see Restatement (Second) of Agency §§ 26, 32, 33, 35, 39, 43, 144, 186 in the Statutory Supplement.*

b. *Apparent authority.* An agent has *apparent authority* to act in a given way on a principal's behalf in relation to a third person, T, if the words or conduct of the principal would lead a reasonable person in T's position to believe that the principal had authorized the agent to so act. Here are three examples:

> *Restatement (Second) of Agency § 8, Illustration 1:* P writes to A directing him to act as his agent for the sale of Blackacre. P sends a copy of this letter to T, a prospective purchaser. A has actual authority to sell Blackacre and, as to T, apparent authority.

> *Illustration 2:* Same facts as in Illustration 1, except that in the letter to A, P adds a postscript, not included in the copy to T, telling A to make no sale until after communication with P. A has no actual authority to sell Blackacre but, as to T, he has apparent authority.

> *Illustration 3:* Same facts as in Illustration 1, except that after A and T have received the letters, P telegraphs a revocation to A. A has no actual authority but, as to T, he has apparent authority to sell Blackacre.

In most cases, actual and apparent authority go hand in hand, as Restatement (Second) of Agency § 8, Illustration 1, supra, suggests. For

* Corporations and Other Business Organizations—Statutes, Rules, Materials, and Forms (Foundation Press; M. Eisenberg ed.).

example, if P Bank appoints A as cashier, and nothing more is said, A will reasonably believe she has the authority that cashiers normally have, and third persons who deal with A will reasonably believe the same thing. Apparent authority becomes salient in such a case if P Bank does not actually give A all the authority that cashiers usually have, and a customer deals with A knowing that A is a cashier, but not knowing that P Bank has placed special limits on A's authority.

The apparent authority of A in the cashier hypothetical is a special type of apparent authority known as *power of position*. "... [A]pparent authority can be created by appointing a person to a position, such as that of manager or treasurer, which carries with it generally recognized duties; to those who know of the appointment there is apparent authority to do the things ordinarily entrusted to one occupying such a position, regardless of unknown limitations which are imposed upon the particular agent.... If a principal puts an agent into, or knowingly permits him to occupy, a position in which according to the ordinary habits of persons in the locality, trade or profession, it is usual for such an agent to have a particular kind of authority, anyone dealing with him is justified in inferring that he has such authority, in the absence of reason to know otherwise." Restatement (Second) of Agency § 27, Comment a, § 49, Comment c.

> *Restatement (Second) of Agency § 49, Illustration 4:* The P bank appoints A as an information clerk, with authority only to answer questions of depositors. During alterations, however, the bank directs A to occupy the space normally occupied by one of the receiving tellers, [with] a sign indicating that it is the "information" window. The sign becomes displaced and T, a depositor in the bank, makes a cash deposit with A, believing that he is a teller. P is bound by this transaction.

On apparent authority, see Restatement (Second) of Agency §§ 27, 49, 159 in the Statutory Supplement.

c. *Agency by estoppel.* Still another type of authority is known as "agency by estoppel." The core of agency by estoppel is described as follows in Restatement (Second) of Agency § 8B:

> (1) A person who is not otherwise liable as a party to a transaction purported to be done on his account, is nevertheless subject to liability to persons who have changed their positions because of their belief that the transaction was entered into by or for him, if

>> (a) he intentionally or carelessly caused such belief, or

>> (b) knowing of such belief and that others might change their positions because of it, he did not take reasonable steps to notify them of the facts.

The concept of agency by estoppel is so close to the concept of apparent authority that for most practical purposes the former concept can be subsumed in the latter.

d. *Inherent authority.* Under the doctrine of *inherent authority*, an agent may bind a principal in certain cases even when the agent had neither actual nor apparent authority. Although the doctrine of inherent authority is relatively well established, its exact contours are not always clear. Restatement (Second) of Agency § 8A provides that "Inherent agency power is a term used . . . to indicate the power of an agent which is derived not from actual authority, apparent authority or estoppel, but solely from the agency relation and exists for the protection of persons harmed by or dealing with a servant or other agent." Section 8A purports to be a definition, but isn't. It states that inherent authority is an agency power that is not derived from actual authority, apparent authority, or estoppel. It states the reason why inherent authority should be recognized. But it doesn't state what inherent authority *is*.

Section 161 of the Restatement concerns the inherent authority of general agents of disclosed or partially disclosed principals. Under Section 161, a disclosed or partially disclosed principal is liable for an act done on his behalf by a general agent, even if the principal had forbidden the agent to do the act, if (i) the act usually accompanies or is incidental to transactions that the agent is authorized to conduct, and (ii) the third person reasonably believes the agent is authorized to do the act. But this leaves open the issue, under what circumstances is a third person reasonable in believing that an agent has authority that, by hypothesis, is beyond the agent's apparent authority?

Section 194 of the Restatement concerns the inherent authority of agents for undisclosed principals. It provides that "A general agent for an undisclosed principal authorized to conduct transactions subjects his principal to liability for acts done on his account, if usual or necessary in such transactions, although forbidden by the principal to do them." Unlike Section 161, Section 194 does not require that the third person reasonably believes the agent is authorized to act. Indeed, such a requirement could not be imposed, because in the case of an undisclosed principal the third person will not know that he is dealing with an agent.

A major rationale of inherent authority in the Restatement (Second) of Agency is based on an analogy to the doctrine of respondeat superior in torts:

> . . . It is inevitable that in doing their work, either through negligence or excess of zeal, agents will harm third persons or will deal with them in unauthorized ways. It would be unfair for an enterprise to have the benefit of the work of its agents without making it responsible to some extent for their excesses and failures to act carefully. The answer of the common law has been the creation of special agency powers or, to phrase it otherwise, the imposition of liability upon the principal because of unauthorized or negligent acts of his servants and other agents. . . .*

Restatement (Second) Agency, § 8A, comment *a*.

* Recall that the terms "master" and "servant" have technical meanings in agency law. (Footnote by ed.)

... [The principal's liability under the doctrine of inherent authority] is based primarily upon the theory that, if one appoints an agent to conduct a series of transactions over a period of time, it is fair that he should bear losses which are incurred when such an agent, although without authority to do so, does something which is usually done in connection with the transactions he is employed to conduct. Such agents can properly be regarded as part of the principal's organization in much the same way as a servant is normally part of the master's business enterprise.... The basis of [inherent authority] is comparable to the liability of a master for the torts of his servant.... In the case of the master, it is thought fair that one who benefits from the enterprise and has a right to control the physical activities of those who make the enterprise profitable, should pay for the physical harm resulting from the errors and derelictions of the servants while doing the kind of thing which makes the enterprise successful. The rules imposing liability upon the principal for some of the contracts and conveyances of a general agent, whether or not a servant, which he is neither authorized nor apparently authorized to make, are based upon a similar public policy. Commercial convenience requires that the principal should not escape liability where there have been deviations from the usually granted authority by persons who are such essential parts of his business enterprise. In the long run it is of advantage to business, and hence to employers as a class, that third persons should not be required to scrutinize too carefully the mandates of permanent or semi-permanent agents who do no more than what is usually done by agents in similar positions.

Restatement (Second) of Agency § 161, Comment.

Under this rationale, the doctrine of inherent authority operates as to contracts in much the same way that the doctrine of respondeat superior operates as to torts, so that the liability of principals for an agent's torts and contracts is treated in a unified way.

An alternative rationale for the doctrine of inherent authority is based on the principal's reasonable expectations. In a world with perfect information, faithful agents will follow all instructions impeccably. In the real world, however, agents acting in good faith will not infrequently deviate from their instructions. Agents, like everyone else, will make mistakes, which may take the form of misinterpreting their instructions or forgetting one of numerous instructions. Furthermore, an agent may reasonably believe that her principal's objective is best served by violating a particular instruction. A principal's instructions to his agent are necessarily given in the present to govern the future. The future, however, may develop in such a way that the agent reasonably believes that if the principal knew all the facts, he would not want the agent to follow a given instruction. Of course, the agent could go back to the principal for further instructions, but often it is infeasible to take that course of action—for example, because a valuable opportunity must be taken immediately or not at all. These real-world facts are reflected in a passage in the Comment to Restatement § 8A:

"It is inevitable that in doing their work, either through negligence or excess of zeal, agents will harm third persons or will deal with them in unauthorized ways. It would be unfair for an enterprise to have the benefit of the work of its agents without making it responsible to some extent for their excesses and failures to act carefully."

Given these realities, the doctrine of inherent authority can be justified on the ground that it is or should be foreseeable to a principal, when he appoints an agent, that as a practical matter the agent acting in good faith for the benefit of the principal is likely to deviate occasionally from instructions. As between the principal, who appointed the agent, who benefits from the agent's activities, and who could or should have foreseen a certain range of deviations from instructions, on the one hand, and the third person who contracts with the agent, on the other, a loss that results from a foreseeable deviation is better placed on the principal.

Under the reasonable-foreseeability rationale, inherent authority might be viewed as simply a special form of *actual* authority. It is the authority to take an action that a person in the principal's position reasonably should have foreseen the agent would be likely to take, even though the action would be in violation of the agent's instructions. The reasonable foreseeability rationale also leads to a test for inherent authority: Would a reasonable person in the *principal's* position have foreseen that, despite his instructions, there was a significant likelihood that the agent would act as he did?

Unlike the Restatement provisions, a definition and test of an agent's authority based on reasonable foreseeability does not limit such authority to general agents. It is true that as a practical matter the application of the test may partly depend on whether an agent is general or special, because it may be reasonably foreseeable that general agents will be especially likely to deviate occasionally from instructions, due to the expansive grant of actual authority that is usually conferred upon such agents. As a matter of principle, however, there is no reason why inherent authority should turn on whether the agent is general or special.

It has been argued that when a third person deals with an agent who exceeded her authority to enter into a contractual transaction, the principal should not be bound because the third person may be deemed at fault for failing to investigate the agent's authority. See Fishman, supra. This argument has no force in the case of an undisclosed principal, and little force in the case of partially disclosed principal: A third person who deals with an agent of an undisclosed principal cannot be deemed at fault for failing to investigate the agent's authority, because the third person does not know that he is dealing with an agent. Similarly, although a third person who deals with the agent of a partially disclosed principal does know he is dealing with an agent, as a practical matter it is difficult or impossible for a third person to investigate the authority of an agent when he does not even know the principal's name.

Even in the case of disclosed principals, the force of the argument is very limited. It seems unlikely that the interests of principals as a class

13

would be served by a rule that gives third persons a powerful incentive to contact the principal every time they consider doing business with agents. It's not easy to see how much benefit there would be in using agents under such a rule, because the principal would end up dealing with every third person himself.

On the issues discussed in this section, see Restatement (Second) of Agency §§ 8A, 159–161A, 194, 195A, 219, 220, 228–231 in the Statutory Supplement.

e. *Ratification.* Even if an agent has neither actual, apparent, nor inherent authority, the principal will be bound to the third person if the agent purported to act on the principal's behalf, and the principal, with knowledge of the material facts, either (1) affirms the agent's conduct by manifesting an intention to treat the agent's conduct as authorized, or (2) engages in conduct that is justifiable only if he has such an intention.

Manifesting an intention to treat the agent's conduct as authorized is sometimes known as *express ratification.* Here is an example.

> *Restatement (Second) of Agency § 84, Illustration 1:* Without power to bind P, A purports to represent him in buying a horse from T. P affirms. P is now a party to the transaction.

Engaging in conduct that is justifiable only if the principal intends to treat the agent's conduct as authorized is sometimes known as *implied ratification.* The most common example is the case where, as a result of the purported agent's transaction, the principal, with knowledge of the facts, receives or retains something to which he would otherwise not be entitled. Here are two examples:

> *Restatement (Second) of Agency § 98, Illustration 1:* P authorizes A to sell a refrigerator at a specified price without a warranty. A, purporting to have authority to do so, contracts with T for the sale of the refrigerator at a lower price than that specified and with a warranty of performance for two years, T paying part of the purchase price. P receives the check given by T, knowing all the facts. The contract as made between A and T is affirmed.

> *Restatement (Second) of Agency § 98, Illustration 2:* P authorizes A to sell a typewriter for $50 in cash. A, purporting to have authority to do so, contracts to sell it to T for $25 and T's old typewriter, which T delivers to A. P receives T's old typewriter, knowing the facts. The transaction between T and A is affirmed.

Ratification need not be communicated to the third person to be effective, although it must be objectively manifested. Restatement (Second) of Agency § 95. However, to be effective a ratification must occur before either (1) the third person has withdrawn, (2) the agreement has otherwise terminated, or (3) the situation has so materially changed that it would be inequitable to bind the third person, and the third person elects not to be bound. See Restatement (Second) of Agency §§ 88, 89.

14   The Comment to Restatement Second of Agency § 52 points out that:

... The concept of ratification ... is unique. It does not conform to the rules of contracts, since it can be accomplished without consideration to or manifestation by the purported principal and without fresh consent by the other party. Further, it operates as if the transaction were complete at the time and place of the first event, rather than the last, as in the normal case of offer and acceptance.

The Comment adds the following rationale for the concept of ratification:

... [T]he best defense of ratification is pragmatic; that it is needed in the prosecution of business. It operates normally to cure minor defects in an agent's authority, minimizing technical defenses and preventing unnecessary law suits. In this aspect, it is a beneficial doctrine, which has been adopted in most systems of law.

A related but different rationale was given by Judge Posner in *Goldstick v. ICM Realty*, 788 F.2d 456, 460 (7th Cir.1986):

... The best explanation [of the concept of ratification] may be that the principal would not have ratified the contract unless he had seen a commercial advantage in doing so, and that the advantage would be less if the ratification had no binding effect. Ordinarily a principal ratifies an agent's unauthorized transaction in order to protect the principal's relationship with the other party to the transaction, usually a customer or supplier: and for ratification to have this protective effect it has to be more than an idle gesture, signifying nothing because unenforceable.

f. *Acquiescence.* A concept that is comparable to, but different from, ratification is authority by *acquiescence.* "[I]f the agent performs a series of acts of a similar nature, the failure of the principal to object to them is an indication that he consents to the performance of similar acts in the future under similar conditions." Restatement (Second) of Agency § 43, Comment b. Suppose, for example, an agent engages in a series of comparable purchases on the principal's behalf. Prior to the first purchase, a reasonable person in the agent's position would not have thought she had authority to enter into such a transaction. Nevertheless, the principal did not object either to that purchase or to a later such purchase when he learned of them. At that point, a reasonable person in the agent's position would assume that the principal approved the agent's engaging in such purchases. Accordingly, the principal's acquiescence gives rise to actual authority. As to third persons who know of the acquiescence, the acquiescence also gives rise to apparent authority.

On the concepts of ratification and acquiescence, see Restatement (Second) of Agency §§ 43, 82–85, 87–90, 93, 94, 97–100A, 143 in the Statutory Supplement.

g. *Termination of agent's authority.* As a general rule, a principal has the *power* to terminate an agent's authority at any time, even if doing so violates a contract between the principal and the agent, and even if it had been agreed that the agent's authority was irrevocable. This rule rests largely on the ground that contracts relating to personal services will not be specifically enforced. (There is an important but limited exception to this rule, which applies to a type of relationship known as an *agency coupled with an interest*. This exception will be discussed in Chapter 6, infra.) Accordingly, a contractual provision under which an agent's authority cannot be terminated by either party normally cannot be specifically enforced. However, such a provision is effective to create *liability* (damages) for wrongful termination. Here is an example:

> *Restatement (Second) of Agency § 118, Illustration 1:* In consideration of A's agreement to advertise and give his best energies to the sale of Blackacre, its owner, P, grants to A "a power of attorney, irrevocable for one year" to sell it. A advertises and spends time trying to sell Blackacre. At the end of three months P informs A that he revokes. A's authority is terminated.

On the revocability of agency powers, see Restatement (Second) of Agency § 118 in the Statutory Supplement.

3. *Liability of Third Person to Principal.* Section 2 considered the liability of a principal to a third person. What is the liability of the third person to the principal? The general rule is that if an agent and a third person enter into a contract under which the agent's principal is liable to the third person, then the third person is liable to the principal. Restatement (Second) of Agency § 292. The major exception is that the third person is not liable to an undisclosed principal if the agent or the principal knew that the third person would not have dealt with the principal if she had known the principal's identity. Id., Comment c.

4. *Liability of Agent to Third Person.*

a. *Where the principal is bound.* Where the agent has actual, apparent, or inherent authority, so that the principal is bound to the third person, the agent's liability to the third person depends in part on whether the principal was disclosed, partially disclosed, or undisclosed.

(i) *Undisclosed principal.* If the principal was undisclosed (that is, if at the time of the transaction the agent purported to act on her own behalf), the general rule is that the agent is bound, even though the principal is bound too. Restatement (Second) of Agency § 322. The theory is that the third person must have expected the agent to be a party to the contract, because that is how the agent presented the transaction. However, there is a quirk in the law here. Under the majority rule, if the third person, after learning of an undisclosed principal's identity, obtains a judgment against the principal, the agent is discharged from liability even if the judgment is not satisfied. Similarly, the undisclosed principal is discharged if the third person obtains a judgment against the agent. Under the minority rule, which is sounder, neither the agent nor the principal is discharged by a judgment against the other, but only by satisfaction of the judgment.

(ii) *Partially disclosed principal.* If the principal was partially disclosed (that is, if at the time of the transaction the third person knew that the agent was acting on behalf of a principal, but did not know the principal's identity), the general rule is that the agent as well as the principal is bound to the third person. Restatement (Second) of Agency § 321. The theory is that if the third person did not know the identity of the principal, and therefore could not investigate the principal's credit or reliability, he probably expected that the agent would be liable, either solely or as a co-promisor or surety. Id., Comment a.

(iii) *Disclosed principal.* Assume now that the principal was disclosed (that is, at the time of the transaction the third person knew that the agent was acting on behalf of a principal and knew the principal's identity). If the principal is bound by the agent's act because the agent had actual, apparent, or inherent authority, or because the principal ratified the act, the general rule is that the agent is not bound to the third person. Restatement (Second) of Agency § 320. The theory is that in such a case the third person did not expect the agent to be bound; he did expect the principal to be bound; and he gets just what he expects.

b. *Where the principal is not bound.* If the principal is *not* bound by the agent's act, because the agent did not have actual, apparent, or inherent authority, the general rule is that the agent is liable to the third person. The agent's liability is usually based on the theory that an agent makes an implied warranty of authority to the third person, although a few authorities have adopted a theory that the agent can be held liable on the contract itself. In principle, the difference between the two theories might lead to a difference in the measure of damages. Under the liability-on-the-contract theory, the third person will recover the gains that he would have derived under the contract—essentially, expectation damages. In contrast, under the implied-warranty theory it might seem that the third person would recover only the losses he suffered by having entered into the transaction—essentially, reliance damages. However, Restatement (Second) of Agency § 329, while adopting the implied-warranty theory, provides for an expectation measure of damages, just as if it had adopted the contract theory: "The third person can recover in damages not only for the harm caused to him by the fact that the agent was unauthorized, but also for the amount by which he would have benefitted had the authority existed." Id., Comment j.

On the agent's liability to the third person, see Restatement (Second) of Agency §§ 320–322, 328–330 in the Statutory Supplement.

5. *Liability of Agent to Principal.* If an agent takes an action that she has no actual authority to perform, but the principal is nevertheless bound because the agent had apparent authority, the agent is liable to the principal for any resulting damages. Restatement (Second) of Agency § 383, Comment e. Whether an agent is liable to the principal for an act that binds the principal by virtue of the agent's inherent but not actual authority is an unsettled point.

6. *Liability of Principal to Agent.* If an agent has acted within her actual authority, the principal is under a duty to indemnify the agent for payments authorized or made necessary in executing the principal's affairs. This includes authorized payments made by the agent on the principal's behalf; payments made by the agent to a third person on contracts upon which the agent was authorized to make herself liable (as where the agent acted on behalf of a partially disclosed or undisclosed principal); payments

of damages to third parties that the agent incurs because of an authorized act that constituted a breach of contract; and expenses in defending actions brought against the agent by third parties because of the agent's authorized conduct.

On the agent's right to indemnification, see Restatement (Second) of Agency §§ 438–440 in the Statutory Supplement.

SECTION 3.   THE AGENT'S DUTY OF LOYALTY

Tarnowski v. Resop

Supreme Court of Minnesota, 1952.
236 Minn. 33, 51 N.W.2d 801.

■ KNUTSON, JUSTICE.

Plaintiff desired to make a business investment. He engaged defendant as his agent to investigate and negotiate for the purchase of a route of coin-operated music machines. On June 2, 1947, relying upon the advice of defendant and the investigation he had made, plaintiff purchased such a business from Phillip Loechler and Lyle Mayer of Rochester, Minnesota, who will be referred to hereinafter as the sellers. The business was located at LaCrosse, Wisconsin, and throughout the surrounding territory. Plaintiff alleges that defendant represented to him that he had made a thorough investigation of the route; that it had 75 locations in operation; that one or more machines were at each location; that the equipment at each location was not more than six months old; and that the gross income from all locations amounted to more than $3,000 per month. As a matter of fact, defendant had made only a superficial investigation and had investigated only five of the locations. Other than that, he had adopted false representations of the sellers as to the other locations and had passed them on to plaintiff as his own. Plaintiff was to pay $30,620 for the business. He paid $11,000 down. About six weeks after the purchase, plaintiff discovered that the representations made to him by defendant were false, in that there were not more than 47 locations; that at some of the locations there were no machines and at others there were machines more than six months old, some of them being seven years old; and that the gross income was far less than $3,000 per month. Upon discovering the falsity of defendant's representations and those of the sellers, plaintiff rescinded the sale. He offered to return what he had received, and he demanded the return of his money. The sellers refused to comply, and he brought suit against them in the district court of Olmsted county. The action was tried, resulting in a verdict of $10,000 for plaintiff. Thereafter, the sellers paid plaintiff $9,500, after which the action was dismissed with prejudice pursuant to a stipulation of the parties.

In this action, brought in Hennepin county, plaintiff alleges that defendant, while acting as agent for him, collected a secret commission from the sellers for consummating the sale, which plaintiff seeks to recover under his first cause of action. In his second cause of action, he seeks to recover damages for [losses caused by defendant's wrong].

1.   With respect to plaintiff's first cause of action, the principle that all profits made by an agent in the course of an agency belonging to the principal, whether they are the fruits of performance or the violation of an agent's duty, is firmly established and universally recognized. Smitz v. Leopold, 51 Minn. 455, 53 N.W. 719. . . .

It matters not that the principal has suffered no damage or even that the transaction has been profitable to him. Raymond Farmers Elevator Co. v. American Surety Co., 207 Minn. 117, 290 N.W. 231, 126 A.L.R. 1351.

The rule and the basis therefor are well stated in Lum v. Clark, 56 Minn. 278, 282, 57 N.W. 662, where, speaking through Mr. Justice Mitchell, we said: "Actual injury is not the principle the law proceeds on, in holding such transactions void. Fidelity in the agent is what is aimed at, and, as a means of securing it, the law will not permit him to place himself in a position in which he may be tempted by his own private interests to disregard those of his principal. . . . It is not material that no actual injury to the company [principal] resulted, or that the policy recommended may have been for its best interest. Courts will not inquire into these matters. It is enough to know that the agent in fact placed himself in such relations that he might be tempted by his own interests to disregard those of his principal. The transaction was nothing more or less than the acceptance by the agent of a bribe to perform his duties in the manner desired by the person who gave the bribe. Such a contract is void. This doctrine rests on such plain principles of law, as well as common business honesty, that the citation of authorities is unnecessary."

The right to recover profits made by the agent in the course of the agency is not affected by the fact that the principal, upon discovering a fraud, has rescinded the contract and recovered that with which he parted. Restatement, Agency, § 407(2). Comment e on Subsection (2) reads: "If an agent has violated a duty of loyalty to the principal so that the principal is entitled to profits which the agent has thereby made, the fact that the principal has brought an action against a third person and has been made whole by such action does not prevent the principal from recovering from the agent the profits which the agent has made. Thus, if the other contracting party has given a bribe to the agent to make a contract with him on behalf of the principal, the principal can rescind the transaction, recovering from the other party anything received by him, or he can maintain an action for damages against him; in either event the principal may recover from the agent the amount of the bribe."

It follows that, insofar as the secret commission of $2,000 received by the agent is concerned, plaintiff had an absolute right thereto, irrespective of any recovery resulting from the action against the sellers for rescision.

2.   Plaintiff's second cause of action is brought to recover damages for (1) losses suffered in the operation of the business prior to rescission; (2) loss of time devoted to operation; (3) expenses in connection with rescission

19

of the sale and investigation therewith; (4) nontaxable expenses in connection with the prosecution of the suit against the sellers; and (5) attorneys' fees in connection with the suit.

The case comes to us on a bill of exceptions. No part of the testimony of the witnesses is included, so we must assume that the evidence establishes the items of damage claimed by plaintiff. Our inquiry is limited to a consideration of the question whether a principal may recover of an agent who has breached his trust the items of damage mentioned after a successful prosecution of an action for rescission against the third parties with whom the agent dealt for his principal.

The general rule is stated in Restatement, Agency, § 407(1), as follows: "If an agent has received a benefit as a result of violating his duty of loyalty, the principal is entitled to recover from him what he has so received, its value, or its proceeds, and also the amount of damage thereby caused, except that if the violation consists of the wrongful disposal of the principal's property, the principal cannot recover its value and also what the agent received in exchange therefor."

In Comment a on Subsection (1) we find the following: "... In either event, whether or not the principal elects to get back the thing improperly dealt with or to recover from the agent its value or the amount of benefit which the agent has improperly received, he is, in addition, entitled to be indemnified by the agent for any loss which has been caused to his interest by the improper transaction. Thus, if the purchasing agent for a restaurant purchases with the principal's money defective food, receiving a bonus therefor, and the use of the food in the restaurant damages the business, the principal can recover from the agent the amount of money improperly expended by him, the bonus which the agent received, and the amount which will compensate for the injury to the business."

The general rule with respect to damages for a tortious act is that "The wrong-doer is answerable for all the injurious consequences of his tortious act, which according to the usual course of events and the general experience were likely to ensue, and which, therefore, when the act was committed, he may reasonably be supposed to have foreseen and anticipated." 1 Sutherland, Damages (4 ed.) § 45, quoted with approval in Sargent v. Mason, 101 Minn. 319, 323, 112 N.W. 255, 257. . . .

Bergquist v. Kreidler, 158 Minn. 127, 196 N.W. 964, involved an action to recover attorneys' fees expended by plaintiffs in an action seeking to enforce and protect their right to the possession of real estate. Defendant, acting as the owner's agent, had falsely represented to plaintiffs that they could have possession on August 1, 1920. It developed after plaintiffs had purchased the premises that a tenant had a lease running to August 1, 1922, on a rental much lower than the actual value of the premises. Defendant (the agent) conceded that plaintiffs were entitled to recover the loss in rent, but contended that attorneys' fees and disbursements expended by plaintiffs in testing the validity of the tenant's lease were not recoverable. In affirming plaintiffs' right to recover we said, 158 Minn. 132, 196 N.W. 966: "... the litigation in which plaintiffs became involved was the direct, legitimate, and a to be expected result of appellant's misrepresentation. The loss sustained by plaintiffs in conducting that litigation 'is plainly traceable' to appellant's wrong and he should make compensation accordingly."

So far as the right to recover attorneys' fees is concerned, the same may be said in this case. Plaintiff sought to return what had been received and demanded a return of his down payment. The sellers refused. He thereupon sued to accomplish this purpose, as he had a right to do, and was successful. His attorneys' fees and expenses of suit were directly traceable to the harm caused by defendant's wrongful act. As such, they are recoverable.

. . . The general rule applicable here is stated in 15 Am.Jur., Damages, § 144, as follows: "It is generally held that where the wrongful act of the defendant has involved the plaintiff in litigation with others or placed him in such relation with others as makes it necessary to incur expense to protect his interest, such costs and expenses, including attorneys' fees, should be treated as the legal consequences of the original wrongful act and may be recovered as damages."

The same is true of the other elements of damage involved. . . .

Affirmed.

––––––

RESTATEMENT (SECOND) OF AGENCY
§§ 13, 387–396, 401, 403, 404, 407

[See Appendix]

––––––

READING v. ATTORNEY–GENERAL, [1951] App.Cas. 507 (H.L.). Reading was a sergeant in the Royal Army Medical Corps during World War II, stationed in Cairo. In 1943, an unidentified man asked Reading whether he would assist in selling cases of whisky and brandy in Cairo, for which he would be paid a few pounds. About a month later Reading was met by a man named Manole, who told Reading that a truck, which Reading was to board, would come at a specified time and place. Reading, dressed in uniform, boarded the truck and conducted it through Cairo. By arrangement he met Manole later on the same day, and received an envelope which contained £2,000. This process was repeated on a number of occasions. In all, Reading was paid around £20,000. The Crown (that is, the English Government) later seized these amounts, on the ground that they had been paid to Reading "for accompanying . . . a loaded lorry in and about Cairo whilst dressed in uniform and thereby falsely representing himself as acting in the course of his military duties . . . in order to avoid police inspection of the said lorry." Reading brought suit to recover the seized amount. Justice Denning, at trial, dismissed Reading's complaint:

   In my judgment, it is a principle of law that if a servant, in violation of his duty of honesty and good faith, takes advantage of his

21

service to make a profit for himself, in this sense, that the assets of which he has control, or the facilities which he enjoys, or the position which he occupies, are the real cause of his obtaining the money, as distinct from being the mere opportunity for getting it, that is to say, if they play the predominant part in his obtaining the money, then he is accountable for it to the master. It matters not that the master has not lost any profit, nor suffered any damage. Nor does it matter that the master could not have done the act himself. It is a case where the servant has unjustly enriched himself by virtue of his service without his master's sanction. It is money which the servant ought not to be allowed to keep, and the law says it shall be taken from him and given to his master, because he got it solely by reason of the position which he occupied as a servant of his master. . . . [Reading] . . . was using his position as a sergeant in His Majesty's Army and the uniform to which his rank entitled him to obtain the money which he received. In my opinion any official position, whether marked by a uniform or not, which enables the holder to earn money by its use gives his master a right to receive the money so earned even though it was earned by a criminal act. "You have earned", the master can say, "money by the use of your position as my servant. It is not for you, who have gained this advantage, to set up your own wrong as a defence to my claim."

The House of Lords affirmed.

Jensen & Meckling, Theory of the Firm: Managerial Behavior, Agency Costs and Ownership Structure

3 J. Financial Economics 305, 308 (1976).

We define an agency relationship as a contract under which one or more persons (the principal(s)) engage another person (the agent) to perform some service on their behalf which involves delegating some decision making authority to the agent. If both parties to the relationship are utility maximizers there is good reason to believe that the agent will not always act in the best interests of the principal. The *principal* can limit divergences from his interest by establishing appropriate incentives for the agent and by incurring monitoring costs designed to limit the aberrant activities of the agent. In addition in some situations it will pay the *agent* to expend resources (bonding costs) to guarantee that he will not take certain actions which would harm the principal or to ensure that the principal will be compensated if he does take such actions. However, it is generally impossible for the principal or the agent at zero cost to ensure that the agent will make optimal decisions from the principal's viewpoint. In most agency relationships the principal and the agent will incur positive monitoring and bonding costs (non-pecuniary as well as pecuniary), and in addition there will be some divergence between the agent's decisions and those decisions which would maximize the welfare of the principal. The dollar equivalent of the reduction in welfare experienced by the principal due to this divergence is also a cost of the agency relationship, and we refer to this latter cost as the "residual loss". We define *agency costs* as the sum of:

(1) the monitoring expenditures by the principal,

(2) the bonding expenditures by the agent,

(3) the residual loss.

CHAPTER II

PARTNERSHIP

INTRODUCTORY NOTE

Although partnership had a rich history under the common law, it has long been governed by statute. Until recently, the relevant statute was the Uniform Partnership Act ("the UPA"), which was promulgated by the National Conference of Commissioners on Uniform State Laws (NCCUSL) in 1914 and was adopted in every state except Louisiana.

In 1994, NCCUSL adopted the Revised Uniform Partnership Act (RUPA), which is intended to supersede the UPA. As of early 2000, RUPA had been enacted in a number of states, but by no means all states. Accordingly, the UPA continues to be important.

Under RUPA § 1006, RUPA normally applies not only to all partnerships formed after RUPA is adopted in any given state but, after a transition period, to all partnerships, even those formed before RUPA was adopted.

The cases and materials in this Section will largely concern the UPA, partly because as of this writing (2000) the UPA is still in effect in many states, partly because RUPA is so new that it has not yet spawned much case law, and partly because RUPA continues many of the rules of the UPA. In general, however, where RUPA makes a material change in a relevant UPA rule the changes will be discussed in a Text Note.

As of 1996, there were 1,116,054 general partnerships in the United States, with an average of 4 partners in each partnership. Alan Zempel, Partnership Returns, 1996, 18 Statistics of Income Bulletin No. 2, at 49–50 (1998).

This chapter will consider the basic partnership form, general partnerships. Two special partnership forms, limited partnerships and limited liability partnerships, will be considered in Chapter 7, infra.

SECTION 1. PARTNERSHIP FORMATION

HILCO PROPERTY SERVICES, INC. v. UNITED STATES, 929 F.Supp. 526 (D.N.H. 1996). "The conduct of the parties and the circumstances surrounding their relationship and transactions control the factual question of whether a partnership existed in cases where the parties have not documented their intentions in a written agreement. . . . Airlines, Inc., 798 F.Supp. 1453, 1455 (D.Nev.1992) (applying UPA) . . . Although 'there is no specific test to determine the existence of a partnership,' Shaw, 798 F.Supp. at 1455, courts consult a variety of factors including whether the parties intended to proceed as partners, have shared profits or losses, had the right to participate in the control of the enterprise, or commonly held real property, see . . . In re Medallion Realty Trust, 103 B.R. 8, 12–14 (Bankr.D.Mass.1989). . . . This non-exhaustive list focuses the inquiry on what actually transpired between the purported partners because the law of partnership 'fixes the legal consequences which flow from the conduct of the parties.' In re Medallion, 103 B.R. at 13 (citations omitted). And although the question of intent is a crucial part of the calculus, 'the only necessary intent . . . is an intent to do those things which constitute a partnership.' Id. Thus,

> [t]he key factor is not the subjective intent of the parties to form a partnership. . . . It is immaterial that the parties do not call their relationship, or believe it to be, a partnership, especially where the rights of third parties are concerned.

Shaw, 798 F.Supp. at 1455 (citations omitted)."

————

ARNOLD v. ERKMANN, 934 S.W.2d 621 (Mo.Ct.App.1996). "A partnership is 'an association of two or more persons to carry on as coowners a business for profit.' . . . The primary criterion [in determining whether a partnership exists] is the parties' intention to enter a relationship which in law constitutes a partnership; intent to form a partnership is not necessary. . . . Indicia of a partnership relationship includes a right to a voice in management of the partnership business, a share of the profits of the partnership business, and a corresponding risk of loss and liability to partnership creditors. . . .

"[The parties in this case made an agreement that] contains language providing for the splitting of profits, allocation of risk, and joint participation in business decisions and obligations over $5,000.00. [Defendant] points out that the agreement specifically disclaims that it creates a partnership in the following language:

> Nothing in this Agreement is intended to nor shall it in fact operate to create an agency, partnership or corporation. . . .

"However, such a recitation is not dispositive of the determination of the existence of a partnership if an intent to enter into a partnership can be found in other provisions of the agreement."

————

UNIFORM PARTNERSHIP ACT §§ 6, 7

REVISED UNIFORM PARTNERSHIP ACT §§ 101(6), 202

[See Appendix]

Martin v. Peyton

New York Court of Appeals, 1927.
246 N.Y. 213, 158 N.E. 77.

Appeal from Supreme Court, Appellate Division, First Department.

Action by Charles S. Martin against William C. Peyton and others. A judgment of the Special Term, entered on the report of a referee in favor of the defendants was affirmed by the Appellate Division (219 App.Div. 297, 220 N.Y.S. 29), and plaintiff appeals. Affirmed.

ANDREWS, J. Much ancient learning as to partnership is obsolete. Today only those who are partners between themselves may be charged for partnership debts by others. (Partnership Law [Cons. Laws, ch. 39], sec. 11.) There is one exception. Now and then a recovery is allowed where in truth such relationship is absent. This is because the debtor may not deny the claim. (Sec. 27.)

Partnership results from contract, express or implied. If denied it may be proved by the production of some written instrument; by testimony as to some conversation; by circumstantial evidence. If nothing else appears the receipt by the defendant of a share of the profits of the business is enough. (Sec. 11.)

Assuming some written contract between the parties the question may arise whether it creates a partnership. If it be complete; if it expresses in good faith the full understanding and obligation of the parties, then it is for the court to say whether a partnership exists. It may, however, be a mere sham intended to hide the real relationship. Then other results follow. In passing upon it effect is to be given to each provision. Mere words will not blind us to realities. Statements that no partnership is intended are not conclusive. If as a whole a contract contemplates an association of two or more persons to carry on as co-owners a business for profit a partnership there is. (Sec. 10.) On the other hand, if it be less than this no partnership exists. Passing on the contract as a whole, an arrangement for sharing profits is to be considered. It is to be given its due weight. But it is to be weighed in connection with all the rest. It is not decisive. It may be merely the method adopted to pay a debt or wages,as interest on a loan or for other reasons.

An existing contract may be modified later by subsequent agreement, oral or written. A partnership may be so created where there was none before. And again, that the original agreement has been so modified may be proved by circumstantial evidence—by showing the conduct of the parties.

In the case before us the claim that the defendants became partners in the firm of Knauth, Nachod & Kuhne, doing business as bankers and brokers, depends upon the interpretation of certain instruments. There is nothing in their subsequent acts determinative of or indeed material upon this question. And we are relieved of questions that sometimes arise. "The plaintiff's position is not," we are told, "that the agreements of June 4, 1921, were a false expression or incomplete expression of the intention of the parties. We say that they express defendants' intention and that that intention was to create a relationship which as a matter of law constitutes a partnership." Nor may the claim of the plaintiff be rested on any question of estoppel. "The plaintiff's claim," he stipulates, "is a claim of actual partnership, not of partnership by estoppel. . . ."

Remitted then, as we are, to the documents themselves, we refer to circumstances surrounding their execution only so far as is necessary to make them intelligible. And we are to remember that although the intention of the parties to avoid liability as partners is clear, although in language precise and definite they deny any design to then join the firm of K.N. & K.; although they say their interests in profits should be construed merely as a measure of compensation for loans, not an interest in profits as such; although they provide that they shall not be liable for any losses or treated as partners, the question still remains whether in fact they agree to so associate themselves with the firm as to "carry on as co-owners a business for profit."

In the spring of 1921 the firm of K.N. & K. found itself in financial difficulties. John R. Hall was one of the partners. He was a friend of Mr. Peyton. From him he obtained the loan of almost $500,000 of Liberty bonds, which K.N. & K. might use as collateral to secure bank advances. This, however, was not sufficient. The firm and its members had engaged in unwise speculations, and it was deeply involved. Mr. Hall was also intimately acquainted with George W. Perkins, Jr., and with Edward W. Freeman. He also knew Mrs. Peyton and Mrs. Perkins and Mrs. Freeman. All were anxious to help him. He, therefore, representing K.N. & K., entered into negotiations with them. While they were pending a proposition was made that Mr. Peyton, Mr. Perkins and Mr. Freeman or some of them should become partners. It met a decided refusal. Finally an agreement was reached. It is expressed in three documents, executed on the same day, all a part of the one transaction. They were drawn with care and are unambiguous. We shall refer to them as "the agreement," "the indenture" and "the option."

We have no doubt as to their general purpose. The respondents were to loan K.N. & K. $2,500,000 worth of liquid securities, which were to be returned to them on or before April 15, 1923. The firm might hypothecate them to secure loans totaling $2,000,000, using the proceeds as its business necessities required. To insure respondents against loss K.N. & K. were to turn over to them a large number of their own securities which may have been valuable, but which were of so speculative a nature that they could not be used as collateral for bank loans. In compensation for the loan the respondents were to receive 40 per cent of the profits of the firm until the return was made, not exceeding, however, $500,000 and not less than $100,000. Merely because the transaction involved the transfer of securities and not of cash does not prevent its being a loan within the meaning of section 11. The respondents also were given an option to join the firm if they or any of them expressed a desire to do so before June 4, 1923.

Many other detailed agreements are contained in the papers. Are they such as may be properly inserted to protect the lenders? Or do they go further? Whatever their purpose, did they in truth associate the respondents with the firm so that they and it together thereafter carried on as co-owners a business for profit? The answer depends upon an analysis of these various provisions.

As representing the lenders, Mr. Peyton and Mr. Freeman are called "trustees." The loaned securities when used as collateral are not to be mingled with other securities of K.N. & K., and the trustees at all times are to be kept informed of all transactions affecting them. To them shall be paid all dividends and income accruing therefrom. They may also substitute for any of the securities loaned securities of equal value. With their consent the firm may sell any of its securities held by the respondents, the proceeds to go, however, to the trustees. In other similar ways the trustees may deal with these same securities, but the securities loaned shall always be sufficient in value to permit of their hypothecation for $2,000,000. If they rise in price the excess may be withdrawn by the defendants. If they fall they shall make good the deficiency.

So far there is no hint that the transaction is not a loan of securities with a provision for compensation. Later a somewhat closer connection with the firm appears. Until the securities are returned the directing management of the firm is to be in the hands of John R. Hall, and his life is to be insured for $1,000,000, and the policies are to be assigned as further collateral security to the trustees. These requirements are not unnatural. Hall was the one known and trusted by the defendants. Their acquaintance with the other members of the firm was of the slightest. These others had brought an old and established business to the verge of bankruptcy. As the respondents knew, they also had engaged in unsafe speculation. The respondents were about to loan $2,500,000 of good securities. As collateral they were to receive others of problematical value. What they required seems but ordinary caution. Nor does it imply an association in the business.

The trustees are to be kept advised as to the conduct of the business and consulted as to important matters. They may inspect the firm books and are entitled to any information they think important. Finally they may veto any business they think highly speculative or injurious. Again we hold this but a proper precaution to safeguard the loan. The trustees may not initiate any transaction as a partner may do. They may not bind the firm by any action of their own. Under the circumstances the safety of the loan depended upon the business success of K.N. & K. This success was likely to be compromised by the inclination of its members to engage in speculation. No longer, if the respondents were to be protected, should it be allowed. The trustees, therefore, might prohibit it, and that their prohibition might be effective, information was to be furnished them. Not dissimilar agreements have been held proper to guard the interests of the lender.

As further security each member of K.N. & K. is to assign to the trustees their interest in the firm. No loan by the firm to any member is permitted and the amount each may draw is fixed. No other distribution of profits is to be made. So that realized profits may be calculated the existing capital is stated to be $700,000, and profits are to be realized as promptly as good business practice will permit. In case the trustees think this is not done, the question is left to them and to Mr. Hall, and if they differ then to an arbitrator. There is no obligation that the firm shall continue the business. It may dissolve at any time. Again we conclude there is nothing here not properly adapted to secure the interest of the respondents as lenders. If their compensation is dependent on a percentage of the profits still provision must be made to define what these profits shall be.

The "indenture" is substantially a mortgage of the collateral delivered by K.N. & K. to the trustees to secure the performance of the "agreement." It certainly does not strengthen the claim that the respondents were partners.

Finally we have the "option." It permits the respondents or any of them or their assignees or nominees to enter the firm at a later date if they desire to do so by buying 50 per cent or less of the interests therein of all or any of the members at a stated price. Or a corporation may, if the respondents and the members agree, be formed in place of the firm. Meanwhile, apparently with the design of protecting the firm business against improper or ill-judged action which might render the option valueless, each member of the firm is to place his resignation in the hands of Mr. Hall. If at any time he and the trustees agree that such resignation should be accepted, that member shall then retire, receiving the value of his interest calculated as of the date of such retirement.

This last provision is somewhat unusual, yet it is not enough in itself to show that on June 4, 1921, a present partnership was created nor taking these various papers as a whole do we reach such a result. It is quite true that even if one or two or three like provisions contained in such a contract do not require this conclusion, yet it is also true that when taken together a point may come where stipulations immaterial separately cover so wide a field that we should hold a partnership exists. As in other branches of the law a question of degree is often the determining factor. Here that point has not been reached. . . .

The judgment appealed from should be affirmed, with costs.

■ CARDOZO, CH. J., POUND, CRANE, LEHMAN, KELLOGG and O'BRIEN, JJ., concur.

29

Judgment affirmed, etc.

———

Lupien v. Malsbenden

Supreme Judicial Court of Maine, 1984.
477 A.2d 746.

■ Before McKusick, C.J., and Nichols, Roberts, Wathen, Glassman and Scholnik, JJ.

■ McKusick, Chief Justice.

Defendant Frederick Malsbenden appeals a judgment of the Superior Court (York County) holding him to partnership liability on a written contract entered into between plaintiff Robert Lupien and one Stephen Cragin doing business as York Motor Mart.[1] The sole issue asserted on appeal is whether the Superior Court erred in its finding that Malsbenden and Cragin were partners in the pertinent part of York Motor Mart's business. We affirm.

On March 5, 1980, plaintiff entered into a written agreement with Stephen Cragin, doing business in the town of York as York Motor Mart, for the construction of a Bradley automobile.[2] Plaintiff made a deposit of $500 towards the purchase price of $8,020 upon signing the contract, and made a further payment of $3,950 one week later on March 12. Both the purchase order of March 5, 1980, and a later bill of sale, though signed by Cragin, identified the seller as York Motor Mart. At the jury-waived trial, plaintiff testified that after he signed the contract he made visits to York Motor Mart on an average of once or twice a week to check on the progress being made on his car. During those visits plaintiff generally dealt with Malsbenden because Cragin was seldom present. On one such visit in April, Malsbenden told plaintiff that it was necessary for the latter to sign over ownership of his pickup truck, which would constitute the balance of the consideration under the contract, so that the proceeds from the sale of the truck could be used to complete construction of the Bradley. When plaintiff complied, Malsbenden provided plaintiff with a rental car, and later with a "demo" model of the Bradley, for his use pending the completion of the vehicle he had ordered. When it was discovered that the "demo" actually belonged to a third person who had entrusted it to York Motor Mart for resale, Malsbenden purchased the vehicle for plaintiff's use. Plaintiff never received the Bradley he had contracted to purchase.

In his trial testimony, defendant Malsbenden asserted that his interest in the Bradley operation of York Motor Mart was only that of a banker. He stated that he had loaned $85,000 to Cragin, without interest, to finance

---

1. Cragin "disappeared" several months before this action was commenced. Plaintiff Lupien originally named Cragin as a co-defendant. However, since Cragin was never served with process, the Superior Court at the behest of both Lupien and defendant Malsbenden dismissed the claim against Cragin.

2. A Bradley automobile is a "kit car" constructed on a Volkswagen chassis.

the Bradley portion of York Motor Mart's business.[3] The loan was to be repaid from the proceeds of each car sold. Malsbenden acknowledged that Bradley kits were purchased with his personal checks and that he had also purchased equipment for York Motor Mart. He also stated that after Cragin disappeared sometime late in May 1980, he had physical control of the premises of York Motor Mart and that he continued to dispose of assets there even to the time of trial in 1983.

The Uniform Partnership Act, adopted in Maine at 31 M.R.S.A. §§ 281–323 (1978 & Supp.1983–1984), defines a partnership as "an association of 2 or more persons ... to carry on as co-owners[4] a business for profit." 31 M.R.S.A. § 286 (1978). Whether a partnership exists is an inference of law based on established facts. *See Dalton v. Austin,* 432 A.2d 774, 777 (Me.1981); *Roux v. Lawand,* 131 Me. 215, 219, 160 A. 756, 757 (1932); *James Bailey Co. v. Darling,* 119 Me. 326, 328, 111 A. 410, 411 (1920). A finding that the relationship between two persons constitutes a partnership may be based upon evidence of an agreement, either express or implied,

> to place their money, effects, labor, and skill, or some or all of them, in lawful commerce or business with the understanding that a community of profits will be shared.... No one factor is alone determinative of the existence of a partnership....

Dalton v. Austin, 432 A.2d at 777; *Cumberland County Power & Light Co. v. Gordon,* 136 Me. 213, 218, 7 A.2d 619, 622 (1939). *See James Bailey Co. v. Darling,* 119 Me. at 328, 111 A. at 411. If the arrangement between the parties otherwise qualifies as a partnership, it is of no matter that the parties did not expressly agree to form a partnership or did not even intend to form one:

> It is possible for parties to intend no partnership and yet to form one. If they agree upon an arrangement which is a partnership in fact, it is of no importance that they call it something else, or that they even expressly declare that they are not to be partners. The law must declare what is the legal import of their agreements, and names go for nothing when the substance of the arrangement shows them to be inapplicable.

James Bailey Co. v. Darling, 119 Me. at 328, 111 A. at 411 (quoting *Beecher v. Bush,* 45 Mich. 188, 193–94, 7 N.W. 785, 785–86 (1881)).

Here the trial justice concluded that, notwithstanding Malsbenden's assertion that he was only a "banker," his "total involvement" in the Bradley operation was that of a partner. The testimony at trial, both

---

3. Malsbenden's testimony indicated that Cragin carried on an automotive repair business at the York Motor Mart that was unrelated to the Bradley operation. Malsbenden testified, without contradiction, that he had no involvement with that other business.

4. As we made clear in *Dalton v. Austin,* 432 A.2d 774, 777 (Me.1981), the term "co-owners" as used in the statute does not necessarily mean joint title to all assets. On the contrary, "the right to participate in control of the business is the essence of co-ownership." *Id.*

respecting Malsbenden's financial interest in the enterprise and his involvement in day-to-day business operations, amply supported the Superior Court's conclusion. Malsbenden had a financial interest of $85,000 in the Bradley portion of York Motor Mart's operations. Although Malsbenden termed the investment a loan, significantly he conceded that the "loan" carried no interest. His "loan" was not made in the form of a fixed payment or payments, but was made to the business, at least in substantial part, in the form of day-to-day purchases of Bradley kits, other parts and equipment, and in the payment of wages. Furthermore, the "loan" was not to be repaid in fixed amounts or at fixed times, but rather only upon the sale of Bradley automobiles.

The evidence also showed that, unlike a banker, Malsbenden had the right to participate in control of the business and in fact did so on a day-to-day basis.[5] According to Urbin Savaria, who worked at York Motor Mart from late April through June 1980, Malsbenden during that time opened the business establishment each morning, remained present through part of every day, had final say on the ordering of parts, paid for parts and equipment, and paid Savaria's salary. On plaintiff's frequent visits to York Motor Mart, he generally dealt with Malsbenden because Cragin was not present. It was Malsbenden who insisted that plaintiff trade in his truck prior to the completion of the Bradley because the proceeds from the sale of the truck were needed to complete the Bradley. When it was discovered that the "demo" Bradley given to plaintiff while he awaited completion of his car actually belonged to a third party, it was Malsbenden who bought the car for plaintiff's use. As of three years after the making of the contract now in litigation, Malsbenden was still doing business at York Motor Mart, "just disposing of property."

Malsbenden and Cragin may well have viewed their relationship to be that of creditor-borrower, rather than a partnership. At trial Malsbenden so asserts, and Cragin's departure from the scene in the spring of 1980 deprives us of the benefit of his view of his business arrangement with Malsbenden. In any event, whatever the intent of these two men as to their respective involvements in the business of making and selling Bradley cars, there is no clear error in the Superior Court's finding that the Bradley car operation represented a pooling of Malsbenden's capital and Cragin's automotive skills, with joint control over the business and intent to share the fruits of the enterprise. As a matter of law, that arrangement amounted to a partnership under 31 M.R.S.A. § 286.

The entry is:

Judgment affirmed.

All concurring.

---

5. Thus its facts clearly distinguish the case at bar from *James Bailey Co. v. Darling,* 119 Me. 326, 332, 111 A. 410, 413 (1920), where although the defendant advanced money for the purchase of automobiles that was to be repaid upon the sale of individual automobiles, the defendant had no control over the business.

NOTE ON THE FORMATION OF PARTNERSHIPS

1. *Formalities.* Corporations, limited partnerships, and limited liability companies can be organized (formed) only if certain formalities are complied with and a filing is made with the state. In contrast, general partnerships can be organized with no formalities and no filing. The absence of a filing requirement reflects in part a conception that partnership status depends on the factual characteristics of a relationship between two or more persons, not on whether the persons think of themselves as having entered into a partnership.

Although no filings are *required* under either the UPA or RUPA, RUPA *permits* certain filings. See, e.g., Note on the Authority of Partners Under RUPA, infra.

2. *The Four-Element Test, Mutual Right of Control, and Loss-Sharing.* It is sometimes said that where there is no express partnership agreement, a relationship will be considered a partnership only if four elements are present—an agreement to share profits, an agreement to share losses, a mutual right of control or management of the business, and a community of interest in the venture. See, e.g., Weingart v. C & W Taylor Partnership, 248 Mont. 76, 809 P.2d 576 (1991); Corpus Christi v. Bayfront Associates, Ltd., 814 S.W.2d 98 (Tex.App.1991). This four-element test departs from the statutory test of both UPA § 6(a) and RUPA § 202, which provide simply that with certain exceptions a partnership is "an association of two or more persons to carry on as co-owners a business for profit," and say nothing about control or loss-sharing.

Although the Comments to both UPA § 6(a) and RUPA § 202 say that "to state that partners are co-owners of a business is to state that they each have the power of ultimate control," in fact even explicit partnership agreements frequently do not involve either ultimate control or loss-sharing for every partner. For example, many partnership agreements vest control in only one or more managing partners, or create elaborate allocations of voting power in which some partners do not share. Similarly, not every partnership agreement provides for loss sharing by every partner. If *explicit* partnership agreements do not always include control and loss-sharing as elements of the partnership relation, why should courts require those elements as a condition to finding an *implicit* partnership?

A better approach is that the presence or absence of the four specified elements, including mutual control and loss-sharing, is evidence, but not a requirement, of a partnership relation. This approach was taken, for example, in Beckman v. Farmer, 579 A.2d 618, 627 (D.C.App.1990), where the court said that "[t]he customary attributes of partnership, such as loss sharing and joint control of decisionmaking are necessary guideposts of inquiry, but none is conclusive." Other cases have held that once profit-sharing has been shown, it is not essential to show that there was an agreement to share in the losses. See Hansford v. Maplewood Station Business Park, 621 N.E.2d 347 (Ind.App.1993); Endsley v. Game–Show Placements, Ltd., 401 N.E.2d 768 (Ind.App.1980). **33**

SECTION 2.   THE LEGAL NATURE OF A PARTNERSHIP

———

UNIFORM PARTNERSHIP ACT § 6

———

REVISED UNIFORM PARTNERSHIP ACT §§ 101(6), 201

[See Appendix]

———

NOTE ON THE LEGAL NATURE OF A PARTNERSHIP: ENTITY OR AGGREGATE STATUS

1. *Entity v. Aggregate.* Individuals may associate in a wide variety of forms, and the issue often arises whether a given form of association has a legal status separate from that of its members. Frequently, this issue is stated in terms of whether a particular form of association is—or is not—a "separate legal entity" or a "legal person" (as opposed to a natural person, that is, an individual). A variety of issues may turn on the answer to this question—for example, whether the association can sue and be sued in its own name, and whether it can hold property in its own right.

In the history of English and American law this issue arose in the context of many different kinds of associations, such as universities, charitable institutions, and even municipalities. In most cases the issue was eventually resolved in a straightforward way, but in the case of partnerships it continued to be vexing. The predominant although not exclusive view under the common law was that a partnership was not an entity, but merely an aggregate of its members, so that a partnership was no more a legal person than was a friendship.

2. *The UPA.* In 1902, when the Conference of Commissioners on Uniform State Laws determined to promulgate a Uniform Partnership Act, Dean James Barr Ames of Harvard Law School was appointed to draft the Act. Subsequently, the Commissioners instructed Dean Ames, at his own urging, to draft the Act on the theory that a partnership is a legal entity. Accordingly, in the drafts submitted by Dean Ames a partnership was defined as *"a legal person* formed by the association of two or more individuals for the purpose of carrying on business with a view to profit," and various provisions of the drafts reflected the entity theory. Dean Ames died before the work was completed, however, and his successor, Dean William Draper Lewis of the University of Pennsylvania Law School, was distinctly unfriendly to the entity view. Ultimately, Dean Lewis convinced the Commissioners to instruct him to draft the Act on the aggregate theory.

UPA Section 6 therefore provides simply that "A partnership is an association of two or more persons to carry on as co-owners a business for profit." Although the language of this provision does not in itself render the issue free from doubt, it is pretty clear that the Act was intended to adopt the aggregate rather than the entity theory of partnership.

However, that is not the end of the story. Having adopted the aggregate theory in principle, in practice the UPA deals with a number of specific issues (such as the ownership of partnership property) *as if* a partnership is an entity. For many purposes, this approach works pretty well. Generally speaking, however, the entity theory of partnership works much better than the aggregate theory. In cases where the UPA treats the partnership as if it is an entity despite the aggregate theory, the results are good but the manner in which the statute reaches those results involves needlessly complex mechanics. In cases where the UPA does not treat the partnership as if it is an entity, the results tend to be bad and in need of legislative revision.

3. *Other Statutes.* The question often arises whether a partnership that operates in a UPA jurisdiction is to be treated as an aggregate or an entity for the purpose of statutes *other* than the UPA. See, e.g., United States v. A & P Trucking Co., 358 U.S. 121 (1958). This question is a matter of legislative intent under the relevant statute. As in all such matters, the answer will depend on the language employed and the purposes manifested in the statute. The fact that the UPA adopts the aggregate theory will be relevant, but not dispositive, in answering that question. A legislature may choose to treat a partnership as an entity for purposes of another statute, even though a partnership is defined as an association under the U.P.A. See,e.g., United States v. A & P Trucking Co., 358 U.S. 121, 79 S.Ct. 203, 3 L.Ed.2d 165 (1958).

4. *RUPA.* In contrast to the UPA, RUPA confers entity status on partnerships. RUPA § 101, like UPA § 6, defines a partnership as "an association of two or more persons to carry on as co-owners a business for profit." However, RUPA § 201 then squarely provides that "A partnership is an entity."

The use of the term "association" in § 101 might lead to some confusion, because it may seem to suggest non-entity status. However, a distinction must be drawn between an "association" and an "aggregate." Any form of business that involves two or more owners can be deemed an association. The question whether the law should treat any given kind of association as a legal entity is a policy issue, or perhaps more accurately, a series of policy issues.

The UPA withheld legal-entity status from partnerships but then created complex rules to arrive at entity-like results on certain issues. RUPA, by conferring entity status on partnerships, is able to drastically simplify many partnership rules, such as those dealing with partnership property and partnership litigation. Nevertheless, entity status does not inherently resolve every issue to which it is relevant. Just as the drafters of the UPA, having denied entity status to partnerships, remained free to

35

(and did) craft rules to reach entity-like results on certain issues, so the drafters of RUPA, having conferred entity status on partnerships, remained free to (and did) craft rules to reach aggregate-like results on certain issues.

To put this differently, no result on any specific partnership-law issue can be "derived" or follows "logically" or "by necessity" from a partnership's legal-entity status under RUPA, any more than any result on any specific issue can be derived, or follows "logically" or "by necessity" from the UPA's denial of that status. Having declared that a partnership is an entity, the drafters of RUPA still had to make policy choices on such issues as whether the partnership could hold property, could sue and be sued in its own name, and so forth. It is true that generally speaking the best rule in many of these areas is one that is consistent with entity status, but it is important not to forget that an independent policy choice must still be made on each issue. The adoption of legal-entity status for partnerships at most simplified the drafting of RUPA and gave a slight push toward certain results.

Thus in one or two areas RUPA itself reaches an aggregate-like result. Most notably, under RUPA, as under the UPA, a partner is individually liable for partnership debts. Under RUPA § 404(b), a partner has a duty of loyalty and care not only to the partnership but to the other partners. Under RUPA § 404(d), a partner's duty of good faith and fair dealing extends both to the partnership and to the other partners.

SECTION 3.   THE ONGOING OPERATION OF PARTNERSHIPS

(a) MANAGEMENT

UNIFORM PARTNERSHIP ACT §§ 18(e), (g), (h), 19, 20

REVISED UNIFORM PARTNERSHIP ACT §§ 103, 401(f), (i), (j), 403

[See Appendix]

Summers v. Dooley

Supreme Court of Idaho, 1971.
94 Idaho 87, 481 P.2d 318.

■ DONALDSON, JUSTICE.

This lawsuit, tried in the district court, involves a claim by one partner against the other for $6,000. The complaining partner asserts that he has been required to pay out more than $11,000 in expenses without any reimbursement from either the partnership funds or his partner. The expenditure in question was incurred by the complaining partner (John Summers, plaintiff-appellant) for the purpose of hiring an additional employee. The trial court denied him any relief except for ordering that he be entitled to one half $966.72 which it found to be a legitimate partnership expense.

The pertinent facts leading to this lawsuit are as follows. Summers entered a partnership agreement with Dooley (defendant-respondent) in 1958 for the purpose of operating a trash collection business. The business was operated by the two men and when either was unable to work, the non-working partner provided a replacement at his own expense. In 1962, Dooley became unable to work and, at his own expense, hired an employee to take his place. In July, 1966, Summers approached his partner Dooley regarding the hiring of an additional employee but Dooley refused. Nevertheless, on his own initiative, Summers hired the man and paid him out of his own pocket. Dooley, upon discovering that Summers had hired an additional man, objected, stating that he did not feel additional labor was necessary and refused to pay for the new employee out of the partnership funds. Summers continued to operate the business using the third man and in October of 1967 instituted suit in the district court for $6,000 against his partner, the gravamen of the complaint being that Summers has been required to pay out more than $11,000 in expenses, incurred in the hiring of the additional man, without any reimbursement from either the partnership funds or his partner. After trial before the court, sitting without a jury, Summers was granted only partial relief[1] and he has appealed. He urges in essence that the trial court erred by failing to conclude that he should be reimbursed for expenses and costs connected in the employment of extra help in the partnership business.

The principal thrust of appellant's contention is that in spite of the fact that one of the two partners refused to consent to the hiring of additional help, nonetheless, the non-consenting partner retained profits earned by the labors of the third man and therefore the non-consenting partner should be estopped from denying the need and value of the employee, and has by his behavior ratified the act of the other partner who hired the additional man.

The issue presented for decision by this appeal is whether an equal partner in a two man partnership has the authority to hire a new employee in disregard of the objection of the other partner and then attempt to charge the dissenting partner with the costs incurred as a result of his unilateral decision.

1. The trial court did award Summers one half of $966.72 which it found to be a legitimate partnership expense.

The State of Idaho has enacted specific statutes with respect to the legal concept known as "partnership." Therefore any solution of partnership problems should logically begin with an application of the relevant code provision.

In the instant case the record indicates that although Summers requested his partner Dooley to agree to the hiring of a third man, such requests were not honored. In fact Dooley made it clear that he was "voting no" with regard to the hiring of an additional employee.

An application of the relevant statutory provisions and pertinent case law to the factual situation presented by the instant case indicates that the trial court was correct in its disposal of the issue since a majority of the partners did not consent to the hiring of the third man. I.C. § 53–318(8) provides:

> "Any difference arising as to ordinary matters connected with the partnership business may be decided by a *majority of the partners....*" (emphasis supplied) ...

The intent of the legislature may be implied from the language used, or inferred on grounds of policy or reasonableness.... A careful reading of the statutory provision indicates that subsection 5 bestows *equal rights in the management and conduct of the partnership business* upon all of the partners. The concept of equality between partners with respect to management of business affairs is a central theme and recurs throughout the Uniform Partnership law, I.C. § 53–301 et seq., which has been enacted in this jurisdiction. Thus the only reasonable interpretation of I.C. § 53–318(8) is that business differences must be decided by a majority of the partners provided no other agreement between the partners speaks to the issues....

In the case at bar one of the partners continually voiced objection to the hiring of the third man. He did not sit idly by and acquiesce in the actions of his partner. Under these circumstances it is manifestly unjust to permit recovery of an expense which was incurred individually and not for the benefit of the partnership but rather for the benefit of one partner.

Judgment affirmed. Costs to respondent.

■ McQUADE, C.J., and McFADDEN, SHEPARD and SPEAR, JJ., concur.

———

QUESTION

Suppose that A, B, and C form a partnership. A contributes 90% of the capital, and by agreement is entitled to 90% of any profits and is responsible for 90% of any losses. B and C each contribute 5% of the capital and by agreement each is entitled to 5% of any profits, and responsible for 5% of any losses. Nothing is said in the agreement concerning how decisions will be made. If A votes one way on an ordinary matter connected with the partnership, and B and C vote another way, who prevails?

———

NOTE ON THE MANAGEMENT OF PARTNERSHIPS

1. *Voting.* The cases and authorities are divided on the issue raised in Summers v. Dooley. In accord with *Summers* is Covalt v. High, 100 N.M. 700, 675 P.2d 999 (App.1983). But see National Biscuit Co. v. Stroud, 249 N.C. 467, 106 S.E.2d 692 (1959).

The rule of UPA § 18(h), that any difference arising as to ordinary matters connected with the partnership business may be decided by a majority of the partners, is "subject to any agreement between them." Partnership agreements often contain provisions vesting management in a managing partner, a managing committee, "senior partners," or some other group composed of less than all the partners, and such agreements override Section 18(h). The same result may be reached even without explicit agreement—for example on the basis of a course of conduct:

> [I]t is ... well settled ... that an agreement for exclusive control of the management of the business by one partner may be implied from the course of conduct of the parties. Here, it was fairly [inferable] from the course of conduct of Parks and Patterson that there was an implied agreement that Parks should be the managing partner.

Parks v. Riverside Ins. Co. of Am., 308 F.2d 175, 180 (10th Cir.1962). Such an implied agreement, if found, would pretty clearly block the nonmanaging partners from objecting to a decision of the managing partners relating to ordinary matters connected with the partnership business solely on the ground that the decision was not arrived at by a majority vote.

RUPA § 401(j) generally follows the voting rules of UPA § 18(h), although there are several differences between the sections. Under UPA § 18(h):

> Any difference arising as to ordinary matters connected with the partnership business may be decided by a majority of the partners; but no act in contravention of any agreement between the partners may be done rightfully without the consent of all the partners.

Under RUPA § 401(j):

> A difference arising as to a matter in the ordinary course of business of a partnership may be decided by a majority of the partners. An act outside the ordinary course of business of a partnership and an amendment to the partnership agreement may be undertaken only with the consent of all of the partners.

RUPA § 401(j) must be read in conjunction with RUPA § 101(5), which defines the term "partnership agreement" to mean "the agreement, written or oral, among the partners concerning the partnership." The Comment to § 101(5) adds:

The definition of "partnership agreement".... is intended to include any agreement among the partners ... concerning either the affairs of the partnership or the conduct of its business.... [T]he agreement may be inferred from the conduct of the parties.

In many partnerships, there is no single document—or no document at all—called a "Partnership Agreement," either because the partnership is itself implicit rather than explicit, or because the partners lack either the inclination or the funds to make a formal agreement. In such cases, under RUPA § 101(5) the "partnership agreement" consists of the fragmentary explicit and implicit agreements that are made from time to time as the partnership relation evolves. Furthermore, even when a partnership does have an explicit and formal "Partnership Agreement," under RUPA § 401(j) unanimity is required not only to depart from this formal agreement, but to depart from any further fragmentary agreement or course of conduct that gives rise to an implied agreement. Thus changes in the way the partnership is actually conducted, not just changes in the way in which it has been explicitly agreed that the partnership will be conducted, may constitute amendments of the partnership agreement for purposes of § 401(j).

Presumably, the term "amendment" in RUPA § 401(j) includes acts in violation of the partnership agreement, as well as changes in the agreement.

Bromberg & Ribstein comment as follows on the language of UPA § 18(b) and RUPA § 401(j):

Under the partnership statutes, it is important to determine on what matters partners have a veto power, and what matters can be decided by majority vote. There is a difference in language between the U.P.A. and R.U.P.A. that bears on this issue, although it is probably not critical in any case. U.P.A.§ 18(h) makes no explicit provision for acts that are neither "ordinary," and which therefore can be decided by a majority vote, nor in "contravention," and therefore must be decided unanimously. R.U.P.A. § 401(j), on the other hand, clarifies that the unanimity requirement applies to both "[a]n act outside the ordinary course of business of a partnership and an amendment to the partnership agreement." This is the effect of the U.P.A., since what is "extraordinary" necessarily depends on the partners' express and implied agreement. The "extraordinary" category has been held to include changing the form of the business entity and substantially altering the rights of the parties. Another example is presented by Paciaroni v. Crane, [408 A.2d 946 (Del.Ch.1979)], in which two of the three partners who owned a race horse wanted to race him despite an injury, while the third owner, the trainer, objected. The court held that the threat to the partnership's only asset made this an extraordinary matter requiring a unanimous vote....

40   Bromberg & Ribstein on Partnership § 6.03(c)(4).

2. *Participation*. Because UPA Section 18(h) provides that partnership action requires a majority vote, what is added by UPA Section 18(e), which provides that all partners have equal rights in the management and conduct of the partnership business? Presumably, the effect of this Section is that absent contrary agreement, every partner must be *consulted* in partnership decisions.

> For a majority of partners to say; We do not care what one partner may say, we, being the majority, will do what we please, is, I apprehend, what this Court will not allow. So, again, with respect to making Mr. *Robertson* the treasurer, Mr. *Const* had a right to be consulted; his opinion might be overruled, and honestly over-ruled, but he ought to have had the question put to him and discussed: In all partnerships ... the partners are bound to be true and faithful to each other: They are to act upon the joint opinion of all, and the discretion and judgment of anyone cannot be excluded: What weight is to be given to it is another question....

Const v. Harris, 37 Eng.Rep. 1191, 1202 (Ch.1824) (Lord Chancellor Eldon). Thus absent contrary agreement, a majority of partners who made decisions without consulting a minority partner would violate § 18(e), even though the majority could have overridden the minority partner after he had been consulted.

RUPA § 401(f) continues the rule of UPA § 18(e), by conferring on each partner the right to participate in management. The Comment to § 401(f) notes that UPA § 18(e) "has been interpreted broadly to mean that, absent contrary agreement, each partner has a continuing right to participate in the management of the partnership and to be informed about the partnership business, even if his assent ... is not required."

NOTE ON WHAT LAW GOVERNS THE INTERNAL AFFAIRS OF PARTNERSHIPS

Legal rules that concern business organizations fall into two general categories: (i) rules that deal with the organization's internal affairs—such as the powers, rights, and duties of the owners, managers, and organs of the organization as among themselves; and (ii) rules that deal with the obligations of the owners, managers, and organs, and of the organization itself, to third persons.

Often, the laws of more than one state might in theory be applied to determine what rules govern an organization's internal affairs. In such cases, the body of law known as *conflict of laws* or *choice of law* determines which state's law governs. In the case of corporations, limited partnerships, and limited liability companies, which are formed by filing organizational documents in a given state, the general choice-of-law rule is that internal affairs are governed by the law of the state in which the corporation is incorporated or in which the limited partnership, or limited liability partnership, or limited liability company is organized. In contrast, the formation of a general partnership does not require the filing of organizational

41

documents. Accordingly, the choice-of-law rule to determine what law governs the internal affairs of general partnerships must depend on other factors. The UPA does not include any provision governing the choice of law for the internal affairs of a general partnership. However, RUPA § 106 provides that a general partnership's internal affairs are governed by the law of the state in which the partnership has its chief executive office.

———

(b) INDEMNIFICATION AND CONTRIBUTION

———

UNIFORM PARTNERSHIP ACT §§ 18(a), (b), (c), (d), (f)

———

REVISED UNIFORM PARTNERSHIP ACT §§ 401(a)–(e), (h)

[See Appendix]

———

NOTE ON INDEMNIFICATION AND CONTRIBUTION

As discussed in Section 5, infra, partners are individually liable to partnership creditors for partnership obligations. As between the partners, however, each partner is liable only for his share of partnership obligations. Thus if one partner pays off a partnership obligation in full (or, for that matter, if he simply pays more than his share), he is entitled to *indemnification* from the *partnership* for the difference between what he paid and his share of the liability.

Indemnification should be distinguished from *contribution*. In a proper case, a partner has a right to be indemnified by the partnership. In contrast, in a proper case the partnership has a right to require *contribution* from one or more *partners*. Thus the obligation to indemnify a partner is a partnership liability, and the obligation to make contribution is a liability of a partner. Partners may, for example, be required to make contribution to fund a partnership obligation to indemnify another partner, so that all partners share a burden that was initially placed on only one. Contribution may also be required for other purposes—in particular, paying off partnership creditors and equalizing capital losses.

"Indemnification resolves the apparent conflict between a partner's joint or joint and several liability, whereby a partner may be called upon to pay the entire amount of partnership debt to third parties under UPA § 15 and RUPA § 306 and the proportionate sharing of profits and losses among the partners under UPA § 18(a) and RUPA § 401(b). A partner who pays or incurs a personal liability to a third party on behalf of the partnership becomes a creditor of the partnership in the amount of the payment or liability, in effect subrogated to the rights of the creditor.... If a going partnership indemnifies the partner, all partners incur a detriment in proportion to their profit shares if the business is profitable, or otherwise according to their loss shares. If the partnership is unable to pay, all partners must contribute to make up the resulting deficit under UPA §§ 18(a) and 40(b)(11) and (d) and RUPA §§ 401(b) and 807(b) according to their loss shares. If the partners are unable to contribute or cannot be sued, the paying partner, rather than the third party, bears the loss." Bromberg & Ribstein on Partnership § 6.02(f).

———

(c) DISTRIBUTIONS, REMUNERATION, AND CAPITAL CONTRIBUTIONS

———

UNIFORM PARTNERSHIP ACT §§ 18(a), (b), (c), (d), (f)

———

REVISED UNIFORM PARTNERSHIP ACT § 401(a)–(e), (h)

[See Appendix]

———

QUESTION

Suppose A, B, and C form a partnership. A contributes 90% of the capital, and B and C each contribute 5%. All work full-time in the partnership business, with roughly equal responsibilities. Nothing is said in the partnership agreement concerning how partnership profits will be divided. If the partnership makes a profit in a given year, how is it to be divided?

———

(d) CAPITAL ACCOUNTS AND DRAWS

———

W. Klein & J. Coffee, Business Organization and Finance 80–84

Seventh ed., 2000.

... CONTRIBUTIONS, ACCOUNTS, AND RETURNS

A.   CAPITAL ACCOUNTS

Suppose that Abe, Bill, Pamela and Morris have formed a partnership for the acquisition and operation of a grocery store. Abe and Bill each are to contribute $15,000 and Pamela $20,000, in cash or in property to be used in the business. Morris will contribute neither cash nor property but will agree to manage the store for five years and will receive a salary slightly lower than what he might earn elsewhere. If the partnership follows customary bookkeeping patterns, its books will show the following information under a heading that is likely to be called "Capital Accounts":

Abe	$15,000
Bill	15,000
Pamela	20,000
Morris	0
Total	$50,000

... In the absence of an agreement to the contrary, if the business were sold for cash, each partner would be entitled to receive an amount equal to his or her capital account, if available. Any excess or deficit would be shared in accordance with each partner's share of gain and loss (a point to be illustrated below).

Capital contribution does not necessarily control the sharing of gain and loss, and shares of gain may differ from shares of loss. For example, our four partners could agree that each will be entitled to an equal 25 percent share of any profits, despite the difference in initial contribution. Indeed, this is the result that will be provided by the Uniform Partnership Act (Sec. 18(a)) in the absence of an agreement to the contrary. At the same time, and again in the absence of an agreement to the contrary, no partner will be entitled to interest on his or her capital account. Losses might be allocated equally among the partners (again, the result in the absence of express agreement) or might be allocated first pro rata among the contributors of initial capital, to the extent of such capital, and then, perhaps, equally among all partners. ...

Suppose that all profits and losses are to be shared equally, and suppose that at the end of the first year of operation the profit (after the payment of Morris's salary) is $20,000, or $5,000 per partner. One way of recording this outcome would be to adjust the capital accounts, which would then appear as follows:

Abe	$20,000 *
Bill	20,000
Pamela	25,000
Morris	5,000
Total	$70,000

*$15,000 initial capital plus $5,000 profit share.

If, on the other hand, the firm experienced a loss of $20,000 in its first year of operations, the capital accounts would be:

Abe	$10,000
Bill	10,000
Pamela	15,000
Morris	(5,000)
Total	$30,000

(Parentheses around a number indicate that it is a negative amount.) If, at this point, the business were sold for exactly the amount of the total capital accounts, $30,000, Morris would be required to contribute $5,000 and the resulting total, $35,000, would then be distributed $10,000 each to Abe and Bill and $15,000 to Pamela. This result may seem to be hard on Morris, and there is some legal authority for relieving him of the debt, at least to the extent that he contributed services without adequate compensation. The issue is one that the partners should think about at the outset. They might well agree that losses are to be shared by the partners in accordance with their initial capital contributions. . . .

B.   DRAW

Thus far we have referred to profits and losses, which are bookkeeping concepts. It is vital to note that profit does not necessarily generate any spare cash. For example, a new retail store may be highly profitable but may need all its profits to expand its inventory. And even if a firm has had profits and does have spare cash, the partners are not automatically entitled to receive a cash payment. There is a separate term—called "draw"—that is used to describe cash distributions to partners. The amount of the draw of each partner is determined by majority vote of the partners (again, in the absence of some other express agreement) and may be more or less than the profit. . . .

Returning now to the bookkeeping effects of a draw, suppose that our grocery store partnership generates an accounting profit of $20,000 in the first year of its operations. . . . We have just seen how this net profit figure can be translated into adjustments to partner capital accounts. Now suppose that there is a draw. Suppose, for example, that the partners agree that each is to be paid $3,000 from partnership funds. The $3,000 would reduce the capital accounts, so they would then be:

Abe	$17,000 *
Bill	17,000
Pamela	22,000
Morris	2,000
Total	$58,000

*$15,000 initial capital account, plus $5,000 profit share, minus $3,000 draw.

Next, assume that there is a loss of $20,000 in the first year, instead of a profit; that the partnership agreement allocates this loss equally among all the partners; and that despite the loss, there is a cash distribution (draw) of $3,000 to each partner. The partnership capital accounts would then be as follows:

Abe	$ 7,000*
Bill	7,000
Pamela	12,000
Morris	(8,000)
Total	$18,000

* $15,000 initial capital account, minus $5,000 loss share, minus $3,000 draw.

45

All of this makes sense if you think about it for a few moments. Bear in mind that the capital accounts are not expected to correspond to values in the firm but instead are merely intended to reflect the relative claims of the partners to the assets of the partnership, which is of importance mostly in the case of withdrawal of a partner or liquidation of the partnership. A partner's share of profit can be thought of as something that he or she has earned and reinvested in the firm. The draw can be thought of as earnings or capital taken out of the firm. The capital account allows us to keep track of relative claims where initial contributions and profit shares differ. The same function is served where, for one reason or another, partners do not draw from the firm amounts strictly in proportion to their profit shares.

C. CAPITAL ACCOUNTS AND VALUE OF A PARTNER'S INTEREST

To illustrate the difference between capital account and value, and the role of the capital account, suppose that the partnership capital accounts stand as follows:

Abe	$17,000
Bill	17,000
Pamela	22,000
Morris	2,000
Total	$58,000

Suppose that the business has increased in value because of the construction of a large housing development nearby. This is the kind of gain that [under the principles of accounting] ordinarily would not be reflected on the partnership books as long as the firm continues to operate with the same owners. Now suppose that the business is sold for $78,000 cash, net of all debts or other obligations. There is a surplus of $20,000 above the amount in the capital accounts (that is, above the amount of the initial contributions increased by profits and decreased by distributions to the partners). This $20,000 can be thought of as previously unrecorded profit; it would be allocated equally among the partners ($5,000 apiece), so that each partner would receive the following amount:

Abe	$22,000 *
Bill	22,000
Pamela	27,000
Morris	7,000
Total	$78,000

*$17,000 current capital account, plus $5,000 share of profit on sale of business.

Finally, assume that the store is sold for less than the amount in the capital accounts—for example, for $38,000. Here there is a previously unrecognized loss of $20,000. In the absence of an agreement to the contrary, the loss would be borne equally by all the partners (again, $5,000 apiece). The relative claims of the partners would therefore be as follows:

Abe	$12,000
Bill	12,000
Pamela	17,000
Morris	(3,000)
Total	$38,000

SECTION 4.   THE AUTHORITY OF A PARTNER

UNIFORM PARTNERSHIP ACT §§ 3, 4(3), 9, 10, 11, 12, 13, 14

REVISED UNIFORM PARTNERSHIP ACT
§§ 301, 302, 303, 304, 305, 306, 308

[See Appendix]

NOTE ON THE AUTHORITY OF PARTNERS UNDER THE UPA

The basic rule governing a partner's actual authority under the UPA is that each partner is an agent of the partnership for the purpose of its business. This rule interacts with the UPA's rule on a partner's apparent authority, which, as the following excerpts show, is both controversial and somewhat ambiguous.

CRANE, THE UNIFORM PARTNERSHIP ACT—A CRITICISM, 28 Harv.L.Rev. 762, 779–80 (1915). "The partner has under this Act authority to bind the partnership by any act 'for apparently carrying on in the usual way the business of the partnership of which he is a member.' This may be taken to mean an act within the apparent course of business as carried on by his particular firm. It has been generally held [before the adoption of the UPA] that not only the course of business of his firm may be relied on as evidence of his authority, but the course of business of other firms in the same locality engaged in the same general line of business. It is submitted that a narrower rule imposes an undue burden on the third person to learn the habits of the particular firm, and because this Act is susceptible of a narrow interpretation the language of the English Act, 'any act for the carrying on in the usual way business of the kind carried on by the firm,' should be substituted."

LEWIS, THE UNIFORM PARTNERSHIP ACT—A REPLY TO MR. CRANE'S CRITICISM [pt. 2], 29 Harv.L.Rev. 291, 299–300 (1916). "[In the drafting of the U.P.A., it was argued,] as Mr. Crane has argued, that to declare that the inquiry should be: 'How is this partnership apparently carried on?' imposes an undue burden on the third person to learn the habits of this particular firm. On the other hand, it was contended that the wording of the English Act was susceptible of the interpretation that a partnership was bound, if the act was a usual act in the business of the kind carried on by the partnership, even though it was apparent that this particular partnership did not carry on the business in that manner. The argument which finally led the Commissioners to adopt the present wording was that it emphasizes the fundamental reason why a partnership is ever bound by an act of a partner not authorized by his co-partners, namely, that partners are bound because they have held him out to do that class of acts. The question therefore which should be determined in each case is, was it an act for apparently carrying on in the usual way the business of the partnership of which he is a member?"

———

BURNS v. GONZALEZ, 439 S.W.2d 128 (Tex.Civ.App.1969). Bosquez and Gonzalez were partners in a business that sold broadcast time on a radio station located in Mexico. The station was owned and operated by a Mexican corporation, Radiodifusora. Bosquez and Gonzalez each owned 50% of Radiodifusora's stock, and Bosquez was its president. In 1957, Radiodifusora made a contract with Burns, which it failed to perform. Subsequently, Bosquez, purporting to act on his own behalf and on behalf of the partnership, executed a $40,000 promissory note payable to Burns, partly in exchange for Burns's promise not to sue Radiodifusora. Burns sued Bosquez and Gonzalez on the note, as partners. Gonzalez argued that Bosquez had no authority to execute the note on the partnership's behalf. In reviewing a jury verdict in favor of defendants, the court stated:

> [Because the] express limitation on the authority of Bosquez was unknown to Burns, then, under the language of [UPA] Sec. 9(1), his act in executing the note would bind the partnership if such act can be classified as an act "for apparently carrying on in the usual way the business of the partnership."
>
> As we interpret Sec. 9(1), the act of a partner binds the firm, absent an express limitation of authority known to the party dealing with such partner, if such act is for the purpose of "apparently carrying on" the business of the partnership in the way in which other firms engaged in the same business in the locality usually transact business, or in the way in which the particular partnership usually transacts its business. In this case, [however,] there is no evidence relating to the manner in which firms engaged in the sale of advertising time on radio stations usually transact business.

———

NOTE ON THE AUTHORITY OF PARTNERS UNDER RUPA

For most practical purposes, the major difference between the UPA and RUPA concerning a partner's authority is that RUPA § 301(1) makes clear, as the UPA did not, that a partnership is bound by an act of the partner for apparently carrying on in the usual way (i) the partnership business or (ii) business *of the kind* carried on by the partnership. The Comment to § 301(1) states:

> Section 301(1).... clarifies that a partner's apparent authority includes acts for carrying on in the ordinary course "business of the kind carried on by the partnership," not just the business of the particular partnership in question. The UPA is ambiguous on this point, but there is some authority for an expanded construction.... See, e.g., Burns v. Gonzalez, 439 S.W.2d 128, 131 (Tex.Civ.App.1969) (dictum)....

The treatment of authority under RUPA also differs from the UPA in certain other respects. For example, RUPA § 302 provides elaborate rules concerning when a transfer of partnership property is binding. In addition:

1. RUPA § 301 makes subtle shifts in determining when a third person's knowledge or notice of a restriction on a partner's authority will be effective to prevent partnership liability from arising. "Under UPA section 9(1), the partnership was not bound by the unauthorized actions of a partner if the third party had 'knowledge' of the partner's lack of authority. Under UPA section 9(1), a third party had knowledge when he or she had actual knowledge or 'when he [or she] has knowledge of such other facts as in the circumstances shows bad faith.' This latter language creates an implied or inquiry notice, the exact parameters of which are ill-defined. Under RUPA, the third party will not be placed under a duty of inquiry or be deemed to have notice from the facts and circumstances. Only actual knowledge or receipt of a notification of a partner's lack of authority will meet the standard." Merrill, Partnership Property and Partnership Authority Under the Revised Uniform Partnership Act, 49 Bus.Law. 83, 88–89 (1993).

2. RUPA § 303 enables a partnership to file a "Statement of Partnership Authority." Under § 303, a *grant* of authority set forth in such a Statement is normally conclusive in favor of third persons, even if they have no actual knowledge of the Statement, unless they have actual knowledge that the partner has no such authority. However, a *limitation* on a partner's authority that is contained in such a Statement, other than a limitation on the partner's authority to transfer real property, will not be effective unless the third party knows of the limitation or the Statement has been delivered to him. A limitation, in a Statement of Partnership Authority, of a partner's authority to transfer partnership real property is effective against all third persons if a certified copy of the Statement is filed in the real-property recording office.

Why would a partnership want to file a Statement that may expand a partner's authority, but will not limit a partner's authority unless it is not only filed but also delivered? One answer is that persons who deal with a partnership may require such a Statement to ensure themselves that the partnership will be bound. Furthermore, "[in] the process of searching for the grant of authority, the third party will acquire actual knowledge of any restriction on authority in a filed statement. [And] the ... partners may protect themselves by delivering the statement to all known creditors, actual or potential." Merrill, supra, at 89.

———

BROMBERG & RIBSTEIN ON PARTNERSHIP § 4.02(a)(4). "It is not clear what is meant by the inclusion of 'apparently' in U.P.A. § 9(1) and R.U.P.A. § 301.... 'Apparently' does probably *expand* liability to include transactions that were not in the usual course but appeared to the plaintiff to be so...."

SECTION 5.   LIABILITY FOR PARTNERSHIP OBLIGATIONS

———

UNIFORM PARTNERSHIP ACT §§ 9, 13, 14, 15, 16, 17, 36

———

REVISED UNIFORM PARTNERSHIP ACT §§ 305, 306, 307, 308

[See Appendix]

———

NOTE ON LIABILITY FOR PARTNERSHIP OBLIGATIONS

1. *UPA.* The provisions of the Uniform Partnership Act governing liability for partnership obligations reflect an amalgam of the entity and aggregate theories. On the one hand, UPA §§ 9, 13, and 14 make "the partnership" liable for defined acts of the partners. It might seem to follow that this liability could be enforced by a suit against the partnership. However, the UPA does not authorize such a suit, because it does not recognize a partnership as an entity, and unless authorized by statute, suit normally cannot be brought against an association that is not an entity. Indeed, the UPA goes to the opposite extreme. Under UPA § 15(a), partners are *jointly and severally* liable for wrongful acts and omissions of the partnership (such as torts) and breaches of trust. Under UPA § 15(b), however, partners are only *jointly* liable "for all other debts and obligations of the partnership." At common law, if an obligation is "joint and several" the obligors can be sued either jointly or separately. If, however, an obligation is only "joint" the obligee must join all the obligors in the same

suit (subject to a few exceptions where jurisdiction over all the obligors cannot be obtained). See C. Clark, Handbook of the Law of Code Pleading 373–74 (2d ed. 1947). Thus under the UPA, an action on a partnership's contractual obligation must be brought against all the partners, and if even one partner is not joined, the action can be dismissed on motion by the partners who were joined.

The inability of a partnership creditor to sue a partnership in its own name, under the UPA, is obviously undesirable, and many states have statutorily patched up the UPA rule by adopting Common Name Statutes, which explicitly allow a partnership to be sued in its own name. An example is N.Y.Civ.Prac.L. & R. § 1025: "Two or more persons conducting a business as a partnership may sue or be sued in the partnership name...." Under such statutes, a judgment is binding on the partnership property and on the individual property of all partners who are served.

The need to join all the partners in a suit to establish liability on a contract claim is also undesirable. Some states address this issue by making all partnership liabilities joint and several, rather than joint. Other states have adopted Joint Debtor Statutes, which provide that a suit against joint obligors can proceed even if some of the obligors are not joined. See, e.g., Cal.Civ.Proc.Code § 410.70. Under such statutes, a judgment is binding on both the joint (partnership) property and on the property of those partners who are served.

2. *RUPA.* Unlike the UPA, RUPA § 307(a) specifically provides that a partnership may both *sue* and *be sued* in its own name. Furthermore, RUPA § 306 provides that partners are jointly and severally liable for *all* obligations of the partnership. However, RUPA adds a new barrier to *collecting* against an individual partner. Under RUPA § 307, a judgment against a partner based on a claim against the partnership normally cannot be satisfied against the partner's individual assets, unless and until a judgment on the same claim has been rendered against the partnership and a writ of execution on the judgment has been returned unsatisfied. To put this differently, RUPA § 307 adopts an exhaustion rule, under which partnership assets must be exhausted before a partner's individual assets can be reached. (The exhaustion rule is made subject to certain exceptions, one of which is that the rule does not apply if the partnership is in bankruptcy.) Thus as the Comment to RUPA § 306 points out, "Joint and several liability under RUPA differs ... from the classic model [of joint and several liability outside RUPA], which permits a judgment creditor to proceed immediately against any of the joint and several judgment debtors."

In effect, RUPA takes an aggregate-like approach to a partner's *liability*, but an entity-like approach to *collecting judgments* based on that liability. (RUPA § 307 also provides that, subject to certain exceptions, a judgment against a partnership is not by itself a judgment against a partner, and cannot be satisfied from a partner's assets unless there is also a judgment against the partner.)

51

SECTION 6.   PARTNERSHIP INTERESTS AND PARTNERSHIP PROPERTY

———

UNIFORM PARTNERSHIP ACT §§ 8, 18(g), 24, 25, 26, 27, 28

———

REVISED UNIFORM PARTNERSHIP ACT §§ 203, 204, 501, 502, 503, 504

[See Appendix]

———

Rapoport v. 55 Perry Co.

New York Supreme Court, Appellate Division, 1975.
50 A.D.2d 54, 376 N.Y.S.2d 147.

Cross appeals from an order of the Supreme Court (HILDA G. SCHWARTZ, J.), entered July 16, 1975 in New York County, which denied a motion by plaintiffs for summary judgment and a cross motion by defendants for summary judgment dismissing the complaint. . . .

■ TILZER, J. In 1969, Simon, Genia and Ury Rapoport entered into a partnership agreement with Morton, Jerome and Burton Parnes, forming the partnership known as 55 Perry Company. Pursuant to the agreement, each of the families owned 50% of the partnership interests. In December of 1974 Simon and Genia Rapoport assigned a 10% interest of their share in the partnership to their adult children, Daniel and Kalia. The Parnes defendants were advised of the assignment and an amended partnership certificate was filed in the County Clerk's office indicating the addition of Daniel and Kalia as partners. However, when the plaintiffs, thereafter, requested the Parnes defendants to execute an amended partnership agreement to reflect the above changes in the partnership, the Parnes refused, taking the position that the partnership agreement did not permit the introduction of new partners without consent of all the existing partners. Thereafter, the plaintiffs Rapoport brought this action seeking a declaration that Simon and Genia Rapoport had an absolute right to assign their interests to their adult children without consent of the defendants and that such assignment was authorized pursuant to paragraph 12 of the partnership agreement. The plaintiffs further sought to have Daniel and Kalia be declared partners in 55 Perry Company and have their names entered upon the books of the partnership as partners. The defendants Parnes interposed an answer, taking the position that the partnership agreement did not permit admission of additional partners without consent of all the existing partners and that the filing of the amended certificate of partnership was unauthorized. After joinder of issue plaintiffs moved for summary judgment and although the defendants did not cross-move for similar relief, such was, nevertheless, requested in their answering papers.

On the motion for summary judgment both parties agreed that there were no issues of fact and that there was only a question of the interpretation of the written documents which should be disposed of as a matter of law by the court. Nevertheless, the court below found that the agreement was ambiguous and that there was a triable issue with respect to the intent of the parties. We disagree and conclude that the agreement is without ambiguity and that pursuant to the terms of the agreement and of the Partnership Law, consent of the Parnes defendants was required in order to admit Daniel Rapoport and Kalia Shalleck to the partnership.

Plaintiffs, in support of their contention that they have an absolute right to assign their interests in the partnership to their adult children and that the children must be admitted to the partnership as partners rely on paragraph 12 of the partnership agreement which provides as follows: "No partner or partners shall have the authority to transfer, sell ... assign or in any way dispose of the partnership realty and/or personalty and shall not have the authority to sell, transfer, assign ... his or their share in this firm, nor enter into any agreement as a result of which any person shall become interested with him in this firm, unless the same is agreed to in writing by a majority of the partners as determined by the percentage of ownership ... except for members of his immediate family who have attained majority, in which case no such consent shall be required." As indicated, plaintiffs argue that the above provision expressly authorizes entry of their adult children into the partnership. Defendants, on the other hand, maintain that paragraph 12 provides only for the right of a partner to assign or transfer a share of the profits in the partnership. We agree with that construction of the agreement.

A reading of the partnership agreement indicates that the parties intended to observe the differences, as set forth in the Partnership Law, between assignees of a partnership interest and the admission into the partnership itself of new partners. The Partnership Law provides that subject to any contrary agreement between the partners, "[n]o person can become a member of a partnership without the consent of all the partners." (Partnership Law, § 40, subd 7.)[2] Subdivision 1 of section 53 of the Partnership Law provides that an assignee of an interest in the partnership is not entitled "to interfere in the management or administration of the partnership business" but is merely entitled to receive "the profits to which the assigning partner would otherwise be entitled." Additionally, section 50 of the Partnership Law indicates the differences between the rights of an assignee and a new partner. That section states that the "property rights of a partner are (a) his rights in specific partnership property, (b) his interest in the partnership, and (c) his right to participate

2. The Partnership Law is New York's version of the UPA. (footnote by ed.)

in the management." On the other hand, as already indicated above, an assignee is excluded in the absence of agreement from interfering in the management of the partnership business and from access to the partnership books and information about partnership transactions. (Partnership Law, § 53.)

The effect, therefore, of the various provisions of the Partnership Law, above discussed, is that unless the parties have agreed otherwise, a person cannot become a member of a partnership without consent of all the partners whereas an assignment of a partnership interest may be made without consent, but the assignee is entitled only to receive the profits of the assigning partner. And, as already stated, the partnership agreement herein clearly took cognizance of the differences between an assignment of an interest in the partnership as compared to the full rights of a partner as set forth in section 50 of the Partnership Law. Paragraph 12 of the agreement by its language has reference to section 53 of the Partnership Law dealing with an "assignment of partner's interest." It (par 12) refers to assignments, encumbrances and agreements "as a result of which any person shall become interested with (the assignor) in this firm." That paragraph does not contain language with respect to admitting a partner to the partnership with all rights to participate in the management of its affairs. Moreover, interpretation of paragraph 12 in this manner is consistent with other provisions of the partnership agreement. For example, in paragraph 15 of the agreement, the following is provided:

> "In the event of the death of any partner the business of this firm shall continue with the heir, or distributee providing he has reached majority, or fiduciary of the deceased partner having the right to succeed the deceased partner with the same rights and privileges and the same obligations, pursuant to all of the terms hereof."

In that paragraph, therefore, there is specific provision to succeed to all the privileges and obligations of a partner—language which is completely absent from paragraph 12.

Accordingly, it appears that contrary to plaintiffs' contention that paragraph 12 was intended to give the parties the right to transfer a full partnership interest to adult children, without consent of all other partners (an agreement which would vary the rights otherwise existing pursuant to Partnership Law, § 40, subd 7) that paragraph was instead intended to limit a partner with respect to his right to assign a partnership interest as provided for under section 53 of the Partnership Law (i.e., the right to profits)—to the extent of prohibiting such assignments without consent of other partners except to children of the existing partners who have reached majority. Therefore, it must be concluded that pursuant to the terms of the partnership agreement, the plaintiffs could not transfer a full partnership interest to their children and that the children only have the rights as assignees to receive a share of the partnership income and profits of their assignors.

Accordingly, the order entered July 16, 1975 should be modified on the law to grant summary judgment in favor of the defendants to the extent of declaring that the partnership agreement does not permit entry into the partnership of new partners, including adult children of the partners who have reached their majority, without consent of all the partners; [and] that the plaintiffs, pursuant to the terms of the agreement, had the right to assign their interests to their adult children but that such children, i.e., Daniel Rapoport and Kalia Shalleck, have not become partners but only have the rights of assignees to receive a share of the partnership income and profits of their assignors. . . .

■ NUNEZ, J. (dissenting). I agree with Special Term that the written partnership agreement providing for the assignment of partners' shares to members of their immediate families without the consent of the other partners is ambiguous and that there is a triable issue as to intent. The agreement being ambiguous, construction is a mixed question of law and fact and resolution thereof to determine the parties' intent should await a trial. . . .

■ STEVENS, P.J., KUPFERMAN and MURPHY, JJ., concur with TILZER, J.; NUNEZ, J., dissents in an opinion. . . .

————

NOTE ON PARTNERSHIP PROPERTY

1. *The UPA.* Property that is used by a partnership may be either partnership property or the property of individual partners that is in effect loaned to the partnership. The issue whether property used by the partnership is partnership property or the property of individual partners may be important for several different reasons. First, the issue may be important for purposes of determining who has the power to transfer the property. Property owned by the partnership can be transferred by the partnership. Property loaned to the partnership cannot be. Second, the issue may be important if creditors of the partnership are competing with creditors of an individual partner, and the question arises whether any given property is owned by the partnership or owned by the partner and loaned to the partnership. Third, the issue may be important if the partnership is dissolved: If property used by the partnership is partnership property, on dissolution the property must be sold along with other partnership assets, and the proceeds of the sale must be distributed among the partners. In contrast, if property used by the partnership is the individual property of a partner, on dissolution the property must normally be returned directly to that partner, rather than sold for the account of all the partners.[1] This third issue may be especially important if the property is crucial to the partnership's business, so that as a practical matter whoever owns the property has the ability to continue the business.

1. But see Pav–Saver Corp. v. Vasso Corp., 143 Ill.App.3d 1013, 97 Ill.Dec. 760, 493 N.E.2d 423 (1986) (wrongfully dissolving partner held not entitled to return of property).

If the aggregate theory of the UPA was strictly applied, a partnership could not own property. Rather, the property that the partners think of as partnership property would as a matter of law be held by the individual partners as joint tenants or tenants in common. For a variety of reasons, such a regime would be wholly impracticable. Accordingly, in the matter of partnership property, as in several other matters, the UPA lays down rules that effectively treat the partnership *as if* it were an entity.

This objective is accomplished largely with smoke and mirrors. UPA § 8 recognizes the concept of "partnership property," and explicitly permits real property to be held in the partnership's name. (Even before the UPA, it was well settled that personal property could be so held.) However, UPA § 25(1) provides that "partnership property" is owned by the *partners,* under the ingenuous nomenclature, *tenancy in partnership.* UPA § 25(2) then systematically strips from the individual partners every incident normally associated with ownership. Under § 25(2)(a), a partner has no right to possess partnership property as an individual. Under § 25(2)(b), a partner cannot individually assign his rights in specific partnership property. Under § 25(2)(c), a partner's rights in specific partnership property cannot be subject to attachment or execution by a creditor of the partner in the latter's individual capacity. Under § 25(2)(d), when the partner dies his right in specific partnership property does not devolve on his heirs or legatees. Under Section 25(2)(e), widows, heirs, and next of kin cannot claim dower, curtesy,or allowances in the partner's right to specific partnership property. In short, under the UPA in theory individual partners own the partnership property, but in practice all the incidents of ownership are vested in the partnership, so that the "tenan[cy] in partnership" rule of the UPA has no real-world significance.

2. *RUPA,* which confers entity status on partnerships, drops the elaborate tenancy-in-partnership apparatus of the UPA. RUPA § 203 provides that "Property acquired by a partnership is property of the partnership and not the partners individually." RUPA § 204 then sets out a series of rules and presumptions concerning whether any given property is partnership property or the separate property of a partner. These provisions are supplemented by § 501, which provides that "A partner is not a co-owner of partnership property and has no interest in partnership property which can be transferred, either voluntarily or involuntarily." The purpose of § 501 is to explicitly abolish the UPA concept of tenancy in partnership.

————

NOTE ON PARTNERSHIP INTERESTS

1. *The Partner's Interest in the Partnership.* Although a partner does not own partnership property under the UPA except in some metaphysical sense, he does own his *interest* in the partnership, that is, his share of the partnership. The net result is a functional two-level ownership structure that is somewhat comparable to the two-level ownership structure in a

corporation. In the case of a corporation, the corporation owns the corporate property, and the shareholder owns her shares in the corporation. In the case of a UPA partnership, in practice (although not in theory) the partnership owns the partnership property, and the partner owns her interest in the partnership.

2. *Assignment.* As compared to ordinary property interests, a partnership interest is conditioned in one very important respect. Normally, the owner of a property interest can freely sell it, and a creditor can freely levy on it. In contrast, although a partnership interest is assignable, a partner cannot make an assignment of his partnership interest that would substitute the transferee as a partner in the transferor's place, because no person can become a partner without the consent of all the partners. Correspondingly, a creditor cannot levy on a partnership interest in such a way as to be substituted as a partner; nor can a creditor recover her debt by selling the partnership interest to a third party who will be substituted as a partner. Accordingly, as pointed out in *Rapoport,* the assignee of a partnership interest does not become a partner (unless all the other partners consent), and has no right to information about the partnership and no right to inspect the partnership books. However, as long as the partnership continues in existence, the assignee of a partnership interest does have a right to receive the distributions to which the assigning partner would otherwise be entitled; and on dissolution the assignee has a right to receive the assigning partner's interest. In practice, despite the limitations on the assignor's rights partnership interests have a fairly high degree of assignability. See A. Bromberg, Enforcement of Partnership Obligations—Who is Sued for The Partnership?, 71 Neb. L. Rev. 143, 240 (1992).

A partner who has assigned her partnership interest remains a partner. However, RUPA § 601(4)(ii) explicitly permits the nonassigning partners to expel the assignor from the partnership, and UPA § 31(c) permits the nonassigning partners to dissolve the partnership as of right even if the partnership is not at will.

3. *Partnership Creditors.*

a. *UPA.* A partner's *separate creditor* (that is a creditor who has extended credit to a partner as an individual, rather than extending credit to a partnership) is in a position somewhat comparable to the assignee of a partnership interest. Under UPA § 28, if such a creditor obtains a judgment, he can get a *charging order* on the partner's partnership interest. Such an order will effectively give the creditor the right to be paid the partnership distributions to which the debtor-partner would be otherwise entitled. The creditor can foreclose on the partnership interest under UPA § 28, and thereby cause its sale. In that case, the buyer of the interest has the right to compel dissolution if (i) the term of the partnership has expired, or (ii) the partnership is at will. Alternatively, the creditor may put the individual partner into bankruptcy, which will result in dissolution of the partnership under UPA § 31(5).

Bromberg & Ribstein on Partnership § 3.05(d)(3)(4) comment as follows on charging orders:

After [a charging order is entered, the debtor partner] continues to be a partner in all respects except distributions and withdrawals from the firm. Moreover, the charging creditor is not yet in the position even of an assignee of the interest. This is apparent because UPA § 28(2) and RUPA § 504 refer to the further step of foreclosure on the debtor partner's partnership interest, which would be necessary only if the interest had not already been assigned to the creditor. By foreclosing, the creditor can obtain a sale of the interest at which the interest is purchased by the creditor or a third party. . . .

Even after foreclosure and sale, the creditor may be far from collecting the debt. At the foreclosure sale only the partner's interest, not specific assets of the partnership, is sold. . . . It is unlikely that the interest will bring a high price from third parties, because of the limited role to which the purchaser is relegated. If the creditor is the purchaser, it will still be entitled only to receive the charged partner's cash flow. Moreover, until dissolution the creditor has no right to an accounting.

One change in the creditor's current status as a result of the foreclosure and sale is that the creditor now owns the partner's entire financial interest in the partnership, including all amounts ultimately due the partner on dissolution after settlement of liabilities. Another is that the purchaser can exercise the assignee's power to seek a judicial dissolution under UPA § 32(2) or RUPA § 801(6) . . . On dissolution, the creditor or other purchaser of the interest at foreclosure can finally obtain whatever share would have come to the debtor partner after payment of all partnership creditors and claims of co-partners.

b. *RUPA.* RUPA § 504 continues UPA § 28 largely unchanged in substance. RUPA § 504 does add some details that are not found in UPA § 28, but for the most part these details are consistent with the case law under § 28. Like the UPA, RUPA § 801(a) provides that a transferee of a partner's transferable interest is entitled to judicial dissolution on the partnership (i) at any time in a partnership at will, and (ii) after the expiration of the partnership's term or the completion of the undertaking in a partnership for a particular undertaking.

4. *Priorities.*

a. *UPA.* A major problem in partnership law concerns the relative priorities of creditors of the partnership (*partnership creditors*) and creditors of a partner in the partner's individual capacity (*separate creditors*). UPA § 40(h) provides that: (i) partnership creditors have priority over separate creditors as to partnership assets, and (ii) separate creditors have priority over partnership creditors as to the individual assets of the partners. See also UPA § 36(4). This rule, which was also in the Bankruptcy Act prior to 1978, is known as the "dual priorities" or "jingle" rule. The rule was widely criticized on the ground that it kept partnership creditors from getting the full benefit of personal liability of the individual partners.

The Bankruptcy Reform Act of 1978 responded to that criticism. Under Chapter 7 of the present Bankruptcy Code, in a partnership bankruptcy the partnership creditors have priority over separate creditors as to partnership assets, but if debts to partnership creditors remain unpaid after partnership assets are exhausted, partnership creditors are put on a parity with separate creditors in dividing up the partner's individual assets. 11 U.S.C. § 723(c). Thus in the usual case, the UPA jingle rule is preempted by the Bankruptcy Code.

    b. *RUPA*. RUPA drops the dual priorities rule of the UPA, to reflect the abolition of the jingle rule in the Bankruptcy Code.

SECTION 7. THE PARTNER'S DUTY OF LOYALTY

UNIFORM PARTNERSHIP ACT § 21

REVISED UNIFORM PARTNERSHIP ACT
§§ 103(a), (b)(3), (5), 104, 403, 404, 405

[See Appendix]

Meinhard v. Salmon

New York Court of Appeals, 1928.
249 N.Y. 458, 164 N.E. 545.

Appeal from a judgment of the Appellate Division of the Supreme Court in the first judicial department, entered June 28, 1928, modifying and affirming as modified a judgment in favor of plaintiff entered upon the report of a referee.

■ CARDOZO, CH. J. On April 10, 1902, Louisa M. Gerry leased to the defendant Walter J. Salmon the premises known as the Hotel Bristol at the northwest corner of Forty-second street and Fifth avenue in the city of New York. The lease was for a term of twenty years, commencing May 1, 1902, and ending April 30, 1922. The lessee undertook to change the hotel building for use as shops and offices at a cost of $200,000. Alterations and additions were to be accretions to the land.

Salmon, while in course of treaty with the lessor as to the execution of the lease, was in course of treaty with Meinhard, the plaintiff, for the necessary funds. The result was a joint venture with terms embodied in a writing. Meinhard was to pay to Salmon half of the moneys requisite to reconstruct, alter, manage and operate the property. Salmon was to pay to

59

Meinhard 40 per cent of the net profits for the first five years of the lease and 50 per cent for the years thereafter. If there were losses, each party was to bear them equally. Salmon, however, was to have sole power to "manage, lease, underlet and operate" the building. There were to be certain pre-emptive rights for each in the contingency of death.

The two were coadventurers, subject to fiduciary duties akin to those of partners (King v. Barnes, 109 N.Y. 267). As to this we are all agreed. The heavier weight of duty rested, however, upon Salmon. He was a coadventurer with Meinhard, but he was manager as well. During the early years of the enterprise, the building, reconstructed, was operated at a loss. If the relation had then ended, Meinhard as well as Salmon would have carried a heavy burden. Later the profits became large with the result that for each of the investors there came a rich return. For each, the venture had its phases of fair weather and of foul. The two were in it jointly, for better or for worse.

When the lease was near its end, Elbridge T. Gerry had become the owner of the reversion. He owned much other property in the neighborhood, one lot adjoining the Bristol Building on Fifth avenue and four lots on Forty-second street. He had a plan to lease the entire tract for a long term to some one who would destroy the buildings then existing, and put up another in their place. In the latter part of 1921, he submitted such a project to several capitalists and dealers. He was unable to carry it through with any of them. Then, in January, 1922, with less than four months of the lease to run, he approached the defendant Salmon. The result was a new lease to the Midpoint Realty Company, which is owned and controlled by Salmon, a lease covering the whole tract, and involving a huge outlay. The term is to be twenty years, but successive covenants for renewal will extend it to a maximum of eighty years at the will of either party. The existing buildings may remain unchanged for seven years. They are then to be torn down, and a new building to cost $3,000,000 is to be placed upon the site. The rental, which under the Bristol lease was only $55,000, is to be from $350,000 to $475,000 for the properties so combined. Salmon personally guaranteed the performance by the lessee of the covenants of the new lease until such time as the new building had been completed and fully paid for.

The lease between Gerry and the Midpoint Realty Company was signed and delivered on January 25, 1922. Salmon had not told Meinhard anything about it. Whatever his motive may have been, he had kept the negotiations to himself. Meinhard was not informed even of the bare existence of a project. The first that he knew of it was in February when the lease was an accomplished fact. He then made demand on the defendants that the lease be held in trust as an asset of the venture, making offer upon the trial to share the personal obligations incidental to the guaranty. The demand was followed by refusal, and later by this suit. A referee gave judgment for the plaintiff, limiting the plaintiff's interest in the lease, however, to 25 per cent. The limitation was on the theory that the plaintiff's equity was to be restricted to one-half of so much of the value of the lease as was contributed or represented by the occupation of the Bristol site. Upon cross-appeals to the Appellate Division, the judgment was modified so as to enlarge the equitable interest to one-half of the whole lease. With this enlargement of plaintiff's interest, there went, of course, a corresponding enlargement of his attendant obligations. The case is now here on an appeal by the defendants.

Joint adventurers, like copartners, owe to one another, while the enterprise continues, the duty of the finest loyalty. Many forms of conduct permissible in a workaday world for those acting at arm's length, are forbidden to those bound by fiduciary ties. A trustee is held to something stricter than the morals of the market place. Not honesty alone, but the punctilio of an honor the most sensitive, is then the standard of behavior. As to this there has developed a tradition that is unbending and inveterate. Uncompromising rigidity has been the attitude of courts of equity when petitioned to undermine the rule of undivided loyalty by the "disintegrating erosion" of particular exceptions (Wendt v. Fischer, 243 N.Y. 439, 444). Only thus has the level of conduct for fiduciaries been kept at a level higher than that trodden by the crowd. It will not consciously be lowered by any judgment of this court.

The owner of the reversion, Mr. Gerry, had vainly striven to find a tenant who would favor his ambitious scheme of demolition and construction. Baffled in the search, he turned to the defendant Salmon in possession of the Bristol, the keystone of the project. He figured to himself beyond a doubt that the man in possession would prove a likely customer. To the eye of an observer, Salmon held the lease as owner in his own right, for himself and no one else. In fact he held it as a fiduciary, for himself and another, sharers in a common venture. If this fact had been proclaimed, if the lease by its terms had run in favor of a partnership, Mr. Gerry, we may fairly assume, would have laid before the partners, and not merely before one of them, his plan of reconstruction. The pre-emptive privilege, or, better, the pre-emptive opportunity, that was thus an incident of the enterprise, Salmon appropriated to himself in secrecy and silence. He might have warned Meinhard that the plan had been submitted, and that either would be free to compete for the award. If he had done this, we do not need to say whether he would have been under a duty, if successful in the competition, to hold the lease so acquired for the benefit of a venture then about to end, and thus prolong by indirection its responsibilities and duties. The trouble about his conduct is that he excluded his coadventurer from any chance to compete, from any chance to enjoy the opportunity for benefit that had come to him alone by virtue of his agency. This chance, if nothing more, he was under a duty to concede. The price of its denial is an extension of the trust at the option and for the benefit of the one whom he excluded.

No answer is it to say that the chance would have been of little value even if seasonably offered. Such a calculus of probabilities is beyond the science of the chancery. Salmon, the real estate operator, might have been preferred to Meinhard, the woolen merchant. On the other hand, Meinhard might have offered better terms, or reinforced his offer by alliance with the

61

wealth of others. Perhaps he might even have persuaded the lessor to renew the Bristol lease alone, postponing for a time, in return for higher rentals, the improvement of adjoining lots. We know that even under the lease as made the time for the enlargement of the building was delayed for seven years. All these opportunities were cut away from him through another's intervention. He knew that Salmon was the manager. As the time drew near for the expiration of the lease, he would naturally assume from silence, if from nothing else, that the lessor was willing to extend it for a term of years, or at least to let it stand as a lease from year to year. Not impossibly the lessor would have done so, whatever his protestations of unwillingness, if Salmon had not given assent to a project more attractive. At all events, notice of termination, even if not necessary, might seem, not unreasonably, to be something to be looked for, if the business was over and another tenant was to enter. In the absence of such notice, the matter of an extension was one that would naturally be attended to by the manager of the enterprise, and not neglected altogether. At least, there was nothing in the situation to give warning to any one that while the lease was still in being, there had come to the manager an offer of extension which he had locked within his breast to be utilized by himself alone. The very fact that Salmon was in control with exclusive powers of direction charged him the more obviously with the duty of disclosure, since only through disclosure could opportunity be equalized. If he might cut off renewal by a purchase for his own benefit when four months were to pass before the lease would have an end, he might do so with equal right while there remained as many years (cf. Mitchell v. Reed, 61 N.Y. 123, 127). He might steal a march on his comrade under cover of the darkness, and then hold the captured ground. Loyalty and comradeship are not so easily abjured. . . .

We have no thought to hold that Salmon was guilty of a conscious purpose to defraud. Very likely he assumed in all good faith that with the approaching end of the venture he might ignore his coadventurer and take the extension for himself. He had given to the enterprise time and labor as well as money. He had made it a success. Meinhard, who had given money, but neither time nor labor, had already been richly paid. There might seem to be something grasping in his insistence upon more. Such recriminations are not unusual when coadventurers fall out. They are not without their force if conduct is to be judged by the common standards of competitors. That is not to say that they have pertinency here. Salmon had put himself in a position in which thought of self was to be renounced, however hard the abnegation. He was much more than a coadventurer. He was a managing coadventurer (Clegg v. Edmondson, 8 D.M. & G. 787, 807). For him and for those like him, the rule of undivided loyalty is relentless and supreme (Wendt v. Fischer, supra; Munson v. Syracuse, etc., R.R. Co., 103 N.Y. 58, 74). A different question would be here if there were lacking any nexus of relation between the business conducted by the manager and the opportunity brought to him as an incident of management (Dean v. MacDowell, 8 Ch.D. 345, 354; Aas v. Benham, 1891, 2 Ch. 244, 258; Latta v. Kilbourn, 150 U.S. 524). For this problem, as for most, there are distinctions of degree. If Salmon had received from Gerry a proposition to lease a building at a location far removed, he might have held for himself the privilege thus acquired, or so we shall assume. Here the subject-matter of the new lease was an extension and enlargement of the subject-matter of the old one. A managing coadventurer appropriating the benefit of such a lease without warning to his partner might fairly expect to be reproached with conduct that was underhand, or lacking, to say the least, in reasonable candor, if the partner were to surprise him in the act of signing the new instrument. Conduct subject to that reproach does not receive from equity a healing benediction.

A question remains as to the form and extent of the equitable interest to be allotted to the plaintiff. The trust as declared has been held to attach to the lease which was in the name of the defendant corporation. We think it ought to attach at the option of the defendant Salmon to the shares of stock which were owned by him or were under his control. The difference may be important if the lessee shall wish to execute an assignment of the lease, as it ought to be free to do with the consent of the lessor. On the other hand, an equal division of the shares might lead to other hardships. It might take away from Salmon the power of control and management which under the plan of the joint venture he was to have from first to last. The number of shares to be allotted to the plaintiff should, therefore, be reduced to such an extent as may be necessary to preserve to the defendant Salmon the expected measure of dominion. To that end an extra share should be added to his half.

Subject to this adjustment, we agree with the Appellate Division that the plaintiff's equitable interest is to be measured by the value of half of the entire lease, and not merely by half of some undivided part. A single building covers the whole area. Physical division is impracticable along the lines of the Bristol site, the keystone of the whole. Division of interests and burdens is equally impracticable. Salmon, as tenant under the new lease, or as guarantor of the performance of the tenant's obligations, might well protest if Meinhard, claiming an equitable interest, had offered to assume a liability not equal to Salmon's, but only half as great. He might justly insist that the lease must be accepted by his coadventurer in such form as it had been given, and not constructively divided into imaginary fragments. What must be yielded to the one may be demanded by the other. The lease as it has been executed is single and entire. If confusion has resulted from the union of adjoining parcels, the trustee who consented to the union must bear the inconvenience (Hart v. Ten Eyck, 2 Johns. Ch. 62). . . .

[Three judges dissented. Andrews, J., who wrote the dissenting opinion, agreed that "(w)ere this a general partnership I should have little doubt as to the correctness of this result assuming the new lease to be an offshoot of the old," but concluded that the parties' joint venture "had in view a very limited object and was to end at a limited time."]

LATTA v. KILBOURN, 150 U.S. 524, 541 (1893). It is "well settled that one partner cannot, directly or indirectly use partnership assets for his own benefit; that he cannot in conducting the business of a partnership, take any profit clandestinely for himself; that he cannot carry on the business of the partnership for his private advantage; that he cannot carry on another business in competition or rivalry with that of the firm, thereby depriving it of the benefit of his time, skill, and fidelity, without being accountable to his copartners for any profit that may accrue to him therefrom; that he cannot be permitted to secure for himself that which it is his duty to obtain, if at all, for the firm of which he is a member; nor can he avail himself of knowledge or information which may be properly regarded as the property of the partnership, in the sense that it is available or useful to the firm for any purpose within the scope of the partnership business."

——————

Birnbaum v. Birnbaum

Court of Appeals of New York, 1989.
73 N.Y. 2d 461, 539 N.E.2d 574, 541 N.Y.S.2d 746.

OPINION OF THE COURT

■ CHIEF JUDGE WACHTLER.

For many years respondent Saul Birnbaum and his brother Bernard Birnbaum engaged in joint real estate enterprises. When Bernard died in 1976, a large portion of his real estate holdings passed to his children, Jay Birnbaum and Ilene Flaum, who are appellants here. An intermixture of familial and economic discord followed, however, between Saul on one side and Jay and Ilene on the other, eventually resulting in a great deal of litigation, of which this case is a small part.

The present dispute involves a shopping center in Cherry Hill, New Jersey, in which Saul has a 50% interest, and in which Jay and Ilene each have a 25% interest, as tenants in common. This property was obtained in 1980 in exchange for another piece of property that had been owned by Saul and Bernard. Soon after acquisition of the Cherry Hill property the tenants in common signed a partnership agreement, naming Saul and Jay managing partners, and requiring that all parties convey their interest in the property to the partnership. Due to conflict between the parties, however, Jay never took an active role in the management of the property, nor did Jay or Ilene convey their interests in the property to the partnership. Nevertheless, through the efforts of Saul the shopping center became an ostensibly profitable endeavor.

The operation and management of the shopping center was a subject of continuous dispute which led to the commencement of numerous actions in the various courts of this State. These actions were consolidated into what essentially became a single accounting proceeding in New York County. From the myriad allegations of the parties in that proceeding, a single issue meriting discussion has filtered its way to this court for review: whether Saul could hire Victoria Tree, who later became his wife, to help develop the property, and properly charge her compensation amounting to hundreds of thousands of dollars to the property, without the consent of Jay and Ilene.

Victoria Tree is not a party in the present actions. The question presented here is whether Saul is entitled to charge Victoria's compensation to the property; we do not have before us the question of whether Victoria is entitled to compensation from Saul personally.

The trial court, confirming a Referee's report, concluded that Victoria's compensation could not be charged to the property. It determined, initially, that Saul personally was not entitled to remuneration for his services in developing the property. The trial court then held that because the services attributed to Victoria were actually part of Saul's fiduciary duty to Jay and Ilene, Victoria was also precluded from receiving compensation from the property, without the consent of Jay and Ilene. The Appellate Division left undisturbed the conclusion that Saul was not entitled to compensation. It reversed the trial court on the issue of payments to Victoria, however, reasoning simply that because Victoria did some work to benefit the property Saul was entitled to charge her compensation to the property. The Appellate Division then certified to this court the question of whether the Appellate Division's order was properly made. We answer this question in the negative.

In the case now before us the lower courts declined to precisely categorize the interests of the parties as partners, joint venturers or tenants in common, although they did conclude that Saul occupied a fiduciary relationship with Jay and Ilene. Jay and Ilene argue here that Saul's role as "patriarch" of the family, along with his duties as either a partner or a tenant in common in the Cherry Hill property gave rise to a fiduciary duty. In contrast, Saul maintains that a partnership exists, which is now in the process of winding up. Partners, however, and particularly managing partners, owe a fiduciary duty to the other partners (see, Meinhard v. Salmon, 249 N.Y. 458, 468). Consequently, even if we accept Saul's characterization of the relationships operating here, the result is the same: he owed a fiduciary duty to Jay and Ilene to protect their interests in the Cherry Hill shopping center.

Saul's financial transactions with Victoria violated his fiduciary duty to Jay and Ilene in two fundamental aspects. First, as a general proposition, absent an agreement to the contrary, partners, joint venturers, and tenants in common look solely to the appreciation of their interest in the endeavor for their financial rewards, and are not entitled to separate compensation for services rendered (see, Levy v. Leavitt, 257 N.Y. 461, 467; Myers v. Bolton, 157 N.Y. 393, 399). Saul does not dispute the lower court's determination that no agreement exists entitling him to compensation for the services he rendered, and thus, personally, he cannot be compensated for the services he provided. Moreover, the trial court's finding, left undisturbed by the Appellate Division, was that the services that are

65

attributed to Victoria are precisely those that Saul was obligated and expected to perform free of individual compensation. Under the facts of this case, Saul acted inconsistently with his obligation to protect the interests of Jay and Ilene, when he charged the property for services that he personally was obligated to perform without direct compensation.

Second, it is elemental that a fiduciary owes a duty of undivided and undiluted loyalty to those whose interests the fiduciary is to protect (e.g., Meinhard v. Salmon, supra, at 463–464; Matter of Rothko, 43 N.Y.2d 305, 319). This is a sensitive and "inflexible" rule of fidelity, barring not only blatant self-dealing, but also requiring avoidance of situations in which a fiduciary's personal interest possibly conflicts with the interest of those owed a fiduciary duty (Matter of Ryan, 291 N.Y. 376, 407). Included within this rule's broad scope is every situation in which a fiduciary, who is bound to single-mindedly pursue the interests of those to whom a duty of loyalty is owed, deals with a person "in such close relation [to the fiduciary] * * * that possible advantage to such other person might * * * consciously or unconsciously" influence the fiduciary's judgment (Albright v. Jefferson County Natl. Bank, 292 N.Y. 31, 39). In this case, Saul's financial relationship with his wife conflicted with his duty to Jay and Ilene and therefore violated the precept of undiluted trust at the core of his responsibilities as a fiduciary.

For these two reasons, therefore, Saul's actions charging the property for Victoria's compensation were inconsistent with his fiduciary obligations, and as such constituted an alteration of his agreement with Jay and Ilene. Consequently, Saul's departure from his basic obligations to Jay and Ilene cannot be countenanced by this court in the absence of both full disclosure and the assent of Jay and Ilene (see, Meinhard v. Salmon, supra, at 467; see also, Phelan v. Middle States Oil Corp., 220 F.2d 593, 603 [Hand, J.]; 2A Scott & Fratcher, Trusts § 170.25 [4th ed.]). The trial court determined that there was neither disclosure nor assent, the Appellate Division did not disturb this conclusion, and, finding support in the record, we are bound also to accept this factual assessment (see, e.g., Alpert v. 28 Williams St. Corp., 63 N.Y.2d 557). Thus we conclude that the trial court properly held that Victoria's compensation could not be charged to the property.

This is not to say, nor would we suggest that a person occupying a position of trust is barred from hiring employees (see, e.g., Partnership Law § 40 [2]). We only reaffirm here the most basic principle that a court will not countenance the behavior of a fiduciary who, without full disclosure and consent, enters into a financial arrangement placing his spouse's interests at odds with the interests of those to whom he owes a duty of undivided loyalty.

Saul argues, however, that in any event a conflict of interest on his part is essentially irrelevant, because Jay and Ilene breached the partnership agreement and thus are not entitled to share in the profits realized from the enterprise. Without passing on the validity of the rule of law Saul seeks to have applied here, neither the trial court nor the Appellate Division found a breach of a partnership agreement on the part of Jay and

Ilene, and, in the record in this court, there is no basis to conclude that such a breach occurred.

We have examined the other issues raised by the parties, and, to the extent they are reviewable by us, we conclude that they were properly determined below.

Accordingly, the order should be modified, with costs to Jay Birnbaum and Ilene Flaum, by reinstating the judgment of Supreme Court, New York County, and, as so modified, affirmed. The certified question should be answered in the negative.

■ JUDGES SIMONS, KAYE, ALEXANDER and TITONE concur; JUDGES HANCOCK, JR., and BELLACOSA taking no part.

Order modified, and, as so modified, affirmed, etc.

NOTE ON SUITS BY A PARTNER AGAINST A PARTNERSHIP

One method by which a partner can vindicate her rights against other partners is by a suit for an accounting. UPA § 22 provides a right to an accounting: (1) when a partner is wrongfully excluded from the business (§ 22(a)); (2) if the right is granted under the partnership agreement (§ 22(b)); (3) for appropriation of an unauthorized benefit in violation of § 21 (§ 22(c)); or (4) or whenever other circumstances render it just and reasonable (§ 22(d)).

However, "cases involving such actions are rare. An action for an accounting ... usually indicates that an atmosphere of mistrust exists in the partnership. In this situation, the easy dissolution permitted under the UPA will often be the appropriate course to follow, particularly if there is no uncompleted term or undertaking." Bromberg & Ribstein on Partnership § 6.08(b).

What about simply suing for the alleged wrong? UPA § 13 provides that "[w]here, by any wrongful conduct or omission of any partner acting in the ordinary course of business of the partnership or with the authority of his co-partners, loss or injury is caused to any person, *not being a partner in the partnership* ... the partnership is liable therefor...." (Emphasis added.) By reason of the italicized phrase, this section is commonly interpreted not to authorize a suit by a partner against a partnership. As a result, the courts have often limited a partner's remedies against the partnership to suits for dissolution or for an accounting. See Beckman v. Farmer, 579 A.2d 618, 649 (D.C.App.1990); Hubbard, Alternative Remedies in Minority Partners' Suits on Partnership Causes of Action, 39 Sw.L.J. 1022 (1986). In *Beckman,* the court justified the rule on the ground that:

> [P]ractical difficulties commend the settlement of accounts before an action at law between partners can be maintained. The value of partners' respective interests cannot be determined while accounts are in flux, but only after partnership liabilities are satisfied, all assets are marshalled, the partners' capital accounts adjusted, and the amount of any surplus ascertained.

67

Id. at 649–50. This justification is unconvincing. It may be true that the complete settlement of accounts is easier at the termination of the partnership, but a partner who wants to make a claim against the partnership is not asking for a complete settlement of accounts.

Given the weak or nonexistent justification of the traditional rule, it is not surprising that the rule is subject to inconsistent and important exceptions:

> The general rule is subject to several exceptions ... [For example, an accounting in] equity may not be necessary when breach of the partnership agreement, wrongful dissolution, fraudulent breach of trust, or misappropriation of money clearly belonging to another partner is charged....

Id. at 650.

2. *RUPA*. RUPA § 305, which is the counterpart of UPA § 13, drops the phrase "not being a partner in the partnership." The Comment states that this change "is intended to permit a partner to sue the partnership on a tort or other theory during the term of the partnership, rather than being limited to the remedies of dissolution and accounting."

SECTION 8. DISSOLUTION (I): DISSOLUTION BY RIGHTFUL ELECTION

UNIFORM PARTNERSHIP ACT §§ 29, 30, 31(1), 38(1), 40

REVISED UNIFORM PARTNERSHIP ACT §§ 601, 602, 603, 701, 801, 802, 803, 804, 807

[See Appendix]

GIRARD BANK v. HALEY, 460 Pa. 237, 332 A.2d 443 (1975). Mrs. Reid, a partner in an at-will UPA partnership, had sent the following letter to the other three partners: "I am terminating the partnership which the four of us entered into on the 28th day of September, 1958." The issue was whether this letter caused a dissolution of the partnership. The chancellor, at trial, held that it did not, because neither in the letter nor at trial did Mrs. Reid offer evidence to justify a termination of the partnership. Reversed.

> In supposing that justification was necessary the learned court below fell into error. Dissolution of a partnership is caused, under § 31

of the [UPA], "by the express will of any partner." The expression of that will need not be supported by any justification. If no "definite term or particular undertaking [is] specified in the partnership agreement," such an at-will dissolution does not violate the agreement between the partners; indeed, an expression of a will to dissolve is effective as a dissolution even if in contravention of the agreement. Ibid. We have recognized the generality of a dissolution at will. If the dissolution results in breach of contract, the aggrieved partners may recover damages for the breach and, if they meet certain conditions, may continue the firm business for the duration of the agreed term or until the particular undertaking is completed. See § 38 of the Act....

The remaining question is whether or not the unilateral dissolution made by Mrs. Reid violated the partnership agreement. The agreement contains no provision fixing a definite term, and the sole "undertaking" to which it refers is that of maintaining and leasing real property. This statement is merely one of general purpose, however, and cannot be said to set forth a "particular undertaking" within the meaning of that phrase as it is used in the Act. A "particular undertaking" under the statute must be capable of accomplishment at some time, although the exact time may be unknown and unascertainable at the date of the agreement. Leasing property, like many other trades or businesses, involves entering into a business relationship which may continue indefinitely; there is nothing "particular" about it. We thus conclude, on the record before us, that the dissolution of the partnership was not in contravention of the agreement.

———

Dreifuerst v. Dreifuerst

Wisconsin Court of Appeals, 1979.
90 Wis.2d 566, 280 N.W.2d 335.

■ Before BROWN, P.J., BODE, J., and ROBERT W. HANSEN, RESERVE JUDGE.

■ BROWN, P.J. The plaintiffs and the defendant, all brothers, formed a partnership. The partnership operated two feed mills, one located at St. Cloud, Wisconsin and one located at Elkhart Lake, Wisconsin. There were no written Articles of Partnership governing this partnership.

On October 4, 1975, the plaintiffs served the defendant with a notice of dissolution and wind-up of the partnership. The action for dissolution and wind-up was commenced on January 27, 1976. The dissolution complaint alleged that the plaintiffs elected to dissolve the partnership. There was no allegation of fault, expulsion or contravention of an alleged agreement as grounds for dissolution. The parties were unable, however, to agree to a winding-up of the partnership.

Hearings on the dissolution were held on October 18, 1976 and March 4, 1977. Testimony was presented regarding the value of the partnership assets and each partner's equity. At the March 4, 1977 hearing, the

69

defendant requested that the partnership be sold pursuant to sec. 178.33(1), Stats., and that the court allow a sale, at which time the partners would bid on the entire property. By such sale, the plaintiffs could continue to run the business under a new partnership, and the defendant's partnership equity could be satisfied in cash.

On February 20, 1978, the trial court, by written decision, denied the defendant's request for a sale and instead divided the partnership assets in-kind according to the valuation presented by the plaintiffs. The plaintiffs were given the physical assets from the Elkhart Lake mill, and the defendant was given the physical assets from the St. Cloud mill. The defendant appeals this order and judgment dividing the assets in-kind.

Under sec. 178.25(1), Stats., a partnership is dissolved when any partner ceases to be associated in the carrying on of the business. The partnership is not terminated, but continues, until the winding-up of the partnership is complete. Sec. 178.25(2), Stats. The action started by the plaintiffs, in this case, was an action for dissolution and wind-up. The plaintiffs were not continuing the partnership and, therefore, secs. 178.36 and 178.37, Stats.,[3] do not apply. The sole question in this case is whether, in the absence of a written agreement to the contrary, a partner, upon dissolution and wind-up of the partnership, can force a sale of the partnership assets.

At the outset, we note, and the parties agree, that the appellant was not in contravention of the partnership agreement since there was no partnership agreement. The partnership was a partnership at will. They also agree there was no written agreement governing distribution of partnership assets upon dissolution and wind-up. The dispute, in this case, is over the authority of the trial court to order in-kind distribution in the absence of any agreement of the partners.

Section 178.33(1), Stats., provides:

> When dissolution is caused in any way, except in contravention of the partnership agreement, each partner, as against his copartners and all persons claiming through them in respect to their interests in the partnership, *unless otherwise agreed,* may have the partnership property applied to discharge its liabilities, and the surplus applied to pay *in cash* the net amount owing to the respective partners. [Emphasis supplied.]

The appellant contends this statute grants him the right to force a sale of the partnership assets in order to obtain his fair share of the partnership assets in cash upon dissolution. He claims that in the absence of an agreement of the partners to in-kind distribution, the trial court had no authority to distribute the assets in-kind. He is entitled to an in-cash settlement after judicial sale.

---

3. Sections 178.36 and 178.37 deal with cases where the partnership is not wound up, but continues after one partner leaves.

The respondents contend the statute does not entitle the appellant to force a sale and grants the trial court the power to distribute the assets in-kind if in-kind distribution is equitably possible and doesn't jeopardize the rights of creditors.

We do not believe that the statute can be read in any way to permit in-kind distribution unless the partners agree to in-kind distribution or unless there is a partnership agreement calling for in-kind distribution at the time of dissolution and wind-up.

A partnership at will is a partnership which has no definite term or particular undertaking and can rightfully be dissolved by the express will of any partner. Sec. 178.26(1)(b), Stats.; J. Crane and A. Bromberg, Law of Partnership § 74(b) (1968) [hereinafter cited as Crane and Bromberg]. In the present case, the respondents wanted to dissolve the partnership. This being a partnership at will, they could rightfully dissolve this partnership with or without the consent of the appellant. In addition, the respondents have never claimed the appellant was in violation of any partnership agreement. Therefore, neither the appellant nor the respondents have wrongfully dissolved the partnership.

Unless otherwise agreed, partners who have not wrongfully dissolved a partnership have a right to wind up the partnership. Sec. 178.32, Stats. Winding-up is the process of settling partnership affairs after dissolution. Winding-up is often called liquidation and involves reducing the assets to cash to pay creditors and distribute to partners the value of their respective interests. Crane and Bromberg, supra, §§ 73 and 80(c). Thus, lawful dissolution (or dissolution which is caused in any way except in contravention of the partnership agreement) gives each partner the right to have the business liquidated and his share of the surplus paid *in cash*. Young v. Cooper, 30 Tenn.App. 55, 203 S.W.2d 376 (1947); sec. 178.33(1), Stats.; Crane and Bromberg, supra, § 83A. In-kind distribution is permissible only in very limited circumstances. If the partnership agreement permits in-kind distribution upon dissolution or wind-up or if, at any time prior to wind-up, all partners agree to in-kind distribution, the court may order in-kind distribution. Logoluso v. Logoluso, 43 Cal.Rptr. 678 (1965); Gathright v. Fulton, 122 Va. 17, 94 S.E. 191, 194 (1917)....

... There was no showing that there were no creditors who would be paid from the proceeds, nor was there a showing that no one other than the partners would be interested in the assets. These factors are important if an in-kind distribution is to be allowed. Section 178.33(1) and § 38 of the Uniform Partnership Act are intended to protect creditors as well as partners. In-kind distributions may affect a creditor's right to collect the debt owed since the assets of the partnership, as a whole, may be worth more than the assets once divided up. Thus, the creditor's ability to collect from the individual partners may be jeopardized. Secondly, if others are interested in the assets, a sale provides a more accurate means of establishing the market value of the assets and, thus, better assuring each partner his share in the value of the assets. Where only the partners are interested in the assets, a fair value can be determined without the necessity of a sale.

71

The sale would be merely the partners bidding with each other without any competition. This process could be accomplished through negotiations or at trial with the court as a final arbitrator of the value of the assets. . . .

However, even assuming the respondents in this case can show that there are no creditors to be paid, no one other than the partners are interested in the assets, and in-kind distribution would be fair to all partners, we cannot read § 38 of the Uniform Partnership Act or sec. 178.33(1), Stats. (the Wisconsin equivalent), as permitting an in-kind distribution under any circumstances, unless all partners agree. The statute and § 38 of the Uniform Partnership Act are quite clear that if a partner may force liquidation, he is entitled to his share of the partnership assets, after creditors are paid *in cash.* . . . We, therefore, must hold the trial court erred in ordering an in-kind distribution of the assets of the partnership.

The last question that arises is whether the appellant can force an actual sale of the assets or whether the trial court can determine the fair market value of the assets and order the respondents to pay the appellant in cash an amount equal to his share in the assets.

As discussed above, a sale is the best means of determining the true fair market value of the assets. Generally, liquidation envisions some form of sale. Since the statutes provide that, unless otherwise agreed, any partner who has not wrongfully dissolved the partnership has the right to wind up the partnership and force liquidation, he likewise has a right to force a sale, unless otherwise agreed. Fortugno v. Hudson Manure Co., 51 N.J.Super. 482, 144 A.2d 207, 218–19 (1958); Young v. Cooper, 30 Tenn. App. 55, 203 S.W.2d 376 (1947). See also Crane and Bromberg, supra, § 83A; 4 Vill.L.Rev. 457 (1959). While judicial sales in some instances may cause economic hardships, these hardships can be avoided by the use of partnership agreements.

By the Court.—Judgment reversed and cause remanded for further proceedings not inconsistent with this opinion.

————

NOTE ON NICHOLES v. HUNT

Nicholes v. Hunt, 273 Or. 255, 541 P.2d 820 (1975), was a case of rightful dissolution of a partnership between Nicholes and Hunt. Hunt had contributed an operating business to the partnership and Nicholes had contributed cash and services. The trial court refused to order a sale of the partnership's assets. Instead, it awarded the operating assets to Hunt, and ordered that Nicholes be paid the value of his partnership interest in cash. Affirmed. "We conclude, as defendant contends and as the trial court found, that the equities lie with the defendant in this case. . . . The defendant conceived and designed the machinery and the method of operation, which was successfully operated for a number of years before formation of the partnership at will." See also Swann v. Mitchell, 435 So.2d 797

(Fla.1983); Wiese v. Wiese, 107 So.2d 208 (Fla.App.1958); Schaefer v. Bork, 413 N.W.2d 873 (Minn.App.1987).

————

NOTE ON DISTRIBUTIONS IN DISSOLUTION, AND ON "SERVICES PARTNERS"

1. *Distributions in Dissolution*. UPA § 40(b) sets out the rules for the distribution of assets after a partnership is dissolved. The first priority is to pay off creditors other than partners. The second priority is to pay off partners for obligations other than capital or profits (for example, a loan that a partner made to the partnership). The third priority is to pay off partners in respect of capital. The fourth priority is to pay off partners in respect of profits. All of these priorities, even those in respect of partnership capital and profits, are defined as "liabilities"—an unusual meaning of that term, which usually refers to debts, not to ownership or equity claims.

Under UPA § 40(d), the partners must contribute the amount necessary to satisfy liabilities as provided in § 18(a). Section 18(a), in turn, provides that each partner shall contribute toward the losses sustained by the partnership, according to his share in the profits. "Losses" in § 18(a) is defined, like "liabilities" in § 40(b), to include losses to capital.

Now suppose that C and S form Partnership P. By agreement, Capital Partner C contributes $100,000 capital, but will not be actively engaged in running the business, while Service Partner S contributes no capital but will spend his full time running the business. Profits are to be shared 50–50, but nothing is said about sharing losses. S performs services of a value of $100,000, which causes an increase in the value of P's gross assets by that amount. After three years, the partnership is dissolved. During these three years, no distribution had been made to either partner and no salary has been paid to S. On dissolution, the partnership's gross assets are worth $200,000, and the partnership owes $100,000 to creditors. C's capital account remains at $100,000. If the value of S's services are not deemed to augment S's capital account, on liquidation the creditors will get $100,000 and C will get $100,000 in respect of his capital account. S will get nothing.

Alternatively, suppose that after all debts to creditors are paid, Partnership P is worth only $50,000; the capital account of Capital Partner C has shrunk from $100,000 to $50,000; and the capital account of Services Partner S is $0. If UPA Section 18(a) is read in a relatively straightforward way, so that S must contribute toward losses of capital according to his share in the profits, then S must contribute $25,000 to equalize the capital loss—that is, to reduce C's capital loss. See Richert v. Handly, 53 Wash.2d 121, 330 P.2d 1079 (1958). The result is that S loses $125,000 ($100,000 in the value of his services, and the $25,000 payment to C). In contrast, C loses $25,000 ($100,000 capital, offset by the $50,000 return of capital and S's $25,000 contribution).

73

These results seem inappropriate. In Schymanski v. Conventz, 674 P.2d 281, 284 (Alaska 1983), the court said, in such a case, that although "[t]he general rule is that, in the absence of an agreement to such effect, a partner contributing only personal services is ordinarily *not* entitled to any share of partnership capital pursuant to dissolution," nevertheless "[p]ersonal services may qualify as capital contributions to a partnership where an express or implied agreement to such effect exists." (Emphasis in original.) This exception makes it easy for a court to get around the general rule, by finding an implied agreement when necessary to avoid a particularly unfair result. See also Parker v. Northern Mixing Co., 756 P.2d 881 (Alaska 1988).

Similarly, in Thompson v. Beth, 14 Wis.2d 271, 111 N.W.2d 171, 175 (1961), the court distinguished between cases in which a partner contributes services only on a "day-to-day" basis, and cases in which "the skill and labor of the partner are his contribution to the capital assets of the partnership." In the former type of case, the court said, the partner's services would not augment his capital account. In the latter type of case, however, the partner's services would augment his capital account. This distinction also leaves a lot of room for a court to get around the general rule by finding that a partner's services were in the latter category rather than the former.

Some cases hold that a special rule applies to joint ventures, and then conclude that the relationship in question was a joint venture rather than a partnership. In Kovacik v. Reed, 49 Cal.2d 166, 169–70, 315 P.2d 314, 315–16 (1957), the court came to the same result by a different path:

> ... Where ... as in the present case, one partner ... contributes the money capital as against the other's skill and labor ... upon loss of the money the party who contributed it is not entitled to recover any part of it from the party who contributed only services.... The rationale ... is that where one party contributes money and the other contributes services, then in the event of a loss each would lose his own capital—the one his money and the other his labor. Another view would be that in such a situation the parties have, by their agreement to share equally in profits, agreed that the values of their contributions—the money on the one hand and the labor on the other—were likewise equal; it would follow that upon the loss, as here, of both money and labor, the parties have shared equally in the losses.

Accord: Becker v. Killarney, 177 Ill.App.3d 793, 127 Ill.Dec. 102, 532 N.E.2d 931 (1988); Snellbaker v. Herrmann, 315 Pa.Super. 520, 462 A.2d 713 (1983) *Kovacik* has been distinguished where the services partner received compensation for his services. See Century Universal Enterprises, Inc. v. Triana Development Corp., 158 Ill.App.3d 182, 110 Ill.Dec. 229, 510 N.E.2d 1260 (1987).

The approach taken in *Kovacik* is sound. If a services-only partner has been fully compensated for his services, it is hard to see why he should not be required to contribute toward making up a capital loss. Otherwise, a capital partner would bear all the partnership's loss and the services-only partner would bear none. But if a services-only partner has not been compensated for his services, then if he must contribute toward the capital loss, he would lose all the value of his services while the capital partner would lose only part of the value of his capital. It is unlikely that the parties would have agreed to this result if they had negotiated on the issue when the partnership was formed. As *Kovacik* suggests, therefore, where a services-only partner has not been compensated for his services, the partners should normally be deemed to have impliedly agreed that she need not contribute to a capital loss.

2. *RUPA.* RUPA § 401(h) continues the rule of UPA § 18. The Comment to § 401(h) makes clear that the rule is intended to apply in the capital-loss context, and provides the following justification for applying the rule to services partners:

> The default rules [of § 401(h)] apply, as does UPA Section 18(a), where one or more of the partners contribute no capital, although there is case law to the contrary. See, e.g., Kovacik v. Reed, 49 Cal.2d 166, 315 P.2d 314 (1957); Becker v. Killarney, 177 Ill.App.3d 793, 532 N.E.2d 931 (1988). It may seem unfair that the contributor of services, who contributes little or no capital, should be obligated to contribute toward the capital loss of the large contributor who contributed no services. In entering a partnership with such a capital structure, the partners should foresee that application of the default rule may bring about unusual results and take advantage of their power to vary by agreement the allocation of capital losses.

This attempt at justification does more to show why RUPA § 401(h) is wrong than why it is right. The Comment begins by frankly recognizing that the result "may seem unfair." It then states that even if the rule is unfair the partners can contract around it. Of course, any rule of partnership law, no matter how foolish, could be "justified" by the argument that it can be contracted around. The point of partnership law, however, should be to make good rules that the parties probably would have agreed to if they had addressed the issue, not to make bad rules that the partners can contract around. Furthermore, many partners don't know partnership law, and therefore won't realize they need to contract around any given rule. Indeed, because persons can be partners without an intention to form a partnership, many partners don't even realize that they are partners, let alone realize that they should consider contracting around any given rule of partnership law.

———

NOTE ON JOINT VENTURES

As pointed out in the Note on Distributions in Dissolution and on Services Partners, supra, some courts have held that a services partner need not contribute toward a capital loss where the enterprise is a "joint venture" rather than a partnership. The line between a joint venture and a partnership is exceedingly thin. "[M]ost courts have [distinguished] between isolated transactions and continuing enterprises by classifying the former as joint ventures." 1 A. Bromberg & L. Ribstein, Partnership 2:42–2:43 (1994).

Some authorities take the position that joint ventures are generally governed by partnership law. See, e.g., id. at 192 ("Whether a [joint venture] is considered a partnership or merely analogized to one, the venturers are governed by the rules applicable to partners"); Comment, The Joint Venture: Problem Child of Partnership, 38 Calif.L.Rev. 860 (1950). In contrast, other commentators argue that joint ventures are not merely a form of partnership, and not entirely subject to partnership rules. See, e.g., Jaeger, Partnership or Joint Venture?, 37 Notre Dame Law. 138 (1961). The same split is found in the cases. Some cases suggest that it makes no legal difference whether an enterprise is characterized as a partnership or a joint venture, while others suggest that special rules apply to joint ventures.

As a realistic matter, what seems to be involved is this: Certain rules of the UPA, such as Section 18(a), produce unsatisfactory results in certain kinds of cases. Courts that want to avoid these results will sometimes do so, if they plausibly can, by holding that a "special rule" applies to joint ventures, and that the enterprise in the case at hand falls within the special rule. In many or most such cases, the desired result could probably be reached, without applying special rules to joint ventures, by finding that the parties had an implied agreement that overrides the relevant rule of the UPA.

The Comment to RUPA § 202 states that "relationships that are called 'joint ventures' are partnerships if they otherwise fit the definition of a partnership. An association is not classified as a partnership, however, simply because it is called a 'joint venture.'"

————

LEFF v. GUNTER, 33 Cal.3d 508, 189 Cal.Rptr. 377, 658 P.2d 740 (1983). "There is an obvious and essential unfairness in one partner's attempted exploitation of a partnership opportunity for his own personal benefit and to the resulting detriment of his copartners. It may be assumed, although perhaps not always easily proven, that such competition with one's own partnership is greatly facilitated by access to relevant information available only to partners. Moreover, it is equally obvious that a formal disassociation of oneself from a partnership does not change this situation unless the interested parties specifically agree otherwise. It is no less a violation of the trust imposed between partners to permit the exploitation of that partnership information and opportunity to the prejudice of one's former associates by the simple expedient of withdrawal from the partnership."

————

ROSENFELD, MEYER & SUSMAN v. COHEN, 146 Cal.App.3d 200, 194 Cal.Rptr. 180 (1983). "[The lower court's] holding that a partner may dissolve a partnership at will in bad faith is not only contrary to *Page v. Page* ... and other cases heretofore cited, but is also contrary to the established principle that even non-fiduciaries must exercise their rights in good faith, deal fairly with each other and refrain from injuring the right of another party to receive the benefits of an agreement or relationship....

"Moreover, the law and motion department's ruling that as a matter of law a partner has the absolute right to dissolve a partnership at will without regard to breach of fiduciary consequences is contrary to the principle that a person may be estopped from exercising rights in bad faith."

––––––

PRENTISS v. SHEFFEL, 20 Ariz.App. 411, 513 P.2d 949 (1973). A and B each owned a 42.5% interest in a partnership, and C owned a 15% interest. A and B fell out with C, and the parties went to court. The trial court concluded that the partnership had been dissolved by the parties' actions, and ordered a sale of the partnership assets. C asked the trial court to order A and B to refrain from bidding for the assets at the judicial sale. The trial court denied the request. Affirmed:

> The principal contention urged by the defendant is that he was *wrongfully* excluded from the management of the partnership, and therefore, because he would in some way be disadvantaged, the plaintiffs should not be allowed to purchase the partnership assets at a judicial sale. The record, however, does not support the defendant's position on two particulars. While the trial court did find that the defendant was excluded from the management of the partnership, there was no indication that such exclusion was done for the wrongful purpose of obtaining the partnership assets in bad faith rather than being merely the result of the inability of the partners to harmoniously function in a partnership relationship.

> Moreover, the defendant has failed to demonstrate how he was injured by the participation of the plaintiffs in the judicial sale. To the contrary, from all the evidence it appears that if the plaintiffs had not participated, the sales price would have been considerably lower. Absent the plaintiff's bid, there would have been only two qualified initial bids, which were $2,076,000 and $2,040,000 respectively. However, with the participation of plaintiffs, whose initial bid was $2,100,000, the final sales price was bid to $2,250,000. Thus it appears that defendant's 15% interest in the partnership was considerably *enhanced* by the plaintiffs' participation.

> The cases the defendant relies upon to support his contention that the plaintiffs should not have been allowed to bid on the partnership assets all deal with instances where, unlike here, a partner has acted in

77

bad faith, engaged in wrongful or fraudulent conduct, or has attempted to avoid paying an adequate consideration for the minority partner's interest.... The defendant characterizes the sale to plaintiffs as a forced sale of his partnership interest. However, defendant was not forced to sell his interest to the plaintiffs. He had the same right to purchase the partnership assets as they did, by submitting the highest bid at the judicial sale. His argument that the plaintiffs were bidding "paper" dollars due to their 85% partnership interest is without force. He too could have bid "paper" dollars to the extent of his 15% interest. Moreover, the fact that the plaintiffs could bid "paper" dollars made it possible, as defendant recognizes in his brief, for them to bid higher than outsiders. As a consequence of this ability to enter a higher bid, the value of the defendant's 15% interest in the sale proceeds increased proportionately.

NOTE ON PARTNERSHIP BREAKUP UNDER THE UPA

One of the most difficult issues in partnership law is how to treat cases in which either a person's status as a partner is terminated, the partnership is to be terminated as a going concern, or both. (The complexity of these issues is illustrated by the fact that they occupy about a third of the text and comment of RUPA.) The difficult substantive issues raised by these issues have been made even more complex by the nomenclature that partnership law has employed. The UPA and RUPA take different strategies toward both the nomenclature and the underlying substantive issues. This Note will focus on dissolution under the UPA. A Note in Section 9, infra, will concern partnership breakup under RUPA.

Before getting directly into the legal issues, it is useful to outline the business economics involved.

Assume that a partnership is to be terminated as a going concern. Typically, the termination process will fall into three phases.

(i) The first phase consists of an event—which may be a decision of a partner or a court—that sets the termination in motion.

(ii) The second phase consists of the process of actually terminating the partnership's business. Inevitably, some period of time must elapse between the moment at which the event that sets termination in motion occurs and the time at which termination of the partnership's business is completed. For example, if the partnership is in the manufacturing business, to terminate the business the partnership will need to pay off its debts, settle its contracts with employees and suppliers, find a purchaser for the factory, and so forth.

(iii) The final phase consists of the completion of the second phase and an end to the partnership as a going concern.

Under the UPA, the first phase is referred to as "dissolution," the second phase is referred to as "winding up," and the third phase is referred to as "termination." The principal draftsman of the UPA explained as follows the manner in which that statute uses the term "dissolution":

> [The term "dissolution" is used in the UPA to designate] a change in the relation of the partners caused by any partner ceasing to be associated in the carrying on of the business. As thus used "dissolution" does not terminate the partnership, it merely ends the carrying on of the business in that partnership. The partnership continues until the winding up of partnership affairs is completed.

Lewis, The Uniform Partnership Act, 24 Yale L.J. 617,626–27 (1915).

To put all of this somewhat differently, "dissolution" is used in the UPA to describe a change in the *legal status* of the partners and the partnership. "Winding-up" is used to describe the *economic* event of liquidation that follows dissolution.

Under the UPA, any termination of a person's status as a partner effects a dissolution of the partnership. It's not easy to see why this should be so when, as often happens, the remaining partners rightfully carry on the partnership's business after one partner has departed. Basically, the UPA's treatment of this issue seems to have been driven by a form of conceptualism. The UPA treats a partnership as an aggregation of persons to carry on business for profit as co-owners, rather than as an entity. Because the UPA treats a partnership as an aggregation, the drafters seemed to have believed that it followed "logically" that any change in the identity of the partners "necessarily" worked a dissolution of the partnership. If a partnership is conceptualized as an aggregation of the partners, and if the partners in Partnership P are A, B, C, and D, then it may have seemed to the drafters of the UPA that if D ceases to be a partner, Partnership P "must be" dissolved, because there is no longer an aggregation of A, B, C, and D. Following this line, UPA § 29 defines dissolution as "the change in the relation of partners caused by any partner ceasing to be associated in the carrying on" of the partnership's business.

The law, however, should not be built on deductive logic, but on policy, morality, and experience. We make rules because they are desirable, not because they are deducible. If a person ceases to be a partner, the law can treat the partnership as either dissolved or not dissolved. Which course the law takes should depend on which treatment better protects expectations and best reflects social policy. This, in turn, depends on what consequences the law should and does attach to dissolution.

Broadly speaking, the law may attach consequences to dissolution (1) among the partners themselves, (2) between the partners as a group and third persons, such as individuals or firms with whom the partnership has contracted, and (3) for tax purposes. The remainder of this Note will consider each of these areas.

1. *Consequences Among the Partners.* Under the UPA, upon the occurrence of dissolution—which, remember, under the UPA means simply that any partner ceases to be a partner—then unless otherwise agreed the partnership normally must sell its assets for cash and distribute the

proceeds of the sale among all the partners. See Dreifuerst v. Dreifuerst, supra. (If, however, a partner, *W*, *wrongfully* causes dissolution, UPA § 38(2)(b) provides that although the *partnership* is dissolved, the remaining partners can continue the partnership's *business*. To do so, the remaining partners must either: (i) Pay *W* the value of her partnership interest (but without counting the value of the partnership's good will), minus any damages caused by the dissolution; or (ii) Put up a bond to secure such a payment, and indemnify *W* against present and future partnership liabilities. See Section 9, infra.)

UPA § 38(1) provides that "[w]hen dissolution is [rightfully] caused ... each partner ... *unless otherwise agreed*, may have the partnership property applied to discharge its liabilities, and the surplus applied to pay in cash the net amount owing to the respective partners." (Emphasis added.) It is well accepted that under the "unless" clause, the partnership agreement can provide that after the termination of a person's status as a partner (and, therefore, after the dissolution of the partnership under the UPA) the remaining partners can continue the partnership *business*, even if the partnership has been dissolved and the dissolution is rightfully caused. See, e.g., Meehan v. Shaughnessy, 404 Mass. 419, 535 N.E.2d 1255 (1989); Adams v. Jarvis, 23 Wis.2d 453, 27 N.W.2d 400 (1964).

Agreements that enable remaining partners to continue the business after dissolution are common, especially in large partnerships, such as law partnerships. Such agreements are usually known as business-continuation agreements or, more simply, continuation agreements. Typically, continuation agreements include not only the right of the remaining partners to continue the partnership's business, but also the terms on which the partner who causes dissolution (or his estate) will be compensated for his partnership interest.

2. *Effect of Dissolution on the Relationship Between the Partnership and Third Parties.* As among the partners, it often won't matter very much whether the withdrawal of a partner does or does not cause dissolution, because as among the partners a continuation agreement can override the substantive effects that dissolution would otherwise have. However, dissolution may also affect the relationship of the partnership to third persons.

For example, suppose that Partnership P, consisting of partners A, B, C, and D, is dissolved by the withdrawal of D, but the business of the partnership is continued by A, B, and C under a continuation agreement. Because P has been dissolved, the partnership of A, B, and C may be deemed a "new" partnership for legal purposes, so that P's assets and agreements, such as leases, licenses, or franchises, must be "transferred" to the new partnership. See Report of the ABA Subcommittee on the Revision of the U.P.A., 43 Bus.Law. 121, 160–62 (1987). In a much remarked-on case, Fairway Development Co. v. Title Insurance Co., 621 F.Supp. 120 (N.D.Ohio 1985), Fairway, a partnership, sued Title Insurance Co. under a title guarantee policy. The policy had been issued at a time when the partners in Fairway were B, S, and W. Subsequently, B and S transferred their partnership interests to W and a third party, V. W and V apparently continued Fairway's business under the Fairway name. The court nevertheless held that Title Insurance was not bound under its policy because the partnership to which it had issued the policy had been legally dissolved.

A debated point under the UPA is whether a partnership agreement can provide not only that the partnership business may be continued after dissolution, but also that the withdrawal of a partner will not cause dissolution, so that the partnership's relation with third parties will not be affected by a partner's withdrawal, as happened in the *Fairway* case. The prevailing (but not unanimous) answer is no, on the ground that UPA § 31 expressly states that "[d]issolution is caused" by the withdrawal of a partner.

3. *Tax Consequences.* The tax-law treatment of dissolution is relatively straightforward, and largely unimpeded by conceptualism. Internal Revenue Code § 708 provides that a partnership's existence does not terminate for tax purposes until either "(A) no part of any business, financial operation, or venture of the partnership continues to be carried on by any of [the] partners in a partnership, or (B) within a twelve-month period there is a sale or exchange of fifty percent or more of the total interest in partnership capital and profits." Accordingly, dissolution under partnership law is normally a non-event for federal income tax purposes. (Warning: Despite IRC § 708, dissolution may have tax effects on a partner who does not continue, or on his estate. Even these effects, however, can normally be avoided by a continuation agreement.)

SECTION 9. DISSOLUTION (II): DISSOLUTION BY JUDICIAL DECREE AND WRONGFUL DISSOLUTION

UNIFORM PARTNERSHIP ACT §§ 31(2), 32, 38(2)

REVISED UNIFORM PARTNERSHIP ACT §§ 601, 602, 603, 701, 801, 802, 803, 804, 807

[See Appendix]

Drashner v. Sorenson

Supreme Court of South Dakota, 1954.
75 S.D.247, 63 N.W.2d 255.

■ SMITH, P.J. In January 1951 the plaintiff, C.H. Drashner, and defendants, A.D. Sorenson and Jacob P. Deis, associated themselves as co-owners in the real estate, loan and insurance business at Rapid City. For a consideration of $7500 they purchased the real estate and insurance agency known as J.

Schumacher Co. located in an office room on the ground floor of the Alex Johnson Hotel building. The entire purchase price was advanced for the partnership by the defendants, but at the time of trial $3,000 of that sum had been repaid to them by the partnership. Although, as will appear from facts presently to be outlined, their operations were not unsuccessful, differences arose and on June 15, 1951 plaintiff commenced this action in which he sought an accounting, dissolution and winding up of the partnership. The answer and counterclaim of defendants prayed for like relief.

The cause came on for trial September 4, 1951. The court among others made the following findings. VII. "That thereafter the plaintiff violated the terms of said partnership agreement, in that he demanded a larger share of the income of the said partnership than he was entitled to receive under the terms of said partnership agreement; that the plaintiff was arrested for reckless driving and served a term in jail for said offense; that the plaintiff demanded that the defendants permit him to draw money for his own personal use out of the moneys held in escrow by the partnership; that the plaintiff spent a large amount of time during business hours in the Brass Rail Bar in Rapid City, South Dakota, and other bars, and neglected his duties in connection with the business of the said partnership. . . . That the plaintiff, by his actions hereinbefore set forth, has made it impossible to carry on the partnership." The conclusions adopted read as follows: I "That the defendants are entitled to continue the partnership and have the value of the plaintiff's interest in the partnership business determined, upon the filing and approval of a good and sufficient bond, conditioned upon the release of the plaintiff from any liability arising out of the said partnership, and further conditioned upon the payment by the defendants to the plaintiff of the value of plaintiffs' interest in the partnership as determined by the Court." II "That in computing the value of the plaintiff's interest in the said partnership, the value of the good will of the business shall not be considered." III "That the value of the partnership shall be finally determined upon a hearing before this Court, . . ." and IV "That the plaintiff shall be entitled to receive one-third of the value of the partnership property owned by the partnership on the 12th day of September, 1951, not including the good will of the business, after the payment of the liabilities of the partnership and the payment to the defendants of the invested capital in the sum of $4,500.00." Judgment was accordingly entered dissolving the partnership as of September 12, 1951.

After hearing at a later date the court found: I "That the value of the said partnership property on the 12th day of September, 1951, was the sum of Four Thousand Four Hundred Ninety-eight and 90/100 Dollars ($4498.90), and on said date there was due and owing by the partnership for accountant's services the sum of Four Hundred Eighty Dollars ($480.00), and that on said date the sum of Four Thousand Five Hundred Dollars ($4500.00) of the capital invested by the defendants had not been returned to the defendants." and II "That there is not sufficient partnership property to reimburse the defendants for their invested capital." Thereupon the court decreed "that the plaintiff had no interest in the property of the said partnership", and that the defendants were the sole owners thereof.

The assignments of error are predicated upon insufficiency of the evidence to support the findings and conclusions. Of these assignments, only those which question whether the court was warranted in finding that (a) the plaintiff caused the dissolution wrongfully, and (b) the value of the partnership property, exclusive of good will, was $4498.90 on the 12th day of September, 1951, merit discussion. A preliminary statement is necessary to place these issues in their framework.

The agreement of the parties contemplated an association which would continue at least until the $7500 advance of defendants had been repaid from the gross earnings of the business. Hence, it was not a partnership at will. Vangel v. Vangel, 116 Cal.App.2d 615, 254 P.2d 919; Zeibak v. Nasser, 12 Cal.2d 1, 82 P.2d 375. In apparent recognition of that fact, both plaintiff and defendants sought dissolution in contravention of the partnership agreement, see SDC 49.0603(2) under SDC 49.0604(1)(d) on the ground that the adverse party had caused the dissolution wrongfully by willfully and persistently committing a breach of the partnership agreement, and by so conducting himself in matters relating to the partnership business as to render impracticable the carrying on of the business in partnership with him.

[The court here quoted U.P.A. Section 38(2)].

From this background we turn to a consideration of the evidence from which the trial court inferred that plaintiff caused the dissolution wrongfully.

The breach between the parties resulted from a continuing controversy over the right of plaintiff to withdraw sufficient money from the partnership to defray his living expenses. Plaintiff was dependent upon his earnings for the support of his family. The defendants had other resources. Plaintiff claimed that he was to be permitted to draw from the earnings of the partnership a sufficient amount to support himself and family. The defendants asserted that there was a definite arrangement for the allocation of the income of the partnership and there was no agreement for withdrawal by plaintiff of more than his allotment under that plan. Defendants' version of the facts was corroborated by a written admission of plaintiff offered in evidence. From evidence thus sharply in conflict, the trial court made a finding, reading as follows: "That the oral partnership agreement between the parties provided that each of the three partners were to draw as compensation one-third of one-half of the commissions earned upon sales made by the partners; that the other one-half of the commissions earned on sales made by the partners and one-half of the commissions earned upon sales made by salesmen employed by the partnership, together with the earnings from the insurance business carried on by the partnership, was to be placed in a fund to be used for the payment of the operating expenses of the partnership, and after the payment of such operating expenses to be used to reimburse the defendants for the capital advanced in the purchase of the Julius Schumacher business and the

83

capital advanced in the sum of Eight Hundred Dollars ($800.00) for the operating expenses of the business.''

As an outgrowth of this crucial difference, there was evidence from which a court could reasonably believe that plaintiff neglected the business and spent too much time in a nearby bar during business hours. At a time when plaintiff had overdrawn his partners and was also indebted to one of defendants for personal advances, he requested $100 and his request was refused. In substance he then said, according to the testimony of the defendant Deis, that he would see that he "gets some money to run on", if they "didn't give it to him he was going to dissolve the partnership and see that he got it." Thereafter plaintiff pressed his claims through counsel, and eventually brought this action to dissolve the partnership. The claim so persistently asserted was contrary to the partnership agreement found by the court.

The foregoing picture of the widening breach between the parties is drawn almost entirely from the evidence of defendants. Of course, plaintiff's version of the agreement of the parties, and of the ensuing differences, if believed, would have supported findings of a different order by the trier of the fact. It cannot be said, we think, that the trial court acted unreasonably in believing defendants, and we think it equally clear the court could reasonably conclude that the insistent and continuing demands of the plaintiff and his attendant conduct rendered it reasonably impracticable to carry on the business in partnership with him. It follows, we are of the opinion, the evidence supports the finding that plaintiff caused the dissolution wrongfully. Zeibak v. Nasser, 12 Cal.2d 1, 82 P.2d 375; Owen v. Cohen, 19 Cal.2d 147, 119 P.2d 713; Meherin v. Meherin, 93 Cal.App.2d 459, 209 P.2d 36; and Vangel v. Vangel, 116 Cal.App.2d 615, 254 P.2d 919.

This brings us to a consideration of the sufficiency of the evidence to support the finding of the court that the property of the partnership was of the value of $4498.90 as of the date of dissolution.

Bitter complaint is made because the trial court refused to consider the good will of this business in arriving at its conclusion. The feeling of plaintiff is understandable. These partners must have placed a very high estimate upon the value of the good will of this agency because they paid Mr. Schumacher $7500 to turn over that office with its very moderate fixtures and its listing of property, together with an agreement that he would not engage in the business in Rapid City for at least two years. No doubt they attached some of this good will value to the location of the business which was under only a month to month letting. Cf. 38 C.J.S., Good Will, § 3, page 951; In re Brown's Will, 242 N.Y. 1, 150 N.E. 581, 44 A.L.R. 510, at page 513. Their estimate of value was borne out by the subsequent history of the business. Its real estate commissions, earned but only partly received, grossed $21,528.25 and its insurance commissions grossed $661.21 in the period January 15 to August 31, 1951. In that period the received commissions paid all expenses, including the commissions of salesmen, retired $3,000 of the $7500 purchase price advanced by defendants, and all of $800 of working capital so advanced, allowed the parties to withdraw $1453.02 each, and accumulated a cash balance of $2221.43. In addition the partnership has commissions due. ... Notwithstanding this indication of the great value of the good will of this business, the statute does not require the court to take it into consideration in valuing the property of the business in these circumstances. The statute provides such a sanction for causing the dissolution of a partnership wrongfully. SDC 49.0610(2)(c)(2) quoted supra. The court applied the statute....

That the $1500 value placed on [the assets other than good will] was conservative we do not question. However, after mature study and reflection we have concluded that the court's finding is not against the clear weight of the evidence appearing in this record. Hence we are not at liberty to disturb it.

The brief of plaintiff includes some discussion of his right to a share in the profits from the date of the dissolution until the final judgment. It does not appear from the record that this claim was presented to the trial court, or that the net profit of the business during that period was evidenced. Because that issue was not presented below, it is not before us.

The judgment of the trial court is affirmed.

All the Judges concur.

NOTE ON WRONGFUL DISSOLUTION

Drashner v. Sorenson illustrates that drastic consequences can befall a wrongfully dissolving partner under the UPA, in the form of (i) damages; (ii) a valuation of his interest that does not reflect the real value of the interest because goodwill is not taken into account; and (iii) a continuation of the business without him. These consequences may have a special impact in a partnership without an expressly specified term. Suppose one of the partners, A, elects to dissolve such a partnership on the theory that the partnership is at will. If the court finds that the partnership is for a term as a matter of implication, A will have dissolved the partnership in contravention of the partnership agreement. The penalties for guessing wrong on whether the court will make such a finding "may act as significant disincentives to dissolution [and may therefore] tend to stabilize the partnership." Hillman, The Dissatisfied Participant in the Solvent Business Venture: A Consideration of the Relative Permanence of Partnerships and Close Corporations, 67 Minn.L.Rev. 1, 34 (1982). For comparable reasons, a partner who believes that other partners have engaged in wrongful conduct is taking a risk if she tries to dissolve a partnership through a self-help election, as opposed to going to court for a decree under UPA Section 32. The other side of the coin, of course, is that judicial proceedings entail delay.

BROMBERG & RIBSTEIN ON PARTNERSHIP

§ 7.06(c), (e).*

(c) Partner Misconduct [as a Ground for Dissolution]

(1) Misconduct as Dissolution Cause Under U.P.A.

The partnership may be dissolved Under the U.P.A. because of the misconduct of a partner. The consequence of such dissolution is that the innocent partners may have the right under U.P.A. § 38(2) to buy out the wrongdoing partner.

The statute defines two types of partner misconduct that may justify dissolution. U.P.A. § 32(1)(c) refers to misconduct that is so serious that it prejudicially affects the business. Such conduct need not be in the course of operating the business, as long as it injures the business, as by jeopardizing the partnership property or credit. Examples include gambling and drug use by a partner.

U.P.A. § 32(1)(d) refers to misconduct "relating to the partnership business" that makes it impractical to carry on the business with the wrongdoing partner. The subsection includes both persistent breach of the partnership agreement and other misconduct, indicating that dissolution is justified on the basis of misconduct that does not constitute a breach of the agreement.

Cases in which dissolution has been decreed on this ground generally have involved conduct that was inconsistent with partner expectations inferred from the parties' particular agreement or from the "standard" agreement provided by the U.P.A.... Thus, for example, it is normally assumed by the partners, in the absence of a specific agreement otherwise, that the partners are to have equal status in terms of voting and access in information (*see* U.P.A. § 18(e) and (h) ...) The courts have accordingly decreed dissolution on basis of denial of access to information such as refusal of an accounting at a time when it should be had pursuant to the partnership agreement. The partners also assume that each partner will devote full attention to the business. Thus, the courts have decreed dissolution when a partner had devoted substantial attention to nonpartnership affairs. Similarly, partnerships have been dissolved when partners breached the implied obligation of fair dealing among partners by enriching themselves at partnership expense (such as fraudulent retention or disposition of funds collected for the partnership property or fraudulent conduct in dealings with a corporation in which the partner is interested) or engaging in outside business, and when a partner refused to cooperate in fulfilling the principal object of the venture. Finally, dissolution has been decreed when misconduct eroded the spirit of cooperation upon which the business was founded.

* Copyright, and reprinted with the permission of, Aspen Law & Business/Panel Publishers.

One particularly important basis of wrongful dissolution is wrongful expulsion of a partner, which is clearly inconsistent with the partners' expectation of continued participation in the firm. In such cases an issue may arise whether the partner was expelled and, if so, whether the expulsion was wrongful.

As indicated by the language of the subsections, dissolution is not justified by an isolated breach of contract or breach of fiduciary duty, as distinguished from *material* misconduct that prevents the carrying on of the business. Moreover, the breach must be willful or persistent. Thus, dissolution will not be ordered for conduct that was at least arguably within the partnership purpose and that was known to but not clearly opposed by the other partners.

The presence or absence of financial harm to the business may be a relevant factor under § 32(1)(c) and (d). U.P.A. § 532(1)(c) requires that the misconduct "affect prejudicially the carrying on of the business." This could be interpreted as a financial harm requirement, but it could also be argued under this language that misconduct may be sufficient if it affects only the interpersonal rather than the financial aspects of the business. Some courts have refused to order dissolution of financially successful partnerships. However, dissolution has been ordered in this situation....

(2) Misconduct as a Cause of Dissociation: R.U.P.A.

R.U.P.A. § 601(5) provides for *dissociation* of a partner upon a judicial determination that the partner has engaged in wrongful conduct. R.U.P.A. § 801(5) provides for *dissociation* for partner conduct that makes it impracticable to carry on the partnership with that partner, or when it is otherwise impracticable to carry on the business. While § 601(5) triggers a right to damages under § 602(c), partner misconduct leading to dissolution under § 801 does not. This distinction is justified to some extent on the ground that dissolution under § 801 is not necessarily based on actionable conduct by the partner. However, this subtle change from the U.P.A. can be expected to cause considerable confusion in the courts, as they attempt to distinguish conduct that causes dissociation and conduct that justifies dissolution, and to ascertain the grounds of judicial decrees for purposes of determining the appropriate relief....

(e) Other Equitable Grounds [for Dissolution]

The court may order dissolution under U.P.A. § 32(1)(f) in situations other than those discussed above when dissolution is "equitable." An example of a situation that might fall within this category is persistent bad business judgment by the defendant partner that does not amount either to incapacity or to misconduct. In this situation, the goals of the association have arguably been frustrated. Similarly, dissolution on equitable grounds may be warranted in the event of partner incapacity if such incapacity does not dissolve the partnership.... Or "equitable" dissolution may be ordered on the basis of partner dissension other than that caused by a partner's misconduct. This approach is particularly useful when there is an unex-

87

pired term so that neither partner has a right to dissolve by express will or withdrawal. . . .

R.U.P.A. § 801(5) provides that the court may dissolve only when it is "it is not otherwise reasonably practicable to carry on the partnership business in conformity with the partnership agreement." This focuses attention on the continuation of the business, which is appropriate when considering whether to dissolve the partnership, rather than on whether a single partner should be able to exit the firm. Moreover, the reference to the partnership agreement confirms that the court should order dissolution only when this would effectuate, rather than frustrate, the partnership agreement. . . .

NOTE ON THE EXPULSION OF A PARTNER

The expulsion of a partner prior to the end of the partnership term without good cause would ordinarily be a wrongful violation of the partnership agreement, and the wrongfully expelled partner would have a right to have the partnership dissolved and liquidated. See UPA §§ 31(1)(d); 32(1)(d), 38(1). In contrast, UPA § 38(1) provides that "if dissolution is caused by the expulsion of a partner, *bona fide under the partnership agreement* and if the expelled partner is discharged from all partnership liabilities, either by payment or agreement . . ., he shall receive in cash only the net amount due him from the partnership." (Emphasis added.) Under this section, a partnership agreement may lawfully provide that a partner can be expelled without cause upon a designated vote of the remaining partners. See Lawlis v. Kightlinger & Gray, 562 N.E.2d 435 (Ind.App.1990); Miller v. Foulston, Siefkin, Powers & Eberhardt, 246 Kan. 450, 790 P.2d 404 (1990).

To fall within UPA § 31(1)(d), an expulsion must be "bona fide." In *Lawlis,* supra, the court stated that "if the power to involuntarily expel partners granted by a partnership agreement is exercised in bad faith or for a 'predatory purpose,' . . . the partnership agreement is violated, giving rise to an action for damages the affected partner has suffered as a result of his expulsion." Id. at 440.

What does "bona fide" or "good faith" mean in this context? It cannot mean that a partner may be expelled only for cause: under such an interpretation, the power to expel a partner under an expulsion provision of a partnership agreement would be no greater than the power to expel a partner even in the absence of an expulsion provision. In *Lawlis,* the court said, "the expelling partners act in 'good faith' regardless of motivation if [the expulsion] does not cause a wrongful withholding of money or property legally due the expelled partner at the time he is expelled." Id. at 443. This seems too restrictive. In Winston & Strawn v. Nosal, 279 Ill.App.3d 231, 664 N.E.2d 239 (1996), Nosal was expelled from a law firm, Winston & Strawn. The expulsion followed (1) Nosal's request for partnership information concerning actions of the partnership's executive committee—in particular, concerning actions of Fairchild, the managing partner—in increasing the compensation and ownership interests of the committee members, and (2) Nosal's threat to sue if his request for information was not granted. Winston & Strawn then brought an action for a declaratory judgment that the expulsion was valid under the partnership agreement. The trial court granted summary judgment for Winston & Strawn. Reversed: It is well-established that a fiduciary relationship exists between partners and that each partner is bound to exercise the utmost good faith and honesty in all matters relating to the partnership business.... *Labovitz v. Dolan*, 189 Ill.App.3d 403, 136 Ill.Dec. 780, 545 N.E.2d 304 (1989)....

Illinois has yet to address the extent of the duty of good faith in the context of partner outplacement or expulsion. Courts in other jurisdictions, however, have concluded that partners owe one another a duty of good faith in the context of expulsion, even where the partnership agreement permits expulsion without cause....

In this case, there is no dispute that the partnership agreement places no restriction upon the expulsion of a partner other than approval by the requisite majority. However, the agreement also grants all partners unrestricted access "to the books and records of the partnership." Access to partnership books is also guaranteed under section 19 of the Act....

Nosal claims that the documents he sought would have revealed the executive committee's plan to retain much of the firm's wealth and management power in the hands of its members. Specifically, the documents would have proven that upon assuming control, and without generally notifying the remaining capital partners, the executive committee dramatically increased the total number of partnership "points," or portions of ownership interest in the firm, and then awarded themselves large increases.

Indeed, the record substantiates that in 1990, the executive committee voted its members considerable increases in individual points which were not given to the remaining capital partners. Nosal's evidence indicates that other capital partners were never notified about this action, and that when Nosal ... sought to learn about it, [he was] repeatedly denied documents expressly guaranteed [to him] under the partnership agreement. We recognize ... testimony that the executive committee had the prerogative to designate the number of points for each capital partner; however, we find nothing in the agreement permitting such self-promoting action as was taken here without the full awareness of the remaining capital partners.

Nosal also alleges that Fairchild intentionally kept such data from him because Nosal could have uncovered evidence of Fairchild's ongoing fraudulent billing scheme subsequently discovered by the firm.

... We note that among the documents sought by Nosal was a firm auditor's internal control report, which arguably could have disclosed questionable billing practices by Fairchild. It cannot be ignored that Nosal's [expulsion] immediately succeeded his ongoing requests for sensitive firm information, and came just days after he presented Fairchild with a draft complaint threatening to sue the firm to enforce his right to examine books and records. The evidence further indicates that it was Fairchild, in his discretion, who was largely instrument in the sudden decision to outplace Nosal despite the fact that just a week before, Nosal was given a favorable review, a compensation increase, and assurances ... that he was not among those to be outplaced.

Fairchild's steadfast refusal of Nosal's access to records, his role in the outplacement, and the fact that it occurred just after Nosal's threatened lawsuit, raise an inference that Nosal was expelled solely because he persisted in invoking rights belonging to him under the partnership agreement and that the reasons advanced by the firm were pretextual. Regardless of the discretion conferred upon partners under a partnership agreement, this does not abrogate their high duty to exercise good faith and fair dealing in the execution of such discretion. Labovitz, 189 Ill.App.3d at 412, 136 Ill.Dec. 780, 545 N.E.2d 304. Nosal has sufficiently raised a triable issue that his expulsion occurred in breach of this duty.

LEVY v. NASSAU QUEENS MEDICAL GROUP, 102 A.D.2d 845, 476 N.Y.S.2d 613, 614 (1984). "While [an expulsion in] bad faith may be actionable, there must be some showing that the partnership acted out of a desire to gain a business or property advantage for the remaining partners.... Policy disagreements do not constitute bad faith 'since at the heart of the partnership concept is the principle that partners may choose with whom they wish to be associated.' "

CRUTCHER v. SMITH, 209 B.R. 347 (Bankr. Ct. E.D. Pa. 1997). "The threshold issue is a factual question of whether the Debtor [Partner] was wrongfully expelled by the Defendants from the partnership, or whether the Debtor caused his own termination from the partnership by failing to fulfill his duties as a partner.... [The Defendant's claim] that the Debtor himself breached the oral partnership agreement and subsequently disassociated himself from the Business, and therefore that his own acts caused dissolution of the partnership in January 1996. In particular, the Defendants claim that the Debtor failed to replace the $500 bad check which he gave to Smith [, one of the partners, and used $110 of partnership funds].....

"However, ... we conclude that the Debtor's alleged wrongful acts were insufficient to trigger a dissolution of the partnership.... ' "[I]t is not for every trivial departure from duty or violation of the articles of partnership, or for every trifling fault or misconduct that courts of equity will interfere and decree a dissolution.' " [Potter v. Brown, 328 Pa. 554, 562, 195 A.901, 904 (1938)], (quoting Story on Partnership, § 287). Although the Debtor's misuse of $110 in partnership funds was technically 'misconduct,' the sum at issue was minimal. The failure to reimburse Smith for [a] $500 bad check was more of a personal wrongful act against Smith than an act against the Business, but arguably was also 'misconduct' inter se the partners. However, the amounts, even when put together, are relatively inconsequential in light of the Business's 1996 gross income of over $200,000. Certainly a $610 offset could have been effected in any future distributions to the partners. We believe that these minor infractions are insufficient to trigger a dissolution of the partnership. . . .

"The Debtor's argument in support of his wrongful expulsion by the Defendants, on the other hand, more logically explains his disassociation from the Business. In essence, the Debtor argues that the Defendants engaged in several definitive steps to ensure his exclusion from the partnership. . . .

" . . . First, the Defendants refused to allow the Debtor to participate in the daily operation of the Business after his hospitalization. Second, upon discovering the Debtor's hospitalization, the Defendants immediately notified [the bank] that there were problems in the partnership and placed an 'alert' on the account which was operative only upon an attempt by the Debtor to withdraw funds from the account. The defendants then proceeded to open a new account bearing only their names. Thus, the Debtor was excluded from all financial matters related to the Business and the partnership in general. . . . Most notably, [the Defendants] did not obtain the Debtor's consent for, nor give him notice of, their purchase of an investment property . . . with partnership funds, thereby depriving the Debtor of any managerial and decision-making authority as a partner.

"These events indicate that the Defendants took unequivocal measures to strip the Debtor of all of his rights as a partner, thereby excluding him from the operation and management of the partnership. The debtor thus has sufficiently established that he was wrongfully expelled from the partnership by the Defendants."

NOTE ON PARTNERSHIP BREAKUP UNDER RUPA

RUPA's provisions on partnership breakup are even more complex than those of the UPA. To begin with nomenclature, RUPA continues to use the terms "dissolution," "winding up," and "termination." However, RUPA adds a new term, "dissociation," to describe the termination of a person's status as a partner.

1. *Events of Dissociation.* Although the term "dissociation" is new, the concept is not. Even under the UPA, a variety of events result in the

termination of a person's status as a partner, and there is a very substantial overlap between the UPA and RUPA concerning the description of those events. For example, RUPA § 602(a) continues the rule of the UPA that every partner has the right to withdraw (dissociate) from the partnership at any time, rightfully or wrongfully, by express will. RUPA § 602(c) provides that a partner who wrongfully dissociates is liable to the partnership and to the other partners for damages caused by the dissociation. Furthermore, if a partner wrongfully dissociates, the partnership can continue without him.

2. *Rightful and Wrongful Dissociation.* RUPA § 602 distinguishes between events of dissociation that involve rightful conduct by the dissociated partner and events of dissociation that involve wrongful conduct. An event of dissociation is rightful unless it is specified as wrongful in § 602(b). The major types of wrongful dissociation are: (i) A dissociation that is in breach of an express provision of the partnership agreement. (ii) A withdrawal of a partner by the partner's express will before the expiration of the partnership term or the completion of an undertaking for which the partnership was formed. (iii) A partner engaged in wrongful conduct that adversely and materially affected the partnership business. (iv) A partner willfully or persistently committed a material breach of the partnership agreement or of a duty of care, loyalty, good faith, and fair dealing owed to the partnership or the other partners under § 404.

The Comment to RUPA § 602 states:

> [Under 602(a)] . . . a partner has the power to dissociate at any time by expressing a will to withdraw, even in contravention of the partnership agreement. The phrase "rightfully or wrongfully" reflects the distinction between a partner's *power* to withdraw in contravention of the partnership agreement and a partner's *right* to do so. In this context, although a partner can not be enjoined from exercising the power to dissociate, the dissociation may be wrongful under subsection (b). . . .
>
> . . . The significance of a wrongful dissociation is that it may give rise to damages under subsection (c) and, if it results in the dissolution of the partnership, the wrongfully dissociating partner is not entitled to participate in winding up the business. . . .

3. *Consequences of Dissociation.* The partnership-breakup provisions of RUPA are driven by functional considerations rather than by the "nature" of a partnership (although the Comments occasionally lapse into conceptual justifications based on the entity theory). Along these lines, RUPA, unlike the UPA, does not provide that every termination of a person's status as a partner—every dissociation—causes dissolution. Instead, the key issue is whether *dissociation* has occurred, and what are the consequences of the kind of dissociation that occurred.

There is an important distinction here between the partnership and the partnership's business. Under the UPA, if the partnership is dissolved because the partnership status of one or more partners is terminated, the remaining partners might continue the business, albeit as a new partnership. For example, the remaining partners might agree on a buyout price with the departing partners, or might buy the partnership business at an auction pursuant to winding up, or might continue the business under a continuation agreement. Under RUPA, the partnership agreement can provide that the departure of a partner does not cause dissolution at all. In fact, under RUPA the dissociation of a partner does not necessarily cause dissolution. For example, upon a wrongful dissociation, or a dissociation by death, the partnership is not dissolved—and therefore the partnership's business continues—unless within ninety days a majority of the remaining partners dissociate or agree to wind up.

Under RUPA, dissociation leads to two forks in the statutory road: winding up under Article 8, or mandatory buyout under Article 7. Which fork must be taken depends on the nature of the event of dissociation.

First Fork: Winding Up. The events of dissociation that require the partnership to be wound up under RUPA are described in § 801. The Official Comment adds:

> ... Under RUPA, not every partner dissociation causes a dissolution of the partnership. Only certain departures trigger a dissolution. The basic rule is that a partnership is dissolved, and its business must be wound up, only upon the occurrence of one of the events listed in Section 801. All other dissociations result in a buyout of the partner's interest under Article 7 and a continuation of the partnership entity and business by the remaining partners.
>
> Section 801 continues two basic rules from the UPA. First, it continues the rule that any member of an *at-will* partnership has the right to force a liquidation. Second, by negative implication, it continues the rule that the partners who wish to continue the business of a *term* partnership can not be forced to liquidate the business by a partner who withdraws prematurely in violation of the partnership agreement.

Second Fork: Buyout. If, upon the dissociation of a partner, winding up is not required under § 801, then RUPA § 701 requires a mandatory buyout of the dissociated partner's interest by the partnership. However, if the dissociation was wrongfully caused by the dissociated partner, § 701(c) provides that the buyout price under § 701(b) is to be reduced by damages for the wrongful dissociation. Furthermore, under § 701(h) a partner who wrongfully dissociates before the expiration of a definite term, or the completion of a particular undertaking, is not entitled to payment of any portion of the buyout price until the expiration of the term or completion of the undertaking, unless the partner establishes to the satisfaction of the court that earlier payment will not cause undue hardship to the business of the partnership. A deferred payment must be adequately secured and bear interest. Under § 701(b), the buyout price of a dissociated partner's interest is the amount that would have been distributable to the dissociating partner if, on the date of dissociation, the assets of the partnership were sold at a price equal to the greater of the liquidation value or the value

93

based on a sale of the entire business as a going concern, without the dissociated partner, and the partnership was wound up as of that date.

SECTION 10. DISSOLUTION (III): AGREEMENTS CONCERNING DISSOLUTION; FIDUCIARY OBLIGATIONS OF DEPARTING PARTNERS

Page v. Page

Supreme Court of California, 1961.
55 Cal.2d 192, 10 Cal.Rptr. 643, 359 P.2d 41.

■ TRAYNOR, J.—Plaintiff and defendant are partners in a linen supply business in Santa Maria, California. Plaintiff appeals from a judgment declaring the partnership to be for a term rather than at will.

The partners entered into an oral partnership agreement in 1949. Within the first two years each partner contributed approximately $43,000 for the purchase of land, machinery, and linen needed to begin the business. From 1949 to 1957 the enterprise was unprofitable, losing approximately $62,000. The partnership's major creditor is a corporation, wholly owned by plaintiff, that supplies the linen and machinery necessary for the day-to-day operation of the business. This corporation holds a $47,000 demand note of the partnership. The partnership operations began to improve in 1958. The partnership earned $3,824.41 in that year and $2,282.30 in the first three months of 1959. Despite this improvement plaintiff wishes to terminate the partnership.

The Uniform Partnership Act provides that a partnership may be dissolved "By the express will of any partner when no definite term or particular undertaking is specified." (Corp.Code, § 15031, subd. (1)(b).) The trial court found that the partnership is for a term, namely, "such reasonable time as is necessary to enable said partnership to repay from partnership profits, indebtedness incurred for the purchase of land, buildings, laundry and delivery equipment and linen for the operation of such business...." Plaintiff correctly contends that this finding is without support in the evidence.

Defendant testified that the terms of the partnership were to be similar to former partnerships of plaintiff and defendant, and that the understanding of these partnerships was that "we went into partnership to start the business and let the business operation pay for itself,—put in so much money, and let the business pay itself out." There was also testimony that one of the former partnership agreements provided in writing that the profits were to be retained until all obligations were paid....

Viewing this evidence most [favorably] for defendant, it proves only that the partners expected to meet current expenses from current income and to recoup their investment if the business were successful.

Defendant contends that such an expectation is sufficient to create a partnership for a term under the rule of Owen v. Cohen, 19 Cal.2d 147, 150 [119 P.2d 713]. In that case. . . . the partners borrowed substantial amounts of money to launch the enterprise and there was an understanding that the loans would be repaid from partnership profits. . . . [T]he court properly held that the partners impliedly promised to continue the partnership for a term reasonably required to allow the partnership to earn sufficient money to accomplish the understood objective. . . .

In the instant case, however, defendant failed to prove any facts from which an agreement to continue the partnership for a term may be implied. The understanding to which defendant testified was no more than a common hope that the partnership earnings would pay for all the necessary expenses. Such a hope does not establish even by implication a "definite term or particular undertaking" as required by section 15031, subdivision (1)(b), of the Corporations Code.

All partnerships are ordinarily entered into with the hope that they will be profitable, but that alone does not make them all partnerships for a term and obligate the partners to continue in the partnerships until all of the losses over a period of many years have been recovered.

Defendant contends that plaintiff is acting in bad faith and is attempting to use his superior financial position to appropriate the now profitable business of the partnership. Defendant has invested $43,000 in the firm, and owing to the long period of losses his interest in the partnership assets is very small. The fact that plaintiff's wholly owned corporation holds a $47,000 demand note of the partnership may make it difficult to sell the business as a going concern. Defendant fears that upon dissolution he will receive very little and that plaintiff, who is the managing partner and knows how to conduct the operations of the partnership, will receive a business that has become very profitable because of the establishment of Vandenberg Air Force Base in its vicinity. Defendant charges that plaintiff has been content to share the losses but now that the business has become profitable he wishes to keep all the gains.

There is no showing in the record of bad faith or that the improved profit situation is more than temporary. In any event these contentions are irrelevant to the issue whether the partnership is for a term or at will. Since, however, this action is for a declaratory judgment and will be the basis for future action by the parties, it is appropriate to point out that defendant is amply protected by the fiduciary duties of copartners.

Even though the Uniform Partnership Act provides that a partnership at will may be dissolved by the express will of any partner (Corp.Code, § 15031, subd. (1)(b)), this power, like any other power held by a fiduciary, must be exercised in good faith.

We have often stated that "Partners are trustees for each other, and in all proceedings connected with the conduct of the partnership every partner is bound to act in the highest good faith to his copartner and may not obtain any advantage over him in the partnership affairs by the slightest misrepresentation, concealment, threat or adverse pressure of any kind." (Llewelyn v. Levi, 157 Cal. 31, 37 [106 P. 219]; Richards v. Fraser, 122 Cal. 456, 460 [55 P. 246]; Yeomans v. Lysfjord, 162 Cal.App.2d 357, 361–362 [327 P.2d 957]; cf. MacIsaac v. Pozzo, 26 Cal.2d 809, 813 [161 P.2d 449]; Corp.Code, § 15021.). . . .

A partner at will is not bound to remain in a partnership, regardless of whether the business is profitable or unprofitable. A partner may not, however, by use of adverse pressure "freeze out" a copartner and appropriate the business to his own use. A partner may not dissolve a partnership to gain the benefits of the business for himself, unless he fully compensates his copartner for his share of the prospective business opportunity. In this regard his fiduciary duties are at least as great as those of a shareholder of a corporation.

In the case of In re Security Finance Co., 49 Cal.2d 370, 376–377 [317 P.2d 1], we stated that although shareholders representing 50 per cent of the voting power have a right under Corporations Code, section 4600, to dissolve a corporation, they may not exercise such right in order "to defraud the other shareholders [citation], to 'freeze out' minority shareholders [citation], or to sell the assets of the dissolved corporation at an inadequate price. [Citation.]"

Likewise in the instant case, plaintiff has the power to dissolve the partnership by express notice to defendant. If, however, it is proved that plaintiff acted in bad faith and violated his fiduciary duties by attempting to appropriate to his own use the new prosperity of the partnership without adequate compensation to his copartner, the dissolution would be wrongful and the plaintiff would be liable as provided by subdivision (2)(a) of Corporations Code, section 15038 (rights of partners upon wrongful dissolution) for violation of the implied agreement not to exclude defendant wrongfully from the partnership business opportunity.

The judgment is reversed.

■ Gibson, C.J., McComb, J., Peters, J., White, J., Dooling, J., and Wood (Parker), J. pro tem., concurred.

Meehan v. Shaughnessy

Supreme Judicial Court of Massachusetts, 1989.
404 Mass. 419, 535 N.E.2d 1255.

■ Before Hennessey, C.J., and Wilkins, Liacos, Lynch and O'Connor, JJ.

■ Hennessey, Chief Justice.

The plaintiffs, James F. Meehan (Meehan) and Leo V. Boyle (Boyle), were partners of the law firm, Parker, Coulter, Daley & White (Parker

Coulter). After Meehan and Boyle terminated their relationship with Parker Coulter to start their own firm, they commenced this action both to recover amounts they claim the defendants, their former partners, owed them under the partnership agreement, and to obtain a declaration as to amounts they owed the defendants for work done at Parker Coulter on cases they removed to their new firm. The defendants (hereinafter collectively Parker Coulter)[1] counterclaimed that Meehan and Boyle violated their fiduciary duties, breached the partnership agreement, and tortiously interfered with their advantageous business and contractual relationships. As grounds for these claims, Parker Coulter asserted that Meehan and Boyle engaged in improper conduct in withdrawing cases and clients from the firm, and in inducing employees to join the new firm of Meehan, Boyle & Cohen, P.C. (MBC). Parker Coulter also filed a third-party action with similar claims against MBC and against Cynthia J. Cohen (Cohen), a former junior partner, and Steven H. Schafer (Schafer), a former associate, who, among others, left the firm to join MBC.

After a jury-waived trial, a Superior Court judge rejected all of Parker Coulter's claims for relief, and found that Meehan and Boyle were entitled to recover amounts owed to them under the partnership agreement. The judge also found, based on the partnership agreement and a quantum meruit theory, that Parker Coulter was entitled to recover from Meehan and Boyle for time billed and expenses incurred on the cases Meehan and Boyle removed to their own firm. Parker Coulter appealed from the judgment, and we granted direct appellate review.

Although we are in agreement with most of the judge's reasoning and conclusions which he reached after lengthy and painstaking proceedings, we nevertheless reverse the judgment entered below and remand for further findings and a hearing, consistent in all respects with this opinion. This result follows from our conclusion, infra, that the judge erred in deciding that Meehan and Boyle acted properly in acquiring consent to remove cases to MBC.[2]

We summarize the facts as found by the judge. Aside from certain conclusions which the judge reached, and which we address in more detail below, the parties agree that these findings were warranted by the evidence. Parker, Coulter, Daley & White is a large partnership which special-

---

1. When a partner leaves a partnership, the partnership is dissolved. G.L. c. 108A, § 29 (1986 ed.). When necessary, we will distinguish between the Parker, Coulter, Daley & White which included Meehan and Boyle as partners, and which has been dissolved, and the current Parker, Coulter, Daley & White, which includes only the defendants as partners.

2. We repeatedly, later in this opinion, refer to "preemptive conduct" of Meehan and Boyle, as well as their "breach of duty."

Undoubtedly these are accurate descriptions, but we do not wish to leave the impression that the MBC attorneys were unfair in the totality of their conduct in departing from the firm. For instance, we recount early in this opinion that Meehan and Boyle left undisturbed with their partners, and made no attempt to claim, a very large amount of business which Meehan had attracted to Parker Coulter.

izes in litigation on behalf of both defendants and plaintiffs. Meehan joined the firm in 1959, and became a partner in 1963; his practice focuses primarily on complex tort litigation, such as product liability and aviation defense work. Boyle joined Parker Coulter in 1971, and became a partner in 1980; he has concentrated on plaintiffs' work. Both have developed outstanding reputations as trial lawyers in the Commonwealth. Meehan and Boyle each were active in the management of Parker Coulter. They each served, for example, on the partnership's executive committee and, as members of this committee, were responsible for considering and making policy recommendations to the general partnership. Boyle was also in charge of the "plaintiffs department" within the firm, which managed approximately 350 cases. At the time of their leaving, Meehan's interest in the partnership was 6% and Boyle's interest was 4.8%.

Meehan and Boyle had become dissatisfied at Parker Coulter. On June 27, 1984, after unsuccessfully opposing the adoption of a firm-wide pension plan, the two first discussed the possibility of leaving Parker Coulter. Another partner met with them to discuss leaving but told them their proposed firm would not be suitable for his type of practice. On July 1, Meehan and Boyle decided to leave Parker Coulter and form their own partnership.

Having decided to establish a new firm, Meehan and Boyle then focused on whom they would invite to join them. The two spoke with Cohen, a junior partner and the de facto head of Parker Coulter's appellate department, about joining the new firm as a partner. They arranged to meet with her on July 5, and told her to keep their conversations confidential. The day before the July 5 meeting, Boyle prepared two lists of what he considered to be his cases. The lists contained approximately eighty to 100 cases, and for each case indicated the status, fee arrangement, estimated settlement value, and potential fee to MBC. Boyle gave these lists to Cohen for her to examine in preparation for the July 5 meeting.

At the July 5 meeting, Meehan and Boyle outlined to Cohen their plans for the new firm, including their intent to offer positions to Schafer, Peter Black (Black), and Warren Fitzgerald (Fitzgerald), who were associates at Parker Coulter. Boyle stated that he hoped the clients he had been representing would go with him to the new firm; Meehan said he would take the aviation work he had at Parker Coulter with him. Both stated that they felt others at Parker Coulter were getting paid as much as or more than they were, but were not working as hard. Cohen decided to consider the offer from Meehan and Boyle, and agreed to keep the plans confidential until formal notice of the separation was given to the partnership. Although the partnership agreement required a notice period of three months, the three decided to give only thirty days' notice. They chose to give shorter notice to avoid what they believed would be an uncomfortable situation at the firm, and possible retaliatory measures by the partnership. Meehan and Boyle had agreed that they would leave Parker Coulter on December 31, 1984, the end of Parker Coulter's fiscal year.

During the first week of August, Cohen accepted the offer to join the new firm as a partner. Her primary reason for leaving Parker Coulter to join MBC was that she enjoyed working with Meehan and Boyle.

In July, 1984, Boyle offered a position at MBC to Schafer, who worked closely with Boyle in the plaintiffs department. Boyle told Schafer to organize his cases, and "to keep an eye towards cases to be resolved in 1985 and to handle these cases for resolution in 1985 rather than 1984." He also told Schafer to make a list of cases he could take with him to MBC, and to keep all their conversations confidential.

Late in the summer of 1984, Meehan asked Black and Fitzgerald to become associates at MBC. Fitzgerald had worked with Meehan in the past on general defense work, and Black worked with Meehan, particularly in the aviation area. Meehan was instrumental in attracting Black, who had previously been employed by U.S. Aviation Underwriters (USAU), to Parker Coulter. Although Black had already considered leaving Parker Coulter, he was concerned about whether USAU would follow him to a small firm like MBC, and wanted to discuss his leaving Parker Coulter with the vice president of USAU. In October, 1984, Black and Meehan met with the USAU vice president in New York. They later received assurances from him that he would be interested in sending USAU business to the proposed new firm. Black then accepted the offer to join MBC. Fitzgerald also accepted. Schafer, Black, and Fitzgerald were the only associates Meehan, Boyle, and Cohen approached concerning the new firm.

During July and the following months, Meehan, Boyle, and Cohen made arrangements for their new practice apart from seeking associates. They began to look for office space and retained an architect. In early fall, a lease was executed on behalf of MBC in the name of MBC Realty Trust. They also retained an attorney to advise them on the formation of the new firm.

Boyle was assigned the task of arranging financing. He prepared a personal financial statement and obtained a bank loan in September, 1984. During that fall, two other loans were made on MBC's credit. Cohen, at the request of an accountant, had been trying to develop projections of MBC's expected revenue in order to obtain long-term financing. The accountant requested a list of cases with indications as to MBC's expected fees for this purpose. In November, Boyle updated and revised the list of cases he expected to take to MBC which he had compiled in July. The November list contained approximately 135 cases. The increase in Boyle's caseload from July to November resulted in part from the departure of a Parker Coulter attorney in early September, 1984. Boyle was in charge of reassigning the cases this attorney worked on. Although another attorney requested transfer of some of these cases, Boyle assigned none to that attorney, and assigned most of the cases to himself and Schafer. Meehan, Cohen, and Black also prepared lists of cases which they anticipated they would remove, and included the potential fee each case would generate for MBC.

Toward the end of November, Boyle prepared form letters to send to clients and referring attorneys as soon as Parker Coulter was notified of the separation. He also drafted a form for the clients to return to him at his home address authorizing him to remove cases to MBC. An outside agency typed these materials on Parker Coulter's letterhead. Schafer prepared similar letters and authorization forms.

While they were planning their departure, from July to approximately December, Meehan, Boyle, Cohen, Schafer, Black, and Fitzgerald all continued to work full schedules. They settled cases appropriately, made reasonable efforts to avoid continuances, tried cases, and worked on discovery. Each generally maintained his or her usual standard of performance.

Meehan and Boyle had originally intended to give notice to Parker Coulter on December 1, 1984. Rumors of their leaving, however, began to circulate before then. During the period from July to early fall, different Parker Coulter partners approached Meehan individually on three separate occasions and asked him if the rumors about his leaving were true. On each occasion, Meehan denied that he was leaving. On November 30, 1984, a partner, Maurice F. Shaughnessy (Shaughnessy), approached Boyle and asked him whether Meehan and Boyle intended to leave the firm. Shaughnessy interpreted Boyle's evasive response as an affirmation of the rumors. Meehan and Boyle then decided to distribute their notice that afternoon, which stated, as their proposed date for leaving, December 31, 1984. A notice was left on the desk of each partner. When Meehan, Boyle, and Cohen gave their notice, the atmosphere at Parker Coulter became "tense, emotional and unpleasant, if not adversarial."

On December 3, the Parker Coulter partners appointed a separation committee and decided to communicate with "important sources of business" to tell them of the separation and of Parker Coulter's desire to continue representing them. Meehan and Boyle asked their partners for financial information about the firm, discussed cases and clients with them, and stated that they intended to communicate with clients and referring attorneys on the cases in which they were involved. Sometime during the week of December 3, the partners sent Boyle a list of cases and requested that he identify the cases he intended to take with him.

Boyle had begun to make telephone calls to referring attorneys on Saturday morning, December 1. He had spoken with three referring attorneys by that date and told them of his departure from Parker Coulter and his wish to continue handling their cases. On December 3, he mailed his previously typed letters and authorization forms, and by the end of the first two weeks of December he had spoken with a majority of referring attorneys, and had obtained authorizations from a majority of clients whose cases he planned to remove to MBC.

Although the partners previously were aware of Boyle's intention to communicate with clients, they did not become aware of the extent of his communications until December 12 or 13. Boyle did not provide his partners with the list they requested of cases he intended to remove until December 17. Throughout December, Meehan, Boyle, and Schafer continued to communicate with referring attorneys on cases they were currently handling to discuss authorizing their transfer to MBC. On December 19,

1984, one of the partners accepted on behalf of Parker Coulter the December 31 departure date and waived the three-month notice period provided for by the partnership agreement. Meehan, Boyle, and Cohen formalized their arrangement as a professional corporation on January 1, 1985.

MBC removed a number of cases from Parker Coulter. Of the roughly 350 contingent fee cases pending at Parker Coulter in 1984, Boyle, Schafer, and Meehan removed approximately 142 to MBC. Meehan advised Parker Coulter that the 4,000 asbestos cases he had attracted to the firm would remain, and he did not seek to take certain other major clients. Black removed thirty-five cases; Fitzgerald removed ten; and Cohen removed three. A provision in the partnership agreement in effect at the separation provided that a voluntarily retiring partner, upon the payment of a "fair charge," could remove "any matter in which the partnership had been representing a client who came to the firm through the personal effort or connection of the retiring partner," subject to the right of the client to stay with the firm. Approximately thirty-nine of the 142 contingent fee cases removed to MBC came to Parker Coulter at least in part through the personal efforts or connections of Parker Coulter attorneys other than Meehan, Boyle, Cohen, Schafer, Black, or Fitzgerald. In all the cases removed to MBC, however, MBC attorneys had direct, existing relationships with the clients. In all the removed cases, MBC attorneys communicated with the referring attorney or with the client directly by telephone or letter. In each case, the client signed an authorization.

Schafer subsequently separated his practice from MBC's. He took with him a number of the cases which had been removed from Parker Coulter to MBC.

Based on these findings, the judge determined that the MBC attorneys did not manipulate cases, or handle them differently as a result of their decision to leave Parker Coulter. He also determined that Parker Coulter failed to prove that the clients whose cases were removed did not freely choose to have MBC represent them. Consequently, he concluded that Meehan and Boyle neither violated the partnership agreement nor breached the fiduciary duty they owed to their partners. In addition, the judge also found that Meehan and Boyle did not tortiously interfere with Parker Coulter's relations with clients or employees. He similarly rejected Parker Coulter's claims against Cohen and Schafer.

1.   Statutory Considerations; the Partnership Agreement.

Before we address Parker Coulter's claims of wrongdoing, we first review the statutory right a partner has to cease his or her association with a partnership, and the statutory right the partner has to assets of the partnership upon leaving. We then examine how the partners in this case have modified these statutory rights in their partnership agreement.

General Laws c. 108A (1986 ed.) governs the formation, conduct, and liquidation of partnerships. Under § 29, a "change in the relation of the partners caused by any partner ceasing to be associated in the carrying on

101

... of the business" results in dissolution of the partnership. The statute enumerates specific changes which cause a dissolution. A partnership may be dissolved at any time, for example, by the express will of a partner. G.L. c. 108A, § 31(1)(b), (2).

Where a partnership agreement provides that the partnership is to continue indefinitely, and the partnership is therefore "at will," a partner has the right to dissolve the partnership, and the dissolution occurs "[w]ithout violation of the agreement between the partners." G.L. c. 108A, § 31(1). See Johnson v. Kennedy, 350 Mass. 294, 298, 214 N.E.2d 276 (1966); Steele v. Estabrook, 232 Mass. 432, 439, 122 N.E. 562 (1919). In a dissolution which occurs "[w]ithout violation of the agreement," the statute expressly defers to the method of dividing the partnership's assets which the parties bargained for in their partnership agreement. G.L. c. 108A, § 38(1). In contrast, where the partnership agreement provides that the partnership is to continue for a definite term, a partner has merely the power to dissolve, and the dissolution occurs "[i]n contravention of the agreement between the partners." G.L. c. 108A, § 31(2). If the dissolution occurs in contravention of the agreement, the dissolving partner is subject to certain damages, and the statute does not expressly allow the partnership agreement to control the division of the partnership's assets. G.L. c. 108A, § 38(2). See generally 2 A.R. Bromberg & L.E. Ribstein, Partnership § 7.02(c) (1988).[3]

In addition to giving a partner the power to dissolve a partnership, and to specifying the effects of a premature dissolution, c. 108A also provides a method for dividing the assets of a dissolved partnership. In the absence of an agreement otherwise, upon dissolution a partner may liquidate the partnership's assets and obtain his or her share of the surplus. G.L. c. 108A, § 38(1). Because it may be impossible to liquidate certain partnership assets immediately, the statute provides that "[o]n dissolution [a] partnership is not terminated, but continues until the winding-up of partnership affairs is completed." G.L. c. 108A, § 30. Each partner has a fiduciary duty to wind up this unfinished partnership business solely for the benefit of the former partnership. G.L. c. 108A, §§ 18(f), 21, 35. See Rosenfeld, Meyer & Susman v. Cohen, 146 Cal.App.3d 200, 216–217, 194 Cal.Rptr. 180 (1983), S.C., 191 Cal.App.3d 1035, 237 Cal.Rptr. 14 (1987); Resnick v. Kaplan, 49 Md.App. 499, 507–508, 434 A.2d 582 (1980), quoting Frates v. Nichols, 167 So.2d 77, 80–81 (Fla.Dist.Ct.App.1964). See generally

---

3. The wrongful conduct described in §§ 31 and 38 consists of dissolving the partnership before its term. We have noted that the dissolution of a partnership at will, "however unseemly in manner and method, [is] not a legal wrong." *Johnson*, supra (citing G.L. c. 108A, § 38[1]). This statement from *Johnson* recognizes that dissolution of a partnership at will is not "wrongful" or "in contravention of the agreement" within the meaning of either § 31 or § 38, and is therefore not a "legal wrong" which would trigger the remedies of § 38(2). See id. We emphasize that the § 38(2) remedy is in addition to, and distinct from, the remedy provided by § 21 for wrongdoing which is not connected with a premature dissolution. Cf. Gaberman, Corporations and Partnerships: Wrongful Dissolution and Damages for Breach of Agreement, 1966 Ann. Survey Mass. Law § 8.8, at 122 (1966) (suggesting that statute can be read to allow no remedy for intentional misconduct at dissolution).

Note, Winding Up Dissolved Law Partnerships: The No–Compensation Rule and Client Choice, 73 Calif.L.Rev. 1597, 1604–1610 (1985). Once the windup is complete, the total value of the dissolved partnership's assets can be determined. Each partner then receives his or her share. G.L. c. 108A, §§ 18, 38(1).

The Parker Coulter partnership agreement provided for rights on a dissolution caused by the will of a partner which are different from those c. 108A provides.[4] Because going concerns are typically destroyed in the dissolution process of liquidation and windup, see J. Crane & A. Bromberg, Partnership 419 (1968), the agreement minimizes the impact of this process. The agreement provides for an allocation to the departing partner of a share of the firm's current net income, and a return of his or her capital contributions. In addition, the agreement also recognizes that a major asset of a law firm is the expected fees it will receive from unfinished business currently being transacted. Instead of assigning a value to the departing partner's interest in this unfinished business, or waiting for the unfinished business to be "wound up" and liquidated, which is the method of division c. 108A provides, the agreement gives the partner the right to remove any case which came to the firm "through the personal effort or connection" of the partner, if the partner compensates the dissolved partnership "for the services to and expenditures for the client."[5] Once the partner has removed a case, the agreement provides that the partner is entitled to retain all future fees in the case, with the exception of the "fair charge" owed to the dissolved firm.[6]

Although the provision in the partnership agreement which divides the dissolved firm's unfinished business does not expressly apply to the removal of cases which did not come to Parker Coulter through the efforts of the departing partner, we believe that the parties intended this provision to apply to these cases also. We interpret this provision to cover these additional cases for two reasons. First, according to the Canons of Ethics and Disciplinary Rules Regulating the Practice of Law (S.J.C. Rule 3:07, Canon 2, as amended through 398 Mass. 1108 [1986]), a lawyer may not participate in an agreement which restricts the right of a lawyer to practice

4. Chapter 108A is intended to be a type of "form contract." See 1 A.R. Bromberg & L.E. Ribstein, Partnership § 1.01(d) (1988). Parties are therefore allowed the freedom to provide for rights at dissolution and during the wind-up period which are different from those provided for in the statute. See G.L. c. 108A, § 38(1).

5. The agreement expressly protects a client's right to choose his or her attorney, by providing that the right to remove a case is "subject to the right of the client to direct that the matter be retained by the continuing firm of remaining partners."

6. The agreement provides that this "fair charge" is a "receivable account of the earlier partnership ... and [is] divided between the remaining partners and the retiring partner on the basis of which they share in the profits of the firm at the time of the withdrawal." This fair charge is thus treated as an asset of the former partnership. Because the partnership, upon the receipt of the fair charge, gives up all future rights to income from the removed case, the partnership's collective interest in the case is effectively "wound up." The fair charge, therefore, is a method of valuing the partnership's unfinished business as it relates to the removed case.

law after the termination of a relationship created by the agreement. One reason for this rule is to protect the public. See Dwyer v. Jung, 133 N.J.Super. 343, 349, 336 A.2d 498 aff'd, 137 N.J.Super. 135, 348 A.2d 208 (1975); Hagen v. O'Connell, Goyak, & Ball, 68 Or.App. 700, 703–704, 683 P.2d 563 (1984); Gray v. Martin, 63 Or.App. 173, 181–182, 663 P.2d 1285 (1983). The strong public interest in allowing clients to retain counsel of their choice outweighs any professional benefits derived from a restrictive covenant. Thus, the Parker Coulter partners could not restrict a departing partner's right to remove any clients who freely choose to retain him or her as their legal counsel. Second, we believe the agreement's carefully drawn provisions governing dissolution and the division of assets indicate the partners' strong intent not to allow the provisions of c. 108A concerning liquidation and wind-up to govern any portion of the dissolved firm's unfinished business.[7] Therefore, based on the partners' intent, and on the prohibition against restrictive covenants between attorneys, we interpret the agreement to provide that, upon the payment of a fair charge, any case may be removed regardless of whether the case came to the firm through the personal efforts of the departing partner. This privilege to remove, as is shown in our later discussion, is of course dependent upon the partner's compliance with fiduciary obligations.

Under the agreement, therefore, a partner who separates his or her practice from that of the firm receives (1) the right to his or her capital contribution, (2) the right to a share of the net income to which the dissolved partnership is currently entitled, and (3) the right to a portion of the firm's unfinished business, and in exchange gives up all other rights in the dissolved firm's remaining assets. As to (3) above, "unfinished business," the partner gives up all right to proceeds from any unfinished business of the dissolved firm which the new, surviving firm retains. Under the agreement, the old firm's unfinished business is, in effect, "wound up" immediately; the departing partner takes certain of the unfinished business of the old, dissolved Parker Coulter on the payment of a "fair charge," and the new, surviving Parker Coulter takes the remainder of the old partnership's unfinished business.[8] The two entities surviving after the dissolution possess "new business," unconnected with that of the old firm, and the former partners no longer have a continuing fiduciary obligation to windup for the benefit of each other the business they shared in their former partnership.

In sum, the statute gives a partner the power to dissolve a partnership at any time. Under the statute, the assets of the dissolved partnership are divided among the former partners through the process of liquidation and windup. The statute, however, allows partners to design their own methods

---

7. The parties have not suggested to us a method, and one is not readily apparent, of applying the statute to only a portion of the firm's unfinished business.

8. A more equitable provision would require that the new, surviving partnership also pay a "fair charge" on the cases it takes from the dissolved partnership. This "fair charge" from the new firm, as is the "fair charge" from the departing partner, would be an asset of the dissolved partnership, in which the departing partner has an interest.

of dividing assets and, provided the dissolution is not premature, expressly states that the partners' method controls. Here, the partners have fashioned a division method which immediately winds up unfinished business, allows for a quick separation of the surviving practices, and minimizes the disruptive impact of a dissolution.

2. Fiduciary Duties; Breach.

We now consider Parker Coulter's claims of wrongdoing. Parker Coulter claims that the judge erred in finding that Meehan, Boyle, Cohen, and Schafer fulfilled their fiduciary duties to the former partnership. In particular, Parker Coulter argues that these attorneys breached their duties (1) by improperly handling cases for their own, and not the partnership's benefit, (2) by secretly competing with the partnership, and (3) by unfairly acquiring from clients and referring attorneys consent to withdraw cases to MBC.[9] We do not agree with Parker Coulter's first two arguments but agree with the third. We first address the claims against Meehan and Boyle, and then turn to those against Cohen and Schafer.

It is well settled that partners owe each other a fiduciary duty of "the utmost good faith and loyalty." Cardullo v. Landau, 329 Mass. 5, 8, 105 N.E.2d 843 (1952). Shelley v. Smith, 271 Mass. 106, 115, 170 N.E. 826 (1930). Holmes v. Darling, 213 Mass. 303, 305, 100 N.E. 611 (1913). As a fiduciary, a partner must consider his or her partners' welfare, and refrain from acting for purely private gain. Shelley, supra. Holmes, supra. Partners thus "may not act out of avarice, expediency or self-interest in derogation of their duty of loyalty." Donahue v. Rodd Electrotype Co. of New England, Inc., 367 Mass. 578, 593, 328 N.E.2d 505 (1975). Meehan and Boyle owed their copartners at Parker Coulter a duty of the utmost good faith and loyalty, and were obliged to consider their copartners' welfare, and not merely their own.

Parker Coulter first argues that Meehan and Boyle violated their fiduciary duty by handling cases for their own benefit, and challenges the judge's finding that no manipulation occurred.[10] Parker Coulter attempts to avoid the burden of demonstrating that this finding is clearly erroneous by

9. Parker Coulter does not claim that Meehan and Boyle wrongfully dissolved the partnership by leaving prematurely. The partnership agreement, although providing that the firm "shall continue indefinitely," required that a partner who leaves to continue practicing elsewhere give three-months' advance notice. This, therefore, may not have been a purely "at will" partnership which a partner has a right to dissolve at any time without triggering the remedies of G.L. c. 108A, § 38(2). See G.L. c. 108A, §§ 31(1), 38. Johnson v. Kennedy, 350 Mass. 294, 298, 214 N.E.2d 276 (1966). Here, Parker Coulter waived compliance with the agreement's three-month notice provision. Meehan and Boyle, therefore, dissolved the partnership "[w]ithout violation of the agreement between the partners." G.L. c. 108A, § 31.

10. The judge found, specifically, that: "MBC, Schafer, Black and Fitzgerald worked full schedules from July to November 30, 1984, and some beyond. There was no manipulation of the cases nor were the cases handled differently as a result of the decision by MBC to leave Parker Coulter. They tried cases, worked on discovery, settled cases and made reasonable efforts to avoid continuances, to try their cases when reached, and settle where appropriate and in general maintain the same level of industry and professionalism that they had always demonstrated."

105

characterizing it as an "inference," and claiming that, as such, it is entitled to no weight. We disagree. The judge's determination was one of fact, and was based on the assessment of the credibility of individuals with personal knowledge of the facts about which they were testifying. We therefore review this finding under the "clearly erroneous" standard. See New England Canteen Serv., Inc. v. Ashley, 372 Mass. 671, 675, 363 N.E.2d 526 (1977).

Parker Coulter also claims that we should disregard the judge's finding of no manipulation because the finding is clearly contradicted by other subsidiary findings, namely that Boyle planned to, and told Schafer to, handle cases for resolution at MBC rather than at Parker Coulter; that Boyle reassigned a number of a departing attorney's cases to himself and Schafer; and that a number of cases which were ready to resolve at Parker Coulter were, in fact, not resolved there. We do not agree that there is a conflict. The judge's finding that Boyle spoke of engaging in improper conduct does not require the conclusion that this conduct actually took place. Similarly, his finding that the reassignment of cases did not establish manipulation is consistent with a determination that the reassignment was based on merit and workload. Furthermore, the judge's finding that the MBC attorneys worked full schedules provides a reason for the delayed resolution of certain cases other than the improper motivation which Parker Coulter urges. Finally, Parker Coulter points to no specific case which the MBC attorneys manipulated for their own benefit. There is thus no contradiction between the judge's findings. We have reviewed the record, and conclude that the judge was warranted in determining that Meehan and Boyle handled cases no differently as a result of their decision to leave Parker Coulter, and that they thus fulfilled their fiduciary duty in this respect.

Parker Coulter next argues that the judge's findings compel the conclusion that Meehan and Boyle breached their fiduciary duty not to compete with their partners by secretly setting up a new firm during their tenure at Parker Coulter. We disagree. We have stated that fiduciaries may plan to compete with the entity to which they owe allegiance, "provided that in the course of such arrangements they [do] not otherwise act in violation of their fiduciary duties." Chelsea Indus. v. Gaffney, 389 Mass. 1, 10, 11–12, 449 N.E.2d 320 (1983). Here, the judge found that Meehan and Boyle made certain logistical arrangements for the establishment of MBC. These arrangements included executing a lease for MBC's office, preparing lists of clients expected to leave Parker Coulter for MBC, and obtaining financing on the basis of these lists. We believe these logistical arrangements to establish a physical plant for the new firm were permissible under Chelsea Indus., especially in light of the attorneys' obligation to represent adequately any clients who might continue to retain them on their departure from Parker Coulter. Canons of Ethics and Disciplinary Rules Regulating the Practice of Law (S.J.C. Rule 3:07, Canon 7, as appearing in 382 Mass. 784 [1981]). There was no error in the judge's determination that this conduct did not violate the partners' fiduciary duty.[11]

Lastly, Parker Coulter argues that the judge's findings compel the conclusion that Meehan and Boyle breached their fiduciary duties by unfairly acquiring consent from clients to remove cases from Parker Coulter. We agree that Meehan and Boyle, through their preparation for obtaining clients' consent, their secrecy concerning which clients they intended to take, and the substance and method of their communications with clients, obtained an unfair advantage over their former partners in breach of their fiduciary duties.

A partner has an obligation to "render on demand true and full information of all things affecting the partnership to any partner." G.L. c. 108A, § 20. See Shelley, supra 271 Mass. at 115, 170 N.E. 826. On three separate occasions Meehan affirmatively denied to his partners, on their demand, that he had any plans for leaving the partnership. During this period of secrecy, Meehan and Boyle made preparations for obtaining removal authorizations from clients. Meehan traveled to New York to meet with a representative of USAU and interest him in the new firm. Boyle prepared form letters on Parker Coulter's letterhead for authorizations from prospective MBC clients. Thus, they were "ready to move" the instant they gave notice to their partners. See BBF, Inc. v. Germanium Power Devices Corp., 13 Mass.App.Ct. 166, 172, 430 N.E.2d 1221 (1982).

On giving their notice, Meehan and Boyle continued to use their position of trust and confidence to the disadvantage of Parker Coulter. The two immediately began communicating with clients and referring attorneys. Boyle delayed providing his partners with a list of clients he intended to solicit until mid-December, by which time he had obtained authorization from a majority of the clients.

Finally, the content of the letter sent to the clients was unfairly prejudicial to Parker Coulter. The ABA Committee on Ethics and Professional Responsibility, in Informal Opinion 1457 (April 29, 1980), set forth ethical standards for attorneys announcing a change in professional association.[12] Because this standard is intended primarily to protect clients, proof

11. Parker Coulter also argues that Meehan and Boyle impermissibly competed with the firm by inducing its employees to join MBC. Because Parker Coulter identifies no specific loss resulting from this claimed breach, see, e.g., Chelsea Indus., supra 389 Mass. at 19 n. 23, 449 N.E.2d 320, (costs of retraining new employees), we need not address this issue.

12. These standards provide the following guidelines for notice to clients:

"(a) the notice is mailed; (b) the notice is sent only to persons with whom the lawyer had an active lawyer-client relationship immediately before the change in the lawyer's professional asso-

ciation; (c) the notice is clearly related to open and pending matters for which the lawyer had direct professional responsibility to the client immediately before the change; (d) the notice is sent promptly after the change; (e) the notice does not urge the client to sever a relationship with the lawyer's former firm and does not recommend the lawyer's employment (although it indicates the lawyer's willingness to continue his responsibility for the matters); (f) the notice makes it clear that the client has the right to decide who will complete or continue the matters; and (g) the notice is brief, dignified, and not disparaging of the lawyer's for-by Parker Coulter of a technical violation of this standard does not aid them in their claims. See Fishman v. Brooks, 396 Mass. 643, 649, 487 N.E.2d 1377 (1986). We will, however, look to this standard for general guidelines as to what partners are entitled to expect from each other concerning their joint clients on the division of their practice. The ethical standard provides that any notice explain to a client that he or she has the right to decide who will continue the representation. Here, the judge found that the notice did not "clearly present to the clients the choice they had between remaining at Parker Coulter or moving to the new firm." By sending a one-side announcement, on Parker Coulter letterhead, so soon after notice of their departure, Meehan and Boyle excluded their partners from effectively presenting their services as an alternative to those of Meehan and Boyle.

Meehan and Boyle could have foreseen that the news of their departure would cause a certain amount of confusion and disruption among their partners. The speed and preemptive character of their campaign to acquire clients' consent took advantage of their partners' confusion. By engaging in these preemptive tactics, Meehan and Boyle violated the duty of utmost good faith and loyalty which they owed their partners. Therefore, we conclude that the judge erred in deciding that Meehan and Boyle acted properly in acquiring consent to remove cases to MBC.

We next consider Parker Coulter's claims against Cohen and Schafer. We have determined that "[e]mployees occupying a position of trust and confidence owe a duty of loyalty to their employer and must protect the interests of their employer." Chelsea Indus., supra 389 Mass. at 11, 449 N.E.2d 320. Cohen was a junior partner, and acting head of Parker Coulter's appellate department. Schafer was an associate responsible for a substantial case load. Both had access to clients and information concerning clients and therefore occupied positions of trust and confidence. We conclude that their participation in the preemptive tactics of Meehan and Boyle violated the duty they owed the partnership.

3. Consequences of Breach.

Before we examine the consequences of the MBC attorneys' breach of duty, we briefly outline what is at stake. If there had been no breach of duty, the assets of the partnership upon dissolution would be divided strictly according to the partnership agreement. Under the agreement, Meehan and Boyle would be entitled to the return of their capital contributions and their share of the dissolved firm's profits. They would also possess the right to remove cases from the old partnership, and to retain all future fees generated by these cases in excess of the fair charge owed to the partnership for work performed there on the removed cases. Because the fair charge is an asset of the dissolved firm under the agreement, Meehan and Boyle would share in this amount according to their respective inter-

mer firm." See also ABA Committee on Ethics and Professional Responsibility Informal Opinion 1466 (Feb. 12, 1981) (extending Informal Opinion 1457 to departing associates as well as partners).

ests in the former partnership. Thus, of the fair charges returned to their former partnership, Meehan and Boyle would receive their combined 10.8% partnership share, and their former partners would receive the remainder.

Parker Coulter essentially argues that, because of their breach of fiduciary duty, Meehan and Boyle forfeit all rights under the partnership agreement. Thus, Parker Coulter contends, Meehan and Boyle are not entitled to their capital contributions or their share of the dissolved partnership's profits. More importantly, according to Parker Coulter, because of their breach Meehan and Boyle have lost the right to retain any fees generated by the cases they removed. Instead, Parker Coulter claims, these fees are owed to them directly. Parker Coulter further argues that, because the third-party defendants, Cohen and Schafer, breached their duty to Parker Coulter, they also owe any fees they may receive on removed cases directly to Parker Coulter. Finally, Parker Coulter contends that the MBC attorneys have forfeited all rights to the compensation they received from July through December, 1984. We reject this extreme remedy. First, we examine the consequences to Meehan and Boyle of their breach; then we turn to Cohen and Schafer.

For Parker Coulter to recover any amount in addition to what it would be entitled to receive upon dissolution under the partnership agreement or the statute, there must be a causal connection between its claimed losses and the breach of duty on the part of the MBC attorneys.... We have concluded that the MBC attorneys unfairly acquired consent from clients. Parker Coulter, therefore, is entitled to recover only those amounts which flow from this breach of duty.

There is no conceivable connection between the attorneys' breach of duty and Parker Coulter's claims to the capital contributions and profit shares of Meehan and Boyle. We have ruled that a partner does not forfeit his or her right to the accrued profits of a partnership by simply breaching the partnership agreement. Fisher v. Fisher, 349 Mass. 675, 677, 212 N.E.2d 222 (1965). Walsh v. Atlantic Assocs., 321 Mass. 57, 64, 71 N.E.2d 580 (1947). The same rule applies to a partner's capital contributions. These amounts are not a form of liquidated damages to which partners can resort in the event of a breach. We conclude, therefore, that Parker Coulter is not entitled to recover these amounts. The judge correctly found that Meehan and Boyle are entitled to a return of their capital contributions (their interest, as determined by the judge, in the partners' reserve account and the partners' capital account), and to the receipt of a portion of the old firm's profits (their interest in the income earned but not distributed account).

We similarly reject Parker Coulter's claims that the MBC attorneys should be required to forfeit all compensation during the period of their breach. Parker Coulter is correct in stating that a fiduciary "can be required to forfeit the right to retain or receive his compensation for conduct in violation of his fiduciary duties." Chelsea Indus. v. Gaffney, 389 Mass. 1, 12, 449 N.E.2d 320 (1983). See Production Mach. Co., supra 327 Mass. at 379, 99 N.E.2d 32; BBF, Inc., supra 13 Mass.App.Ct. at 177, 430

N.E.2d 1221. Parker Coulter fails to consider, however, that a fiduciary may be required "to repay only that portion of his compensation, if any, that was in excess of the worth of his services to his employer." Chelsea Indus., supra. Here, the judge found that throughout the period in question the MBC attorneys worked as hard, and were as productive as they had always been. This finding was warranted, and is unchallenged by Parker Coulter. In these circumstances, we conclude that the value of the MBC attorneys' services was equal to their compensation. Parker Coulter, therefore, is not entitled to this relief.

Parker Coulter's claim that it is entitled to all fees from removed cases, however, rests on a different footing from its claims to compensation, capital contributions, and profit shares. We therefore examine more closely Parker Coulter's allegations of a causal connection between the breach of duty and its loss of clients.

Although the judge found that the MBC attorneys did not breach their fiduciary duties in acquiring consent from clients, he nonetheless stated, as an alternative ground for denying relief on this claim, that Parker Coulter had shown no causal connection between the departing attorneys' acts and its loss of clients. He ruled that Parker Coulter failed to show that clients who left the firm would have remained had the plaintiffs and third-party defendants acted properly. Parker Coulter argues that the standard of causation the judge imposed was too strict. We agree that the judge's ruling placed an inappropriate burden on Parker Coulter.

In these circumstances, it is appropriate to place on the party who improperly removed the case the burden of proving that the client would have consented to removal in the absence of any breach of duty. See Knolls v. Gilchrist Co., 362 Mass. 642, 651, 289 N.E.2d 879 (1972) (where goods are damaged in bailee's hands, bailor is relieved of traditional burden of proving bailee's negligence, and burden is on bailee to prove that loss was not caused by any lack of due care). See also William Rodman & Sons v. State Tax Comm'n, 373 Mass. 606, 611, 368 N.E.2d 1382 (1977) (application of rule to cigarette stamper-wholesaler). We have recognized that shifting the burden of proof may be justified on policy grounds because it encourages a defendant both to preserve information concerning the circumstances of the plaintiff's injury and to use best efforts to fulfill any duty he or she may owe the plaintiff. See William Rodman & Sons, supra. Based on similar reasoning, courts in other jurisdictions have shifted the burden of proof in cases involving a breach of fiduciary duty. Once it is established that a partner or corporate manager has engaged in self-dealing, or has acquired a corporate or partnership opportunity, these courts require the fiduciary to prove that his or her actions were intrinsically fair, and did not result in harm to the corporation or partnership. See Ohio Drill & Tool Co. v. Johnson, 498 F.2d 186, 195 (6th Cir.1974) (interpreting Ohio common law); Fliegler v. Lawrence, 361 A.2d 218, 221 (Del.1976); Newton v. Hornblower, Inc., 224 Kan. 506, 518, 582 P.2d 1136 (1978); Huffington v. Upchurch, 532 S.W.2d 576, 579 (Tex.1976).

We conclude that Meehan and Boyle had the burden of proving no causal connection between their breach of duty and Parker Coulter's loss of clients.... Proof of the circumstances of the preparations for obtaining authorizations and of the actual communications with clients was more accessible to Meehan and Boyle than to Parker Coulter. Furthermore, requiring these partners to disprove causation will encourage partners in the future to disclose seasonably and fully any plans to remove cases. This disclosure will allow the partnership and the departing partner an equal opportunity to present to clients the option of continuing with the partnership or retaining the departing partner individually.[13]

We remand the case to the Superior Court for findings consistent with our conclusion that the MBC attorneys bear the burden of proof. We emphasize that we do not remand the case for the presentation of additional evidence on this issue. At trial, both parties argued whether the MBC attorneys' actions in removing cases affected the clients' right to choose, and introduced a substantial amount of evidence bearing on clients' reasons for selecting MBC. The parties have had a full opportunity to present evidence concerning what might have influenced clients' decisions, and are not now entitled to a further evidentiary hearing on this issue.

To guide the judge on remand in his reexamination of the record and his subsidiary findings, we briefly outline factors relevant to determining whether a client freely chose MBC and, thus, whether the MBC attorneys met their burden of disproving a causal relationship between their preemptive tactics and the removal of the case. We note at the outset that the partnership agreement's specific terms offer no direct assistance in resolving this issue. It is true that the partnership agreement provides that a departing partner has the right to remove any case which came to the partnership through his or her personal efforts or connections. Resorting to this provision alone to determine which cases were properly removed, however, is inappropriate. The partnership agreement states that the right to remove is subject to the client's right freely to choose who will continue handling his or her case. Thus, the parties expressly bargained with each other that they would allow a client a free choice. To give effect, therefore, to the entire agreement of the parties before us, there must be some examination of a client's reasons for choosing to retain MBC.

Although the record contains no evidence as to the actual preference of a particular client, expressed and unaffected by the MBC attorneys' improper communications, the record is replete with circumstantial evidence bearing on this issue. Circumstantial factors relevant to whether a client freely exercised his or her right to choose include the following: (1) who was responsible for initially attracting the client to the firm;[14] (2) who

13. As between the attorneys, a mutual letter, from both the partnership and the departing partner, outlining the separation plans and the clients' right to choose, would be an appropriate means of opening the discussion between the attorneys and their clients concerning the clients' choice of continuing representation.

14. As shown above, while specific provisions of the partnership agreement do not directly assist in resolving the causation issue, who was responsible for generating a

managed the case at the firm; (3) how sophisticated the client was and whether the client made the decision with full knowledge;[15] and (4) what was the reputation and skill of the removing attorneys. Therefore, the judge is to reexamine the record and his subsidiary findings in light of the factors we have identified, and to reach a conclusion as to whether Meehan and Boyle have met their burden of proof on each of the removed cases. With the burden of proof on Meehan and Boyle, Parker Coulter will prevail if the evidence is in balance. Trustees of Forbes Library v. Labor Relations Comm'n, 384 Mass. 559, 566, 428 N.E.2d 124 (1981).

In those cases, if any, where the judge concludes, in accordance with the above analysis, that Meehan and Boyle have met their burden, we resolve the parties' dispute over fees solely under the partnership agreement.[16] Under the agreement's terms, as we have interpreted them, Meehan and Boyle owe a fair charge to their former partnership for its "services to and expenditures for" the clients in these matters. Meehan and Boyle are entitled to their combined 10.8% partnership share of this amount, and their former partners are entitled to the remainder. We agree with the judge that a "fair charge" on a removed case consists of the firm's unreimbursed expenses plus the rate billed per hour by members of the firm multiplied by the hours expended on the case.[17] In fixing this hourly

case is nonetheless a significant factor. The attorney to whom a case is directly referred, or whose personal efforts and connections brought the case to the firm, generally has a significant, close relationship with the client or referring attorney. The partnership agreement in this case attests to the significance of this relationship within the profession. Approximately 100 of the 142 contingent fee cases removed to MBC originally were brought to Parker Coulter entirely by the efforts of Meehan, Boyle, or Schafer, and were managed solely by an MBC attorney within Parker Coulter.

On the contrary, approximately thirty-nine of the contingent fee cases, although managed by an MBC attorney, were brought to the firm entirely by a Parker Coulter attorney or were brought to the firm by a Parker Coulter attorney in conjunction with an MBC attorney. We identify these cases as the judge did. The judge found that twenty-four of the contingent fee cases removed to MBC did not originally come to Parker Coulter through the efforts or connections of an MBC attorney, or were not originally referred to an MBC attorney.... The judge found that fifteen contingent fee cases came to Parker Coulter only in part through the efforts of an MBC attorney.... The judge made no specific findings as to how three of the cases came to Parker Coulter....

15. In a minor number of removed cases, the insurance defense cases, the judge found the client was sophisticated, and made the decision to retain MBC with full knowledge of the circumstances. In this situation, other factors, such as who originally brought the client in, may become less significant.

16. As we noted above, Parker Coulter does not claim that Meehan and Boyle dissolved the partnership prematurely.

17. MBC attorneys removed from Parker Coulter a number of insurance company cases, where the fee is determined on an hourly basis, and a number of contingent fee cases, where the fee does not depend on the time involved. Deciding that billable hours is a fair charge on contingent fee cases has two effects which are arguably unfair both to Parker Coulter and to MBC. If the client is unsuccessful, MBC will nonetheless have reimbursed Parker Coulter for services which generated no contingent fee. Conversely, if the client is successful, MBC will retain all the potential "windfall" of the amount by which the contingent fee exceeds MBC's investment of time in the case and its payment of a fair charge to Parker Coulter. Treating a contingent fee case as if the fee were determined on an hourly basis is justified here, however, because the parties did not bargain otherwise.

rate, the firm made a determination that the time charged was reasonable and fair compensation for the services rendered. We conclude, therefore, that, in accordance with the partnership agreement, Meehan and Boyle must reimburse their former partnership for time billed and expenses incurred at that firm on all cases which were fairly removed.[18] We further conclude that, under the agreement, Meehan and Boyle have the right to retain all fees generated by these cases in excess of the fair charge.[19]

We now address the correct remedy in those cases, if any, which the judge determines Meehan and Boyle unfairly removed. In light of a conclusion that Meehan and Boyle have failed to prove that certain clients would not have preferred to stay with Parker Coulter, granting Parker Coulter merely a fair charge on these cases pursuant to the partnership agreement would not make it whole. We turn, therefore, to c. 108A. Section 21 of c. 108A provides: "Every partner must account to the partnership for any benefit, and hold as trustee for it any profits derived by him without the consent of the other partners from any transaction connected with the formation, conduct or liquidation of the partnership...." We have consistently applied this statute, and held that a partner must account for any profits which flow from a breach of fiduciary duty. Shulkin v. Shulkin, 301 Mass. 184, 192–193, 16 N.E.2d 644 (1938). Shelley v. Smith, 271 Mass. 106, 118, 170 N.E. 826 (1930). See Holmes v. Darling, 213 Mass. 303, 100 N.E. 611 (1913) (common law rule). Cf. Production Mach. Co. v. Howe, 327 Mass. 372, 378, 99 N.E.2d 32 (1951) (similar remedy for corporate fiduciary's breach); Durfee v. Durfee & Channing, Inc., 323 Mass. 187, 198, 80 N.E.2d 522 (1948) (same). We have reasoned that this rule requiring the imposition of a constructive trust "does not rest [merely] upon the narrow ground of injury or damage to the [partnership] resulting from a betrayal of confidence, but upon a broader foundation of a wise public policy that, for the purpose of removing all temptation, extinguishes all possibility of profit flowing from a breach of the confidence imposed by the fiduciary relation." Durfee, supra at 198–199, 80 N.E.2d 522, quoting Guth v. Loft, Inc., 23

---

18. Parker Coulter does not argue that Cohen or Schafer is responsible for any portion of this fair charge. We therefore do not address this issue. Mass.R.A.P. 16(a)(4), as amended, 367 Mass. 921 (1975).

19. Parker Coulter claims that, even if there were no breach of duty, the provision concerning the division of unfinished business on dissolution is unenforceable because the parties reached no agreement as to a fair charge. Consequently, Parker Coulter argues, c. 108A applies which, they claim, requires MBC to wind up all removed cases for the benefit of the former partnership. These arguments are unconvincing. First, if c. 108A were to apply, both the Parker Coulter defendants and MBC would be obligated to wind up all business originated in Parker Coulter for the benefit of the dissolved firm. G.L. c.

108A, §§ 18(f), 21, 35. See Jewel v. Boxer, 156 Cal.App.3d 171, 177–178, 203 Cal.Rptr. 13 (1984); Resnick v. Kaplan, 49 Md.App. 499, 507, 434 A.2d 582 (1982). Second, a contractual term requiring future negotiations as to specific details (a so-called "agreement to agree") is not unenforceable merely because such negotiations break down. As long as the contract, or reference to trade practice, provides "some objective method" for determining the missing term "independent of either party's mere wish or desire, ... the court will fill the gaps." Metro–Goldwyn–Mayer, Inc. v. Scheider, 40 N.Y.2d 1069, 1071, 392 N.Y.S.2d 252, 360 N.E.2d 930 (1976). The term "fair charge," given trade practice and evidence of a reasonable hourly billing rate, is sufficiently definite.

Del.Ch. 255, 270, 5 A.2d 503 (1939). Under this rule, "the innocent partner is to be put as nearly as possible in the same position which he would have occupied if there had been no wrongdoing." Shulkin, supra 301 Mass. at 193, 16 N.E.2d 644, quoted with approval in Zimmerman v. Bogoff, 402 Mass. 650, 661, 524 N.E.2d 849 (1988). We do not, however, seek to "deprive the wrong-doing partner of any participation in the fruits of his wrongful actions" (emphasis added). Shulkin, supra 301 Mass. at 193, 16 N.E.2d 644. We merely require that the fruits be shared among the parties as if they had been "earned by the partnership in the usual course of its business." Id.

Meehan and Boyle breached the duty they owed to Parker Coulter. If the judge determines that, as a result of this breach, certain clients left the firm, Meehan and Boyle must account to the partnership for any profits they receive on these cases pursuant to c. 108A, in addition to paying the partnership a fair charge on these cases pursuant to the agreement. The "profit" on a particular case is the amount by which the fee received from the case exceeds the sum of (1) any reasonable overhead expenses MBC incurs in resolving the case, see Jewel v. Boxer, 156 Cal.App.3d 171, 180, 203 Cal.Rptr. 13 (1984); Ellerby v. Spiezer, 138 Ill.App.3d 77, 83, 92 Ill.Dec. 602, 485 N.E.2d 413 (1985), and (2) the fair charge it owes under the partnership agreement. We emphasize that reasonable overhead expenses on a particular case are not the equivalent of the amount represented by the hours MBC attorneys have expended on the case multiplied by their hourly billing rate. Reasonable overhead expenses are to include only MBC's costs in generating the fee, and are not to include any profit margin for MBC. We treat this profit on a particular case as if it had been earned in the usual course of business of the partnership which included Meehan and Boyle as partners. Shulkin, supra 301 Mass. at 193, 16 N.E.2d 644. Failing to treat this profit as if it had been earned by Meehan or Boyle while at their former partnership would exclude Meehan and Boyle from participating in the fruits of their labors and, more importantly, would provide Parker Coulter with an unjustified windfall. Parker Coulter would receive a windfall because there is no guarantee that the profit would have been generated had the case not been handled at MBC. Meehan's and Boyle's former partners are thus entitled to their portion of the fair charge on each of the unfairly removed cases (89.2%), and to that amount of profit from an unfairly removed case which they would have enjoyed had the MBC attorneys handled the case at Parker Coulter (89.2%). Id.

The MBC attorneys argue that any remedy which grants Parker Coulter a recovery in excess of a fair charge on cases removed impermissibly infringes on an attorney's relationship with clients and reduces his or her incentive to use best efforts on their behalf. We agree that punitive measures may infringe on a client's right to adequate representation, and to counsel of his or her own choosing. Cf. Jewel, supra 156 Cal.App.3d at 178, 203 Cal.Rptr. 13 (how fee distributed among former partners of no concern to client); Ellerby, supra 138 Ill.App.3d at 81, 92 Ill.Dec. 602, 485 N.E.2d 413 (same). We believe, however, that the remedy we impose does not suffer from the MBC attorneys' claimed defects. Under the constructive trust we impose, Meehan and Boyle will receive a share of the fruits of their efforts in the unfairly removed cases which is the same as that which they would have enjoyed at Parker Coulter. We note, moreover, that incentives other than profit motivate attorneys. These incentives include an attorney's ethical obligations to the client and the profession, and a concern for his or her reputation. See generally 2 A.R. Bromberg & L.E. Ribstein, Partnership § 7.08, at 7:85 (1988).

Furthermore, the MBC attorneys' argument would provide us with no mechanism to enforce the partners' fiduciary duties. Imposition of a narrowly tailored constructive trust will enforce the obligations resulting from a breach of duty and will not harm the innocent clients. We conclude, therefore, that Meehan and Boyle hold in a constructive trust for the benefit of the former partnership the profits they have derived or may derive from any cases which they unfairly removed.

We now address the consequences to Cohen and Schafer of their breach of fiduciary duty. The judge found that Cohen participated in the removal of some insurance defense cases, and that Schafer participated in the removal of a number of contingent fee cases. Therefore, we conclude that Schafer must hold in a constructive trust for the benefit of the former partnership any profits, as we have defined this term, which he has received or may receive in his separate practice from cases which the judge determines were unfairly removed. Cohen also must hold any profits she has received or may receive from unfairly removed cases in a similar constructive trust. Although Cohen and Schafer were not parties to the partnership agreement, and thus were not contractually bound to remove cases fairly, we believe their fiduciary duties require this result. See Chelsea Indus. v. Gaffney, 389 Mass. 1, 11–12, 449 N.E.2d 320 (1983).[20]

4. Conclusion and Order.

In sum, we conclude that the MBC attorneys' breach of duty consisted of their method of acquiring consent from clients to remove cases. We therefore limit Parker Coulter's recovery to only those losses which were caused by this breach of duty, but place on the MBC attorneys the burden of disproving causation. On remand, the judge is to determine, based on the record and his findings as they now stand, whether the MBC attorneys have met their burden as to each case removed from Parker Coulter. A constructive trust for the benefit of the former partnership is to be imposed on any profits which Meehan, Boyle, Cohen, or Schafer receive on cases which the judge determines they unfairly removed. Because the fair charge which Meehan and Boyle owe on all removed cases is an asset of the former partnership, and because the constructive trust we impose is for the benefit of the former partnership, each former partner is entitled to his or her

---

20. We dismiss Parker Coulter's claims of tortious interference with its relations with clients and employees. Parker Coulter seeks the same damages from these claimed wrongs as it sought from its breach of fiduciary duty claims, namely all fees from the cases removed to MBC. We have determined the portion of these fees to which Parker Coulter is entitled. Therefore, we do not consider further its claims of tortious interference.

partnership share of these amounts. The Parker Coulter defendants are thus entitled to 89.2% of the fair charges on all removed cases, and 89.2% of the profits from the unfairly removed cases; Meehan and Boyle are entitled to 6% and 4.8%, respectively, of these amounts. Additionally, under the agreement's terms, Meehan and Boyle are to receive the return of their capital contributions and their profit shares.

The judgment below is reversed and the case is remanded to the Superior Court (1) for findings, in accordance with the factors we have identified, as to which cases were unfairly removed, (2) for a further evidentiary hearing to determine the reasonable overhead and thus the "profits" on the cases, if any, which were unfairly removed, and (3) for entry of a new judgment dispositive of all issues.

SO ORDERED.

CHAPTER III

LIMITED PARTNERSHIPS, LIMITED LIABILITY COMPANIES, AND LIMITED LIABILITY PARTNERSHIPS

Although the different forms of business organization vary in a number of respects, traditionally the predominant considerations in selecting a form of organization have been taxation and liability. Owners want minimum taxation and maximum protection against individual liability. For many years, the major choice of prospective owners was between corporations and partnerships. Corporations offered maximum protection against liability; partnerships (for reasons to be explained in this Chapter) normally offered minimum taxation. In recent years, however, new, alternative forms of unincorporated business organization have emerged that offer both protection against liability and minimum taxation. Three of these forms will be considered in this Chapter, in the order in which they evolved: limited partnerships, limited liability companies, and limited liability partnerships.

SECTION 1. LIMITED PARTNERSHIPS

Limited partnerships are not a new form of business organization. They are included in this chapter, rather than Chapter 2 (Partnership) for two reasons. First, recent changes in the administration of the Internal Revenue Code have affected several forms, including limited partnerships, in a way that makes it useful to consider these forms together. Second, although the limited partnership is an old form, in recent times there have been important changes in liability issues concerning limited partnerships. Both the liability and the tax developments will be considered in this section.

(a) THE UNIFORM LIMITED PARTNERSHIP ACTS

Over the course of time, the Commissioners on Uniform State Laws have promulgated several uniform limited partnership acts.

In 1916, the Commissioners promulgated the original Uniform Limited Partnership Act. It was adopted in every state except Louisiana.

In 1976, the Commissioners promulgated a replacement for the Uniform Limited Partnership Act, called the Revised Uniform Partnership Act.

The new Act modernized the prior Act and reflected the influence of the corporate model. It has been widely but not universally adopted.

In 1985, the Commissioners amended the Revised Uniform Limited Partnership Act in a number of important respects. The states are still in the process of adopting these amendments.

In the balance of this Section, the 1916 Act will be referred to as the ULPA, and the 1976 Act, as amended in 1985, will be referred to as RULPA.

(b) FORMATION OF A LIMITED PARTNERSHIP

REVISED UNIFORM LIMITED PARTNERSHIP ACT §§ 101, 201, 302, 403

[See Appendix]

NOTE

Unlike general partnerships, limited partnerships are basically creatures of statute, although they have nonstatutory historical antecedents. RULPA § 101 defines a limited partnership as "a partnership formed by two or more persons under the provisions of Section ... having as members one or more general partners and one or more limited partners." RULPA § 201 provides that in order to form a limited partnership a certificate of limited partnership must be filed in the office of the Secretary of State. The certificate must state the name of the limited partnership, the name and business address of each general partner, the latest date upon which the limited partnership is to dissolve, and the name and address of the agent for service of process.

(c) LIABILITY OF LIMITED PARTNERS

REVISED UNIFORM LIMITED PARTNERSHIP ACT § 303

[See Appendix]

Gateway Potato Sales v. G.B. Investment Co.

Court of Appeals of Arizona, 1991.
170 Ariz. 137, 822 P.2d 490.

■ TAYLOR, JUDGE.

Gateway Potato Sales (Gateway), a creditor of Sunworth Packing Limited Partnership (Sunworth Packing), brought suit to recover payment for goods it had supplied to the limited partnership. Gateway sought recovery from Sunworth Packing, from Sunworth Corporation as general partner, and from G.B. Investment Company (G.B. Investment) as a limited partner, pursuant to Arizona Revised Statutes Annotated (A.R.S.) § 29–319. Under § 29–319, a limited partner may become liable for the obligations of the limited partnership under certain circumstances in which the limited partner has taken part in the control of the business.

G.B. Investment moved for summary judgment, urging that there was no evidence that the circumstances described in A.R.S. § 29–319 had occurred in this case. It argued that, as a limited partner, it was not liable to the creditors of the limited partnership except to the extent of its investment. The trial court agreed, granting G.B. Investment's motion for summary judgment.

Gateway appeals from the judgment and the denial of its motion for reconsideration, arguing the existence of conflicting evidence of material facts relating to the participation of the limited partner in the control of the partnership business. We agree and reverse the grant of summary judgment.

FACTS

On review from the trial court's order granting summary judgment, the facts are viewed in the light most favorable to the party against whom judgment is entered. Dolezal v. Carbrey, 161 Ariz. 365, 366, 778 P.2d 1261, 1262 (1989). Sunworth Corporation and G.B. Investment formed Sunworth Packing in November 1985 for the purpose of engaging in potato farming in Arizona. The limited partnership certificate and agreement of Sunworth Packing, filed with the office of the Arizona Secretary of State, specified Sunworth Corporation as the general partner and G.B. Investment Company as the limited partner. The agreement recited that the limited partner would not participate in the control of the business. The agreement further stated that the limited partner would not become liable to the creditors of the partnership, except to the extent of its initial contribution and any liability it may incur with an Arizona bank as a signatory party or guarantor of a loan and/or line of credit.

In late 1985, Robert C. Ellsworth, the president of Sunworth Corporation, called Robert Pribula, the owner of Gateway, located in Minnesota, to see if Gateway would supply Sunworth Packing with seed potatoes. Pribula hesitated to supply the seed potatoes without receiving assurance of payment because Pribula was aware that Ellsworth had previously undergone bankruptcy. Pribula, however, decided to sell the seed potatoes to Sunworth Packing after being assured by Ellsworth that he was in partnership with a large financial institution, G.B. Investment Company, and that G.B. Investment was providing the financing, was actively involved in the operation of the business, and had approved the purchase of the seed potatoes. Thereafter, from February 1986 through April 1986, Gateway sold substantial quantities of seed potatoes to Sunworth Packing.

119

While supplying the seed potatoes, Pribula believed that he was doing business with a general partnership (i.e., Sunworth Packing Company, formed by Sunworth Corporation and G.B. Investment Company). The sales documents used by the parties specified "Sunworth Packing Company" as the name of the partnership. Pribula was neither aware of the true name of the partnership nor that it was a limited partnership.

All of Gateway's dealings were with Ellsworth. Pribula neither contacted G.B. Investment prior to selling the seed potatoes to the limited partnership nor did he otherwise attempt to verify any of the statements Ellsworth had made about G.B. Investment's involvement. The only direct contact between G.B. Investment and Gateway occurred some time after the sale of the seed potatoes. It is, however, disputed whether G.B. Investment ever provided any assurance of payment to Gateway.

G.B. Investment's vice-president, Darl Anderson, testified in his affidavit that G.B. Investment had exerted no control over the daily management and operation of the limited partnership, Sunworth Packing. This testimony was contradicted, however, by the affidavit testimony of Ellsworth which was presented by Gateway in opposing G.B. Investment's motion for summary judgment. According to Ellsworth, G.B. Investment's employees, Darl Anderson and Thomas McHolm, controlled the day-to-day affairs of the limited partnership and made Ellsworth account to them for nearly everything he did. This day-to-day contact included but was not limited to approval of most of the significant operational decisions and expenditures and the use and management of partnership funds without Ellsworth's involvement.[1]

Ellsworth testified further that he had described G.B. Investment's control of the business operation to Pribula. Pribula confirmed that Ells-

---

1. Ellsworth described with some specificity the ways in which G.B. Investment's control was exerted:

a. During the early months of the Partnership, Thomas McHolm and/or Darl Anderson were at the Partnership's offices on a daily basis directing the operation of the Partnership, and thereafter, they were at the Partnership's offices at least 2–3 times per week reviewing the operations of the business, directing changes in operations, and instructing me to make certain changes in operating the Partnership's affairs;

b. G.B. Investment Company was solely responsible for obtaining a $150,000.00 line-of-credit loan for the Partnership with Valley National Bank of Arizona, and it also signed documents guaranteeing the repayment of the loan;

c. As the President of the general partner, I was not permitted to make any significant independent business decisions concerning the operations of the Partnership, but was directed to have all business decisions approved with Darl Anderson and/or Thomas McHolm, or was directed to carry out decisions made by Darl Anderson and/or Thomas McHolm. For example, instead of using Partnership funds to pay certain creditors and suppliers, I was directed by Darl Anderson and/or Thomas McHolm to use the Partnership funds to purchase additional machinery and equipment;

d. Prior to constructing improvements to the packaging facilities of the Partnership, Thomas McHolm and/or Darl Anderson had to approve all construction bids, individually selected some of the suppliers and subcontractors, and individually selected the equipment to be installed;

worth had informed him that G.B. Investment's employees, McHolm and Anderson, were at the partnership's office on a frequent basis, that Ellsworth reported directly to them, that daily operations of the partnership were reviewed by representatives of G.B. Investment, and that Ellsworth had to get their approval before making certain business decisions.

DISCUSSION

Gateway argues that sufficient questions of fact exist which preclude the granting of summary judgment in favor of G.B. Investment. We will

e. Thomas McHolm and/or Darl Anderson dictated the accounting procedures to be followed by the Partnership, reviewed the Partnership's books and accounts almost continually, dictated that the Partnership use the same accounting firm as that of G.B. Investment Company to do the Partnership accounting tasks, undertook the responsibility of having prepared all Partnership tax forms and returns, and I only signed tax returns after they had been prepared by G.B. Investment Company's accountants and reviewed by Darl Anderson or some other employee/agent of G.B. Investment Company;

f. During a great portion of the duration of the Partnership, Thomas McHolm and/or Darl Anderson oversaw the daily operations of the Partnership because I had to have all expenditures approved by Thomas McHolm and/or Darl Anderson and Darl Anderson had to approve and sign checks issued by the Partnership, including without limitation payroll checks and invoices for telephone charges, utilities, publications, interest payments, bank card charges, supplies, etc. Copies of a sampling of the invoices and the corresponding checks are attached hereto as Exhibit 2;

g. After it was decided to add a hydro-cooler to the processing and packaging facilities of the Partnership, Thomas McHolm individually selected the refrigeration equipment and chose the contractor to install the refrigeration equipment on the hydrocooler, and even saw to it that G.B. Investment Company (not the Partnership) directly paid the contractor for all of his services;

h. Thomas McHolm insisted that the Partnership use a particular supplier, to-wit: Allied Packaging, to supply packaging materials to the Partnership, he further took an active role in reviewing and modifying the art work for use on the packaging items, and personally approved the bid submitted for the art work;

i. At least on two separate occasions, approximately in August, 1986 and again in November, 1986, Darl Anderson caused sums of monies (approximately $8,000 and $7,000 respectively) to be withdrawn from the Partnership account (No. 2270–8018) with Valley National Bank without the prior knowledge or consent of myself, as the President of the general partner of the Partnership. These monies were paid directly to G.B. Investment, and the withdrawals caused other checks of the Partnership to be dishonored due to insufficient funds and left the Partnership without sufficient funds to meet its payroll obligations;

j. Darl Anderson and/or Thomas McHolm caused certain expenses of the Partnership to be paid directly by G.B. Investment Company, to-wit: refrigeration equipment; and

k. After the Partnership defaulted on its loan payments to Valley National Bank, a loan which had been guaranteed by G.B. Investment Company, Darl Anderson, without my knowledge or consent, instructed the Valley National Bank to proceed with declaring the loan to be in default and to pursue its remedies under its Security Agreement with the Partnership, to-wit: to sell the equipment and machinery that it held as collateral at a foreclosure auction. At the foreclosure auction held on March 3, 1987, by Valley National Bank, Darl Anderson, on behalf of G.B. Investment Company, bought the equipment and machinery previously owned by Sunworth Corporation.

121

affirm the trial court's grant of summary judgment if there is no genuine issue of material fact in dispute and the moving party is entitled to judgment as a matter of law. Orme School v. Reeves, 166 Ariz. 301, 305, 802 P.2d 1000, 1004 (1990).

Subsection (a) of A.R.S. § 29–319 sets forth the general rule that a limited partner who is not also a general partner is not liable for the obligations of the limited partnership.

> [A] limited partner is not liable for the obligations of a limited partnership unless he is also a general partner or, in addition to the exercise of his rights and powers as a limited partner, he takes part in the control of the business. However, if the limited partner's participation in the control of the business is not substantially the same as the exercise of the powers of a general partner, he is liable only to persons who transact business with the limited partnership with actual knowledge of his participation in control.

In responding to the motion for summary judgment, Gateway urged the trial court to find that Gateway had presented a fact question of G.B. Investment's liability to it under A.R.S. § 29–319(a). Gateway argued that the statute imposes liability on a limited partner whose participation in the control of the business is substantially the same as the exercised power of a general partner. Gateway further argued that even if the person transacting business with the limited partnership did not know of the limited partner's participation in control, there is liability. Alternatively, Gateway argued that the statute imposes liability when the powers exercised in controlling the business might fall short of being "substantially the same as the exercise of powers of a general partner," but the person transacting business with the limited partnership had actual knowledge of the participation in control. Gateway asserted that the evidence it was presenting in response to the motion for summary judgment raised issues of material fact as to whether either of these situations had occurred. If either had occurred, Gateway argued, it would be entitled to recover from the limited partner, G.B. Investment.

In granting G.B. Investment's motion for summary judgment, the trial court gave two reasons for concluding that G.B. Investment could not be found liable under A.R.S. § 29–319(a) as a matter of law. First, as we interpret the trial court's comments, it read the statute as having a threshold requirement—that is, under all circumstances, a creditor of the limited partnership must have contact with the limited partner in order to impose liability on the limited partner. The evidence before the trial court showed that Gateway merely relied upon the statements made by Ellsworth, president of the general partner, and that Gateway did not contact G.B. Investment prior to transacting business with the limited partnership. Based upon these facts, the trial court concluded that liability could not be imposed upon G.B. Investment. The trial court's minute entry states, in relevant part:

> [I]t is undisputed that the plaintiff contracted with and sold seed potatoes to the limited partnership, without any direct contact with the

movant. In other words, at the time the sale with the limited partnership was consummated and completed—plaintiff can not by the posture of the evidence—be said to have been a person who, while transacting business with the limited partnership, did so with actual knowledge of defendant G.B. Investment Company's participation in control with the limited partnership or its general partner.

Consequently, plaintiff fails to leap the first "hurdle"; and neither the court nor the trier-of-fact need review plaintiff's factual assertions regarding "safe harbor" excesses or violations, if any, under A.R.S. § 29–319(B). The only purported contact between plaintiff and defendant G.B. Investment Company occurred in the fall of 1986, well after the last of the seed potatoes were delivered by plaintiff to the limited partnership.

Notwithstanding the representations made by Robert C. Ellsworth, as the president of the general partner, Sunworth Corporation, regarding the movant, plaintiff admits it never directly contacted the movant, to inquire into or verify Ellsworth's authority to bind the movant by such representations.

The court finds, given the present record, that movant G.B. Investment has no liability to plaintiff arising from movant being a limited partner in Sunworth Packing Limited Partnership.

After reaching this conclusion, the trial court also found that no specific facts had been presented which would support the application of A.R.S. § 29–319 so as to impose liability on G.B. Investment. As the minute entry states:

> The court further finds that while the statutory protection extended to limited partners is not absolute, there are no specific facts included within the plaintiff's response, supporting statement of facts, and supporting affidavits, which would support the applicability of A.R.S. § 29–319(A) so as to impose liability in favor of plaintiff and against the movant G.B. Investment.

To the extent that the trial court's ruling may have been based on a belief that a limited partner could never be liable under the statute unless the creditor had contact with the limited partner and learned directly from him of his participation and control of the business, we believe that ruling to be in error.

In A.R.S. § 29–319(a), the legislature stopped short of expressly stating that if the limited partner's participation in the control of the business is substantially the same as the exercise of the powers of a general partner, he is liable to persons who transact business with a limited partnership even though they have no knowledge of his participation and control. It has made this statement by implication, though, by stating to the opposite effect that "if the limited partner's participation in the control of the business is not substantially the same as the exercise of the powers of a general partner, he is liable only to persons who transact business with the

123

limited partnership with actual knowledge of his participation in control." A.R.S. § 29–319(a).

We believe this interpretation is strengthened by an examination of the legislative history of Arizona's limited partnership statute. It is further strengthened by the legislature's refusal to modify this statute to correspond to the Revised Uniform Limited Partnership Act, as amended in 1985. Prior to 1982, Arizona's limited partnership statute was patterned after the Uniform Limited Partnership Act (ULPA), which was drafted in 1916. Section 7 of the ULPA provided that "[a] limited partner shall not become liable as a general partner unless, in addition to the exercise of his rights and powers as a limited partner, he takes part in the control of the business." Uniform Limited Partnership Act § 7, 6 U.L.A. 559 (1969).[3]

The Revised Uniform Limited Partnership Act (RULPA) was drafted in 1976. Revised Uniform Limited Partnership Act, 6 U.L.A. 239, 240 (Supp. 1991). In 1982, the Arizona legislature adopted the RULPA after repealing its enactment of the ULPA. See 1982 Ariz.Sess.Laws, ch. 192, § 1 (effective July 24, 1982). Presently, A.R.S. § 29–319(a), dealing with a limited partner's liability to third parties, is very similar to the 1976 version of section 303(a) of the RULPA which stated:

> Except as provided in subsection (d), a limited partner is not liable for the obligations of a limited partnership unless he is also a general partner or, and in addition to the exercise of his rights and powers as a limited partner, he takes part in the control of the business. However, if the limited partner's participation in the control of the business is not substantially the same as the exercise of the powers of a general partner, he is liable only to persons who transact business with the limited partnership with actual knowledge of his participation in control.

Revised Uniform Limited Partnership Act § 303(a), 6 U.L.A. 239, 325 (Supp.1991). The drafters' comment to section 303 explained that limited partners exercising all of the powers of a general partner would not escape liability by avoiding direct dealings with third parties. The comment stated:

> Section 303 makes several important changes in Section 7 of the prior uniform law. The first sentence of Section 303(a) carries over the basic test from former Section 7 whether the limited partner "takes part in the control of the business" in order to ensure that judicial decisions under the prior uniform law remain applicable to the extent not expressly changed. The second sentence of Section 303(a) reflects a wholly new concept. Because of the difficulty of determining when the "control" line has been overstepped, it was thought it unfair to impose general partner's liability on a limited partner except to the extent that a third party had knowledge of his participation in control of the

---

3. The language of Arizona's then § 29–307 was taken verbatim from section 7 of the ULPA. For the text of Arizona's Uniform Limited Partnership Act, since repealed, see Uniform Limited Partnership Act, 1943 Ariz.Sess.Laws 124, reprinted in A.R.S. §§ 29–301 to–366 app. (1989) (as amended).

business. On the other hand, in order to avoid permitting a limited partner to exercise all of the powers of a general partner while avoiding any direct dealings with third parties, the "is not substantially the same as" test was introduced. . . .

Id. at 326 cmt.

In 1985, the drafters of the RULPA backtracked from the position taken in section 303(a) of the 1976 Act. The new amendments reflect a reluctance to hold a limited partner liable if the limited partner had no direct contact with the creditor. The 1985 revised RULPA section 303(a) was amended to provide as follows:

> Except as provided in Subsection (d), a limited partner is not liable for the obligations of a limited partnership unless he is also a general partner or, in addition to the exercise of his rights and powers as a limited partner, he participates in the control of the business. However, if the limited partner participates in the control of the business, he is liable only to persons who transact business with the limited partnership reasonably believing, based upon the limited partner's conduct, that the limited partner is a general partner.

Id. at 325 (emphasis added). The comment to section 303 was also revised to explain the reason for the amendment. The revised comment states:

> Section 303 makes several important changes in Section 7 of the 1916 Act. The first sentence of Section 303(a) differs from the text of Section 7 of the 1916 Act in that it speaks of participating (rather than taking part) in the control of the business; this was done for the sake of consistency with the second sentence of Section 303(a), not to change the meaning of the text. It is intended that judicial decisions interpreting the phrase "takes part in the control of the business" under the prior uniform law will remain applicable to the extent that a different result is not called for by other provisions of Section 303 and other provisions of the Act. The second sentence of Section 303(a) reflects a wholly new concept in the 1976 Act that has been further modified in the 1985 Act. It was adopted partly because of the difficulty of determining when the "control" line has been overstepped, but also (and more importantly) because of a determination that it is not sound public policy to hold a limited partner who is not also a general partner liable for the obligations of the partnership except to persons who have done business with the limited partnership reasonably believing, based on the limited partner's conduct, that he is a general partner. . . .

Id. at 326 cmt. (emphasis added).

The Arizona legislature, however, has not revised A.R.S. § 29–319(a) to correspond to the section 303 amendments. The Arizona statute continues to impose liability on a limited partner whenever the "substantially the same as" test is met, even though the creditor has no knowledge of the limited partner's control. It follows then that no contact between the creditor and the limited partner is required to impose liability.

Moreover, whereas section 303 of the RULPA states that the creditor's reasonable belief must be "based upon the limited partner's conduct," under A.R.S. § 29–319 the only requirement is that the creditor has had "actual knowledge of [the limited partner's] participation in control." The statute does not state that this knowledge must be based upon the limited partner's conduct. The comments to the original version of section 303 of the RULPA, from which Arizona's statute is taken, make it clear that only when the "substantially the same as" test is met is direct contact not a requirement. Conversely, if the "substantially the same as" test is not met, direct contact is required. Under the facts presented in this case, Gateway had no direct contact with G.B. Investment until after the sales were concluded. We conclude, therefore, that G.B. Investment would be liable only if the "substantially the same as" test was met.

Whether a limited partner has exercised the degree of control that will make him liable to a creditor has always been a factual question. This is so regardless of whether the particular statute involved is patterned after section 7 of the ULPA or after section 303 of the RULPA. E.g., Alzado v. Blinder, Robinson & Co., 752 P.2d 544 (Colo.1988); Gast v. Petsinger, 228 Pa.Super. 394, 323 A.2d 371 (1974); Holzman v. DeEscamilla, 86 Cal. App.2d 858, 195 P.2d 833 (1948). Our current Arizona statute lists activities that a limited partner may undertake without participating in controlling the business. It also states that other activities may be excluded from the definition of such control. Where activities do not fall within the "safe harbor" of A.R.S. § 29–319(b), it is necessary for a trier-of-fact to determine whether such activities amount to "control." In the absence of actual knowledge of the limited partner's participation in the control of the partnership business, there must be evidence from which a trier-of-fact might find not only control, but control that is "substantially the same as the exercise of powers of a general partner."

We conclude that the evidence Gateway presented in this case should have allowed it to withstand summary judgment. The affidavit testimony of Ellsworth raises the issue whether he was merely a puppet for the limited partner, G.B. Investment. While a few of the activities Ellsworth listed may have fallen within the protected areas listed in A.R.S. § 29–319(b), others did not. Ellsworth's detailed statement raises substantial issues of material facts.

Viewing the facts in the light most favorable to Gateway, we cannot say as a matter of law that G.B. Investment was entitled to summary judgment. We conclude that Gateway is entitled to a determination by trial of the extent of control exercised by G.B. Investment over Sunworth Packing.

For the foregoing reasons, we reverse the judgment of the trial court and remand for further proceedings.

■ EHRLICH, P.J., and CLABORNE, J., concur.

(d) CORPORATE GENERAL PARTNERS

NOTE ON CORPORATE GENERAL PARTNERS

It seems likely that the plaintiff in *Gateway* sued the limited partner, rather than the general partner, because the sole general partner was a corporation with limited assets. Ordinarily, shareholders are not liable for their corporation's debts. Therefore, if both Gateway and the corporate general partner had insufficient assets to pay the debt to the plaintiff, the plaintiff would have been unable to collect on Gateway's debt unless the limited partner was liable.

RULPA §§ 303(b)(1) and 402(9) explicitly recognize that a corporation can be a general partner in a limited partnership. In addition, RULPA § 303(b) provides that "[a] limited partner does not participate in the control of the business . . . by . . . being an officer, director, or shareholder of a general partner that is a corporation. . . ."

Although a director or officer of a corporate general partner is not liable for the debts of a limited partnership merely because he participates in the control of the partnership's business in that capacity, he may become liable if the corporate officers fail to maintain their corporate-officer identity in conducting partnership affairs, or if corporate assets are inter-mingled with partnership assets, or if the corporation is not sufficiently capitalized. See Mursor Buildings, Inc. v. Crown Mountain Apartment Associates, 467 F.Supp. 1316 (D.V.I. (1978)); Western Camps, Inc. v. Riverway Ranch Enterprises, 70 Cal.App.3d 714, 138 Cal.Rptr. 918 (1977). See generally Chapter 4, Section 6.

In Gonzalez v. Chalpin, 77 N.Y.2d 74, 564 N.Y.S.2d 702, 565 N.E.2d 1253 (1990), decided under the ULPA (the predecessor of RULPA), the court held that if a limited partner, who is also an officer and sole owner of the corporate general partner, takes part in the control of the limited partnership's business, she has the burden of proving "that any relevant actions taken were performed solely in the capacity as officer of the general partner." It is doubtful that this approach would be followed under RULPA.

In re USACafes, L.P. Litigation

Court of Chancery of Delaware, 1991.
600 A.2d 43.

■ ALLEN, CHANCELLOR.

These consolidated actions arise out of the October 1989 purchase by Metsa Acquisition Corp. of substantially all of the assets of USACafes, L.P., a Delaware limited partnership (the "Partnership") at a cash price of $72.6

million or $10.25 per unit. Plaintiffs are holders of limited partnership units. They bring these cases as class actions on behalf of all limited partnership unitholders except defendants. The relief sought includes, inter alia, the imposition of constructive trusts on certain funds received by defendants in connection with the Metsa sale and an award of damages to the class resulting from the sale.

The Partnership was formed in the 1986 reorganization of the business of USACafes, Inc., a Nevada corporation. Also formed as part of that reorganization was USACafes General Partner, Inc. (the "General Partner"), a Delaware corporation that acts as the general partner of the Partnership. Both the Partnership and the General Partner are named as defendants in this action. A second category of defendants is composed of Sam and Charles Wyly, brothers who together own all of the stock of the General Partner, sit on its board, and who also personally, directly or indirectly, own 47% of the limited partnership units of the Partnership. Sam Wyly chairs the Board of the General Partner.

The third category of defendants are four other individuals who sit on the board of directors of the General Partner. All of these persons are alleged to have received substantial cash payments, loan forgiveness, or other substantial personal benefits in connection with the 1989 Metsa purchase.

The last of the defendants is Metsa, the buyer of the Partnership's assets. Metsa is not alleged to be related in any way to the Wylys or any other defendant except as a buyer in the transaction under review.

The Theories of the Amended Complaint

The amended complaint arrays four theories of liability against these defendants. The first and most central theory involves an alleged breach of the duty of loyalty. In essence, it claims that the sale of the Partnership's assets was at a low price, favorable to Metsa, because the directors of the General Partner all received substantial side payments that induced them to authorize the sale of the Partnership assets for less than the price that a fair process would have yielded. Specifically, it is alleged that, in connection with the sale, (1) the Wylys received from Metsa more than $11 million in payments (or promises to pay in the future) which were disguised as consideration for personal covenants not to compete; (2) the General Partner (which the Wylys wholly own) received a $1.5 million payment right in consideration of the release of a claim that plaintiffs assert was non-existent; (3) defendant Rogers, a director of the General Partner and President of the Partnership was forgiven the payment of a $956,169 loan from the Partnership and was given an employment agreement with the Partnership that contemplated a one million dollar cash payment in the event, then imminent, of a "change in control"; (4) defendant Tuley, also a director of the General Partner, was forgiven repayment of a $229,701 loan; and (5) the other directors were given employment agreements providing for a $60,000 payment in the event of a change in control. In sum, it is alleged that between $15 and $17 million was or will be paid to the directors and officers of the General Partner by or with the approval of Metsa; those payments are alleged to constitute financial inducements to the directors of the General Partner to refrain from searching for a higher offer to the Partnerships. Plaintiffs add that, even assuming that Metsa was the buyer willing to pay the best price, some part at least of these "side payments" should have gone to the Partnership.

The second theory of liability reflected in the amended complaint asserts that the General Partner was (or the directors of the General Partner were) not sufficiently informed to make a valid business judgment on the sale. This theory focuses upon the absence of shopping of the Partnership's assets, or of any post-agreement market check procedure, and on the alleged weakness of the investment banker's opinion. Thus, this claim is that the defendants were uninformed when they authorized the sale to Metsa.

The third theory of liability is asserted on behalf of a class of limited partnership unitholders who held stock in the predecessor Nevada corporation—USACafes, Inc.—and who were issued partnership units pursuant to the reorganization of the USACafes business into the limited partnership form. It is alleged that those persons were misled by a December 5, 1986, prospectus (the "Prospectus"), disseminated in conjunction with the issuance of the partnership units,[1] into believing, reasonably, that, under the then proposed and later adopted structure, any sale of substantially all of the Partnership assets would require the affirmative vote of a majority of all unitholders. The relief apparently sought on this theory is the judicial recognition of an implied right to vote on the Metsa transaction (which has long since closed) or rescission of it in absence of such a vote.

The last theory in the amended complaint is the only one asserted against Metsa, the buyer. It charges that Metsa knowingly participated in the other defendants' alleged breaches of duty in connection with the sale by offering and making (or, in the case of the forgiveness of partnership debt, in agreeing to) personal payments to those controlling the General Partner designed to induce those persons to breach fiduciary duties they owed to the limited partners. Plaintiffs claim that this course of action makes Metsa jointly liable for wrongs done to the class or injuries suffered by class members out of this transaction.

* * *

The Pending Motions

... [T]he Wyly defendants and the other director defendants move under Rule 12(b)(6) to dismiss the breach of fiduciary duty claims in the amended complaint asserting that, while the General Partner admittedly did owe fiduciary duties to the limited partners, they as directors of the General Partner owe no such duties to those persons. The whole remedy of

---

1. The prospectus did not seek a share-holders' vote, but rather informed the share-holders that the reorganization would be approved by shareholder action by consent.

the limited partners for breach of the duties of loyalty and care, it is said, is against the General Partner only and not its directors. . . .

[The gist of] the director defendants' motion to dismiss for failure to state a claim with respect to the sale of the Partnership's assets. . . . is the assertion that the directors of the General Partner owed the limited partners no duty of loyalty or care. In their view their only duty of loyalty was to the General Partner itself and to its shareholders (i.e., the Wyly brothers). Thus, in alleging that the director defendants breached duties of loyalty and care running to them, the directors say the limited partners have asserted a legal nullity.

In my opinion the assertion by the directors that the independent existence of the corporate General Partner is inconsistent with their owing fiduciary duties directly to limited partners is incorrect. Moreover, even were it correct, their position on this motion would have to be rejected in any event because the amended complaint expressly alleges that they personally participated in the alleged breach by the General Partner itself, which admittedly did owe loyalty to the limited partners.

The first basis of this holding is the more significant. While I find no corporation law precedents directly addressing the question whether directors of a corporate general partner owe fiduciary duties to the partnership and its limited partners, the answer to it seems to be clearly indicated by general principles and by analogy to trust law. I understand the principle of fiduciary duty, stated most generally, to be that one who controls property of another may not, without implied or express agreement, intentionally use that property in a way that benefits the holder of the control to the detriment of the property or its beneficial owner. There are, of course, other aspects—a fiduciary may not waste property even if no self interest is involved and must exercise care even when his heart is pure—but the central aspect of the relationship is, undoubtedly, fidelity in the control of property for the benefit of another.[2] See generally Robert Flannigan, The Fiduciary Obligation, 9 Oxford J. Legal St. 285 (1989).

The law of trusts represents the earliest and fullest expression of this principle in our law, but courts of equity have extended it appropriately to achieve substantial justice in a wide array of situations. Thus, corporate directors, even though not strictly trustees, were early on regarded as fiduciaries for corporate stockholders. E.g., Koehler v. Black River Falls Iron Co., 67 U.S. (2 Black) 715, 17 L.Ed. 339 (1862); Wardell v. Union Pac. R.R. Co., 103 U.S. 651, 26 L.Ed. 509 (1880). When control over corporate property was recognized to be in the hands of shareholders who controlled the enterprise, the fiduciary obligation was found to extend to such persons as well. Allied Chemical & Dye Corp. v. Steel & Tube Co., 14 Del.Ch. 1, 120 A. 486, 491 (1923).

2. Thus, for example, a borrower of money is not considered a fiduciary for the lender simply because she is bound to return the principle sum plus interest. The "property" is held by the borrower for her own benefit.

While the parties cite no case treating the specific question whether directors of a corporate general partner are fiduciaries for the limited partnership, a large number of trust cases do stand for a principle that would extend a fiduciary duty to such persons in certain circumstances. The problem comes up in trust law because modernly corporations may serve as trustees of express trusts. Thus, the question has arisen whether directors of a corporate trustee may personally owe duties of loyalty to cestui que trusts of the corporation. A leading authority states the accepted answer:

> The directors and officers of [a corporate trustee] are certainly under a duty to the beneficiaries not to convert to their own use property of the trust administered by the corporation.... Furthermore, the directors and officers are under a duty to the beneficiaries of trusts administered by the corporation not to cause the corporation to misappropriate the property.... The breach of trust need not, however, be a misappropriation.... Any officer [director cases are cited in support here] who knowingly causes the corporation to commit a breach of trust causing loss ... is personally liable to the beneficiary of the trust....
>
> Moreover, a director or officer of a trust institution who improperly acquires an interest in the property of a trust administered by the institution is subject to personal liability. He is accountable for any profit.... Even where the trustee [itself] is not liable, however, because it had no knowledge that the director was making the purchase ..., the director ... is liable to the beneficiaries.... The directors and officers are in a fiduciary relation not merely to the [corporation] ... but to the beneficiaries of the trust administered by the [corporation].

4 A. Scott & W. Fratcher, The Law of Trusts § 326.3, at 304–306 (4th ed. 1989) (citing cases) ["Scott on Trusts"].

The theory underlying fiduciary duties is consistent with recognition that a director of a corporate general partner bears such a duty towards the limited partnership. That duty, of course, extends only to dealings with the partnership's property or affecting its business, but, so limited, its existence seems apparent in any number of circumstances. Consider, for example, a classic self-dealing transaction: assume that a majority of the board of the corporate general partner formed a new entity and then caused the general partner to sell partnership assets to the new entity at an unfairly small price, injuring the partnership and its limited partners. Can it be imagined that such persons have not breached a duty to the partnership itself? And does it not make perfect sense to say that the gist of the offense is a breach of the equitable duty of loyalty that is placed upon a fiduciary? It appears true that the same result might be rationalized as aider and abettor liability, but I am unsure what such indirection would add that is useful where a self-dealing transaction or other diversion of partnership property is alleged. Indeed in some instances, for example the use by a director of confidential information concerning the partnership's business not yet known by the board of the general partner, there may be no breach of loyalty or care by the general partner itself to abet, yet there may be director liability to the partnership by the director. Cf. cases cited at 4 Scott on Trusts § 326.3, at n. 7.

Two courts have, in fact, held a sole shareholder/director of a corporate general partner personally liable for breach of fiduciary duty to limited partners, although without much discussion of the issue here considered. See Tobias v. First City National Bank and Trust Co., 709 F.Supp. 1266, 1277–78 (S.D.N.Y.1989); Remenchik v. Whittington, Tex.Ct.App., 757 S.W.2d 836 (1988); see also In re Integrated Resources, Inc., Case No. 90–B–10411 (CB) (Bankr.S.D.N.Y. Oct. 22, 1990) (controlling shareholder held liable).

While these authorities extend the fiduciary duty of the general partner to a controlling shareholder, they support as well, the recognition of such duty in directors of the General Partner who, more directly than a controlling shareholder, are in control of the partnership's property. It is not necessary here to attempt to delineate the full scope of that duty. It may well not be so broad as the duty of the director of a corporate trustee.[3] But it surely entails the duty not to use control over the partnership's property to advantage the corporate director at the expense of the partnership. That is what is alleged here.

The amended complaint contains the following allegations:

16.   The General Partner and its directors, the named individual defendants, are in a fiduciary relationship with the plaintiffs and the other Unitholders of USACafes. . . .

17.   . . . Through their unit ownership and executive positions [the director defendants] have dominated and controlled the affairs of USACafes. Among other things, they have . . . failed to adequately solicit or consider alternative proposals for USACafes, have failed to negotiate in good faith to enhance Unitholders' values and, instead, have agreed to sell all of its assets to Metsa, which will result in the minority limited partners receiving the grossly inadequate price of $10.25 per Unit. As inducement to the individual defendants to agree to the Metsa proposal, Metsa offered to pay and the individual defendants agreed to accept, certain additional payments (approximately $17 million) that were not offered to the classes. . . .

19.   The individual defendants and the General Partner participated in the wrongdoing complained of in order to divert the valuable assets of USACafes for their own benefit by entering into highly favorable compensation arrangements with Metsa as part of the liquidation of USACafes.

I therefore conclude that the amended complaint does allege facts which if true establish that the director defendants have breached fiduciary obligations imposed upon them as directors of a Delaware corporation or

---

3. For example, I imply nothing on such questions as whether a director of a corporate general partner might be held liable directly to the partnership on a "corporate" opportunity theory or for waste of partnership assets (two possible consequences of characterizing such persons as fiduciaries for the partnership).

have participated in a breach of such duties by the General Partner. The amended complaint does, in my opinion, state a claim upon which relief can be granted. . . .

The motions of the individual defendants, the General Partner, and the Partnership to dismiss the claims arising out of the sale of the Partnership's assets is denied. . . .

———

As of 1996, there were 311,600 limited partnerships in the United States, with an average of 32 partners in each partnership. Alan Zempel, Partnership Returns, 1996, 18 Statistics of Income Bulletin No. 2, at 49–50 (1998).

———

NOTE ON THE TAXATION OF UNINCORPORATED BUSINESS ORGANIZATIONS

Taxation is a major issue in the choice of business form. There are two basic patterns of business taxation under the Internal Revenue Code, which may be called firm taxation and flow-through taxation.

Under *firm taxation*, a business firm is taxable on its income. Accordingly, if the firm has income or expenses, or gains or losses, those items go into the firm's taxable income, not into the owners' taxable income. If the firm then makes distributions to its owners out of after-tax income, the owners ordinarily pay taxes on those distributions. This is sometimes referred to as "double taxation."

Under *flow-through* taxation, a firm is not subject to taxation. Instead, all of the firm's income and expenses, and gains and losses, are taxable directly to the firm's owners. Distributions are not taxed. There is no "double taxation" effect. If the firm has losses, the owners can utilize the losses to offset their income from other sources.

Whether firm taxation or flow-through taxation is preferable for the owners of an enterprise depends in any given case on corporate and individual tax rates, the owners' circumstances, and other variables. Generally speaking, under present tax rates, owners of an enterprise will ordinarily regard flow-through taxation as preferable to firm taxation.

Historically, a firm-taxation pattern applied more or less automatically to corporations, and a flow-through taxation pattern applied more or less automatically to partnerships. Until recently, however, it was often less clear which type of taxation would be applied to forms of business organization that are intermediate between general partnerships and corporations—forms such as the limited partnership.

This issue has now been resolved by the IRS's "check-the-box" Regulations. Under these Regulations, any domestic unincorporated business that

133

constitutes an "eligible entity" can elect either flow-through taxation or firm (corporate) taxation. If an eligible entity has two or more owners, it will be taxed as a partnership—that is, it will be taxed under the partnership provisions of the Internal Revenue Code. If an eligible entity has only one owner, the entity will be disregarded for tax purposes—that is, all of the entity's income and expenses and gains and losses will be attributed to the owner.

Generally speaking, an eligible entity is any business entity other than a corporation or a business entity that is specifically made taxable as corporation under the Internal Revenue Code. The most important entity in the latter category is the *master limited partnership*. Essentially, a master limited partnership is a limited partnership whose limited-partnership interests are publicly traded—that is, traded on an established securities market, or readily tradeable on a secondary market. With certain exceptions, under the Internal Revenue Code publicly traded limited partnerships are taxed as corporations, and cannot elect partnership taxation.

There is another important respect in which the tax comparison of the traditional forms has been blurred. Just as publicly traded limited partnerships are now normally taxed like corporations, so the Internal Revenue Code provides a route through which partnership-tax treatment can be achieved by certain corporate enterprises. Subchapter S of the Code (I.R.C. §§ 1361–1379) permits the owners of qualifying corporations to elect a special tax status under which the corporation and its shareholders receive flow-though taxation that is comparable (although not identical) to partnership taxation, The taxable income of an S corporation is computed essentially as if the corporation were an individual. With some exceptions, items of income, loss, deduction, and credit are passed through to the shareholders on a pro rata basis, and added to or subtracted from each shareholder's gross income.

Among the conditions for making and maintaining a Subchapter S election are the following: (1) The corporation may not have more than seventy-five shareholders. (2) The corporation may not have more than one class of stock. (3) All the shareholders must be individuals or qualified estates or trusts. (4) No shareholder may be a nonresident alien. The amount of the corporation's assets and income is immaterial under Subchapter S.

As of 1995, there were 4,474,000 corporations in the United States. Almost half—2,153,000—were S corporations. United States Bureau of the Census, Statistical Abstract of the United States (1998).

SECTION 2. LIMITED LIABILITY COMPANIES

UNIFORM LIMITED LIABILITY COMPANY ACT §§ 101, 103, 201–203, 301–303, 404, 405, 408, 409

[See Appendix]

DELAWARE LIMITED LIABILITY COMPANY ACT §§ 18–101, 18–107, 18–201, 18–206, 18–301, 18–303, 18–401, 18–402, 18–504

[See Appendix]

NOTE ON LIMITED LIABILITY COMPANIES

Limited liability companies (LLCs) are noncorporate entities that are created under special statutes that combine elements of corporation and partnership law. As under corporation law, the owners (*members*) of LLCs have limited liability. As under partnership law, an LLC has great freedom to structure its internal governance by agreement. Like a corporation, an LLC is an entity, so that it can, for example, hold property and sue and be sued in its own name. LLCs come in two flavors: member-managed LLCs, which are managed by their members, and manager-managed LLCs, which are managed by managers who may or may not be members.

The LLC is a relatively new form. As a result, the LLC statutes are still evolving and the case law is still sparse.

Moreover, unlike the limited partnership statutes of the various states, which tend to follow RULPA, the LLC statutes are highly variable. Part (although not all) of the reason for this variability is explained by tax issues. At the time LLCs first evolved, alternative forms of business organization (that is, alternative to general partnerships and corporations) were not automatically entitled to the benefits of partnership taxation. Instead, whether any given firm that was cast in an alternative unincorporated form, such as an LLC, qualified for partnership taxation, depended on whether or not the firm had a certain number of characteristics that were deemed by the Internal Revenue Service to be "critical corporate characteristics," such as continuity of life and transferability of ownership interests.

The original LLC statutes were partly shaped by this tax rule. Some of the statutes were highly flexible, and allowed each LLC to choose its own characteristics. Other statutes, however, made certain LLC characteristics mandatory, in an effort to ensure that LLCs created under the statute would be bulletproof against an attack based on the IRS's characteristic-counting test.

Under the new, check-the-box approach to the taxation of alternative forms of business organization, no special purpose is served by making a statute bulletproof, rather than flexible. It is therefore to be expected that bulletproof LLC statutes will converge with flexible LLC statutes.

135

This Note will describe the central characteristics of LLCs in terms of prevailing statutory patterns. Bear in mind that as to any given characteristic there will usually be some LLC statutes that fall outside the major patterns this Note describes.

1. *Formation; Articles of Organization; Powers.* An LLC is formed by filing articles of organization in a designated state office—usually, the office of the Secretary of State. (Some statutes use the term *certificate of organization* rather than the term *articles of organization.*) Most statutes allow LLCs to be formed by a single person. The articles must include the name of the LLC, the address of its principal place of business or registered office in the State, and the name and address of its agent for service of process. Many or most statutes also require the articles to state: (1) The purpose of the LLC. (2) If the LLC is to be manager-managed, the names of the initial managers. If the LLC is to be member-managed, the names of its initial members. (3) The duration of the LLC or the latest date on which it is to dissolve. Many statutes also require the articles to include various kinds of additional information, the nature of which varies considerably.

Most statutes either (i) provide that LLCs have all powers necessary to effectuate their purposes or (ii) contain an exhaustive laundry list of an LLC's powers.

2. *Operating Agreements.* An LLC's articles of organization are usually very sketchy. In most LLCs, the critical foundational instrument document is the *operating agreement.* This is an agreement among the members concerning the LLC's affairs. (Some statutes use the term *limited liability agreement* rather than the term *operating agreement.*) The operating agreement typically provides for the governance of the LLC, its capitalization, the admission and withdrawal of members, and distributions. The statutes vary on whether an operating agreement must be in writing.

3. *Management.* Almost all of the LLC statutes provide as a default rule, which prevails unless agreed otherwise, that an LLC is to be managed by its members. A few statutes provide as a default rule that an LLC is to be managed by managers—who may but need not be members—unless otherwise agreed. Most of the statutes provide that the statutory default rule can be varied only by a provision in the LLC's articles of organization, but some provide that the statutory default rule can be varied in the operating agreement. One way to vary the statutory rule is to completely reverse it—either by providing for manager management in a state where the default rule is member management, or by providing for member management in a state where the default rule is manager management. Another way to vary the statutory default rule is to distribute management functions between members and managers.

4. *Voting by Members.* About half the statutes provide as a default rule that members vote per capita—that is, one vote per member—unless otherwise agreed. This is like the partnership default rule. About half provide that members vote pro rata, that is, by financial interest, unless otherwise agreed. This is the usual rule in corporations. Normally, members act by a majority vote, per capita or pro rata as the case may be.

However, some of the statutes require a unanimous vote for certain designated actions.

5. *Agency Powers.*

a. *Member-managed LLCs.* Under a majority of the statutes, the apparent authority of a member of a member-managed LLC is comparable to the apparent authority of a partner—that is, each member has power to bind the LLC for any act that is for apparently carrying on the business of the LLC in the usual or ordinary way. Even if an action is not in the usual or ordinary way, the remaining members may confer on a given member actual authority to bind the LLC to an action or a type of action. Conversely, the remaining members may withdraw the actual authority of a member to take a certain kind of action that is in the ordinary or usual way. In that case, if the member takes such an action the LLC will be bound by virtue of the member's apparent authority, but the member may be obliged to indemnify the LLC for any loss that results from her contravention of the other members' decision.

b. *Manager-managed LLCs.* In manager-managed firms, the rules concerning authority are comparable to those in the corporations—that is, typically only the managers have apparent authority to bind the firm. Members of a manager-managed LLC have no apparent authority to bind the LLC, just as shareholders have no apparent authority to bind a corporation. Most of the statutes provide that a manager in a manager-managed LLC has partner-like apparent authority.

6. *Inspection of Books and Records.* The statutes generally provide that members are entitled to access to the LLC's books and records or to specified books and records. Some statutes include an explicit provision that the inspection must be for a proper purpose. Such a limitation might or might not be read into other statutes.

7. *Fiduciary Duties.* The fiduciary duties of managers and members of LLCs are largely unspecified by the LLC statutes, just as the fiduciary duties of directors, officers, and shareholders are largely unspecified by the corporate statutes. Presumably, the courts in deciding LLC cases involving fiduciary duties will borrow very heavily from the corporate and partnership case-law.

Despite the lack of extensive specification, the LLC statutes, like the corporate and partnership statutes, do include important provisions concerning particular issues of fiduciary duty. For example, most although not all of the statutes specify the elements of the duty of care. (Some statutes provide that a manager will be liable only for gross negligence, bad faith, recklessness, or equivalent conduct. Others require a manager to act as would a prudent person in similar circumstances.) Many of the LLC statutes, like most corporate statutes, also provide mechanisms for the authorization of self-interested transactions.

The most striking divergence between the LLC statutes and the corporate and partnership statutes is that some of the LLC statutes, at least on their face, permit the operating agreement to waive all fiduciary

137

duties. There is support in both corporate law and partnership law for giving effect to the informed approval of specific self-interested transactions by the disinterested shareholders or partners. There is also support in corporate and partnership law for giving effect to contractual rules that allow a fiduciary to engage in specific types of conduct that would constitute a breach of the duty of loyalty in the absence of the rule. An example is a rule that allows the fiduciary to take certain kinds of corporate opportunities. In general, however, corporate law and partnership law do not permit an advance waiver of the entire duty of loyalty. How the courts will respond to waivers of the duty of loyalty in the LLC context—if any such waivers are actually adopted—remains to be seen.

Some of the statutes specifically provide that in a manager-managed LLC a member who is not also a manager owes no duties to the LLC or the other members solely by reason of being a member.

8. *Derivative Actions*. Most of the statutes explicitly permit members of LLCs to bring derivative actions on the LLC's behalf based on a breach of fiduciary duties. Even where the statute does not explicitly permit such actions, courts are highly likely to permit them, on analogy to corporation and limited-partnership law, and because a failure to do so might allow fiduciaries who were in control of an LLC to violate their fiduciary duties without any sanction.

9. *Distributions*. Most LLC statutes provide that in the absence of an agreement to the contrary, distributions to members are to be made pro rata according to the members' contributions, on analogy to corporation law, rather than per capita (the default rule in partnership law). Some of the statutes, however, provide that in the absence of agreement, distributions are to be on a per capita basis.

10. *Members' Interests*. A member of an LLC has financial rights, and may also have governance rights as a member—that is, apart from any governance rights she may have as a manager in a manager-managed LLC. A member's *financial* rights include her right to receive distributions. A member's governance rights include her right, if any, to participate in management, to vote on certain issues, and to be supplied with information. Some but not all statutes provide a list of actions that require member approval, at least in the absence of a contrary provision in the organic documents.

Most statutes define a member's *interest* in an LLC to consist of the member's financial rights. A few define a member's interest to include her governance rights.

Generally speaking, a member of an LLC can freely transfer her financial rights by transferring her interest in the LLC. Governance rights are treated differently. A number of statutes provide that a member can transfer her governance rights only with the unanimous consent of the other members. Some statutes provide that in the absence of an agreement to the contrary, a member can transfer her governance rights with the approval of a majority of the other members, or a majority of other members' financial interests, depending on the statute. Some statutes provide that a member can transfer governance rights, even without the unanimous or majority consent of the other members, if the articles of organization or operating agreement so provides.

It is clear that a member who assigns her interest normally cannot *assign* her governance rights, but it is not always clear whether an assigning member *retains* her governance rights. Some statutes provide that a member who assigns her membership interest loses her membership status. Some statutes provide that a member who assigns her membership interest loses her membership status if and when the assignee becomes a member. Some statutes provide that if a member assigns her membership interest, the remaining members can remove the assignor as a member. Some statutes don't speak to the issue.

If a member of an LLC assigns her interest in the LLC as a *pledge* to secure a debt, rather than in an outright sale, and if the creditor gets a judgment against the member, the creditor can get a charging order against the member's interest. A charging order gives the creditor the right to the member's share of any distributions. See PB Real Estate, Inc. v. DEM II Properties, infra.

11. *Liability.* All of the LLC statutes provide that the members and managers of an LLC are not liable for the LLC's debts, obligations, and other liabilities. It is highly likely that the courts will develop a form of piercing-the-veil doctrine applicable to LLCs. See Hollowell v. Orleans Regional Hospital, infra.

12. *Disassociation.* The LLC statutes vary considerably in their treatment of disassociation, that is, the termination of a member's interest in an LLC other than by the member's voluntary transfer of her interest. The statutes typically provide that the death, bankruptcy, or lawful expulsion of a member results in her disassociation. A number of statutes provide that a member either has (i) the right to withdraw (or "resign") at any time; (ii) the power although not necessarily the right to withdraw at any time; or (iii) the right to withdraw at any time unless otherwise provided in the operating agreement. However, a majority of the statutes do not explicitly provide a right or power to dissociate, although in some cases the right or power might be inferred from other statutory provisions.

———

As of 1996, there were 221,000 LLCs in the United States, with an average of 4 members in each LLC. The number of LLCs is growing rapidly. There were 17,000 LLCs in 1993, 48,000 LLCs in 1994, and 119,000 LLCs in 1995. Alan Zempel, Partnership Returns, 1996, 18 Statistics of Income Bulletin No. 2, at 49–50 (1998).

———

PB Real Estate, Inc. v. DEM II Properties

Appellate Court of Connecticut, 1998.
50 Conn.App. 741, 719 A.2d 73.

■ SHEA, JUDGE.

The Connecticut Limited Liability Company Act, General Statutes §§ 34–100 to 34–242, inclusive, was adopted in 1993 and is generally similar to the model act promulgated in 1995 by the Uniform Laws Commissioners. "The allure of the limited liability company is its unique ability to bring together in a single business organization the best features of all other business forms—properly structured, its owners obtain both a corporate-styled liability shield and the pass-through tax benefits of a partnership." Unif. Limited Liability Company Act, prefatory note, 6A U.L.A. 426 (1995). The central issue in this appeal is the extent to which that liability shield protects the interest of a member of a limited liability company against a judgment creditor when the basis for the judgment is an obligation unrelated to the activities of the company. Under the circumstances of this case, we conclude that it raises no barrier to the satisfaction of such a judgment from the member's interest in the company.

After obtaining a deficiency judgment resulting from a mortgage foreclosure against the defendants, Edward J. Botwick, David J. Kurzawa and DEM II Properties, the plaintiff, PB Real Estate, Inc., applied, pursuant to General Statutes (Rev. to 1995) § 34–66(1),[2] for a charging order directed to Botwick & Kurzawa, LLC, a limited liability company (LLC) engaged in the practice of law. The plaintiff was attempting to satisfy the judgment from any payments becoming due to the individual defendants, each of whom owns one half of the LLC. The trial court granted the application and directed the LLC to pay to the plaintiff "present and future shares of any and all distributions, credits, drawings, or payments due[3] to the defendant[s] ... until the judgment is satisfied in full...." The order also directed the LLC to furnish to the plaintiff for examination a copy of the LLC agreement and various financial information.

2. General Statutes (Rev. to 1995) § 34–66(1) provides: "On due application to a competent court by any judgment creditor of a partner, the court which entered the judgment, order, or decree, or any other court, may charge the interest of the debtor partner with payment of the unsatisfied amount of such judgment debt with interest thereon; and may then or later appoint a receiver of his share of the profits, and of any other money due or to fall due to him in respect of the partnership, and make all other orders, directions, accounts and inquiries which the debtor partner might have made, or which the circumstances of the case may require." This provision was repealed by No. 95–341 of the 1995 Public Acts, which became effective on July 1, 1997. The plaintiff's motion for a charging order was granted on November 11, 1996.

3. The trial court observed that the phrase, "distributions, credits, drawings, or payments due" in the charging order may be broader than the definition of a member's limited liability company interest in General Statutes § 34–101(10), "a member's share of the profits and losses of the limited liability company and a member's right to receive distributions of the limited liability company's assets...." The court restricted the scope of the turnover order to payments found to have been "distributions."

Pursuant to General Statutes § 52–356b (b), the plaintiff applied for a turnover order, claiming that the LLC had not fully complied with the charging order because the 1996 profit and loss statement indicated that a portion of the item designated on the statement as "legal staff" expense appeared to have been paid to the defendants, contrary to the directive in the charging order that all distributions should be paid to the plaintiff. After an evidentiary hearing, the trial court granted the application for a turnover order. The LLC appeals from that order and raises two issues: (1) whether certain payments it made to the defendants, the sole owners, managers and members of the LLC, were properly the subject of a turnover order; and (2) whether the turnover order exceeds the scope of the statute authorizing such orders with respect to an LLC. We resolve both issues against the LLC and affirm the order of the trial court.

I

The trial court found that, since the date of the charging order, the LLC had paid approximately $28,000 to each of two defendants. The court rejected the defendants' claim that those payments were merely compensation for their services to the LLC as lawyers and were similar to the wages paid to other employees of the firm. The payments to the defendants were not shown in the "salary" column of the business record where payments to employees of the law firm are recorded but were listed separately under their initials. The 1996 tax returns of the individual defendants indicated that they received little or no wages, but they reported significant earnings from self-employment. The trial court concluded that the payments made by the law firm to the defendants were "distributions" that were subject to the charging order.

The LLC does not dispute the underlying facts on which the trial court relied in reaching that conclusion. Even without such a concession, we conclude that the evidence adequately supports the facts set forth in the memorandum of decision. The LLC contends, nevertheless, that several provisions of the Connecticut Limited Liability Company Act preclude the conclusion that the challenged payments were distributions.

II

The LLC claims that the trial court incorrectly failed to limit the turnover order to the "rights of an assignee of the member's limited liability company interest," as provided by General Statutes § 34–171 in defining the rights of a judgment creditor. That statute provides that, "[t]o the extent so charged, the judgment creditor has only the rights of an assignee of the member's limited liability company interest." The phrase, "[l]imited liability company membership interest," is defined by General Statutes § 34–101(10) to mean "a member's share of the profits and losses of the limited liability company and a member's right to receive distributions of the limited liability company's assets, unless otherwise provided in the operating agreement." The operating agreement for the LLC provides that "all distributions . . . shall be made at such time as determined by the Manager," who consists solely of the two owners. They maintain that they

141

have authorized no distributions, and therefore, the court's finding that the $28,000 each of them has received was a distribution is contrary to General Statutes § 34–158, which provides in part that "[a] member is entitled to receive distributions . . . from a limited liability company to the extent and at the times or upon the happening of the events specified in the operating agreement or at the times determined by the members or managers pursuant to section 34–142."[8]

It defies common sense for the defendants, who jointly comprise the "Manager," to contend that the payments they made to themselves from the assets of their LLC do not constitute distributions, simply because they never voted to order such distributions. The operating agreement requires that distributions "shall be made at such time as determined by the Manager," but does not specify any formal procedure for authorizing distributions. General Statutes § 34–142(a) requires "the affirmative vote, approval or consent of . . . more than one-half by number of the managers" to decide matters connected with the LLC, but these are alternatives. The defendants can hardly deny that they approved or consented to the payments they received from the LLC, which they own and control. Neither § 34–142(a) nor General Statutes § 34–158, which authorizes distributions "at the times determined by the members or managers pursuant to section 34–142," raises any barrier to the finding of the court that the payments to the defendants constituted distributions subject to the charging order they have disregarded.

Furthermore, the definition in § 34–101(10) of a member's limited liability company interest, which § 34–171 makes available for satisfaction of a judgment, includes "a member's share of the profits and losses" of the company as well as "distributions of the . . . company's assets. . . . " Although the defendants at trial presented a profit and loss statement for 1996 showing a net profit of only $23.44, that result was achieved only by treating the payments of $28,000 to each of them as expenses for wages. If those payments were neither distributions, as the defendants contend, nor wages, as the trial court found, they would have to be considered profits. The plaintiff claims that, as an assignee of the defendants' shares thereof, it would be entitled to satisfy its deficiency judgment from those profits even if the payments made to the defendants had not been approved in accordance with the operating agreement. The defendants contend, however, that General Statutes § 34–170(a)(2), providing that "an assignment entitles the assignee to receive, to the extent assigned, only the distributions to which the assignor would be entitled" indicates otherwise. The trial court did not consider the issue of a possible inconsistency between that provision and the definition of a member's interest in § 34–101(10), nor shall we do so in view of our agreement with the court's conclusion

---

8. General Statutes § 34–142(a) provides in relevant part that "the affirmative vote, approval or consent of . . . more than one-half by number of the managers, if management of the limited liability company is vested in managers, shall be required to decide any matter connected with the business or affairs of the limited liability company."

that the payments received by the defendants were distributions subject to the charging order.

The judgment issuing the turnover order is affirmed.

In this opinion the other judges concurred.

———

Hollowell v. Orleans Regional Hospital

United States District Court, E.D. Louisiana 1998.
1998 WL 283298 (E.D.La.).

■ LEMMON, J. . . .

I. BACKGROUND

A. PROCEDURAL

Plaintiffs Lisa Hollowell, Terrence Pierce and Emma Chess filed this class action suit on behalf of themselves and others similarly situated against defendants Orleans Regional Hospital ("ORH"), Success Counseling Services, North Louisiana Regional Hospital ("NLRH"), Magnolia Health Systems ("MHS"), Precision Incorporated Systems ("Precision), . . . New Orleans Rehabilitation Services ("NORS"), North Louisiana Regional Hospital Partnership ("NLRHP"), William C. Windham, John Turner, [and] Richard Williams. . . . Plaintiffs allege that they were laid off by the defendants without proper notice in violation of the provisions of the Worker Adjustment and Retraining Notification ("WARN") Act, 29 U.S.C. §§ 2101 to 2109. . . . United States District Judge Marcel Livaudais certified this case as a class action before transferring this case to this division.

Defendants filed a Motion for Summary Judgment and plaintiffs filed a Cross-Motion for Partial Summary Judgment. . . .

B. FACTUAL

Plaintiffs allege the following facts. ORH was a Medicaid funded hospital in New Orleans which provided psychiatric and substance abuse treatment for children and adolescents. ORH was a limited liability company under Louisiana law whose members were NLRH, Precision, and NORS. ORH was operated by NLRHP, a partnership under Louisiana law consisting of NLRH and Precision. William Windham and John Turner were each fifty percent shareholders of NLRH and Richard Williams was the sole shareholder of Precision. MHS, another limited liability company under Louisiana law whose members consisted of NLRH and Precision, served as a management company for NLRH and ORH.

As Louisiana began implementing regulatory changes in its Medicaid reimbursement policies, ORH made several changes to its operating procedures, including providing outpatient services. These services were provided by Success Counseling Services, who "employed" a number of ORH employees. As regulatory changes began to affect admission and length of stay regulations in psychiatric hospitals, the patient census at ORH began to drop and consequently, ORH began discharging employees. Ultimately, ORH shut down its operations on November 3, 1995....

II. CROSS–MOTIONS FOR SUMMARY JUDGMENT

The WARN Act consists of Sections 2101 to 2109 of Title 29 of the United States Code. Section 2101(a) requires an "employer" to serve written notice to "employees" who suffer an "employment loss" as a result of a "plant closing" or "mass layoff" at least sixty-days prior to the "plant closing" or "mass layoff." In their Motion for Summary Judgment and in opposition to plaintiffs' Motion for Partial Summary Judgment, defendants argue that ... defendants Turner, Williams, Windham, as individuals, are not "employers" as that term is defined in Section 2101; that ORH is not an "employer" as that term is defined in Section 2101; [and] that all of the defendants did not constitute a "single business enterprise" within the meaning of the WARN Act.... In support of their Motion for Partial Summary Judgment and in opposition to defendants' Motion for Summary Judgment, plaintiffs argue that ... all of the defendants constitute a "single business enterprise"; and that defendants Turner, Williams, and Windham are directly liable in their individual capacities as "employers" as that term is defined in Section 2101, and are indirectly liable for ORH's WARN Act violations.

[The court held that an individual may not be held directly liable for WARN Act violations.]

Under Louisiana law, [however,] an individual may be held liable for the debts of a corporation under certain circumstances. Thus, while the WARN Act may not provide direct liability for individuals, under Louisiana law an individual may be held liable for damages sustained as a result of a corporation's unlawful acts, if the business entity is merely an "alter ego" of the individual. In United States v. Clinical Leasing Service, Inc. 982 F.2d 900 (5th Cir.1992), the Fifth Circuit noted that Louisiana courts focus on the following five elements in deciding whether in fact a corporation is merely an "alter ego" of an individual:

(1) commingling of corporate and shareholder funds;

(2) failure to follow statutory formalities for incorporation and the transaction of corporate affairs;

(3) undercapitalization of the corporation;

(4) failure to provide separate bank accounts and bookkeeping records; and

(5) failure to hold regular shareholder or director meetings.

Clinical Leasing Servs., 982 F.2d at 902.[11] In this manner, Louisiana law permits plaintiffs to hold individuals liable for the debts of a corporation. See generally Glenn G. Morris, Piercing the Corporate Veil in Louisiana, 52 LA.L.REV. 271 (1991). Louisiana law also permits plaintiffs to hold

---

11. Clinical Leasing Services did not involve a WARN Act claim.

individual shareholders of a corporation liable for the debts of a corporation where the individuals act through the corporation to "commit fraud or deceit on a third party." McDonough Marine Servs. v. Doucet, 694 So.2d 305, 308 (La.Ct.App. 1st Cir.1996).

ORH is a limited liability company rather than a corporation. No case has yet explicitly held that the "veil" of protection from liability afforded by the limited liability company form of business in Louisiana may be "pierced" in the same manner as the "veil" of protection afforded Louisiana corporations. However, commentators throughout the nation appear to agree that the limited liability company "veil" may be "pierced" in the same manner as the corporate "veil."[8] More specifically, several commentators appear to assume that indeed a Louisiana limited liability company's "veil" may be pierced.[9] As Professor Kalinka notes in her Louisiana Civil Law Treatise on Louisiana Limited Liability Companies and Partnerships, "[t]he same policy considerations in piercing the veil of a corporation apply to an LLC." Susan Kalinka, Louisiana Liability Companies & Partnerships: a Guide to Business and Tax Planning § 1.32, at 64 (1997), in 9 Louisiana Civil Law Treatise (1997). However, Professor Kalinka cautions that the analyses between corporate veil piercing and limited liability company veil piercing may not completely overlap, noting that "[b]ecause the Louisiana LLC law requires fewer formalities such as annual elections of directors, keeping minutes, or holding meetings, failure to follow these formalities should not serve as grounds for piercing the veil of an LLC." Id.

With this caveat in mind, this court holds that under Louisiana law the "veil" of protection afforded ORH by its Limited Liability Company form may be "pierced" if in fact ORH was operating as the "alter ego" of ORH's members or if ORH's members were committing fraud or deceit on third parties through ORH. Moreover, the veil provided by the corporate status of ORH's members may also be pierced in like fashion. These questions necessarily involve a fact-intensive review of the relationships among all of

---

8. See, e.g., See Karin Schwindt, Comment, Limited Liability Companies: Issues in Member Liability, 44 UCLA L. REV. 1541 (1997); Robert B. Thompson, The Limits of Liability in the New Limited Liability Entities, 32 WAKE FOREST L.REV. 1 (1997); Rachel Maizes, Limited Liability Companies: A Critique, 70 ST. JOHN'S L.REV. 575 (1996); Eric Fox, Note, Piercing the Veil of Limited Liability Companies, 62 GEO. WASH. L.REV. 1143 (1994); Wayne M. Gazur & Neil M. Goff, Assessing the Limited Liability Company, 41 CASE W. RES. L.REV. 387, 403 (1991); Robert R. Keatinge, et al. The Limited Liability Company: A Study of the Emerging Entity, 47 BUS. LAW. 375, 445 (1992); Curtis J. Braukmann, Comment, Limited Liability Companies, 39 KAN. L.REV. 967, 992 (1991).

9. See J. William Callison & Maureen A. Sullivan, Limited Liability Companies: a State-by-state Guide to Law & Practice at § 15.28 (1996 & Supp.1997) ("[T]o the extent that the corporate law concept of 'piercing the corporate veil' applies to Louisiana LLCs, members can be liable to creditors who are able to pierce the corporate-type protection afforded by the LLC. Courts might pierce the LLC form and hold members personally liable if respect for the LLC form would work injustice."); Susan Kalinka, The Louisiana Limited Liability Company After the "Check–The–Box", 57 LA. L.REV. 715, 794 (1997) ("a court may use a veil-piercing theory to hold members of an LLC liable for the LLC's obligations, especially if the LLC is thinly capitalized or under-insured. The limitations on a member's liability under the Louisiana LLC Law should be retained.").

the members of ORH in order to make a determination of whether ORH was the "alter ego" of its members or, alternatively, whether ORH's members were using ORH to commit fraud. Accordingly, the court declines to grant summary judgment to any of the defendants, or in favor of the plaintiffs, on the plaintiffs' "veil piercing" claims.

F. "SINGLE BUSINESS ENTERPRISE"

In addition to holding the ORH's codefendants, including the individual defendants and ORH's members, liable for ORH's debts by "piercing" ORH's and/or its members' "veils," ORH's codefendants, but not the individual defendants, may be held directly liable for violating the WARN Act if they, along with ORH, are considered to be a single "business enterprise" within the meaning of the WARN Act. Section 639.3(a)(2) of Title 20 of the Code of Federal Regulations sets forth the factors to be considered in deciding whether to treat subsidiaries and parent companies as a single "business enterprise" under Section 2101(a)(1):

> Under existing legal rules, independent contractors and subsidiaries which are wholly or partially owned by a parent company are treated as separate employers or as part of the parent or contracting company depending upon the degree of their independence from the parent. Some of the factors to be considered in making this determination are (i) common ownership, (ii) common directors and/or officers, (iii) de facto exercise of control, (iv) unity of personnel policies emanating from a common source, and (v) the dependency of operations.

The Department of Labor has expounded on this regulation by stating:

> Several commenters raised questions about the definition of "[i]ndependent contractors and subsidiaries" in § 639.3(a)(2). Some of these commenters suggested that the definition should be simplified to treat subsidiaries as separate employers as long as they are "bona fide separate and distinct companies and hold themselves out to the public as such"; or to define as separate companies entities that have separate payroll functions. One commenter requested special treatment for the garment industry because of the peculiar relationship of jobbers and contractors within that industry. Another commenter suggested that the regulation also should recognize the doctrine of joint employer status, as that doctrine has been developed under the NLRA. A commenter suggested that the National Mediation Board should be recognized as the authority for determining whether companies covered by the Railway Labor Act (RLA) are separate. Another commenter stated that the rule on subsidiaries also should apply to operating divisions.

> The intent of the regulatory provision relating to independent contractors and subsidiaries is not to create a special definition of these terms for WARN purposes; the definition is intended only to summarize existing law that has developed under State Corporations laws and such statutes as the NLRA, the Fair Labor Standards Act (FLSA) and the Employee Retirement Income Security Act (ERISA). The Depart-

ment does not believe that there is any reason to attempt to create new law in this area especially for WARN purposes when relevant concepts of State and federal law adequately cover the issue. Thus, no change has been made in the definition. Similarly, the regulation is not intended to foreclose any application of existing law or to identify the source of legal authority for making determinations of whether related entities are separate. To the extent that existing law recognizes the joint employer doctrine or the special situation of the garment industry, nothing in the regulation prevents application of that law. Nor does the regulation preclude recognition of the National Mediation Board as an authoritative decision maker for entities covered under the RLA. Neither does the regulation preclude treatment of operating divisions as separate entities if such divisions could be so defined under existing law.

54 Fed.Reg. 16045 (April 10, 1989) (alteration in original).

In determining whether several entities should be treated as a "single business enterprise" for purposes of WARN Act liability, courts have looked to state corporate law, other federal labor laws, and the above quoted regulations. See United Paperworkers v. Alden Corrugated Container, 901 F.Supp. 426, 437 (D.Mass.1995) (discussing the caselaw). Thus, the determination whether several entities are to be treated as a "single business enterprise" for purposes of WARN Act liability overlaps, in no small degree, the factors to be considered in determining whether ORH's "veil" may be "pierced." Therefore, for the same reasons that summary judgment is inappropriate on plaintiffs' "veil piercing" claims, summary judgment is also inappropriate on plaintiffs' WARN Act claims against the non-ORH defendants....

... Accordingly, the following issues remain for trial:

(1) Plaintiffs' damages;

(2) Whether any or all the non-ORH defendants,[10] excluding the individual defendants, and ORH operated a "single business enterprise" in light of the following factors:

(a) common ownership;

(b) common directors and/or officers;

(c) de facto exercise of control;

(d) unity of personnel policies emanating from a common source; and

(e) the dependency of operations.

(3) Whether ORH was the "alter ego" of any or all of the non-ORH defendants, including the individual defendants, and whether the members of ORH were the "alter egos" of their shareholders, in light of the following factors:

---

10. The "non-ORH defendants" are Success Counseling Services, NLRH, MHS, Precision, NLRHP, William C. Windham, John Turner, and Richard Williams.

(a) commingling of funds;

(b) failure to follow statutory formalities for formation and the transaction affairs;

(c) undercapitalization;

(d) failure to provide separate bank accounts and bookkeeping records; and

(e) failure to hold regular required meetings.

(4) Whether ORH's members acted through ORH to commit fraud or deceit, and whether the shareholders of ORH's members acted in similar fashion. . . .

McConnell v. Hunt Sports Enterprises

Court of Appeals of Ohio, 1999.
132 Ohio App.3d 657, 725 N.E.2d 1193.

On June 17, 1997, John H. McConnell and Wolfe Enterprises, Inc. filed a complaint for declaratory judgment in the Franklin County Court of Common Pleas against Hunt Sports Enterprises, Hunt Sports Enterprises, L.L.C., Hunt Sports Group, L.L.C. ("Hunt Sports Group") and Columbus Hockey Limited ("CHL"). CHL was a limited liability company formed under R.C. Chapter 1705. A brief background of the events leading up to the formation of CHL and the subsequent discord among certain of its members follows.

In 1996, the National Hockey League ("NHL") determined it would be accepting applications for new hockey franchises. In April 1996, Gregory S. Lashutka, the mayor of Columbus, received a phone call from an NHL representative inquiring as to Columbus's interest in a hockey team. As a result, Mayor Lashutka asked certain community leaders who had been involved in exploring professional sports in Columbus to pursue the possibility of applying for an NHL hockey franchise. Two of these persons were Ronald A. Pizzuti and McConnell.

Pizzuti began efforts to recruit investors in a possible franchise. Pizzuti approached Lamar Hunt, principal of Hunt Sports Group, as to Hunt's interest in investing in such a franchise for Columbus. Hunt was already the operating member of the Columbus Crew, a professional soccer team whose investors included Hunt Sports Group, Pizzuti, McConnell, and Wolfe Enterprises, Inc. Hunt expressed an interest in participating in a possible franchise. The deadline for applying for an NHL expansion franchise was November 1, 1996.

On October 31, 1996, CHL was formed when its articles of organization were filed with the secretary of state pursuant to R.C. 1705.04. The members of CHL were McConnell, Wolfe Enterprises, Inc., Hunt Sports

Group, Pizzuti Sports Limited, and Buckeye Hockey, L.L.C.[1] Each member made an initial capital contribution of $25,000. CHL was subject to an operating agreement that set forth the terms between the members. Pursuant to section 2.1 of CHL's operating agreement, the general character of the business of CHL was to invest in and operate a franchise in the NHL.

On or about November 1, 1996, an application was filed with the NHL on behalf of the city of Columbus. In the application, the ownership group was identified as CHL, and the individuals in such group were listed as Pizzuti Sports Limited, McConnell, Wolfe Enterprises, Inc. and Hunt Sports Group. A $100,000 check from CHL was included as the application fee. Also included within the application package was Columbus's plan for an arena to house the hockey games. There was no facility at the time, and the proposal was to build a facility that would be financed, in large part, by a three-year countywide one-half percent sales tax. The sales tax issue would be on the May 1997 ballot.

On May 6, 1997, the sales tax issue failed. The day after, Mayor Lashutka met with Hunt, and other opportunities were discussed. The mayor also spoke with Gary Bettman, commissioner of the NHL, and they discussed whether an alternate plan for an arena was possible. Also on May 7, 1997, Dimon McPherson, chairman and chief executive officer of Nationwide Insurance Enterprise ("Nationwide"), met with Hunt, and they discussed the possibility of building the arena despite the failure of the sales tax issue. McPherson testified that he chose Hunt because: "[w]ell, he was the visible, obvious, only person that was involved in trying to bring NHL hockey to Columbus. There was really no one else to turn to." Hunt was interested, and Nationwide began working on an arena plan. On or about May 9, 1997, the mayor spoke with Bettman and let him know that alternate plans would be pursued, and Mr. Bettman gave Columbus until June 4, 1997 to come up with a plan.

By May 28, 1997, Nationwide had come up with a plan to finance an arena privately and on such date, Nationwide representatives met with representatives of Hunt Sports Group. Hunt Sports Group did not accept Nationwide's lease proposal. McPherson told Hunt that City Council would be meeting on Monday, June 2, 1997 to vote on an ordinance that, in general terms, included an authorization for the city to enter into an agreement with Nationwide to build a downtown arena. Nationwide informed Hunt Sports Group that it needed an answer by Friday, May 30, 1997 as to whether, in general terms, the lease proposal was acceptable. On May 29, 1997, Nationwide representatives again met with representatives of Hunt Sports Group. Again, Hunt Sports Group indicated that the lease proposal was unacceptable and that the NHL team would lose millions with

---

1. In its answer and counterclaim, Hunt Sports Group averred that Ameritech was also a member of CHL. Ameritech's name does not appear on Schedule A of the operating agreement; however, the record reflects that Ameritech contributed $25,000 to CHL and was considered a member of CHL. Ameritech's membership status is not an issue in this appeal.

this proposal. The June 4, 1997 NHL deadline was discussed. Hunt Sports Group stated that it would continue to evaluate the proposal, and it wanted the weekend to do so. Nationwide informed appellant that it needed an answer by close of business Friday, May 30.

On May 30, 1997, McPherson called McConnell and requested that they meet and discuss "where [they] were on the arena." McPherson "could see that the situation now was slipping away, and [he] just didn't want that to happen," so he went to see McConnell for advice and counsel. McConnell testified that the conversation was "totally out of the blue. [McPherson] said that Nationwide was going to finance and build an arena, and that he had offered the Hunt group the opportunity to pick up the lease and bring a franchise in. That was news to me. It was out of the blue." McPherson told McConnell about appellant's rejection of the lease proposal and discussed the NHL's June 4 deadline. McConnell stated that if Hunt would not step up and lease the arena and, therefore, get the franchise, McConnell would. Hunt Sports Group did not contact Nationwide on May 30, 1997.

On Saturday, May 31, McPherson told Nationwide's board of directors that there was not yet a lease commitment but that if Hunt Sports Group did not lease the arena, McConnell would. On Monday, June 2, 1997, City Council passed the resolution that set forth the terms for Nationwide to build an arena downtown. Also on June 2, 1997, McPherson met with Bettman and told him that Nationwide would be building an arena in downtown Columbus. McPherson also told Bettman that if need be, McConnell would purchase the franchise on his own. On or about Tuesday, June 3, McConnell was informed that appellant [Hunt] had not yet accepted the lease proposal. On June 3, Hunt spoke with Robert J. Woodward, Jr., executive vice-president and chief investment officer of Nationwide and asked him to fax a copy of the ordinance passed by City Council. On that same date, Hunt Sports Group told Nationwide that it still found the terms of the lease to be unacceptable. On June 3 or June 4, McConnell, in a conversation with the NHL, orally agreed to apply for a hockey franchise for Columbus. On June 4, McPherson returned a call from Hunt, and Hunt informed McPherson that he was still interested in pursuing an agreement with Nationwide.

On June 4, 1997, the NHL franchise expansion committee met. Bettman informed the committee that Nationwide would build an arena, and McConnell was prepared to go forward with the franchise even if he had to do it himself. The committee was told that Hunt Sports Group's involvement was an open issue, but McConnell as an owner was more than adequate. The expansion committee recommended Columbus to the NHL board of governors as one of four cities to be granted a franchise.

On June 5, 1997, the NHL sent Hunt a letter requesting that he let them know by Monday, June 9, 1997 whether he was going forward with his franchise application. In a June 6, 1997 letter to the NHL, Hunt responded that CHL intended to pursue the franchise application. Hunt informed the NHL that he had arranged a meeting with the members of

CHL to be held on June 9, 1997. Hunt indicated that the application was contingent upon entering into an appropriate lease for a hockey facility.

On June 9, 1997, a meeting took place at Pizzuti's office. Those present at the meeting included: McConnell, Hunt, Pizzuti, John F. Wolfe, chairman of Wolfe Enterprises, Inc., and representatives of Buckeye Hockey, L.L.C. and Ameritech. The NHL required that the ownership group be identified and that such ownership group sign a lease term sheet by June 9, 1997. Brian Ellis, president and chief operating officer of Nationwide, presented the lease term sheet to those present at the meeting, left the meeting and went to a different room.

Hunt indicated the lease was unacceptable. Ameritech and Buckeye Hockey, L.L.C. indicated that if Hunt found it unacceptable then they too found it unacceptable. Pizzuti and Wolfe agreed to participate along with McConnell. John Christie, president of JMAC, Inc., the personal investment company of the McConnell family, left the meeting and joined Ellis. Christie informed Ellis that McConnell had accepted the term sheet and was signing it in his individual capacity. The term sheet contained a signature line for "Columbus Hockey Limited" as the franchise owner. Ellis phoned his secretary and had her omit the name "Columbus Hockey Limited" on her computer from under the signature line and fax the change to Ellis at Pizzuti's office. McConnell then signed the term sheet as the owner of the franchise. Christie faxed the signed lease term sheet to Bettman that day along with a cover letter and a description of the ownership group. Such ownership group was identified as: John H. McConnell, majority owner, Pizzuti Sports, L.L.C., John F. Wolfe and "[u]p to seven (7) other members." The cover letter indicated that the attached material signified an amendment to the November 1, 1996 application from the city.

On June 17, 1997, the NHL expansion committee recommended to the NHL board of governors that Columbus be awarded a franchise with McConnell's group as owner of the franchise. On the same date, the complaint in the case at bar was filed. On or about June 25, 1997, the NHL board of governors awarded Columbus a franchise with McConnell's group ["COLHOC"] as owner. Hunt Sports Group, Buckeye Hockey, L.L.C. and Ameritech have no ownership interest in the hockey franchise. . . .

In their complaint, McConnell and Wolfe Enterprises, Inc. requested a declaration that section 3.3 of the CHL operating agreement allowed members of CHL to compete with CHL. Specifically, McConnell and Wolfe Enterprises, Inc. sought a declaration that under the operating agreement, they were permitted to participate in COLHOC and obtain the franchise. . . .

On June 23, 1997, Hunt Sports Group filed an answer and counterclaim on its behalf and on behalf on CHL. The counterclaim was asserted against McConnell and alleged breach of contract, breach of fiduciary duty and interference with prospective business relationships.

151

On July 3, 1997, McConnell and Wolfe Enterprises, Inc. filed a motion for summary judgment as to count one of the first amended complaint (declaratory judgment as to section 3.3 of the operating agreement) and as to counts one through five of the counterclaim [which included breach of fiduciary duty and tortious interference with business relationships]. . . . On October 31, 1997, the trial court rendered a decision, granting summary judgment in favor of McConnell and Wolfe Enterprises, Inc. on count one of the . . . complaint and on [certain] counts. . . . of the counterclaim. Specifi- cally, the trial court found that section 3.3 of the operating agreement was clear and unambiguous and allowed McConnell and Wolfe Enterprises, Inc. to compete against CHL and obtain the NHL franchise. In addition, the trial court found McConnell did not breach the operating agreement by competing against CHL. The claims that remained included . . . breach of fiduciary duty and interference with prospective business relationships. . . .

A jury trial was held in May 1998 on [certain counts of the] com- plaint. . . . On May 15, 1998, the trial court rendered a decision, granting McConnell and Wolfe Enterprises, Inc.'s motion for directed verdicts on counts three and four of the . . . complaint. . . .

Summary judgment is appropriate when, construing the evidence most strongly in favor of the nonmoving party, (1) there is no genuine issue of material fact, (2) the moving party is entitled to judgment as a matter of law, and (3) reasonable minds can come to but one conclusion, that conclusion being adverse to the nonmoving party. . . .

As indicated above, count one of the . . . complaint sought a declaration that section 3.3 of CHL's operating agreement allowed members to compete against CHL to obtain an NHL franchise. Appellees contend section 3.3 is plain and unambiguous and allows what occurred here—COLHOC compet- ing for and obtaining the NHL franchise. Appellant asserts, in part, that the trial court's interpretation of section 3.3 was incorrect and that section 3.3 is ambiguous and subject to different interpretations. Therefore, appel- lant contends extrinsic evidence should have been considered, and such evidence would have shown the parties did not intend section 3.3 to mean members could compete against CHL and take away CHL's only pur- pose. . . .

Section 3.3 of the operating agreement states:

"Members May Compete. Members shall not in any way be prohib- ited from or restricted in engaging or owning an interest in any other business venture of any nature, including any venture which might be competitive with the business of the Company."

Appellant emphasizes the word "other" in the above language and states, in essence, that it means any business venture that is different from the business of the company. Appellant points out that under section 2.1 of the operating agreement, the general character of the business is "to invest in and operate a franchise in the National Hockey League." Hence, appel- lant contends that members may only engage in or own an interest in a venture that is not in the business of investing in and operating a franchise with the NHL.

Appellant's interpretation of section 3.3 goes beyond the plain language of the agreement and adds words or meanings not stated in the provision. Section 3.3, for example, does not state "[m]embers shall not be prohibited from or restricted in engaging or owning an interest in any other business venture that is different from the business of the company." Rather, section 3.3 states: "any other business venture of any nature." (Emphasis added.) It then adds to this statement: "including any venture which might be competitive with the business of the Company." The words "any nature" could not be broader, and the inclusion of the words "any venture which might be competitive with the business of the Company" makes it clear that members were not prohibited from engaging in a venture that was competitive with CHL's investing in and operating an NHL franchise. Contrary to appellant's contention, the word "other" simply means a business venture other than CHL. The word "other" does not limit the type of business venture in which members may engage.

Hence, section 3.3 did not prohibit appellees from engaging in activities that may have been competitive with CHL, including appellees' participation in COLHOC. Accordingly, summary judgment in favor of appellees was appropriate, and appellees were entitled to a declaration that section 3.3 of the operating agreement permitted appellees to request and obtain an NHL hockey franchise to the exclusion of CHL.

Appellant next contends that the trial court erred in granting summary judgment in favor of appellees on [count one] of appellant's counterclaim. Count one of the counterclaim alleged McConnell breached the operating agreement by forming COLHOC for the sole purpose of competing directly with CHL's application for an NHL franchise. . . .

. . . [T]here are no genuine issues of material fact, appellees are entitled to judgment as a matter of law and reasonable minds could only conclude that section 3.3 of the operating agreement allowed appellees to request and obtain an NHL franchise to the exclusion of CHL, McConnell did not breach the operating agreement by forming COLHOC and competing against CHL. . . . Therefore, summary judgment in favor of appellees on count one of the . . . complaint and on [count one] of appellant's counterclaim was appropriate. . . .

. . . [T]he trial court was correct in stating that it could not be considered a breach of fiduciary duty, in and of itself, to compete against CHL because the operating agreement allowed such competition. Contract provisions may affect the scope of fiduciary duties, and as such, the trial court was correct to indicate that the method of competing, not the competing itself, may constitute a breach of fiduciary duty. . . .

. . . In the case at bar, a limited liability company is involved which, like a partnership, involves a fiduciary relationship. Normally, the presence of such a relationship would preclude direct competition between members of the company. However, here we have an operating agreement that by its

153

very terms allows members to compete with the business of the company. Hence, the question we are presented with is whether an operating agreement of a limited liability company may, in essence, limit or define the scope of the fiduciary duties imposed upon its members. We answer this question in the affirmative. . . .

Here, the injury complained of by appellant was, essentially, appellees competing with CHL and obtaining the NHL franchise. The operating agreement constitutes the undertaking of the parties herein. In becoming members of CHL, appellant and appellees agreed to abide by the terms of the operating agreement, and such agreement specifically allowed competition with the company by its members. As such, the duties created pursuant to such undertaking did not include a duty not to compete. Therefore, there was no duty on the part of appellees to refrain from subjecting appellant to the injury complained of herein. . . .

[The evidence also] does not show that appellees tortiously interfered with appellant's prospective business relationships with Nationwide and the NHL. The evidence does not show that appellees induced or otherwise purposely caused Nationwide and the NHL to not enter into or continue a business relationship with appellant. Indeed, and as indicated above, the evidence shows that McConnell stated he would lease the arena and obtain the franchise only if appellant did not. It was only after appellant rejected the lease proposal on several occasions that McConnell stepped in. Appellant had yet another opportunity on June 9, 1997 to participate in the Nationwide arena lease and the NHL franchise. Appellant again found the lease proposal unacceptable, and without a signed lease term sheet, there would have been no franchise from the NHL.

McPherson testified that Nationwide would accept a lease agreement with whomever the successful franchise applicant was. In addition, it is clear from Bettman's testimony that the NHL was still considering appellant as a potential franchise owner up until the last moment. Again, the evidence does not show that appellees' actions constituted an intentional interference with appellant's business relationships. It must be noted that appellees had the right to compete against CHL. However, even given such right, McConnell did not approach Nationwide or the NHL. Nationwide approached McConnell only after appellant indicated the lease terms were unacceptable. In short, it was appellant's actions that caused the termination of any relationship or potential relationship it had with Nationwide and the NHL.

In conclusion, there was not sufficient material evidence presented at trial so as to create a factual question for the jury on the issues of breach of fiduciary duty and tortious interference with business relationships. Therefore, a directed verdict in favor of appellees ... was appropriate. . . .

■ BOWMAN, J., concurs.

■ PEGGY L. BRYANT, J., concurs in part and dissents in part.*

---

* Judge Bryant dissented on an issue concerning attorneys' fees. The majority's disposition of that issue is not included in the text. (Footnote by ed.).

SECTION 3.   LIMITED LIABILITY PARTNERSHIPS

UNIFORM PARTNERSHIP ACT §§ 101(5), 306(c), 1001

[See Appendix]

TEXAS LIMITED LIABILITY PARTNERSHIP ACT

[See Appendix]

NOTE ON LIMITED LIABILITY PARTNERSHIPS

Another important new form of business organization is the limited liability partnership ("LLP"). Essentially, LLPs are general partnerships, with one core difference and several ancillary differences. The core difference is that, as the name indicates, the liability of general partners of a limited liability partnership is less extensive than the liability of a general partner. Although the statutes vary, generally speaking a partner in an LLP is not personally liable for *all* partnership obligations, but only for obligations arising from her own activities—with the exception, under some LLP statutes, that she is also liable for activities closely related to her, for contractual obligations, or both. This core idea is articulated differently under different statutes, and the precise liability of a partner in an LLP will depend on the statute.

Under the LLP statutes, the liability of a partner in an LLP is "limited" only in the sense that the partner is not personally liable for *all* of the LLP's obligations. A partner in an LLP *is* personally liable for certain obligations, and as to those obligations a partner's liability is unlimited—that is, a partner is personally liable for those obligations to the entire extent of her wealth.

An ancillary difference between ordinary general partnerships and LLPs is that under some LLP statutes there is a tradeoff for limited liability, in the form of a requirement of a minimum amount of liability insurance or segregated funds. Another ancillary difference between LLPs and ordinary general partnerships is that LLPs must be registered with the appropriate state office.

*

APPENDIX

RESTATEMENT (SECOND) OF AGENCY

(Selected Sections)

Chapter 1

INTRODUCTORY MATTERS

TOPIC 1. DEFINITIONS

TOPIC 3. ESSENTIAL CHARACTERISTICS OF RELATION

TOPIC 4. AGENCY DISTINGUISHED FROM OTHER RELATIONS

Chapter 2

CREATION OF RELATION

TOPIC 1. MUTUAL CONSENT AND CONSIDERATION

TOPIC 3. CAPACITY OF PARTIES TO RELATION

Chapter 3

CREATION AND INTERPRETATION OF AUTHORITY AND APPARENT AUTHORITY

TOPIC 1. METHODS OF MANIFESTING CONSENT

TOPIC 2. INTERPRETATION OF AUTHORITY AND APPARENT AUTHORITY

TITLE A. AUTHORITY

Chapter 13

DUTIES AND LIABILITIES OF AGENT TO PRINCIPAL

TOPIC 1. DUTIES

TOPIC 2. LIABILITIES

Chapter 14

DUTIES AND LIABILITIES OF PRINCIPAL TO AGENT

TOPIC 1. CONTRACTUAL AND RESTITUTIONAL DUTIES AND LIABILITIES

Chapter 1

INTRODUCTORY MATTERS

TOPIC 1. DEFINITIONS

§ 1. Agency; Principal; Agent

(1) Agency is the fiduciary relation which results from the manifestation of consent by one person to another that the other shall act on his behalf and subject to his control, and consent by the other so to act.

(2) The one for whom action is to be taken is the principal.

(3) The one who is to act is the agent.

§ 2. Master; Servant; Independent Contractor

(1) A master is a principal who employs an agent to perform service in his affairs and who controls or has the right to control the physical conduct of the other in the performance of the service.

(2) A servant is an agent employed by a master to perform service in his affairs whose physical conduct in the performance of the service is controlled or is subject to the right to control by the master.

(3) An independent contractor is a person who contracts with another to do something for him but who is not controlled by the other nor subject to the other's right to control with respect to his physical conduct in the performance of the undertaking. He may or may not be an agent.

Comment:

   a. Servants and non-servant agents. A master is a species of principal, and a servant is a species of agent. . . .

   b. Servant contrasted with independent contractor. The word "servant" is used in contrast with "independent contractor". The latter term includes all persons who contract to do something for another but who are not servants in doing the work undertaken. An agent who is not a servant is, therefore, an independent contractor when he contracts to act on account of the principal. Thus, a broker who contracts to sell goods for his principal is an independent contractor as distinguished from a servant. Although, under some circumstances, the principal is bound by the broker's unauthorized contracts and representations, the principal is not liable to third persons for tangible harm resulting from his unauthorized physical conduct within the scope of the employment, as the principal would be for similar conduct by a servant; nor does the principal have the duties or immunities of a master towards the broker. Although an agent who contracts to act and who is not a servant is therefore an independent contractor, not all independent contractors are agents. Thus, one who contracts for a stipulated price to build a house for another and who reserves no direction over the conduct of the work is an independent contractor; but he is not an agent, since he is not a fiduciary, has no power to make the one employing him a party to a transaction, and is subject to no control over his conduct. ...

c. Servants not necessarily menials. As stated more fully in Section 220, the term servant does not denote menial or manual service. Many servants perform exacting work requiring intelligence rather than muscle. Thus the officers of a corporation or a ship, the interne in a hospital, all of whom give their time to their employers, are servants equally with the janitor and others performing manual labor. ...

§ 3. General Agent; Special Agent

(1) A general agent is an agent authorized to conduct a series of transactions involving a continuity of service.

(2) A special agent is an agent authorized to conduct a single transaction or a series of transactions not involving continuity of service.

§ 4. Disclosed Principal; Partially Disclosed Principal; Undisclosed Principal

(1) If, at the time of a transaction conducted by an agent, the other party thereto has notice that the agent is acting for a principal and of the principal's identity, the principal is a disclosed principal.

(2) If the other party has notice that the agent is or may be acting for a principal but has no notice of the principal's identity, the principal for whom the agent is acting is a partially disclosed principal.

(3) If the other party has no notice that the agent is acting for a principal, the one for whom he acts is an undisclosed principal.

§ 7. Authority

Authority is the power of the agent to affect the legal relations of the principal by acts done in accordance with the principal's manifestations of consent to him.

§ 8. Apparent Authority

Apparent authority is the power to affect the legal relations of another person by transactions with third persons, professedly as agent for the other, arising from and in accordance with the other's manifestations to such third persons.

§ 8A. Inherent Agency Power

Inherent agency power is a term used in the restatement of this subject to indicate the power of an agent which is derived not from authority, apparent authority or estoppel, but solely from the agency relation and exists for the protection of persons harmed by or dealing with a servant or other agent.

§ 8B. Estoppel; Change of Position

(1) A person who is not otherwise liable as a party to a transaction purported to be done on his account, is nevertheless subject to liability to persons who have changed their positions because of their belief that the transaction was entered into by or for him, if

(a) he intentionally or carelessly caused such belief, or

(b) knowing of such belief and that others might change their positions because of it, he did not take reasonable steps to notify them of the facts.

(2) An owner of property who represents to third persons that another is the owner of the property or who permits the other so to represent, or who realizes that third persons believe that another is the owner of the property, and that he could easily inform the third persons of the facts, is subject to the loss of the property if the other disposes of it to third persons who, in ignorance of the facts, purchase the property or otherwise change their position with reference to it.

(3) Change of position, as the phrase is used in the restatement of this subject, indicates payment of money, expenditure of labor, suffering a loss or subjection to legal liability.

TOPIC 3. ESSENTIAL CHARACTERISTICS OF RELATION

§ 13. Agent as a Fiduciary

An agent is a fiduciary with respect to matters within the scope of his agency.

§ 14. Control by Principal

A principal has the right to control the conduct of the agent with respect to matters entrusted to him.

TOPIC 4. AGENCY DISTINGUISHED FROM OTHER RELATIONS

§ 14H. Agents or Holders of a Power Given for Their Benefit

One who holds a power created in the form of an agency authority, but given for the benefit of the power holder or of a third person, is not an agent of the one creating the power.

§ 14O. Security Holder Becoming a Principal

A creditor who assumes control of his debtor's business for the mutual benefit of himself and his debtor, may become a principal, with liability for the acts and transactions of the debtor in connection with the business.

Chapter 2

CREATION OF RELATION

TOPIC 1. MUTUAL CONSENT AND CONSIDERATION

§ 15. Manifestations of Consent

An agency relation exists only if there has been a manifestation by the principal to the agent that the agent may act on his account, and consent by the agent so to act.

TOPIC 3. CAPACITY OF PARTIES TO RELATION

§ 23. Agent Having Interests Adverse to Principal

One whose interests are adverse to those of another can be authorized to act on behalf of the other; it is a breach of duty for him so to act without revealing the existence and extent of such adverse interests.

Chapter 3

CREATION AND INTERPRETATION OF AUTHORITY AND APPARENT AUTHORITY

TOPIC 1. METHODS OF MANIFESTING CONSENT

§ 26. Creation of Authority: General Rule

Except for the execution of instruments under seal or for the performance of transactions required by statute to be authorized in a particular way, authority to do an act can be created by written or spoken words or other conduct of the principal which, reasonably interpreted, causes the agent to believe that the principal desires him so to act on the principal's account.

§ 27. Creation of Apparent Authority: General Rule

Except for the execution of instruments under seal or for the conduct of transactions required by statute to be authorized in a particular way, apparent authority to do an act is created as to a third person by written or spoken words or any other conduct of the principal which, reasonably interpreted, causes the third person to believe that the principal consents to have the act done on his behalf by the person purporting to act for him.

TOPIC 2. INTERPRETATION OF AUTHORITY AND APPARENT AUTHORITY

TITLE A. AUTHORITY

§ 32. Applicability of Rules for Interpretation of Agreements

Except to the extent that the fiduciary relation between principal and agent requires special rules, the rules for the interpretation of contracts apply to the interpretation of authority.

§ 33. General Principle of Interpretation

An agent is authorized to do, and to do only, what it is reasonable for him to infer that the principal desires him to do in the light of the principal's manifestations and the facts as he knows or should know them at the time he acts.

Comment:

a. Authority an ambulatory power. The agency relation is normally the result of a contract and is always the result of an agreement between the parties. For the purpose of interpreting the words used, the effect of customs and all similar matters, the normal rules for the interpretation of contracts are applicable, as stated in Section 32. Nevertheless, an agreement creating an agency relation has elements different from those of other contracts. The implicit, basic understanding of the parties to the agency relation is that the agent is to act only in accordance with the principal's desires as manifested to him.... Whatever the original agreement or authority may have been, he is authorized at any given moment to do, and to do only, what he reasonably believes the principal desires him to do, in the light of what he knows or should know of the principal's purpose and the existing circumstances....

Illustrations:

1. P, a mill owner, directs A, his purchasing agent, to purchase a large quantity of raw material, to be used in executing an order for goods. The following day the order for goods is rescinded, as A learns. Without inquiry as to whether or not P still wishes the material, A has no authority to purchase the raw material.

2. P, the owner of a factory running on half time for lack of orders, before leaving for his vacation, directs his purchasing agent to "put in our usual monthly coal supply of 1000 tons." The following day a large order comes in which will immediately put the factory on full running time. It may be found that A is authorized to purchase sufficient coal to keep the factory running, this depending upon whether or not P can easily be reached, the

167

amount of discretion usually given to A, the condition of P's bank balance, and other factors.

3. Same facts as in Illustration 2, except that P is present when the large order is received. A has no authority to order more than 1000 tons.

b. Authority distinct from contract of agency. An agent is a fiduciary under a duty to obey the will of the principal as he knows it or should know it. This will may change, either with or without a change in events. Whatever it is at any given time, if the agent has reason to know it, his duty is not to act contrary to it. The fact that in changing his mind the principal is violating his contract with the agent does not diminish the agent's duty of obedience to it. Hence the rule applicable to the interpretation of authority must be as flexible as the will of the principal may be. Thus, whether or not the agent is authorized to do a particular act at a particular time depends, not only on what the principal told the agent, but upon a great variety of other factors, including changes in the situation after the instructions were given. The interpretation of authority, therefore, differs in this respect from the interpretation of a contract, even the contract of agency.

The agent's authority may therefore be increased, diminished, become dormant or be destroyed, not only by further manifestations by the principal but also by the happening of events, dependent, in many situations, upon what the agent knows or should know as to the principal's purposes. This does not mean that the agent can do anything merely because he believes it to be of advantage to the principal. Nor does it mean that the agent is authorized to act if he believes the principal would authorize him to act if he knew the facts. The agent's scope of authority is limited to the authorized subject matter and the kind of transaction contemplated. An agent of a dealer in property, whose function is limited to selling, is not authorized to buy property even if he reasonably believes the principal would authorize its purchase if he knew of the opportunity. The ordinary store manager, in the absence of an emergency, is not authorized to borrow, even though he knows the principal would welcome the opportunity.

It is in accordance with this continuous comparison between the communication to the agent and the circumstances under which he acts, that his authority may broaden ... or may be diminished, suspended or terminated ..., however irrevocable the terms in which the authority is expressed. Whether or not the principal is liable for a breach of contract for revoking the authority, nevertheless he can do so. ... Further, because the agent is under a duty to protect the principal's interests within the authorized field, if the circumstances are or become ambiguous, either intrinsically or because of extrinsic facts, and he cannot communicate with the principal, the agent is authorized to act reasonably in accordance with the facts as he knows or should know them. ...

§ 35. When Incidental Authority Is Inferred

Unless otherwise agreed, authority to conduct a transaction includes authority to do acts which are incidental to it, usually accompany it, or are reasonably necessary to accomplish it.

§ 39. Inference That Agent Is to Act Only for Principal's Benefit

Unless otherwise agreed, authority to act as agent includes only authority to act for the benefit of the principal.

§ 43. Acquiescence by Principal in Agent's Conduct

(1) Acquiescence by the principal in conduct of an agent whose previously conferred authorization reasonably might include it, indicates that the conduct was authorized; if clearly not included in the authorization, acquiescence in it indicates affirmance.

(2) Acquiescence by the principal in a series of acts by the agent indicates authorization to perform similar acts in the future.

TITLE B. APPARENT AUTHORITY

§ 49. Interpretation of Apparent Authority Compared with Interpretation of Authority

The rules applicable to the interpretation of authority are applicable to the interpretation of apparent authority except that:

> (a) manifestations of the principal to the other party to the transaction are interpreted in light of what the other party knows or should know instead of what the agent knows or should know ....

. . .

Chapter 4

RATIFICATION

TOPIC 1. DEFINITIONS

§ 82. Ratification

Ratification is the affirmance by a person of a prior act which did not bind him but which was done or professedly done on his account, whereby the act, as to some or all persons, is given effect as if originally authorized by him.

> c. *A unique concept.* The concept of ratification ... is unique. It does not conform to the rules of contracts, since it can be accomplished without consideration to or manifestation by the purported principal and without fresh consent by the other party. Further, it operates as if the transaction were complete at the time and place of the first event, rather than the last, as in the normal case of offer and acceptance. It does not conform to the rules of torts, since the ratifier may become responsible for a harm which was not caused by him, his

169

property or his agent. It can not be justified on a theory of restitution, since the ratifier may not have received a benefit, nor the third person a deprivation. Nor is ratification dependent upon a doctrine of estoppel, since there may be ratification although neither the agent nor the other party suffer a loss resulting from a statement of affirmance or a failure to disavow. However, in some cases in which ratification is claimed, the principal's liability can be based upon unjust enrichment or estoppel, either in addition to or as alternative to his liability based on ratification. See §§ 103, 140.

d. *Justification.* That the doctrine of ratification may at times operate unfairly must be admitted, since it gives to the purported principal an election to blow hot or cold upon a transaction to which, in contract cases, the other party normally believes himself to be bound. But this hardship is minimized by denying a power to ratify when it would obviously be unfair. See §§ 88–90. Further, if the transaction is not ratified normally the pseudo-agent is responsible; if not, it is because the third party knew, or agreed to take the risk, of lack of authority by the agent. In many cases, the third person is a distinct gainer as where the purported principal ratifies a tort or a loan for which he was not liable and for which he receives nothing. This result is not, however, unjust, since although the creation of liability against the ratifier may run counter to established tort or contract principles, the liability is self-imposed. Even one who ratifies to protect his business reputation or who retains unwanted goods rather than defend a law suit, chooses ratification as preferable to the alternative. Further, the sometimes-derided doctrine of relation back not only is one used in other parts of the law, but it tends to give the parties what they wanted or said they wanted. If it sometimes halogens that a mistaken or over-zealous agent is relieved from liability to the third person, the net result causes no harm to anyone. However, perhaps the best defense of ratification is pragmatic; that it is needed in the prosecution of business. It operates normally to cure minor defects in an agent's authority, minimizing technical defenses and preventing unnecessary law suits. In this aspect, it is a beneficial doctrine, which has been adopted in most systems of law.

§ 83. Affirmance

Affirmance is either

(a) a manifestation of an election by one on whose account an unauthorized act has been done to treat the act as authorized, or

(b) conduct by him justifiable only if there were such an election.

TOPIC 2. WHEN AFFIRMANCE RESULTS IN RATIFICATION

§ 84. What Acts Can Be Ratified

(1) An act which, when done, could have been authorized by a purported principal, or if an act of service by an intended principal, can be ratified if, at the time of affirmance, he could authorize such an act.

(2) An act which, when done, the purported or intended principal could not have authorized, he cannot ratify, except an act affirmed by a legal representative whose appointment relates back to or before the time of such act.

§ 85. Purporting to Act as Agent as a Requisite for Ratification

(1) Ratification does not result from the affirmance of a transaction with a third person unless the one acting purported to be acting for the ratifier.

(2) An act of service not involving a transaction with a third person is subject to ratification if, but only if, the one doing the act intends or purports to perform it as the servant of another.

§ 87. Who Can Affirm

To become effective as ratification, the affirmance must be by the person identified as the principal at the time of the original act or, if no person was then identified, by the one for whom the agent intended to act.

§ 88. Affirmance After Withdrawal of Other Party or Other Termination of Original Transaction

To constitute ratification, the affirmance of a transaction must occur before the other party has manifested his withdrawal from it either to the purported principal or to the agent, and before the offer or agreement has otherwise terminated or been discharged.

§ 89. Affirmance After Change of Circumstances

If the affirmance of a transaction occurs at a time when the situation has so materially changed that it would be inequitable to subject the other party to liability thereon, the other party has an election to avoid liability.

§ 90. Affirmance After Rights Have Crystallized

If an act to be effective in creating a right against another or to deprive him of a right must be performed before a specific time, an affirmance is not effective against the other unless made before such time.

TOPIC 3.   WHAT CONSTITUTES AFFIRMANCE

§ 93. Methods and Formalities of Affirmance

(1) Except as stated in Subsection (2), affirmance can be established by any conduct of the purported principal manifesting that he consents to be a party to the transaction, or by conduct justifiable only if there is ratification.

(2) Where formalities are requisite for the authorization of an act, its affirmance must be by the same formalities in order to constitute a ratification.

(3) The affirmance can be made by an agent authorized so to do.

§ 94. Failure to Act as Affirmance

An affirmance of an unauthorized transaction can be inferred from a failure to repudiate it.

§ 97. Bringing Suit or Basing Defense as Affirmance

There is affirmance if the purported principal, with knowledge of the facts, in an action in which the third person or the purported agent is an adverse party:

> (a) brings suit to enforce promises which were part of the unauthorized transaction or to secure interests which were the fruit of such transaction and to which he would be entitled only if the act had been authorized; or

> (b) bases a defense upon the unauthorized transaction as though it were authorized; or

> (c) continues to maintain such suit or base such defense.

§ 98. Receipt of Benefits as Affirmance

The receipt by a purported principal, with knowledge of the facts, of something to which he would not be entitled unless an act purported to be done for him were affirmed, and to which he makes no claim except through such act, constitutes an affirmance unless at the time of such receipt he repudiates the act. If he repudiates the act, his receipt of benefits constitutes an affirmance at the election of the other party to the transaction.

§ 99. Retention of Benefits as Affirmance

The retention by a purported principal, with knowledge of the facts and before he has changed his position, of something which he is not entitled to retain unless an act purported to be done on his account is affirmed, and to which he makes no claim except through such act, constitutes an affirmance unless at the time of such retention he repudiates the act. Even if he repudiates the act, his retention constitutes an affirmance at the election of the other party to the transaction.

TOPIC 4. LIABILITIES

§ 100. Effect of Ratification; In General

[T]he liabilities resulting from ratification are the same as those resulting from authorization if, between the time when the original act was performed and when it was affirmed, there has been no change in the capacity of the principal or third person or in the legality of authorizing or performing the original act.

§ 100A. Relation Back in Time and Place

The liabilities of the parties to a ratified act or contract are determined in accordance with the law governing the act or contract at the time and place it was done or made. Whether the conduct of the purported principal is an affirmance depends upon the law at the time and place when and where the principal consents or acts.

Chapter 5

TERMINATION OF AGENCY POWERS

TOPIC 1. TERMINATION OF AUTHORITY

TITLE B. TERMINATION BY MUTUAL CONSENT, REVOCATION, OR RENUNCIATION

§ 118. Revocation or Renunciation

Authority terminates if the principal or the agent manifests to the other dissent to its continuance.

Comment:

   a. Such termination by act of the principal is revocation; by act of the agent, it is renunciation.

   b. Power to revoke or renounce. The principal has power to revoke and the agent has power to renounce, although doing so is in violation of a contract between the parties and although the authority is expressed to be irrevocable. A statement in a contract that the authority cannot be terminated by either party is effective only to create liability for its wrongful termination.

Illustrations:

   1. In consideration of A's agreement to advertise and give his best energies to the sale of Blackacre, its owner, P, grants to A "a power of attorney, irrevocable for one year" to sell it. A advertises and spends time trying to sell Blackacre. At the end of three months P informs A that he revokes. A's authority is terminated.

   2. In consideration of $1000 and A's promise to endeavor to sell, P grants to A for a period of one year a power of attorney to sell property, with compensation at 25 per cent. of the selling price, the power of attorney ending with this phrase: "Hereby intending and agreeing that this power shall be irrevocable during one year, and that during this period A shall have a power coupled with an interest which shall not be affected by my death or other circumstances." At the end of three months P informs A that he revokes. A's authority is terminated.

173

Comment:

   c. *Liabilities.* If there is a contract between principal and agent that the authority shall not be revoked or renounced, a party who revokes or renounces, unless privileged by the conduct of the other or by supervening circumstances, is subject to liability to the other. . . .

   d. *Non-agency powers.* A power in the form of an agency authority given for the protection of a person described as an agent, but who is not one, is not an agency authority and cannot be revoked by the power giver; if such a power is held for the benefit of a third person, it can be terminated neither by revocation nor renunciation. See § 139. . . .

         . . .

TOPIC 5.   TERMINATION OF POWERS GIVEN AS SECURITY

§ 138.   Definition

   A power given as security is a power to affect the legal relations of another, created in the form of an agency authority, but held for the benefit of the power holder or a third person and given to secure the performance of a duty or to protect a title, either legal or equitable, such power being given when the duty or title is created or given for consideration.

Comment:

   a. A power given as security arises when a person manifests consent that the one to whom it is given can properly act to create liability against him, or to dispose of some of his interests, or to perfect or otherwise protect a title already in the power holder or in the person for whom he is to act. If the power is given as security for the performance of a duty, it must be supported by consideration, but consideration is not necessary if the power is in aid of and accompanies a transfer of a title to the power holder.

   b. *Distinguished from authority.* A power given as security is one held for the benefit of a person other than the power giver. . . .

         . . .

§ 139.   Termination of Powers Given as Security

   (1) Unless otherwise agreed, a power given as security is not terminated by:

      (a) revocation by the creator of the power;

      (b) surrender by the holder of the power, if he holds for the benefit of another;

      (c) the loss of capacity during the lifetime of either the creator of the power or the holder of the power; or

(d) the death of the holder of the power, or, if the power is given as security for a duty which does not terminate at the death of the creator of the power, by his death.

(2) A power given as security is terminated by its surrender by the beneficiary, if of full capacity; or by the happening of events which, by its terms, discharges the obligations secured by it, or which makes its execution illegal or impossible.

Chapter 6

LIABILITY OF PRINCIPAL TO THIRD PERSONS; CONTRACTS AND CONVEYANCES

TOPIC 1. GENERAL PRINCIPLES

§ 140. Liability Based Upon Agency Principles

The liability of the principal to a third person upon a transaction conducted by an agent, or the transfer of his interests by an agent, may be based upon the fact that:

(a) the agent was authorized;

(b) the agent was apparently authorized; or

(c) the agent had a power arising from the agency relation and not dependent upon authority or apparent authority.

§ 143. Effect of Ratification

Upon ratification with knowledge of the material facts, the principal becomes responsible for contracts and conveyances made for him by one purporting to act on his account as if the transaction had been authorized, if there has been no supervening loss of capacity by the principal or change in the law which would render illegal the authorization or performance of such a transaction.

TOPIC 2. DISCLOSED OR PARTIALLY DISCLOSED PRINCIPAL

TITLE A. CREATION OF LIABILITY BY AUTHORIZED ACTS

§ 144. General Rule

A disclosed or partially disclosed principal is subject to liability upon contracts made by an agent acting within his authority if made in proper form and with the understanding that the principal is a party.

TITLE C. CREATION OF LIABILITY BY UNAUTHORIZED ACTS

§ 159. Apparent Authority

A disclosed or partially disclosed principal is subject to liability upon contracts made by an agent acting within his apparent authority if made in proper form and with the understanding that the apparent principal is a party. The rules as to the liability of a principal for authorized acts, are applicable to unauthorized acts which are apparently authorized.

§ 160. Violation of Secret Instructions

A disclosed or partially disclosed principal authorizing an agent to make a contract, but imposing upon him limitations as to incidental terms intended not to be revealed, is subject to liability upon a contract made in violation of such limitations with a third person who has no notice of them.

§ 161. Unauthorized Acts of General Agent

A general agent for a disclosed or partially disclosed principal subjects his principal to liability for acts done on his account which usually accompany or are incidental to transactions which the agent is authorized to conduct if, although they are forbidden by the principal, the other party reasonably believes that the agent is authorized to do them and has no notice that he is not so authorized.

§ 161A. Unauthorized Acts of Special Agents

A special agent for a disclosed or partly disclosed principal has no power to bind his principal by contracts or conveyances which he is not authorized or apparently authorized to make, unless the principal is estopped, or unless:

> (a) the agent's only departure from his authority or apparent authority is
>
> > i.   in naming or disclosing the principal, or
> >
> > ii. in having an improper motive, or
> >
> > iii. in being negligent in determining the facts upon which his authority is based, or
> >
> > iv. in making misrepresentations; or
>
> (b) the agent is given possession of goods or commercial documents with authority to deal with them.

TITLE D.   DEFENSES AND LIABILITY AFFECTED
BY SUBSEQUENT EVENTS

§ 179. Rights Between Third Person and Agent

Unless otherwise agreed, the liability of a disclosed or partially disclosed principal is not affected by any rights or liabilities existing between the other party and the agent at the time the contract is made.

§ 180. Defenses of Principal—In General

A disclosed or partially disclosed principal is entitled to all defenses arising out of a transaction between his agent and a third person. He is not entitled to defenses which are personal to the agent.

TOPIC 3. UNDISCLOSED PRINCIPAL

TITLE A. CREATION OF LIABILITY BY AUTHORIZED ACTS

§ 186. General Rule

An undisclosed principal is bound by contracts and conveyances made on his account by an agent acting within his authority, except that the principal is not bound by a contract which is under seal or which is negotiable, or upon a contract which excludes him.

TITLE B. CREATION OF LIABILITY BY UNAUTHORIZED ACTS

§ 194. Acts of General Agents

A general agent for an undisclosed principal authorized to conduct transactions subjects his principal to liability for acts done on his account, if usual or necessary in such transactions, although forbidden by the principal to do them.

§ 195. Acts of Manager Appearing to Be Owner

An undisclosed principal who entrusts an agent with the management of his business is subject to liability to third persons with whom the agent enters into transactions usual in such businesses and on the principal's account, although contrary to the directions of the principal.

§ 195A. Unauthorized Acts of Special Agents

A special agent for an undisclosed principal has no power to bind his principal by contracts or conveyances which he is not authorized to make unless:

    (a) the agent's only departure from his authority is

        (i) in not disclosing his principal, or

        (ii) in having an improper motive, or

        (iii) in being negligent in determining the facts upon which his authority is based, or

        (iv) in making misrepresentations; or

    (b) the agent is given possession of goods or commercial documents with authority to deal with them.

TITLE C. DEFENSES AND LIABILITY AFFECTED BY SUBSEQUENT EVENTS

§ 203. Defenses of Undisclosed Principal—In General

An undisclosed principal is entitled to all defenses arising out of a transaction with an agent, but not defenses which are personal to the agent.

§ 205. Power of Agent to Modify Contract Before Disclosure of Principal

Until the existence of the principal is disclosed, an agent who has made a contract for an undisclosed principal has power to cancel the contract and to modify it with binding effect upon the principal if the contract or conveyance, as modified, is authorized or is within the inherent power of the agent to make.

Chapter 7

LIABILITY OF PRINCIPAL TO THIRD PERSON; TORTS

TOPIC 2. LIABILITY FOR AUTHORIZED CONDUCT OR CONDUCT INCIDENTAL THERETO

TITLE B. TORTS OF SERVANTS

§ 219. When Master is Liable for Torts of His Servants

(1) A master is subject to liability for the torts of his servants committed while acting in the scope of their employment.

(2) A master is not subject to liability for the torts of his servants acting outside the scope of their employment, unless:

(a) the master intended the conduct or the consequences, or

(b) the master was negligent or reckless, or

(c) the conduct violated a non-delegable duty of the master, or

(d) the servant purported to act or to speak on behalf of the principal and there was reliance upon apparent authority, or he was aided in accomplishing the tort by the existence of the agency relation.

WHO IS A SERVANT

§ 220. Definition of Servant

(1) A servant is a person employed to perform services in the affairs of another and who with respect to the physical conduct in the performance of the services is subject to the other's control or right to control.

(2) In determining whether one acting for another is a servant or an independent contractor, the following matters of fact, among others, are considered:

(a) the extent of control which, by the agreement, the master may exercise over the details of the work;

(b) whether or not the one employed is engaged in a distinct occupation or business;

(c) the kind of occupation, with reference to whether, in the locality, the work is usually done under the direction of the employer or by a specialist without supervision;

(d) the skill required in the particular occupation;

(e) whether the employer or the workman supplies the instrumentalities, tools, and the place of work for the person doing the work;

(f) the length of time for which the person is employed;

(g) the method of payment, whether by the time or by the job;

(h) whether or not the work is a part of the regular business of the employer;

(i) whether or not the parties believe they are creating the relation of master and servant; and

(j) whether the principal is or is not in business.

SCOPE OF EMPLOYMENT

§ 228. General Statement

(1) Conduct of a servant is within the scope of employment if, but only if:

(a) it is of the kind he is employed to perform;

(b) it occurs substantially within the authorized time and space limits;

(c) it is actuated, at least in part, by a purpose to serve the master, and

(d) if force is intentionally used by the servant against another, the use of force is not unexpectable by the master.

(2) Conduct of a servant is not within the scope of employment if it is different in kind from that authorized, far beyond the authorized time or space limits, or too little actuated by a purpose to serve the master.

§ 229. Kind of Conduct Within Scope of Employment

(1) To be within the scope of the employment, conduct must be of the same general nature as that authorized, or incidental to the conduct authorized.

(2) In determining whether or not the conduct, although not authorized, is nevertheless so similar to or incidental to the conduct authorized as to be within the scope of employment, the following matters of fact are to be considered:

(a) whether or not the act is one commonly done by such servants;

(b) the time, place and purpose of the act;

(c) the previous relations between the master and the servant;

179

(d) the extent to which the business of the master is apportioned between different servants;

(e) whether or not the act is outside the enterprise of the master or, if within the enterprise, has not been entrusted to any servant;

(f) whether or not the master has reason to expect that such an act will be done;

(g) the similarity in quality of the act done to the act authorized;

(h) whether or not the instrumentality by which the harm is done has been furnished by the master to the servant;

(i) the extent of departure from the normal method of accomplishing an authorized result; and

(j) whether or not the act is seriously criminal.

§ 230. Forbidden Acts

An act, although forbidden, or done in a forbidden manner, may be within the scope of employment.

§ 231. Criminal or Tortious Acts

An act may be within the scope of employment although consciously criminal or tortious.

TITLE C. AGENTS' TORTS—LIABILITY NOT DEPENDENT UPON RELATION OF MASTER AND SERVANT

IN GENERAL

§ 250. Non-liability for Physical Harm by Non-servant Agents

A principal is not liable for physical harm caused by the negligent physical conduct of a non-servant agent during the performance of the principal's business, if he neither intended nor authorized the result nor the manner of performance, unless he was under a duty to have the act performed with due care.

Chapter 10

LIABILITY OF THIRD PERSON TO PRINCIPAL

TOPIC 1. CONTRACTS; DISCLOSED AGENCY

§ 292. General Rule

The other party to a contract made by an agent for a disclosed or partially disclosed principal, acting within his authority, apparent authority or other agency power, is liable to the principal as if he had contracted directly with the principal, unless the principal is excluded as a party by the form or terms of the contract.

§ 298. Defenses of Other Party

The other party to a contract made by an agent on behalf of a disclosed or partially disclosed principal has all the defenses which he would have had against the principal if the principal had made the contract under the same circumstances.

§ 299. Rights Between Other Party and Agent

Unless otherwise agreed, the liability of the other party to a disclosed or partially disclosed principal upon a contract made by an agent is not affected by any rights or liabilities then existing between the other party and the agent.

TOPIC 2. CONTRACTS; UNDISCLOSED AGENCY

§ 302. General Rule

A person who makes a contract with an agent of an undisclosed principal, intended by the agent to be on account of his principal and within the power of such agent to bind his principal, is liable to the principal as if the principal himself had made the contract with him, unless he is excluded by the form or terms of the contract, unless his existence is fraudulently concealed or unless there is set-off or a similar defense against the agent.

§ 303. Principal Excluded From Transaction

A person with whom an agent makes a contract on account of an undisclosed principal is not liable in an action at law brought upon the contract by such principal:

> (a) if the contract is in the form of a sealed or negotiable instrument; or

> (b) if the terms of the contract exclude liability to any undisclosed principal or to the particular principal.

§ 306. Rights Between Other Party and Agent

(1) If the agent has been authorized to conceal the existence of the principal, the liability to an undisclosed principal of a person dealing with the agent within his power to bind the principal is diminished by any claim which such person may have against the agent at the time of making the contract and until the existence of the principal becomes known to him, if he could set off such claim in an action against the agent.

(2) If the agent is authorized only to contract in the principal's name, the other party does not have set-off for a claim due him from the agent unless the agent has been entrusted with the possession of chattels which he disposes of as directed or unless the principal has otherwise misled the third person into extending credit to the agent.

§ 308. Defenses of Other Party

In an action by an undisclosed principal against the other party to a contract, the other party has all the defenses, except those of a purely procedural nature:

(a) which he would have had against the principal if the principal had made the contract under the same circumstances,

(b) which he had against the agent until the discovery of the principal, unless the agent was authorized to contract only in the principal's name.

TOPIC 5. EFFECT OF RATIFICATION

§ 319. General Rule

Where a purported servant or other agent has entered into a transaction with a third person, its ratification by the purported master or other principal has the same effect upon the liabilities of the third person to the principal as an original authorization.

Chapter 11

LIABILITY OF AGENT TO THIRD PERSONS

TOPIC 1. CONTRACTS AND CONVEYANCES

TITLE A. AGENT A PARTY TO A TRANSACTION CONDUCTED BY HIMSELF

§ 320. Principal Disclosed

Unless otherwise agreed, a person making or purporting to make a contract with another as agent for a disclosed principal does not become a party to the contract.

§ 321. Principal Partially Disclosed

Unless otherwise agreed, a person purporting to make a contract with another for a partially disclosed principal is a party to the contract.

§ 322. Principal Undisclosed

An agent purporting to act upon his own account, but in fact making a contract on account of an undisclosed principal, is a party to the contract.

§ 326. Principal Known to Be Nonexistent or Incompetent

Unless otherwise agreed, a person who, in dealing with another, purports to act as agent for a principal whom both know to be nonexistent or wholly incompetent, becomes a party to such a contract.

Comment:

. . .

b. Promoters. The classic illustration of the rule stated in this Section is the promoter. When a promoter makes an agreement with another on behalf of a corporation to be formed, the following alternatives may represent the intent of the parties:

(1) They may understand that the other party is making a revocable offer to the nonexistent corporation which will result in a contract if the corporation is formed and accepts the offer prior to withdrawal. This is the normal understanding.

(2) They may understand that the other party is making an irrevocable offer for a limited time. Consideration to support the promise to keep the offer open can be found in an express or limited promise by the promoter to organize the corporation and use his best efforts to cause it to accept the offer.

(3) They may agree to a present contract by which the promoter is bound, but with an agreement that his liability terminates if the corporation is formed and manifests its willingness to become a party. There can be no ratification by the newly formed corporation, since it was not in existence when the agreement was made. . . .

(4) They may agree to a present contract on which, even though the corporation becomes a party, the promoter remains liable either primarily or as surety for the performance of the corporation's obligation.

Which one of these possible alternatives, or variants thereof, is intended is a matter of interpretation on the facts of the individual case.

TITLE B. AGENT NOT PARTY TO TRANSACTION CONDUCTED BY HIMSELF

§ 328. Liability of Authorized Agent for Performance of Contract

An agent, by making a contract only on behalf of a competent disclosed or partially disclosed principal whom he has power so to bind, does not thereby become liable for its nonperformance.

§ 329. Agent Who Warrants Authority

A person who purports to make a contract, conveyance or representation on behalf of another who has full capacity but whom he has no power to bind, thereby becomes subject to liability to the other party thereto upon an implied warranty of authority, unless he has manifested that he does not make such warranty or the other party knows that the agent is not so authorized.

§ 330. Liability for Misrepresentation of Authority

A person who tortiously misrepresents to another that he has authority to make a contract, conveyance, or representation on behalf of a principal whom he has no power to bind, is subject to liability to the other in an action of tort for loss caused by reliance upon such misrepresentation.

TITLE C. DEFENSES AND EFFECTS OF SUBSEQUENT EVENTS

§ 333. Rights Between Other Party and Principal

Unless otherwise agreed, the liability of an agent upon a contract between a third person and the principal to which the agent is a party is not affected by any rights or liabilities existing between the third person and the principal not arising from the transaction, except that, with the consent of the principal, the agent can set off a claim which the principal would have in an action brought against him.

§ 334. Defenses of Agent—In General

In an action against an agent upon a contract between a third person and the principal to which the agent is a party, the agent has all the defenses which arise out of the transaction itself and also those which he has personally against the third person; defenses which are personal to the principal are not available to the agent.

§ 335. Agent Surety for Principal

In an action brought against an agent upon a contract to which the agent is a party but under which the primary duty of performance rests upon the principal, the agent has the defenses available to a surety.

§ 336. Election by Other Party to Hold Principal; Agency Disclosed

Unless otherwise agreed, the agent of a disclosed or partially disclosed principal who is a party to a contract made by another with such principal is not relieved from liability upon the contract by the determination of the other party to look to the principal alone, nor, unless the agent and the principal are joint contractors, by the fact that the other gets a judgment against the principal. He is relieved from liability to the extent that he is prejudiced thereby if he changes his position in justifiable reliance upon a manifestation of the other that he will look solely to the principal for performance.

§ 337. Election by Other Party to Hold Principal; Agency Undisclosed

An agent who has made a contract on behalf of an undisclosed principal is not relieved from liability by the determination of the other party thereto to look to the principal alone for the performance of the contract. He is discharged from liability if the other obtains a judgment against the principal, or, to the extent that he is prejudiced thereby, if he changes his position in justifiable reliance upon the other's manifestation that he will look solely to the principal for payment.

Chapter 13

DUTIES AND LIABILITIES OF AGENT TO PRINCIPAL

TOPIC 1. DUTIES

TITLE B. DUTIES OF SERVICE AND OBEDIENCE

§ 377. Contractual Duties

A person who makes a contract with another to perform services as an agent for him is subject to a duty to act in accordance with his promise.

§ 379. Duty of Care and Skill

(1) Unless otherwise agreed, a paid agent is subject to a duty to the principal to act with standard care and with the skill which is standard in the locality for the kind of work which he is employed to perform and, in addition, to exercise any special skill that he has.

(2) Unless otherwise agreed, a gratuitous agent is under a duty to the principal to act with the care and skill which is required of persons not agents performing similar gratuitous undertakings for others.

TITLE C. DUTIES OF LOYALTY

§ 387. General Principle

Unless otherwise agreed, an agent is subject to a duty to his principal to act solely for the benefit of the principal in all matters connected with his agency.

§ 388. Duty to Account for Profits Arising Out of Employment

Unless otherwise agreed, an agent who makes a profit in connection with transactions conducted by him on behalf of the principal is under a duty to give such profit to the principal.

Comment:

a. Ordinarily, the agent's primary function is to make profits for the principal, and his duty to account includes accounting for any unexpected and incidental accretions whether or not received in violation of duty. Thus, an agent who, without the knowledge of the principal, receives something in connection with, or because of, a transaction conducted for the principal, has a duty to pay this to the principal even though otherwise he has acted with perfect fairness to

185

the principal and violates no duty of loyalty in receiving the amount. . . .

Illustrations:

1. A, a real estate broker acting for P, the seller, in order to assure himself of his commission, makes a contract with T, a purchaser, by which, if T cancels the contract with P, as he is given the right to do, T is to pay A the amount of A's commission. T repudiates the contract with P but pays A. A holds his commission as a constructive trustee for P.

2. P authorizes A to sell land held in A's name for a fixed sum. A makes a contract to sell the land to T, who makes a deposit which is to be forfeited if the transaction is not carried out. T forfeits the amount. A sells the land to another person at the price fixed by P. A is under a duty to account to P for the amount received from T. . . .

Comment:

b.   Gratuities to agent. An agent can properly retain gratuities received on account of the principal's business if, because of custom or otherwise, an agreement to this effect is found. Except in such a case, the receipt and retention of a gratuity by an agent from a party with interests adverse to those of the principal is evidence that the agent is committing a breach of duty to the principal by not acting in his interests.

Illustrations:

4. A, the purchasing agent for the P railroad, purchases honestly and for a fair price fifty trucks from T, who is going out of business. In gratitude for A's favorable action and without ulterior motive or agreement, T makes A a gift of a car. A holds the automobile as a constructive trustee for P, although A is not otherwise liable to P. . . .

Comment:

c.   Use of confidential information. An agent who acquires confidential information in the course of his employment or in violation of his duties has a duty not to use it to the disadvantage of the principal. . . . He also has a duty to account for any profits made by the use of such information, although this does not harm the principal. Thus, where a corporation has decided to operate an enterprise at a place where land values will be increased because of such operation, a corporate officer who takes advantage of his special knowledge to buy land in the vicinity is accountable for the profits he makes, even though such purchases have no adverse effect upon the enterprise. So, if he has "inside" information that the corporation is about to purchase or sell securities, or to declare or to pass a dividend, profits made by him in stock transactions undertaken because of his knowledge are held in constructive trust for the principal. He is also liable for profits made by selling confidential information to third persons, even though the principal is not adversely affected.

§ 389. Acting as Adverse Party Without Principal's Consent

Unless otherwise agreed, an agent is subject to a duty not to deal with his principal as an adverse party in a transaction connected with his agency without the principal's knowledge.

Comment:

a. The rule stated in this Section applies to transactions which the agent conducts for his principal, dealing therein with himself, and also to transactions in which the agent deals with his principal, who acts in person or through another agent; it is applicable to transactions in which the agent is acting entirely for himself and to those in which he has such a substantial interest that it reasonably might affect his judgment. Thus, an agent who is appointed to sell or to give advice concerning sales violates his duty if, without the principal's knowledge, he sells to himself or purchases from the principal through the medium of a "straw," or induces his principal to sell to a corporation in which he has a large concealed interest....

. . .

c. Where no harm to principal. The rule stated in this Section is not based upon the existence of harm to the principal in the particular case. It exists to prevent a conflict of opposing interests in the minds of agents whose duty it is to act solely for the benefit of their principals. The rule applies, therefore, even though the transaction between the principal and the agent is beneficial to the principal. Thus, in the absence of a known custom or an agreement, an agent employed to sell at the market price cannot, without disclosure to the principal, properly buy the goods on his own account, even though he pays a higher price for them than the principal could obtain elsewhere. The rule applies also although the transaction is a public sale and the price received is above that stated by the principal to be adequate. Likewise, ordinarily, an agent appointed to buy or to sell at a fixed price violates his duty to the principal if, without the principal's acquiescence, he buys from or sells the specified article to himself at the specified price, even though it is impossible to obtain more or as much. However, if a broker is employed to sell property with an agreement that he is to retain all above a specified price, it may be inferred that the transaction gives him an option to purchase at that price without notice to the principal that he is acting for himself....

. . .

§ 390. Acting as Adverse Party With Principal's Consent

An agent who, to the knowledge of the principal, acts on his own account in a transaction in which he is employed has a duty to deal fairly with the principal and to disclose to him all facts which the agent knows or should know would reasonably affect the principal's judgment, unless the principal has manifested that he knows such facts or that he does not care to know them.

Comment:

 a. Facts to be disclosed. One employed as agent violates no duty to the principal by acting for his own benefit if he makes a full disclosure of the facts to an acquiescent principal and takes no unfair advantage of him. Before dealing with the principal on his own account, however, an agent has a duty, not only to make no misstatements of fact, but also to disclose to the principal all relevant facts fully and completely. A fact is relevant if it is one which the agent should realize would be likely to affect the judgment of the principal in giving his consent to the agent to enter into the particular transaction on the specified terms. Hence, the disclosure must include not only the fact that the agent is acting on his own account (see § 389), but also all other facts which he should realize have or are likely to have a bearing upon the desirability of the transaction from the viewpoint of the principal. This includes, in the case of sales to him by the principal, not only the price which can be obtained, but also all facts affecting the desirability of sale, such as the likelihood of a higher price being obtained later, the possibilities of dealing with the property in another way, and all other matters which a disinterested and skillful agent advising the principal would think reasonably relevant.

 If the principal has limited business experience, an agent cannot properly fail to give such information merely because the principal says he does not care for it; the agent's duty of fair dealing is satisfied only if he reasonably believes that the principal understands the implications of the transaction.

Illustrations:

 1. P employs A to sell Blackacre for $1,000. A, having sought a customer, is unable to find one and reports such fact to P. He then states that he is willing to pay $1,000, telling P truthfully that he believes that a better sale might be made later in view of the chance that the locality will develop. A pays P $1,000. A month later, A sells the land for $1,500. In the absence of other facts, A has violated no duty to P.

 2. P employs A to purchase a suitable manufacturing site for him. A owns one which is suitable and sells it to P at the fair price of $25,000, telling P all relevant facts except that, a short time previously, he purchased the land for $15,000. The transaction can be rescinded by P. . . .

Comment:

    c. Fairness. The agent must not take advantage of his position to persuade the principal into making a hard or improvident bargain. If the agent is one upon whom the principal naturally would rely for advice, the fact that the agent discloses that he is acting as an adverse party does not relieve him from the duty of giving the principal impartial advice based upon a carefully formed judgment as to the principal's interests. If he cannot or does not wish to do so, he has a duty to see that the principal secures the advice of a competent and disinterested third person. An agent who is in a close confidential relation to the principal, such as a family attorney, has the burden of proving that a substantial gift to him was not the result of undue influence. Even though an agent employed to sell is not in such a position, payment of less than the reasonable market value for property he buys from the principal is evidence that the bargain was unfair. If the principal is not in a dependent position, however, and the agent fully performs his duties of disclosure, a transaction of purchase and sale between them is not voidable merely because the principal receives an inadequate price or pays too great a price.

Illustrations:

    4. P, a young physician with some inherited wealth and no business experience, places his property in charge of A to manage. Desiring a particular piece of land which represents a large share of P's assets, A waits until there is a slump in the price of land and, believing correctly that the slump is only temporary, suggests to P that it be sold, offering as an incentive that P's income from his profession will increase and that, although the price to be obtained is low, P can well afford to get more enjoyment from the proceeds now than from a larger amount later. P thereupon agrees to sell to A at a price which is as much as could be obtained at that time for the property. It may be found that A violated his duty of dealing fairly with P.

    5. Same facts as in Illustration 4, except that A provides P with an independent experienced adviser, who gives disinterested advice, setting out the possibilities of accretion in values. It may be found that A has satisfied his duty of loyalty....

. . .

    e. Agreements for compensation. A person is not ordinarily subject to a fiduciary duty in making terms as to compensation with a prospective principal....

. . .

§ 391. Acting for Adverse Party Without Principal's Consent

    Unless otherwise agreed, an agent is subject to a duty to his principal not to act on behalf of an adverse party in a transaction connected with his agency without the principal's knowledge.

§ 392. Acting for Adverse Party With Principal's Consent

An agent who, to the knowledge of two principals, acts for both of them in a transaction between them, has a duty to act with fairness to each and to disclose to each all facts which he knows or should know would reasonably affect the judgment of each in permitting such dual agency, except as to a principal who has manifested that he knows such facts or does not care to know them.

§ 393. Competition as to Subject Matter of Agency

Unless otherwise agreed, an agent is subject to a duty not to compete with the principal concerning the subject matter of his agency.

§ 394. Acting for One With Conflicting Interests

Unless otherwise agreed, an agent is subject to a duty not to act or to agree to act during the period of his agency for persons whose interests conflict with those of the principal in matters in which the agent is employed.

§ 395. Using or Disclosing Confidential Information

Unless otherwise agreed, an agent is subject to a duty to the principal not to use or to communicate information confidentially given him by the principal or acquired by him during the course of or on account of his agency or in violation of his duties as agent, in competition with or to the injury of the principal, on his own account or on behalf of another, although such information does not relate to the transaction in which he is then employed, unless the information is a matter of general knowledge.

§ 396. Using Confidential Information After Termination of Agency

Unless otherwise agreed, after the termination of the agency, the agent:

(a) has no duty not to compete with the principal;

(b) has a duty to the principal not to use or to disclose to third persons, on his own account or on account of others, in competition with the principal or to his injury, trade secrets, written lists of names, or other similar confidential matters given to him only for the principal's use or acquired by the agent in violation of duty. The agent is entitled to use general information concerning the method of business of the principal and the names of the customers retained in his memory, if not acquired in violation of his duty as agent;

(c) has a duty to account for profits made by the sale or use of trade secrets and other confidential information, whether or not in competition with the principal;

(d) has a duty to the principal not to take advantage of a still subsisting confidential relation created during the prior agency relation.

TOPIC 2. LIABILITIES

§ 401. Liability for Loss Caused

An agent is subject to liability for loss caused to the principal by any breach of duty.

§ 403. Liability for Things Received in Violation of Duty of Loyalty

If an agent receives anything as a result of his violation of a duty of loyalty to the principal, he is subject to a liability to deliver it, its value, or its proceeds, to the principal.

§ 404. Liability for Use of Principal's Assets

An agent who, in violation of duty to his principal, uses for his own purposes or those of a third person assets of the principal's business is subject to liability to the principal for the value of the use. If the use predominates in producing a profit he is subject to liability, at the principal's election, for such profit; he is not, however, liable for profits made by him merely by the use of time which he has contracted to devote to the principal unless he violates his duty not to act adversely or in competition with the principal.

Comment:

a. The rule stated in this Section applies whether or not the agent uses the principal's facilities or other assets in competition with him. It applies irrespective of any harm done to the things used and irrespective of the use which the principal would have made of them.

Illustration:

1. P employs A to take care of the horses which P uses for driving purposes. P does not use them for a month and, during this period, without P's consent, A rents the horses to various persons who benefit the horses by the exercise thereby given them. A is subject to liability to P for the amount which he has received as rental.

Comment:

b. What are assets of the principal. The agent is subject to liability not only for the use of tangible things but also for the use of trade secrets, good-will, credit, and other intangible assets of the principal. Thus, an agent is subject to liability if, in selling his own goods, he uses the principal's trade-mark in territory in which the

191

trade-mark is known but in which the principal does not sell and does not intend to sell similar goods.

Although the right to the services of an agent is a business asset of the principal, the agent's liability for profits made by his use of the principal's assets does not include a liability for profits made by him during hours which he should have devoted to the principal's service, unless he has thereby violated a fiduciary duty owed by him to the principal.

Illustration:

2. P employs A to give his full time to P as a bookkeeper. A uses portions of the time which he should have devoted to P's service in keeping the books for another employer, deriving thereby a greater salary than he receives from P. P cannot recover from A the amount of salary which A receives from the other employer.

c. *Whether use of principal's assets predominates.* Whether or not the use of assets of the principal predominates in producing a profit is a question of fact. Where an agent conducts a business upon the principal's premises, the location and facilities of the principal or the services of the agent may predominate in the creation of profits. If a ship captain uses the ship to carry heavy packages of his own, by selling which he makes a substantial profit, the owner is entitled to it; if the captain carries a box of trinkets for personal sale at ports of call, the ivory he thereby obtains does not necessarily go to the shipowner.

Illustration:

3. A soldier uses his official uniform and position to smuggle forbidden goods into a friendly country and thereby makes large profits. The country by which he is employed is entitled to the profits.

Comment:

d. *Other remedies of principal.* In addition to the rights which the principal has under the rule stated in this Section, the principal may have a cause of action for breach of contract or for a tort by the agent, or he may be entitled to a decree declaring a constructive trust in the specific proceeds of the use of an asset. These rights may be in the alternative or they may be cumulative, in accordance with the rules stated in Section 407. Thus, if the agent improperly uses the principal's chattels, the principal is entitled to recover their value, plus any damages caused to the business by their use, if the use amounts to a conversion; or he can recover the chattels in specie together with any profit which the agent has made from them, plus any damage to them or to the business caused by their use.

§ 407. Principal's Choice of Remedies

(1) If an agent has received a benefit as a result of violating his duty of loyalty, the principal is entitled to recover from him what he has so received, its value, or its proceeds, and also the amount of damage thereby caused; except that, if the violation consists of the wrongful disposal of the principal's property, the principal cannot recover its value and also what the agent received in exchange therefor.

(2) A principal who has recovered damages from a third person because of an agent's violation of his duty of loyalty is entitled nevertheless to obtain from the agent any profit which the agent improperly received as a result of the transaction.

Chapter 14

DUTIES AND LIABILITIES OF PRINCIPAL TO AGENT

TOPIC 1. CONTRACTUAL AND RESTITUTIONAL DUTIES AND LIABILITIES

TITLE A. INTERPRETATION OF CONTRACTS AND LIABILITIES THEREUNDER

§ 438. Duty of Indemnity; The Principle

(1) A principal is under a duty to indemnify the agent in accordance with the terms of the agreement with him.

(2) In the absence of terms to the contrary in the agreement of employment, the principal has a duty to indemnify the agent where the agent

   (a) makes a payment authorized or made necessary in executing the principal's affairs or, unless he is officious, one beneficial to the principal, or

   (b) suffers a loss which, because of their relation, it is fair that the principal should bear.

§ 439. When Duty of Indemnity Exists

Unless otherwise agreed, a principal is subject to a duty to exonerate an agent who is not barred by the illegality of his conduct to indemnify him for:

   (a) authorized payments made by the agent on behalf of the principal;

   (b) payments upon contracts upon which the agent is authorized to make himself liable, and upon obligations arising from the possession or ownership of things which he is authorized to hold on account of the principal;

(c) payments of damages to third persons which he is required to make on account of the authorized performance of an act which constitutes a tort or a breach of contract;

(d) expenses of defending actions by third persons brought because of the agent's authorized conduct, such actions being unfounded but not brought in bad faith; and

(e) payments resulting in benefit to the principal, made by the agent under such circumstances that it would be inequitable for indemnity not to be made.

§ 440. When No Duty of Indemnity

Unless otherwise agreed, the principal is not subject to a duty to indemnify an agent:

(a) for pecuniary loss or other harm, not of benefit to the principal, arising from the performance of unauthorized acts or resulting solely from the agent's negligence or other fault; or

(b) if the principal has otherwise performed his duties to the agent, for physical harm caused by the performance of authorized acts, for harm suffered as a result of torts, other than the tortious institution of suits, committed upon the agent by third persons because of his employment, or for harm suffered by the refusal of third persons to deal with him; or

(c) if the agent's loss resulted from an enterprise which he knew to be illegal.

§ 442. Period of Employment

Unless otherwise agreed, mutual promises by principal and agent to employ and to serve create obligations to employ and to serve which are terminable upon notice by either party; if neither party terminates the employment, it may terminate by lapse of time or by supervening events.

RESTATEMENT (THIRD) OF AGENCY

TENTATIVE DRAFT NO. 1
(2000)

TABLE OF CONTENTS

CHAPTER ONE

INTRODUCTORY MATTERS

Topic 1

DEFINITIONS AND TERMINOLOGY

CHAPTER 2

PRINCIPLES OF ATTRIBUTION

Topic 1

ACTUAL AUTHORITY

Topic 2

APPARENT AUTHORITY

Topic 3

RESPONDEAT SUPERIOR

Topic 4

RELATED DOCTRINES

CHAPTER 1

INTRODUCTORY MATTERS

Topic 1.
DEFINITIONS AND TERMINOLOGY

§ 1.01 Agency Defined

Agency is the fiduciary relationship that arises when one person (the "principal") manifests consent to another person (the "agent") that the agent shall act on the principal's behalf and subject to the principal's control, and the agent consents so to act.

§ 1.02 Manifestation

A person manifests consent or intention through written or spoken words or other conduct if the person has notice that another will infer such consent or intention from the words or conduct.

§ 1.03 Terminology

(1) *Co-agents; superior and subordinate agent.* Co-agents have agency relationships with the same principal. A superior co-agent has the right, conferred by the principal, to direct a subordinate co-agent. A co-agent may be appointed by the principal or by another agent actually or apparently authorized by the principal to do so. Within an organization, a superior co-agent may exercise the authority to appoint a co-agent on behalf of the principal.

(2) *Disclosed, undisclosed, and unidentified principals.*

(a) *Disclosed principal.* A principal is disclosed if, at the time the third party and the agent interact, the third party has notice that the agent is acting for a principal and has notice of the principal's identity.

(b) *Undisclosed principal.* A principal is undisclosed if, at the time the third party and the agent interact, the third party has no notice that the agent is acting for a principal.

(c) *Unidentified principal.* A principal is unidentified if, at the time the third party and the agent interact, the third party has notice that the agent is acting for a principal but does not have notice of the principal's identity.

(3) *Dual agent.* A dual agent acts on behalf of more than one principal with regard to the same transaction.

(4) *Gratuitous agent.* A gratuitous agent undertakes or promises to undertake service without a right to receive compensation or other consideration.

(5) *Notice.* A person has notice of a fact if the individual knows it, has reason to know it, or should know it.

(6) *Person.* A person is (a) an individual; (b) an organization or association of persons that has legal capacity to possess rights and incur

obligations, including a corporation, a general, limited, or limited liability partnership, a limited liability company, a joint venture, or a foundation; (c) a government or political subdivision, or an instrumentality or entity created by government; (d) any form of trust or estate; or (e) any other legal or commercial entity.

(7) *Power of attorney.* A power of attorney is an instrument with which a principal appoints an agent with authority to act to the extent specified in the instrument.

(8) *Subagent.* A subagent is a person appointed by an agent empowered to do so, to perform functions undertaken by the agent for the principal, but for whose conduct the agent agrees with the principal to be primarily responsible.

(9) *Trustee and agent-trustee.* A trustee is a holder of property who is subject to fiduciary duties to deal with the property for the benefit of charity or for one or more persons, at least one of whom is not the sole trustee. An agent-trustee is a trustee subject to the control of the settlor or of one or more beneficiaries.

§ 1.04 Parties' Usage and Characterization Not Controlling

An agency relationship arises only when the factors stated in § 1.01 are present. Any characterization of the relationship in an agreement between parties or in the context of industry or popular usage is not controlling. . . .

CHAPTER 2

PRINCIPLES OF ATTRIBUTION

Topic 1.
ACTUAL AUTHORITY

§ 2.01 Actual Authority

An agent acts with actual authority in affecting the principal's legal relations if, at the time of taking action, the agent reasonably believes, in accordance with the principal's manifestations to the agent, that the principal wishes the agent so to act.

Comment . . .

b. Terminology. . . .

The term "inherent agency power," used in Restatement Second, Agency and defined therein by § 8A, is not used in this Restatement. Inherent agency power is defined as "a term used . . . to indicate the power of an agent which is derived not from authority, apparent authority or estoppel, but solely from the agency relation and exists for the protection of persons named by or dealing with a servant or agent." Other doctrines stated in this Restatement encompass the justifications underpinning § 8A, including the centrality of interpretation by the agent to the agent's relationship with the principal, as well as the doctrines of apparent authority, estoppel, and restitution.

c. Rationale. Actual authority is a consequence of the principal's expressive conduct toward the agent, through which the principal manifests consent to be affected by the agent's action, and the agent's reasonable understanding of the principal's manifestation. The agent's actions manifest the agent's consent to act on the principal's behalf, as does any separate manifestation of assent by the agent. When the agent acts with actual authority, the agent's power to affect the principal's legal relations with third parties is coextensive with the agent's right to do so, which actual authority creates. In contrast, although an agent who acts with apparent authority also affects the principal's legal relations, the agent lacks the right to do so, and the agent's act is not rightful as toward the principal.

The focal point for determining whether an agent acted with actual authority is the agent's understanding at the time the agent acted. Although it is commonly said that the principal grants or confers actual authority, the principal's initial manifestation to the agent may often be modified or supplemented by subsequent manifestations from the principal and by other developments that the agent should reasonably consider in determining what the principal wishes to be done.

Illustrations:

1. P gives A a written power of attorney authorizing A to sell a piece of property owned by P. P subsequently says to A, "Don't sell the property. Lease it instead." After P's statement, A has actual authority only to lease.

2. Same facts as Illustration 1, except that A overhears P say to a third party that P no longer wishes to sell the property and wishes A to lease it. A has actual authority only to lease because A knows P does not wish the property to be sold....

If the principal states directions to the agent in general or open-ended terms, the agent will have to exercise discretion in determining the specific acts to be performed to a greater degree than if the principal's statement specifies in detail what the agent should do. It should be foreseeable to the principal that an agent's exercise of discretion may not result in the decision the principal would make individually. Regardless of the detail in the principal's statements or other conduct, the agent's duty is to interpret them reasonably to further purposes of the principal that the agent knows or should know, in light of facts that the agent knows or should know when the agent acts. When the principal's instructions are ambiguous, or if circumstances change, it will often be reasonable for the agent to seek clarification from the principal rather than speculating about the principal's wishes....

§ 2.02 Scope of Actual Authority

(1) The agent has actual authority with respect to acts or types of acts designated in the principal's manifestations to the agent, as well as acts necessary or incidental to achieving the principal's objectives.

(2) The agent should interpret the principal's manifestations in light of any meaning known by the agent to be ascribed by the principal and, in the absence of any meaning known to the agent, reasonably in light of the context, including facts known to the agent and the agent's fiduciary duty to the principal.

(3) The agent's understanding of the principal's objectives should reflect the principal's manifestations to the agent and the inferences reasonably to be drawn from the circumstances creating the agency.

Comment ...

d. Agent's reasonable understanding of principal's manifestation.... The agent does not have actual authority to do an act if the agent does not reasonably believe the principal has consented to its commission. Whether an agent's belief is reasonable is determined from the viewpoint of a reasonable person in the agent's situation under circumstances of which the agent has notice....

The context in which the principal and the agent interact frames the reasonableness of the agent's understanding of the principal's objectives and includes the nature of the principal's business or the principal's personal situation. The agent's authority encompasses acts necessary to accomplish the end the principal has directed that the agent achieve. In exigent circumstances not known to the principal, the agent may reasonably believe that the principal would wish the agent to act beyond the specifics detailed by the principal.

Illustrations:

2. P Corporation employs A as the Facilities Manager at an amusement park owned by P Corporation. A reports to B, P Corporation's Vice President for Leisure Activities. B directs A to arrange for the reseeding of the badly deteriorated lawn adjacent to the park's entrance. B also directs A to complete the reseeding by the end of the week. A purchases grass seed and directs grounds keepers to schedule time for reseeding. A then learns that the park location is in the path of a forecasted hurricane. A has actual authority to postpone the reseeding.

3. Same facts as Illustration 2, except weather conditions do not interrupt the reseeding. A knows that the lawn could be reseeded either at much higher cost to achieve turf conditions suitable for a golf course, or at lower cost to achieve conditions that are visually attractive but not suitable for use as a golf course. Absent other manifestations from B, or other knowledge of P Corporation's practices, A lacks actual authority to reseed to

199

achieve the golf course standard. In light of the use P Corporation will make of the lawn, it is not reasonable for A to believe that P Corporation's objectives require that the lawn be usable as a golf course.

... The principal's situation, if known to the agent at the time the agent acts, may affect the agent's authority to do a particular act. Additionally, the principal may revoke or limit authority subsequent to granting it. The agent's understanding at the time the agent acts is controlling. If the agent knows that the principal's reason for previously authorizing the agent to do an act is no longer operative, the agent does not have actual authority to do the act. . . .

The agent's understanding of the principal's interests and objectives is an element of the agent's reasonable interpretation of the principal's conduct. If a literal interpretation of the principal's communication to the agent would authorize an act inconsistent with the principal's interests or objectives known to the agent, it is open to question whether the agent's literal interpretation is reasonable.

Illustration:

8. P, a toy designer, employs A as an agent to present P's designs to toy manufacturers. P says to A, "Before you show the design, sign whatever forms the manufacturer requires." A knows that P's practice is to retain all copyright and other intellectual property interests in P's designs. It is not reasonable for A to interpret P's instruction to authorize A to sign a form that assigns or releases all of P's interests in the design to T, a toy manufacturer. A therefore does not have actual authority to sign such a form. A has apparent authority as defined in § 2.03 only if based on P's conduct it is reasonable for T to believe that A has authority to sign the form. . . .

e. *Interpretation by agent.* . . .

The principal's ability to communicate with the agent is a basic component of the principal's exercise of the right of control. In particular, the principal has the opportunity to state instructions to the agent with clarity and specificity. Moreover, much that underlies the occurrence of the risk that the agent will depart from instructions is within the principal's control. The principal's instructions may be insufficiently clear in their import to enable the agent to discern what acts the principal wishes the agent to do or to refrain from doing. The principal's instructions, albeit clear as far as they go, may be incomplete in some significant respect, or the instructions may reasonably be understood by the agent to authorize the agent's exercise of discretion. Moreover, an agent may depart from instructions because the agent interprets the instructions from a perspective that differs in significant respects from the perspective from which the principal would interpret the identical language. Although not all factors that underlie such differences in perspective are always within the principal's control, in

200

significant respects the principal makes decisions that shape the viewpoint from which the agent interprets instructions.

Occasionally it may be open to doubt what the principal's instructions mean, even when they are interpreted literally. As a result, the agent may interpret them differently from the interpretation the principal would have preferred. The agent's fiduciary duty to the principal obliges the agent to interpret the principal's manifestations so as to infer, in a reasonable manner, what the principal desires to be done in light of facts that the agent knows or should know at the time of acting. Within this basic framework, however, it is not surprising that more than one reasonable interpretation of instructions might be possible. Not all agents are equally gifted in their capacity for reasonable interpretation, especially when the instructions themselves are not specific or when the principal has not furnished the agent with a separate instruction that specifies how to resolve doubtful cases.

The principal may take steps that, by reducing ambiguity or other lack of clarity, reduce the risk that the agent's actions will deviate from the principal's wishes, interests, or objectives. Giving the agent a formal written set of instructions reduces the agent's discretion and potential to err in determining what actions to take. The principal may also reduce the risk of deviation by monitoring the agent, for example by requiring prompt checks on the agent's actions by a superior co-agent or an external auditor. How an organizational principal structures itself, including titles given to individuals and habitual patterns of interaction among them, may also reduce the risk of deviation by orienting individuals to defined roles and organizationally-specified constraints on action.

However, an organizational principal, like any principal, is at risk of misunderstanding and misinterpretation. Very detailed instructions may be so complex that lapses occur because the agent's attentiveness slips. Prolix instructions may cause some agents to decide that certain instructions may be ignored as trivial or as unwittingly imposed obstacles to achieving what the agent perceives the principal's overriding objective to be. An agent is not privileged to disregard instructions unless the agent reasonably believes that the principal wishes the agent to do so. If third parties with whom the agent interacts reasonably believe the agent to be authorized, the doctrine of apparent authority, defined in § 2.03, may apply to protect the third party. It does not protect the agent who departs from instructions....

An agent who knowingly contravenes or exceeds the principal's instructions may believe that to do so best serves the principal's interests. The agent may believe that circumstances have changed since the initial instructions and that, were the principal to reconsider the matter, different instructions would be given. Unless it is reasonable for the agent to believe that the principal wishes the agent to construe the instructions in light of changed circumstances, the agent lacks authority to act contrary to instructions.

201

Illustrations:

16. P retains A, directing A to buy Blackacre but to offer no more than $250,000. A then learns that Blackacre has increased substantially in value and, if purchased for $300,000, would represent a bargain. It is financially feasible for P to pay $300,00 for Blackacre. A does not have actual authority to offer more than $250,000 for Blackacre.

17. Same facts as Illustration 16, except that Blackacre is to be sold at an auction in which the successful bidder will be required to deposit a check in an amount equal to ten percent of the bid. P gives A a blank check to use in making the deposit. A does not have actual authority to bid more than $250,000 for Blackacre.

18. Same facts as Illustration 16, except that P owns and operates a golf course on land that almost entirely surrounds Blackacre. A has notice of P's long term business plan to enhance the aesthetic and athletic quality of the course and thereby make it more profitable. At the auction of Blackacre, A learns for the first time that there will be one other bidder, B. A also learns that B's plan for using Blackacre is to construct a cement factory on it. A is unable to contact P to relay this information and receive further instructions. A succeeds in purchasing Blackacre for P by bidding $260,000. A acted with actual authority.

It is often feasible for the agent to contact the principal to inquire what the principal now wishes to be done. In an era of rapid electronic communication, it is often both cheap and easy for the agent to make inquiry before proceeding. The agent's inquiry gives the principal the opportunity to clarify or supplement the prior instructions. However, the agent may believe it infeasible to contact the principal for clarification, or that the advantage promised by the transaction will be lost if the agent does not conclude it promptly. Unless the agent has a basis reasonably to believe that the principal does not wish to resolve the question, the agent should attempt to contact the principal, prior to exercising discretion to disregard prior instructions. If the principal does not respond to the agent's inquiry, and viewed objectively the action then taken by the agent reasonably serves the principal's interests as the agent could best discern them, the agent acted with actual authority.

The principal's instructions may not address prior occasions on which the agent has contravened the principal's instructions. On prior occasions the principal may have affirmatively approved of the agent's unauthorized act or silently acquiesced in it by failing to voice affirmative disapproval. The history is likely to influence the agent's subsequent interpretation of instructions; if the principal's subsequent instructions do not address the history, the agent may well infer from the principal's silence that the principal will not demand compliance with the instructions to any degree greater than the principal has done in the past. It is a question of fact whether the agent is reasonable in drawing such an inference. It will probably not be reasonable if the principal has recently renewed the instructions or newly emphasized the importance of complying with them.

The agent may believe, whether correctly or erroneously, that the agent knows the principal's best interests better than does the principal; what appears to be hubris on the agent's part may well emerge when the agent in fact has greater expertise or knowledge than does the principal as to matters within the scope of the agency relationship. Agents are often said to depart from their instructions due to an "excess of zeal." One explanation for this phenomenon is that just advanced, that is, the agent's belief in a superior knowledge of the principal's best interests. Additionally, agents sometimes exhibit an "excess of zeal" because they have information about the principal's situation that differs from the principal's own information and beliefs based upon it. Matters that seem urgent or imperative to the agent may seem less so to the principal, whose knowledge will often be broader in scope and whose time horizon will often extend farther into the future than will the agent's. Such differences in perspective may well be aggravated by the incentive structure embedded in the agent's relationship with the principal. Lapses from instructions may well follow if the agent's compensation is contingent on the volume of transactions concluded by the agent, or is derivative of their dollar value, or if the agent fears the principal will terminate the agency relationship if the agent does not achieve success. Regardless of the explanation for the lapse, the agent does not have authority to disregard instructions unless it is reasonable for the agent to believe that the principal wishes the agent to do so.

Illustrations:

19. The vice president (VP) of P Corporation, in charge of P Corporation's information technology, enters into negotiations with T Corporation to buy a new computer system. Before the VP begins negotiations with T Corporation, the board of directors of P Corporation authorizes the expenditure of up to $5 million on a new computer system. The CEO of P Corporation then directs the VP not to buy a computer system from T Corporation because the CEO has been told by other CEOs that T Corporation's products demand a high level of user sophistication. The VP believes that the CEO has underestimated the computer skills of P Corporation's work force and enters into a contract with T Corporation to buy a computer system for $4 million dollars. The VP did not have actual authority to enter into a transaction specifically forbidden by the CEO.

20. Same facts as Illustration 19, except that the VP, additionally, has good reason to believe that the computer system is a

bargain at the $4 million price. The VP does not have actual authority to contract to buy it.

f. Explicit instructions. The principal may direct the agent to do a specific act or forbid a particular act. The agent's fiduciary duty to the principal obliges the agent to interpret the principal's instructions so as to infer, in a reasonable manner, what the principal would wish the agent to do in light of facts the agent knows or should know at the time of acting.

Although the agent's task of interpretation is often straightforward, given instructions of such specificity, the principal's language does not interpret itself, and circumstances may require the agent to exercise discretion in ascertaining the principal's wishes. Suppose the principal (P), the owner of a menagerie, makes a statement that P believes directs the general manager of the menagerie (A) to buy no more horses. If A enters into an agreement to buy another horse for the menagerie, A did not act with actual authority unless A reasonably believed that P wished the purchase to be made.

Consider the variety of explanations for A's purchase of the horse on P's account despite what appears to be P's direction to the contrary. First, P's statement might not have expressed P's wishes clearly. Perhaps P said, "I'm not into horses anymore," which is not a categorical statement of an instruction to A. If A sought clarification from P, P might have responded, "What I meant was, buy no more horses." A's purchase of the additional horse would be unauthorized. A might, however, reasonably believe that no clarification was necessary, if perhaps A believed that P meant to discontinue P's private use of horses, separate from the menagerie business. A's belief is not reasonable, though, in the absence of some reason to ascribe that interpretation to P's statement. A might fail to seek clarification from P if logistics make it difficult or impossible to do so or if P seems too rushed or distracted to explain further. It is a question of fact whether A's failure is reasonable under the circumstances.

Suppose P said to A originally (or in response to A's request for clarification): "Buy no more horses." This instruction, clear on its face, might nonetheless leave A in doubt in some circumstances. P's language does not itself define the word "horse," and does not eliminate A's need to interpret P's language to determine whether P intends to prohibit A's purchase of, say, a pony or a zebra or toy horses for sale in the menagerie's gift shop. A's interpretation will not be reasonable unless it takes into account A's prior experience with P which is likely to reveal how P uses language when referring to the menagerie.

Moreover, A might wonder how absolutely or unconditionally to interpret P's instruction. Would it contravene the instruction to buy an additional horse after the death of one of the horses on display in the menagerie? Should A understand P to mean that the value of an additional horse, relative to the sale price, is totally irrelevant? Must A pass on the opportunity to buy an especially valuable horse at a very low price? Although A may believe that P's best interests would be served by ignoring the literal interpretation of P's instruction, unless A has reason to believe that P wishes A to do so, it is not reasonable for A to disregard the instruction rather than contacting P, if feasible, for further clarification.

A might decide to contravene P's instruction if A believes it to be a mistake from the standpoint of the business interest of the menagerie itself. Although A's departure from P's instructions may well be understandable, it is not consistent with the focus of A's duty of loyalty, which is owed to P and not to the menagerie itself. A lacks authority to depart from P's instructions to serve A's perception of what is required to further the interests of the menagerie itself.

Regardless of the breadth or narrowness with which the principal has conveyed authority to the agent, an agent's actual authority extends only to acts that the agent reasonably believes the principal has authorized or wishes the agent to do. The fiduciary character of the agency relationship shapes the agent's permissible interpretation of authority, disallowing an interpretation that is inconsistent with interests of the principal that the agent knows or should know. . . .

Topic 2.
APPARENT AUTHORITY

§ 2.03 Apparent Authority

Apparent authority is the power to affect a principal's legal relations with third parties held by an agent or other actor, when a third party reasonably believes the actor has authority to act on behalf of the principal and that belief is traceable to the principal's manifestations. When an agent holds a position within an organization, or has been placed in charge of a transaction or situation, a third party acts reasonably in believing that the agent has authority to do acts consistent with the position the agent occupies absent knowledge of circumstances that would lead a reasonable third party to inquire into the existence, extent, or nature of the agent's authority.

Topic 3.
RESPONDEAT SUPERIOR

§ 2.04 Respondeat Superior

An employer is subject to liability for torts committed by employees while acting in the scope of their employment.

Topic 4.
RELATED DOCTRINES

§ 2.05 Estoppel to Deny Authority

A person, not otherwise liable as a party to a transaction purportedly done on that person's account, is subject to liability to persons who justifiably change position because they believe the transaction to be on the person's account, if

(1) the person intentionally or carelessly caused such belief, or

(2) knowing of such belief and that it might induce others to change their positions, the person did not take reasonable steps to notify them of the facts.

§ 2.06 Estoppel of Undisclosed Principal

An undisclosed principal may not rely on instructions given an agent that qualify or reduce the agent's authority to less than the authority a third party would reasonably believe the agent to have under the same circumstances if the principal had been disclosed.

Comment ...

b. Terminology. The situation encompassed by this rule is more precisely one of "undisclosed agency" because the third party does not know that the actor in question is acting as an agent, not a principal. The rule stated in this section is an instance of "inherent agency power," a term used in Restatement Second, Agency § 8A, and arguably an instance of "usual authority" as that term is defined by secondary authority in the United Kingdom. In this Restatement, the terms "inherent agency power" and "usual authority" are not used....

c. Rationale....

The rule stated in this section, like the doctrine of apparent authority, protects third parties by backstopping actual authority when circumstances might otherwise permit the principle opportunistically to speculate at the expense of third parties. See § 2.03, Comment c. Apparent authority itself is not present when the principal is undisclosed because no manifestation has been made that the actor with whom the third party interacts has authority to act as an agent. If the agent operates a business under the agent's name, the appearance to the third party may be that the agent owns the business and that its assets will be available to satisfy business-related obligations incurred by the agent. The opportunity for speculation provided the principal would emerge when the principal has limited the agent's authority, and the agent enters into a contract exceeding the agent's actual authority. Then, if the contract is advantageous to the principal, neither the principal nor the agent will raise the agent's lack of authority, and the third party will lack reason to know of it. On the other hand, if the contract then is disadvantageous to the principal, the principal may assert lack of authority as a defense.

The doctrine allocates to the principal the risk that the agent will deviate from the principal's instructions and do acts that are consistent with the position the agent occupies, which are acts that third parties would anticipate an agent in such a position would have authority to do and may well be acts that are foreseeable to the principal. Such acts are especially likely to be foreseeable when they are consistent with the agent's position although they contravene the principal's instructions. It is true that a third party who deals with an actor, lacking notice that the actor is someone's agent, does not expect the liability of any person in addition to the immediate actor with whom the third party deals. Estoppel's perspective is broader, if less well defined. The question is whether it is unjust, in particular circumstances, to permit a principal who has chosen to deal through an agent but to remain undisclosed to have the benefit of restrictions on the agent's authority. In the instance in which the rule is applicable, it is unlikely that the third party will inquire into the status of the immediate actor or seek to identify the existence of restrictions on that actor's right to interact with legal consequences for the third party. The need to make such inquiries, in the circumstances to which this doctrine applies, is unlikely to occur to a reasonable third party, and making the inquiry may be difficult or its costs may seem excessive relative to the magnitude of the individual transaction.

The doctrine encompasses deviations from actual authority of a sort that would not lead a reasonable third party to make separate inquiry into the scope of the agent's authority. Such deviations are foreseeable to the principal and are likely not to be contested by any principal, whether or not undisclosed, when they appear likely to benefit the principal.

Illustrations:

1. P buys a medical supplies business owned and run for many years by A. P employs A as general manager, telling A to keep P's ownership a secret. P tells A to sell no supplies at a discount except with P's prior approval. As is customary in the trade, A offers T Hospital a standard discount in exchange for a large order. T Hospital accepts the offer made by A. P is bound to sell to T Hospital on the terms to which A agreed. Had T known that A acted as an agent on behalf of a principal, T would reasonably believe that an agent in A's position had authority to offer the standard discount....

§ 2.07 Restitution of Benefit

A principal who receives a benefit from a third party that results from the action of an agent, or a person who appears to be an agent, must make restitution if the principal would otherwise be unjustly enriched.

UNIFORM PARTNERSHIP ACT

PART I. PRELIMINARY PROVISIONS

208

PART I

PRELIMINARY PROVISIONS

§ 1. Name of Act

This act may be cited as Uniform Partnership Act.

§ 2. Definition of Terms

In this act, "Court" includes every court and judge having jurisdiction in the case.

"Business" includes every trade, occupation, or profession.

"Person" includes individuals, partnerships, corporations, and other associations.

"Bankrupt" includes bankrupt under the Federal Bankruptcy Act or insolvent under any state insolvent act.

"Conveyance" includes every assignment, lease, mortgage, or encumbrance.

"Real property" includes land and any interest or estate in land.

§ 3. Interpretation of Knowledge and Notice

(1) A person has "knowledge" of a fact within the meaning of this act not only when he has actual knowledge thereof, but also when he has knowledge of such other facts as in the circumstances shows bad faith.

(2) A person has "notice" of a fact within the meaning of this act when the person who claims the benefit of the notice:

(a) States the fact to such person, or

* Omitted.

(b) Delivers through the mail, or by other means of communication, a written statement of the fact to such person or to a proper person at his place of business or residence.

§ 4. Rules of Construction

(1) The rule that statutes in derogation of the common law are to be strictly construed shall have no application to this act.

(2) The law of estoppel shall apply under this act.

(3) The law of agency shall apply under this act.

(4) This act shall be so interpreted and construed as to effect its general purpose to make uniform the law of those states which enact it.

(5) This act shall not be construed so as to impair the obligations of any contract existing when the act goes into effect, nor to affect any action or proceedings begun or right accrued before this act takes effect.

§ 5. Rules for Cases Not Provided for in This Act

In any case not provided for in this act the rules of law and equity, including the law merchant, shall govern.

PART II

NATURE OF PARTNERSHIP

§ 6. Partnership Defined

(1) A partnership is an association of two or more persons to carry on as co-owners a business for profit.

(2) But any association formed under any other statute of this state, or any statute adopted by authority, other than the authority of this state, is not a partnership under this act, unless such association would have been a partnership in this state prior to the adoption of this act; but this act shall apply to limited partnerships except in so far as the statutes relating to such partnerships are inconsistent herewith.

§ 7. Rules for Determining the Existence of a Partnership

In determining whether a partnership exists, these rules shall apply:

(1) Except as provided by section 16 persons who are not partners as to each other are not partners as to third persons.

(2) Joint tenancy, tenancy in common, tenancy by the entireties, joint property, common property, or part ownership does not of itself establish a partnership, whether such co-owners do or do not share any profits made by the use of the property.

(3) The sharing of gross returns does not of itself establish a partnership, whether or not the persons sharing them have a joint or common right or interest in any property from which the returns are derived.

(4) The receipt by a person of a share of the profits of a business is prima facie evidence that he is a partner in the business, but no such inference shall be drawn if such profits were received in payment:

(a) As a debt by installments or otherwise,

(b) As wages of an employee or rent to a landlord,

(c) As an annuity to a widow or representative of a deceased partner,

(d) As interest on a loan, though the amount of payment vary with the profits of the business,

(e) As the consideration for the sale of a good-will of a business or other property by installments or otherwise.

§ 8. Partnership Property

(1) All property originally brought into the partnership stock or subsequently acquired by purchase or otherwise, on account of the partnership, is partnership property.

(2) Unless the contrary intention appears, property acquired with partnership funds is partnership property.

(3) Any estate in real property may be acquired in the partnership name. Title so acquired can be conveyed only in the partnership name.

(4) A conveyance to a partnership in the partnership name, though without words of inheritance, passes the entire estate of the grantor unless a contrary intent appears.

PART III

RELATIONS OF PARTNERS TO PERSONS DEALING WITH THE PARTNERSHIP

§ 9. Partner Agent of Partnership as to Partnership Business

(1) Every partner is an agent of the partnership for the purpose of its business, and the act of every partner, including the execution in the partnership name of any instrument, for apparently carrying on in the usual way the business of the partnership of which he is a member binds the partnership, unless the partner so acting has in fact no authority to act for the partnership in the particular matter, and the person with whom he is dealing has knowledge of the fact that he has no such authority.

(2) An act of a partner which is not apparently for the carrying on of the business of the partnership in the usual way does not bind the partnership unless authorized by the other partners.

(3) Unless authorized by the other partners or unless they have abandoned the business, one or more but less than all the partners have no authority to:

(a) Assign the partnership property in trust for creditors or on the assignee's promise to pay the debts of the partnership,

(b) Dispose of the good-will of the business,

(c) Do any other act which would make it impossible to carry on the ordinary business of a partnership,

(d) Confess a judgment,

(e) Submit a partnership claim or liability to arbitration or reference.

(4) No act of a partner in contravention of a restriction on authority shall bind the partnership to persons having knowledge of the restriction.

§ 10. Conveyance of Real Property of the Partnership

(1) Where title to real property is in the partnership name, any partner may convey title to such property by a conveyance executed in the partnership name; but the partnership may recover such property unless the partner's act binds the partnership under the provisions of paragraph (1) of section 9, or unless such property has been conveyed by the grantee or a person claiming through such grantee to a holder for value without knowledge that the partner, in making the conveyance, has exceeded his authority.

(2) Where title to real property is in the name of the partnership, a conveyance executed by a partner, in his own name, passes the equitable interest of the partnership, provided the act is one within the authority of the partner under the provisions of paragraph (1) of section 9.

(3) Where title to real property is in the name of one or more but not all the partners, and the record does not disclose the right of the partnership, the partners in whose name the title stands may convey title to such property, but the partnership may recover such property if the partners' act does not bind the partnership under the provisions of paragraph (1) of section 9, unless the purchaser or his assignee, is a holder for value, without knowledge.

(4) Where the title to real property is in the name of one or more or all the partners, or in a third person in trust for the partnership, a conveyance executed by a partner in the partnership name, or in his own name, passes the equitable interest of the partnership, provided the act is one within the authority of the partner under the provisions of paragraph (1) of section 9.

(5) Where the title to real property is in the names of all the partners a conveyance executed by all the partners passes all their rights in such property.

§ 11. Partnership Bound by Admission of Partner

An admission or representation made by any partner concerning partnership affairs within the scope of his authority as conferred by this act is evidence against the partnership.

§ 12. Partnership Charged With Knowledge of or Notice to Partner

Notice to any partner of any matter relating to partnership affairs, and the knowledge of the partner acting in the particular matter, acquired while a partner or then present to his mind, and the knowledge of any other partner who reasonably could and should have communicated it to the acting partner, operate as notice to or knowledge of the partnership, except in the case of a fraud on the partnership committed by or with the consent of that partner.

§ 13. Partnership Bound by Partner's Wrongful Act

Where, by any wrongful act or omission of any partner acting in the ordinary course of the business of the partnership or with the authority of his co-partners, loss or injury is caused to any person, not being a partner in the partnership, or any penalty is incurred, the partnership is liable therefor to the same extent as the partner so acting or omitting to act.

§ 14. Partnership Bound by Partner's Breach of Trust

The partnership is bound to make good the loss:

(a) Where one partner acting within the scope of his apparent authority receives money or property of a third person and misapplies it; and

(b) Where the partnership in the course of its business receives money or property of a third person and the money or property so received is misapplied by any partner while it is in the custody of the partnership.

§ 15. Nature of Partner's Liability

All partners are liable

(a) Jointly and severally for everything chargeable to the partnership under sections 13 and 14.

(b) Jointly for all other debts and obligations of the partnership; but any partner may enter into a separate obligation to perform a partnership contract.

§ 16. Partner by Estoppel

(1) When a person, by words spoken or written or by conduct, represents himself, or consents to another representing him to any one, as a partner in an existing partnership or with one or more persons not actual partners, he is liable to any such person to whom such representation has been made, who has, on the faith of such representation, given credit to the actual or apparent partnership, and if he has made such representation or consented to its being made in a public manner he is liable to such person, whether the representation has or has not been made or communicated to such person so giving credit by or with the knowledge of the apparent partner making the representation or consenting to its being made.

(a) When a partnership liability results, he is liable as though he were an actual member of the partnership.

(b) When no partnership liability results, he is liable jointly with the other persons, if any, so consenting to the contract or representation as to incur liability, otherwise separately.

(2) When a person has been thus represented to be a partner in an existing partnership, or with one or more persons not actual partners, he is an agent of the persons consenting to such representation to bind them to the same extent and in the same manner as though he were a partner in fact, with respect to persons who rely upon the representation. Where all the members of the existing partnership consent to the representation, a partnership act or obligation results; but in all other cases it is the joint act or obligation of the person acting and the persons consenting to the representation.

§ 17. Liability of Incoming Partner

A person admitted as a partner into an existing partnership is liable for all the obligations of the partnership arising before his admission as though he had been a partner when such obligations were incurred, except that this liability shall be satisfied only out of partnership property.

PART IV

RELATIONS OF PARTNERS TO ONE ANOTHER

§ 18. Rules Determining Rights and Duties of Partners

The rights and duties of the partners in relation to the partnership shall be determined, subject to any agreement between them, by the following rules:

(a) Each partner shall be repaid his contributions, whether by way of capital or advances to the partnership property and share equally in the profits and surplus remaining after all liabilities, including those to partners, are satisfied; and must contribute towards the losses, whether of capital or otherwise, sustained by the partnership according to his share in the profits.

(b) The partnership must indemnify every partner in respect of payments made and personal liabilities reasonably incurred by him in the ordinary and proper conduct of its business, or for the preservation of its business or property.

(c) A partner, who in aid of the partnership makes any payment or advance beyond the amount of capital which he agreed to contribute, shall be paid interest from the date of the payment or advance.

(d) A partner shall receive interest on the capital contributed by him only from the date when repayment should be made.

(e) All partners have equal rights in the management and conduct of the partnership business.

(f) No partner is entitled to remuneration for acting in the partnership business, except that a surviving partner is entitled to reasonable compensation for his services in winding up the partnership affairs.

(g) No person can become a member of a partnership without the consent of all the partners.

(h) Any difference arising as to ordinary matters connected with the partnership business may be decided by a majority of the partners; but no act in contravention of any agreement between the partners may be done rightfully without the consent of all the partners.

§ 19. Partnership Books

The partnership books shall be kept, subject to any agreement between the partners, at the principal place of business of the partnership, and every partner shall at all times have access to and may inspect and copy any of them.

§ 20. Duty of Partners to Render Information

Partners shall render on demand true and full information of all things affecting the partnership to any partner or the legal representative of any deceased partner or partner under legal disability.

§ 21. Partner Accountable as a Fiduciary

(1) Every partner must account to the partnership for any benefit, and hold as trustee for it any profits derived by him without the consent of the other partners from any transaction connected with the formation, conduct, or liquidation of the partnership or from any use by him of its property.

(2) This section applies also to the representatives of a deceased partner engaged in the liquidation of the affairs of the partnership as the personal representatives of the last surviving partner.

§ 22. Right to an Account

Any partner shall have the right to a formal account as to partnership affairs:

(a) If he is wrongfully excluded from the partnership business or possession of its property by his co-partners,

(b) If the right exists under the terms of any agreement,

(c) As provided by section 21,

(d) Whenever other circumstances render it just and reasonable.

§ 23. Continuation of Partnership Beyond Fixed Term

(1) When a partnership for a fixed term or particular undertaking is continued after the termination of such term or particular undertaking without any express agreement, the rights and duties of the partners remain the same as they were at such termination, so far as is consistent with a partnership at will.

(2) A continuation of the business by the partners or such of them as habitually acted therein during the term, without any settlement or liquidation of the partnership affairs, is prima facie evidence of a continuation of the partnership.

PART V

PROPERTY RIGHTS OF A PARTNER

§ 24. Extent of Property Rights of a Partner

The property rights of a partner are (1) his rights in specific partnership property, (2) his interest in the partnership, and (3) his right to participate in the management.

§ 25. Nature of a Partner's Right in Specific Partnership Property

(1) A partner is co-owner with his partners of specific partnership property holding as a tenant in partnership.

(2) The incidents of this tenancy are such that:

(a) A partner, subject to the provisions of this act and to any agreement between the partners, has an equal right with his partners to possess specific partnership property for partnership purposes; but he has no right to possess such property for any other purpose without the consent of his partners.

(b) A partner's right in specific partnership property is not assignable except in connection with the assignment of rights of all the partners in the same property.

(c) A partner's right in specific partnership property is not subject to attachment or execution, except on a claim against the partnership. When partnership property is attached for a partnership debt the partners, or any of them, or the representatives of a deceased partner, cannot claim any right under the homestead or exemption laws.

(d) On the death of a partner his right in specific partnership property vests in the surviving partner or partners, except where the deceased was the last surviving partner, when his right in such property vests in his legal representative. Such surviving partner or partners, or the legal representative of the last surviving partner, has no right to possess the partnership property for any but a partnership purpose.

(e) A partner's right in specific partnership property is not subject to dower, curtesy, or allowances to widows, heirs, or next of kin.

§ 26. Nature of Partner's Interest in the Partnership

A partner's interest in the partnership is his share of the profits and surplus, and the same is personal property.

§ 27. Assignment of Partner's Interest

(1) A conveyance by a partner of his interest in the partnership does not of itself dissolve the partnership, nor, as against the other partners in the absence of agreement, entitle the assignee, during the continuance of the partnership, to interfere in the management or administration of the partnership business or affairs, or to require any information or account of partnership transactions, or to inspect the partnership books; but it merely entitles the assignee to receive in accordance with his contract the profits to which the assigning partner would otherwise be entitled.

(2) In case of a dissolution of the partnership, the assignee is entitled to receive his assignor's interest and may require an account from the date only of the last account agreed to by all the partners.

§ 28. Partner's Interest Subject to Charging Order

(1) On due application to a competent court by any judgment creditor of a partner, the court which entered the judgment, order, or decree, or any other court, may charge the interest of the debtor partner with payment of the unsatisfied amount of such judgment debt with interest thereon; and may then or later appoint a receiver of his share of the profits, and of any other money due or to fall due to him in respect of the partnership, and make all other orders, directions, accounts and inquiries which the debtor partner might have made, or which the circumstances of the case may require.

(2) The interest charged may be redeemed at any time before foreclosure, or in case of a sale being directed by the court may be purchased without thereby causing a dissolution:

(a) With separate property, by any one or more of the partners, or

(b) With partnership property, by any one or more of the partners with the consent of all the partners whose interests are not so charged or sold.

(3) Nothing in this act shall be held to deprive a partner of his right, if any, under the exemption laws, as regards his interest in the partnership.

PART VI

DISSOLUTION AND WINDING UP

§ 29. Dissolution Defined

The dissolution of a partnership is the change in the relation of the partners caused by any partner ceasing to be associated in the carrying on as distinguished from the winding up of the business.

Official Comment

... In this act dissolution designates the point in time when the partners cease to carry on the business together; termination is the point in time when all the partnership affairs are wound up; winding up, the process of settling partnership affairs after dissolution.

§ 30. Partnership Not Terminated by Dissolution

On dissolution the partnership is not terminated, but continues until the winding up of partnership affairs is completed.

§ 31. Causes of Dissolution

Dissolution is caused:

(1) Without violation of the agreement between the partners,

(a) By the termination of the definite term or particular undertaking specified in the agreement,

(b) By the express will of any partner when no definite term or particular undertaking is specified,

(c) By the express will of all the partners who have not assigned their interests or suffered them to be charged for their separate debts, either before or after the termination of any specified term or particular undertaking,

(d) By the expulsion of any partner from the business bona fide in accordance with such a power conferred by the agreement between the partners;

(2) In contravention of the agreement between the partners, where the circumstances do not permit a dissolution under any other provision of this section, by the express will of any partner at any time;

(3) By any event which makes it unlawful for the business of the partnership to be carried on or for the members to carry it on in partnership;

(4) By the death of any partner;

(5) By the bankruptcy of any partner or the partnership;

(6) By decree of court under section 32.

Official Comment

Paragraph (2) will settle a matter on which at present considerable confusion and uncertainty exists. The paragraph as drawn allows a partner to dissolve a partnership in contravention of the agreement between the partners. . . .

The relation of partners is one of agency. The agency is such a personal one that equity cannot enforce it even where the agreement provides that the partnership shall continue for a definite time. The power of any partner to terminate the relation, even though in doing so he breaks a contract, should, it is submitted, be recognized.

The rights of the parties upon a dissolution in contravention of the agreement are safeguarded by section 38(2), infra.

§ 32. Dissolution by Decree of Court

(1) On application by or for a partner the court shall decree a dissolution whenever:

(a) A partner has been declared a lunatic in any judicial proceeding or is shown to be of unsound mind,

(b) A partner becomes in any other way incapable of performing his part of the partnership contract,

(c) A partner has been guilty of such conduct as tends to affect prejudicially the carrying on of the business,

(d) A partner wilfully or persistently commits a breach of the partnership agreement, or otherwise so conducts himself in matters relating to the partnership business that it is not reasonably practicable to carry on the business in partnership with him,

(e) The business of the partnership can only be carried on at a loss,

(f) Other circumstances render a dissolution equitable.

(2) On the application of the purchaser of a partner's interest under sections 28 or 29: [1]

(a) After the termination of the specified term or particular undertaking,

(b) At any time if the partnership was a partnership at will when the interest was assigned or when the charging order was issued.

§ 33. General Effect of Dissolution on Authority of Partner

Except so far as may be necessary to wind up partnership affairs or to complete transactions begun but not then finished, dissolution terminates all authority of any partner to act for the partnership,

(1) With respect to the partners,

(a) When the dissolution is not by the act, bankruptcy or death of a partner; or

(b) When the dissolution is by such act, bankruptcy or death of a partner, in cases where section 34 so requires.

(2) With respect to persons not partners, as declared in section 35.

§ 34. Right of Partner to Contribution From Co-partners After Dissolution

Where the dissolution is caused by the act, death or bankruptcy of a partner, each partner is liable to his co-partners for his share of any liability created by any partner acting for the partnership as if the partnership had not been dissolved unless

(a) The dissolution being by act of any partner, the partner acting for the partnership had knowledge of the dissolution, or

---

1. So in original. Probably should read "sections 27 or 28."

(b) The dissolution being by the death or bankruptcy of a partner, the partner acting for the partnership had knowledge or notice of the death or bankruptcy.

§ 35. Power of Partner to Bind Partnership to Third Persons After Dissolution

(1) After dissolution a partner can bind the partnership except as provided in Paragraph (3)

(a) By any act appropriate for winding up partnership affairs or completing transactions unfinished at dissolution;

(b) By any transaction which would bind the partnership if dissolution had not taken place, provided the other party to the transaction

(I) Had extended credit to the partnership prior to dissolution and had no knowledge or notice of the dissolution; or

(II) Though he had not so extended credit, had nevertheless known of the partnership prior to dissolution, and, having no knowledge or notice of dissolution, the fact of dissolution had not been advertised in a newspaper of general circulation in the place (or in each place if more than one) at which the partnership business was regularly carried on.

(2) The liability of a partner under Paragraph (1b) shall be satisfied out of partnership assets alone when such partner had been prior to dissolution

(a) Unknown as a partner to the person with whom the contract is made; and

(b) So far unknown and inactive in partnership affairs that the business reputation of the partnership could not be said to have been in any degree due to his connection with it.

(3) The partnership is in no case bound by any act of a partner after dissolution

(a) Where the partnership is dissolved because it is unlawful to carry on the business, unless the act is appropriate for winding up partnership affairs; or

(b) Where the partner has become bankrupt; or

(c) Where the partner has no authority to wind up partnership affairs; except by a transaction with one who

(I) Had extended credit to the partnership prior to dissolution and had no knowledge or notice of his want of authority; or

(II) Had not extended credit to the partnership prior to dissolution, and, having no knowledge or notice of his want of authority, the fact of his want of authority has not been advertised in the manner provided for advertising the fact of dissolution in Paragraph (1bII).

(4) Nothing in this section shall affect the liability under Section 16 of any person who after dissolution represents himself or consents to another

representing him as a partner in a partnership engaged in carrying on business.

§ 36. Effect of Dissolution on Partner's Existing Liability

(1) The dissolution of the partnership does not of itself discharge the existing liability of any partner.

(2) A partner is discharged from any existing liability upon dissolution of the partnership by an agreement to that effect between himself, the partnership creditor and the person or partnership continuing the business; and such agreement may be inferred from the course of dealing between the creditor having knowledge of the dissolution and the person or partnership continuing the business.

(3) Where a person agrees to assume the existing obligations of a dissolved partnership, the partners whose obligations have been assumed shall be discharged from any liability to any creditor of the partnership who, knowing of the agreement, consents to a material alteration in the nature or time of payment of such obligations.

(4) The individual property of a deceased partner shall be liable for all obligations of the partnership incurred while he was a partner but subject to the prior payment of his separate debts.

§ 37. Right to Wind Up

Unless otherwise agreed the partners who have not wrongfully dissolved the partnership or the legal representative of the last surviving partner, not bankrupt, has the right to wind up the partnership affairs; provided, however, that any partner, his legal representative or his assignee, upon cause shown, may obtain winding up by the court.

§ 38. Rights of Partners to Application of Partnership Property

(1) When dissolution is caused in any way, except in contravention of the partnership agreement, each partner, as against his co-partners and all persons claiming through them in respect of their interests in the partnership, unless otherwise agreed, may have the partnership property applied to discharge its liabilities, and the surplus applied to pay in cash the net amount owing to the respective partners. But if dissolution is caused by expulsion of a partner, bona fide under the partnership agreement and if the expelled partner is discharged from all partnership liabilities, either by payment or agreement under section 36(2), he shall receive in cash only the net amount due him from the partnership.

(2) When dissolution is caused in contravention of the partnership agreement the rights of the partners shall be as follows:

(a) Each partner who has not caused dissolution wrongfully shall have,

I.   All the rights specified in paragraph (1) of this section, and

II.   The right, as against each partner who has caused the dissolution wrongfully, to damages for breach of the agreement.

(b) The partners who have not caused the dissolution wrongfully, if they all desire to continue the business in the same name, either by themselves or jointly with others, may do so, during the agreed term for the partnership and for that purpose may possess the partnership property, provided they secure the payment by bond approved by the court, or pay to any partner who has caused the dissolution wrongfully, the value of his interest in the partnership at the dissolution, less any damages recoverable under clause (2aII) of this section, and in like manner indemnify him against all present or future partnership liabilities.

(c) A partner who has caused the dissolution wrongfully shall have:

I.   If the business is not continued under the provisions of paragraph (2b) all the rights of a partner under paragraph (1), subject to clause (2aII), of this section,

II.   If the business is continued under paragraph (2b) of this section the right as against his co-partners and all claiming through them in respect of their interests in the partnership, to have the value of his interest in the partnership, less any damages caused to his co-partners by the dissolution, ascertained and paid to him in cash, or the payment secured by bond approved by the court, and to be released from all existing liabilities of the partnership; but in ascertaining the value of the partner's interest the value of the good-will of the business shall not be considered.

Official Comment

The right given to each partner, where no agreement to the contrary has been made, to have his share of the surplus paid to him in cash makes certain an existing uncertainty. At present it is not certain whether a partner may or may not insist on a physical partition of the property remaining after third persons have been paid.

§ 39. Rights Where Partnership Is Dissolved for Fraud or Misrepresentation

Where a partnership contract is rescinded on the ground of the fraud or misrepresentation of one of the parties thereto, the party entitled to rescind is, without prejudice to any other right, entitled,

(a) To a lien on, or a right of retention of, the surplus of the partnership property after satisfying the partnership liabilities to third persons for any sum of money paid by him for the purchase of an interest in the partnership and for any capital or advances contributed by him; and

(b) To stand, after all liabilities to third persons have been satisfied, in the place of the creditors of the partnership for any payments made by him in respect of the partnership liabilities; and

(c) To be indemnified by the person guilty of the fraud or making the representation against all debts and liabilities of the partnership.

§ 40. Rules for Distribution

In settling accounts between the partners after dissolution, the following rules shall be observed, subject to any agreement to the contrary:

(a) The assets of the partnership are:

I. The partnership property,

II. The contributions of the partners necessary for the payment of all the liabilities specified in clause (b) of this paragraph.

(b) The liabilities of the partnership shall rank in order of payment, as follows:

I. Those owing to creditors other than partners,

II. Those owing to partners other than for capital and profits,

III. Those owing to partners in respect of capital,

IV. Those owing to partners in respect of profits.

(c) The assets shall be applied in order of their declaration in clause (a) of this paragraph to the satisfaction of the liabilities.

(d) The partners shall contribute, as provided by section 18(a) the amount necessary to satisfy the liabilities; but if any, but not all, of the partners are insolvent, or, not being subject to process, refuse to contribute, the other partners shall contribute their share of the liabilities, and, in the relative proportions in which they share the profits, the additional amount necessary to pay the liabilities.

(e) An assignee for the benefit of creditors or any person appointed by the court shall have the right to enforce the contributions specified in clause (d) of this paragraph.

(f) Any partner or his legal representative shall have the right to enforce the contributions specified in clause (d) of this paragraph, to the extent of the amount which he has paid in excess of his share of the liability.

(g) The individual property of a deceased partner shall be liable for the contributions specified in clause (d) of this paragraph.

(h) When partnership property and the individual properties of the partners are in possession of a court for distribution, partnership creditors shall have priority on partnership property and separate creditors on individual property, saving the rights of lien or secured creditors as heretofore.

(i) Where a partner has become bankrupt or his estate is insolvent the claims against his separate property shall rank in the following order:

I. Those owing to separate creditors,

II. Those owing to partnership creditors,

III. Those owing to partners by way of contribution.

§ 41. Liability of Persons Continuing the Business in Certain Cases

(1) When any new partner is admitted into an existing partnership, or when any partner retires and assigns (or the representative of the deceased partner assigns) his rights in partnership property to two or more of the partners, or to one or more of the partners and one or more third persons, if the business is continued without liquidation of the partnership affairs, creditors of the first or dissolved partnership are also creditors of the partnership so continuing the business.

(2) When all but one partner retire and assign (or the representative of a deceased partner assigns) their rights in partnership property to the remaining partner, who continues the business without liquidation of partnership affairs, either alone or with others, creditors of the dissolved partnership are also creditors of the person or partnership so continuing the business.

(3) When any partner retires or dies and the business of the dissolved partnership is continued as set forth in paragraphs (1) and (2) of this section, with the consent of the retired partners or the representative of the deceased partner, but without any assignment of his right in partnership property, rights of creditors of the dissolved partnership and of the creditors of the person or partnership continuing the business shall be as if such assignment had been made.

(4) When all the partners or their representatives assign their rights in partnership property to one or more third persons who promise to pay the debts and who continue the business of the dissolved partnership, creditors of the dissolved partnership are also creditors of the person or partnership continuing the business.

(5) When any partner wrongfully causes a dissolution and the remaining partners continue the business under the provisions of section 38(2b), either alone or with others, and without liquidation of the partnership affairs, creditors of the dissolved partnership are also creditors of the person or partnership continuing the business.

(6) When a partner is expelled and the remaining partners continue the business either alone or with others, without liquidation of the partnership affairs, creditors of the dissolved partnership are also creditors of the person or partnership continuing the business.

(7) The liability of a third person becoming a partner in the partnership continuing the business, under this section, to the creditors of the dissolved partnership shall be satisfied out of partnership property only.

(8) When the business of a partnership after dissolution is continued under any conditions set forth in this section the creditors of the dissolved partnership, as against the separate creditors of the retiring or deceased partner or the representative of the deceased partner, have a prior right to any claim of the retired partner or the representative of the deceased partner against the person or partnership continuing the business, on account of the retired or deceased partner's interest in the dissolved

partnership or on account of any consideration promised for such interest or for his right in partnership property.

(9) Nothing in this section shall be held to modify any right of creditors to set aside any assignment on the ground of fraud.

(10) The use by the person or partnership continuing the business of the partnership name, or the name of a deceased partner as part thereof, shall not of itself make the individual property of the deceased partner liable for any debts contracted by such person or partnership.

§ 42. Rights of Retiring or Estate of Deceased Partner When the Business Is Continued

When any partner retires or dies, and the business is continued under any of the conditions set forth in section 41(1, 2, 3, 5, 6), or section 38(2b) without any settlement of accounts as between him or his estate and the person or partnership continuing the business, unless otherwise agreed, he or his legal representative as against such persons or partnership may have the value of his interest at the date of dissolution ascertained, and shall receive as an ordinary creditor an amount equal to the value of his interest in the dissolved partnership with interest, or, at his option or at the option of his legal representative, in lieu of interest, the profits attributable to the use of his right in the property of the dissolved partnership; provided that the creditors of the dissolved partnership as against the separate creditors, or the representative of the retired or deceased partner, shall have priority on any claim arising under this section, as provided by section 41(8) of this act.

§ 43. Accrual of Actions

The right to an account of his interest shall accrue to any partner, or his legal representative, as against the winding up partners or the surviving partners or the person or partnership continuing the business, at the date of dissolution, in the absence of any agreement to the contrary.

REVISED UNIFORM PARTNERSHIP ACT (1997)

ARTICLE 1. GENERAL PROVISIONS

ARTICLE 2. NATURE OF PARTNERSHIP

ARTICLE 3. RELATIONS OF PARTNERS TO PERSONS DEALING WITH PARTNERSHIP

ARTICLE 4. RELATIONS OF PARTNERS TO EACH OTHER AND TO PARTNERSHIP

ARTICLE 5. TRANSFEREES AND CREDITORS OF PARTNER

ARTICLE 6. PARTNER'S DISSOCIATION

ARTICLE 1

GENERAL PROVISIONS

SECTION 101. DEFINITIONS.

In this [Act]:

(1) "Business" includes every trade, occupation, and profession.

(2) "Debtor in bankruptcy" means a person who is the subject of:

(i) an order for relief under Title 11 of the United States Code or a comparable order under a successor statute of general application; or

(ii) a comparable order under federal, state, or foreign law governing insolvency.

(3) "Distribution" means a transfer of money or other property from a partnership to a partner in the partner's capacity as a partner or to the partner's transferee.

(4) "Foreign limited liability partnership" means a partnership that:

(i) is formed under laws other than the laws of this State; and

(ii) has the status of a limited liability partnership under those laws.

(5) "Limited liability partnership" means a partnership that has filed a statement of qualification under Section 1001 and does not have a similar statement in effect in any other jurisdiction.

(6) "Partnership" means an association of two or more persons to carry on as co-owners a business for profit formed under Section 202, predecessor law, or comparable law of another jurisdiction.

(7) "Partnership agreement" means the agreement, whether written, oral, or implied, among the partners concerning the partnership, including amendments to the partnership agreement.

(8) "Partnership at will" means a partnership in which the partners have not agreed to remain partners until the expiration of a definite term or the completion of a particular undertaking.

(9) "Partnership interest" or "partner's interest in the partnership" means all of a partner's interests in the partnership, including the partner's transferable interest and all management and other rights.

(10) "Person" means an individual, corporation, business trust, estate, trust, partnership, association, joint venture, government, governmental

subdivision, agency, or instrumentality, or any other legal or commercial entity.

(11) "Property" means all property, real, personal, or mixed, tangible or intangible, or any interest therein.

(12) "State" means a State of the United States, the District of Columbia, the Commonwealth of Puerto Rico, or any territory or insular possession subject to the jurisdiction of the United States.

(13) "Statement" means a statement of partnership authority under Section 303, a statement of denial under Section 304, a statement of dissociation under Section 704, a statement of dissolution under Section 805, a statement of merger under Section 907, a statement of qualification under Section 1001, a statement of foreign qualification under Section 1102, or an amendment or cancellation of any of the foregoing.

(14) "Transfer" includes an assignment, conveyance, lease, mortgage, deed, and encumbrance.

Comment: ...

The definition of a "foreign limited liability partnership" includes a partnership formed under the laws of another state, foreign country, or other jurisdiction provided it has the status of a limited liability partnership in the other jurisdiction. Since the scope and nature of foreign limited liability partnership liability shields may vary in different jurisdictions, the definition avoids reference to similar or comparable laws. Rather, the definition incorporates the concept of a limited liability partnership in the foreign jurisdiction, however defined in that jurisdiction. The reference to formation "under laws other than the laws of this State" makes clear that the definition includes partnerships formed in foreign countries as well as in another state.

The definition of a "limited liability partnership" makes clear that a partnership may adopt the special liability shield characteristics of a limited liability partnership simply by filing a statement of qualification under Section 1001. A partnership may file the statement in this State regardless of where formed. When coupled with the governing law provisions of Section 106(b), this definition simplifies the choice of law issues applicable to partnerships with multi-state activities and contacts. Once a statement of qualification is filed, a partnership's internal affairs and the liability of its partners are determined by the law of the State where the statement is filed. See Section 106(b). The partnership may not vary this particular requirement. See Section 103(b)(9).

The reference to a "partnership" in the definition of a limited liability partnership makes clear that the RUPA definition of the term rather than the UPA concept controls for purposes of a limited liability partnership. Section 101(6) defines a "partnership" as "an association of two or more persons to carry on as co-owners a business for profit formed under Section 202, predecessor law, or comparable law of

229

another jurisdiction." Section 202(b) further provides that "an association formed under a statute other than this [Act], a predecessor statute, or a comparable statute of another jurisdiction is not a partnership under this [Act]." This language was intended to clarify that a limited partnership is not a RUPA general partnership. It was not intended to preclude the application of any RUPA general partnership rules to limited partnerships where limited partnership law otherwise adopts the RUPA rules. See Comments to Section 202(b) and Prefatory Note.

The effect of these definitions leaves the scope and applicability of RUPA to limited partnerships to limited partnership law, not to sever the linkage between the two Acts in all cases. Certain provisions of RUPA will continue to govern limited partnerships by virtue of Revised Uniform Limited Partnership Act (RULPA) Section 1105 which provides that "in any case not provided for in this [Act] the provisions of the Uniform Partnership Act govern." The RUPA partnership definition includes partnerships formed under the UPA. Therefore, the limited liability partnership rules will govern limited partnerships "in any case not provided for" in RULPA. Since RULPA does not provide for any rules applicable to a limited partnership becoming a limited liability partnership, the limited liability partnership rules should apply to limited partnerships that file a statement of qualification.

Partner liability deserves special mention. RULPA Section 403(b) provides that a general partner of a limited partnership "has the liabilities of a partner in a partnership without limited partners." Thus limited partnership law expressly references general partnership law for general partner liability and does not separately consider the liability of such partners. The liability of a general partner of a limited partnership that becomes a LLLP would therefore be the liability of a general partner in an LLP and would be governed by Section 306. The liability of a limited partner in a LLLP is a more complicated matter. RULPA Section 303(a) separately considers the liability of a limited partner. Unless also a general partner, a limited partner is not liable for the obligations of a limited partnership unless the partner participates in the control of the business and then only to persons reasonably believing the limited partner is a general partner. Therefore, arguably limited partners in a LLLP will have the specific RULPA Section 303(c) liability shield while general partners will have a superior Section 306(c) liability shield. In order to clarify limited partner liability and other linkage issues, states that have adopted RUPA, these limited liability partnership rules, and RULPA may wish to consider an amendment to RULPA. A suggested form of such an amendment is:

SECTION 1107. LIMITED LIABILITY LIMITED PARTNERSHIP.

(a) A limited partnership may become a limited liability partnership by:

(1) obtaining approval of the terms and conditions of the limited partnership becoming a limited liability limited partnership by the vote necessary to amend the limited partnership agreement except, in the case of a limited partnership agreement that expressly considers contribution obligations, the vote necessary to amend those provisions;

(2) filing a statement of qualification under Section 1001(c) of the Uniform Partnership Act (1994); and

(3) complying with the name requirements of Section 1002 of the Uniform Partnership Act (1994).

(b) A limited liability limited partnership continues to be the same entity that existed before the filing of a statement of qualification under Section 1001(c) of the Uniform Partnership Act (1994).

(c) Sections 306(c) and 307(f) of the Uniform Partnership Act (1994) apply to both general and limited partners of a limited liability limited partnership. . . .

The definition of "partnership agreement" is adapted from Section 101(9) of RULPA. The RUPA definition is intended to include the agreement among the partners, including amendments, concerning either the affairs of the partnership or the conduct of its business. It does not include other agreements between some or all of the partners, such as a lease or loan agreement. The partnership agreement need not be written; it may be oral or inferred from the conduct of the parties.

Any partnership in which the partners have not agreed to remain partners until the expiration of a definite term or the completion of a particular undertaking is a "partnership at will." The distinction between an "at-will" partnership and a partnership for "a definite term or the completion of a particular undertaking" is important in determining the rights of dissociating and continuing partners following the dissociation of a partner. See Sections 601, 602, 701(b), 801(a), 802(b), and 803.

It is sometimes difficult to determine whether a partnership is at will or is for a definite term or the completion of a particular undertaking. Presumptively, every partnership is an at-will partnership. See, e.g., Stone v. Stone, 292 So.2d 686 (La.1974); Frey v. Hauke, 171 Neb. 852, 108 N.W.2d 228 (1961). To constitute a partnership for a term or a particular undertaking, the partners must agree (i) that the partnership will continue for a definite term or until a particular undertaking is completed *and* (ii) that they will remain partners until the expiration of the term or the completion of the undertaking. Both are necessary for a term partnership; if the partners have the unrestricted right, as distinguished from the power, to withdraw from a partnership formed

231

for a term or particular undertaking, the partnership is one at will, rather than a term partnership.

To find that the partnership is formed for a definite term or a particular undertaking, there must be clear evidence of an agreement among the partners that the partnership (i) has a minimum or maximum duration or (ii) terminates at the conclusion of a particular venture whose time is indefinite but certain to occur. See, e.g., Stainton v. Tarantino, 637 F.Supp. 1051 (E.D.Pa.1986) (partnership to dissolve no later than December 30, 2020); Abel v. American Art Analog, Inc., 838 F.2d 691 (3d Cir.1988) (partnership purpose to market an art book); 68th Street Apts., Inc. v. Lauricella, 362 A.2d 78 (N.J.Super.Ct.1976) (partnership purpose to construct an apartment building). A partnership to conduct a business which may last indefinitely, however, is an at-will partnership, even though there may be an obligation of the partnership, such as a mortgage, which must be repaid by a certain date, absent a specific agreement that no partner can rightfully withdraw until the obligation is repaid. See, e.g., Page v. Page, 55 Cal.2d 192, 359 P.2d 41 (1961) (partnership purpose to operate a linen supply business); Frey v. Hauke, supra (partnership purpose to contract and operate a bowling alley); Girard Bank v. Haley, 460 Pa. 237, 332 A.2d 443 (1975) (partnership purpose to maintain and lease buildings).

"Partnership interest" or "partner's interest in the partnership" is defined to mean all of a partner's interests in the partnership, including the partner's transferable interest and all management and other rights. A partner's "transferable interest" is a more limited concept and means only his share of the profits and losses and right to receive distributions, that is, the partner's economic interests. See Section 502 and Comment. . . .

SECTION 102. KNOWLEDGE AND NOTICE.

(a) A person knows a fact if the person has actual knowledge of it.

(b) A person has notice of a fact if the person:

(1) knows of it;

(2) has received a notification of it; or

(3) has reason to know it exists from all of the facts known to the person at the time in question.

(c) A person notifies or gives a notification to another by taking steps reasonably required to inform the other person in ordinary course, whether or not the other person learns of it.

(d) A person receives a notification when the notification:

(1) comes to the person's attention; or

(2) is duly delivered at the person's place of business or at any other place held out by the person as a place for receiving communications.

(e) Except as otherwise provided in subsection (f), a person other than an individual knows, has notice, or receives a notification of a fact for purposes of a particular transaction when the individual conducting the transaction knows, has notice, or receives a notification of the fact, or in any event when the fact would have been brought to the individual's attention if the person had exercised reasonable diligence. The person exercises reasonable diligence if it maintains reasonable routines for communicating significant information to the individual conducting the transaction and there is reasonable compliance with the routines. Reasonable diligence does not require an individual acting for the person to communicate information unless the communication is part of the individual's regular duties or the individual has reason to know of the transaction and that the transaction would be materially affected by the information.

(f) A partner's knowledge, notice, or receipt of a notification of a fact relating to the partnership is effective immediately as knowledge by, notice to, or receipt of a notification by the partnership, except in the case of a fraud on the partnership committed by or with the consent of that partner.

Comment: ...

A person "knows" a fact only if that person has actual knowledge of it. Knowledge is cognitive awareness. That is solely an issue of fact. This is a change from the UPA Section 3(1) definition of "knowledge" which included the concept of "bad faith" knowledge arising from other known facts.

"Notice" is a lesser degree of awareness than "knows" and is based on a person's: (i) actual knowledge; (ii) receipt of a notification; or (iii) reason to know based on actual knowledge of other facts and the circumstances at the time. The latter is the traditional concept of inquiry notice.

Generally, under RUPA, statements filed pursuant to Section 105 [Execution, Filing, and Recording of Documents] do not constitute constructive knowledge or notice, except as expressly provided in the Act. See Section 301(1) (generally requiring knowledge of limitations on partner's apparent authority). Properly recorded statements of limitation on a partner's authority, on the other hand, generally constitute constructive knowledge with respect to the transfer of real property held in the partnership name. See Sections 303(d)(1), 303(e), 704(b), and 805(b)....

A notification is not required to be in writing. That is a change from UPA Section 3(2)(b). As under the UCC, the time and circumstances under which a notification may cease to be effective are not determined by RUPA....

SECTION 103. EFFECT OF PARTNERSHIP AGREEMENT; NON-WAIVABLE PROVISIONS.

(a) Except as otherwise provided in subsection (b), relations among the partners and between the partners and the partnership are governed by the partnership agreement. To the extent the partnership agreement does not otherwise provide, this [Act] governs relations among the partners and between the partners and the partnership.

(b) The partnership agreement may not:

(1) vary the rights and duties under Section 105 except to eliminate the duty to provide copies of statements to all of the partners;

(2) unreasonably restrict the right of access to books and records under Section 403(b);

(3) eliminate the duty of loyalty under Section 404(b) or 603(b)(3), but:

(i) the partnership agreement may identify specific types or categories of activities that do not violate the duty of loyalty, if not manifestly unreasonable; or

(ii) all of the partners or a number or percentage specified in the partnership agreement may authorize or ratify, after full disclosure of all material facts, a specific act or transaction that otherwise would violate the duty of loyalty;

(4) unreasonably reduce the duty of care under Section 404(c) or 603(b)(3);

(5) eliminate the obligation of good faith and fair dealing under Section 404(d), but the partnership agreement may prescribe the standards by which the performance of the obligation is to be measured, if the standards are not manifestly unreasonable;

(6) vary the power to dissociate as a partner under Section 602(a), except to require the notice under Section 601(1) to be in writing;

(7) vary the right of a court to expel a partner in the events specified in Section 601(5);

(8) vary the requirement to wind up the partnership business in cases specified in Section 801(4), (5), or (6);

(9) vary the law applicable to a limited liability partnership under Section 106(b); or

(10) restrict rights of third parties under this [Act].

Comment:

1. The general rule under Section 103(a) is that relations among the partners and between the partners and the partnership are governed by the partnership agreement. See Section 101(5). To the extent that the partners fail to agree upon a contrary rule, RUPA provides the default rule. Only the rights and duties listed in Section

103(b), and implicitly the corresponding liabilities and remedies under Section 405, are mandatory and cannot be waived or varied by agreement beyond what is authorized. Those are the only exceptions to the general principle that the provisions of RUPA with respect to the rights of the partners *inter se* are merely default rules, subject to modification by the partners. All modifications must also, of course, satisfy the general standards of contract validity. See Section 104.

2. Under subsection (b)(1), the partnership agreement may not vary the requirements for executing, filing, and recording statements under Section 105, except the duty to provide copies to all the partners. A statement that is not executed, filed, and recorded in accordance with the statutory requirements will not be accorded the effect prescribed in the Act, except as provided in Section 303(d).

3. Subsection (b)(2) provides that the partnership agreement may not unreasonably restrict a partner or former partner's access rights to books and records under Section 403(b). It is left to the courts to determine what restrictions are reasonable. See Comment 2 to Section 403. Other information rights in Section 403 can be varied or even eliminated by agreement.

4. Subsection[s] (b)(3) through (5) are intended to ensure a fundamental core of fiduciary responsibility. Neither the fiduciary duties of loyalty or care, nor the obligation of good faith and fair dealing, may be eliminated entirely. However, the statutory requirements of each can be modified by agreement, subject to the limitation[s] stated in subsection[s] (b)(3) through (5).

There has always been a tension regarding the extent to which a partner's fiduciary duty of loyalty can be varied by agreement, as contrasted with the other partners' consent to a particular and known breach of duty. On the one hand, courts have been loathe to enforce agreements broadly "waiving" in advance a partner's fiduciary duty of loyalty, especially where there is unequal bargaining power, information, or sophistication. For this reason, a very broad provision in a partnership agreement in effect negating any duty of loyalty, such as a provision giving a managing partner complete discretion to manage the business with no liability except for acts and omissions that constitute wilful misconduct, will not likely be enforced. See, e.g., Labovitz v. Dolan, 189 Ill.App.3d 403, 136 Ill.Dec. 780, 545 N.E.2d 304 (1989). On the other hand, it is clear that the remaining partners can "consent" to a particular conflicting interest transaction or other breach of duty, after the fact, provided there is full disclosure.

RUPA attempts to provide a standard that partners can rely upon in drafting exculpatory agreements. It is not necessary that the agreement be restricted to a particular transaction. That would require bargaining over every transaction or opportunity, which would be excessively burdensome. The agreement may be drafted in terms of types or categories of activities or transactions, but it should be reasonably specific.

A provision in a real estate partnership agreement authorizing a partner who is a real estate agent to retain commissions on partnership property bought and sold by that partner would be an example of a "type or category" of activity that is not manifestly unreasonable and thus should be enforceable under the Act. Likewise, a provision authorizing that partner to buy or sell real property for his own account without prior disclosure to the other partners or without first offering it to the partnership would be enforceable as a valid category of partnership activity.

Ultimately, the courts must decide the outer limits of validity of such agreements, and context may be significant. It is intended that the risk of judicial refusal to enforce manifestly unreasonable exculpatory clauses will discourage sharp practices while accommodating the legitimate needs of the parties in structuring their relationship.

5. Subsection (b)(3)(i) permits the partners, in their partnership agreement, to identify specific types or categories of partnership activities that do not violate the duty of loyalty. A modification of the statutory standard must not, however, be manifestly unreasonable. This is intended to discourage overreaching by a partner with superior bargaining power since the courts may refuse to enforce an overly broad exculpatory clause. See, e.g., Vlases v. Montgomery Ward & Co., 377 F.2d 846, 850 (3d Cir.1967) (limitation prohibits unconscionable agreements); PPG Industries, Inc. v. Shell Oil Co., 919 F.2d 17, 19 (5th Cir.1990) (apply limitation deferentially to agreements of sophisticated parties).

Subsection (b)(3)(ii) is intended to clarify the right of partners, recognized under general law, to consent to a known past or anticipated violation of duty and to waive their legal remedies for redress of that violation. This is intended to cover situations where the conduct in question is not specifically authorized by the partnership agreement. It can also be used to validate conduct that might otherwise not satisfy the "manifestly unreasonable" standard. Clause (ii) provides that, after full disclosure of all material facts regarding a specific act or transaction that otherwise would violate the duty of loyalty, it may be authorized or ratified by the partners. That authorization or ratification must be unanimous unless a lesser number or percentage is specified for this purpose in the partnership agreement.

6. Under subsection (b)(4), the partners' duty of care may not be unreasonably reduced below the statutory standard set forth in Section 404(d), that is, to refrain from engaging in grossly negligent or reckless conduct, intentional misconduct, or a knowing violation of law.

For example, partnership agreements frequently contain provisions releasing a partner from liability for actions taken in good faith and in the honest belief that the actions are in the best interests of the partnership and indemnifying the partner against any liability incurred in connection with the business of the partnership if the partner acts in a good faith belief that he has authority to act. Many partnership agreements reach this same result by listing various activities and stating that the performance of these activities is deemed not to constitute gross negligence or wilful misconduct. These types of provisions are intended to come within the modifications authorized by subsection (b)(4). On the other hand, absolving partners of intentional misconduct is probably unreasonable. As with contractual standards of loyalty, determining the outer limit in reducing the standard of care is left to the courts.

The standard may, of course, be increased by agreement to one of ordinary care or an even higher standard of care.

7. Subsection (b)(5) authorizes the partners to determine the standards by which the performance of the obligation of good faith and fair dealing is to be measured. The language of subsection (b)(5) is based on UCC Section 1–102(3). The partners can negotiate and draft specific contract provisions tailored to their particular needs (e.g., five days notice of a partners' meeting is adequate notice), but blanket waivers of the obligation are unenforceable....

8. Section 602(a) continues the traditional UPA Section 31(2) rule that every partner has the power to withdraw from the partnership at any time, which power can not be bargained away. Section 103(b)(6) provides that the partnership agreement may not vary the power to dissociate as a partner under Section 602(a), except to require that the notice of withdrawal under Section 601(1) be in writing....

9. Under subsection (b)(7), the right of a partner to seek court expulsion of another partner under Section 601(5) can not be waived or varied (e.g., requiring a 90–day notice) by agreement. Section 601(5) refers to judicial expulsion on such grounds as misconduct, breach of duty, or impracticability.

10. Under subsection (b)(8), the partnership agreement may not vary the right of partners to have the partnership dissolved and its business wound up under Section 801(4), (5), or (6). Section 801(4) provides that the partnership must be wound up if its business is unlawful. Section 801(5) provides for judicial winding up in such circumstances as frustration of the firm's economic purpose, partner misconduct, or impracticability. Section 801(6) accords standing to transferees of an interest in the partnership to seek judicial dissolution of the partnership in specified circumstances.

11. Subsection (b)(9) makes clear that a limited liability partnership may not designate the law of a State other than the State where it filed its statement of qualification to govern its internal affairs and the liability of its partners. See Sections 101(5), 106(b), and 202(a). Therefore, the selection of a state within which to file a statement of qualification has important choice of law ramifications, particularly where the partnership was formed in another state. See Comments to Section 106(b)....

SECTION 104. SUPPLEMENTAL PRINCIPLES OF LAW.

(a) Unless displaced by particular provisions of this [Act], the principles of law and equity supplement this [Act].

(b) If an obligation to pay interest arises under this [Act] and the rate is not specified, the rate is that specified in [applicable statute].

Comment:

The principles of law and equity supplement RUPA unless displaced by a particular provision of the Act.... These supplementary principles encompass not only the law of agency and estoppel and the law merchant mentioned in the UPA, but all of the other principles listed in UCC Section 1–103: the law relative to capacity to contract, fraud, misrepresentation, duress, coercion, mistake, bankruptcy, and other common law validating or invalidating causes, such as unconscionability. No substantive change from either the UPA or the UCC is intended....

SECTION 105. EXECUTION, FILING, AND RECORDING OF STATEMENTS.

(a) A statement may be filed in the office of [the Secretary of State]. A certified copy of a statement that is filed in an office in another State may be filed in the office of [the Secretary of State]. Either filing has the effect provided in this [Act] with respect to partnership property located in or transactions that occur in this State.

(b) A certified copy of a statement that has been filed in the office of the [Secretary of State] and recorded in the office for recording transfers of real property has the effect provided for recorded statements in this [Act]. A recorded statement that is not a certified copy of a statement filed in the office of the [Secretary of State] does not have the effect provided for recorded statements in this [Act].

(c) A statement filed by a partnership must be executed by at least two partners. Other statements must be executed by a partner or other person authorized by this [Act]. An individual who executes a statement as, or on behalf of, a partner or other person named as a partner in a statement shall personally declare under penalty of perjury that the contents of the statement are accurate.

(d) A person authorized by this [Act] to file a statement may amend or cancel the statement by filing an amendment or cancellation that names the partnership, identifies the statement, and states the substance of the amendment or cancellation.

(e) A person who files a statement pursuant to this section shall promptly send a copy of the statement to every nonfiling partner and to any other person named as a partner in the statement. Failure to send a copy of a statement to a partner or other person does not limit the effectiveness of the statement as to a person not a partner.

(f) The [Secretary of State] may collect a fee for filing or providing a certified copy of a statement. The [officer responsible for] recording transfers of real property may collect a fee for recording a statement.

Comment:

1. Section 105 is new. It mandates the procedural rules for the execution, filing, and recording of the various "statements" (see Section 101(11)) authorized by RUPA. . . .

No filings are mandatory under RUPA. In all cases, the filing of a statement is optional and voluntary. A system of mandatory filing and disclosure for partnerships, similar to that required for corporations and limited partnerships, was rejected for several reasons. First, RUPA is designed to accommodate the needs of small partnerships, which often have unwritten or sketchy agreements and limited resources. Furthermore, inadvertent partnerships are also governed by the Act, as the default form of business organization, in which case filing would be unlikely.

The RUPA filing provisions are, however, likely to encourage the voluntary use of partnership statements. There are a number of strong incentives for the partnership or the partners to file statements or for third parties, such as lenders or transferees of partnership property, to compel them to do so.

Only statements that are executed, filed, and, if appropriate (such as the authority to transfer real property), recorded in conformity with Section 105 have the legal consequences accorded statements by RUPA. The requirements of Section 105 cannot be varied in the partnership agreement, except the duty to provide copies of statements to all the partners. See Section 103(b)(1). . . .

SECTION 106. GOVERNING LAW.

(a) Except as otherwise provided in subsection (b), the law of the jurisdiction in which a partnership has its chief executive office governs relations among the partners and between the partners and the partnership.

(b) The law of this State governs relations among the partners and between the partners and the partnership and the liability of partners for an obligation of a limited liability partnership.

Comment:

The subsection (a) internal relations rule is new. . . .

RUPA looks to the jurisdiction in which a partnership's chief executive office is located to provide the law governing the internal relations among the partners and between the partners and the partnership. The concept of the partnership's "chief executive office" is drawn from UCC Section 9–103(3)(d). It was chosen in lieu of the State of organization because no filing is necessary to form a general partnership, and thus the situs of its organization is not always clear, unlike a limited partnership, which is organized in the State where its certificate is filed.

The term "chief executive office" is not defined in the Act, nor is it defined in the UCC. Paragraph 5 of the Official Comment to UCC Section 9–103(3)(d) explains:

> "Chief executive office" ... means the place from which in fact the debtor manages the main part of his business operations.... Doubt may arise as to which is the "chief executive office" of a multi-state enterprise, but it would be rare that there could be more than two possibilities.... [The rule] will be simple to apply in most cases....

In the absence of any other clear rule for determining a partnership's legal situs, it seems convenient to use that rule for choice of law purposes as well.

The choice-of-law rule provided by Section 106 is only a default rule, and the partners may by agreement select the law of another State to govern their internal affairs, subject to generally applicable conflict of laws requirements. For example, where the partners may not resolve a particular issue by an explicit provision of the partnership agreement, such as the rights and duties set forth in Section 103(b), the law chosen will not be applied if the partners or the partnership have no substantial relationship to the chosen State or other reasonable basis for their choice or if application of the law of the chosen State would be contrary to a fundamental policy of a State that has a materially greater interest than the chosen State. See Restatement (Second) of Conflict of Laws § 187(2) (1971). The partners must ... select only one State to govern their internal relations. They cannot select one State for some aspects of their internal relations and another State for others.

Contrasted with the variable choice-of-law rule provided by subsection (a), the law of the State where a limited liability partnership files its statement of qualification applies to such a partnership and may not be varied by the agreement of the partners. See Section 103(b)(9). Also, a partnership that files a statement of qualification in another state is not defined as a limited liability partnership in this state. See Section 101(5). Unlike a general partnership which may be formed without any filing, a partnership may only become a limited liability partnership by filing a statement of qualification. Therefore, the situs of its organization is clear. Because it is often unclear where a general partnership is actually formed, the decision to file a statement of qualification in a particular state constitutes a choice-of-law for the partnership which cannot be altered by the partnership agreement. See Comments to Section 103(b)(9). If the partnership agreement of an existing partnership specifies the law of a particular state as its governing law, and the partnership thereafter files a statement of qualification in another state, the partnership agreement choice is no longer controlling. In such cases, the filing of a statement of qualification "amends" the partnership agreement on this limited matter. Accordingly, if a statement of qualification is revoked or canceled for a limited liability partnership, the law of the state of filing would continue to apply unless the partnership agreement thereafter altered the applicable law rule.

SECTION 107. PARTNERSHIP SUBJECT TO AMENDMENT OR REPEAL OF [ACT].

A partnership governed by this [Act] is subject to any amendment to or repeal of this [Act].

Comment:

The reservation of power provision is new. It is adapted from Section 1.02 of the Revised Model Business Corporation Act (RMBCA) and Section 1106 of RULPA.

As explained in the Official Comment to the RMBCA, the genesis of those provisions is Trustees of Dartmouth College v. Woodward, 17 U.S. (4 Wheat) 518 (1819), which held that the United States Constitution prohibits the application of newly enacted statutes to existing corporations, while suggesting the efficacy of a reservation of power provision. Its purpose is to avoid any possible argument that a legal entity created pursuant to statute or its members have a contractual or vested right in any specific statutory provision and to ensure that the State may in the future modify its enabling statute as it deems appropriate and require existing entities to comply with the statutes as modified.

ARTICLE 2

NATURE OF PARTNERSHIP

Section 201.   Partnership As Entity.
Section 202.   Formation of Partnership.
Section 203.   Partnership Property.
Section 204.   When Property Is Partnership Property.

SECTION 201. PARTNERSHIP AS ENTITY.

(a) A partnership is an entity distinct from its partners.

(b) A limited liability partnership continues to be the same entity that existed before the filing of a statement of qualification under Section 1001.

Comment:

RUPA embraces the entity theory of the partnership. In light of the UPA's ambivalence on the nature of partnerships, the explicit statement provided by subsection (a) is deemed appropriate as an expression of the increased emphasis on the entity theory as the dominant model. *But see* Section 306 (partners' liability joint and

241

several unless the partnership has filed a statement of qualification to become a limited liability partnership).

Giving clear expression to the entity nature of a partnership is intended to allay previous concerns stemming from the aggregate theory, such as the necessity of a deed to convey title from the "old" partnership to the "new" partnership every time there is a change of cast among the partners. Under RUPA, there is no "new" partnership just because of membership changes. That will avoid the result in cases such as Fairway Development Co. v. Title Insurance Co., 621 F.Supp. 120 (N.D.Ohio 1985), which held that the "new" partnership resulting from a partner's death did not have standing to enforce a title insurance policy issued to the "old" partnership.

Subsection (b) makes clear that the explicit entity theory provided by subsection (a) applies to a partnership both before and after it files a statement of qualification to become a limited liability partnership. Thus, just as there is no "new" partnership resulting from membership changes, the filing of a statement of qualification does not create a "new" partnership. The filing partnership continues to be the same partnership entity that existed before the filing. Similarly, the amendment or cancellation of a statement of qualification under Section 105(d) or the revocation of a statement of qualification under Section 1003(c) does not terminate the partnership and create a "new" partnership. See Section 1003(d). Accordingly, a partnership remains the same entity regardless of a filing, cancellation, or revocation of a statement of qualification.

SECTION 202. FORMATION OF PARTNERSHIP.

(a) Except as otherwise provided in subsection (b), the association of two or more persons to carry on as co-owners a business for profit forms a partnership, whether or not the persons intend to form a partnership.

(b) An association formed under a statute other than this [Act], a predecessor statute, or a comparable statute of another jurisdiction is not a partnership under this [Act].

(c) In determining whether a partnership is formed, the following rules apply:

(1) Joint tenancy, tenancy in common, tenancy by the entireties, joint property, common property, or part ownership does not by itself establish a partnership, even if the co-owners share profits made by the use of the property.

(2) The sharing of gross returns does not by itself establish a partnership, even if the persons sharing them have a joint or common right or interest in property from which the returns are derived.

(3) A person who receives a share of the profits of a business is presumed to be a partner in the business, unless the profits were received in payment:

(i) of a debt by installments or otherwise;

(ii) for services as an independent contractor or of wages or other compensation to an employee;

(iii) of rent;

(iv) of an annuity or other retirement or health benefit to a beneficiary, representative, or designee of a deceased or retired partner;

(v) of interest or other charge on a loan, even if the amount of payment varies with the profits of the business, including a direct or indirect present or future ownership of the collateral, or rights to income, proceeds, or increase in value derived from the collateral; or

(vi) for the sale of the goodwill of a business or other property by installments or otherwise.

Comment:

1. Section 202 combines UPA Sections 6 and 7. The traditional UPA Section 6(1) "definition" of a partnership is recast as an operative rule of law. No substantive change in the law is intended. The UPA "definition" has always been understood as an operative rule, as well as a definition. The addition of the phrase, "whether or not the persons intend to form a partnership," merely codifies the universal judicial construction of UPA Section 6(1) that a partnership is created by the association of persons whose intent is to carry on as co-owners a business for profit, regardless of their subjective intention to be "partners." Indeed, they may inadvertently create a partnership despite their expressed subjective intention not to do so. The new language alerts readers to this possibility.

As under the UPA, the attribute of co-ownership distinguishes a partnership from a mere agency relationship. A business is a series of acts directed toward an end. Ownership involves the power of ultimate control. To state that partners are co-owners of a business is to state that they each have the power of ultimate control. See Official Comment to UPA § 6(1). On the other hand, as subsection (c)(1) makes clear, passive co-ownership of property by itself, as distinguished from the carrying on of a business, does not establish a partnership.

2. Subsection (b) provides that business associations organized under other statutes are not partnerships. Those statutory associations include corporations, limited partnerships, and limited liability companies. That continues the UPA concept that general partnership is the residual form of for profit business association, existing only if another form does not.

A limited partnership is not a partnership under this definition. Nevertheless, certain provisions of RUPA will continue to govern

243

limited partnerships because RULPA itself, in Section 1105, so requires "in any case not provided for" in RULPA. For example, the rules applicable to a limited liability partnership will generally apply to limited partnerships. See Comment to Section 101(5) (definition of a limited liability partnership). In light of ... RULPA Section 1105, UPA Section 6(2), which provides that limited partnerships are governed by the UPA, is redundant and has not been carried over to RUPA. It is also more appropriate that the applicability of RUPA to limited partnerships be governed exclusively by RULPA. For example, a RULPA amendment may clarify certain linkage questions regarding the application of the limited liability partnership rules to limited partnerships. See Comment to Section 101(5) for a suggested form of such an amendment....

Relationships that are called "joint ventures" are partnerships if they otherwise fit the definition of a partnership. An association is not classified as a partnership, however, simply because it is called a "joint venture."

An unincorporated nonprofit organization is not a partnership under RUPA, even if it qualifies as a business, because it is not a "for profit" organization.

3. Subsection (c) provides three rules of construction that apply in determining whether a partnership has been formed under subsection (a). They are largely derived from UPA Section 7, and to that extent no substantive change is intended. The sharing of profits is recast as a rebuttable presumption of a partnership, a more contemporary construction, rather than as prima facie evidence thereof. The protected categories, in which receipt of a share of the profits is not presumed to create a partnership, apply whether the profit share is a single flat percentage or a ratio which varies, for example, after reaching a dollar floor or different levels of profits.

Like its predecessor, RUPA makes no attempt to answer in every case whether a partnership is formed. Whether a relationship is more properly characterized as that of borrower and lender, employer and employee, or landlord and tenant is left to the trier of fact. As under the UPA, a person may function in both partner and nonpartner capacities....

SECTION 203. PARTNERSHIP PROPERTY.

Property acquired by a partnership is property of the partnership and not of the partners individually.

Comment:

All property acquired by a partnership, by transfer or otherwise, becomes partnership property and belongs to the partnership as an entity, rather than to the individual partners. This expresses the substantive result of UPA Sections 8(1) and 25.

Neither UPA Section 8(1) nor RUPA Section 203 provides any guidance concerning when property is "acquired by" the partnership. That problem is dealt with in Section 204. . . .

SECTION 204. WHEN PROPERTY IS PARTNERSHIP PROPERTY.

(a) Property is partnership property if acquired in the name of:

(1) the partnership; or

(2) one or more partners with an indication in the instrument transferring title to the property of the person's capacity as a partner or of the existence of a partnership but without an indication of the name of the partnership.

(b) Property is acquired in the name of the partnership by a transfer to:

(1) the partnership in its name; or

(2) one or more partners in their capacity as partners in the partnership, if the name of the partnership is indicated in the instrument transferring title to the property.

(c) Property is presumed to be partnership property if purchased with partnership assets, even if not acquired in the name of the partnership or of one or more partners with an indication in the instrument transferring title to the property of the person's capacity as a partner or of the existence of a partnership.

(d) Property acquired in the name of one or more of the partners, without an indication in the instrument transferring title to the property of the person's capacity as a partner or of the existence of a partnership and without use of partnership assets, is presumed to be separate property, even if used for partnership purposes.

Comment: . . .

3. Ultimately, it is the intention of the partners that controls whether property belongs to the partnership or to one or more of the partners in their individual capacities, at least as among the partners themselves. RUPA sets forth two rebuttable presumptions that apply when the partners have failed to express their intent.

First, under subsection (c), property purchased with partnership funds is presumed to be partnership property, notwithstanding the name in which title is held. The presumption is intended to apply if partnership credit is used to obtain financing, as well as the use of partnership cash or property for payment. Unlike the rule in subsection (b), under which property is *deemed* to be partnership property if the partnership's name or the partner's capacity as a partner is disclosed in the instrument of conveyance, subsection (c) raises only a *presumption* that the property is partnership property if it is purchased with partnership assets.

245

That presumption is also subject to an important caveat. Under Section 302(b), partnership property held in the name of individual partners, without an indication of their capacity as partners or of the existence of a partnership, that is transferred by the partners in whose name title is held to a purchaser without knowledge that it is partnership property is free of any claims of the partnership.

Second, under subsection (d), property acquired in the name of one or more of the partners, without an indication of their capacity as partners and without use of partnership funds or credit, is presumed to be the partners' separate property, even if used for partnership purposes. In effect, it is presumed in that case that only the use of the property is contributed to the partnership. . . .

ARTICLE 3

RELATIONS OF PARTNERS TO PERSONS DEALING WITH PARTNERSHIP

SECTION 301. PARTNER AGENT OF PARTNERSHIP.

Subject to the effect of a statement of partnership authority under Section 303:

(1) Each partner is an agent of the partnership for the purpose of its business. An act of a partner, including the execution of an instrument in the partnership name, for apparently carrying on in the ordinary course the partnership business or business of the kind carried on by the partnership binds the partnership, unless the partner had no authority to act for the partnership in the particular matter and the person with whom the partner was dealing knew or had received a notification that the partner lacked authority.

(2) An act of a partner which is not apparently for carrying on in the ordinary course the partnership business or business of the kind carried on by the partnership binds the partnership only if the act was authorized by the other partners.

Comment: . . .

2. Section 301(1) retains the basic principles reflected in UPA Section 9(1). It declares that each partner is an agent of the partnership and that, by virtue of partnership status, each partner has apparent authority to bind the partnership in ordinary course transac-

tions. The effect of Section 301(1) is to characterize a partner as a general managerial agent having both actual and apparent authority co-extensive in scope with the firm's ordinary business, at least in the absence of a contrary partnership agreement.

Section 301(1) effects two changes from UPA Section 9(1). First, it clarifies that a partner's apparent authority includes acts for carrying on in the ordinary course "business of the kind carried on by the partnership," not just the business of the particular partnership in question. The UPA is ambiguous on this point, but there is some authority for an expanded construction in accordance with the so-called English rule. See, e.g., Burns v. Gonzalez, 439 S.W.2d 128, 131 (Tex.Civ.App.1969) (dictum); Commercial Hotel Co. v. Weeks, 254 S.W. 521 (Tex.Civ.App.1923). No substantive change is intended by use of the more customary phrase "carrying on in the ordinary course" in lieu of the UPA phrase "in the usual way." The UPA and the case law use both terms without apparent distinction.

The other change from the UPA concerns the allocation of risk of a partner's lack of authority. RUPA draws the line somewhat differently from the UPA.

Under UPA Section 9(1) and (4), only a person with knowledge of a restriction on a partner's authority is bound by it. Section 301(1) provides that a person who has received a notification of a partner's lack of authority is also bound. The meaning of "receives a notification" is explained in Section 102(d). Thus, the partnership may protect itself from unauthorized acts by giving a notification of a restriction on a partner's authority to a person dealing with that partner. A notification may be effective upon delivery, whether or not it actually comes to the other person's attention. To that extent, the risk of lack of authority is shifted to those dealing with partners.

On the other hand, as used in the UPA, the term "knowledge" embodies the concept of "bad faith" knowledge arising from other known facts. As used in RUPA, however, "knowledge" is limited to actual knowledge. See Section 102(a). Thus, RUPA does not expose persons dealing with a partner to the greater risk of being bound by a restriction based on their purported reason to know of the partner's lack of authority from all the facts they did know. Compare Section 102(b)(3) (notice).

With one exception, this result is not affected even if the partnership files a statement of partnership authority containing a limitation on a partner's authority. Section 303(f) makes clear that a person dealing with a partner is not deemed to know of such a limitation merely because it is contained in a filed statement of authority. Under Section 303(e), however, all persons are deemed to know of a limitation on the authority of a partner to transfer real property contained in a recorded statement. Thus, a recorded limitation on authority concerning real property constitutes constructive knowledge of the limitation to the whole world.

3. Section 301(2) is drawn directly from UPA Section 9(2), with conforming changes to mirror the new language of subsection (1). Subsection (2) makes it clear that the partnership is bound by a partner's actual authority, even if the partner has no apparent authority. Section 401(j) requires the unanimous consent of the partners for a grant of authority outside the ordinary course of business, unless the partnership agreement provides otherwise. Under general agency principles, the partners can subsequently ratify a partner's unauthorized act. See Section 104(a).

4. UPA Section 9(3) contains a list of five extraordinary acts that require unanimous consent of the partners before the partnership is bound. RUPA omits that section. That leaves it to the courts to decide the outer limits of the agency power of a partner. Most of the acts listed in UPA Section 9(3) probably remain outside the apparent authority of a partner under RUPA, such as disposing of the goodwill of the business, but elimination of a statutory rule will afford more flexibility in some situations specified in UPA Section 9(3). In particular, it seems archaic that the submission of a partnership claim to arbitration always requires unanimous consent. See UPA § 9(3)(e). . . . .

SECTION 302. TRANSFER OF PARTNERSHIP PROPERTY.

(a) Partnership property may be transferred as follows:

(1) Subject to the effect of a statement of partnership authority under Section 303, partnership property held in the name of the partnership may be transferred by an instrument of transfer executed by a partner in the partnership name.

(2) Partnership property held in the name of one or more partners with an indication in the instrument transferring the property to them of their capacity as partners or of the existence of a partnership, but without an indication of the name of the partnership, may be transferred by an instrument of transfer executed by the persons in whose name the property is held.

(3) Partnership property held in the name of one or more persons other than the partnership, without an indication in the instrument transferring the property to them of their capacity as partners or of the existence of a partnership, may be transferred by an instrument of transfer executed by the persons in whose name the property is held.

(b) A partnership may recover partnership property from a transferee only if it proves that execution of the instrument of initial transfer did not bind the partnership under Section 301 and:

(1) as to a subsequent transferee who gave value for property transferred under subsection (a)(1) and (2), proves that the subsequent transferee knew or had received a notification that the person who executed the instrument of initial transfer lacked authority to bind the partnership; or

(2) as to a transferee who gave value for property transferred under subsection (a)(3), proves that the transferee knew or had received a notification that the property was partnership property and that the person who executed the instrument of initial transfer lacked authority to bind the partnership.

(c) A partnership may not recover partnership property from a subsequent transferee if the partnership would not have been entitled to recover the property, under subsection (b), from any earlier transferee of the property.

(d) If a person holds all of the partners' interests in the partnership, all of the partnership property vests in that person. The person may execute a document in the name of the partnership to evidence vesting of the property in that person and may file or record the document.

SECTION 303. STATEMENT OF PARTNERSHIP AUTHORITY.

(a) A partnership may file a statement of partnership authority, which:

(1) must include:

(i) the name of the partnership;

(ii) the street address of its chief executive office and of one office in this State, if there is one;

(iii) the names and mailing addresses of all of the partners or of an agent appointed and maintained by the partnership for the purpose of subsection (b); and

(iv) the names of the partners authorized to execute an instrument transferring real property held in the name of the partnership; and

(2) may state the authority, or limitations on the authority, of some or all of the partners to enter into other transactions on behalf of the partnership and any other matter.

(b) If a statement of partnership authority names an agent, the agent shall maintain a list of the names and mailing addresses of all of the partners and make it available to any person on request for good cause shown.

(c) If a filed statement of partnership authority is executed pursuant to Section 105(c) and states the name of the partnership but does not contain all of the other information required by subsection (a), the statement nevertheless operates with respect to a person not a partner as provided in subsections (d) and (e).

(d) Except as otherwise provided in subsection (g), a filed statement of partnership authority supplements the authority of a partner to enter into transactions on behalf of the partnership as follows:

(1) Except for transfers of real property, a grant of authority contained in a filed statement of partnership authority is conclusive in favor of a person who gives value without knowledge to the contrary,

so long as and to the extent that a limitation on that authority is not then contained in another filed statement. A filed cancellation of a limitation on authority revives the previous grant of authority.

(2) A grant of authority to transfer real property held in the name of the partnership contained in a certified copy of a filed statement of partnership authority recorded in the office for recording transfers of that real property is conclusive in favor of a person who gives value without knowledge to the contrary, so long as and to the extent that a certified copy of a filed statement containing a limitation on that authority is not then of record in the office for recording transfers of that real property. The recording in the office for recording transfers of that real property of a certified copy of a filed cancellation of a limitation on authority revives the previous grant of authority.

(e) A person not a partner is deemed to know of a limitation on the authority of a partner to transfer real property held in the name of the partnership if a certified copy of the filed statement containing the limitation on authority is of record in the office for recording transfers of that real property.

(f) Except as otherwise provided in subsections (d) and (e) and Sections 704 and 805, a person not a partner is not deemed to know of a limitation on the authority of a partner merely because the limitation is contained in a filed statement.

(g) Unless earlier canceled, a filed statement of partnership authority is canceled by operation of law five years after the date on which the statement, or the most recent amendment, was filed with the [Secretary of State].

Comment:

1. Section 303 is new. It provides for an optional statement of partnership authority specifying the names of the partners authorized to execute instruments transferring real property held in the name of the partnership. It may also grant supplementary authority to partners, or limit their authority, to enter into other transactions on behalf of the partnership. The execution, filing, and recording of statements is governed by Section 105....

2. The most important goal of the statement of authority is to facilitate the transfer of real property held in the name of the partnership. A statement must specify the names of the partners authorized to execute an instrument transferring that property.

Under subsection (d)(2), a recorded grant of authority to transfer real property held in the name of the partnership is conclusive in favor of a transferee for value without actual knowledge to the contrary....

Under subsection (e), third parties are deemed to know of a recorded limitation on the authority of a partner to transfer real property held in the partnership name. Since transferees are bound under Section 301 by knowledge of a limitation on a partner's authority, they are bound by such a recorded limitation. Of course, a transferee with actual knowledge of a limitation on a partner's authority is bound under Section 301, whether or not there is a recorded statement of limitation.

3. A statement of partnership authority may have effect beyond the transfer of real property held in the name of the partnership. Under subsection (a)(2), a statement of authority may contain any other matter the partnership chooses, including a grant of authority, or a limitation on the authority, of some or all of the partners to enter into other transactions on behalf of the partnership. Since Section 301 confers authority on all partners to act for the partnership in ordinary matters, the real import of such a provision is to grant extraordinary authority, or to limit the ordinary authority, of some or all of the partners.

The effect given to such a provision is different from that accorded a provision regarding the transfer of real property. Under subsection (d)(1), a filed grant of authority is binding on the partnership, in favor of a person who gives value without actual knowledge to the contrary, unless limited by another filed statement. That is the same rule as for statements involving real property under subsection 301(d)(2). There is, however, no counterpart to subsection (e) regarding a filed limitation of authority. To the contrary, subsection (f) makes clear that filing a limitation of authority does not operate as constructive knowledge of a partner's lack of authority with respect to non-real property transactions.

Under Section 301, only a third party who knows or has received a notification of a partner's lack of authority in an ordinary course transaction is bound. Thus, a limitation on a partner's authority to transfer personal property or to enter into other non-real property transactions on behalf of the partnership, contained in a filed statement of partnership authority, is effective only against a third party who knows or has received a notification of it. The fact of the statement being filed has no legal significance in those transactions, although the filed statement is a potential source of actual knowledge to third parties.

4. It should be emphasized that Section 303 concerns the authority of partners to bind the partnership to third persons. As among the partners, the authority of a partner to take any action is governed by the partnership agreement, or by the provisions of RUPA governing the relations among partners, and is not affected by the filing or recording of a statement of partnership authority....

SECTION 304. STATEMENT OF DENIAL.

A partner or other person named as a partner in a filed statement of partnership authority or in a list maintained by an agent pursuant to Section 303(b) may file a statement of denial stating the name of the partnership and the fact that it is being denied, which may include denial of a person's authority or status as a partner. A statement of denial is a limitation on authority as provided in Section 303(d) and (e).

SECTION 305. PARTNERSHIP LIABLE FOR PARTNER'S AC-TIONABLE CONDUCT.

(a) A partnership is liable for loss or injury caused to a person, or for a penalty incurred, as a result of a wrongful act or omission, or other actionable conduct, of a partner acting in the ordinary course of business of the partnership or with authority of the partnership.

(b) If, in the course of the partnership's business or while acting with authority of the partnership, a partner receives or causes the partnership to receive money or property of a person not a partner, and the money or property is misapplied by a partner, the partnership is liable for the loss.

Comment:

Section 305(a), which is derived from UPA Section 13, imposes liability on the partnership for the wrongful acts of a partner acting in the ordinary course of the partnership's business or otherwise within the partner's authority. The scope of the section has been expanded by deleting from UPA Section 13, "not being a partner in the partnership." This is intended to permit a partner to sue the partnership on a tort or other theory during the term of the partnership, rather than being limited to the remedies of dissolution and an accounting. See also Comment 2 to Section 405.

The section has also been broadened to cover no-fault torts by the addition of the phrase, "or other actionable conduct."

The partnership is liable for the actionable conduct or omission of a partner acting in the ordinary course of its business or "with the authority of the partnership." This is intended to include a partner's apparent, as well as actual, authority....

Section 305(b).... imposes strict liability on the partnership for the misapplication of money or property received by a partner in the course of the partnership's business or otherwise within the scope of the partner's actual authority.

SECTION 306. PARTNER'S LIABILITY.

(a) Except as otherwise provided in subsection (b), all partners are liable jointly and severally for all obligations of the partnership unless otherwise agreed by the claimant or provided by law.

(b) A person admitted as a partner into an existing partnership is not personally liable for any partnership obligation incurred before the person's admission as a partner.

(c) An obligation of a partnership incurred while the partnership is a limited liability partnership, whether arising in contract, tort, or otherwise, is solely the obligation of the partnership. A partner is not personally liable, directly or indirectly, by way of contribution or otherwise, for such a partnership obligation solely by reason of being or so acting as a partner. This subsection applies notwithstanding anything inconsistent in the partnership agreement that existed immediately before the vote required to become a limited liability partnership under Section 1001(b).

Comment:

1. Section 306(a) changes the UPA rule by imposing joint and several liability on the partners for all partnership obligations where the partnership is not a limited liability partnership. Under UPA Section 15, partners' liability for torts is joint and several, while their liability for contracts is joint but not several. About ten States that have adopted the UPA already provide for joint and several liability. The UPA reference to "debts and obligations" is redundant, and no change is intended by RUPA's reference solely to "obligations."

Joint and several liability under RUPA differs, however, from the classic model, which permits a judgment creditor to proceed immediately against any of the joint and several judgment debtors. Generally, Section 307(d) requires the judgment creditor to exhaust the partnership's assets before enforcing a judgment against the separate assets of a partner. . . .

3. Subsection (c) alters classic joint and several liability of general partners for obligations of a partnership that is a limited liability partnership. Like shareholders of a corporation and members of a limited liability company, partners of a limited liability partnership are not personally liable for partnership obligations incurred while the partnership liability shield is in place solely because they are partners. As with shareholders of a corporation and members of a limited liability company, partners remain personally liable for their personal misconduct.

In cases of partner misconduct, Section 401(c) sets forth a partnership's obligation to indemnify the culpable partner where the partner's liability was incurred in the ordinary course of the partnership's business. When indemnification occurs, the assets of both the partnership and the culpable partner are available to a creditor. However, Sections 306(c), 401(b), and 807(b) make clear that a partner who is not otherwise liable under Section 306(c) is not obligated to contribute assets to the partnership in excess of agreed contributions to share the loss with the culpable partner. (See Comments to Sections 401(b) and 807(b) regarding a slight variation in the context of priority of payment of partnership obligations.) Accordingly, Section 306(c) makes clear that an innocent partner is not personally liable for specified partnership obligations, directly or indirectly, by way of contribution or otherwise.

Although the liability shield protections of Section 306(c) may be modified in part or in full in a partnership agreement (and by way of private contractual guarantees), the modifications must constitute an intentional waiver of the liability protections. See Sections 103(b),

253

104(a), and 902(b). Since the mere act of filing a statement of qualification reflects the assumption that the partners intend to modify the otherwise applicable partner liability rules, the final sentence of subsection (c) makes clear that the filing negates inconsistent aspects of the partnership agreement that existed immediately before the vote to approve becoming a limited liability partnership. The negation only applies to a partner's personal liability for future partnership obligations. The filing however has no effect as to previously created partner obligations to the partnership in the form of specific capital contribution requirements.

Inter se contribution agreements may erode part or all of the effects of the liability shield. For example, Section 807(f) provides that an assignee for the benefit of creditors of a partnership or a partner may enforce a partner's obligation to contribute to the partnership. The ultimate effect of such contribution obligations may make each partner jointly and severally liable for all partnership obligations— even those incurred while the partnership is a limited liability partnership. Although the final sentence of subsection (c) negates such provisions existing before a statement of qualification is filed, it will have no effect on any amendments to the partnership agreement after the statement is filed. . . .

SECTION 307. ACTIONS BY AND AGAINST PARTNERSHIP AND PARTNERS.

(a) A partnership may sue and be sued in the name of the partnership.

(b) An action may be brought against the partnership and, to the extent not inconsistent with section 306, any or all of the partners in the same action or in separate actions.

(c) A judgment against a partnership is not by itself a judgment against a partner. A judgment against a partnership may not be satisfied from a partner's assets unless there is also a judgment against the partner.

(d) A judgment creditor of a partner may not levy execution against the assets of the partner to satisfy a judgment based on a claim against the partnership unless the partner is personally liable for the claim under Section 306 and:

(1) a judgment based on the same claim has been obtained against the partnership and a writ of execution on the judgment has been returned unsatisfied in whole or in part;

(2) the partnership is a debtor in bankruptcy;

(3) the partner has agreed that the creditor need not exhaust partnership assets;

(4) a court grants permission to the judgment creditor to levy execution against the assets of a partner based on a finding that partnership assets subject to execution are clearly insufficient to satisfy the judgment, that exhaustion of partnership assets is excessively

burdensome, or that the grant of permission is an appropriate exercise of the court's equitable powers; or

(5) liability is imposed on the partner by law or contract independent of the existence of the partnership.

(e) This section applies to any partnership liability or obligation resulting from a representation by a partner or purported partner under Section 308.

Comment:

1. Section 307 is new. Subsection (a) provides that a partnership may sue and be sued in the partnership name. That entity approach is designed to simplify suits by and against a partnership.

At common law, a partnership, not being a legal entity, could not sue or be sued in the firm name. The UPA itself is silent on this point, so in the absence of another enabling statute, it is generally necessary to join all the partners in an action against the partnership.

Most States have statutes or rules authorizing partnerships to sue or be sued in the partnership name. Many of those statutes, however, are found in the state provisions dealing with civil procedure rather than in the partnership act....

3. Subsection (c) provides that a judgment against the partnership is not, standing alone, a judgment against the partners, and it cannot be satisfied from a partner's personal assets unless there is a judgment against the partner. Thus, a partner must be individually named and served, either in the action against the partnership or in a later suit, before his personal assets may be subject to levy for a claim against the partnership.

RUPA leaves it to the law of judgments, as did the UPA, to determine the collateral effects to be accorded a prior judgment for or against the partnership in a subsequent action against a partner individually....

SECTION 308. LIABILITY OF PURPORTED PARTNER.

(a) If a person, by words or conduct, purports to be a partner, or consents to being represented by another as a partner, in a partnership or with one or more persons not partners, the purported partner is liable to a person to whom the representation is made, if that person, relying on the representation, enters into a transaction with the actual or purported partnership. If the representation, either by the purported partner or by a person with the purported partner's consent, is made in a public manner, the purported partner is liable to a person who relies upon the purported partnership even if the purported partner is not aware of being held out as a partner to the claimant. If partnership liability results, the purported partner is liable with respect to that liability as if the purported partner were a partner. If no partnership liability results, the purported partner is liable with respect to that liability jointly and severally with any other person consenting to the representation.

(b) If a person is thus represented to be a partner in an existing partnership, or with one or more persons not partners, the purported partner is an agent of persons consenting to the representation to bind them to the same extent and in the same manner as if the purported partner were a partner, with respect to persons who enter into transactions in reliance upon the representation. If all of the partners of the existing partnership consent to the representation, a partnership act or obligation results. If fewer than all of the partners of the existing partnership consent to the representation, the person acting and the partners consenting to the representation are jointly and severally liable.

(c) A person is not liable as a partner merely because the person is named by another in a statement of partnership authority.

(d) A person does not continue to be liable as a partner merely because of a failure to file a statement of dissociation or to amend a statement of partnership authority to indicate the partner's dissociation from the partnership.

(e) Except as otherwise provided in subsections (a) and (b), persons who are not partners as to each other are not liable as partners to other persons.

ARTICLE 4

RELATIONS OF PARTNERS TO EACH OTHER AND TO PARTNERSHIP

Section 401. Partner's Rights and Duties.
Section 402. Distributions in Kind.
Section 403. Partner's Rights and Duties With Respect to Information.
Section 404. General Standards of Partner's Conduct.
Section 405. Actions by Partnership and Partners.
Section 406. Continuation of Partnership Beyond Definite Term or Particular Undertaking.

SECTION 401. PARTNER'S RIGHTS AND DUTIES.

(a) Each partner is deemed to have an account that is:

(1) credited with an amount equal to the money plus the value of any other property, net of the amount of any liabilities, the partner contributes to the partnership and the partner's share of the partnership profits; and

(2) charged with an amount equal to the money plus the value of any other property, net of the amount of any liabilities, distributed by the partnership to the partner and the partner's share of the partnership losses.

(b) Each partner is entitled to an equal share of the partnership profits and is chargeable with a share of the partnership losses in proportion to the partner's share of the profits.

(c) A partnership shall reimburse a partner for payments made and indemnify a partner for liabilities incurred by the partner in the ordinary course of the business of the partnership or for the preservation of its business or property.

(d) A partnership shall reimburse a partner for an advance to the partnership beyond the amount of capital the partner agreed to contribute.

(e) A payment or advance made by a partner which gives rise to a partnership obligation under subsection (c) or (d) constitutes a loan to the partnership which accrues interest from the date of the payment or advance.

(f) Each partner has equal rights in the management and conduct of the partnership business.

(g) A partner may use or possess partnership property only on behalf of the partnership.

(h) A partner is not entitled to remuneration for services performed for the partnership, except for reasonable compensation for services rendered in winding up the business of the partnership.

(i) A person may become a partner only with the consent of all of the partners.

(j) A difference arising as to a matter in the ordinary course of business of a partnership may be decided by a majority of the partners. An act outside the ordinary course of business of a partnership and an amendment to the partnership agreement may be undertaken only with the consent of all of the partners.

(k) This section does not affect the obligations of a partnership to other persons under Section 301.

Comment: ...

3. Subsection (b) establishes the default rules for the sharing of partnership profits and losses. The UPA Section 18(a) rules that profits are shared equally and that losses, whether capital or operating, are shared in proportion to each partner's share of the profits are continued. Thus, under the default rule, partners share profits per capita and not in proportion to capital contribution as do corporate shareholders or partners in limited partnerships. Compare RULPA Section 504. With respect to losses, the qualifying phrase, "whether capital or operating," has been deleted as inconsistent with contemporary partnership accounting practice and terminology; no substantive change is intended.

If partners agree to share profits other than equally, losses will be shared similarly to profits, absent agreement to do otherwise. That rule, carried over from the UPA, is predicated on the assumption that partners would likely agree to share losses on the same basis as profits, but may fail to say so. Of course, by agreement, they may share losses on a different basis from profits.

The default rules apply, as does UPA Section 18(a), where one or more of the partners contribute no capital, although there is case law to the contrary. See, e.g., Kovacik v. Reed, 49 Cal.2d 166, 315 P.2d 314 (1957); Becker v. Killarney, 177 Ill.App.3d 793, 523 N.E.2d 467 (1988). It may seem unfair that the contributor of services, who contributes little or no capital, should be obligated to contribute toward the capital loss of the large contributor who contributed no services. In entering a partnership with such a capital structure, the partners should foresee that application of the default rule may bring about unusual results and take advantage of their power to vary by agreement the allocation of capital losses.

Subsection (b) provides that each partner "is chargeable" with a share of the losses, rather than the UPA formulation that each partner shall "contribute" to losses. Losses are charged to each partner's account as provided in subsection (a)(2). It is intended to make clear that a partner is not obligated to contribute to partnership losses before his withdrawal or the liquidation of the partnership, unless the partners agree otherwise. In effect, unless related to an obligation for which the partner is not personally liable under Section 306(c), a partner's negative account represents a debt to the partnership unless the partners agree to the contrary. Similarly, each partner's share of the profits is credited to his account under subsection (a)(1). Absent an agreement to the contrary, however, a partner does not have a right to receive a current distribution of the profits credited to his account, the interim distribution of profits being a matter arising in the ordinary course of business to be decided by majority vote of the partners.

However, where a liability to contribute at dissolution and winding up relates to a partnership obligation governed by the limited liability rule of Section 306(c), a partner is not obligated to contribute additional assets even at dissolution and winding up. See Section 807(b). In such a case, although a partner is not personally liable for the partnership obligation, that partner's interest in the partnership remains at risk. See also Comment to Section 401(c) relating to indemnification.

In the case of an operating limited liability partnership, the Section 306 liability shield may be partially eroded where the limited liability partnership incurs both shielded and unshielded liabilities. Where the limited liability partnership uses its assets to pay shielded liabilities before paying unshielded liabilities, each partner's obligation to contribute to the limited liability partnership for that partner's share of the unpaid and unshielded obligations at dissolution and winding up remains intact. The same issue is less likely to occur in the context of the termination of a limited liability partnership since a partner's contribution obligation is based only on that partner's share of unshielded obligations and the partnership will ordinarily use the contributed assets to pay unshielded claims first as they were the basis of the contribution obligations. See Comments to Section 807(b).

4. Subsection (c) is derived from UPA Section 18(b) and provides that the partnership shall reimburse partners for payments made and indemnify them for liabilities incurred in the ordinary course of the partnership's business or for the preservation of its business or property. Reimbursement and indemnification is an obligation of the partnership. Indemnification may create a loss toward which the partners must contribute. Although the right to indemnification is usually enforced in the settlement of accounts among partners upon dissolution and winding up of the partnership business, the right accrues when the liability is incurred and thus may be enforced during the term of the partnership in an appropriate case. See Section 405 and Comment. A partner's right to indemnification under this Act is not affected by the partnership becoming a limited liability partnership. Accordingly, partners continue to share partnership losses to the extent of partnership assets....

7. Under subsection (f), each partner has equal rights in the management and conduct of the business. It is based on UPA Section 18(e), which has been interpreted broadly to mean that, absent contrary agreement, each partner has a continuing right to participate in the management of the partnership and to be informed about the partnership business even if his assent to partnership business decisions is not required. There are special rules regarding the partner vote necessary to approve a partnership becoming (or canceling its status as) a limited liability partnership. See Section 1001(b)....

11. Subsection (j) continues with one important clarification the UPA Section 18(h) scheme of allocating management authority among the partners. In the absence of an agreement to the contrary, matters arising in the ordinary course of the business may be decided by a majority of the partners. Amendments to the partnership agreement and matters outside the ordinary course of the partnership business require unanimous consent of the partners. Although the text of the UPA is silent regarding extraordinary matters, courts have generally required the consent of all partners for those matters. See, e.g., Paciaroni v. Crane, 408 A.2d 946 (Del.Ch.1989); Thomas v. Marvin E. Jewell & Co., 232 Neb. 261, 440 N.W.2d 437 (1989); Duell v. Hancock, 83 A.D.2d 762, 443 N.Y.S.2d 490 (1981)....

SECTION 402. DISTRIBUTIONS IN KIND.

A partner has no right to receive, and may not be required to accept, a distribution in kind.

Comment: ...

This section is complemented by Section 807(a) which provides that, in winding up the partnership business on dissolution, any surplus after the payment of partnership obligations must be applied to pay in cash the net amount distributable to each partner.

SECTION 403. PARTNER'S RIGHTS AND DUTIES WITH RESPECT TO INFORMATION.

(a) A partnership shall keep its books and records, if any, at its chief executive office.

(b) A partnership shall provide partners and their agents and attorneys access to its books and records. It shall provide former partners and their agents and attorneys access to books and records pertaining to the period during which they were partners. The right of access provides the opportunity to inspect and copy books and records during ordinary business hours. A partnership may impose a reasonable charge, covering the costs of labor and material, for copies of documents furnished.

(c) Each partner and the partnership shall furnish to a partner, and to the legal representative of a deceased partner or partner under legal disability:

(1) without demand, any information concerning the partnership's business and affairs reasonably required for the proper exercise of the partner's rights and duties under the partnership agreement or this [Act]; and

(2) on demand, any other information concerning the partnership's business and affairs, except to the extent the demand or the information demanded is unreasonable or otherwise improper under the circumstances.

Comment: ...

2. ... A partner's right to inspect and copy the partnership's books and records is not conditioned on the partner's purpose or motive. Compare RMBCA Section 16.02(c)(1) (shareholder must have proper purpose to inspect certain corporate records). A partner's unlimited personal liability justifies an unqualified right of access to the partnership books and records. An abuse of the right to inspect and copy might constitute a violation of the obligation of good faith and fair dealing for which the other partners would have a remedy. See Sections 404(d) and 405.

Under Section 103(b)(2), a partner's right of access to partnership books and records may not be unreasonably restricted by the partnership agreement. Thus, to preserve a partner's core information rights despite unequal bargaining power, an agreement limiting a partner's right to inspect and copy partnership books and records is subject to judicial review. Nevertheless, reasonable restrictions on access to partnership books and records by agreement are authorized. For example, a provision in a partnership agreement denying partners access to the compensation of other partners should be upheld, absent any abuse such as fraud or duress. ...

3. ... Paragraph (2) continues the UPA rule that partners are entitled, on demand, to any other information concerning the partnership's business and affairs. The demand may be refused if either the

demand or the information demanded is unreasonable or otherwise improper. That qualification is new to the statutory formulation. The burden is on the partnership or partner from whom the information is requested to show that the demand is unreasonable or improper....

The Section 403(c) information rights can be waived or varied by agreement of the partners, since there is no Section 103(b) limitation on the variation of those rights as there is with respect to the Section 403(b) access rights to books and records. See Section 103(b)(2).

SECTION 404. GENERAL STANDARDS OF PARTNER'S CONDUCT.

(a) The only fiduciary duties a partner owes to the partnership and the other partners are the duty of loyalty and the duty of care set forth in subsections (b) and (c).

(b) A partner's duty of loyalty to the partnership and the other partners is limited to the following:

(1) to account to the partnership and hold as trustee for it any property, profit, or benefit derived by the partner in the conduct and winding up of the partnership business or derived from a use by the partner of partnership property, including the appropriation of a partnership opportunity;

(2) to refrain from dealing with the partnership in the conduct or winding up of the partnership business as or on behalf of a party having an interest adverse to the partnership; and

(3) to refrain from competing with the partnership in the conduct of the partnership business before the dissolution of the partnership.

(c) A partner's duty of care to the partnership and the other partners in the conduct and winding up of the partnership business is limited to refraining from engaging in grossly negligent or reckless conduct, intentional misconduct, or a knowing violation of law.

(d) A partner shall discharge the duties to the partnership and the other partners under this [Act] or under the partnership agreement and exercise any rights consistently with the obligation of good faith and fair dealing.

(e) A partner does not violate a duty or obligation under this [Act] or under the partnership agreement merely because the partner's conduct furthers the partner's own interest.

(f) A partner may lend money to and transact other business with the partnership, and as to each loan or transaction the rights and obligations of the partner are the same as those of a person who is not a partner, subject to other applicable law.

(g) This section applies to a person winding up the partnership business as the personal or legal representative of the last surviving partner as if the person were a partner.

Comment:

1. Section 404 is new. The title, "General Standards of Partner's Conduct," is drawn from RMBCA Section 8.30. Section 404 is both comprehensive and exclusive. In that regard, it is structurally different from the UPA which touches only sparingly on a partner's duty of loyalty and leaves any further development of the fiduciary duties of partners to the common law of agency. Compare UPA Sections 4(3) and 21.

Section 404 begins by stating that the **only** fiduciary duties a partner owes to the partnership and the other partners are the duties of loyalty and care set forth in subsections (b) and (c) of the Act. Those duties may not be waived or eliminated in the partnership agreement, but the agreement may identify activities and determine standards for measuring performance of the duties, if not manifestly unreasonable. See Sections 103(b)(3)–(5). . . .

[2.] Under Section 103(b)(3), the partnership agreement may not "eliminate" the duty of loyalty. Section 103(b)(3)(i) expressly empowers the partners, however, to identify specific types or categories of activities that do not violate the duty of loyalty, if not manifestly unreasonable. As under UPA Section 21, the other partners may also consent to a specific act or transaction that otherwise violates one of the rules. For the consent to be effective under Section 103(b)(3)(ii), there must be full disclosure of all material facts regarding the act or transaction and the partner's conflict of interest. See Comment 5 to Section 103.

3. Subsection (c) is new and establishes the duty of care that partners owe to the partnership and to the other partners. There is no statutory duty of care under the UPA, although a common law duty of care is recognized by some courts. See, e.g., Rosenthal v. Rosenthal, 543 A.2d 348, 352 (Me.1988) (duty of care limited to acting in a manner that does not constitute gross negligence or wilful misconduct).

The standard of care imposed by RUPA is that of gross negligence, which is the standard generally recognized by the courts. See, e.g., Rosenthal v. Rosenthal, supra. Section 103(b)(4) provides that the duty of care may not be eliminated entirely by agreement, but the standard may be reasonably reduced. See Comment 6 to Section 103.

4. Subsection (d) is also new. It provides that partners have an obligation of good faith and fair dealing in the discharge of all their duties, including those arising under the Act, such as their fiduciary duties of loyalty and care, and those arising under the partnership agreement. The exercise of any rights by a partner is also subject to the obligation of good faith and fair dealing. The obligation runs to the partnership and to the other partners in all matters related to the conduct and winding up of the partnership business.

The obligation of good faith and fair dealing is a contract concept, imposed on the partners because of the consensual nature of a partnership. See Restatement (Second) of Contracts § 205 (1981). It is not characterized, in RUPA, as a fiduciary duty arising out of the partners' special relationship. Nor is it a separate and independent obligation. It is an ancillary obligation that applies whenever a partner discharges a duty or exercises a right under the partnership agreement or the Act.

The meaning of "good faith and fair dealing" is not firmly fixed under present law. "Good faith" clearly suggests a subjective element, while "fair dealing" implies an objective component. It was decided to leave the terms undefined in the Act and allow the courts to develop their meaning based on the experience of real cases. . . .

In some situations the obligation of good faith includes a disclosure component. Depending on the circumstances, a partner may have an affirmative disclosure obligation that supplements the Section 403 duty to render information.

Under Section 103(b)(5), the obligation of good faith and fair dealing may not be eliminated by agreement, but the partners by agreement may determine the standards by which the performance of the obligation is to be measured, if the standards are not manifestly unreasonable. See Comment 7 to Section 103.

5. Subsection (e) is new and deals expressly with a very basic issue on which the UPA is silent. A partner as such is not a trustee and is not held to the same standards as a trustee. Subsection (e) makes clear that a partner's conduct is not deemed to be improper merely because it serves the partner's own individual interest.

That admonition has particular application to the duty of loyalty and the obligation of good faith and fair dealing. It underscores the partner's rights as an owner and principal in the enterprise, which must always be balanced against his duties and obligations as an agent and fiduciary. For example, a partner who, with consent, owns a shopping center may, under subsection (e), legitimately vote against a proposal by the partnership to open a competing shopping center.

6. Subsection (f) authorizes partners to lend money to and transact other business with the partnership and, in so doing, to enjoy the same rights and obligations as a nonpartner. That language is drawn from RULPA Section 107. The rights and obligations of a partner doing business with the partnership as an outsider are expressly made subject to the usual laws governing those transactions. They include, for example, rules limiting or qualifying the rights and remedies of inside creditors, such as fraudulent transfer law, equitable subordination, and the law of avoidable preferences, as well as general debtor-creditor law. The reference to "other applicable law" makes clear that subsection (f) is not intended to displace those laws, and thus they are preserved under Section 104(a).

It is unclear under the UPA whether a partner may, for the partner's own account, purchase the assets of the partnership at a foreclosure sale or upon the liquidation of the partnership. Those

263

purchases are clearly within subsection (f)'s broad approval. It is also clear under that subsection that a partner may purchase partnership assets at a foreclosure sale, whether the partner is the mortgagee or the mortgagee is an unrelated third party. Similarly, a partner may purchase partnership property at a tax sale. The obligation of good faith requires disclosure of the partner's interest in the transaction, however. . . .

SECTION 405.   ACTIONS BY PARTNERSHIP AND PARTNERS.

(a) A partnership may maintain an action against a partner for a breach of the partnership agreement, or for the violation of a duty to the partnership, causing harm to the partnership.

(b) A partner may maintain an action against the partnership or another partner for legal or equitable relief, with or without an accounting as to partnership business, to:

(1) enforce the partner's rights under the partnership agreement;

(2) enforce the partner's rights under this [Act], including:

(i) the partner's rights under Sections 401, 403, or 404;

(ii) the partner's right on dissociation to have the partner's interest in the partnership purchased pursuant to Section 701 or enforce any other right under [Article] 6 or 7; or

(iii) the partner's right to compel a dissolution and winding up of the partnership business under Section 801 or enforce any other right under [Article] 8; or

(3) enforce the rights and otherwise protect the interests of the partner, including rights and interests arising independently of the partnership relationship.

(c) The accrual of, and any time limitation on, a right of action for a remedy under this section is governed by other law. A right to an accounting upon a dissolution and winding up does not revive a claim barred by law.

Comment:

1.   Section 405(a) is new and reflects the entity theory of partnership. It provides that the partnership itself may maintain an action against a partner for any breach of the partnership agreement or for the violation of any duty owed to the partnership, such as a breach of fiduciary duty.

2.   Section 405(b) is the successor to UPA Section 22, but with significant changes. At common law, an accounting was generally not available before dissolution. That was modified by UPA Section 22 which specifies certain circumstances in which an accounting action is available without requiring a partner to dissolve the partnership. Section 405(b) goes far beyond the UPA rule. It provides that, during the term of the partnership, partners may maintain a variety of legal

or equitable actions, including an action for an accounting, as well as a final action for an accounting upon dissolution and winding up. It reflects a new policy choice that partners should have access to the courts during the term of the partnership to resolve claims against the partnership and the other partners, leaving broad judicial discretion to fashion appropriate remedies. . . .

Under subsection (b), a partner may bring a direct suit against the partnership or another partner for almost any cause of action arising out of the conduct of the partnership business. That eliminates the present procedural barriers to suits between partners filed independently of an accounting action. In addition to a formal account, the court may grant any other appropriate legal or equitable remedy. Since general partners are not passive investors like limited partners, RUPA does not authorize derivative actions, as does RULPA Section 1001. . . .

3. Generally, partners may limit or contract away their Section 405 remedies. They may not, however, eliminate entirely the remedies for breach of those duties that are mandatory under Section 103(b). See Comment 1 to Section 103. . . .

SECTION 406. CONTINUATION OF PARTNERSHIP BEYOND DEFINITE TERM OR PARTICULAR UNDERTAKING.

(a) If a partnership for a definite term or particular undertaking is continued, without an express agreement, after the expiration of the term or completion of the undertaking, the rights and duties of the partners remain the same as they were at the expiration or completion, so far as is consistent with a partnership at will.

(b) If the partners, or those of them who habitually acted in the business during the term or undertaking, continue the business without any settlement or liquidation of the partnership, they are presumed to have agreed that the partnership will continue.

ARTICLE 5

TRANSFEREES AND CREDITORS OF PARTNER

SECTION 501. PARTNER NOT CO–OWNER OF PARTNERSHIP PROPERTY.

A partner is not a co-owner of partnership property and has no interest in partnership property which can be transferred, either voluntarily or involuntarily.

Comment:

Section 501 provides that a partner is not a co-owner of partnership property and has no interest in partnership property that can be transferred, either voluntarily or involuntarily. Thus, the section abolishes the UPA Section 25(1) concept of tenants in partnership and reflects the adoption of the entity theory. Partnership property is owned by the entity and not by the individual partners. See also Section 203, which provides that property transferred to or otherwise acquired by the partnership is property of the partnership and not of the partners individually....

Adoption of the entity theory also has the effect of protecting partnership property from execution or other process by a partner's personal creditors. That continues the result under UPA Section 25(2)(c). Those creditors may seek a charging order under Section 504 to reach the partner's transferable interest in the partnership....

SECTION 502. PARTNER'S TRANSFERABLE INTEREST IN PARTNERSHIP.

The only transferable interest of a partner in the partnership is the partner's share of the profits and losses of the partnership and the partner's right to receive distributions. The interest is personal property.

Comment:

Section 502 continues the UPA Section 26 concept that a partner's only transferable interest in the partnership is the partner's share of profits and losses and right to receive distributions, that is, the partner's financial rights. The term "distribution" is defined in Section 101(3)....

Under Section 503(b)(3), a transferee of a partner's transferable interest has standing to seek judicial dissolution of the partnership business.

A partner has other interests in the partnership that may not be transferred, such as the right to participate in the management of the business. Those rights are included in the broader concept of a "partner's interest in the partnership." See Section 101(9).

SECTION 503. TRANSFER OF PARTNER'S TRANSFERABLE INTEREST.

(a) A transfer, in whole or in part, of a partner's transferable interest in the partnership:

(1) is permissible;

(2) does not by itself cause the partner's dissociation or a dissolution and winding up of the partnership business; and

(3) does not, as against the other partners or the partnership, entitle the transferee, during the continuance of the partnership, to

participate in the management or conduct of the partnership business, to require access to information concerning partnership transactions, or to inspect or copy the partnership books or records.

(b) A transferee of a partner's transferable interest in the partnership has a right:

(1) to receive, in accordance with the transfer, distributions to which the transferor would otherwise be entitled;

(2) to receive upon the dissolution and winding up of the partnership business, in accordance with the transfer, the net amount otherwise distributable to the transferor; and

(3) to seek under Section 801(6) a judicial determination that it is equitable to wind up the partnership business.

(c) In a dissolution and winding up, a transferee is entitled to an account of partnership transactions only from the date of the latest account agreed to by all of the partners.

(d) Upon transfer, the transferor retains the rights and duties of a partner other than the interest in distributions transferred.

(e) A partnership need not give effect to a transferee's rights under this section until it has notice of the transfer.

(f) A transfer of a partner's transferable interest in the partnership in violation of a restriction on transfer contained in the partnership agreement is ineffective as to a person having notice of the restriction at the time of transfer.

Comment:

1. ... Subsection (a)(1) states explicitly that a partner has the right to transfer his transferable interest in the partnership. The term "transfer" is used throughout RUPA in lieu of the term "assignment." See Section 101(10).

Subsection (a)(2) continues the UPA Section 27(1) rule that an assignment of a partner's interest in the partnership does not of itself cause a winding up of the partnership business. Under Section 601(4)(ii), however, a partner who has transferred substantially all of his partnership interest may be expelled by the other partners....

4. Subsection (d) is new. It makes clear that unless otherwise agreed the partner whose interest is transferred retains all of the rights and duties of a partner, other than the right to receive distributions. That means the transferor is entitled to participate in the management of the partnership and remains personally liable for all partnership obligations, unless and until he withdraws as a partner, is expelled under Section 601(4)(ii), or is otherwise dissociated under Section 601....

6. Subsection (f) is new and provides that a transfer of a partner's transferable interest in the partnership in violation of a restric-

tion on transfer contained in a partnership agreement is ineffective as to a person with timely notice of the restriction. Under Section 103(a), the partners may agree among themselves to restrict the right to transfer their partnership interests. Subsection (f) makes explicit that a transfer in violation of such a restriction is ineffective as to a transferee with notice of the restriction. See Section 102(b) for the meaning of "notice." RUPA leaves to general law and the UCC the issue of whether a transfer in violation of a valid restriction is effective as to a transferee without notice of the restriction.

Whether a particular restriction will be enforceable, however, must be considered in light of other law. See 11 U.S.C. § 541(c)(1) (property owned by bankrupt passes to trustee regardless of restrictions on transfer); UCC § 9–318(4) (agreement between account debtor and assignor prohibiting creation of security interest in a general intangible or requiring account debtor's consent is ineffective); Battista v. Carlo, 57 Misc.2d 495, 293 N.Y.S.2d 227 (1968) (restriction on transfer of partnership interest subject to rules against unreasonable restraints on alienation of property) (dictum); Tupper v. Kroc, 88 Nev. 146, 494 P.2d 1275 (1972) (partnership interest subject to charging order even if partnership agreement prohibits assignments). Cf. Tu–Vu Drive–In Corp. v. Ashkins, 61 Cal.2d 283, 38 Cal.Rptr. 348, 391 P.2d 828 (1964) (restraints on transfer of corporate stock must be reasonable). Even if a restriction on the transfer of a partner's transferable interest in a partnership were held to be unenforceable, the transfer might be grounds for expelling the partner-transferor from the partnership under Section 601(5)(ii).

7. Other rules that apply in the case of transfers include Section 601(4)(ii) (expulsion of partner who transfers substantially all of partnership interest); Section 601(6) (dissociation of partner who makes an assignment for benefit of creditors); and Section 801(6) (transferee has standing to seek judicial winding up).

SECTION 504. PARTNER'S TRANSFERABLE INTEREST SUBJECT TO CHARGING ORDER.

(a) On application by a judgment creditor of a partner or of a partner's transferee, a court having jurisdiction may charge the transferable interest of the judgment debtor to satisfy the judgment. The court may appoint a receiver of the share of the distributions due or to become due to the judgment debtor in respect of the partnership and make all other orders, directions, accounts, and inquiries the judgment debtor might have made or which the circumstances of the case may require.

(b) A charging order constitutes a lien on the judgment debtor's transferable interest in the partnership. The court may order a foreclosure of the interest subject to the charging order at any time. The purchaser at the foreclosure sale has the rights of a transferee.

(c) At any time before foreclosure, an interest charged may be redeemed:

(1) by the judgment debtor;

(2) with property other than partnership property, by one or more of the other partners; or

(3) with partnership property, by one or more of the other partners with the consent of all of the partners whose interests are not so charged.

(d) This [Act] does not deprive a partner of a right under exemption laws with respect to the partner's interest in the partnership.

(e) This section provides the exclusive remedy by which a judgment creditor of a partner or partner's transferee may satisfy a judgment out of the judgment debtor's transferable interest in the partnership.

ARTICLE 6

PARTNER'S DISSOCIATION

Section 601. Events Causing Partner's Dissociation.
Section 602. Partner's Power to Dissociate; Wrongful Dissociation.
Section 603. Effect of Partner's Dissociation.

SECTION 601. EVENTS CAUSING PARTNER'S DISSOCIATION.

A partner is dissociated from a partnership upon the occurrence of any of the following events:

(1) the partnership's having notice of the partner's express will to withdraw as a partner [upon the date of notice] or on a later date specified by the partner;

(2) an event agreed to in the partnership agreement as causing the partner's dissociation;

(3) the partner's expulsion pursuant to the partnership agreement;

(4) the partner's expulsion by the unanimous vote of the other partners if:

(i) it is unlawful to carry on the partnership business with that partner;

(ii) there has been a transfer of all or substantially all of that partner's transferable interest in the partnership, other than a transfer for security purposes, or a court order charging the partner's interest, which has not been foreclosed;

(iii) within 90 days after the partnership notifies a corporate partner that it will be expelled because it has filed a certificate of dissolution or the equivalent, its charter has been revoked, or its right to conduct business has been suspended by the jurisdiction of its incorporation, [and] there is no revocation of the certificate of dissolution or no reinstatement of its charter or its right to conduct business; or

269

(iv) a partnership that is a partner has been dissolved and its business is being wound up;

(5) on application by the partnership or another partner, the partner's expulsion by judicial determination because:

(i) the partner engaged in wrongful conduct that adversely and materially affected the partnership business;

(ii) the partner willfully or persistently committed a material breach of the partnership agreement or of a duty owed to the partnership or the other partners under Section 404; or

(iii) the partner engaged in conduct relating to the partnership business which makes it not reasonably practicable to carry on the business in partnership with the partner;

(6) the partner's:

(i) becoming a debtor in bankruptcy;

(ii) executing an assignment for the benefit of creditors;

(iii) seeking, consenting to, or acquiescing in the appointment of a trustee, receiver, or liquidator of that partner or of all or substantially all of that partner's property; or

(iv) failing, within 90 days after the appointment, to have vacated or stayed the appointment of a trustee, receiver, or liquidator of the partner or of all or substantially all of the partner's property obtained without the partner's consent or acquiescence, or failing within 90 days after the expiration of a stay to have the appointment vacated;

(7) in the case of a partner who is an individual:

(i) the partner's death;

(ii) the appointment of a guardian or general conservator for the partner; or

(iii) a judicial determination that the partner has otherwise become incapable of performing the partner's duties under the partnership agreement;

(8) in the case of a partner that is a trust or is acting as a partner by virtue of being a trustee of a trust, distribution of the trust's entire transferable interest in the partnership, but not merely by reason of the substitution of a successor trustee;

(9) in the case of a partner that is an estate or is acting as a partner by virtue of being a personal representative of an estate, distribution of the estate's entire transferable interest in the partnership, but not merely by reason of the substitution of a successor personal representative; or

(10) termination of a partner who is not an individual, partnership, corporation, trust, or estate.

Comment:

1. RUPA dramatically changes the law governing partnership breakups and dissolution. An entirely new concept, "dissociation," is used in lieu of the UPA term "dissolution" to denote the change in the relationship caused by a partner's ceasing to be associated in the carrying on of the business. "Dissolution" is retained but with a different meaning. See Section 802. The entity theory of partnership provides a conceptual basis for continuing the firm itself despite a partner's withdrawal from the firm.

Under RUPA, unlike the UPA, the dissociation of a partner does not necessarily cause a dissolution and winding up of the business of the partnership. Section 801 identifies the situations in which the dissociation of a partner causes a winding up of the business. Section 701 provides that in all other situations there is a buyout of the partner's interest in the partnership, rather than a windup of the partnership business. In those other situations, the partnership entity continues, unaffected by the partner's dissociation.

A dissociated partner remains a partner for some purposes and still has some residual rights, duties, powers, and liabilities. Although Section 601 determines when a partner is dissociated from the partnership, the consequences of the partner's dissociation do not all occur at the same time. Thus, it is more useful to think of a dissociated partner as a partner for some purposes, but as a former partner for others. For example, see Section 403(b) (former partner's access to partnership books and records). The consequences of a partner's dissociation depend on whether the partnership continues or is wound up, as provided in Articles 6, 7 and 8.

Section 601 enumerates all of the events that cause a partner's dissociation....

2. Section 601(1) provides that a partner is dissociated when the partnership has notice of the partner's express will to withdraw as a partner, unless a later date is specified by the partner. If a future date is specified by the partner, other partners may dissociate before that date; specifying a future date does not bind the others to remain as partners until that date. See also Section 801(2)(i).

Section 602(a) provides that a partner has the power to withdraw at any time. The power to withdraw is immutable under Section 103(b)(6), with the exception that the partners may agree the notice must be in writing. This continues the present rule that a partner has the power to withdraw at will, even if not the right. See UPA Section 31(2). Since no writing is required to create a partner relationship, it was felt unnecessarily formalistic, and a trap for the unwary, to require a writing to end one. If a written notification is given, Section 102(d) clarifies when it is deemed received.

RUPA continues the UPA "express will" concept, thus preserving existing case law. Section 601(1) clarifies existing law by providing

271

that the partnership must have notice of the partner's expression of will before the dissociation is effective. See Section 102(b) for the meaning of "notice." ...

4. Section 601(3) provides that a partner may be expelled by the other partners pursuant to a power of expulsion contained in the partnership agreement. That continues the basic rule of UPA Section 31(1)(d). The expulsion can be with or without cause. As under existing law, the obligation of good faith under Section 404(d) does not require prior notice, specification of cause, or an opportunity to be heard. See Holman v. Coie, 11 Wash.App. 195, 522 P.2d 515, cert. denied, 420 U.S. 984 (1974).

5. Section 601(4) empowers the partners, by unanimous vote, to expel a partner for specified causes, even if not authorized in the partnership agreement. This changes the UPA Section 31(1)(d) rule that authorizes expulsion only if provided in the partnership agreement. A partner may be expelled from a term partnership, as well as from a partnership at will. Under Section 103(a), the partnership agreement may change or abolish the partners' power of expulsion....

Subsection (4)(ii) provides that a partner may be expelled for transferring substantially all of his transferable interest in the partnership, other than as security for a loan. (He may, however, be expelled upon foreclosure.) This rule is derived from UPA Section 31(1)(c). To avoid the presence of an unwelcome transferee, the remaining partners may dissolve the partnership under Section 801(2)(ii), after first expelling the transferor partner....

6. ... Subsection (5)(iii) provides for judicial expulsion of a partner who engaged in conduct relating to the partnership business that makes it not reasonably practicable to carry on the business in partnership with that partner. Expulsion for such misconduct makes the partner's dissociation wrongful under Section 602(a)(ii) and may also support a judicial decree of dissolution under Section 801(5)(ii).

7. Section 601(6) provides that a partner is dissociated upon becoming a debtor in bankruptcy or upon taking or suffering other action evidencing the partner's insolvency or lack of financial responsibility....

Initially, upon the filing of the bankruptcy petition, the debtor partner's transferable interest in the partnership will pass to the bankruptcy trustee as property of the estate under Section 541(a)(1) of the Bankruptcy Code, notwithstanding any restrictions on transfer provided in the partnership agreement. In most Chapter 7 cases, that will result in the eventual buyout of the partner's interest.

The application of various provisions of the federal Bankruptcy Code to Section 601(6)(i) is unclear. In particular, there is uncertainty as to the validity of UPA Section 31(5), and thus its RUPA counterpart, under Sections 365(e) and 541(c)(1) of the Bankruptcy Code. Those sections generally invalidate so-called *ipso facto* laws that cause a termination or modification of the debtor's contract or property rights because of the bankruptcy filing. As a consequence, RUPA Section 601(6)(i), which provides for a partner's dissociation by operation of law upon becoming a debtor in bankruptcy, may be invalid under the Supremacy Clause. . . .

8. UPA Section 31(4) provides for the dissolution of a partnership upon the death of any partner, although by agreement the remaining partners may continue the partnership business. RUPA Section 601(7)(i), on the other hand, provides for dissociation upon the death of a partner who is an individual, rather than dissolution of the partnership. . . . Normally, under RUPA, the deceased partner's transferable interest in the partnership will pass to his estate and be bought out under Article 7. . . .

SECTION 602. PARTNER'S POWER TO DISSOCIATE; WRONGFUL DISSOCIATION.

(a) A partner has the power to dissociate at any time, rightfully or wrongfully, by express will pursuant to Section 601(1).

(b) A partner's dissociation is wrongful only if:

(1) it is in breach of an express provision of the partnership agreement; or

(2) in the case of a partnership for a definite term or particular undertaking, before the expiration of the term or the completion of the undertaking;

(i) the partner withdraws by express will, unless the withdrawal follows within 90 days after another partner's dissociation by death or otherwise under Section 601(6) through (10) or wrongful dissociation under this subsection;

(ii) the partner is expelled by judicial determination under Section 601(5);

(iii) the partner is dissociated by becoming a debtor in bankruptcy; or

(iv) in the case of a partner who is not an individual, trust other than a business trust, or estate, the partner is expelled or otherwise dissociated because it willfully dissolved or terminated.

(c) A partner who wrongfully dissociates is liable to the partnership and to the other partners for damages caused by the dissociation. The liability is in addition to any other obligation of the partner to the partnership or to the other partners.

Comment:

1. Subsection (a) states explicitly what is implicit in UPA Section 31(2) and RUPA Section 601(1)—that a partner has the power to dissociate at any time by expressing a will to withdraw, even in contravention of the partnership agreement. The phrase "rightfully

273

or wrongfully" reflects the distinction between a partner's *power* to withdraw in contravention of the partnership agreement and a partner's *right* to do so. In this context, although a partner can not be enjoined from exercising the power to dissociate, the dissociation may be wrongful under subsection (b).

2. Subsection (b) provides that a partner's dissociation is wrongful only if it results from one of the enumerated events. The significance of a wrongful dissociation is that it may give rise to damages under subsection (c) and, if it results in the dissolution of the partnership, the wrongfully dissociating partner is not entitled to participate in winding up the business under Section 804.

Under subsection (b), a partner's dissociation is wrongful if (1) it breaches an express provision of the partnership agreement or (2), in a term partnership, before the expiration of the term or the completion of the undertaking (i) the partner voluntarily withdraws by express will, except a withdrawal following *another* partner's wrongful dissociation or dissociation by death or otherwise under Section 601(6) through (10); (ii) the partner is expelled for misconduct under Section 601(5); (iii) the partner becomes a debtor in bankruptcy (see Section 101(2)); or (iv) a partner that is an entity (other than a trust or estate) is expelled or otherwise dissociated because its dissolution or termination was willful. Since subsection (b) is merely a default rule, the partnership agreement may eliminate or expand the dissociations that are wrongful or modify the effects of wrongful dissociation.

The exception in subsection (b)(2)(i) is intended to protect a partner's reactive withdrawal from a term partnership after the premature departure of another partner, such as the partnership's rainmaker or main supplier of capital, under the same circumstances that may result in the dissolution of the partnership under Section 801(2)(i). Under that section, a term partnership is dissolved 90 days after the bankruptcy, incapacity, death (or similar dissociation of a partner that is an entity), or wrongful dissociation of any partner, unless a majority in interest (see Comment 5(i) to Section 801 for a discussion of the term "majority in interest") of the remaining partners agree to continue the partnership. Under Section 602(b)(2)(i), a partner's exercise of the right of withdrawal by express will under those circumstances is rendered "rightful," even if the partnership is continued by others, and does not expose the withdrawing partner to damages for wrongful dissociation under Section 602(c).

A partner wishing to withdraw prematurely from a term partnership for any other reason, such as another partner's misconduct, can avoid being treated as a wrongfully dissociating partner by applying to a court under Section 601(5)(iii) to have the offending partner expelled. Then, the partnership could be dissolved under Section 801(2)(i) or the remaining partners could, by unanimous vote, dissolve the partnership under Section 801(2)(ii).

3. Subsection (c) provides that a wrongfully dissociating partner is liable to the partnership and to the other partners for any damages caused by the wrongful nature of the dissociation. That liability is in addition to any other obligation of the partner to the partnership or to the other partners. For example, the partner would be liable for any damage caused by breach of the partnership agreement or other misconduct. The partnership might also incur substantial expenses resulting from a partner's premature withdrawal from a term partnership, such as replacing the partner's expertise or obtaining new financing. The wrongfully dissociating partner would be liable to the partnership for those and all other expenses and damages that are causally related to the wrongful dissociation.

Section 701(c) provides that any damages for wrongful dissociation may be offset against the amount of the buyout price due to the partner under Section 701(a), and Section 701(h) provides that a partner who wrongfully dissociates from a term partnership is not entitled to payment of the buyout price until the term expires.

Under UPA Section 38(2)(c)(II), in addition to an offset for damages, the goodwill value of the partnership is excluded in determining the value of a wrongfully dissociating partner's partnership interest. Under RUPA, however, unless the partnership's goodwill is damaged by the wrongful dissociation, the value of the wrongfully dissociating partner's interest will include any goodwill value of the partnership. If the firm's goodwill is damaged, the amount of the damages suffered by the partnership and the remaining partners will be offset against the buyout price. See Section 701 and Comments.

SECTION 603. EFFECT OF PARTNER'S DISSOCIATION.

(a) If a partner's dissociation results in a dissolution and winding up of the partnership business, [Article] 8 applies; otherwise, [Article] 7 applies.

(b) Upon a partner's dissociation:

(1) the partner's right to participate in the management and conduct of the partnership business terminates, except as otherwise provided in Section 803;

(2) the partner's duty of loyalty under Section 404(b)(3) terminates; and

(3) the partner's duty of loyalty under Section 404(b)(1) and (2) and duty of care under Section 404(c) continue only with regard to matters arising and events occurring before the partner's dissociation, unless the partner participates in winding up the partnership's business pursuant to Section 803.

Comment:

1. Section 603(a) is a "switching" provision. It provides that, after a partner's dissociation, the partner's interest in the partnership must be purchased pursuant to the buyout rules in Article 7 *unless*

there is a dissolution and winding up of the partnership business under Article 8. Thus, a partner's dissociation will always result in either a buyout of the dissociated partner's interest or a dissolution and winding up of the business.

By contrast, under the UPA, every partner dissociation results in the dissolution of the partnership, most of which trigger a right to have the business wound up unless the partnership agreement provides otherwise. See UPA § 38. The only exception in which the remaining partners have a statutory right to continue the business is when a partner wrongfully dissolves the partnership in breach of the partnership agreement. See UPA § 38(2)(b).

2. Section 603(b) is new and deals with some of the internal effects of a partner's dissociation. Subsection (b)(1) makes it clear that one of the consequences of a partner's dissociation is the immediate loss of the right to participate in the management of the business, unless it results in a dissolution and winding up of the business. In that case, Section 804(a) provides that all of the partners who have not wrongfully dissociated may participate in winding up the business.

Subsection[s] (b)(2) and (3) clarify a partner's fiduciary duties upon dissociation. No change from current law is intended. With respect to the duty of loyalty, the Section 404(b)(3) duty not to compete terminates upon dissociation, and the dissociated partner is free immediately to engage in a competitive business, without any further consent. With respect to the partner's remaining loyalty duties under Section 404(b) and duty of care under Section 404(c), a withdrawing partner has a continuing duty after dissociation, but it is limited to matters that arose or events that occurred before the partner dissociated. For example, a partner who leaves a brokerage firm may immediately compete with the firm for new clients, but must exercise care in completing on-going client transactions and must account to the firm for any fees received from the old clients on account of those transactions. As the last clause makes clear, there is no contraction of a dissociated partner's duties under subsection (b)(3) if the partner thereafter participates in the dissolution and winding up the partnership's business.

ARTICLE 7

PARTNER'S DISSOCIATION WHEN BUSINESS NOT WOUND UP

SECTION 701. PURCHASE OF DISSOCIATED PARTNER'S INTEREST.

(a) If a partner is dissociated from a partnership without resulting in a dissolution and winding up of the partnership business under Section 801, the partnership shall cause the dissociated partner's interest in the partnership to be purchased for a buyout price determined pursuant to subsection (b).

(b) The buyout price of a dissociated partner's interest is the amount that would have been distributable to the dissociating partner under Section 807(b) if, on the date of dissociation, the assets of the partnership were sold at a price equal to the greater of the liquidation value or the value based on a sale of the entire business as a going concern without the dissociated partner and the partnership were wound up as of that date. Interest must be paid from the date of dissociation to the date of payment.

(c) Damages for wrongful dissociation under Section 602(b), and all other amounts owing, whether or not presently due, from the dissociated partner to the partnership, must be offset against the buyout price. Interest must be paid from the date the amount owed becomes due to the date of payment.

(d) A partnership shall indemnify a dissociated partner whose interest is being purchased against all partnership liabilities, whether incurred before or after the dissociation, except liabilities incurred by an act of the dissociated partner under Section 702.

(e) If no agreement for the purchase of a dissociated partner's interest is reached within 120 days after a written demand for payment, the partnership shall pay, or cause to be paid, in cash to the dissociated partner the amount the partnership estimates to be the buyout price and accrued interest, reduced by any offsets and accrued interest under subsection (c).

(f) If a deferred payment is authorized under subsection (h), the partnership may tender a written offer to pay the amount it estimates to be the buyout price and accrued interest, reduced by any offsets under subsection (c), stating the time of payment, the amount and type of security for payment, and the other terms and conditions of the obligation.

(g) The payment or tender required by subsection (e) or (f) must be accompanied by the following:

(1) a statement of partnership assets and liabilities as of the date of dissociation;

(2) the latest available partnership balance sheet and income statement, if any;

(3) an explanation of how the estimated amount of the payment was calculated; and

(4) written notice that the payment is in full satisfaction of the obligation to purchase unless, within 120 days after the written notice, the dissociated partner commences an action to determine the buyout

price, any offsets under subsection (c), or other terms of the obligation to purchase.

(h) A partner who wrongfully dissociates before the expiration of a definite term or the completion of a particular undertaking is not entitled to payment of any portion of the buyout price until the expiration of the term or completion of the undertaking, unless the partner establishes to the satisfaction of the court that earlier payment will not cause undue hardship to the business of the partnership. A deferred payment must be adequately secured and bear interest.

(i) A dissociated partner may maintain an action against the partnership, pursuant to Section 405(b)(2)(ii), to determine the buyout price of that partner's interest, any offsets under subsection (c), or other terms of the obligation to purchase. The action must be commenced within 120 days after the partnership has tendered payment or an offer to pay or within one year after written demand for payment if no payment or offer to pay is tendered. The court shall determine the buyout price of the dissociated partner's interest, any offset due under subsection (c), and accrued interest, and enter judgment for any additional payment or refund. If deferred payment is authorized under subsection (h), the court shall also determine the security for payment and other terms of the obligation to purchase. The court may assess reasonable attorney's fees and the fees and expenses of appraisers or other experts for a party to the action, in amounts the court finds equitable, against a party that the court finds acted arbitrarily, vexatiously, or not in good faith. The finding may be based on the partnership's failure to tender payment or an offer to pay or to comply with subsection (g).

Comment:

1. Article 7 is new and provides for the buyout of a dissociated partner's interest in the partnership when the partner's dissociation does not result in a dissolution and winding up of its business under Article 8. See Section 603(a). If there is no dissolution, the remaining partners have a right to continue the business and the dissociated partner has a right to be paid the value of his partnership interest. These rights can, of course, be varied in the partnership agreement. See Section 103. A dissociated partner has a continuing relationship with the partnership and third parties as provided in Sections 603(b), 702, and 703. See also Section 403(b) (former partner's access to partnership books and records).

2. Subsection (a) provides that, if a partner's dissociation does not result in a windup of the business, the partnership shall cause the interest of the dissociating partner to be purchased for a buyout price determined pursuant to subsection (b). The buyout is mandatory. The "cause to be purchased" language is intended to accommodate a purchase by the partnership, one or more of the remaining partners, or a third party. . . .

3. Subsection (b) provides how the "buyout price" is to be determined. The terms "fair market value" or "fair value" were not used because they are often considered terms of art having a special meaning depending on the context, such as in tax or corporate law. "Buyout price" is a new term. It is intended that the term be developed as an independent concept appropriate to the partnership buyout situation, while drawing on valuation principles developed elsewhere.

Under subsection (b), the buyout price is the amount that would have been distributable to the dissociating partner under Section 807(b) if, on the date of dissociation, the assets of the partnership were sold at a price equal to the greater of liquidation value or going concern value without the departing partner. Liquidation value is not intended to mean distress sale value. Under general principles of valuation, the hypothetical selling price in either case should be the price that a willing and informed buyer would pay a willing and informed seller, with neither being under any compulsion to deal. The notion of a minority discount in determining the buyout price is negated by valuing the business as a going concern. Other discounts, such as for a lack of marketability or the loss of a key partner, may be appropriate, however.

Since the buyout price is based on the value of the business at the time of dissociation, the partnership must pay interest on the amount due from the date of dissociation until payment to compensate the dissociating partner for the use of his interest in the firm. Section 104(b) provides that interest shall be at the legal rate unless otherwise provided in the partnership agreement....

UPA Section 38(2)(c)(II) provides that the good will of the business not be considered in valuing a wrongfully dissociating partner's interest. The forfeiture of good will rule is implicitly rejected by RUPA. See Section 602(c) and Comment 3.

The Section 701 rules are merely default rules. The partners may, in the partnership agreement, fix the method or formula for determining the buyout price and all of the other terms and conditions of the buyout right. Indeed, the very right to a buyout itself may be modified, although a provision providing for a complete forfeiture would probably not be enforceable. See Section 104(a).

4. Subsection (c) provides that the partnership may offset against the buyout price all amounts owing by the dissociated partner to the partnership, whether or not presently due, including any damages for wrongful dissociation under Section 602(c). This has the effect of accelerating payment of amounts not yet due from the departing partner to the partnership, including a long-term loan by the partnership to the dissociated partner. Where appropriate, the amounts not yet due should be discounted to present value. A dissociating partner, on the other hand, is not entitled to an add-on for amounts owing to him by the partnership. Thus, a departing partner who has made a

long-term loan to the partnership must wait for repayment, unless the terms of the loan agreement provide for acceleration upon dissociation.

It is not intended that the partnership's right of setoff be construed to limit the amount of the damages for the partner's wrongful dissociation and any other amounts owing to the partnership to the value of the dissociated partner's interest. Those amounts may result in a net sum due to the partnership from the dissociated partner.

5. Subsection (d) follows the UPA Section 38 rule and provides that the partnership must indemnify a dissociated partner against all partnership liabilities, whether incurred before or after the dissociation, except those incurred by the dissociated partner under Section 702.

6. Subsection (e) provides that, if no agreement for the purchase of the dissociated partner's interest is reached within 120 days after the dissociated partner's written demand for payment, the partnership must pay, or cause to be paid, in cash the amount it estimates to be the buyout price, adjusted for any offsets allowed and accrued interest. Thus, the dissociating partner will receive in cash within 120 days of dissociation the undisputed minimum value of the partner's partnership interest. If the dissociated partner claims that the buyout price should be higher, suit may thereafter be brought as provided in subsection (i) to have the amount of the buyout price determined by the court. This is similar to the procedure for determining the value of dissenting shareholders' shares under RMBCA Sections 13.20–13.28.

The "cause to be paid" language of subsection (a) is repeated here to permit either the partnership, one or more of the continuing partners, or a third-party purchaser to tender payment of the estimated amount due.

7. Subsection (f) provides that, when deferred payment is authorized in the case of a wrongfully dissociating partner, a written offer stating the amount the partnership estimates to be the purchase price should be tendered within the 120–day period, even though actual payment of the amount may be deferred, possibly for many years.... The dissociated partner is entitled to know at the time of dissociation what amount the remaining partners think is due, including the estimated amount of any damages allegedly caused by the partner's wrongful dissociation that may be offset against the buyout price....

9. Subsection (h) replaces UPA Section 38(2)(c) and provides a somewhat different rule for payment to a partner whose dissociation before the expiration of a definite term or the completion of a particular undertaking is wrongful under Section 602(b). Under subsection (h), a wrongfully dissociating partner is not entitled to receive any portion of the buyout price before the expiration of the term or completion of the undertaking, unless the dissociated partner establishes to the satisfaction of the court that earlier payment will not

cause undue hardship to the business of the partnership. In all other cases, there must be an immediate payment in cash.

10. Subsection (i) provides that a dissociated partner may maintain an action against the partnership to determine the buyout price, any offsets, or other terms of the purchase obligation. The action must be commenced within 120 days after the partnership tenders payment of the amount it estimates to be due or, if deferred payment is authorized, its written offer. This provision creates a 120–day "cooling off" period. It also allows the parties an opportunity to negotiate their differences after disclosure by the partnership of its financial statements and other required information.

If the partnership fails to tender payment of the estimated amount due (or a written offer, if deferred payment is authorized), the dissociated partner has one year after written demand for payment in which to commence suit.

If the parties fail to reach agreement, the court must determine the buyout price of the partner's interest, any offsets, including damages for wrongful dissociation, and the amount of interest accrued. If payment to a wrongfully dissociated partner is deferred, the court may also require security for payment and determine the other terms of the obligation. . . .

SECTION 702. DISSOCIATED PARTNER'S POWER TO BIND AND LIABILITY TO PARTNERSHIP.

(a) For two years after a partner dissociates without resulting in a dissolution and winding up of the partnership business, the partnership, including a surviving partnership under [Article] 9, is bound by an act of the dissociated partner which would have bound the partnership under Section 301 before dissociation only if at the time of entering into the transaction the other party:

(1) reasonably believed that the dissociated partner was then a partner;

(2) did not have notice of the partner's dissociation; and

(3) is not deemed to have had knowledge under Section 303(e) or notice under Section 704(c).

(b) A dissociated partner is liable to the partnership for any damage caused to the partnership arising from an obligation incurred by the dissociated partner after dissociation for which the partnership is liable under subsection (a).

Comment:

1. Section 702 deals with a dissociated partner's lingering apparent authority to bind the partnership in ordinary course partnership transactions and the partner's liability to the partnership for any loss caused thereby. It also applies to partners who withdraw incident to a merger under Article 9. See Section 906(e).

A dissociated partner has no *actual* authority to act for the partnership. See Section 603(b)(1). Nevertheless, in order to protect innocent third parties, Section 702(a) provides that the partnership remains bound, for two years after a partner's dissociation, by that partner's acts that would, before his dissociation, have bound the partnership under Section 301 if, and only if, the other party to the transaction reasonably believed that he was still a partner, did not have notice of the partner's dissociation, and is not deemed to have had knowledge of the dissociation under Section 303(e) or notice thereof under Section 704(c).

Under Section 301, every partner has *apparent* authority to bind the partnership by any act for carrying on the partnership business in the ordinary course, unless the other party knows that the partner has no actual authority to act for the partnership or has received a notification of the partner's lack of authority. Section 702(a) continues that general rule for two years after a partner's dissociation, subject to three modifications.

After a partner's dissociation, the general rule is modified, first, by requiring the other party to show reasonable reliance on the partner's status as a partner. Section 301 has no explicit reliance requirement, although the partnership is bound only if the partner purports to act on its behalf. Thus, the other party will normally be aware of the partnership and presumably the partner's status as such.

The second modification is that, under Section 702(a), the partnership is not bound if the third party has *notice* of the partner's dissociation, while under the general rule of Section 301 the partnership is bound unless the third party *knows* of the partner's lack of authority. Under Section 102(b), a person has "notice" of a fact if he knows or has reason to know it exists from all the facts that are known to him or he has received a notification of it. Thus, the partnership may protect itself by sending a notification of the dissociation to a third party, and a third party may, in any event, have a duty to inquire further based on what is known. That provides the partnership with greater protection from the unauthorized acts of a dissociated partner than from those of partners generally.

The third modification of the general apparent authority rule under Section 702(a) involves the effect of a statement of dissociation. Section 704(c) provides that, for the purposes of Sections 702(a)(3) and 703(b)(3), third parties are deemed to have notice of a partner's dissociation 90 days after the filing of a statement of dissociation. Thus, the filing of a statement operates as constructive notice of the dissociated partner's lack of authority after 90 days, conclusively terminating the dissociated partner's Section 702 apparent authority. . . .

Under RUPA, therefore, a partnership should notify all known creditors of a partner's dissociation and may, by filing a statement of dissociation, conclusively limit to 90 days a dissociated partner's lingering agency power. Moreover, under Section 703(b), a dissociated partner's lingering liability for post-dissociation partnership liabilities may be limited to 90 days by filing a statement of dissociation. These incentives should encourage both partnerships and dissociating partners to file statements routinely. Those transacting substantial business with partnerships can protect themselves from the risk of dealing with dissociated partners, or relying on their credit, by checking the partnership records at least every 90 days.

2. Section 702(b) is a corollary to subsection (a) and provides that a dissociated partner is liable to the partnership for any loss resulting from an obligation improperly incurred by the partner under subsection (a). In effect, the dissociated partner must indemnify the partnership for any loss, meaning a loss net of any gain from the transaction. The dissociated partner is also personally liable to the third party for the unauthorized obligation.

SECTION 703. DISSOCIATED PARTNER'S LIABILITY TO OTHER PERSONS.

(a) A partner's dissociation does not of itself discharge the partner's liability for a partnership obligation incurred before dissociation. A dissociated partner is not liable for a partnership obligation incurred after dissociation, except as otherwise provided in subsection (b).

(b) A partner who dissociates without resulting in a dissolution and winding up of the partnership business is liable as a partner to the other party in a transaction entered into by the partnership, or a surviving partnership under [Article] 9, within two years after the partner's dissociation, only if at the time of entering into the transaction the other party:

(1) reasonably believed that the dissociated partner was then a partner;

(2) did not have notice of the partner's dissociation; and

(3) is not deemed to have had knowledge under Section 303(e) or notice under Section 704(c).

(c) By agreement with the partnership creditor and the partners continuing the business, a dissociated partner may be released from liability for a partnership obligation.

(d) A dissociated partner is released from liability for a partnership obligation if a partnership creditor, with notice of the partner's dissociation but without the partner's consent, agrees to a material alteration in the nature or time of payment of a partnership obligation.

SECTION 704. STATEMENT OF DISSOCIATION.

(a) A dissociated partner or the partnership may file a statement of dissociation stating the name of the partnership and that the partner is dissociated from the partnership.

283

(b) A statement of dissociation is a limitation on the authority of a dissociated partner for the purposes of Section 303(d) and (e).

(c) For the purposes of Sections 702(a)(3) and 703(b)(3), a person not a partner is deemed to have notice of the dissociation 90 days after the statement of dissociation is filed.

SECTION 705. CONTINUED USE OF PARTNERSHIP NAME.

Continued use of a partnership name, or a dissociated partner's name as part thereof, by partners continuing the business does not of itself make the dissociated partner liable for an obligation of the partners or the partnership continuing the business.

ARTICLE 8

WINDING UP PARTNERSHIP BUSINESS

SECTION 801. EVENTS CAUSING DISSOLUTION AND WINDING UP OF PARTNERSHIP BUSINESS.

A partnership is dissolved, and its business must be wound up, only upon the occurrence of any of the following events:

(1) in a partnership at will, the partnership's having notice from a partner, other than a partner who is dissociated under Section 601(2) through (10), of that partner's express will to withdraw as a partner [as of the time of the notice], or on a later date specified by the partner;

(2) in a partnership for a definite term or particular undertaking:

(i) within 90 days after a partner's dissociation by death or otherwise under Section 601(6) through (10) or wrongful dissociation under Section 602(b), the express will of at least half of the remaining partners to wind up the partnership business, for which purpose a partner's rightful dissociation pursuant to Section 602(b)(2)(i) constitutes the expression of that partner's will to wind up the partnership business;

(ii) the express will of all of the partners to wind up the partnership business; or

(iii) the expiration of the term or the completion of the undertaking;

(3) an event agreed to in the partnership agreement resulting in the winding up of the partnership business;

(4) an event that makes it unlawful for all or substantially all of the business of the partnership to be continued, but a cure of illegality within 90 days after notice to the partnership of the event is effective retroactively to the date of the event for purposes of this section;

(5) on application by a partner, a judicial determination that:

(i) the economic purpose of the partnership is likely to be unreasonably frustrated;

(ii) another partner has engaged in conduct relating to the partnership business which makes it not reasonably practicable to carry on the business in partnership with that partner; or

(iii) it is not otherwise reasonably practicable to carry on the partnership business in conformity with the partnership agreement; or

(6) on application by a transferee of a partner's transferable interest, a judicial determination that it is equitable to wind up the partnership business:

(i) after the expiration of the term or completion of the undertaking, if the partnership was for a definite term or particular undertaking at the time of the transfer or entry of the charging order that gave rise to the transfer; or

(ii) at any time, if the partnership was a partnership at will at the time of the transfer or entry of the charging order that gave rise to the transfer.

Comment:

1. Under UPA Section 29, a partnership is dissolved every time a partner leaves. That reflects the aggregate nature of the partnership under the UPA. Even if the business of the partnership is continued by some of the partners, it is technically a new partnership. The dissolution of the old partnership and creation of a new partnership causes many unnecessary problems....

RUPA's move to the entity theory is driven in part by the need to prevent a technical dissolution or its consequences. Under RUPA, not every partner dissociation causes a dissolution of the partnership. Only certain departures trigger a dissolution. The basic rule is that a partnership is dissolved, and its business must be wound up, only upon the occurrence of one of the events listed in Section 801. All other dissociations result in a buyout of the partner's interest under Article 7 and a continuation of the partnership entity and business by the remaining partners. See Section 603(a).

With only three exceptions, the provisions of Section 801 are merely default rules and may by agreement be varied or eliminated as grounds for dissolution. The first exception is dissolution under Section 801(4) resulting from carrying on an illegal business. The other two exceptions cover the power of a court to dissolve a partnership under Section 801(5) on application of a partner and under Section 801(6) on application of a transferee.....

2. Under RUPA, "dissolution" is merely the commencement of the winding up process. The partnership continues for the limited purpose of winding up the business. In effect, that means the scope of the partnership business contracts to completing work in process and taking such other actions as may be necessary to wind up the business. Winding up the partnership business entails selling its assets, paying its debts, and distributing the net balance, if any, to the partners in cash according to their interests. The partnership entity continues, and the partners are associated in the winding up of the business until winding up is completed. When the winding up is completed, the partnership entity terminates.

3. Section 801 continues two basic rules from the UPA. First, it continues the rule that any member of an *at-will* partnership has the right to force a liquidation. Second, by negative implication, it continues the rule that the partners who wish to continue the business of a *term* partnership can not be forced to liquidate the business by a partner who withdraws prematurely in violation of the partnership agreement.....

4. Section 801(1) provides that a partnership at will is dissolved and its business must be wound up upon the partnership's having notice of a partner's express will to withdraw as a partner, unless a later effective date is specified by the partner.....

If, after dissolution, none of the partners wants the partnership wound up, Section 802(b) provides that, with the consent of all the partners, including the withdrawing partner, the remaining partners may continue the business. In that event, although there is a technical dissolution of the partnership and, at least in theory, a temporary contraction of the scope of the business, the partnership entity continues and the scope of its business is restored. See Section 802(b) and Comment 2.

5. Section 801(2) provides three ways in which a term partnership may be dissolved before the expiration of the term:

(i) Subsection (2)(i) provides for dissolution after a partner's dissociation by death or otherwise under Section 601(6) to (10) or wrongful dissociation under Section 602(b), if within 90 days after the dissociation at least half of the remaining partners express their will to dissolve the partnership. Thus if a term partnership had six partners and one of the partners dies or wrongfully dissociates before the end of the term, the partnership will, as a result of the dissociation, be dissolved only if three of the remaining five partners affirmatively vote in favor of dissolution within 90 days after the dissociation.* This

* Prior to August 1997, Section 801(2)(i) provided that upon the dissociation of a part-ner in a term partnership by death or other-wise under Section 601(6) through (10)

reactive dissolution of a term partnership protects the remaining partners where the dissociating partner is crucial to the successful continuation of the business. The corresponding UPA Section 38(2)(b) rule requires unanimous consent of the remaining partners to continue the business, thus giving each partner an absolute right to a reactive liquidation. Under [the 1994 revision of RUPA], if the partnership is continued by the majority, any dissenting partner who wants to withdraw may do so rightfully under the exception to Section 602(b)(2)(i), in which case his interest in the partnership will be bought out under Article 7. By itself, however, a partner's vote not to continue the business is not necessarily an expression of the partner's will to withdraw, and a dissenting partner may still elect to remain a partner and continue in the business.

The Section 601 dissociations giving rise to a reactive dissolution are: (6) a partner's bankruptcy or similar financial impairment; (7) a partner's death or incapacity; (8) the distribution by a trust-partner of its entire partnership interest; (9) the distribution by an estate-partner of its entire partnership interest; and (10) the termination of an entity-partner. Any dissociation during the term of the partnership that is wrongful under Section 602(b), including a partner's voluntary withdrawal, expulsion or bankruptcy, also gives rise to a reactive dissolution. Those statutory grounds may be varied by agreement or the reactive dissolution may be abolished entirely.

Under Section 601(6)(i), a partner is dissociated upon becoming a debtor in bankruptcy. The bankruptcy of a partner or of the partnership is not, however, an event of dissolution under Section 801. That is a change from UPA Section 31(5). A partner's bankruptcy does, however, cause dissolution of a term partnership under Section 801(2)(i), unless a majority in interest of the remaining partners thereafter agree to continue the partnership. Affording the other partners the option of buying out the bankrupt partner's interest avoids the necessity of winding up a term partnership every time a partner becomes a debtor in bankruptcy.

Similarly, under Section 801(2)(i), the death of any partner will result in the dissolution of a term partnership, only if at least half of the remaining partners express their will to wind up the partnership's business. If dissolution does occur, the deceased partner's transferable

or wrongful dissociation under 602(b) the partnership would dissolve unless "a majority in interest of the remaining partners (including partners who have rightfully dissociated pursuant to Section 602(b)(2)(i)) agree to continue the partnership." This language was thought to be necessary for a term partnership to lack continuity of life under the Internal Revenue Act tax classification regulations. These regulations were repealed effective January 1, 1997. The current language, approved at the 1997 annual meeting of the National Conference of Commissioners on Uniform State Laws, allows greater continuity in a term partnership than the prior version of this subsection and UPA Section 38(2)(b). (Footnote by NCCUSL).

interest in the partnership passes to his estate and must be bought out under Article 7. See Comment 8 to Section 601.

(ii) Section 801(2)(ii) provides that a term partnership may be dissolved and wound up at any time by the express will of all the partners. That is merely an expression of the general rule that the partnership agreement may override the statutory default rules and that the partnership agreement, like any contract, can be amended at any time by unanimous consent.

UPA Section 31(1)(c) provides that a term partnership may be wound up by the express will of all the partners whose transferable interests have not been assigned or charged for a partner's separate debts. That rule reflects the belief that the remaining partners may find transferees very intrusive. This provision has been deleted, however, because the liquidation is easily accomplished under Section 801(2)(ii) by first expelling the transferor partner under Section 601(4)(ii).

(iii) Section 801(2)(iii) is based on UPA Section 31(1)(a) and provides for winding up a term partnership upon the expiration of the term or the completion of the undertaking.

Subsection (2)(iii) must be read in conjunction with Section 406. Under Section 406(a), if the partners continue the business after the expiration of the term or the completion of the undertaking, the partnership will be treated as a partnership at will. Moreover, if the partners continue the business without any settlement or liquidation of the partnership, under Section 406(b) they are presumed to have agreed that the partnership will continue, despite the lack of a formal agreement. The partners may also agree to ratify all acts taken since the end of the partnership's term.

6. Section 801(3) provides for dissolution upon the occurrence of an event specified in the partnership agreement as resulting in the winding up of the partnership business. The partners may, however, agree to continue the business and to ratify all acts taken since dissolution.

7. Section 801(4) continues the basic rule in UPA Section 31(3) and provides for dissolution if it is unlawful to continue the business of the partnership, unless cured. The "all or substantially all" proviso is intended to avoid dissolution for insubstantial or innocent regulatory violations. If the illegality is cured within 90 days after notice to the partnership, it is effective retroactively for purposes of this section. The requirement that an uncured illegal business be wound up cannot be varied in the partnership agreement. See Section 103(b)(8).

8. Section 801(5) provides for judicial dissolution on application by a partner. It is based in part on UPA Section 32(1), and the language comes in part from RULPA Section 802. A court may order a partnership dissolved upon a judicial determination that: (i) the economic purpose of the partnership is likely to be unreasonably

frustrated; (ii) another partner has engaged in conduct relating to the partnership business which makes it not reasonably practicable to carry on the business in partnership with that partner; or (iii) it is not otherwise reasonably practicable to carry on the partnership business in conformity with the partnership agreement. The court's power to wind up the partnership under Section 801(5) cannot be varied in the partnership agreement. See Section 103(b)(8).

RUPA deletes UPA Section 32(1)(e) which provides for dissolution when the business can only be carried on at a loss. That provision might result in a dissolution contrary to the partners' expectations in a start-up or tax shelter situation, in which case "book" or "tax" losses do not signify business failure. Truly poor financial performance may justify dissolution under subsection (5)(i) as a frustration of the partnership's economic purpose.

RUPA also deletes UPA Section 32(1)(f) which authorizes a court to order dissolution of a partnership when "other circumstances render a dissolution equitable." That provision was regarded as too open-ended and, given RUPA's expanded remedies for partners, unnecessary. No significant change in result is intended, however, since the interpretation of UPA Section 32(1)(f) is comparable to the specific grounds expressed in subsection (5). *See, e.g., Karber v. Karber,* 145 Ariz. 293, 701 P.2d 1 (Ct.App.1985) (partnership dissolved on basis of suspicion and ill will, citing UPA §§ 32(1)(d) and (f)); *Fuller v. Brough,* 159 Colo. 147, 411 P.2d 18 (1966) (not equitable to dissolve partnership for trifling causes or temporary grievances that do not render it impracticable to carry on partnership business); *Lau v. Wong,* 1 Haw.App. 217, 616 P.2d 1031 (1980) (partnership dissolved where business operated solely for benefit of managing partner).

9. Section 801(6) provides for judicial dissolution on application by a transferee of a partner's transferable interest in the partnership, including the purchaser of a partner's interest upon foreclosure of a charging order. It is based on UPA Section 32(2) and authorizes dissolution upon a judicial determination that it is equitable to wind up the partnership business (i) after the expiration of the partnership term or completion of the undertaking or (ii) at any time, if the partnership were a partnership at will at the time of the transfer or when the charging order was issued. The requirement that the court determine that it is equitable to wind up the business is new. The rights of a transferee under this section cannot be varied in the partnership agreement. *See* Section 103(b)(8).

SECTION 802. PARTNERSHIP CONTINUES AFTER DISSOLUTION.

(a) Subject to subsection (b), a partnership continues after dissolution only for the purpose of winding up its business. The partnership is terminated when the winding up of its business is completed.

289

(b) At any time after the dissolution of a partnership and before the winding up of its business is completed, all of the partners, including any dissociating partner other than a wrongfully dissociating partner, may waive the right to have the partnership's business wound up and the partnership terminated. In that event:

(1) the partnership resumes carrying on its business as if dissolution had never occurred, and any liability incurred by the partnership or a partner after the dissolution and before the waiver is determined as if dissolution had never occurred; and

(2) the rights of a third party accruing under Section 804(1) or arising out of conduct in reliance on the dissolution before the third party knew or received a notification of the waiver may not be adversely affected.

Comment:

1. Section 802(a) is derived from UPA Section 30 and provides that a partnership continues after dissolution only for the purpose of winding up its business, after which it is terminated. RUPA continues the concept of "termination" to mark the completion of the winding up process. Since no filing or other formality is required, the date will often be determined only by hindsight. No legal rights turn on the partnership's termination or the date thereof. Even after termination, if a previously unknown liability is asserted, all of the partners are still liable.

2. Section 802(b) makes explicit the right of the remaining partners to continue the business after an event of dissolution if all of the partners, including the dissociating partner or partners, waive the right to have the business wound up and the partnership terminated. Only those "dissociating" partners whose dissociation was the immediate cause of the dissolution must waive the right to have the business wound up. The consent of wrongfully dissociating partners is not required.

3. Upon waiver of the right to have the business wound up, paragraph (1) of the subsection provides that the partnership entity may resume carrying on its business as if dissolution had never occurred, thereby restoring the scope of its business to normal. "Resumes" is intended to mean that acts appropriate to winding up, authorized when taken, are in effect ratified, and the partnership remains liable for those acts, as provided explicitly in paragraph (2)....

SECTION 803. RIGHT TO WIND UP PARTNERSHIP BUSINESS.

(a) After dissolution, a partner who has not wrongfully dissociated may participate in winding up the partnership's business, but on application of any partner, partner's legal representative, or transferee, the [designate the appropriate court], for good cause shown, may order judicial supervision of the winding up.

(b) The legal representative of the last surviving partner may wind up a partnership's business.

(c) A person winding up a partnership's business may preserve the partnership business or property as a going concern for a reasonable time, prosecute and defend actions and proceedings, whether civil, criminal, or administrative, settle and close the partnership's business, dispose of and transfer the partnership's property, discharge the partnership's liabilities, distribute the assets of the partnership pursuant to Section 807, settle disputes by mediation or arbitration, and perform other necessary acts.

SECTION 804. PARTNER'S POWER TO BIND PARTNERSHIP AFTER DISSOLUTION.

Subject to Section 805, a partnership is bound by a partner's act after dissolution that:

(1) is appropriate for winding up the partnership business; or

(2) would have bound the partnership under Section 301 before dissolution, if the other party to the transaction did not have notice of the dissolution.

SECTION 805. STATEMENT OF DISSOLUTION.

(a) After dissolution, a partner who has not wrongfully dissociated may file a statement of dissolution stating the name of the partnership and that the partnership has dissolved and is winding up its business.

(b) A statement of dissolution cancels a filed statement of partnership authority for the purposes of Section 303(d) and is a limitation on authority for the purposes of Section 303(e).

(c) For the purposes of Sections 301 and 804, a person not a partner is deemed to have notice of the dissolution and the limitation on the partners' authority as a result of the statement of dissolution 90 days after it is filed.

(d) After filing and, if appropriate, recording a statement of dissolution, a dissolved partnership may file and, if appropriate, record a statement of partnership authority which will operate with respect to a person not a partner as provided in Section 303(d) and (e) in any transaction, whether or not the transaction is appropriate for winding up the partnership business.

Comment:

1. Section 805 is new. Subsection (a) provides that, after an event of dissolution, any partner who has not wrongfully dissociated may file a statement of dissolution on behalf of the partnership. The filing and recording of a statement of dissolution is optional. The execution, filing, and recording of the statement is governed by Section 105. The legal consequences of filing a statement of dissolution are similar to those of a statement of dissociation under Section 704....

SECTION 806. PARTNER'S LIABILITY TO OTHER PARTNERS AFTER DISSOLUTION.

(a) Except as otherwise provided in subsection (b) and Section 306, after dissolution a partner is liable to the other partners for the partner's share of any partnership liability incurred under Section 804.

(b) A partner who, with knowledge of the dissolution, incurs a partnership liability under Section 804(2) by an act that is not appropriate for winding up the partnership business is liable to the partnership for any damage caused to the partnership arising from the liability.

Comment: ...

Subsection (a) provides that, except as provided in Section 306(a) and subsection (b), after dissolution each partner is liable to the other partners by way of contribution for his share of any partnership liability incurred under Section 804. That includes not only obligations that are appropriate for winding up the business, but also obligations that are inappropriate if within the partner's apparent authority. Consistent with other provisions of this Act, Section 806(a) makes clear that a partner does not have a contribution obligation with regard to limited liability partnership obligations for which the partner is not liable under Section 306. See Comments to Section 401(b)....

Section 806 is merely a default rule and may be varied in the partnership agreement. See Section 103(a).

SECTION 807. SETTLEMENT OF ACCOUNTS AND CONTRIBUTIONS AMONG PARTNERS.

(a) In winding up a partnership's business, the assets of the partnership, including the contributions of the partners required by this section, must be applied to discharge its obligations to creditors, including, to the extent permitted by law, partners who are creditors. Any surplus must be applied to pay in cash the net amount distributable to partners in accordance with their right to distributions under subsection (b).

(b) Each partner is entitled to a settlement of all partnership accounts upon winding up the partnership business. In settling accounts among the partners, the profits and losses that result from the liquidation of the partnership assets must be credited and charged to the partners' accounts. The partnership shall make a distribution to a partner in an amount equal to any excess of the credits over the charges in the partner's account. A partner shall contribute to the partnership an amount equal to any excess of the charges over the credits in the partner's account but excluding from the calculation charges attributable to an obligation for which the partner is not personally liable under Section 306.

(c) If a partner fails to contribute the full amount required under subsection (b), all of the other partners shall contribute, in the proportions in which those partners share partnership losses, the additional amount necessary to satisfy the partnership obligations for which they are personally liable under Section 306. A partner or partner's legal representative may recover from the other partners any contributions the partner makes to the extent the amount contributed exceeds that partner's share of the partnership obligations for which the partner is personally liable under Section 306.

(d) After the settlement of accounts, each partner shall contribute, in the proportion in which the partner shares partnership losses, the amount necessary to satisfy partnership obligations that were not known at the time of the settlement and for which the partner is personally liable under Section 306.

(e) The estate of a deceased partner is liable for the partner's obligation to contribute to the partnership.

(f) An assignee for the benefit of creditors of a partnership or a partner, or a person appointed by a court to represent creditors of a partnership or a partner, may enforce a partner's obligation to contribute to the partnership.

Comment:

1. Section 807 provides the default rules for the settlement of accounts and contributions among the partners in winding up the business. It is derived in part from UPA Sections 38(1) and 40.

2. Subsection (a) continues the rule in UPA Section 38(1) that, in winding up the business, the partnership assets must first be applied to discharge partnership liabilities to creditors. For this purpose, any required contribution by the partners is treated as an asset of the partnership. After the payment of all partnership liabilities, any surplus must be applied to pay in cash the net amount due the partners under subsection (b) by way of a liquidating distribution.

RUPA continues the "in-cash" rule of UPA Section 38(1) and is consistent with Section 402, which provides that a partner has no right to receive, and may not be required to accept, a distribution in kind, unless otherwise agreed. The in-cash rule avoids the valuation problems that afflict unwanted in-kind distributions.

The partnership must apply its assets to discharge the obligations of partners who are creditors on a parity with other creditors. See Section 404(f).... In effect, that abolishes the priority rules in UPA Section 40(b) and (c) which subordinate the payment of inside debt to outside debt. Both RULPA and the RMBCA do likewise. See RULPA § 804; RMBCA §§ 6.40(f), 14.05(a). Ultimately, however, a partner whose "debt" has been repaid by the partnership is personally liable, as a partner, for any outside debt remaining unsatisfied, unlike a limited partner or corporate shareholder. Accordingly, the obligation to contribute sufficient funds to satisfy the claims of outside creditors may result in the equitable subordination of inside debt when partnership assets are insufficient to satisfy all obligations to non-partners.

RUPA in effect abolishes the "dual priority" or "jingle" rule of UPA Section 40(h) and (i). Those sections gave partnership creditors priority as to partnership property and separate creditors priority as to separate property. The jingle rule has already been preempted by the Bankruptcy Code, at least as to Chapter 7 partnership liquidation proceedings. Under Section 723(c) of the Bankruptcy Code, and under RUPA, partnership creditors share pro rata with the partners' individual creditors in the assets of the partners' estates.

3. Subsection (b) provides that each partner is entitled to a settlement of all partnership accounts upon winding up. It also establishes the default rules for closing out the partners' accounts. First, the profits and losses resulting from the liquidation of the partnership assets must be credited or charged to the partners' accounts, according to their respective shares of profits and losses. Then, the partnership must make a final liquidating distribution to those partners with a positive account balance. That distribution should be in the amount of the excess of credits over the charges in the account. Any partner with a negative account balance must contribute to the partnership an amount equal to the excess of charges over the credits in the account provided the excess relates to an obligation for which the partner is personally liable under Section 306. The partners may, however, agree that a negative account does not reflect a debt to the partnership and need not be repaid in settling the partners' accounts.

Section 807(b) makes clear that a partner's contribution obligation to a partnership in dissolution only considers the partner's share of obligations for which the partner was personally liable under Section 306 ("unshielded obligations"). See Comments to Section 401(b) (partner contribution obligation to an operating partnership). Properly determined under this Section, the total required partner contributions will be sufficient to satisfy the partnership's total unshielded obligations. In special circumstances where a partnership has both shielded and unshielded obligations and the [partners] required contributions are used to first pay shielded partnership obligations, the partners may be required to make further contributions to satisfy the partnership unpaid unshielded obligations. The proper resolution of this matter is left to debtor-creditor law as well as the law governing the fiduciary obligations of the partners. See Section 104(a).

RUPA eliminates the distinction in UPA Section 40(b) between the liability owing to a partner in respect of capital and the liability owing in respect of profits. Section 807(b) speaks simply of the right of a partner to a liquidating distribution. That implements the logic of RUPA Sections 401(a) and 502 under which contributions to capital and shares in profits and losses combine to determine the right to distributions. The partners may, however, agree to share "operating" losses differently from "capital" losses, thereby continuing the UPA distinction.

4. Subsection (c) continues the UPA Section 40(d) rule that solvent partners share proportionately in the shortfall caused by insolvent partners who fail to contribute their proportionate share. The partnership may enforce a partner's obligation to contribute. See Section 405(a). A partner is entitled to recover from the other partners any contributions in excess of that partner's share of the partnership's liabilities. See Section 405(b)(iii).

5. Subsection (d) provides that, after settling the partners' accounts, each partner must contribute, in the proportion in which he shares losses, the amount necessary to satisfy partnership obligations that were not known at the time of the settlement. That continues the basic rule of UPA Section 40(d) and underscores that the obligation to contribute exists independently of the partnership's books of account. It specifically covers the situation of a partnership liability that was unknown when the partnership books were closed. . . .

ARTICLE 9

CONVERSIONS AND MERGERS

SECTION 901. DEFINITIONS.

In this [article]:

(1) "General partner" means a partner in a partnership and a general partner in a limited partnership.

(2) "Limited partner" means a limited partner in a limited partnership.

(3) "Limited partnership" means a limited partnership created under the [State Limited Partnership Act], predecessor law, or comparable law of another jurisdiction.

(4) "Partner" includes both a general partner and a limited partner.

Comment: . . .

2. As Section 908 makes clear, the requirements of Article 9 are not mandatory, and a partnership may convert or merge in any other manner provided by law. Article 9 is merely a "safe harbor." If the requirements of the article are followed, the conversion or merger is legally valid. Since most States have no other established procedure

for the conversion or merger of partnerships, it is likely that the Article 9 procedures will be used in virtually all cases....

SECTION 902. CONVERSION OF PARTNERSHIP TO LIMITED PARTNERSHIP.

(a) A partnership may be converted to a limited partnership pursuant to this section.

(b) The terms and conditions of a conversion of a partnership to a limited partnership must be approved by all of the partners or by a number or percentage specified for conversion in the partnership agreement.

(c) After the conversion is approved by the partners, the partnership shall file a certificate of limited partnership in the jurisdiction in which the limited partnership is to be formed.   The certificate must include:

(1) a statement that the partnership was converted to a limited partnership from a partnership;

(2) its former name; and

(3) a statement of the number of votes cast by the partners for and against the conversion and, if the vote is less than unanimous, the number or percentage required to approve the conversion under the partnership agreement.

(d) The conversion takes effect when the certificate of limited partnership is filed or at any later date specified in the certificate.

(e) A general partner who becomes a limited partner as a result of the conversion remains liable as a general partner for an obligation incurred by the partnership before the conversion takes effect.   If the other party to a transaction with the limited partnership reasonably believes when entering the transaction that the limited partner is a general partner, the limited partner is liable for an obligation incurred by the limited partnership within 90 days after the conversion takes effect.   The limited partner's liability for all other obligations of the limited partnership incurred after the conversion takes effect is that of a limited partner as provided in the [State Limited Partnership Act].

SECTION 903. CONVERSION OF LIMITED PARTNERSHIP TO PARTNERSHIP.

(a) A limited partnership may be converted to a partnership pursuant to this section.

(b) Notwithstanding a provision to the contrary in a limited partnership agreement, the terms and conditions of a conversion of a limited partnership to a partnership must be approved by all of the partners.

(c) After the conversion is approved by the partners, the limited partnership shall cancel its certificate of limited partnership.

(d) The conversion takes effect when the certificate of limited partnership is canceled.

(e) A limited partner who becomes a general partner as a result of the conversion remains liable only as a limited partner for an obligation incurred by the limited partnership before the conversion takes effect. Except as otherwise provided in Section 306, the partner is liable as a general partner for an obligation of the partnership incurred after the conversion takes effect.

SECTION 904. EFFECT OF CONVERSION; ENTITY UN-CHANGED.

(a) A partnership or limited partnership that has been converted pursuant to this [article] is for all purposes the same entity that existed before the conversion.

(b) When a conversion takes effect:

(1) all property owned by the converting partnership or limited partnership remains vested in the converted entity;

(2) all obligations of the converting partnership or limited partnership continue as obligations of the converted entity; and

(3) an action or proceeding pending against the converting partnership or limited partnership may be continued as if the conversion had not occurred.

SECTION 905. MERGER OF PARTNERSHIPS.

(a) Pursuant to a plan of merger approved as provided in subsection (c), a partnership may be merged with one or more partnerships or limited partnerships.

(b) The plan of merger must set forth:

(1) the name of each partnership or limited partnership that is a party to the merger;

(2) the name of the surviving entity into which the other partnerships or limited partnerships will merge;

(3) whether the surviving entity is a partnership or a limited partnership and the status of each partner;

(4) the terms and conditions of the merger;

(5) the manner and basis of converting the interests of each party to the merger into interests or obligations of the surviving entity, or into money or other property in whole or part; and

(6) the street address of the surviving entity's chief executive office.

(c) The plan of merger must be approved:

(1) in the case of a partnership that is a party to the merger, by all of the partners, or a number or percentage specified for merger in the partnership agreement; and

297

(2) in the case of a limited partnership that is a party to the merger, by the vote required for approval of a merger by the law of the State or foreign jurisdiction in which the limited partnership is organized and, in the absence of such a specifically applicable law, by all of the partners, notwithstanding a provision to the contrary in the partnership agreement.

(d) After a plan of merger is approved and before the merger takes effect, the plan may be amended or abandoned as provided in the plan.

(e) The merger takes effect on the later of:

(1) the approval of the plan of merger by all parties to the merger, as provided in subsection (c);

(2) the filing of all documents required by law to be filed as a condition to the effectiveness of the merger; or

(3) any effective date specified in the plan of merger.

Comment:

Section 905 provides a "safe harbor" for the merger of a general partnership and one or more general or limited partnerships. The surviving entity may be either a general or a limited partnership. . . .

SECTION 906.　EFFECT OF MERGER.

(a) When a merger takes effect:

(1) the separate existence of every partnership or limited partnership that is a party to the merger, other than the surviving entity, ceases;

(2) all property owned by each of the merged partnerships or limited partnerships vests in the surviving entity;

(3) all obligations of every partnership or limited partnership that is a party to the merger become the obligations of the surviving entity; and

(4) an action or proceeding pending against a partnership or limited partnership that is a party to the merger may be continued as if the merger had not occurred, or the surviving entity may be substituted as a party to the action or proceeding.

(b) The [Secretary of State] of this State is the agent for service of process in an action or proceeding against a surviving foreign partnership or limited partnership to enforce an obligation of a domestic partnership or limited partnership that is a party to a merger. The surviving entity shall promptly notify the [Secretary of State] of the mailing address of its chief executive office and of any change of address. Upon receipt of process, the [Secretary of State] shall mail a copy of the process to the surviving foreign partnership or limited partnership.

(c) A partner of the surviving partnership or limited partnership is liable for:

(1) all obligations of a party to the merger for which the partner was personally liable before the merger;

(2) all other obligations of the surviving entity incurred before the merger by a party to the merger, but those obligations may be satisfied only out of property of the entity; and

(3) except as otherwise provided in Section 306, all obligations of the surviving entity incurred after the merger takes effect, but those obligations may be satisfied only out of property of the entity if the partner is a limited partner.

(d) If the obligations incurred before the merger by a party to the merger are not satisfied out of the property of the surviving partnership or limited partnership, the general partners of that party immediately before the effective date of the merger shall contribute the amount necessary to satisfy that party's obligations to the surviving entity, in the manner provided in Section 807 or in the [Limited Partnership Act] of the jurisdiction in which the party was formed, as the case may be, as if the merged party were dissolved.

(e) A partner of a party to a merger who does not become a partner of the surviving partnership or limited partnership is dissociated from the entity, of which that partner was a partner, as of the date the merger takes effect. The surviving entity shall cause the partner's interest in the entity to be purchased under Section 701 or another statute specifically applicable to that partner's interest with respect to a merger. The surviving entity is bound under Section 702 by an act of a general partner dissociated under this subsection, and the partner is liable under Section 703 for transactions entered into by the surviving entity after the merger takes effect.

SECTION 907. STATEMENT OF MERGER.

(a) After a merger, the surviving partnership or limited partnership may file a statement that one or more partnerships or limited partnerships have merged into the surviving entity.

(b) A statement of merger must contain:

(1) the name of each partnership or limited partnership that is a party to the merger;

(2) the name of the surviving entity into which the other partnerships or limited partnership were merged;

(3) the street address of the surviving entity's chief executive office and of an office in this State, if any; and

(4) whether the surviving entity is a partnership or a limited partnership.

(c) Except as otherwise provided in subsection (d), for the purposes of Section 302, property of the surviving partnership or limited partnership which before the merger was held in the name of another party to the merger is property held in the name of the surviving entity upon filing a statement of merger.

(d) For the purposes of Section 302, real property of the surviving partnership or limited partnership which before the merger was held in the name of another party to the merger is property held in the name of the surviving entity upon recording a certified copy of the statement of merger in the office for recording transfers of that real property.

(e) A filed and, if appropriate, recorded statement of merger, executed and declared to be accurate pursuant to Section 105(c), stating the name of a partnership or limited partnership that is a party to the merger in whose name property was held before the merger and the name of the surviving entity, but not containing all of the other information required by subsection (b), operates with respect to the partnerships or limited partnerships named to the extent provided in subsections (c) and (d).

SECTION 908. NONEXCLUSIVE.

This [article] is not exclusive. Partnerships or limited partnerships may be converted or merged in any other manner provided by law.

[ARTICLE] 10

LIMITED LIABILITY PARTNERSHIP

Section 1001.   Statement of Qualification.
Section 1002.   Name.
Section 1003.   Annual Report.

SECTION 1001. STATEMENT OF QUALIFICATION.

(a) A partnership may become a limited liability partnership pursuant to this section.

(b) The terms and conditions on which a partnership becomes a limited liability partnership must be approved by the vote necessary to amend the partnership agreement except, in the case of a partnership agreement that expressly considers contribution obligations, the vote necessary to amend those provisions.

(c) After the approval required by subsection (b), a partnership may become a limited liability partnership by filing a statement of qualification. The statement must contain:

(1) the name of the partnership;

(2) the street address of the partnership's chief executive office and, if different, the street address of an office in this State, if any;

(3) if there is no office in this State, the name and street address of the partnership's agent for service of process who must be an individual resident of this State or any other person authorized to do business in this State;

(4) a statement that the partnership elects to be a limited liability partnership; and

(5) a deferred effective date, if any.

(d) The status of a partnership as a limited liability partnership is effective on the later of the filing of the statement or a date specified in the statement. The status remains effective, regardless of changes in the partnership, until it is canceled pursuant to Section 105(d) or revoked pursuant to Section 1003.

(e) The status of a partnership as a limited liability partnership and the liability of its partners is not affected by errors or later changes in the information required to be contained in the statement of qualification under subsection (c).

(f) The filing of a statement of qualification establishes that a partnership has satisfied all conditions precedent to the qualification of the partnership as a limited liability partnership.

(g) An amendment or cancellation of a statement of qualification is effective when it is filed or on a deferred effective date specified in the amendment or cancellation.

Comment:

Any partnership may become a limited liability partnership by filing a statement of qualification. See Comments to Sections 101(6) and 202(b) regarding a limited partnership filing a statement of qualification to become a limited liability limited partnership. Section 1001 sets forth the required contents of a statement of qualification. The section also sets forth requirements for the approval of a statement of qualification, establishes the effective date of the filing (and any amendments) which remains effective until canceled or revoked, and provides that the liability of the partners of a limited liability partnership is not affected by errors or later changes in the statement information.

Subsection (b) provides that the terms and conditions on which a partnership becomes a limited liability partnership must ... generally be approved by the vote necessary to amend the partnership agreement. This means that the act of becoming a limited liability partnership is equivalent to an amendment of the partnership agreement. Where the partnership agreement is silent as to how it may be amended, the subsection (b) vote requires the approval of every partner. Since the limited liability partnership rules are not intended to increase the vote necessary to amend the partnership agreement, where the partnership agreement specifically sets forth an amendment process, that process may be used. Where a partnership agreement sets forth several amendment procedures depending upon the nature of the amendment, the required vote will be that necessary to amend the contribution obligations of the partners. The specific "contribution" vote is preferred because the filing of the statement directly affects partner contribution obligations. Therefore, the language "considers contribution" should be broadly interpreted to include any amendment vote that indirectly affects any partner's contribution obligation such as a partner's obligation to "indemnify" other partners.

301

The unanimous vote default rule reflects the significance of a partnership becoming a limited liability partnership. In general, upon such a filing each partner is released from the personal contribution obligation imposed under this Act in exchange for relinquishing the right to enforce the contribution obligations of other partners under this Act. See Comments to Sections 306(c) and 401(b). The wisdom of this bargain will depend on many factors including the relative risks of the partners' duties and the assets of the partnership.

Subsection (c) sets forth the information required in a statement of qualification. The [information] must include the name of the partnership which must comply with Section 1002 to identify the partnership as a limited liability partnership. The statement must also include the address of the partnership's chief executive office and, if different, the street address of any other office in this State. A statement must include the name and street address of an agent for service of process only if it does not have any office in this State.

As with other statements, a statement of qualification must be filed in the office of the Secretary of State. See Sections 101(13) and 105(a). Accordingly, a statement of qualification is executed, filed, and otherwise regarded as a statement under this Act. For example, a copy of a filed statement must be sent to every nonfiling partner unless otherwise provided in the partnership agreement. See Sections 105(e) and 103(b)(1). A statement of qualification must be executed by at least two partners under penalties of perjury that the contents of the statement are accurate. See Section 105(c). A person who files the statement must promptly send a copy of the statement to every nonfiling partner but failure to send the copy does not limit the effectiveness of the filed statement to a nonpartner. Section 105(e). The filing must be accompanied by the fee required by the Secretary of State. Section 105(f).

Subsection (d) makes clear that once a statement is filed and effective, the status of the partnership as a limited liability partnership remains effective until the partnership status is either canceled or revoked "regardless of changes in the partnership." Accordingly, a partnership that dissolves but whose business is continued under a business continuation agreement retains its status as a limited liability partnership without the need to refile a new statement. Also, limited liability partnership status remains even though a partnership may be dissolved, wound up, and terminated. Even after the termination of the partnership, the former partners of a terminated partnership would not be personally liable for partnership obligations incurred while the partnership was a limited liability partnership.

Subsection (d) also makes clear that limited liability partnership status remains effective until actual cancellation under Section 1003 or revocation under Section 105(d). Ordinarily the terms and conditions of becoming a limited liability partnership must be approved by the vote necessary to amend the partnership agreement. See Sections

1001(b), 306(c), and 401(j). Since the statement of cancellation may be filed by a person authorized to file the original statement of qualification, the same vote necessary to approve the filing of the statement of qualification must be obtained to file the statement of cancellation. See Section 105(d).

Subsection (f) provides that once a statement of qualification is executed and filed under subsection (c) and Section 105, the partnership assumes the status of a limited liability partnership. This status is intended to be conclusive with regard to third parties dealing with the partnership. It is not intended to affect the rights of partners. For example, a properly executed and filed statement of qualification conclusively establishes the limited liability shield described in Section 306(c). If the partners executing and filing the statement exceed their authority, the internal abuse of authority has no effect on the liability shield with regard to third parties. Partners may challenge the abuse of authority for purposes of establishing the liability of the culpable partners but may not effect the liability shield as to third parties. Likewise, third parties may not challenge the existence of the liability shield because the decision to file the statement lacked the proper vote. As a result, the filing of the statement creates the liability shield even when the required subsection (b) vote is not obtained.

SECTION 1002. NAME.

The name of a limited liability partnership must end with "Registered Limited Liability Partnership", "Limited Liability Partnership", "R.L.L.P.", "L.L.P.", "RLLP," or "LLP".

Comment:

The name provisions are intended to alert persons dealing with a limited liability partnership of the presence of the liability shield. Because many jurisdictions have adopted the naming concept of a "registered" limited liability partnership, this aspect has been retained. These name requirements also distinguish limited partnerships and general partnerships that become limited liability partnerships because the new name must be at the end of and in addition to the general or limited partnership's regular name. See Comments to Section 101(6). Since the name identification rules of this section do not alter the regular name of the partnership, they do not disturb historic notions of apparent authority of partners in both general and limited partnerships.

SECTION 1003. ANNUAL REPORT.

(a) A limited liability partnership, and a foreign limited liability partnership authorized to transact business in this State, shall file an annual report in the office of the [Secretary of State] which contains:

303

(1) the name of the limited liability partnership and the State or other jurisdiction under whose laws the foreign limited liability partnership is formed;

(2) the current street address of the partnership's chief executive office and, if different, the current street address of an office in this State, if any; and

(3) if there is no current office in this State, the name and street address of the partnership's current agent for service of process who must be an individual resident of this State or any other person authorized to do business in this State.

(b) An annual report must be filed between [January 1 and April 1] of each year following the calendar year in which a partnership files a statement of qualification or a foreign partnership becomes authorized to transact business in this State.

(c) The [Secretary of State] may administratively revoke the statement of qualification of a partnership that fails to file an annual report when due or to pay the required filing fee. The [Secretary of State] shall provide the partnership at least 60 days' written notice of intent to revoke the statement. The notice must be mailed to the partnership at its chief executive office set forth in the last filed statement of qualification or annual report. The notice must specify the annual report that has not been filed, the fee that has not been paid, and the effective date of the revocation. The revocation is not effective if the annual report is filed and the fee is paid before the effective date of the revocation.

(d) A revocation under subsection (c) only affects a partnership's status as a limited liability partnership and is not an event of dissolution of the partnership.

(e) A partnership whose statement of qualification has been administratively revoked may apply to the [Secretary of State] for reinstatement within two years after the effective date of the revocation. The application must state:

(1) the name of the partnership and the effective date of the revocation; and

(2) that the ground for revocation either did not exist or has been corrected.

(f) A reinstatement under subsection (e) relates back to and takes effect as of the effective date of the revocation, and the partnership's status as a limited liability partnership continues as if the revocation had never occurred.

Comment:

Section 1003 sets forth the requirements of an annual report that must be filed by all limited liability partnerships and any foreign limited liability partnership authorized to transact business in this State. See Sections 101(5) (definition of a limited liability partnership) and 101(4) (definition of a foreign limited liability partnership). The failure of a limited liability partnership to file an annual report is a basis for the Secretary of State to administratively revoke its statement of qualification. See Section 1003(c). A foreign limited liability partnership that fails to file an annual report may not maintain an action or proceeding in this State. See Section 1103(a).

Subsection (a) generally requires that an annual report contain the same information required in a statement of qualification. Compare Sections 1001(a) and 1003(a). The differences are that the annual report requires disclosure of the state of formation of a foreign limited liability partnership but deletes the delayed effective date and limited liability partnership election statement provisions of a statement of qualification. As such, the annual report serves to update the information required in a statement of qualification. Under subsection (b), the annual report must be filed between January 1 and April 1 of each calendar year following the year in which a statement of qualification was filed or a foreign limited liability partnership becomes authorized to transact business. This timing requirement means that a limited liability partnership must make an annual filing and may not prefile multiple annual reports in a single year.

Subsection (c) sets forth the procedure for the Secretary of State to administratively revoke a partnership's statement of qualification for the failure to file an annual report when due or pay the required filing fee. The Secretary of State must provide a partnership at least 60 days' written notice of the intent to revoke the statement. The notice must be mailed to the partnership at the address of its chief executive office set forth in the last filed statement or annual report and must state the grounds for revocation as well as the effective date of revocation. The revocation is not effective if the stated problem is cured before the stated effective date.

Under subsection (d), a revocation only terminates the partnership's status as a limited liability partnership but is not an event of dissolution of the partnership itself. Where revocation occurs, a partnership may apply for reinstatement under subsection (e) within two years after the effective date of the revocation. The application must state that the grounds for revocation either did not exist or have been corrected. The Secretary of State may grant the application on the basis of the statements alone or require proof of correction. Under subsection (f), when the application is granted, the reinstatement relates back to and takes effect as of the effective date of the revocation. The relation back doctrine prevents gaps in a reinstated partnership's liability shield. See Comments to Section 306(c).

[ARTICLE] 11

FOREIGN LIMITED LIABILITY PARTNERSHIP

305

SECTION 1101.   LAW GOVERNING FOREIGN LIMITED LIABILITY PARTNERSHIP.

(a) The laws under which a foreign limited liability partnership is formed govern relations among the partners and between the partners and the partnership and the liability of partners for obligations of the partnership.

(b) A foreign limited liability partnership may not be denied a statement of foreign qualification by reason of any difference between the laws under which the partnership was formed and the laws of this State.

(c) A statement of foreign qualification does not authorize a foreign limited liability partnership to engage in any business or exercise any power that a partnership may not engage in or exercise in this State as a limited liability partnership.

Comment:

Section 1101 provides that the laws where a foreign limited liability partnership is formed rather than the laws of this State govern both the internal relations of the partnership and liability of its partners for the obligations of the partnership. See Section 101(4) (definition of a foreign limited liability partnership). Section 106(b) provides that the laws of this State govern the internal relations of a domestic limited liability and the liability of its partners for the obligations of the partnership. See Sections 101(5) (definition of a domestic limited liability partnership). A partnership may therefore choose the laws of a particular jurisdiction by filing a statement of qualification in that jurisdiction. But there are limitations on this choice.

Subsections (b) and (c) together make clear that although a foreign limited liability partnership may not be denied a statement of foreign qualification simply because of a difference between the laws of its foreign jurisdiction and the laws of this State, it may not engage in any business or exercise any power in this State that a domestic limited liability partnership may not engage in or exercise. Under subsection (c), a foreign limited liability partnership that engages in a business or exercises a power in this State that a domestic may not engage in or exercise, does so only as an ordinary partnership without the benefit of the limited liability partnership liability shield set forth in Section 306(c). In this sense, a foreign limited liability partnership is treated the same as a domestic limited liability partnership. Also, the Attorney General may maintain an action to restrain a foreign limited liability partnership from transacting an unauthorized business in this State. See Section 1105.

SECTION 1102. STATEMENT OF FOREIGN QUALIFICATION.

(a) Before transacting business in this State, a foreign limited liability partnership must file a statement of foreign qualification. The statement must contain:

(1) the name of the foreign limited liability partnership which satisfies the requirements of the State or other jurisdiction under whose laws it is formed and ends with "Registered Limited Liability Partnership", "Limited Liability Partnership", "R.L.L.P.", "L.L.P.", "RLLP," or "LLP";

(2) the street address of the partnership's chief executive office and, if different, the street address of an office in this State, if any;

(3) if there is no office in this State, the name and street address of the partnership's agent for service of process who must be an individual resident of this State or any other person authorized to do business in this State; and

(4) a deferred effective date, if any.

(b) The status of a partnership as a foreign limited liability partnership is effective on the later of the filing of the statement of foreign qualification or a date specified in the statement. The status remains effective, regardless of changes in the partnership, until it is canceled pursuant to Section 105(d) or revoked pursuant to Section 1003.

(c) An amendment or cancellation of a statement of foreign qualification is effective when it is filed or on a deferred effective date specified in the amendment or cancellation.

Comment:

Section 1102 provides that a foreign limited liability partnership must file a statement of foreign qualification before transacting business in this State. The section also sets forth the information required in the statement. As with other statements, a statement of foreign qualification must be filed in the office of the Secretary of State. See Sections 101(13), 105(a), and 1001(c). Accordingly, a statement of foreign qualification is executed, filed, and otherwise regarded as a statement under this Act. See Section 101(13) (definition of a statement includes a statement of foreign qualification).

Subsection (a) generally requires the same information in a statement of foreign qualification as is required in a statement of qualification. Compare Sections 1001(c). The statement of foreign qualification must include a name that complies with the requirements for domestic limited liability partnership under Section 1002 and must include the address of the partnership's chief executive office and, if different, the street address of any other office in this State. If a foreign limited liability partnership does not have any office in this State, the statement of foreign qualification must include the name and street address of an agent for service of process.   **307**

As with a statement of qualification, a statement of foreign qualification (and amendments) is effective when filed or at a later specified filing date. Compare Sections 1102(b) and (c) with Sections 1001(e) and (h). Likewise, a statement of foreign qualification remains effective until canceled by the partnership or revoked by the Secretary of State, regardless of changes in the partnership. See Sections 105(d) (statement cancellation) and Section 1003 (revocation for failure to file annual report or pay annual filing fee) and compare Sections 1102(b) and 1001(e). Statement of qualification provisions regarding the relationship of the status of a foreign partnership relative to its initial filing of a statement are governed by foreign law and are therefore omitted from this section. See Sections 1001(f) (effect of errors and omissions) and (g) (filing establishes all conditions precedent to qualification).

SECTION 1103. EFFECT OF FAILURE TO QUALIFY.

(a) A foreign limited liability partnership transacting business in this State may not maintain an action or proceeding in this State unless it has in effect a statement of foreign qualification.

(b) The failure of a foreign limited liability partnership to have in effect a statement of foreign qualification does not impair the validity of a contract or act of the foreign limited liability partnership or preclude it from defending an action or proceeding in this State.

(c) Limitations on personal liability of partners are not waived solely by transacting business in this State without a statement of foreign qualification.

(d) If a foreign limited liability partnership transacts business in this State without a statement of foreign qualification, the [Secretary of State] is its agent for service of process with respect to [claims for relief] arising out of the transaction of business in this State.

Comment:

Section 1103 makes clear that the only consequence of a failure to file a statement of foreign qualification is that the foreign limited liability partnership will not be able to maintain an action or proceeding in this State. The partnership's contracts remain valid, it may defend an action or proceeding, personal liability of the partners is not waived, and the Secretary of State is the agent for service of process with respect to claims arising out of transacting business in this State. Sections 1103(b)–(d). Once a statement of foreign qualification is filed, the Secretary of State may revoke the statement for failure to file an annual report but the partnership has the right to cure the failure for two years. See Section 1003(c) and (e). Since the failure to file a statement of foreign qualification has no impact on the liability shield of the partners, a revocation of a statement of foreign qualification also has no impact on the liability shield created under foreign laws. Compare Sections 1103(c) and 1003(f) (revocation of the statement of qualification of a domestic limited liability partnership removes partner liability shield unless filing problems cured within two years).

SECTION 1104. ACTIVITIES NOT CONSTITUTING TRANSACTING BUSINESS.

(a) Activities of a foreign limited liability partnership which do not constitute transacting business within the meaning of this [article] include:

(1) maintaining, defending, or settling an action or proceeding;

(2) holding meetings of its partners or carrying on any other activity concerning its internal affairs;

(3) maintaining bank accounts;

(4) maintaining offices or agencies for the transfer, exchange, and registration of the partnership's own securities or maintaining trustees or depositories with respect to those securities;

(5) selling through independent contractors;

(6) soliciting or obtaining orders, whether by mail or through employees or agents or otherwise, if the orders require acceptance outside this State before they become contracts;

(7) creating or acquiring indebtedness, mortgages, or security interests in real or personal property;

(8) securing or collecting debts or foreclosing mortgages or other security interests in property securing the debts, and holding, protecting, and maintaining property so acquired;

(9) conducting an isolated transaction that is completed within 30 days and is not one in the course of similar transactions of like nature; and

(10) transacting business in interstate commerce.

(b) For purposes of this [article], the ownership in this State of income-producing real property or tangible personal property, other than property excluded under subsection (a), constitutes transacting business in this State.

(c) This section does not apply in determining the contacts or activities that may subject a foreign limited liability partnership to service of process, taxation, or regulation under any other law of this State.

Comment:

Because the Attorney General may restrain a foreign limited liability partnership from transacting an unauthorized business in this State and a foreign partnership may not maintain an action or proceeding in this State, the concept of "transacting business" in this State is important. To provide more certainty, subsection (a) sets forth ten separate categories of activities that do not constitute transacting business. Subsection (c) makes clear that the section only considers the definition of "transacting business" and as no impact on whether a

309

foreign limited liability partnership's activities in this State subject it to service of process, taxation, or regulation under any other law of this State.

SECTION 1105.   ACTION BY [ATTORNEY GENERAL].

The [Attorney General] may maintain an action to restrain a foreign limited liability partnership from transacting business in this State in violation of this [article].

Comment:

Section 1105 makes clear that the Attorney General may restrain a foreign limited liability from transacting an unauthorized business in this State. As a threshold matter, a foreign limited liability partnership must be "transacting business" in this State within the meaning of Section 1104. Secondly, the business transacted in this State must be that which could not be engaged in by a domestic limited liability partnership. See Section 1101(c). The fact that a foreign limited liability partnership has a statement of foreign qualification does not permit it to engage in any unauthorized business in this State or impair the power of the Attorney General to restrain the foreign partnership from engaging in the unauthorized business. See Section 1101(c).

ARTICLE 12

MISCELLANEOUS PROVISIONS

SECTION 1201. UNIFORMITY OF APPLICATION AND CON- STRUCTION.

This [Act] shall be applied and construed to effectuate its general purpose to make uniform the law with respect to the subject of this [Act] among States enacting it.

SECTION 1202.   SHORT TITLE.

This [Act] may be cited as the Uniform Partnership Act (1994).

SECTION 1203.   SEVERABILITY CLAUSE.

If any provision of this [Act] or its application to any person or circumstance is held invalid, the invalidity does not affect other provisions or applications of this [Act] which can be given effect without the invalid provision or application, and to this end the provisions of this [Act] are severable.

SECTION 1204. EFFECTIVE DATE.

This [Act] takes effect _____.

SECTION 1205. REPEALS.

Effective January 1, 199__, the following acts and parts of acts are repealed: [the State Partnership Act as amended and in effect immediately before the effective date of this Act].

SECTION 1206. APPLICABILITY.

(a) Before January 1, 199__, this [Act] governs only a partnership formed:

(1) after the effective date of this [Act], unless that partnership is continuing the business of a dissolved partnership under [Section 41 of the prior Uniform Partnership Act]; and

(2) before the effective date of this [Act], that elects, as provided by subsection (c), to be governed by this [Act].

(b) After January 1, 199__, this [Act] governs all partnerships.

(c) Before January 1, 199__, a partnership voluntarily may elect, in the manner provided in its partnership agreement or by law for amending the partnership agreement, to be governed by this [Act]. The provisions of this [Act] relating to the liability of the partnership's partners to third parties apply to limit those partners' liability to a third party who had done business with the partnership within one year preceding the partnership's election to be governed by this [Act], only if the third party knows or has received a notification of the partnership's election to be governed by this [Act].

SECTION 1207. SAVINGS CLAUSE.

This [Act] does not affect an action or proceeding commenced or right accrued before this [Act] takes effect.

FORM OF PARTNERSHIP AGREEMENT

by
JACK S. JOHAL, ERIK S. SCHIMMELBUSCH & HILTON S. WILLIAMS

The following Annotated Form of Partnership Agreement was drafted by Jack S. Johal, Erik S. Schimmelbusch, and Hilton S. Williams. The form was originally published in the State Bar of California's Business Law News, Summer 1997, at p. 15.

The Form was prepared with California partnerships in mind, but since the California statute is based on RUPA (although it differs from RUPA in certain respects), the Form would by and large be an appropriate starting-point for drafting a partnership agreement under most or all versions of RUPA. As originally published, the form made cross-references to the California statute. For ease of use in this Supplement, the editor of the Supplement has inserted, in place of the California cross-references, cross-references to RUPA.

General Partnership Agreement for

_____,

a California General Partnership

This Agreement of General Partnership (**"Agreement"**), dated for reference purposes only _____, 19__ (**"Effective Date"**), is entered into by and between the parties listed on the signature pages of this Agreement (collectively referred to as **"Partners"** and individually as **"Partner"**).

AGREEMENT

1. FORMATION AND ORGANIZATION.

1.1 <u>Formation</u>. The Partners hereby form a general partnership (**"Partnership"**) pursuant to the laws of the State of California, which Partnership shall be governed by and in accordance with the Uniform Partnership Act of 1994, (**"Partnership Act"**).

1.2 <u>Name</u>. The Partnership's name shall be "_____" and the Partnership's business shall continue to be conducted under said name.

1.3 <u>Principal Place of Business</u>. The Partnership's principal place of business shall be located at (i) _____, or (ii) such other place or places in California as a majority interest of the Partners may select from time to time upon written notice thereof to the other Partners.

1.4 <u>Business</u>. The Partnership's business shall be to _____

The Partnership shall have the power to do all acts and things in furtherance of and incidental to the foregoing business.

1.5 Filings.

1.5.1 Fictitious Business Name. As soon after the Effective Date as is reasonably practicable, the Partners shall execute, file, and publish an appropriate fictitious business name statement for the Partnership in accordance with the California Business and Professions Code.

1.5.2 Statement of Partnership Authority. As soon after the Effective Date as is reasonably practicable, the Partners shall (i) sign, acknowledge and verify a statement of partnership authority pursuant to RUPA § 303, (ii) file such statement in the Secretary of State's office, and (iii) cause said statement to be recorded in each county in California in which the Partnership owns or contemplates owning real property or any interest in real property. Promptly following any change in the Partners of the Partnership, the Partners shall amend such statement, file such statement with the Secretary of State's office and cause said amended statement to be recorded in each county in California in which the Partnership owns or contemplates owning real property or any interest in real property.[3]

1.5.3 Percentage Interests. As used in this Agreement, a Partner's **"Percentage Interest"** shall mean the percentage set forth below opposite such Partner's name:

_____ ___%

_____ ___%

As used in this Agreement, **"Percentage Interests"** shall mean the aggregate of all such percentages, unless the context requires otherwise. **"Majority Interest"** shall mean those Partners who hold a majority of the Percentage Interests which all Partners hold.

1.6 Term. The Partnership shall commence upon the Effective Date and shall continue for a period of forty (40) years thereafter, unless sooner terminated in accordance with Section 10 below.

2. CAPITAL CONTRIBUTIONS.

2.1 Initial Capital.

2.1.1 Partner #1. Upon the formation of the Partnership, Partner #1 shall contribute cash in the amount of One Hundred Thousand Dollars ($100,000) to the Partnership. Partner #1 shall receive a corresponding credit to its Capital Account.

---

3. *Comment:* Pursuant to RUPA § 303(a), a partnership may file a Statement of Partnership Authority with the Secretary of State. The Statement may specify the authority, or limitations on authority, of some or all of the partners to enter into transactions on behalf of the partnership. A filed Statement of Partnership Authority binds the partnership in favor of third parties who lack knowledge contrary to the statements in the document as to personal property transactions, and as to real property transactions if the Statement is recorded in the office for recording transfers of that property.

2.1.2   Partner #2.   Upon the formation of the Partnership, Partner #2 shall contribute to the Partnership all of its right, title, and interest in and to that certain real property described on the attached Exhibit "___."   The Partners agree that such property has a net fair market value of One Hundred Thousand Dollars ($100,000).   Partner #2 shall receive a credit to its Capital Account equal to such net fair market value.

2.1.3   Partner #3.   Upon the formation of the Partnership, Partner #3 shall contribute to the Partnership all of his or her right to acquire that certain real property described on the attached Exhibit "___" pursuant to that certain Purchase Agreement, dated April 1, 1995, by and between Partner #3 and John Doe.   The Partners agree that such right has a net fair market value of One Hundred Thousand Dollars ($100,000).   Partner #3 shall receive a credit to his or her Capital Account equal to such value.

2.1.4   As used in this agreement, **"Capital Contribution"** shall mean any cash or its equivalent in property, both real and personal, contributed to the capital of the Partnership.

2.2   Additional Capital.   No Partner shall be required to make any additional Capital Contributions.   To the extent *[unanimously or by Majority Interest]* approved by the Partners, from time to time, the Partners may be permitted to make additional Capital Contributions if and to the extent they so desire, and if the Partners determine that such additional Capital Contributions are necessary or appropriate for the conduct of the Partnership's business *[including, without limitation, expansion or diversification]*. In that event, the Partners shall have the opportunity, but not the obligation, to participate in such Capital Contributions on a pro rata basis in accordance with their Percentage Interests.   Each Partner shall receive a credit to its Capital Account in the amount of any additional capital which it contributes to the Partnership.   Immediately following such Capital Contributions, the Percentage Interests shall be adjusted by the Partners to reflect the new relative proportions of the Capital Accounts of the Partners.

2.3   Capital Accounts.   The Partnership shall establish and maintain an individual capital account (**"Capital Account"**) for each Partner in accordance with [Internal Revenue Code Treasury] Regulations Section 1.704–1(b)(2)(iv).[4]   If a Partner transfers all or part of its Partnership

---

4. *Comment:* For tax purposes, allocations of income, gain, loss, deduction and credit must be made in accordance with the partners' respective interests in the partnership. I.R.C. § 704. Allocations which have substantial economic effect are deemed to be in accordance with the partners' respective interests for these purposes. Allocations will have economic effect if the partnership agreement incorporates the "safe harbor" provisions, set forth in Treasury Regulations Section 1.704–1(b)(2). Pursuant to such "safe harbor" provisions, (i) capital accounts must be maintained in accordance with Treasury Regulations Section 1.704–1(b)(2)(iv), (ii) liquidating distributions must be made in accordance with positive capital account balances, and (iii) each partner must be obligated to restore any deficit balance in its capital account upon liquidation of its interest in the

Interest in accordance with this Agreement, such Partner's Capital Account attributable to the transferred Partnership Interest shall carry over to the new owner of such Partnership Interest pursuant to Regulations Section 1.704–1(b)(2)(iv)(1).

2.4 No Interest. No Partner shall be entitled to interest on the unreturned portion of his capital contributions.

2.5 Withdrawal of Partner or Capital. No Partner may withdraw as a partner of, or withdraw capital from, the Partnership without the consent of a Majority Interest of the Partners.[5]

2.6 Return of Capital. No Partner guarantees the return of another Partner's capital contributions.

3. DISTRIBUTIONS.

3.1 Cash Available for Distribution. As used in this Agreement, the term **"Cash Available for Distribution"** shall mean the amount of cash which *[all or a Majority Interest]* of the Partners deem available for distribution to the Partners, taking into account, among other factors, (i) all Partnership obligations then due and payable (including any compensation payable to the Partners in accordance with Section 5.6 below), (ii) anticipated Partnership expenditures, and (iii) those amounts which the Partners deem reasonably necessary, in [their] sole discretion, to place into reserves to satisfy customary and usual costs and claims with respect to the Partnership's business.

3.2 Manner of Distribution. The Partnership shall distribute Cash Available For Distribution to the Partners in the following order of priority:

(a) First, to the Partners, pro rata, in accordance with the amount of capital which the Partners have contributed to the Partnership, until each Partner has received distributions under this subsection (a) which, in the aggregate, equal one hundred percent (100%) of the capital which such Partner has contributed to the Partnership; and

(b) Thereafter, to the Partners, pro rata, in accordance with their respective Percentage Interests.

3.3 Time of Distribution. The Partnership shall distribute Cash Available For Distribution to the Partners pursuant to Section 3.2 above in such amounts and at such times as *[all or a Majority Interest]* of the Partners shall determine.

partnership. In lieu of a deficit restoration requirement, the partnership agreement can include "qualified income offset" and corresponding "loss limitation" provisions drafted to comply with treasury Regulations Section 1.704–1(b)(2)(ii)(d). In order to ensure that allocations will be respected for tax purposes, the partnership agreement should contain a provision which requires capital accounts to be maintained in accordance with Treasury Regulations Section 1.704–1(b)(2)(iv), as well as provisions which satisfy the remaining "safe harbor" requirements.

5. *See* Section 9 of the Agreement concerning dissociation.

315

3.4 Withholding. The Partnership shall withhold and pay all [state] withholding taxes in accordance with the provisions [of state law].

4. PROFITS AND LOSSES.

4.1 Determination of Profits and Losses. Partnership profits and losses shall be determined in accordance with Internal Revenue Code Sections 703 and 704, as amended ("**Code**"), and the Treasury Regulations promulgated thereunder.

4.2 Allocation of Profits and Losses. *[RUPA § 401(b)]*

4.2.1 Losses. Subject to Section 4.3 below, Partnership losses shall be allocated to the Partners in the following order of priority:

(a) First, to the Partners in the amount of any profits previously allocated to them pursuant to Section 4.2.2(b) below (to the extent such profits have not been offset by prior loss allocations under this subsection (a));

(b) Second, to the Partners, pro rata, in proportion to their positive Capital Account balances, until no Partner has a positive Capital Account balance; and

(c) Thereafter, to the Partners, pro rata, in accordance with their respective Percentage Interests.

4.2.2 Profits. Subject to Section 4.3 below, Partnership profits shall be allocated to the Partners in the following order of priority:

(a) First, to the Partners in the amount of any losses previously allocated to them pursuant to Sections 4.2.1(b) and 4.2.1(c) above (to the extent such losses have not been offset by prior profit allocations under this subsection (a)); and

(b) Thereafter, to the Partners, pro rata, in accordance with their respective Percentage Interests.

4.3 Special Allocations.

4.3.1 Minimum Gain Chargeback. If there is a net decrease in "Partnership Minimum Gain" (as defined in Treasury Regulations Section 1.704–2(d)) during any fiscal year of the Partnership, each Partner shall be specially allocated items of Partnership income and gain for such fiscal year (and, if necessary, in subsequent fiscal years) in an amount equal to the portion of such Partner's share of the net decrease in Partnership Minimum Gain that is allocable to the disposition of any Partnership property which is subject to a "Nonrecourse Liability" (as defined in Treasury Regulations Section 1.752–1(a)(2)), which share of such net decrease shall be determined in accordance with Treasury Regulations Section 1.704–2(g)(2). Allocations pursuant to this Section 4.3.1 shall be made in proportion to the respective amounts required to be allocated to each Partner under this Section 4.3.1. The items to be so allocated shall be determined in accordance with Treasury Regulations Section 1.704–2(f). This Section 4.3.1 is intended to comply and shall be interpreted consistently with the minimum gain chargeback requirement contained in Treasury Regulations Section 1.704–2(f).

4.3.2 <u>Chargeback of Minimum Gain Attributable To Partner Nonrecourse Debt</u>. If there is a net decrease in Partnership Minimum Gain attributable to a "Partner Nonrecourse Debt" (as defined in Treasury Regulations Section 1.704–2(b)(4)) during any Partnership fiscal year, each Partner who has a share of the Partnership Minimum Gain attributable to such Partner Nonrecourse Debt (determined in accordance with Treasury Regulations Section 1.704–2(i)(5)) shall be specially allocated items of Partnership income and gain for such fiscal year (and, if necessary, in subsequent fiscal years) in an amount equal to that portion of such Partner's share of the net decrease in Partnership Minimum Gain attributable to such Partner Nonrecourse Debt that is allocable to the disposition of Partnership property subject to such Partner Nonrecourse Debt (which share of such net decrease shall be determined in accordance with Treasury Regulations Section 1.704–2(i)(5)). Allocations pursuant to this Section 4.3.2 shall be made in proportion to the respective amounts required to be allocated to each Partner under this Section 4.3.2. The items to be so allocated shall be determined in accordance with Treasury Regulations Section 1.704–2(i)(4). This Section 4.3.2 is intended to comply and shall be interpreted consistently with the minimum gain chargeback requirement contained in Treasury Regulations Section 1.704–2(i)(4).

4.3.3 <u>Nonrecourse Deductions</u>. Any nonrecourse deductions (as defined in Treasury Regulations Section 1.704–2(b)(1)) for any fiscal year or other period shall be specially allocated to the Partners, pro rata, in accordance with their respective Percentage Interests.

4.3.4 <u>Partner Nonrecourse Deductions</u>. Any items of Partnership loss, deduction, or [Internal Revenue] Code Section 705(a)(2)(B) expenditures attributable to a Partner Nonrecourse Debt for any fiscal year or other period shall be specially allocated to the Partner who bears the economic risk of loss with respect to the Partner Nonrecourse Debt to which such items of Partnership loss, deduction, or Code Section 705(a)(2)(B) expenditures are attributable in accordance with Treasury Regulations Section 1.704–2(i).

4.4 <u>Code Section 704(c) Allocations</u>. Notwithstanding Sections 4.2 and 4.3 above, in accordance with Code Section 704(c) and the Treasury Regulations promulgated thereunder, income, gain, loss, and deduction with respect to any Partnership property contributed to the capital of the Partnership shall be allocated between the Partners so as to take account of any variation between the adjusted basis of such property to the Partnership for federal income tax purposes and its fair market value on the date of contribution. Allocations pursuant to this Section 4.4 are solely for purposes of federal, state, and local taxes. As such, they shall not affect or in any way be taken into account in computing a Partner's Capital Account or share of profits, losses, or other items of distributions pursuant to this Agreement.

5. MANAGEMENT AND AUTHORITY.

5.1 Participation by Partners. Except as expressly provided otherwise in this Agreement, (i) each Partner shall participate in the control, management and direction of the Partnership's business, and (ii) all Partnership matters shall be decided by a Majority Interest of the Partners. *[RUPA § 401(f)]* [6]

5.2 Fiduciary Duties. Each Partner owes to the Partnership the duty of loyalty and the duty of care. Accordingly, each Partner shall (i) account to the Partnership for any property, profit, or benefit obtained by such Partner in the conduct of the Partnership's business, and (ii) refrain from dealing with the Partnership as or on behalf of a party having an adverse interest to that of the Partnership.[7]

5.3 Rights and Responsibilities. The Partners shall be responsible for the day-to-day management and operation of the Partnership's business. In addition, all things to be done by the Partnership shall be, except as expressly provided otherwise in this Agreement, decided by a Majority Interest of the Partners including the following *[RUPA § 401(j)]*:

  (a) Execute all contracts, notes, deeds of trust, grant deeds, agreements for sale, escrow instructions, releases, easements, and other documents and instruments in connection with the Partnership's business;

6. *Comment:* Under RUPA, in the absence of a contrary agreement, each partner has equal rights in the management and conduct of the partnership business, and may possess partnership property only on behalf of the partnership. A majority of the partners may resolve a difference arising as to a matter in the ordinary course of business of the partnership; however, an act outside the ordinary course of business and/or an amendment to the partnership agreement requires the consent of all of the partners. *See* Section 5.4 below, providing for decisions to be made by unanimous vote of the partners with respect to matters in the ordinary course of the partnership's business.

7. *Comment:* RUPA sets forth specific duties owed by a partner to the partnership and the other partners. The two principal duties that a partner owes to the partnership and the other partners are (i) the duty of loyalty, and (ii) the duty of care. The duty of loyalty includes (i) the duty to account to the partnership for any property, profit, or benefit obtained by the partner in the conduct of the partnership business or from the use of partnership property or information including the appropriation of a partnership opportunity; (ii) the duty to refrain from dealing with the partnership in the conduct or winding up of the partnership business as or on behalf of a party having an interest adverse to the partnership; and (iii) the duty to refrain from competing with the partnership in the conduct of the partnership business before the partnership's dissolution. A partner's duty of care to the partnership and the other partners is limited to refraining from engaging in grossly negligent or reckless conduct, intentional misconduct, or a knowing violation of law. Certain provisions of RUPA regarding fiduciary duties may not be varied by the partnership agreement. The partnership agreement may not eliminate the duty of loyalty. If not manifestly unreasonable, however, the partnership agreement may (i) identify specific types or categories of activities that do not violate the duty of loyalty; or (ii) provide that a specified percentage of the partners may authorize or ratify, after full disclosure of all material facts, a specific act or transaction that would otherwise violate the duty of loyalty. In addition, the partnership agreement may not unreasonably reduce the duty of care or eliminate the obligation of good faith and fair dealing. The partnership agreement may, however, prescribe the standards by which the performance of the obligation is to be measured, provided that such standards are not manifestly unreasonable.

318

(b) [Sell,] lease, exchange or otherwise dispose of all or any part of the Partnership's property;

(c) Exercise the Partnership's rights and fulfill the Partnership's obligations with respect to any partnership in which the Partnership is a partner, whether such rights and obligations are conferred by law or set forth in the governing instrument for such other partnership;

(d) Employ or discharge, at the Partnership's expense, ... agents, employees, independent contractors, attorneys, and/or accountants;

(e) Operate and maintain Partnership property;

(f) Obtain insurance necessary for the proper protection of the Partnership and the Partners; and

(g) Adjust any and all claims against the Partnership.

5.4 Unanimous Consent Required. Notwithstanding Section 5.3 above, none of the following shall be effected without the unanimous prior written consent of all Partners [RUPA § 401(j)]

(a) Admit an additional Partner to the Partnership;

(b) Borrow money on behalf of the Partnership in excess of _____;

(c) Prepay (in whole or in part), refinance, increase, modify, or extend any Partnership obligation;

(d) Pledge, hypothecate or otherwise encumber all or any part of the Partnership's assets;

(e) Dissolve the Partnership;

(f) Assign the Partnership's property in trust for creditors or on the assignee's promise to pay the Partnership's debts;

(g) Confess a judgment;

(h) Do any act which would make it impossible for the Partners to carry on the ordinary business of the Partnership;

(i) Submit a Partnership claim or liability to arbitration or reference; ...

(j) Authorize the merger [RUPA §§ 905–907] [8] with, or conversion [RUPA §§ 901–904] [9] into, a foreign or domestic other business entity[; or]

8. Comment: RUPA provides for the merger of one or more partnerships into one partnership or any other number of business entities provided that the entities that are parties to the merger are permitted under the laws of their respective states of organization to effect the merger. Each party must approve an Agreement containing (i) terms and conditions of the merger; (ii) name and place of organization of the surviving entity; (iii) the manner of converting interests; (iv) any other details or provisions as are required by the laws under which constituent entities are organized; and (v) any other desired provisions.

A Statement of Merger may be filed pursuant to RUPA § 915 to evidence a merger in which (i) only partnerships are involved; and (ii) a domestic partnership is a party and no other party is a domestic entity. Although it is optional, a Statement of Merger should be filed whenever a constituent partnership owns real property and recorded in each county in which real property is owned.

319

(k) Do any act in contravention of this Agreement.

5.5 <u>Time and Opportunities</u>. The Partners shall devote to the Partnership such time as is reasonably necessary to carry out their respective obligations under this Agreement. During the term of this Partnership, each Partner may engage in any business activity for his own profit or advantage without the other Partners' consent, provided such other activity is not in competition with the Partnership's business. *[RUPA § 404(b)(3)]*

5.6 <u>Expenses</u>. Each Partner shall be entitled to reimbursement from the Partnership for those out-of-pocket expenses which such Partner reasonably incurs in the proper conduct of the Partnership's business. Each Partner shall itemize all such expenses in reasonable detail.

Upon a merger, the separate existence of the non-surviving entities ceases, and the surviving entity succeeds to all rights and property of the non-surviving entities without further act or deed and is subject to the obligations of the disappearing entities.

9. *Comment:* RUPA provides that a partnership may be converted into a domestic limited partnership, limited liability company, or a foreign other business entity if each of the partners would, pursuant to the proposed conversion, receive a percentage interest in the profits and capital of the converted business entity equal to the partner's percentage interest in profits and capital of the converting partnership as of the effective time of the conversion. The conversion may be effected only if (i) the law under which the new entity will exist expressly permits the formation of such new entity pursuant to a conversion; and (ii) the partnership complies with all of the requirements of such other law that applies to the conversion of such other business entity.

The partnership must approve a plan of conversion that states (i) the terms and conditions of the conversion; (ii) the place of the organization of the converted entity and of the converting partnership; (iii) the name of the converted entity after conversion, if different from that of the converting partnership; (iv) the manner of converting the partnership interests of each of the partners into securities of or interests in the converted entity; (v) the provisions of the governing document for the converted entity to which the holders of interest in the converted entity are to be bound; (vi) any other details or provisions required by law under which the converted entity is organized; and (vii) any other details or provisions desired by the parties.

An entity that converts into another entity is for all purposes considered the same entity that existed prior to the conversion. When a conversion takes effect, all of the following apply: (i) all rights and property of the converting entity remain vested in the converted entity; (ii) all debts, liabilities and obligations of the converting entity continue as debts, liabilities and obligations of the converted entity; (iii) all rights of creditors and liens upon the property of the converting entity are preserved and remain enforceable against the converted entity; and (iv) any action or proceeding pending by or against the converting entity may be continued against the converted entity as if the conversion had never occurred.

The personal liability of a partner of a converting partnership is unchanged regarding all obligations for which the partner was personally liable prior to the conversion. Similarly, a partner of a partnership that converted from another business entity is liable for any obligations of the converting other business entity for which the partner was personally liable prior to the conversion....

320

5.7 <u>Compensation</u>.

    5.7.1 <u>In General</u>. Except as expressly provided otherwise in this Section, no Partner shall be entitled to receive compensation for services rendered to the Partnership, unless such compensation is approved in writing by *[all or a Majority Interest]* of the Partners. *[RUPA § 401(h)]*

    5.7.2 <u>Contracts With Partners and Affiliates</u>. The Partnership may enter into contracts with a Partner or an affiliate of a Partner for the performance of services upon such terms and conditions as the Partners deem to be in the Partnership's best interests; provided, however, such contracts must provide for commercially reasonable fees, compensation, and/or other monetary payments.[10]

    5.7.3 <u>Tax Treatment</u>. Any compensation which the Partnership pays to a Partner in accordance with this Section shall be treated as a payment made to one who is not a partner under Code Section 707(a) or 707(c).

5.8 <u>Indemnification</u>. The Partnership shall bear the cost of all expenditures and liabilities which the Partners incur in the proper conduct of the Partnership's business. The Partnership, to the extent of its assets, shall indemnify, defend and hold harmless a Partner from and against any and all liabilities of every kind, arising in any manner out of or in connection with the operation of the Partnership's business, except as to those matters arising by reason of such Partner's fraud, gross negligence, willful misconduct, or breach of fiduciary duty.

6. ACCOUNTING AND BANKING.

6.1 <u>Fiscal Year</u>. The fiscal year of the Partnership shall be the calendar year.

6.2 <u>Accounting Method</u>. The Partnership's books shall be kept on the method of accounting which the Partners select, provided the Partnership is entitled under the Code to use such method of accounting. The Partnership shall prepare, or cause to be prepared, financial statements for financial reporting purposes on such method of accounting in accordance with those accounting principles used to prepare the Partnership's federal income tax returns, consistently applied.

6.3 <u>Books and Records</u>. The Partners shall keep, or cause to be kept, (i) accurate records of all transactions entered into with respect to the Partnership's business, and (ii) accurate books and accounts with respect to the Partnership's management and operation. The Partners shall (i) maintain the Partnership's books of account and other records at the Partnership's principal place of business, and (ii) make such documents available at ordinary business hours for inspection and copying by each Partner or its designated representative. Any copies which a Partner

---

10. *Comment:* Partners should be advised that notwithstanding the foregoing provision, they must ensure that if they or their affiliates enter into contracts with the Partnership, that they do not violate the duties of loyalty and care discussed above with respect to Section 5.2.

makes of the documents specified herein shall be at such Partner's expense. *[RUPA § 403]*

6.4 <u>Bank Accounts</u>. The Partners shall open and thereafter maintain a separate bank account(s) in the Partnership's name, in which all Partnership funds shall be deposited. All withdrawals from the Partnership's bank account(s) shall be made only by checks requiring the signature of such person or persons as *[all or a Majority Interest]* of the Partners shall designate.

6.5 <u>Tax Matters</u>.

6.5.1 <u>Tax Returns</u>. The Partners shall prepare and file, or cause to be prepared and filed, at the Partnership's expense, all federal and state tax returns on behalf of the Partnership in a timely manner.

6.5.2 <u>Tax Elections</u>. The Partners may cause the Partnership to make any tax elections available to the Partnership under the Code or any state revenue or taxation law.

7. TRANSFERS OF PARTNERSHIP INTERESTS.

7.1 <u>General Prohibition</u>. No Partner may sell, assign, pledge, hypothecate, or otherwise transfer or encumber all or any part of its interest in the Partnership without the other Partners' prior written consent, which consent may be withheld for any reason or for no reason at all. Any attempted sale, assignment, pledge, hypothecation, or other transfer or encumbrance of a Partner's interest in the Partnership in violation of this Section 7.1 shall be invalid. As such, it shall neither (i) relieve the transferor Partner of any of its obligations under this Agreement, nor (ii) entitle the transferee to any rights as a partner of the Partnership, as such rights are set forth in this Agreement and/or conferred by law.

7.2 <u>Permitted Transfers</u>. A Partner *[without the other Partners' consent]* may, transfer all or any part of his interest in the Partnership in trust for the benefit of himself, his spouse, his children, or grandchildren, or any combination thereof, provided (i) such Partner is a trustee or co-trustee of such trust, and (ii) such Partner, as trustee or co-trustee, agrees in writing to abide by the terms and conditions of this Agreement.

7.3 <u>Transferee As Partner</u>. Any transferee which acquires an interest in the Partnership in accordance with Sections 7.1 or 7.2 above shall satisfy each of the following conditions:

(a) The transferee must execute a written agreement whereby such transferee agrees to be bound by all of the terms, conditions, restrictions, and limitations set forth in this Agreement;

(b) The spouse of such transferee, if any, must consent in writing to be bound by all of the terms, conditions, restrictions, and limitations set forth in this Agreement; and

(c) The transferee must reimburse the Partnership for all reasonable legal and accounting fees and other costs which the Partnership must pay as a result of the transaction.

7.4 Status of Transferee. Upon the satisfaction of those conditions set forth in Section 7.3 above, the transferee shall succeed to the Partnership interest of the transferor Partner in the same capacity as the transferor Partner held in the Partnership. Accordingly, the transferee shall acquire all rights and obligations with respect to title, management, capital, allocations, and distributions which the transferor Partner held in the Partnership, as such rights and obligations are set forth in this Agreement and/or conferred by law. If any of the conditions set forth in Section 7.3 above are not satisfied or waived in writing by the Partners, then (i) the transferor Partner shall not be relieved of any of its obligations as a Partner of the Partnership (as such obligations are set forth in this Agreement and/or conferred by law), and (ii) the transferee shall not be entitled to any rights of a Partner under this Agreement, other than the right to receive as much of the transferor Partner's share of Partnership profits, losses and distributions to which the transferor Partner otherwise would be entitled under this Agreement.[11] *[RUPA § 503]*

7.5 Transfers By Operation of Law. Any party who acquires any interest in the Partnership by operation of law, including by death or court decree, shall not be entitled to vote or otherwise participate in the Partnership's business.

8. ADDITIONAL PARTNERS.

8.1 Admission. A person or entity may be admitted as an additional Partner in the Partnership only with the written consent of all Partners, which consent may be withheld for any reason or for no reason at all. *[RUPA § 401(i)]*

8.2 Amendment. Upon the admission of an additional Partner pursuant to Section 8.1 above, each Partner (including the additional Partner) shall execute an amendment to this Agreement (i) evidencing the additional Partner's consent to be bound by all of the provisions contained in this Agreement, and (ii) reflecting the Partners' new Percentage Interests.

9. DISSOCIATION OF A PARTNER.

A Partner shall cease to be a Partner, and shall be deemed "dissociated" within the meaning of [RUPA §§ 601–603], upon the occurrence of any of the events described in Section 9.1 below.

---

11. *Comment:* RUPA § 502 provides that a partner's only "transferable interest" in the partnership under RUPA is the partner's share of the profits, losses, and distributions. The interest is characterized as personal property. Although a partner may transfer his or her interest in the partnership, RUPA § 503(a) provides that such transfer does not (i) by itself cause the partner's dissociation or a dissolution of the partnership; or (ii) entitle the transferee to participate in the management or conduct of the partnership business; or (iii) entitle the transferee to access to partnership information or inspect or copy the partnership books or records. Despite these limitations, a transferee has a right to (i) receive distributions to which the transferor would otherwise be entitled; (ii) receive a net amount otherwise distributable to the transferor upon the dissolution and winding up of the partnership's business; and (iii) seek a judicial determination that it is equitable to wind up the partnership business.

9.1   Events of Dissociation. The following events shall result in a Partner's dissociation from the Partnership *[RUPA § 601]*:

(a) Such Partner's expulsion pursuant to the unanimous vote of the other Partners;

(b) Such Partner's expulsion pursuant to an order of a court of competent jurisdiction;

(c) Such Partner becomes a debtor in bankruptcy;

(d) In the case of a Partner who is an individual, such Partner's death or incapacity;

(e) In the case of a Partner that is a trust or an estate, the distribution of the trust's or estate's entire transferable interest in the Partnership; or

(f) The termination of a Partner who is not an individual, partnership, corporation, trust, or estate.[12]

9.2   Wrongful Dissociation.

9.2.1   Events Causing Wrongful Dissociation. A Partner's dissociation shall be deemed wrongful if such dissociation (i) resulted from an event described in paragraphs (b), (c), (e) or (f) of Section 9.1 above, or (ii) resulted from an event not described in Section 9.1 above.[13] *[RUPA § 602]*

9.2.2   Liability of Wrongfully Dissociated Partner. A Partner who wrongfully dissociates is liable to the Partnership and to the other Partners for any damages caused by such wrongful dissociation, and such liability is in addition to any other obligation owed by the Partner to the Partnership.[14] *[RUPA § 602(c)]*

12. *Comment:* Under the UPA, the death or withdrawal of a partner automatically triggered a dissolution of the partnership. Accordingly, the termination of a partner's relationship with the partnership was discussed only in the context of dissolution. In contrast, RUPA treats the dissolution of a partnership and the withdrawal of a partner as two separate concepts. The withdrawal of a partner from a partnership is referred to as "dissociation" in RUPA. RUPA § 601 lists events, which include those described above, which result in a partner's dissociation. In addition, the partnership agreement may identify other events causing a partner's dissociation.

13. *Comment:* A partner has the power to dissociate at any time by express will, irrespective of whether such dissociation is rightful or wrongful. A partner's dissociation is wrongful if it is in breach of an express provision of the partnership agreement.

Dissociation is also wrongful if, in the case of a partnership for a definite term or particular undertaking, (i) the partner withdraws by express will (except as specified under limited circumstances); (ii) the partner is expelled by judicial determination; (iii) the partner is dissociated by becoming a debtor in bankruptcy; or (iv) in the case of a partner who is not an individual, trust other than a business trust, or estate, the partner is expelled or dissociated because it willfully dissolved or terminated. A partner who wrongfully dissociates is liable to the partnership and to the other partners for any damages caused by such wrongful dissociation, and such liability is in addition to any other obligation owed by the partner to the partnership. Accordingly, the partnership agreement may specify additional consequences of a partner's wrongful dissociation.

14. *Comment:* The language contained in Section 9.2.2 mirrors the language of

9.3 <u>Liability of Dissociated Partner.</u> A dissociated Partner is liable to the Partnership for any obligation incurred prior to that Partner's dissociation. A dissociated Partner may be liable for a transaction entered into by the Partnership within two years after the Partner's dissociation, provided the requirements set forth in RUPA § 703(b) are satisfied.[15] *[RUPA § 702]*

10. DISSOLUTION AND TERMINATION OF PARTNERSHIP.

10.1 <u>Events of Dissolution.</u>[16] The Partnership shall dissolve upon the occurrence of any of the following events:

(a) The expiration of the Partnership's term, as set forth in Section 1.6 above;[17] *[RUPA § 801(2)(iii)]*

(b) The Partners' unanimous written consent to dissolve the Part-

---

RUPA § 602(c). Under RUPA, a partner's liability for wrongfully dissociating, as described above, is in addition to any other obligation owed by the partner to the partnership. Accordingly, a wrongfully dissociating partner will be held liable for any other breach of the partnership agreement and the partnership agreement may specify additional consequences of a partner's wrongful dissociation.

15. *Comment:* Under RUPA, a partner is not discharged from liability for a partnership obligation incurred before dissociation merely because he or she has dissociated from the partnership. Generally, a dissociated partner is not liable for partnership obligations incurred after dissociation. A dissociated partner may, however, be liable to a third party for transactions entered into by the partnership within two years after the partner's dissociation, if (i) the other party reasonably believed that the dissociated partner was then a partner; (ii) the other party did not have notice of the partner's dissociation; and (iii) the other party is not deemed to have had knowledge or notice by reason of the filing of a Statement of Partnership Authority or Statement of Dissociation. A dissociated partner may be released from liability for a partnership obligation by agreement with the partnership creditor and the partners continuing the partnership business. In addition, a dissociated partner is released from liability for a partnership obligation if a partnership creditor, with notice of the partner's dissociation but without the partner's consent, agrees to a material alteration in the form of nature or time of payment of a partnership obligation.

16. *Comment:* In a partnership at will, RUPA provides that the partnership will dis-

solve by the express will of at least half of the partners, including partners, other than wrongfully dissociating partners, who have dissociated within the preceding 90 days and for which purpose such dissociation constitutes an expression of that partner's will to dissolve and wind up the partnership business.

Regardless of whether a partnership is at will or for a definite term or undertaking, RUPA provides that the partnership will be dissolved and must be wound up upon the occurrence of (i) an event agreed to in the partnership agreement; (ii) an event that makes it unlawful for all or substantially all of the business of the partnership to be continued, unless such illegality is cured within 90 days after notice to the partnership of such event; or (iii) on application by a partner, a judicial determination that any of the following provisions of RUPA § 801 apply: (1) the partnership's economic purpose is likely to be frustrated; (2) another partner has engaged in conduct relating to the partnership business that makes it not reasonably practicable to carry on the business in partnership with that partner, or (3) it is not otherwise reasonably practical to conduct the partnership business in conformity with the partnership agreement.

17. *Comment:* In a partnership for a definite term, dissolution is triggered by (i) the expiration of 90 days after a partner's dissociation by several specified events, including, without limitation, a partner's death, bankruptcy, or wrongful dissociation, unless before that time a majority in interest of the partners (including partners who have rightfully dissociated) agree to continue the partnership; (ii) the expiration of the term.

nership;[18] *[RUPA § 801(2)(ii)]*

(c)The sale, transfer or other disposition of all or substantially all of the Partnership's assets;

(d) The occurrence of any event which makes it unlawful for the Partners to carry on the Partnership's business; *[RUPA § 801(4)]* or

(e) Whenever a court of competent jurisdiction so properly decrees.[19] *[RUPA § 801(5)]*

10.2 <u>Winding–Up</u>. Upon the Partnership's dissolution, the Partnership's business shall be wound up within a reasonable period of time, its assets liquidated, a final accounting made, and the Partnership's books closed. The Partners shall liquidate the Partnership's real property in an orderly fashion over a reasonable period of time pursuant to established real estate practices.[20] *[RUPA §§ 801–807]*

10.3 <u>Manner of Distribution</u>. Those proceeds which the Partnership derives from the liquidation of its assets shall be applied and distributed in the following order of priority:

18. *Comment:* Where the partnership is for a definite term, RUPA § 801(2)(ii) requires the express will of all of the partners to wind up the partnership business.

19. *Comment:* To obtain a judicial decree that a partnership should be dissolved, a partner must make application for such decree, and the court must determine that one of the requirements contained in RUPA § 801 is fulfilled (See, footnote 13). In addition, a partnership is dissolved if, on application by a transferee of a partner's interest, a judicial determination is made that it is equitable to wind up the partnership business after the expiration of the term or completion of the undertaking, provided that the partnership was for a definite term or specific undertaking at the time of the transfer or entry of the charging order that gave rise to the transfer.

20. *Comment:* Any partner who has not dissociated may participate in winding up the partnership's business. Upon application by any partner, however, a court may order judicial supervision of the winding up. The person winding up the partnership's business may do the following:

(i) preserve the partnership business or property as a going concern for a reasonable time; (ii) prosecute and defend actions and proceedings, whether civil, criminal, or administrative; (iii) settle and close the partnership's business; (iv) dispose of and transfer the partnership's property; (v) discharge the partnership's liabilities; (vi) distribute the partnership's assets; (vii) settle disputes by mediation or arbitration; and (viii) perform other necessary acts.

Under limited circumstances, a partnership may be bound by acts that occur during the winding up process. A partnership is bound by a partner's act after dissolution that is (i) appropriate for winding up the partnership's business; or (ii) would have bound the partnership before dissolution, if the other party to the transaction did not have notice of the dissolution.

RUPA provides that a partner who has not wrongfully dissociated may file a statement of dissolution stating, (i) the name of the partnership as filed with the Secretary of State; (ii) any identification number issued by the Secretary of State; and (iii) that the partnership has dissolved and is winding up its business. A Statement of Dissolution cancels a filed Statement of Partnership Authority, and is a limitation on authority for purposes of RUPA § 303(e). A third party is deemed to have notice of the dissolution and limitation of a partner's authority as a result of the Statement of Dissolution 90 days after it is filed.

After filing a Statement of Dissolution, a dissolved partnership may file and, if appropriate, record a Statement of Partnership Authority that will be valid with respect to any transaction, whether or not the transaction is appropriate for winding up the partnership's business.

(a) First, to the payment of expenses of liquidation and Partnership debts owing to creditors other than Partners;

(b) Second, to the payment of any Partnership debts owing to Partners; and

(c) Thereafter, to the Partners in accordance with their positive Capital Account balances, after taking into account income and loss allocations for the Partnership taxable year during which liquidation occurs. These liquidating distributions shall be made by the end of the Partnership taxable year in which the Partnership is liquidated, or, if later, within ninety (90) days after the date of such liquidation.

10.4 <u>Deficit Restoration Requirement</u>. If, upon liquidation, any Partner has a deficit balance in his Capital Account, after taking into account all Capital Account adjustments for the Partnership taxable year during which liquidation occurs, such Partner shall contribute cash to the capital of the Partnership in the amount necessary to eliminate such deficit balance by the end of the Partnership taxable year during which liquidation occurs or, if later, within ninety (90) days after the date of such liquidation. *[RUPA § 807(b)]*

10.5 <u>Termination</u>. Immediately after the application and distribution of liquidation proceeds in accordance with Section 10.3 above, the Partnership shall terminate.[21]

11. MISCELLANEOUS.

11.1 <u>Amendment</u>. This Agreement is subject to amendment only with the written consent of those Partners whose consent is required under this Agreement to accomplish the action reflected in such amendment.

11.2 <u>Binding Effect</u>. Subject to the restrictions set forth herein, this Agreement shall be binding upon the Partners and their respective successors, assigns, representatives, and beneficiaries.

11.3 <u>Captions and Headings</u>. Captions and headings used in this Agreement are for convenience purposes only. As such, they shall not control, affect, modify, amend or change the meaning and/or construction of any term or provision contained in this Agreement.

11.4 <u>Counterparts and Facsimiles</u>. The Partners may execute this Agreement simultaneously, in any number of counterparts, or on facsimile copies, each of which shall be deemed an original, but all of which together shall constitute one and the same Agreement.

11.5 <u>Entire Agreement</u>. This Agreement contains the Partners' entire agreement and supersedes any prior oral or written agreements among them with respect to the subject matter contained herein. There are no representations, agreements, arrangements, or understandings (oral or

---

21. *Comment:* RUPA provides that a partnership continues after dissolution only for the purpose of winding up its business. The partnership is terminated when the winding [up is completed].

written) among the Partners relating to the subject matter of this Agreement which are not fully expressed herein.

11.6 <u>Further Documents</u>. Each party agrees to execute, with acknowledgment and affidavit if required, any and all documents in writing which may be required under this Agreement.

11.7 <u>Governing Law</u>. This Agreement, together with the Partners' respective rights and obligations hereunder, shall be governed by and construed in accordance with the laws of the State of California.

11.8 <u>Notices</u>. Any notice required or permitted hereunder shall be given in writing and shall be deemed effectively given upon (i) personal delivery, (ii) twenty-four (24) hours after deposit with Federal Express or a comparable express courier, addressed to a party at the address set forth below his signature hereto, or (iii) forty-eight (48) hours after deposit in the United States mail, by certified mail, return receipt requested, postage prepaid, addressed to a Partner at the address set forth below his signature hereto. A Partner may designate another address for notice purposes upon written notice thereof to the Partnership.

11.9 <u>Partition—No Right</u>. No Partner shall have any right to seek or demand (i) partition of all or any part of the Partnership's assets, or (ii) any specific Partnership assets upon the liquidation of the Partnership.

11.10 <u>Prevailing Party's Fees</u>. If any party commences an action against another party to interpret or enforce any of the terms of this Agreement, or because of the other party's breach of any provision set forth in this Agreement, the losing party shall pay to the prevailing party reasonable attorneys' fees, costs and expenses, court costs and other costs of action incurred in connection with the prosecution or defense of such action, whether or not the action is prosecuted to a final judgment. For purposes of this Agreement, the terms "attorneys' fees" or "attorneys' fees and costs" shall mean the fees and expenses of counsel to the parties hereto, which may include, without limitation, printing, photostating, duplicating and other expenses, air freight charges, and fees billed for law clerks, paralegals, librarians and others not admitted to the bar but performing services under the supervision of an attorney. The terms "attorneys' fees" or "attorneys' fees and costs" shall also include, without limitation, all such fees and expenses incurred with respect to appeals, arbitrations and bankruptcy proceedings, and whether or not any action or proceeding is brought with respect to the matter for which said fees and expenses were incurred. The term "attorney" shall have the same meaning as the term "counsel."

11.11 <u>Pronouns and Gender</u>. Any pronouns or references used in this Agreement shall be deemed to include the masculine, feminine, or neuter gender, as appropriate. Any expression in the singular or plural shall, if appropriate in the context, include both the singular and the plural.

11.12 <u>Recitals and Exhibits</u>. All recitals set forth in this Agreement and all exhibits referenced in this Agreement are incorporated into this Agreement by this reference.

11.13 <u>Severability</u>. If a court of competent jurisdiction finds any provision in this Agreement to be invalid, such invalidity shall not affect the remainder of the Agreement. In such event, the invalid provision shall be deemed severed therefrom and the remainder of the Agreement shall remain enforceable in accordance with its terms and of full force and effect.

11.14 <u>Third Parties—No Interest</u>. Nothing in this Agreement (whether express or implied) is intended to or shall (i) confer any rights or remedies under or by reason of this Agreement on any persons other than the parties hereto and their respective successors and assigns, (ii) relieve or discharge the obligation or liability of any third person to any party hereto, or (iii) give any third person any right of subrogation or action against any party to this Agreement.

11.15 <u>Waiver</u>. A party's waiver of any breach of any provision contained in this Agreement shall not constitute a continuing waiver or a waiver of any subsequent breach of such provision or any other provision contained in this Agreement.

11.16 <u>Time of Essence</u>. Time is of the essence of this Agreement and all terms, covenants, conditions and provisions set forth in this Agreement.

12. EXECUTION.

IN WITNESS WHEREOF, the Partners have executed this Agreement effective as of the Effective Date as set forth in the Agreement.

Date: _____

_____

Signature

_____

Typed Name

_____

Residence Address

Date: _____

_____

Signature

_____

Typed Name

_____

Residence Address

13. CONSENT OF SPOUSES.

We certify that:

(1) We are the spouses of the persons who signed the foregoing Partnership Agreement and who constitute the members of the Partnership described in that Agreement.

(2) We have read and approve the provisions of that Partnership Agreement, including but not limited to those relating to the purchase, sale, or other disposition of the interest of a deceased, retiring, withdrawing, or terminating partner.

(3) We agree to be bound by and accept those provisions of that Partnership Agreement in lieu of all other interests we, or any of us, may have in that Partnership, whether the interest be community property or otherwise.

(4) Our spouses shall have the full power of management of their interests in the Partnership, including any portion of those interests that are our community property, and they have the full right, without our further approval, to exercise their voting rights as partners in the Partnership, to execute any amendments to the Partnership Agreement, and to sell, transfer, encumber, and deal in any manner with those Partnership interests, including any portion of those interests that are our community property.

Executed on Date: _____, at: _____, California.

_____
Signature

_____
Typed Name

_____
Signature

_____
Typed Name

UNIFORM LIMITED PARTNERSHIP ACT (1976) WITH 1985 AMENDMENTS

ARTICLE 1.   GENERAL PROVISIONS

ARTICLE 2.   FORMATION; CERTIFICATE OF LIMITED PARTNERSHIP

ARTICLE 3.   LIMITED PARTNERS

ARTICLE 4.   GENERAL PARTNERS

ARTICLE 5.   FINANCE

ARTICLE 6.   DISTRIBUTIONS AND WITHDRAWAL

* Omitted.

ARTICLE 1

GENERAL PROVISIONS

§ 101. Definitions

As used in this [Act], unless the context otherwise requires:

(1) "Certificate of limited partnership" means the certificate referred to in Section 201, and the certificate as amended or restated.

332   * Omitted.

(2) "Contribution" means any cash, property, services rendered, or a promissory note or other binding obligation to contribute cash or property or to perform services, which a partner contributes to a limited partnership in his capacity as a partner.

(3) "Event of withdrawal of a general partner" means an event that causes a person to cease to be a general partner as provided in Section 402.

(4) "Foreign limited partnership" means a partnership formed under the laws of any state other than this State and having as partners one or more general partners and one or more limited partners.

(5) "General partner" means a person who has been admitted to a limited partnership as a general partner in accordance with the partnership agreement and named in the certificate of limited partnership as a general partner.

(6) "Limited partner" means a person who has been admitted to a limited partnership as a limited partner in accordance with the partnership agreement.

(7) "Limited partnership" and "domestic limited partnership" mean a partnership formed by two or more persons under the laws of this State and having one or more general partners and one or more limited partners.

(8) "Partner" means a limited or general partner.

(9) "Partnership agreement" means any valid agreement, written or oral, of the partners as to the affairs of a limited partnership and the conduct of its business.

(10) "Partnership interest" means a partner's share of the profits and losses of a limited partnership and the right to receive distributions of partnership assets.

(11) "Person" means a natural person, partnership, limited partnership (domestic or foreign), trust, estate, association, or corporation.

(12) "State" means a state, territory, or possession of the United States, the District of Columbia, or the Commonwealth of Puerto Rico.

§ 102. Name

The name of each limited partnership as set forth in its certificate of limited partnership:

(1) shall contain without abbreviation the words "limited partnership";

(2) may not contain the name of a limited partner unless (i) it is also the name of a general partner or the corporate name of a corporate general partner, or (ii) the business of the limited partnership had been carried on under that name before the admission of that limited partner;

(3) may not be the same as, or deceptively similar to, the name of any corporation or limited partnership organized under the laws of this State or licensed or registered as a foreign corporation or limited partnership in this State; and

(4) may not contain the following words [here insert prohibited words]....

§ 105. Records to Be Kept

(a) Each limited partnership shall keep at the office referred to in Section 104(1) the following:

(1) a current list of the full name and last known business address of each partner, separately identifying the general partners (in alphabetical order) and the limited partners (in alphabetical order);

(2) a copy of the certificate of limited partnership and all certificates of amendment thereto, together with executed copies of any powers of attorney pursuant to which any certificate has been executed;

(3) copies of the limited partnership's federal, state and local income tax returns and reports, if any, for the three most recent years;

(4) copies of any then effective written partnership agreements and of any financial statements of the limited partnership for the three most recent years; and

(5) unless contained in a written partnership agreement, a writing setting out:

(i) the amount of cash and a description and statement of the agreed value of the other property or services contributed by each partner and which each partner has agreed to contribute;

(ii) the times at which or events on the happening of which any additional contributions agreed to be made by each partner are to be made;

(iii) any right of a partner to receive, or of a general partner to make, distributions to a partner which include a return of all or any part of the partner's contribution; and

(iv) any events upon the happening of which the limited partnership is to be dissolved and its affairs wound up.

(b) Records kept under this section are subject to inspection and copying at the reasonable request and at the expense of any partner during ordinary business hours.

§ 106. Nature of Business

A limited partnership may carry on any business that a partnership without limited partners may carry on except [here designate prohibited activities].

§ 107. Business Transactions of Partner With Partnership

Except as provided in the partnership agreement, a partner may lend money to and transact other business with the limited partnership and, subject to other applicable law, has the same rights and obligations with respect thereto as a person who is not a partner.

ARTICLE 2

FORMATION; CERTIFICATE OF LIMITED PARTNERSHIP

§ 201. Certificate of Limited Partnership

(a) In order to form a limited partnership, a certificate of limited partnership must be executed and filed in the office of the Secretary of State. The certificate shall set forth:

(1) the name of the limited partnership;

(2) the address of the office and the name and address of the agent for service of process required to be maintained by Section 104;

(3) the name and the business address of each general partner;

(4) the latest date upon which the limited partnership is to dissolve; and

(5) any other matters the general partners determine to include therein.

(b) A limited partnership is formed at the time of the filing of the certificate of limited partnership in the office of the Secretary of State or at any later time specified in the certificate of limited partnership if, in either case, there has been substantial compliance with the requirements of this section.

Comment

The 1985 Act requires far fewer matters to be set forth in the certificate of limited partnership than did Section 2 of the 1916 Act and Section 201 of the 1976 Act. This is in recognition of the fact that the partnership agreement, not the certificate of limited partnership, has become the authoritative and comprehensive document for most limited partnerships, and that creditors and potential creditors of the partnership do and should refer to the partnership agreement and to other information furnished to them directly by the partnership and by others, not to the certificate of limited partnership, to obtain facts concerning the capital and finances of the partnership and other matters of concern. Subparagraph (b), which is based upon the 1916 Act, has been retained to make it clear that existence of the limited partnership depends only upon compliance with this section. Its continued existence is not dependent upon compliance with other provisions of this Act.

§ 202. Amendment to Certificate

(a) A certificate of limited partnership is amended by filing a certificate of amendment thereto in the office of the Secretary of State. The certificate shall set forth:

(1) the name of the limited partnership;

(2) the date of filing the certificate; and

(3) the amendment to the certificate.

(b) Within 30 days after the happening of any of the following events, an amendment to a certificate of limited partnership reflecting the occurrence of the event or events shall be filed:

(1) the admission of a new general partner;

(2) the withdrawal of a general partner; or

(3) the continuation of the business under Section 801 after an event of withdrawal of a general partner.

(c) A general partner who becomes aware that any statement in a certificate of limited partnership was false when made or that any arrangements or other facts described have changed, making the certificate inaccurate in any respect, shall promptly amend the certificate.

(d) A certificate of limited partnership may be amended at any time for any other proper purpose the general partners determine.

(e) No person has any liability because an amendment to a certificate of limited partnership has not been filed to reflect the occurrence of any event referred to in subsection (b) of this section if the amendment is filed within the 30–day period specified in subsection (b).

(f) A restated certificate of limited partnership may be executed and filed in the same manner as a certificate of amendment. . . .

§ 204. Execution of Certificates

(a) Each certificate required by this Article to be filed in the office of the Secretary of State shall be executed in the following manner:

(1) an original certificate of limited partnership must be signed by all general partners;

(2) a certificate of amendment must be signed by at least one general partner and by each other general partner designated in the certificate as a new general partner; and

(3) a certificate of cancellation must be signed by all general partners.

(b) Any person may sign a certificate by an attorney-in-fact, but a power of attorney to sign a certificate relating to the admission of a general partner must specifically describe the admission.

(c) The execution of a certificate by a general partner constitutes an affirmation under the penalties of perjury that the facts stated therein are true.

§ 206. Filing in Office of Secretary of State

(a) Two signed copies of the certificate of limited partnership and of any certificates of amendment or cancellation (or of any judicial decree of amendment or cancellation) shall be delivered to the Secretary of State. A person who executes a certificate as an agent or fiduciary need not exhibit evidence of his [or her] authority as a prerequisite to filing. Unless the Secretary of State finds that any certificate does not conform to law, upon receipt of all filing fees required by law he [or she] shall:

(1) endorse on each duplicate original the word "Filed" and the day, month, and year of the filing thereof;

(2) file one duplicate original in his [or her] office; and

(3) return the other duplicate original to the person who filed it or his [or her] representative.

(b) Upon the filing of a certificate of amendment (or judicial decree of amendment) in the office of the Secretary of State, the certificate of limited partnership shall be amended as set forth therein, and upon the effective date of a certificate of cancellation (or a judicial decree thereof), the certificate of limited partnership is cancelled.

§ 207. Liability for False Statement in Certificate

If any certificate of limited partnership or certificate of amendment or cancellation contains a false statement, one who suffers loss by reliance on the statement may recover damages for the loss from:

(1) any person who executes the certificate, or causes another to execute it on his behalf, and knew, and any general partner who knew or should have known, the statement to be false at the time the certificate was executed; and

(2) any general partner who thereafter knows or should have known that any arrangement or other fact described in the certificate has changed, making the statement inaccurate in any respect within a sufficient time before the statement was relied upon reasonably to have enabled that general partner to cancel or amend the certificate, or to file a petition for its [judicial] cancellation or amendment . . . .

§ 208. Scope of Notice

The fact that a certificate of limited partnership is on file in the office of the Secretary of State is notice that the partnership is a limited partnership and the persons designated therein as general partners are general partners, but it is not notice of any other fact.

Comment

. . . By stating that the filing of a certificate of limited partnership only results in notice of the general liability of the general partners, Section 208 obviates the concern that third parties may be held to have notice of special provisions set forth in the certificate. While this section is designed to preserve by implication the limited liability of limited partners, the implicit protection provided is not intended to change any liability of a limited partner which may be created by his action or inaction under the law of estoppel, agency, fraud or the like.

§ 209. Delivery of Certificates to Limited Partners

Upon the return by the Secretary of State pursuant to Section 206 of a certificate marked "Filed," the general partners shall promptly deliver or mail a copy of the certificate of limited partnership and each certificate of amendment or cancellation to each limited partner unless the partnership agreement provides otherwise.

ARTICLE 3

LIMITED PARTNERS

§ 301. Admission of Limited Partners

(a) A person becomes a limited partner:

(1) at the time the limited partnership is formed; or

(2) at any later time specified in the records of the limited partnership for becoming a limited partner.

(b) After the filing of a limited partnership's original certificate of limited partnership, a person may be admitted as an additional limited partner:

(1) in the case of a person acquiring a partnership interest directly from the limited partnership, upon compliance with the partnership agreement or, if the partnership agreement does not so provide, upon the written consent of all partners; and

(2) in the case of an assignee of a partnership interest of a partner who has the power, as provided in Section 704, to grant the assignee the right to become a limited partner, upon the exercise of that power and compliance with any conditions limiting the grant or exercise of the power.

§ 302. Voting

Subject to Section 303, the partnership agreement may grant to all or a specified group of the limited partners the right to vote (on a per capita or other basis) upon any matter.

Comment

Section 302 first appeared in the 1976 Act, and must be read together with subdivision (b)(6) of Section 303. Although the 1916 Act did not speak specifically of the voting powers of limited partners, it was not uncommon for partnership agreements to grant such powers to limited partners. Section 302 is designed only to make it clear that the partnership agreement may grant such power to limited partners. If such powers are granted to limited partners beyond the "safe harbor" of subdivision (6) or (8) of Section 303(b), a court may (but of course need not) hold that, under the circumstances, the limited partners have participated in "control of the business" within the meaning of Section 303(a). Section 303(c) makes clear that the exercise of powers beyond the ambit of Section 303(b) is not ipso facto to be taken as taking part in the control of the business.

§ 303. Liability to Third Parties

(a) Except as provided in subsection (d), a limited partner is not liable for the obligations of a limited partnership unless he [or she] is also a general partner or, in addition to the exercise of his [or her] rights and powers as a limited partner, he [or she] participates in the control of the business. However, if the limited partner participates in the control of the business, he [or she] is liable only to persons who transact business with the limited partnership reasonably believing, based upon the limited partner's conduct, that the limited partner is a general partner.

(b) A limited partner does not participate in the control of the business within the meaning of subsection (a) solely by doing one or more of the following:

(1) being a contractor for or an agent or employee of the limited partnership or of a general partner or being an officer, director, or shareholder of a general partner that is a corporation;

(2) consulting with and advising a general partner with respect to the business of the limited partnership;

(3) acting as surety for the limited partnership or guaranteeing or assuming one or more specific obligations of the limited partnership;

(4) taking any action required or permitted by law to bring or pursue a derivative action in the right of the limited partnership;

(5) requesting or attending a meeting of partners;

(6) proposing, approving, or disapproving, by voting or otherwise, one or more of the following matters:

(i) the dissolution and winding up of the limited partnership;

(ii) the sale, exchange, lease, mortgage, pledge, or other transfer of all or substantially all of the assets of the limited partnership;

(iii) the incurrence of indebtedness by the limited partnership other than in the ordinary course of its business;

(iv) a change in the nature of the business;

(v) the admission or removal of a general partner;

(vi) the admission or removal of a limited partner;

(vii) a transaction involving an actual or potential conflict of interest between a general partner and the limited partnership or the limited partners;

(viii) an amendment to the partnership agreement or certificate of limited partnership; or

(ix) matters related to the business of the limited partnership not otherwise enumerated in this subsection (b), which the partnership agreement states in writing may be subject to the approval or disapproval of limited partners;

(7) winding up the limited partnership pursuant to Section 803; or

(8) exercising any right or power permitted to limited partners under this [Act] and not specifically enumerated in this subsection (b).

(c) The enumeration in subsection (b) does not mean that the possession or exercise of any other powers by a limited partner constitutes participation by him [or her] in the business of the limited partnership.

(d) A limited partner who knowingly permits his [or her] name to be used in the name of the limited partnership, except under circumstances permitted by Section 102(2), is liable to creditors who extend credit to the limited partnership without actual knowledge that the limited partner is not a general partner.

Comment

... The second sentence of Section 303(a) .... was adopted partly because of the difficulty of determining when the "control" line has been overstepped, but also (and more importantly) because of a determination that it is not sound public policy to hold a limited partner who is not also a general partner liable for the obligations of the partnership except to persons who have done business with the limited partnership reasonably believing, based on the limited partner's conduct, that he is a general partner. Paragraph (b) is intended to provide a "safe harbor" by enumerating certain activities which a limited partner may carry on for the partnership without being deemed to have taken part in control of the business. This "safe harbor" list has been expanded beyond that set out in the 1976 Act to reflect case law and statutory developments and more clearly to assure that limited partners are not subjected to general liability where such liability is inappropriate. Paragraph (d) is derived from Section 5 of the 1916 Act, but adds as a condition to the limited partner's liability the requirement that a limited partner must have knowingly permitted his name to be used in the name of the limited partnership.

§ 304. Person Erroneously Believing Himself [or Herself] Limited Partner

(a) Except as provided in subsection (b), a person who makes a contribution to a business enterprise and erroneously but in good faith believes that he [or she] has become a limited partner in the enterprise is not a general partner in the enterprise and is not bound by its obligations by reason of making the contribution, receiving distributions from the enterprise, or exercising any rights of a limited partner, if, on ascertaining the mistake, he [or she]:

(1) causes an appropriate certificate of limited partnership or a certificate of amendment to be executed and filed; or

(2) withdraws from future equity participation in the enterprise by executing and filing in the office of the Secretary of State a certificate declaring withdrawal under this section.

(b) A person who makes a contribution of the kind described in subsection (a) is liable as a general partner to any third party who transacts business with the enterprise (i) before the person withdraws and an appropriate certificate is filed to show withdrawal, or (ii) before an appropriate certificate is filed to show that he [or she] is not a general partner, but in either case only if the third party actually believed in good faith that the person was a general partner at the time of the transaction.

§ 305. Information

Each limited partner has the right to:

(1) inspect and copy any of the partnership records required to be maintained by Section 105; and

(2) obtain from the general partners from time to time upon reasonable demand (i) true and full information regarding the state of the business and financial condition of the limited partnership, (ii) promptly after becoming available, a copy of the limited partnership's federal, state, and local income tax returns for each year, and (iii) other information regarding the affairs of the limited partnership as is just and reasonable.

ARTICLE 4

GENERAL PARTNERS

§ 401. Admission of Additional General Partners

After the filing of a limited partnership's original certificate of limited partnership, additional general partners may be admitted as provided in writing in the partnership agreement or, if the partnership agreement does not provide in writing for the admission of additional general partners, with the written consent of all partners.

§ 402. Events of Withdrawal

Except as approved by the specific written consent of all partners at the time, a person ceases to be a general partner of a limited partnership upon the happening of any of the following events:

(1) the general partner withdraws from the limited partnership as provided in Section 602;

(2) the general partner ceases to be a member of the limited partnership as provided in Section 702;

(3) the general partner is removed as a general partner in accordance with the partnership agreement;

341

(4) unless otherwise provided in writing in the partnership agreement, the general partner: (i) makes an assignment for the benefit of creditors; (ii) files a voluntary petition in bankruptcy; (iii) is adjudicated a bankrupt or insolvent; (iv) files a petition or answer seeking for himself [or herself] any reorganization, arrangement, composition, readjustment, liquidation, dissolution, or similar relief under any statute, law, or regulation; (v) files an answer or other pleading admitting or failing to contest the material allegations of a petition filed against him [or her] in any proceeding of this nature; or (vi) seeks, consents to, or acquiesces in the appointment of a trustee, receiver, or liquidator of the general partner or of all or any substantial part of his [or her] properties;

(5) unless otherwise provided in writing in the partnership agreement, [120] days after the commencement of any proceeding against the general partner seeking reorganization, arrangement, composition, readjustment, liquidation, dissolution, or similar relief under any statute, law, or regulation, the proceeding has not been dismissed, or if within [90] days after the appointment without his [or her] consent or acquiescence of a trustee, receiver, or liquidator of the general partner or of all or any substantial part of his [or her] properties, the appointment is not vacated or stayed or within [90] days after the expiration of any such stay, the appointment is not vacated;

(6) in the case of a general partner who is a natural person,

(i) his [or her] death; or

(ii) the entry of an order by a court of competent jurisdiction adjudicating him [or her] incompetent to manage his [or her] person or his [or her] estate;

(7) in the case of a general partner who is acting as a general partner by virtue of being a trustee of a trust, the termination of the trust (but not merely the substitution of a new trustee);

(8) in the case of a general partner that is a separate partnership, the dissolution and commencement of winding up of the separate partnership;

(9) in the case of a general partner that is a corporation, the filing of a certificate of dissolution, or its equivalent, for the corporation or the revocation of its charter; or

(10) in the case of an estate, the distribution by the fiduciary of the estate's entire interest in the partnership.

Comment

Section 402 expands considerably the provisions of Section 20 of the 1916 Act, which provided for dissolution in the event of the retirement, death or insanity of a general partner. Subdivisions (1), (2) and (3) recognize that the general partner's agency relationship is terminable at will, although it may result in a breach of the partnership agreement giving rise to an action for damages. Subdivisions (4) and (5) reflect a judgment that, unless the limited partners agree otherwise, they ought to have the power to rid themselves of a general partner who is in such dire financial straits that he is the subject of proceedings under the National Bankruptcy Code or a similar provision of law. Subdivisions (6) through (10) simply elaborate on the notion of death in the case of a general partner who is not a natural person. . . .

§ 403. General Powers and Liabilities

(a) Except as provided in this [Act] or in the partnership agreement, a general partner of a limited partnership has the rights and powers and is subject to the restrictions of a partner in a partnership without limited partners.

(b) Except as provided in this [Act], a general partner of a limited partnership has the liabilities of a partner in a partnership without limited partners to persons other than the partnership and the other partners. Except as provided in this [Act] or in the partnership agreement, a general partner of a limited partnership has the liabilities of a partner in a partnership without limited partners to the partnership and to the other partners.

§ 404. Contributions by General Partner

A general partner of a limited partnership may make contributions to the partnership and share in the profits and losses of, and in distributions from, the limited partnership as a general partner. A general partner also may make contributions to and share in profits, losses, and distributions as a limited partner. A person who is both a general partner and a limited partner has the rights and powers, and is subject to the restrictions and liabilities, of a general partner and, except as provided in the partnership agreement, also has the powers, and is subject to the restrictions, of a limited partner to the extent of his [or her] participation in the partnership as a limited partner.

§ 405. Voting

The partnership agreement may grant to all or certain identified general partners the right to vote (on a per capita or any other basis), separately or with all or any class of the limited partners, on any matter.

ARTICLE 5

FINANCE

§ 501. Form of Contribution

The contribution of a partner may be in cash, property, or services rendered, or a promissory note or other obligation to contribute cash or property or to perform services.

§ 502. Liability for Contribution

(a) A promise by a limited partner to contribute to the limited partnership is not enforceable unless set out in a writing signed by the limited partner.

(b) Except as provided in the partnership agreement, a partner is obligated to the limited partnership to perform any enforceable promise to contribute cash or property or to perform services, even if he [or she] is unable to perform because of death, disability, or any other reason. If a partner does not make the required contribution of property or services, he [or she] is obligated at the option of the limited partnership to contribute cash equal to that portion of the value, as stated in the partnership records required to be kept pursuant to Section 105, of the stated contribution which has not been made.

(c) Unless otherwise provided in the partnership agreement, the obligation of a partner to make a contribution or return money or other property paid or distributed in violation of this [Act] may be compromised only by consent of all partners. Notwithstanding the compromise, a creditor of a limited partnership who extends credit or otherwise acts in reliance on that obligation after the partner signs a writing which reflects the obligation, and before the amendment or cancellation thereof to reflect the compromise, may enforce the original obligation.

§ 503. Sharing of Profits and Losses

The profits and losses of a limited partnership shall be allocated among the partners, and among classes of partners, in the manner provided in writing in the partnership agreement. If the partnership agreement does not so provide in writing, profits and losses shall be allocated on the basis of the value, as stated in the partnership records required to be kept pursuant to Section 105, of the contributions made by each partner to the extent they have been received by the partnership and have not been returned.

§ 504. Sharing of Distributions

Distributions of cash or other assets of a limited partnership shall be allocated among the partners and among classes of partners in the manner provided in writing in the partnership agreement. If the partnership agreement does not so provide in writing, distributions shall be made on the basis of the value, as stated in the partnership records required to be kept pursuant to Section 105, of the contributions made by each partner to the extent they have been received by the partnership and have not been returned.

ARTICLE 6

DISTRIBUTIONS AND WITHDRAWAL

§ 601. Interim Distributions

Except as provided in this Article, a partner is entitled to receive distributions from a limited partnership before his [or her] withdrawal from the limited partnership and before the dissolution and winding up thereof to the extent and at the times or upon the happening of the events specified in the partnership agreement.

§ 602. Withdrawal of General Partner

A general partner may withdraw from a limited partnership at any time by giving written notice to the other partners, but if the withdrawal violates the partnership agreement, the limited partnership may recover from the withdrawing general partner damages for breach of the partnership agreement and offset the damages against the amount otherwise distributable to him [or her].

§ 603. Withdrawal of Limited Partner

A limited partner may withdraw from a limited partnership at the time or upon the happening of events specified in writing in the partnership agreement. If the agreement does not specify in writing the time or the events upon the happening of which a limited partner may withdraw or a definite time for the dissolution and winding up of the limited partnership, a limited partner may withdraw upon not less than six months' prior written notice to each general partner at his [other] address on the books of the limited partnership at its office in this State.

§ 604. Distribution Upon Withdrawal

Except as provided in this Article, upon withdrawal any withdrawing partner is entitled to receive any distribution to which he [or she] is entitled under the partnership agreement and, if not otherwise provided in the agreement, he [or she] is entitled to receive, within a reasonable time after withdrawal, the fair value of his [or her] interest in the limited partnership as of the date of withdrawal based upon his [or her] right to share in distributions from the limited partnership.

§ 605. Distribution in Kind

Except as provided in writing in the partnership agreement, a partner, regardless of the nature of his [or her] contribution, has no right to demand and receive any distribution from a limited partnership in any form other than cash. Except as provided in writing in the partnership agreement, a partner may not be compelled to accept a distribution of any asset in kind from a limited partnership to the extent that the percentage of the asset distributed to him [or her] exceeds a percentage of that asset which is equal to the percentage in which he [or she] shares in distributions from the limited partnership.

§ 606. Right to Distribution

At the time a partner becomes entitled to receive a distribution, he [or she] has the status of, and is entitled to all remedies available to, a creditor of the limited partnership with respect to the distribution.

§ 607. Limitations on Distribution

A partner may not receive a distribution from a limited partnership to the extent that, after giving effect to the distribution, all liabilities of the limited partnership, other than liabilities to partners on account of their partnership interests, exceed the fair value of the partnership assets.

§ 608. Liability Upon Return of Contribution

(a) If a partner has received the return of any part of his [or her] contribution without violation of the partnership agreement or this [Act], he [or she] is liable to the limited partnership for a period of one year thereafter for the amount of the returned contribution, but only to the extent necessary to discharge the limited partnership's liabilities to creditors who extended credit to the limited partnership during the period the contribution was held by the partnership.

(b) If a partner has received the return of any part of his [or her] contribution in violation of the partnership agreement or this [Act], he [or she] is liable to the limited partnership for a period of six years thereafter for the amount of the contribution wrongfully returned.

(c) A partner receives a return of his [or her] contribution to the extent that a distribution to him [or her] reduces his [or her] share of the fair value of the net assets of the limited partnership below the value, as set forth in the partnership records required to be kept pursuant to Section 105, of his contribution which has not been distributed to him [or her].

ARTICLE 7

ASSIGNMENT OF PARTNERSHIP INTERESTS

§ 701. Nature of Partnership Interest

A partnership interest is personal property.

§ 702. Assignment of Partnership Interest

Except as provided in the partnership agreement, a partnership interest is assignable in whole or in part. An assignment of a partnership interest does not dissolve a limited partnership or entitle the assignee to become or to exercise any rights of a partner. An assignment entitles the assignee to receive, to the extent assigned, only the distribution to which the assignor would be entitled. Except as provided in the partnership agreement, a partner ceases to be a partner upon assignment of all his [or her] partnership interest.

§ 703. Rights of Creditor

On application to a court of competent jurisdiction by any judgment creditor of a partner, the court may charge the partnership interest of the partner with payment of the unsatisfied amount of the judgment with interest. To the extent so charged, the judgment creditor has only the rights of an assignee of the partnership interest. This [Act] does not deprive any partner of the benefit of any exemption laws applicable to his [or her] partnership interest.

§ 704. Right of Assignee to Become Limited Partner

(a) An assignee of a partnership interest, including an assignee of a general partner, may become a limited partner if and to the extent that (i) the assignor gives the assignee that right in accordance with authority described in the partnership agreement, or (ii) all other partners consent.

(b) An assignee who has become a limited partner has, to the extent assigned, the rights and powers, and is subject to the restrictions and liabilities, of a limited partner under the partnership agreement and this [Act]. An assignee who becomes a limited partner also is liable for the obligations of his [or her] assignor to make and return contributions as provided in Articles 5 and 6. However, the assignee is not obligated for liabilities unknown to the assignee at the time he [or she] became a limited partner.

(c) If an assignee of a partnership interest becomes a limited partner, the assignor is not released from his [or her] liability to the limited partnership under Sections 207 and 502.

§ 705. Power of Estate of Deceased or Incompetent Partner

If a partner who is an individual dies or a court of competent jurisdiction adjudges him [or her] to be incompetent to manage his [or her] person or his [or her] property, the partner's executor, administrator, guardian, conservator, or other legal representative may exercise all of the partner's rights for the purpose of settling his [or her] estate or administering his [or her] property, including any power the partner had to give an assignee the right to become a limited partner. If a partner is a corporation, trust, or other entity and is dissolved or terminated, the powers of that partner may be exercised by its legal representative or successor.

ARTICLE 8

DISSOLUTION

§ 801. Nonjudicial Dissolution

A limited partnership is dissolved and its affairs shall be wound up upon the happening of the first to occur of the following:

(1) at the time specified in the certificate of limited partnership;

(2) upon the happening of events specified in writing in the partnership agreement;

(3) written consent of all partners;

(4) an event of withdrawal of a general partner unless at the time there is at least one other general partner and the written provisions of the

partnership agreement permit the business of the limited partnership to be carried on by the remaining general partner and that partner does so, but the limited partnership is not dissolved and is not required to be wound up by reason of any event of withdrawal, if, within 90 days after the withdrawal, all partners agree in writing to continue the business of the limited partnership and to the appointment of one or more additional general partners if necessary or desired; or

(5) entry of a decree of judicial dissolution under Section 802.

§ 802. Judicial Dissolution

On application by or for a partner the [designate the appropriate court] court may decree dissolution of a limited partnership whenever it is not reasonably practicable to carry on the business in conformity with the partnership agreement.

§ 803. Winding Up

Except as provided in the partnership agreement, the general partners who have not wrongfully dissolved a limited partnership or, if none, the limited partners, may wind up the limited partnership's affairs; but the [designate the appropriate court] court may wind up the limited partnership's affairs upon application of any partner, his [or her] legal representative, or assignee.

§ 804. Distribution of Assets

Upon the winding up of a limited partnership, the assets shall be distributed as follows:

(1) to creditors, including partners who are creditors, to the extent permitted by law, in satisfaction of liabilities of the limited partnership other than liabilities for distributions to partners under Section 601 or 604;

(2) except as provided in the partnership agreement, to partners and former partners in satisfaction of liabilities for distributions under Section 601 or 604; and

(3) except as provided in the partnership agreement, to partners first for the return of their contributions and secondly respecting their partnership interests, in the proportions in which the partners share in distributions. . . .

ARTICLE 10

DERIVATIVE ACTIONS

§ 1001. Right of Action

A limited partner may bring an action in the right of a limited partnership to recover a judgment in its favor if general partners with authority to do so have refused to bring the action or if an effort to cause those general partners to bring the action is not likely to succeed.

§ 1002. Proper Plaintiff

In a derivative action, the plaintiff must be a partner at the time of bringing the action and (i) must have been a partner at the time of the transaction of which he [or she] complains or (ii) his [or her] status as a partner must have devolved upon him [or her] by operation of law or pursuant to the terms of the partnership agreement from a person who was a partner at the time of the transaction.

§ 1003. Pleading

In a derivative action, the complaint shall set forth with particularity the effort of the plaintiff to secure initiation of the action by a general partner or the reasons for not making the effort.

§ 1004. Expenses

If a derivative action is successful, in whole or in part, or if anything is received by the plaintiff as a result of a judgment, compromise, or settlement of an action or claim, the court may award the plaintiff reasonable expenses, including reasonable attorney's fees, and shall direct him [or her] to remit to the limited partnership the remainder of those proceeds received by him [or her].

ARTICLE 11

MISCELLANEOUS

§ 1105. Rules for Cases Not Provided for in This [Act]

In any case not provided for in this [Act] the provisions of the Uniform Partnership Act govern.

RE–RULPA
PROPOSED REVISION OF REVISED
UNIFORM LIMITED PARTNERSHIP
ACT
(March 2000 Draft)

NOTE: The proposed revision of RULPA—sometimes known as Re–RULPA, is scheduled for first reading by the National Conference of Commissioners on Uniform State Laws in 2000, and for possible final approval in 2001.

TABLE OF CONTENTS

351

Prefatory Note

Re-RULPA's Overall Approach

Re–RULPA is a "stand alone" act, "de-linked" from the general partnership act. To be able to stand alone, Re–RULPA incorporates many provisions from RUPA and some from ULLCA. As a result, Re–RULPA is far longer and more complex than RULPA.

353

Re–RULPA is being drafted for a business world in which limited liability partnerships and limited liability companies can meet many of the needs formerly met by limited partnerships. Re–RULPA therefore targets two types of enterprises that seem largely beyond the scope of LLPs and LLCs: (i) sophisticated, manager-entrenched commercial deals whose participants commit for the long term, and (ii) estate planning arrangements (family limited partnerships). Re–RULPA accordingly assumes that, more often than not, people utilizing the act will want:

- strong centralized management, strongly entrenched, and
- passive investors with little right to exit the entity

Re–RULPA's rules, and particularly its default rules, have been designed to reflect these assumptions. . . .

[ARTICLE] 1
GENERAL PROVISIONS

SECTION 101. SHORT TITLE. This [Act] may be cited as the Revised Uniform Limited Partnership Act (20___).

SECTION 102. DEFINITIONS. In this [Act]:

(1) "Business" means any lawful activity, whether or not carried on for profit.

(2) "Certificate of limited partnership" means the certificate referred to in Section 201 and the certificate as amended or restated.

(3) "Contribution" means any benefit provided by a person to a limited partnership in order to become a partner or in the person's capacity as a partner.

(4) "Debtor in bankruptcy" means a person who is the subject of:

(A) an order for relief under Title 11 of the United States Code or a comparable order under a successor statute of general application; or

(B) a comparable order under federal, state, or foreign law governing insolvency.

(5) "Designated office" means:

(A) with respect to a limited partnership, the office that a limited partnership is required to maintain under Section 114; and

(B) with respect to a foreign limited partnership, its principal office.

(6) "Distribution" means a transfer of money or other property from a limited partnership to a partner in the partner's capacity as a partner or to a transferee on account of a transferable interest owned by the transferee.

(7) "Domestic limited partnership" means a limited partnership formed under this [Act]. The term includes a limited liability limited partnership. The term does not include a foreign limited partnership or foreign limited liability limited partnership.

354 (8) "Entity" means a person other than an individual.

(9) "Foreign limited partnership" means a partnership formed under the laws of a jurisdiction other than this State and required by those laws to have as partners one or more general partners and one or more limited partners. The term includes a foreign limited liability limited partnership.

(10) "Foreign limited liability limited partnership" means a foreign limited partnership whose general partners are protected from liability for the obligations of the foreign limited partnership under a provision similar to Section 404(c).

(11) "General partner" means:

(A) with respect to a domestic limited partnership, a person who has been admitted to a limited partnership as a general partner under Section 401; and

(B) with respect to a foreign limited partnership, a person that has rights, powers and obligations similar to those of a general partner in a domestic limited partnership.

(12) "Limited liability limited partnership" means a limited partnership whose certificate of limited partnership does not include a statement made pursuant to Section 404(b).

(13) "Limited partner" means:

(A) with respect to a domestic limited partnership, a person who has been admitted to a limited partnership as a limited partner under Section 301; and

(B) with respect to a foreign limited partnership, a person that has rights, powers and obligations similar to those of a limited partner in a domestic limited partnership.

(14) "Limited partnership", except in the phrase "foreign limited partnership", means a domestic limited partnership.

(15) "Ownership interest" means an owner's proprietary interest in a business organization.

(16) "Partner" means a limited or general partner.

(17) "Partnership agreement" means a valid agreement, written or oral, of the partners as to the affairs of a limited partnership and the conduct of its business.

(18) "Person" means an individual, corporation, business trust, estate, trust, partnership, limited liability company, association, joint venture, government, governmental subdivision, agency, or instrumentality, or any other legal or commercial entity.

(19) "Principal office" means the office where the principal executive office of a domestic or foreign limited partnership is located, whether or not the office is located in this State.

(20) "Record" means information that is inscribed on a tangible medium or that is stored in an electronic or other medium and is retrievable in perceivable form.

(21) "Required records" means the records that a limited partnership is required to maintain under Section 106.

(22) "Sign" means to identify a record, whether in writing, electronically, or otherwise, by means of a signature, mark, or other symbol, with intent to authenticate the record.

(23) "State" means a State of the United States, the District of Columbia, the Commonwealth of Puerto Rico, or any territory or insular possession subject to the jurisdiction of the United States.

(24) "Transfer" includes an assignment, conveyance, deed, bill of sale, lease, mortgage, security interest, encumbrance, and gift.

(25) "Transferable interest" means a partner's share of the profits and losses of the limited partnership and the partner's right to receive distributions.

(26) "Transferee" means a person to whom all or part of a transferable interest has been transferred, whether or not the transferor is a partner.

SECTION 103. KNOWLEDGE AND NOTICE.

(a) A person knows a fact if the person has actual knowledge of it.

(b) Except as otherwise provided in subsections (c) and (d), a person has notice of a fact if the person:

(1) knows of it;

(2) has received a notification of it; or

(3) has reason to know it exists from all of the facts known to the person at the time in question

(c) Subject to subsection (d), a certificate of limited partnership on file in the [office of the Secretary of State] is notice that the partnership is a limited partnership and the persons designated in the certificate as general partners are general partners but is not notice of any other fact.

(d) A person has notice:

(1) of another person's dissociation as a general partner, 90 days after the effective date of an amendment to the certificate of limited partnership which states that the other person has dissociated or 90 days after the effective date of a statement of dissociation pertaining to that other person, whichever occurs first;

(2) of a limited partnership's dissolution, 90 days after the effective date of an amendment to the certificate of limited partnership stating that the limited partnership is dissolved;

(3) of a limited partnership's termination, 90 days after the effective date of a statement of termination;

(4) of a limited partnership's conversion under [Article] 11[,] 90 days after the effective date of the articles of conversion; and

(5) of a merger under [Article] 11, 90 days after the effective date of the articles of merger.

(e) A person notifies or gives a notification to another by taking steps reasonably required to inform the other person in ordinary course, whether or not the other person learns of it.

(f) A person receives a notification when the notification:

(1) comes to the person's attention; or

(2) is duly delivered at the person's place of business or at any other place held out by the person as a place for receiving communications.

(g) Except as otherwise provided in subsection (h), an entity knows, has notice, or receives a notification of a fact for purposes of a particular transaction when the individual conducting the transaction for the entity knows, has notice, or receives a notification of the fact, or in any event when the fact would have been brought to the individual's attention if the entity had exercised reasonable diligence. An entity exercises reasonable diligence if it maintains reasonable routines for communicating significant information to the individual conducting the transaction for the entity and there is reasonable compliance with the routines. Reasonable diligence does not require an individual acting for the entity to communicate information unless the communication is part of the individual's regular duties or the individual has reason to know of the transaction and that the transaction would be materially affected by the information.

(h) A general partner's knowledge, notice, or receipt of a notification of a fact relating to the limited partnership is effective immediately as knowledge by, notice to, or receipt of a notification by the limited partnership, except in the case of a fraud on the limited partnership committed by or with the consent of the general partner. A limited partner's knowledge, notice, or receipt of a notification of a fact relating to the limited partnership is not effective as knowledge by, notice to, or receipt of a notification by the limited partnership.

SECTION 104. NATURE AND DURATION OF ENTITY; WHEN PARTNER PROPER PARTY.

(a) A limited partnership is an entity distinct from its partners.

(b) A partner is not a proper party to a proceeding by or against a limited partnership except when:

(1) an object of the proceeding is to determine or enforce a partner's right against or liability to the limited partnership;

(2) the proceeding includes a claim that the partner is personally liable under Section 404 or 405 or on some basis not dependent on the partner's status as partner; or

(3) the partner is bringing a derivative action under [Article] 10.

357

(c) A limited partnership remains the same entity regardless of whether its certificate of limited partnership includes or ceases to include a statement made under Section 404(b).

(d) A limited partnership has a perpetual duration.

SECTION 105. PURPOSE AND POWERS.

(a) A limited partnership may be organized under this [Act] for any lawful purpose.

(b) A limited partnership has the same powers as an individual to do all things necessary or convenient to carry on its business, including the power to:

(1) sue and be sued and defend in its own name, including an action against a partner for a breach of the partnership agreement, or for the violation of a duty to the partnership, causing harm to the partnership;

(2) purchase, receive, lease, or otherwise acquire, and own, hold, improve, use, and otherwise deal with real or personal property, or any legal or equitable interest in property, wherever located;

(3) sell, convey, mortgage, grant a security interest in, lease, exchange, and otherwise encumber or dispose of all or any part of its property;

(4) purchase, receive, subscribe for, or otherwise acquire, own, hold, vote, use, sell, mortgage, lend, grant a security interest in, or otherwise dispose of and deal in and with, ownership interests in or obligations of any other entity;

(5) make contracts and guarantees, incur liabilities, borrow money, issue its notes, bonds, and other obligations, which may be convertible into or include the option to purchase other securities of the limited partnership, and secure any of its obligations by a mortgage on or a security interest in any of its property, franchises, or income;

(6) lend money, invest and reinvest its money, and receive and hold real and personal property as security for repayment;

(7) be a promoter, partner, member, associate, or manager of any partnership, joint venture, trust, or other entity;

(8) conduct its business, locate offices, and exercise the powers granted by this [Act] within or without this State;

(9) appoint officers, employees, and agents of the limited partnership, define their duties, fix their compensation, and lend them money and credit;

(10) pay pensions and establish pension plans, pension trusts, profit sharing plans, bonus plans, option plans, and benefit or incentive plans for any or all of its current or former partners, officers, employees, and agents;

(11) make donations for the public welfare or for charitable, scientific, or educational purposes; and

(12) make payments or donations, or do any other act, not inconsistent with law, that furthers the business of the limited partnership.

SECTION 106. GOVERNING LAW. The law of this State governs relations among the partners and between the partners and the limited partnership and the liability of partners for an obligation of a limited partnership.

SECTION 107. SUPPLEMENTAL PRINCIPLES OF LAW.

(a) Unless displaced by particular provisions of this [Act], the principles of law and equity supplement this [Act].

(b) If an obligation to pay interest arises under this [Act] and the rate is not specified, the rate is that specified in [applicable statute].

SECTION 108. NAME.

(a) The name of a limited partnership must contain "limited liability limited partnership" or the abbreviation "LLLP" or "L.L.L.P." and may contain the name of any partner. Subject to Section 905, the same requirements apply to the name of a foreign limited partnership authorized to transact business in this State.

(b) Unless authorized by subsections (c) and (d), the name of a limited partnership and, subject to Section 905, of a foreign limited partnership authorized to transact business in this State, must be distinguishable upon the records of the [Secretary of State] from:

(1) the name of any entity incorporated, organized, or authorized to transact business in this State; and

(2) any name reserved or registered under Section 109 or 906 or [insert citations to other State laws allowing the reservation or registration of business names, including fictitious name statutes].

(c) A domestic or foreign limited partnership may apply to the [Secretary of State] for authorization to use a name that is not distinguishable upon the records of the [Secretary of State] from one or more of the names described in subsection (b). The [Secretary of State] shall authorize use of the name applied for if, as to each conflicting name:

(1) the present user, registrant, or owner of the conflicting name consents to the use in a signed record and submits an undertaking in form satisfactory to the [Secretary of State] to change the conflicting name to a name that is distinguishable upon the records of the [Secretary of State] from the name applied for and from all of the names described in subsection (b); or

(2) the applicant delivers to the [Secretary of State] a certified copy of the final judgment of a court of competent jurisdiction establishing the applicant's right to use in this State the name applied for.

(d) A domestic or foreign limited partnership may use a name, including a fictitious name, shown upon the records of the [Secretary of State] as being used by another entity, if the domestic or foreign limited partnership proposing to use the name:

(1) has merged with the other entity;

(2) has been formed by reorganization with the other entity;

(3) has been converted from the other entity; or

(4) has acquired substantially all of the assets, including the name, of the other entity.

SECTION 109. RESERVATION OF NAME.

(a) Subject to Section 108, the exclusive right to the use of a name may be reserved by:

(1) a person intending to organize a limited partnership under this [Act] and to adopt that name;

(2) a domestic limited partnership or any foreign limited partnership authorized to transact business in this State which, in either case, intends to adopt that name;

(3) a foreign limited partnership intending to obtain a certificate of authority to transact business in this State and adopt that name;

(4) a person intending to organize a foreign limited partnership and intending to have it obtain a certificate of authority to transact business in this State and adopt that name;

(5) a foreign limited partnership formed under the name: and

(6) a foreign limited partnership formed under a name that does not comply with Section 108(a), but the named reserved under this paragraph may differ from the foreign limited partnership's name only as necessary to comply with Section 108(a).

(b) The reservation must be made by filing with the [Secretary of State] an application, signed by the applicant, to reserve a specified name. If the [Secretary of State] finds that the name is available for use by a domestic or foreign limited partnership, the [Secretary of State] shall reserve the name for the exclusive use of the applicant for a period of 120 days. An applicant who has so reserved a name may reserve the same name for additional 120–day periods. A person having a current reservation for a name may not file for another 120–day period pertaining to the same name until 90 days have elapsed in the current reservation. The right to the exclusive use of a reserved name may be transferred to any other person by filing in the [office of the Secretary of State] a notice of the transfer, signed by the applicant for whom the name was reserved and specifying the name and address of the person to whom the transfer was made.

SECTION 110. EFFECT OF PARTNERSHIP AGREEMENT; NONWAIVABLE PROVISIONS.

(a) Except as otherwise provided in subsection (b), the partnership agreement governs relations among the partners and between the partners and the partnership. To the extent the partnership agreement does not otherwise provide, this [Act] governs relations among the partners and between the partners and the partnership.

(b) The partnership agreement may not:

(1) vary the law applicable to a limited partnership under Section 106;

(2) vary the rights and duties under Section 204;

(3) unreasonably restrict the right to information under Sections 305 and 407, but the partnership agreement may impose reasonable limitations on the availability and use of information obtained under those sections and may define appropriate remedies, including liquidated damages, for a breach of any reasonable limitation on use;

(4) eliminate the duty of loyalty under Section 408, but the partnership agreement may:

(A) identify specific types or categories of activities that do not violate the duty of loyalty, if not manifestly unreasonable; and

(B) specify the number or percentage of partners or disinterested general partners that may authorize or ratify, after full disclosure of all material facts, a specific act or transaction that otherwise would violate the duty of loyalty;

(5) unreasonably reduce the duty of care under Section 408(c);

(6) eliminate the obligation of good faith and fair dealing under Sections 306(c) and 408(d), but the partnership agreement may prescribe the standards by which the performance of the obligation is to be measured, if the standards are not manifestly unreasonable;

(7) vary the power of a person to dissociate as a general partner under Section 604, except to require that the notice under Section 603(1) be in writing;

(8) vary the right of a court to expel a partner in the events specified in Sections 601(5) and 603(b)(5);

(9) vary the right of a court to decree dissolution in the circumstances specified in Section 802;

(10) vary the requirement to wind up the partnership's business as specified in Section 803(a);

(11) unreasonably restrict the right to bring a derivative action under [Article] 10;

(12) restrict the right of a partner to approve a merger or conversion under Section 1110;

(13) restrict rights of a third party under this [Act].

SECTION 111. REQUIRED RECORDS.

(a) A limited partnership shall maintain at its designated office the following required records:

(1) a current list showing the full name and last known address of each partner, separately identifying the general partners, in alphabetical order, and the limited partners, in alphabetical order;

(2) a copy of the certificate of limited partnership and all amendments to the certificate, together with signed copies of any powers of attorney pursuant to which any certificate or amendment has been signed;

(3) a copy of any filed articles of conversion or merger;

(4) a copy of the limited partnership's federal, state, and local income tax returns and reports, if any, for the three most recent years;

(5) a copy of any written partnership agreements and any written amendments to any of those agreements and of any financial statements of the limited partnership for the three most recent years;

(6) a copy of the three most recent annual reports delivered by the limited partnership to the [Secretary of State] pursuant to Section 210;

(7) a copy of any record made by the limited partnership during the past three years of any consents given by or votes taken of any partner pursuant to this [Act] or the partnership agreement; and

(8) unless contained in a written partnership agreement, a writing setting out:

(A) the amount of cash, and a description and statement of the agreed value of the other benefits, contributed by each partner and which each partner has agreed to contribute;

(B) the times at which or events on the happening of which any additional contributions agreed to be made by each partner are to be made;

(C) for any person who is both a general partner and a limited partner, a specification of what transferable interest the person owns in each capacity; and

(D) any events upon the happening of which the limited partnership is to be dissolved and its affairs wound up.

(b) Sections 305 and 407 govern access to the records required by this section.

SECTION 112. BUSINESS TRANSACTIONS OF PARTNER WITH PARTNERSHIP. A partner may lend money to and transact other business with the limited partnership and, subject to other law, has the same rights and obligations with respect thereto as a person who is not a partner.

SECTION 113. DUAL CAPACITY. A person may be both a general partner and a limited partner. A person who is both a general and limited partner has the rights, powers, duties, and obligations provided by this [Act] and the partnership agreement in each of those capacities. When the person acts as a general partner, the person is subject to the obligations and restrictions under this [Act] and the partnership agreement for general partners. When the person acts as a limited partner, the person is subject to the obligations and restrictions under this [Act] and the partnership agreement for limited partners.

SECTION 114. OFFICE AND AGENT FOR SERVICE OF PROCESS.

(a) A limited partnership shall designate and continuously maintain in this State:

    (1) an office, which need not be a place of its business in this State; and

    (2) an agent for service of process.

(b) A foreign limited partnership shall designate and continuously maintain in this State an agent for service of process.

(c) An agent for service of process must be an individual resident of this State, a domestic entity, or a foreign entity authorized to do business in this State.

SECTION 115. CHANGE OF DESIGNATED OFFICE OR AGENT FOR SERVICE OF PROCESS. A limited partnership or foreign limited partnership may change its designated office, agent for service of process, or the address of its agent for service of process, by delivering to the [Secretary of State] for filing a statement of change which sets forth:

    (1) the name of the domestic or foreign limited partnership;

    (2) the street address of its current designated office;

    (3) if the current designated office is to be changed, the street address of the new designated office;

    (4) the name and address of its current agent for service of process; and

    (5) if the current agent for service of process or street address of that agent is to be changed, the new address or the name and street address of the new agent for service of process.

SECTION 116. RESIGNATION OF AGENT FOR SERVICE OF PROCESS.

(a) An agent for service of process of a limited partnership or foreign limited partnership may resign by delivering to the [Secretary of State] for filing a record of the statement of resignation.

(b) After filing a statement of resignation, the [Secretary of State] shall mail a copy to the designated office and another copy to the limited partnership at its principal office if the address of that office appears in the records of the [Secretary of State].

(c) An agency is terminated on the 31st day after the statement is filed in the [office of the Secretary of State].

SECTION 117. SERVICE OF PROCESS.

(a) An agent for service of process appointed by a limited partnership or a foreign limited partnership is an agent of the limited partnership or foreign limited partnership for service of any process, notice, or demand required or permitted by law to be served upon the limited partnership or foreign limited partnership.

(b) If a limited partnership or foreign limited partnership fails to appoint or maintain an agent for service of process in this State or the agent for service of process cannot with reasonable diligence be found at the agent's address, the [Secretary of State] is an agent of the limited partnership or foreign limited partnership upon whom process, notice, or demand may be served.

(c) Service of any process, notice, or demand on the [Secretary of State] may be made by delivering to and leaving with the [Secretary of State], the [Assistant Secretary of State], or clerk having charge of the limited partnership department of the [office of the Secretary of State] duplicate copies of the process, notice, or demand. If the process, notice, or demand is served on the [Secretary of State], the [Secretary of State] shall forward one of the copies by registered or certified mail, return receipt requested, to the limited partnership or foreign limited partnership at its designated office. Service is effected under this subsection at the earliest of:

(1) the date the limited partnership or foreign limited partnership receives the process, notice, or demand;

(2) the date shown on the return receipt, if signed on behalf of the limited partnership or foreign limited partnership; or

(3) five days after its deposit in the mail, if mailed postpaid and correctly addressed.

(d) The [Secretary of State] shall keep a record of all processes, notices, and demands served pursuant to this section and record the time of and the action taken regarding the service.

(e) This section does not affect the right to serve process, notice, or demand in any manner otherwise provided by law.

SECTION 118. CONSENT AND PROXIES OF PARTNERS.

(a) Action requiring the consent or vote of partners under this [Act] may be taken without a meeting.

(b) A [limited] partner may appoint a proxy to vote or otherwise act for the limited partner by signing an appointment instrument, either personally or by the limited partner's attorney in fact.

[ARTICLE] 2
FORMATION; CERTIFICATE OF LIMITED
PARTNERSHIP AND OTHER FILINGS
SECTION 201. CERTIFICATE OF LIMITED PARTNERSHIP.

(a) In order to form a limited partnership, a certificate of limited partnership must be executed and filed in the [office of the Secretary of State]. The certificate must include:

(1) the name of the limited partnership;

(2) the address of the initial designated office and the name and address of the initial agent for service of process;

(3) the name and the address of each general partner;

(4) if one or more of the general partners, or categories of general partners, are liable for the limited partnership's debts and obligations under Section 404(b), a statement to that effect; and

(5) any additional information required by [Article] 11.

(b) A certificate of limited partnership may also contain any other matters, but may not vary the nonwaivable provisions of this [Act] in Section 110.

(c) Subject to subsection (b), if any provision of a partnership agreement is inconsistent with the certificate of limited partnership or with a filed statement of dissociation, termination or change, or filed articles of conversion or merger:

(1) the partnership agreement prevails as to partners and transferees; and

(2) the certificate of limited partnership, statement of dissociation, termination, or change, or articles of conversion or merger prevails as to persons, other than partners and transferees, who reasonably rely on the filed record to their detriment.

(d) A limited partnership is formed at the time of the filing of the certificate of limited partnership in the [office of the Secretary of State] or, subject to Section 206(d), at any later time specified in the certificate of limited partnership if, in either case, there has been substantial compliance with the requirements of this section.

SECTION 202. AMENDMENT OR RESTATEMENT OF CERTIFICATE.

(a) A certificate of limited partnership may be amended by filing an amendment in the [office of the Secretary of State] or pursuant to [Article] 11. An amendment and filing made as provided in [Article] 11 must each set forth:

(1) the name of the limited partnership;

(2) the date of filing the certificate; and

(3) the changes the amendment makes to the certificate.

(b) A limited partnership shall file an amendment to a certificate of limited partnership reflecting the occurrence of any of these events:

(1) the admission of a new general partner;

(2) the dissociation of a person as a general partner;

(3) the appointment of a person to wind up the limited partnership's business under Section 803(b) or (c).

(c) A general partner who becomes aware that any statement in a certificate of limited partnership was false when made or that any arrangements or other facts described have changed, making the certificate inaccurate in any respect, shall promptly:

(1) cause the certificate to be amended; or

(2) if appropriate, file a statement of change pursuant to Section 115 or a statement of correction pursuant to Section 207.

(d) A certificate of limited partnership may be amended at any time for any other proper purpose the general partners determine.

(e) A restated certificate of limited partnership may be filed in the same manner as an amendment.

SECTION 203. STATEMENT OF TERMINATION.

A dissolved limited partnership that has completed winding up may file in the [office of the Secretary of State] a statement of termination that sets forth:

(1) the name of the limited partnership;

(2) the date of filing of its original certificate of limited partnership;

(3) the effective date of termination, which must be a date certain and is subject to Section 206(d), if the statement is not to be effective upon filing; and

(4) any other information the general partners filing the statement determine.

SECTION 204. SIGNING OF RECORDS.

(a) Each record pertaining to a domestic or foreign limited partnership and filed pursuant to this Act in the [office of the Secretary of State] must be signed in the following manner:

(1) An original certificate of limited partnership must be signed by all general partners listed in the certificate.

(2) An amendment making, modifying or deleting a statement under Section 404(b) must be signed by all general partners listed in the certificate.

(3) An amendment designating as general partner a person admitted under Section 801(3)(B) following the dissociation of a limited partnership's last general partner must be signed by that person.

(4) An amendment required by Section 803(b) or (d) following the appointment of a person to wind up the dissolved limited partnership's business must be signed by that person.

(5) Any other amendment must be signed by:

(A) at least one general partner listed in the certificate;

(B) each other person designated in the amendment as a new general partner; and

(C) each person who the amendment indicates has dissociated as a general partner, unless:

> (i) the person is deceased or a guardian or general conservator has been appointed for the person and the amendment so states; or

> (ii) the person has previously filed a statement of dissociation.

(6) A restated certificate of limited partnership must be signed by at least one general partner listed in the certificate, and to the extent the restated certificate effects a change under any other paragraph of this subsection the certificate must be signed in a manner that satisfies that paragraph.

(7) A statement of termination must be signed by all general partners listed in the certificate or, if the certificate of a dissolved limited partnership lists no general partners, by the person appointed under section 803(b) or 803(c) to wind up the dissolved limited partnership's business.

(8) Articles of conversion must be signed by each general partner listed in the certificate of limited partnership.

(9) Articles of merger must be signed as provided in Section 1108(a).

(10) Any other record signed by or on behalf of a limited partnership must be signed by at least one general partner listed in the certificate.

(11) A statement by a person pursuant to Section 605(4) stating that the person has dissociated as a general partner must be signed by that person.

(12) A statement of withdrawal by a person pursuant to Section 307 must be signed by that person.

(13) A record signed by or on behalf of a foreign limited partnership must be signed by at least one general partner of the foreign limited partnership.

(b) Any person may sign by an attorney in fact any record to be filed pursuant to this [Act].

SECTION 205. FILING BY JUDICIAL ACT.

(a) If a person required by [this Act] to sign any record fails or refuses to do so, any other person who is adversely affected by the failure or refusal may petition the [appropriate court] to order the person to sign the record or order the [Secretary of State] to file the record unsigned. If the adversely affected person is not the limited partnership or foreign limited partnership to which the record pertains, the adversely affected person must make that limited partnership or foreign limited partnership a party to the action.

(b) A person adversely affected may seek both remedies provided in subsection (a) in the same action, in the alternative. If the court finds that it is proper for the record to be signed and that a person required by [this Act] to sign the record has failed or refused to do so, the court shall order the person to sign the record or order the [Secretary of State] to file an appropriate record unsigned, which is effective without being signed.

SECTION 206. FILING IN [OFFICE OF SECRETARY OF STATE].

(a) A record authorized to be filed under this [Act] must be in a medium permitted by the [Secretary of State] and must be delivered to the [office of the Secretary of State]. Unless the [Secretary of State] determines that a record fails to comply as to form with the filing requirements of this [Act], and if all filing fees have been paid, the [Secretary of State] shall file the record and:

(1) for a statement of dissociation, send:

(A) a receipt for the statement and the fees to the person whom the statement indicates has dissociated as a general partner; and

(B) a copy of the statement and receipt to the limited partnership;

(2) for a statement of withdrawal, send:

(A) a receipt for the statement and the fees to the person on whose behalf the record was filed; and

(B) if the statement refers to an existing limited partnership, a copy of the statement and receipt to the limited partnership; and

(3) for all other records, send a receipt for the record and the fees to the person on whose behalf the record was filed.

(b) Upon request and payment of a fee, the [Secretary of State] shall send to the requester a certified copy of the requested record.

(c) Except as otherwise provided in subsection (d), a record accepted for filing by the [Secretary of State] is effective:

(1) at the time of filing on the date it is filed, as evidenced by the [Secretary of State's] endorsement of the date and time on the record; or

(2) at the time specified in the record as its effective time on the date it is filed.

(d) A record may specify a delayed effective time and date, and if it does so the record becomes effective at the time and on the date specified. If a delayed effective date is specified but the time is not specified, the record is effective at the close of business on that date. If a delayed effective date is later than the 90th day after the record is filed, the record is effective on the 90th day.

SECTION 207. CORRECTING FILED RECORD.

(a) A limited partnership or foreign limited partnership may correct a record filed by the [Secretary of State] if at the time of filing the record contained false or erroneous information or was defectively signed.

(b) A record is corrected by:

(1) preparing a statement of correction that:

(A) describes the record, including its filing date, or attaches a copy of it to the statement of correction;

(B) specifies the incorrect information and the reason it is incorrect or the manner in which the signing was defective; and

(C) corrects the incorrect information or defective signing; and

(2) delivering the corrected record to the [Secretary of State] for filing.

(c) A statement of correction is effective retroactively on the effective date of the record the statement corrects, but the statement is effective when filed:

(1) for the purposes of Section 103(c) and (d); and

(2) as to persons relying on the uncorrected record and adversely affected by the correction.

SECTION 208. LIABILITY FOR FALSE INFORMATION IN RECORD.

(a) If a record filed under this [Act] contains false information, a person who suffers loss by reliance on the information may recover damages for the loss from:

(1) a person who signed the record, or caused another to sign it on the person's behalf, and knew the statement to be false at the time the record was signed; and

(2) a general partner who has notice that the information is false within a sufficient time before the information was relied upon to have reasonably enabled that general partner to effect an amendment under Section 202 or file a statement of change pursuant to Section 115, a petition pursuant to Section 205, or a statement of correction pursuant to Section 207.

(b) The signing of a record authorized or required to be filed under this [Act] constitutes an affirmation under the penalties of perjury that the facts stated in the record are true.

SECTION 209. CERTIFICATE OF EXISTENCE OR AUTHORIZATION.

(a) A person may request the [Secretary of State] to furnish a certificate of existence for a limited partnership or a certificate of authorization for a foreign limited partnership.

(b) A certificate of existence for a limited partnership must state:

(1) the limited partnership's name;

(2) that it is duly formed under the laws of this State and the date of formation;

(3) whether all fees, taxes and penalties due to the [Secretary of State] under this [Act] or other law have been paid;

(4) whether its most recent annual report required by Section 210 has been filed with the [Secretary of State];

(5) that no statement of termination has been filed; and

(6) other facts of record in the [office of the Secretary of State] which may be requested by the applicant.

(c) A certificate of authorization for a foreign limited partnership must state:

(1) the foreign limited partnership's name and any alternate name adopted under Section 905(a) for use in this State;

(2) that it is authorized to transact business in this State;

(3) whether all fees, taxes and penalties due to the [Secretary of State] under this [Act] or other law have been paid;

(4) whether its most recent annual report required by Section 210 has been filed with the [Secretary of State];

(5) that its certificate of authority to transact business has not been revoked and a certificate of cancellation has not been filed; and

(6) other facts of record in the [office of the Secretary of State] which may be requested by the applicant.

(d) Subject to any qualification stated in the certificate, a certificate of existence or authorization issued by the [Secretary of State] may be relied upon as conclusive evidence that the domestic or foreign limited partnership is in existence or is authorized to transact business in this State.

SECTION 210. ANNUAL REPORT FOR [SECRETARY OF STATE].

(a) A limited partnership, and a foreign limited partnership authorized to transact business in this State, shall deliver to the [Secretary of State] for filing an annual report that sets forth:

(1) the name of the limited partnership or foreign limited partnership, including any alternate name adopted under Section 905(a), and the State or other jurisdiction under whose law the domestic or foreign limited partnership is formed;

(2) the address of its designated office and the name and address of its agent for service of process in this State; and

(3) in the case of a limited partnership, the address of its principal office.

(b) Information in an annual report must be current as of the date the annual report is signed on behalf of the limited partnership.

(c) The first annual report must be delivered to the [Secretary of State] between [January 1 and April 1] of the year following the calendar year in which a limited partnership was formed or a foreign limited partnership was authorized to transact business. Subsequent annual reports must be delivered to the [Secretary of State] between [January 1 and April 1] of the ensuing calendar years.

(d) If an annual report does not contain the information required in subsection (a), the [Secretary of State] shall promptly notify the reporting limited partnership or foreign limited partnership and return the report to it for correction. If the report is corrected to contain the information required in subsection (a) and delivered to the [Secretary of State] within 30 days after the effective date of the notice, it is timely filed.

(e) If a filed annual report contains an address of a designated office or the name or address of an agent for service of process that differs from the information shown upon the records of the [Secretary of State] immediately before the filing, the annual report's differing information is considered a statement of change under Section 115.

[ARTICLE] 3
LIMITED PARTNERS

SECTION 301. ADMISSION OF LIMITED PARTNERS. A person becomes a limited partner as provided in the partnership agreement, as the result of a merger or conversion under [Article] 11 or with the consent of all the partners.

SECTION 302. NO RIGHT OR POWER AS LIMITED PARTNER TO BIND LIMITED PARTNERSHIP. A limited partner has neither the right nor the power as a limited partner to act for or bind the limited partnership.

SECTION 303. NO LIABILITY AS LIMITED PARTNER TO THIRD PARTIES. A limited partner is not liable for a debt, obligation, or other liability of the limited partnership solely by reason of being a limited partner, even if the limited partner participates in the management and control of the limited partnership.

SECTION 304. MANAGEMENT RIGHTS OF LIMITED PARTNERS.

(a) A limited partner has no right to participate in the management of the limited partnership, except for:

(1) amendment to the partnership agreement under subsection (b);

(2) authorization or ratification under Section 110(b)(3)(B) of acts or transactions that would otherwise violate the duty of loyalty;

371

(3) a decision under subsection (b) to authorize the limited partnership to amend its certificate of limited partnership to include, modify or delete a statement under Section 404(b);

(4) access to the required records and other information under Section 305;

(5) admission of a new partner under Sections 301(b), 401 or 801(3)(B);

(6) a decision under Section 502(c) to compromise a claim against a partner;

(7) expulsion of a limited partner under Section 601(b)(4) or a general partner under Section 603(4);

(8) a decision under Section 703(c)(3) to use limited partnership property to redeem an interest subject to a charging order;

(9) a decision under Section 801(2) whether to dissolve the limited partnership;

(10) a decision under Section 801(3)(A)(ii) whether to dissolve the limited partnership following the dissociation of a general partner;

(11) a decision under Section 801(3)(B) whether to continue the limited partnership and appoint a new general partner following the dissociation of the limited partnership's last general partner;

(12) a decision under Section 803(b) to appoint a person to wind up the dissolved limited partnership's business;

(13) application to a court pursuant to Section 803(c) for the appointment of a person to wind up the dissolved limited partnership's business;

(14) the bringing of a derivative action under [Article] 10; and

(15) approval under [Article] 11 of a plan of conversion or merger.

(b) The consent of each partner is necessary to:

(1) amend the partnership agreement; and

(2) authorize a limited partnership to amend its certificate of limited partnership to include, modify or delete a statement under Section 404(b).

SECTION 305. LIMITED PARTNER'S AND FORMER LIMITED PARTNER'S RIGHT TO INFORMATION.

(a) On 10 days' written demand to the limited partnership, a limited partner may inspect and copy the required records during regular business hours in the limited partnership's designated office. A partner making demand pursuant to this subsection need not demonstrate, state, or have any particular purpose for seeking the information.

(b) A limited partner may, during regular business hours and at a reasonable location specified by the limited partnership, obtain from the limited partnership and inspect and copy true and full information regarding the state of the business and financial condition of the limited partnership and other information regarding the affairs of the limited partnership as is just and reasonable if:

(1) the limited partner seeks the information for a purpose reasonably related to the partner's interest as a limited partner;

(2) the limited partner makes a written demand on the limited partnership, describing with reasonable particularity the information sought and the purpose for seeking the information; and

(3) the information sought is directly connected to the limited partner's purpose.

(c) Within 10 days after receiving a demand pursuant to subsection (b), the limited partnership shall in writing inform the limited partner who made the demand:

(1) what information the limited partnership will provide in response to the demand;

(2) when and where the limited partnership will provide that information; and

(3) if the limited partnership declines to provide any demanded information, the limited partnership's reasons for declining.

(d) Subject to subsection (f), a person dissociated as a limited partner may inspect and copy a required record during regular business hours in the limited partnership's designated office if:

(1) the record pertains to the period during which the person was a limited partner;

(2) the person seeks the information in good faith; and

(3) the person meets the requirements stated in subsection (b).

(e) The limited partnership shall respond to a demand made pursuant to subsection (d) in the same manner as provided in subsection (c).

(f) If an individual who is a limited partner dies, Section 704 applies.

(g) The limited partnership may impose reasonable limitations on the use of information obtained under this section. In a dispute concerning the reasonableness of a restriction under this subsection, the limited partnership has the burden of proving reasonableness.

(h) A limited partnership may charge a limited partner or person dissociated as a limited partner who makes a demand under this section reasonable costs of copying, limited to the costs of labor and material.

(i) A limited partner or person dissociated as a limited partner may exercise the rights stated in this section through an attorney or other agent. In that event, any limitations on availability and use under subsection (g) apply both to the limited partner or person and to the attorney or other agent. The rights stated in this section extend to the legal representative of a person under legal disability who is a limited partner or person dissociated as a limited partner. The rights stated in this section do not

373

extend to a transferee, but subsection (d) creates rights for a person dissociated as a limited partner and subsection (f) recognizes the rights of the executor or administrator of a deceased limited partner.

SECTION 306. LIMITED DUTIES OF LIMITED PARTNERS.

(a) Except as otherwise provided in subsection (b), a limited partner does not owe any fiduciary duty to the limited partnership or to any other partner.

[two different versions of subsection (b) follow; Drafting Committee is to choose between them]

Version #1 (pro tanto; from ULLCA)— (b) A limited partner who pursuant to the limited partnership agreement exercises some or all of the rights of a general partner in the management and conduct of the limited partnership's business is held to the standards of conduct for a general partner to the extent that the limited partner exercises the managerial authority vested in a general partner by this [Act].

Version #2 (pro tanto) (inspired by RMBCA)— (b) To the extent the partnership agreement vests the discretion or powers of a general partner in a limited partner, that limited partner has the duties of a general partner with respect to the vested discretion or powers.

[end of different versions]

(c) A limited partner shall discharge duties to the partnership and the other partners under this [Act] or under the partnership agreement and exercise rights consistently with the obligation of good faith and fair dealing. The obligation stated in this subsection displaces any obligation of good faith and fair dealing at common law or otherwise.

(d) A limited partner does not violate a duty or obligation under this [Act] merely because the limited partner's conduct furthers the limited partner's own interest.

SECTION 307. PERSON ERRONEOUSLY BELIEVING SELF LIMITED PARTNER.

(a) Except as otherwise provided in subsection (b), a person who makes an investment in a business enterprise and erroneously but in good faith believes that the person has become a limited partner in the enterprise is not liable for its obligations by reason of making the investment, receiving distributions from the enterprise, or exercising any rights of or appropriate to a limited partner, if, on ascertaining the mistake, the person:

(1) causes an appropriate certificate of limited partnership, amendment, or statement of correction to be signed and filed; or

(2) withdraws from future equity participation in the enterprise by signing and filing in the [office of the Secretary of State] a statement of withdrawal under this section.

(b) A person who makes an investment of the kind described in subsection (a) is liable to the same extent as a general partner to any third party who transacts business with the enterprise (i) before the person withdraws and an appropriate statement of withdrawal is filed, or (ii) before an appropriate certificate, amendment, or statement of correction is filed to show that the person is not a general partner, but in either case only if the third party actually believed in good faith that the person was a general partner at the time of the transaction.

(c) If a person makes a diligent effort in good faith to comply with subsection (a)(1) and is unable to cause the appropriate certificate of limited partnership or amendment to be executed and filed, the person has the right to withdraw from the enterprise pursuant to subsection (a)(2) even if otherwise the withdrawal would breach an agreement with others who are or have agreed to become co-owners of the enterprise.

[ARTICLE] 4
GENERAL PARTNERS

SECTION 401. ADMISSION OF GENERAL PARTNERS. A person becomes a general partner as provided in the partnership agreement, under Section 801(3)(B) following the dissociation of a limited partnership's last general partner, as the result of a conversion or merger under [Article] 11 or with the consent of all the partners.

SECTION 402. GENERAL PARTNER AGENT OF LIMITED PARTNERSHIP.

(a) Each general partner is an agent of the limited partnership for the purpose of its business. An act of a general partner, including the execution of an instrument in the partnership's name, for apparently carrying on in the ordinary course the limited partnership's business or business of the kind carried on by the limited partnership binds the limited partnership, unless the general partner did not have authority to act for the limited partnership in the particular matter and the person with whom the general partner was dealing knew, had received a notification, or had notice under Section 103(d) that the general partner lacked authority.

(b) An act of a general partner which is not apparently for carrying on in the ordinary course the limited partnership's business or business of the kind carried on by the limited partnership binds the limited partnership only if the act was authorized by all the other partners.

SECTION 403. LIMITED PARTNERSHIP LIABLE FOR GENERAL PARTNER'S ACTIONABLE CONDUCT.

(a) A limited partnership is liable for loss or injury caused to a person, or for a penalty incurred, as a result of a wrongful act or omission, or other actionable conduct, of a general partner acting in the ordinary course of business of the limited partnership or with authority of the limited partnership.

(b) If, in the course of the limited partnership's business or while acting with authority of the limited partnership, a general partner receives or causes the limited partnership to receive money or property of a person not a partner, and the money or property is misapplied by a general partner, the limited partnership is liable for the loss.

SECTION 404. GENERAL PARTNER'S LIABILITY.

(a) Except as otherwise provided in subsection (b), the debts, obligations, and liabilities of a limited partnership, whether arising in contract, tort, or otherwise, are solely the debts, obligations, and liabilities of the limited partnership. A general partner is not personally liable for a debt, obligation, or liability of the limited partnership solely by reason of being or acting as a general partner.

(b) All or specified general partners, or specified categories of general partners, of a limited partnership are liable in their capacity as general partners for all or specified debts, obligations, or liabilities of the limited partnership if:

(1) a provision to that effect is contained in the certificate of limited partnership; and

(2) a general partner so liable has consented in writing to the provision or to be bound by the provision.

SECTION 405. ACTIONS BY AND AGAINST PARTNERSHIP AND PARTNERS.

(a) An action may be brought against the limited partnership and, to the extent not inconsistent with Sections 104(a) and 404, any or all of the general partners may be joined in the same action or separate actions may be brought.

(b) A judgment against a limited partnership is not by itself a judgment against a general partner. A judgment against a limited partnership may not be satisfied from a general partner's assets unless there is also a judgment against the general partner.

(c) A judgment creditor of a general partner may not levy execution against the assets of the general partner to satisfy a judgment based on a claim against the limited partnership, unless the partner is personally liable for the claim under Section 404 and:

(1) a judgment based on the same claim has been obtained against the limited partnership and a writ of execution on the judgment has been returned unsatisfied in whole or in part;

(2) the limited partnership is a debtor in bankruptcy;

(3) the general partner has agreed that the creditor need not exhaust limited partnership assets;

(4) a court grants permission to the judgment creditor to levy execution against the assets of a general partner based on a finding that limited partnership assets subject to execution are clearly insufficient to satisfy the judgment, that exhaustion of limited partnership assets is excessively burdensome, or that the grant of permission is an appropriate exercise of the court's equitable powers; or

(5) liability is imposed on the general partner by law or contract independent of the existence of the limited partnership.

SECTION 406. MANAGEMENT RIGHTS OF GENERAL PARTNERS.

(a) Each general partner has equal rights in the management and conduct of the limited partnership's business. Except for matters listed in Section 304(a), any matter relating to the business of the limited partnership may be exclusively decided by the general partner or, if there is more than one general partner, by a majority of the general partners.

(b) Action requiring the consent or vote of general partners under this [Act] may be taken without a meeting.

(c) A general partner may appoint a proxy to vote or otherwise act for the general partner by signing an appointive instrument, either personally or by the general partner's attorney in fact.

(d) A limited partnership shall reimburse a general partner for payments made and indemnify a general partner for liabilities incurred by the general partner in the ordinary course of the business of the partnership or for the preservation of its business or property.

(e) A limited partnership shall reimburse a general partner for an advance to the limited partnership beyond the amount of capital the general partner agreed to contribute.

(f) A payment or advance made by a general partner which gives rise to an obligation of the limited partnership under subsection (d) or (e) constitutes a loan to the limited partnership which accrues interest from the date of the payment or advance.

(g) A general partner is not entitled to remuneration for services performed for the partnership.

SECTION 407. GENERAL PARTNER'S AND FORMER GENERAL PARTNER'S RIGHT TO INFORMATION.

(a) Without having to demonstrate, state, or have any particular purpose for seeking the information, a general partner may during regular business hours inspect and copy:

(1) in the limited partnership's required office, the required records; and

(2) at a reasonable location specified by the limited partnership any other records maintained by the limited partnership regarding the limited partnership's business, affairs, and financial condition.

(b) Each general partner and the limited partnership shall furnish to a general partner:

(1) without demand, any information concerning the limited partnership's business and affairs reasonably required for the proper exercise of the general partner's rights and duties under the partnership agreement or this [Act]; and

(2) on demand, any other information concerning the limited partnership's business and affairs, except to the extent the demand or the information demanded is unreasonable or otherwise improper under the circumstances.

(c) Subject to subsection (e), on 10 days' written demand to the limited partnership, a person dissociated as a general partner may have access to a record described in subsection (a) at the location stated in subsection (a) if:

(1) the record pertains to the period during which the person was a general partner;

(2) the person seeks the record in good faith; and

(3) the person meets the requirements stated in Section 305(b).

(d) The limited partnership shall respond to a demand made pursuant to subsection (c) in the same manner as provided in Section 305(c).

(e) If an individual who is a general partner dies, Section 704 applies.

(f) The limited partnership may impose reasonable limitations on the use of information under this section. In any dispute concerning the reasonableness of a restriction under this subsection, the limited partnership has the burden of proving reasonableness.

(g) A limited partnership may charge a person dissociated as a general partner who makes a demand under this section reasonable costs of copying, limited to the costs of labor and material.

(h) A general partner or person dissociated as a general partner may exercise the rights stated in this section through an attorney or other agent. In that event, any limitation on availability and use under subsection (f) apply to the attorney or other agent as well as to the general partner or person dissociated as a general partner. The rights stated in this section extend to the legal representative of a person who has dissociated as a general partner because of death or legal disability. The rights stated in this section do not extend to a transferee, but subsection (c) creates rights for a dissociated general partner and subsection (e) recognizes the rights of the executor or administrator of a deceased limited partner.

SECTION 408. GENERAL STANDARDS OF GENERAL PARTNER'S CONDUCT.

(a) The only fiduciary duties that a general partner owes to the limited partnership and the other partners are the duty of loyalty and the duty of care stated in subsections (b) and (c).

(b) A general partner's duty of loyalty to the limited partnership and the other partners is limited to the following:

(1) to account to the limited partnership and hold as trustee for it any property, profit, or benefit derived by the general partner in the conduct and winding up of the limited partnership's business or derived from a use by the general partner of limited partnership

property, including the appropriation of a limited partnership opportunity;

(2) to refrain from dealing with the limited partnership in the conduct or winding up of the limited partnership's business as or on behalf of a party having an interest adverse to the limited partnership; and

(3) to refrain from competing with the limited partnership in the conduct of the limited partnership's business before the dissolution of the limited partnership.

(c) A general partner's duty of care to the limited partnership and the other partners in the conduct and winding up of the limited partnership's business is limited to refraining from engaging in grossly negligent or reckless conduct, intentional misconduct, or a knowing violation of law.

(d) A general partner shall discharge the duties to the partnership and the other partners under this [Act] or under the partnership agreement and exercise any rights consistently with the obligation of good faith and fair dealing. The obligation stated in this subsection displaces any obligation of good faith and fair dealing at common law or otherwise.

(e) A general partner does not violate a duty or obligation under this [Act] or under the partnership agreement merely because the general partner's conduct furthers the general partner's own interest.

(f) A general partner is relieved of liability imposed by law for violation of the standards prescribed by subsections (b) through (e) to the extent of the managerial authority delegated to one or more of the limited partners by the partnership agreement.

[ARTICLE] 5
CONTRIBUTIONS, PROFITS, AND DISTRIBUTIONS

SECTION 501. FORM OF CONTRIBUTION. A contribution of a partner may consist of tangible or intangible property or other benefit to the limited partnership, including money, promissory notes, services performed, or other agreements to contribute cash or property, or contracts for services to be performed.

SECTION 502. LIABILITY FOR CONTRIBUTION.

(a) A partner's obligation to contribute money, property, or other benefit to, or to perform services for, a limited partnership is not excused by the member's death, disability, or other inability to perform personally.

(b) If a partner does not make a promised contribution of property or services, the partner is obligated at the option of the limited partnership to contribute money equal to that portion of the value, as stated in the required records, of the stated contribution which has not been made.

(c) The obligation of a partner to make a contribution or return money or other property paid or distributed in violation of this [Act] may be compromised only by consent of all partners. A creditor of a limited partnership who extends credit or otherwise acts in reliance on an obli-

379

gation described in subsection (a), and without notice of any compromise under this subsection, may enforce the original obligation.

SECTION 503. ALLOCATION OF PROFITS AND LOSSES. The profits and losses of a limited partnership are allocated among the partners on the basis of the value, as stated in the required records, of the contributions made by each partner to the extent those contributions have been received by the limited partnership.

SECTION 504. SHARING OF DISTRIBUTIONS. Any distributions made by a limited partnership are in proportion to the partners' allocation of profits and losses in effect when the limited partnership decides to make the distribution.

SECTION 505. INTERIM DISTRIBUTIONS. A partner does not have a right to any distribution before the dissolution and winding up of the limited partnership unless the limited partnership decides to make an interim distribution.

SECTION 506. NO DISTRIBUTION ON ACCOUNT OF DISSO-CIATION. A person has no right to receive any distribution on account of dissociation.

SECTION 507. DISTRIBUTION IN KIND. A partner has no right to demand or receive any distribution from a limited partnership in any form other than cash. A limited partnership may distribute an asset in kind, subject to Section 813(b) and only to the extent that each partner receives a percentage of the asset equal to the partner's share of distributions.

SECTION 508. RIGHT TO DISTRIBUTION. At the time a partner becomes entitled to receive a distribution, the partner has the status of, and is entitled to all remedies available to, a creditor of the limited partnership with respect to the distribution. However, the limited partnership's obligation to make a distribution is subject to offset for any amount owed to the limited partnership by the partner or dissociated partner on whose account the distribution is made.

SECTION 509. LIMITATIONS ON DISTRIBUTION.

(a) A limited partnership may not make a distribution in violation of the partnership agreement.

(b) A limited partnership may not make a distribution if after the distribution:

(1) the limited partnership would not be able to pay its debts as they become due in the ordinary course of business; or

(2) the limited partnership's total assets would be less than the sum of its total liabilities plus the amount that would be needed, if the limited partnership were to be dissolved, wound up, and terminated at the time of the distribution, to satisfy the preferential rights upon dissolution, winding up, and termination of partners whose preferential rights are superior to those of persons receiving the distribution.

(c) A limited partnership may base a determination that a distribution is not prohibited under subsection (b) on financial statements prepared on the basis of accounting practices and principles that are reasonable in the circumstances or on a fair valuation or other method that is reasonable in the circumstances.

(d) Except as otherwise provided in subsection (g), the effect of a distribution under subsection (b) is measured:

(1) in the case of distribution by purchase, redemption, or other acquisition of a transferable interest in the limited partnership, as of the date money or other property is transferred or debt incurred by the limited partnership; and

(2) in all other cases, as of the date:

(A) the distribution is authorized, if the payment occurs within 120 days after that date; or

(B) the payment is made, if payment occurs more than 120 days after that date.

(e) A limited partnership's indebtedness to a partner incurred by reason of a distribution made in accordance with this section is at parity with the limited partnership's indebtedness to its general, unsecured creditors.

(f) A limited partnership's indebtedness, including indebtedness issued in connection with or as part of a distribution, is not considered a liability for purposes of determinations under subsection (b) if the terms of the indebtedness provide that payment of principal and interest are made only to the extent that a distribution could then be made to partners under this section.

(g) If indebtedness is issued as a distribution, each payment of principal or interest on the indebtedness is treated as a distribution, the effect of which is measured on the date the payment is made.

SECTION 510. LIABILITY FOR IMPROPER DISTRIBUTIONS.

(a) A general partner who votes for or assents to a distribution made in violation of Section 509 is personally liable to the limited partnership for the amount of the distribution which exceeds the amount that could have been distributed without the violation if it is established that in voting for or assenting to the distribution the general partner failed to comply with Section 509(c) or 408.

(b) A partner or transferee who knew a distribution was made in violation of Section 509 is personally liable to the limited partnership, but only to the extent that the distribution received by the partner or transferee exceeded the amount that could have been properly paid under Section 509.

(c) A general partner against whom an action is brought under subsection (a) may:

(1) implead in the action any other person who as a general partner voted for or assented to the distribution in violation of subsection (a) and compel contribution from that person; and

(2) implead in the action any person who received a distribution in violation of subsection (b) and compel contribution from that person in the amount that person received in violation of subsection (b).

(d) A proceeding under this section is barred unless it is commenced within two years after the distribution.

[ARTICLE] 6

DISSOCIATION

SECTION 601. DISSOCIATION AS A LIMITED PARTNER.

(a) A person does not have a right to dissociate as a limited partner before the termination of the limited partnership.

(b) A person is dissociated from a limited partnership as a limited partner upon the occurrence of any of the following events:

(1) the limited partnership's having notice of the person's express will to withdraw as a limited partner or on a later date specified by the person;

(2) an event agreed to in the partnership agreement as causing the person's dissociation as a limited partner;

(3) the person's expulsion as a limited partner pursuant to the partnership agreement;

(4) the person's expulsion as a limited partner by the unanimous vote of the other partners if:

(A) it is unlawful to carry on the limited partnership's business with that person as a limited partner;

(B) there has been a transfer of all of the person's transferable interest in the limited partnership, other than a transfer for security purposes, or a court order charging the person's interest, which has not been foreclosed;

(C) the person is a corporation and, within 90 days after the limited partnership notifies the person that it will be expelled as a limited partner because it has filed a certificate of dissolution or the equivalent, its charter has been revoked, or its right to conduct business has been suspended by the jurisdiction of its incorporation, there is no revocation of the certificate of dissolution or no reinstatement of its charter or its right to conduct business; or

(D) the person is a limited liability company or partnership that has been dissolved and whose business is being wound up;

(5) on application by the limited partnership, the person's expulsion as a limited partner by judicial determination because:

(A) the person engaged in wrongful conduct that adversely and materially affected the limited partnership's business;

(B) the person willfully or persistently committed a material breach of the partnership agreement or of the obligation of good faith and fair dealing under Section 306(c); or

(C) the person engaged in conduct relating to the limited partnership's business which makes it not reasonably practicable to carry on the business with the person as limited partner;

(6) in the case of a person who is an individual, the person's death;

(7) in the case of a person that is a trust or is acting as a limited partner by virtue of being a trustee of a trust, distribution of the trust's entire transferable interest in the limited partnership, but not merely by reason of the substitution of a successor trustee;

(8) in the case of a person that is an estate or is acting as a limited partner by virtue of being a personal representative of an estate, distribution of the estate's entire transferable interest in the limited partnership, but not merely by reason of the substitution of a successor personal representative;

(9) termination of a limited partner that is not an individual, partnership, limited liability company, corporation, trust, or estate;

(10) the limited partnership's participation in a merger or conversion under [Article] 11, if the limited partnership:

(A) is not the converted or surviving entity; or

(B) is the converted or surviving entity but, as a result of the conversion or merger, the person ceases to be a limited partner.

SECTION 602. EFFECT OF DISSOCIATION AS A LIMITED PARTNER.

Upon a person's dissociation as a limited partner,

(1) subject to section 704, the person has no further rights as a limited partner;

(2) the person's obligation of good faith and fair dealing as a limited partner under Section 306(c) continues only as to matters arising and events occurring before the dissociation;

(3) subject to Section 704 and [Article] 11, any transferable interest owned by the person in the person's capacity as a limited partner immediately before dissociation is owned by the person as a mere transferee; and

(4) the dissociation does not of itself discharge the person from any obligation to the limited partnership or the other partners which the person incurred while a limited partner.

SECTION 603. DISSOCIATION AS A GENERAL PARTNER. A person is dissociated from a limited partnership as a general partner upon the occurrence of any of the following events:

383

(1) the limited partnership's having notice of the person's express will to withdraw as a general partner or on a later date specified by the person;

(2) an event agreed to in the partnership agreement as causing the person's dissociation as a general partner;

(3) the person's expulsion as a general partner pursuant to the partnership agreement;

(4) the person's expulsion as a general partner by the unanimous vote of the other partners if:

(A) it is unlawful to carry on the limited partnership's business with that person as a general partner;

(B) there has been a transfer of all or substantially all of the person's transferable interest in the limited partnership, other than a transfer for security purposes, or a court order charging the person's interest, which has not been foreclosed;

(C) the person is a corporation and, within 90 days after the limited partnership notifies the person that it will be expelled as a general partner because it has filed a certificate of dissolution or the equivalent, its charter has been revoked, or its right to conduct business has been suspended by the jurisdiction of its incorporation, there is no revocation of the certificate of dissolution or no reinstatement of its charter or its right to conduct business; or

(D) the person is a limited liability company or partnership that has been dissolved and whose business is being wound up;

(5) on application by the limited partnership, the person's expulsion as a general partner by judicial determination because:

(A) the person engaged in wrongful conduct that adversely and materially affected the limited partnership affairs;

(B) the person willfully or persistently committed a material breach of the partnership agreement or of a duty owed to the partnership or the other partners under Section 408; or

(C) the person engaged in conduct relating to the limited partnership's business which makes it not reasonably practicable to carry on the affairs of the limited partnership with the person as a general partner;

(6) the person's:

(A) becoming a debtor in bankruptcy;

(B) execution of an assignment for the benefit of creditors;

(C) seeking, consenting to, or acquiescing in the appointment of a trustee, receiver, or liquidator of that partner or of all or substantially all of that general partner's property; or

(D) failure, within 90 days after the appointment, to have vacated or stayed the appointment of a trustee, receiver, or liquidator of the general partner or of all or substantially all of the person's property obtained without the person's consent or acquiescence, or failing within 90 days after the expiration of a stay to have the appointment vacated;

(7) in the case of a person who is an individual:

(A) the person's death;

(B) the appointment of a guardian or general conservator for the person; or

(C) a judicial determination that the person has otherwise become incapable of performing the person's duties as a general partner under the partnership agreement;

(8) in the case of a person that is a trust or is acting as a general partner by virtue of being a trustee of a trust, distribution of the trust's entire transferable interest in the limited partnership, but not merely by reason of the substitution of a successor trustee;

(9) in the case of a person that is an estate or is acting as a general partner by virtue of being a personal representative of an estate, distribution of the estate's entire transferable interest in the limited partnership, but not merely by reason of the substitution of a successor personal representative;

(10) termination of a general partner that is not an individual, partnership, limited liability company, corporation, trust, or estate;

(11) the limited partnership's participation in a merger or conversion under [Article] 11, if the limited partnership:

(A) is not the converted or surviving entity; or

(B) is the converted or surviving entity but, as a result of the conversion or merger, the person ceases to be a general partner.

SECTION 604. PERSON'S POWER TO DISSOCIATE AS GENERAL PARTNER; WRONGFUL DISSOCIATION.

(a) A person has the power to dissociate as a general partner at any time, rightfully or wrongfully, by express will pursuant to Section 603(1).

(b) A person's dissociation as a general partner is wrongful only if:

(1) it is in breach of an express provision of the partnership agreement; or

(2) it occurs before the termination of the limited partnership, and:

(A) the person withdraws as a general partner by express will;

(B) the person is expelled as a general partner by judicial determination under Section 603(5);

(C) the person is dissociated as a general partner by becoming a debtor in bankruptcy; or

(D) in the case of a person that is not an individual, trust other than a business trust, or estate, the person is expelled or otherwise dissociated as a general partner because it willfully dissolved or terminated.

(c) A person who wrongfully dissociates as a general partner is liable to the limited partnership and, subject to Section 1001, to the other partners for damages caused by the dissociation. The liability is in addition to any other obligation of the general partner to the limited partnership or to the other partners.

SECTION 605. EFFECT OF DISSOCIATION AS A GENERAL PARTNER. Upon a person's dissociation as a general partner:

(1) the person's right to participate as a general partner in the management and conduct of the partnership's business terminates;

(2) the person's duty of loyalty as a general partner under Section 408(b)(3) terminates;

(3) the person's duty of loyalty as a general partner under Section 408(b)(1) and (2) and duty of care under Section 408(c) continue only with regard to matters arising and events occurring before the person's dissociation as a general partner;

(4) the person shall sign, at the request of the limited partnership, an amendment to the certificate of limited partnership which states that the person has dissociated, and may sign and file a statement of dissociation pertaining to the person;

(5) subject to Section 704 and [Article] 11, any transferable interest owned by the person immediately before dissociation in the person's capacity as a general partner is owned by the person as a mere transferee; and

(6) the dissociation does not of itself discharge the person from any obligation to the limited partnership or the other partners which the person incurred while a general partner.

SECTION 606. DISSOCIATED GENERAL PARTNER'S POW-ER TO BIND AND LIABILITY TO PARTNERSHIP BEFORE DIS-SOLUTION.

(a) After a person is dissociated as a general partner and before the limited partnership is dissolved, converted under [Article] 11 or merged out of existence under [Article 11], the limited partnership is bound by an act of the person only if:

(1) the act would have bound the limited partnership under Section 402 before the dissociation; and

(2) at the time the other party enters into the transaction:

(A) less than two years has passed since the dissociation; and

(B) the other party does not have notice of the dissociation and reasonably believes that the person is a general partner.

(b) If a limited partnership incurs an obligation under subsection (a), the person dissociated as a general partner is liable:

(1) to the limited partnership for any damage caused to the limited partnership arising from that obligation; and

(2) if a general partner or a person dissociated as a general partner is liable for that obligation, then to that general partner or other person for any damage caused to that general partner or other person arising from that liability.

SECTION 607. DISSOCIATED GENERAL PARTNER'S LIABILITY TO OTHER PERSONS.

(a) A person's dissociation as a general partner does not of itself discharge the person's liability as a general partner for a limited partnership's obligation incurred before dissociation. Except as otherwise provided in subsections (b) and (c), the person is not liable for a limited partnership's obligation incurred after dissociation.

(b) A person whose dissociation as a general partner resulted in a dissolution and winding up of the limited partnership's business is liable to the same extent as a general partner under Section 404 on an obligation incurred by the limited partnership under Section 804.

(c) A person who has dissociated as a general partner but whose dissociation did not result in a dissolution and winding up of the limited partnership's business is liable to the same extent as a general partner under Section 404 on a transaction entered into after the dissociation by the limited partnership, only if:

(1) a general partner would be liable on the transaction; and

(2) at the time the other party enters into the transaction:

(A) less than two years has passed since the dissociation; and

(B) the other party does not have notice of the dissociation and reasonably believes that the person is a general partner.

(d) By agreement with the limited partnership's creditor and the limited partnership, a person dissociated as a general partner may be released from liability for a limited partnership's obligation.

(e) A person dissociated as a general partner is released from liability for a limited partnership's obligation if a limited partnership's creditor, with notice of the person's dissociation as a general partner but without the person's consent, agrees to a material alteration in the nature or time of payment of the limited partnership's obligation.

[ARTICLE] 7
TRANSFERABLE INTERESTS AND RIGHTS OF TRANSFEREES AND CREDITORS

SECTION 701. PARTNER'S TRANSFERABLE INTEREST. The only transferable interest of a partner is the partner's allocation of the profits and losses of the partnership and the partner's right to receive distributions. The interest is personal property.

SECTION 702. TRANSFER OF PARTNER'S TRANSFERABLE INTEREST.

(a) A transfer, in whole or in part, of a partner's transferable interest in the limited partnership:

(1) is permissible;

(2) does not by itself cause the partner's dissociation or a dissolution and winding up of the limited partnership's business; and

(3) does not, as against the other partners or the limited partnership, entitle the transferee, during the continuance of the limited partnership, to participate in the management or conduct of the limited partnership's business, to require access to information concerning the limited partnership's transactions, or to inspect or copy the limited partnership's books or records.

(b) A transferee of a partner's transferable interest in the limited partnership has a right:

(1) to receive, in accordance with the transfer, distributions to which the transferor would otherwise be entitled; and

(2) to receive upon the dissolution and winding up of the limited partnership's business, in accordance with the transfer, the net amount otherwise distributable to the transferor.

(c) In a dissolution and winding up, a transferee is entitled to an account of the limited partnership's transactions only from the date of dissolution.

(d) Upon transfer, the transferor retains the rights and duties of a partner other than the interest in distributions transferred, including the transferor's liability to the limited partnership under Sections 208 and 502.

(e) A limited partnership need not give effect to a transferee's rights under this section until it has notice of the transfer.

(f) A transfer of a partner's transferable interest in the limited partnership in violation of a restriction on transfer contained in the partnership agreement is ineffective as to a person having notice of the restriction at the time of transfer.

(g) A transferee who becomes a partner with respect to a transferable interest is liable for the transferor's obligations under Sections 502 and 510. However, the transferee is not obligated for liabilities unknown to the transferee at the time the transferee became a partner.

SECTION 703. RIGHTS OF CREDITOR OF PARTNER OR TRANSFEREE.

(a) On application to a court of competent jurisdiction by any judgment creditor of a partner or transferee, the court may charge the transferable interest of the judgment debtor with payment of the unsatisfied amount of the judgment with interest. To the extent so charged, the judgment creditor has only the rights of a transferee. The court may appoint a receiver of the share of the distributions due or to become due to the judgment debtor in respect of the partnership and make all other orders, directions, accounts, and inquiries the judgment debtor might have made or which the circumstances of the case may require to give effect to the charging order.

(b) A charging order constitutes a lien on the judgment debtor's transferable interest. The court may order a foreclosure upon the interest subject to the charging order at any time. The purchaser at the foreclosure sale has the rights of a transferee.

(c) At any time before foreclosure, an interest charged may be redeemed:

(1) by the judgment debtor;

(2) with property other than limited partnership property, by one or more of the other partners; or

(3) with limited partnership property, by the limited partnership with the consent of all partners whose interests are not so charged.

(d) This [Act] does not deprive any partner or transferee of the benefit of any exemption laws applicable to the partner's or transferee's transferable interest.

(e) This section provides the exclusive remedy by which a judgment creditor of a partner or transferee may satisfy a judgment out of the judgment debtor's transferable interest.

SECTION 704. POWER OF ESTATE OF DECEASED PARTNER. If a partner who is an individual dies, the deceased partner's executor, administrator, or other legal representative may exercise the rights of a transferee as provided in Section 702 and, for the purposes of settling the estate, may exercise the rights of a current limited partner under Section 305.

[ARTICLE] 8
DISSOLUTION

SECTION 801. NONJUDICIAL DISSOLUTION. A limited partnership is dissolved, and its business must be wound up, only upon the occurrence of any of the following events:

(1) the happening of an event specified in writing in the partnership agreement;

(2) written consent of all general partners and of limited partners owning a majority of the interests in profit owned by persons as limited partners;

(3) after the dissociation of a person as a general partner:

(A) if the limited partnership has at least one remaining general partner,

(i) the limited partnership's having notice within 90 days after the dissociation of the express will of any remaining general partner to dissolve the limited partnership; or

(ii) written consent to dissolve the limited partnership given within 90 days after the dissociation by limited partners owning a majority of the interests in profit owned by persons as limited partners immediately following the dissociation; or

(B) if the limited partnership has no remaining general partner, the passage of 90 days after the dissociation unless within that 90 days partners owning a majority of the interests in profit owned by limited partners immediately following the dissociation consent to continue the business and to admit at least one general partner and at least one person is admitted as a general partner in accordance with that consent;

(4) the passage of 90 days after the dissociation of the limited partnership's last limited partner, unless before the end of the 90 days the limited partnership admits at least one limited partner;

(5) the signing of a declaration of dissolution by the [Secretary of State] under Section 810(b); or

(6) entry of a decree of judicial dissolution under Section 802.

SECTION 802. JUDICIAL DISSOLUTION. On application by or for a partner the [appropriate court] court may decree dissolution of a limited partnership if it is not reasonably practicable to carry on the business in conformity with the partnership agreement.

SECTION 803. WINDING UP.

(a) A limited partnership continues after dissolution only for the purpose of winding up its business. In winding up its business the limited partnership may amend its certificate of limited partnership to state that the limited partnership is dissolved, preserve the limited partnership's business or property as a going concern for a reasonable time, prosecute and defend actions and proceedings, whether civil, criminal, or administrative, settle and close the limited partnership's business, dispose of and transfer the limited partnership's property, discharge the limited partnership's liabilities, distribute the assets of the limited partnership under Section 813, settle disputes by mediation or arbitration, file a statement of termination under Section 203, and perform other necessary acts.

(b) If a dissolved limited partnership has no general partners, limited partners owning a majority of the interests in profit owned by partners may appoint a person to wind up the dissolved limited partnership's business. A person appointed under this subsection:

(1) has the powers of a general partner under Section 804; and

(2) shall promptly amend the certificate of limited partnership to:

(A) state that the limited partnership has no general partner and that the person has been appointed to wind up the limited partnership; and

(B) give the address of the person.

(c) On the application of any partner, a court may order judicial supervision of the winding up, including the appointment of a person to wind up the dissolved limited partnership's business, if:

(1) a limited partnership has no general partner and within a reasonable time following the dissolution no person has been appointed pursuant to subsection (b); or

(2) the applicant establishes other good cause.

SECTION 804. POWER OF GENERAL PARTNER AND PERSON DISSOCIATED AS GENERAL PARTNER TO BIND PARTNERSHIP AFTER DISSOLUTION.

(a) A limited partnership is bound by a general partner's act after dissolution which:

(1) is appropriate for winding up the limited partnership's business; or

(2) would have bound the partnership under Section 402 before dissolution, if the other party to the transaction did not have notice of the dissolution.

(b) A person dissociated as a general partner binds a limited partnership through an act occurring after dissolution if:

(1) at the time the other party enters into the transaction:

(A) less than two years has passed since the person's dissociation as a general partner; and

(B) the other party does not have notice of the dissociation and reasonably believes that the person is a general partner; and

(2) the act:

(A) is appropriate for winding up the limited partnership's business; or

(B) would have bound the limited partnership under Section 402 before dissolution and at the time the other party enters into the transaction the other party does not have notice of the dissolution.

SECTION 805. LIABILITY AFTER DISSOLUTION OF GENERAL PARTNER AND PERSON DISSOCIATED AS GENERAL PARTNER TO LIMITED PARTNERSHIP, OTHER GENERAL PARTNERS, AND PERSONS DISSOCIATED AS GENERAL PARTNER.

(a) If a general partner having knowledge of the dissolution causes a limited partnership to incur an obligation under Section 804(a) by an act that is not appropriate for winding up the partnership's business, the general partner is liable:

(1) to the limited partnership for any damage caused to the limited partnership arising from the obligation; and

(2) if another general partner or a person dissociated as a general partner is liable for the obligation, then to that other general partner

or person for any damage caused to that other general partner or person arising from that liability.

(b) If a person dissociated as a general partner causes a limited partnership to incur an obligation under Section 804(b), the person is liable:

(1) to the limited partnership for any damage caused to the limited partnership arising from the obligation; and

(2) if a general partner or another person dissociated as a general partner is liable for that obligation, to that general partner or other person for any damage caused to that general partner or other person arising from that liability.

SECTION 806. KNOWN CLAIMS AGAINST DISSOLVED LIMITED PARTNERSHIP.

(a) A dissolved limited partnership may dispose of the known claims against it by following the procedure described in this section.

(b) A dissolved limited partnership shall notify its known claimants in writing of the dissolution. The notice must:

(1) specify the information required to be included in a claim;

(2) provide a mailing address to which the claim is to be sent;

(3) state the deadline for receipt of the claim, which may not be less than 120 days after the date the written notice is received by the claimant;

(4) state that the claim will be barred if not received by the deadline; and

(5) unless the limited partnership's certificate of limited partnership has never contained a statement under Section 404(b), state that the barring of a claim against the limited partnership will also bar any corresponding claim against any present or dissociated general partner which is based on Section 404(b).

(c) A claim against a dissolved limited partnership is barred if the requirements of subsection (b) are met and:

(1) the claim is not received by the specified deadline; or

(2) in the case of a claim that is timely received but rejected by the dissolved limited partnership, the claimant does not commence a proceeding to enforce the claim against the limited partnership within 90 days after the receipt of the notice of the rejection.

(d) In this section, "claim" does not include a contingent liability or a claim based on an event occurring after the effective date of dissolution.

SECTION 807. OTHER CLAIMS AGAINST DISSOLVED LIMITED PARTNERSHIP.

(a) A dissolved limited partnership may publish notice of its dissolution and request persons having claims against the limited partnership to present them in accordance with the notice.

(b) The notice must:

(1) be published at least once in a newspaper of general circulation in the [county] in which the dissolved limited partnership's principal office is located or, if it has none in this State, in which the limited partnership's designated office is or was last located;

(2) describe the information required to be contained in a claim and provide a mailing address to which the claim is to be sent;

(3) state that a claim against the limited partnership is barred unless a proceeding to enforce the claim is commenced within five years after publication of the notice; and

(4) unless the limited partnership's certificate of limited partnership has never contained a statement under Section 404(b), state that the barring of a claim against the limited partnership will also bar any corresponding claim against any present or dissociated general partner which is based on Section 404.

(c) If a dissolved limited partnership publishes a notice in accordance with subsection (b), the claim of each of the following claimants is barred unless the claimant commences a proceeding to enforce the claim against the dissolved limited partnership within five years after the publication date of the notice:

(1) a claimant who did not receive written notice under Section 806;

(2) a claimant whose claim was timely sent to the dissolved limited partnership but not acted on; and

(3) a claimant whose claim is contingent or based on an event occurring after the effective date of dissolution.

(d) A claim not barred under this section may be enforced:

(1) against the dissolved limited partnership, to the extent of its undistributed assets;

(2) if the assets have been distributed in liquidation, against a partner or transferee to the extent of that person's proportionate share of the claim or the limited partnership's assets distributed to the partner or transferee in liquidation, whichever is less, but a person's total liability for all claims under this paragraph may not exceed the total amount of assets distributed to the person as part of the winding up of the dissolved limited partnership; or

(3) against any person liable on the claim under Section 404.

SECTION 808. EFFECT OF CLAIMS BAR ON PERSONAL LIABILITY OF PARTNERS AND DISSOCIATED PARTNERS. If Section 806 or 807 bars a claim against a dissolved limited partnership, any corresponding claim under Section 404 is also barred.

SECTION 809. GROUNDS FOR ADMINISTRATIVE DISSOLUTION. The [Secretary of State] may commence a proceeding to dissolve a limited partnership administratively if the limited partnership does not:

(1) pay any fees, taxes, or penalties due to the [Secretary of State] under this [Act] or other law within 60 days after they are due; or

(2) deliver its annual report to the [Secretary of State] within 60 days after it is due.

SECTION 810. PROCEDURE FOR AND EFFECT OF ADMINISTRATIVE DISSOLUTION.

(a) If the [Secretary of State] determines that a ground exists for administratively dissolving a limited partnership, the [Secretary of State] shall enter a record of the determination and serve the limited partnership with a copy of the record.

(b) If within 60 days after service of the copy the limited partnership does not correct each ground for dissolution or demonstrate to the reasonable satisfaction of the [Secretary of State] that each ground determined by the [Secretary of State] does not exist, the [Secretary of State] shall administratively dissolve the limited partnership by signing a declaration of dissolution that recites the grounds for dissolution and its effective date. The [Secretary of State] shall file the original of the declaration and serve the limited partnership with a copy of the declaration.

(c) A limited partnership administratively dissolved continues its existence but may carry on only business necessary to wind up and liquidate its business and affairs under Sections 803 and 813 |spaceŒ and to notify claimants under Sections 806 and 807.

(d) The administrative dissolution of a limited partnership does not terminate the authority of its agent for service of process.

SECTION 811. REINSTATEMENT FOLLOWING ADMINISTRATIVE DISSOLUTION.

(a) A limited partnership administratively dissolved may apply to the [Secretary of State] for reinstatement within two years after the effective date of dissolution. The application must:

(1) recite the name of the limited partnership and the effective date of its administrative dissolution;

(2) state that the ground or grounds for dissolution either did not exist or have been eliminated; and

(3) state that the limited partnership's name satisfies the requirements of Section 108.

(b) If the [Secretary of State] determines that the application contains the information required by subsection (a) and that the information is correct, the [Secretary of State] shall cancel the declaration of dissolution and prepare a declaration of reinstatement that recites this determination and the effective date of reinstatement, file the original of the declaration of reinstatement, and serve the limited partnership with a copy.

(c) When reinstatement is effective, it relates back to and takes effect as of the effective date of the administrative dissolution and the limited partnership may resume its business as if the administrative dissolution had never occurred.

SECTION 812. APPEAL FROM DENIAL OF REINSTATE-MENT.

(a) If the [Secretary of State] denies a limited partnership's application for reinstatement following administrative dissolution, the [Secretary of State] shall serve the limited partnership with a record that explains the reason or reasons for denial.

(b) The limited partnership may appeal from the denial of reinstatement to the [appropriate court] within 30 days after service of the notice of denial is perfected. The limited partnership appeals by petitioning the court to set aside the dissolution and attaching to the petition copies of the [Secretary of State's] declaration of dissolution, the company's application for reinstatement, and the [Secretary of State's] notice of denial.

(c) The court may summarily order the [Secretary of State] to reinstate the dissolved limited partnership or may take other action the court considers appropriate.

SECTION 813. SETTLING OF ACCOUNTS AND DISTRIBUTION OF ASSETS.

(a) In winding up a limited partnership's business, the assets of the limited partnership, including the contributions required by this section, must be applied to discharge its obligations to creditors, including, to the extent permitted by law, partners who are creditors.

(b) Any surplus remaining after the limited partnership complies with subsection (a) is paid in cash as a distribution.

(c) If the limited partnership's assets are insufficient to discharge all of its obligations under section (a), with respect to each undischarged obligation incurred when certificate of limited partnership contained a provision authorized by Section 404(b):

(1) each person who was a general partner and bound by that provision when the obligation was incurred and who has not been released from that obligation under Section 607 shall contribute to the limited partnership for the purpose of enabling the limited partnership to discharge that obligation and the contribution due from each of those persons is in proportion to the allocation of limited-partnership losses in effect for each of those persons when the obligation was incurred;

(2) if a person fails to contribute the full amount required under paragraph (1) with respect to an undischarged limited partnership's obligation, the other persons required to contribute by paragraph (1) on account of that obligation shall contribute the additional amount necessary to discharge the obligation and the additional contribution due from each of those other persons is in proportion to the allocation of limited partnership losses in effect for each of those other persons when the obligation was incurred; and

(3) if a person fails to make the additional contribution required by paragraph (2), further additional contributions are due and are determined in the same manner as provided in that paragraph.

(d) A person who makes an additional contribution under subsection (c)(2) or(3) may recover from any person whose failure to contribute under subsection (c)(1) or (2) necessitated the additional contribution. A person may not recover under this subsection more than the amount additionally contributed. A person's liability under this subsection may not exceed the amount the person failed to contribute.

(e) The estate of a deceased person is liable for the person's obligations under this section.

(f) An assignee for the benefit of creditors of a limited partnership or a partner, or a person appointed by a court to represent creditors of a limited partnership or a partner, may enforce a person's obligation to contribute under subsection (c).

[ARTICLE] 9

FOREIGN LIMITED PARTNERSHIPS

SECTION 901. GOVERNING LAW

(a) The laws of the State or other jurisdiction under which a foreign limited partnership is organized govern its organization and internal affairs and the liability of its partners.

(b) A foreign limited partnership may not be denied a certificate of authority by reason of any difference between the laws of the jurisdiction under which the foreign limited partnership is organized and the laws of this State.

(c) A certificate of authority does not authorize a foreign limited partnership to engage in any business or exercise any power that a limited partnership may not engage in or exercise in this State.

SECTION 902. APPLICATION FOR CERTIFICATE OF AUTHORITY.

(a) A foreign limited partnership may apply for a certificate of authority to transact business in this State by delivering an application to the [Secretary of State] for filing. The application must state:

(1) the name of the foreign limited partnership and, if that name does not comply with Section 108, an alternate name adopted pursuant to Section 905(a).

(2) the name of the State or country under whose law it is organized;

(3) the street address of its principal office, and if the laws of the jurisdiction under which the foreign limited partnership is organized require the foreign limited partnership to maintain an office in that jurisdiction, the street address of that required office;

(4) the name and street address of its initial agent for service of process in this State;

(5) the name and address of each of its general partners;

(6) whether the foreign limited partnership is a foreign limited liability limited partnership.

(b) A foreign limited partnership shall deliver with the completed application a certificate of existence or a record of similar import authenticated by the [Secretary of State] or other official having custody of limited partnership's records in the State or country under whose law it is organized.

SECTION 903. ACTIVITIES NOT CONSTITUTING TRANSACTING BUSINESS.

(a) Activities of a foreign limited partnership that do not constitute transacting business in this State within the meaning of this [article] include:

(1) maintaining, defending, or settling an action or proceeding;

(2) holding meetings of its partners or carrying on any other activity concerning its internal affairs;

(3) maintaining bank accounts;

(4) maintaining offices or agencies for the transfer, exchange, and registration of the foreign limited partnership's own securities or maintaining trustees or depositories with respect to those securities;

(5) selling through independent contractors;

(6) soliciting or obtaining orders, whether by mail or electronic means or through employees or agents or otherwise, if the orders require acceptance outside this State before they become contracts;

(7) creating or acquiring indebtedness, mortgages, or security interests in real or personal property;

(8) securing or collecting debts or enforcing mortgages or other security interests in property securing the debts, and holding, protecting, and maintaining property so acquired;

(9) conducting an isolated transaction that is completed within 30 days and is not one in the course of similar transactions of a like manner; and

(10) transacting business in interstate commerce.

(b) For purposes of this [article], the ownership in this State of income-producing real property or tangible personal property, other than property excluded under subsection (a), constitutes transacting business in this State.

(c) This section does not apply in determining the contacts or activities that may subject a foreign limited partnership to service of process, taxation, or regulation under any other law of this State.

SECTION 904. ISSUANCE OF CERTIFICATE OF AUTHORI-TY. Unless the [Secretary of State] determines that an application for a certificate of authority fails to comply as to form with the filing requirements of this [Act], the [Secretary of State], upon payment of all filing fees, shall file the application, file a certificate of authority to transact business in this State and send a conformed copy of the certificate, together with a receipt for the fees to the foreign limited partnership or its representative.

SECTION 905. NONCOMPLYING NAME OF FOREIGN LIMITED PARTNERSHIP.

(a) A foreign limited partnership whose name does not comply with Section 108 may not obtain a certificate of authority until it adopts, for the purpose of transacting business in this State, an alternate name that complies with Section 108. A foreign limited partnership that adopts an alternate name under this subsection and then obtains a certificate of authority with that name need not comply with [fictitious name statute]. After obtaining a certificate of authority with an alternate name, a foreign limited partnership must transact business in this State under that name.

(b) If a foreign limited partnership authorized to transact business in this State changes its name to one that does not comply with Section 108, it may not thereafter transact business in this State until it complies with subsection (a) and obtains an amended certificate of authority.

SECTION 906. REVOCATION OF CERTIFICATE OF AUTHORITY.

(a) A certificate of authority of a foreign limited partnership to transact business in this State may be revoked by the [Secretary of State] in the manner provided in subsection (b) if the foreign limited partnership fails to:

(1) pay any fees, taxes, or penalties due to the [Secretary of State] under this [Act] or other law within 60 days after they are due;

(2) deliver its annual report required under Section 210 to the [Secretary of State] within 60 days after it is due;

(3) appoint and maintain an agent for service of process as required by Section 114(b); or

(4) file a statement of a change under Section 115 within [to be determined] days after a change has occurred in the name or address of the agent.

(b) The [Secretary of State] may not revoke a certificate of authority of a foreign limited partnership unless the [Secretary of State] sends the foreign limited partnership notice of the revocation, at least 60 days before its effective date, by a record addressed to its agent for service of process in this State, or if the foreign limited partnership fails to appoint and maintain a proper agent in this State, addressed to the foreign limited partnership's designated office. The notice must specify the cause for the revocation of the certificate of authority. The authority of the foreign limited partnership to transact business in this State ceases on the effective date of the revocation unless the foreign limited partnership cures the failure before that date.

SECTION 907. CANCELLATION OF CERTIFICATE OF AUTHORITY; EFFECT OF FAILURE TO HAVE CERTIFICATE.

(a) A foreign limited partnership may cancel its certificate of authority to transact business in this State by filing in the office of the [Secretary of State] a certificate of cancellation.

(b) A foreign limited partnership transacting business in this State may not maintain an action or proceeding in this State unless it has a certificate of authority to transact business in this State.

(c) The failure of a foreign limited partnership to have a certificate of authority to transact business in this State does not impair the validity of a contract or act of the foreign limited partnership or prevent the foreign limited partnership from defending an action or proceeding in this State.

(d) A partner of a foreign limited partnership is not liable for the obligations of the foreign limited partnership solely by reason of the foreign limited partnership's having transacted business in this State without a certificate of authority. (e) If a foreign limited partnership transacts business in this State without a certificate of authority or cancels its certificate of authority, it appoints the [Secretary of State] as its agent for service of process for rights of action arising out of the transaction of business in this State.

SECTION 908. ACTION BY [ATTORNEY GENERAL]. The [Attorney General] may maintain an action to restrain a foreign limited partnership from transacting business in this State in violation of this [article].

[ARTICLE] 10
ACTIONS BY PARTNERS
SECTION 1001. DIRECT ACTIONS BY PARTNERS.

(a) Subject to subsection (b), a partner may maintain a direct action against the partnership or another partner for legal or equitable relief, with or without an accounting as to partnership's business, to:

(1) enforce the partner's rights under the partnership agreement;

(2) enforce the partner's rights under this [Act]; or

(3) enforce the rights and otherwise protect the interests of the partner, including rights and interests arising independently of the partnership relationship.

(b) A partner bringing a direct action under this section must plead and prove an actual or threatened injury that is not solely the result of an injury suffered or threatened to be suffered by the limited partnership.

(c) The accrual of, and any time limitation on, a right of action for a remedy under this section is governed by other law. A right to an accounting upon a dissolution and winding up does not revive a claim barred by law.

SECTION 1002. DERIVATIVE ACTION. A partner may bring a derivative action to enforce a right of a limited partnership if:

(1) the partner first makes a demand on the general partners, requesting that they cause the limited partnership to bring an action to enforce the right, and the general partners do not bring the action within a reasonable time; or

(2) a demand will be futile.

SECTION 1003. PROPER PLAINTIFF. In a derivative action, the plaintiff must be a partner at the time of bringing the action and:

(1) the plaintiff must have been a partner when the conduct giving rise to action occurred; or

(2) the plaintiff's status as a partner must have devolved upon the plaintiff by operation of law or pursuant to the terms of the partnership agreement from a person who was a partner at the time of the conduct.

SECTION 1004. PLEADING. In a derivative action, the complaint must state with particularity:

(1) the date and content of plaintiff's demand and the general partners' response to the demand; or

(2) why demand is excused as futile.

SECTION 1005. PROCEEDS AND EXPENSES.

(a) Except as otherwise provided in subsection (b):

(1) any proceeds or other benefits of a derivative action, whether by judgment, compromise, or settlement, belong to the limited partnership and not to the derivative plaintiff;

(2) if the derivative plaintiff receives any of those proceeds, the derivative plaintiff shall immediately remit them to the limited partnership.

(b) If a derivative action is successful in whole or in part, the court may award the plaintiff reasonable expenses, including reasonable attorney's fees, from the recovery of the limited partnership.

[ARTICLE] 11
CONVERSIONS AND MERGERS

SECTION 1101. DEFINITIONS. In this [article]:

(1) ''Business organization'' means a domestic or foreign general partnership, including a limited liability partnership, a limited partnership, including a limited liability limited partnership, a limited liability company, a business trust, a corporation, and any other entity having owners and ownership interests under its governing statute.

(2) ''Constituent business organization'' means a business organization that is party to a merger.

(3) "Converted business organization" means the business organization into which a converting business organization converts pursuant to Section 1102.

(4) "Converting business organization" means a business organization that converts into another business organization pursuant to Section 1102.

(5) "General partner" means a general partner of a limited partnership.

(6) "Governing statute" of a business organization means the statute under which the organization is incorporated, organized, formed, or created and which governs the internal affairs of the organization.

(7) "Organizational documents" means:

(A) for a domestic or foreign general partnership, its partnership agreement;

(B) for a limited partnership and a foreign limited partnership, its certificate of limited partnership and partnership agreement;

(C) for a domestic or foreign limited liability company, its articles of organization and operating agreement;

(D) for a business trust, its agreement of trust and declaration of trust;

(E) for a domestic or foreign corporation, its articles of incorporation, bylaws, and other agreements among its shareholders which are authorized by its governing statute; and

(F) for any other business organization, the basic records that create the business organization and determine its internal governance and the relations among its owners.

(8) "Owner" means:

(A) with respect to a general or limited partnership, a partner;

(B) with respect to a limited liability company, a member;

(C) with respect to a business trust, the owner of a beneficial interest in the trust;

(D) with respect to a corporation, a shareholder; and

(E) with respect to any other business organization, a person who has an ownership interest in the organization.

(9) "Owner's liability" means personal liability for a debt, obligation, or liability of a business organization which is imposed on an owner:

(A) by the organization's governing statute solely by reason of the owner's capacity as owner; or

(B) by the organization's organizational documents under a provision of the organization's governing statute authorizing those documents to make one or more specified owners or categories of owners liable in their capacity as owners for all or specified debts, obligations, or liabilities of the business organization.

(10) "Person dissociated as a general partner" means a person dissociated as a general partner of a limited partnership.

(11) "Surviving business organization" means a business organization into which one or more other business organizations are merged. A surviving business organization may preexist the merger or be created by the merger.

SECTION 1102. CONVERSION.

(a) A business organization other than a limited partnership may convert to a limited partnership, and a limited partnership may convert to another business organization pursuant to Sections 1102 through 1105 and a plan of conversion, if:

(1) those sections are not inconsistent with the governing statute of the other business organization; and

(2) the other business organization complies with its governing statute in effecting the conversion.

(b) The plan of conversion must include:

(1) the name and form of the business organization before conversion;

(2) the name and form of the business organization after conversion; and

(3) the terms and conditions of the conversion; and

(4) the organizational documents of the converted business organization.

SECTION 1103. ACTION ON PLAN OF CONVERSION BY LIMITED PARTNERSHIP.

(a) If a converting business organization is a limited partnership, subject to Section 1110 all the partners must approve the plan of conversion.

(b) After a conversion is approved, and at any time before a filing is made under Section 1104, a converting business organization that is a limited partnership may amend the plan or abandon the planned conversion subject to any contractual rights:

(1) as provided in the plan; and

(2) except as prohibited by the plan, by the same consent as was required to approve the plan.

SECTION 1104. FILINGS REQUIRED; EFFECTIVE DATE.

(a) After a plan of conversion is approved:

(1) if the converting business organization is a limited partnership, the limited partnership shall file with the [Secretary of State] articles of conversion, which must include:

(A) a statement that the limited partnership has been converted into another business organization;

(B) the name and form of that business organization and the jurisdiction of its governing statute;

(C) the date the conversion is effective according to the governing statute of converted business organization;

(D) a statement that the conversion was approved as required by this [Act]; and

(E) a statement that the conversion was approved as required by the governing statute of the converted business organization; and

(2) if the converting business organization is a not a limited partnership, the converting business organization shall file with the [Secretary of State] a certificate of limited partnership, which must include, in addition to the information required by Section 201:

(A) a statement that the limited partnership was converted from another form of business organization;

(B) the name and form of that business organization and the jurisdiction of its governing statute; and

(C) a statement that the conversion was approved in a manner that complied with the business organization's governing statute.

(b) A conversion becomes effective:

(1) if the converted business organization is a limited partnership, when the certificate of limited partnership takes effect; and

(2) if the converted business organization is not a limited partnership, as provided by the governing statute of the converted business organization.

SECTION 1105. EFFECT OF CONVERSION.

(a) A business organization that has been converted pursuant to this [article] is for all purposes the same entity that existed before the conversion.

(b) When a conversion takes effect:

(1) all property owned by the converting business organization vests in the converted business organization;

(2) all debts, liabilities, and other obligations of the converting business organization continue as obligations of the converted business organization;

(3) an action or proceeding pending by or against the converting business organization may be continued as if the conversion had not occurred;

(4) except as prohibited by other law, all of the rights, privileges, immunities, powers, and purposes of the converting business organization vest in the converted business organization; and

(5) except as otherwise agreed, if the converting business organization is a limited partnership the conversion does not dissolve the limited partnership for the purpose of [Article] 8.

(c) A converted business organization that is a foreign entity consents to the jurisdiction of the courts of this State to enforce any obligation owed by the converting business organization, if before the conversion the converting business organization was subject to suit in this State on that obligation. A converted business organization that is a foreign entity and not authorized to transact business in this State appoints the [Secretary of State] as its agent for service of process for the purposes of enforcing an obligation under this subsection. Service on the [Secretary of State] under this subsection is made in the same manner and with the same consequences as stated in Section 117(c) and (d).

SECTION 1106. MERGER.

(a) A limited partnership may merge with one or more other constituent business organizations pursuant to Sections 1106 through 1109 and a plan of merger, if:

(1) those sections are not inconsistent with the governing statute of each of the other constituent business organizations; and

(2) each of the other constituent business organizations complies with its governing statute in effecting the merger.

(b) The plan of merger must include:

(1) the name and form of each constituent business organization;

(2) the name and form of the surviving business organization and, if the surviving business organization is to be created by the merger, a statement to that effect;

(3) the terms and conditions of the merger;

(4) if the surviving business organization is to be created by the merger, the surviving business organization's organizational documents; and

(5) if the surviving business organization is not to be created by the merger, any amendments to be made by the merger to the surviving business organization's organizational documents.

SECTION 1107. ACTION ON PLAN OF MERGER BY LIMITED PARTNERSHIP.

(a) Subject to Section 1110, all the partners of a constituent business organization that is a limited partnership must approve the plan of merger.

(b) After a merger is approved, and at any time before a filing is made under Section 1108, a constituent business organization that is a limited partnership may amend the or abandon the planned merger, subject to any contractual rights:

(1) as provided in the plan; and

(2) except as prohibited by the plan, by the same consent as was required to approve the plan; and

SECTION 1108. FILINGS REQUIRED; EFFECTIVE DATE.

(a) After each constituent business organization has approved a merger, articles of merger must be signed on behalf of:

(1) each preexisting constituent business organization that is a limited partnership, by each general partner listed in the certificate of limited partnership; and

(2) each preexisting constituent business organization that is not a limited partnership, by a duly authorized representative.

(b) The articles of merger must include:

(1) the name and form of each constituent business organization and the jurisdiction of its governing statute;

(2) the name and form of the surviving business organization, the jurisdiction of its governing statute and, if the surviving business organization is created by the merger, a statement to that effect;

(3) the date the merger is effective;

(4) if the surviving business organization is to be created by the merger:

(A) if it will be a limited partnership, the limited partnership's certificate of limited partnership; or

(B) if it will be a business organization other than a limited partnership, the organizational document that creates the business organization;

(5) if the surviving business organization preexists the merger, any amendments provided for in the plan of merger for the organizational document that created the business organization; and

(6) a statement as to each constituent business organization that the merger was approved as required by the business organization's governing statute;

(7) any additional information required by the governing statute of any constituent business organization

(c) Each constituent business organization that is a limited partnership shall file the articles of merger in the [office of the Secretary of State].

(d) A merger becomes effective under this [article] upon the later of:

(1) compliance with subsection (c) and the performance of any acts required to effectuate the merger under the governing statute of each constituent business organization; or

(2) subject to Section 206, a later date specified in the articles of merger.

SECTION 1109. EFFECT OF MERGER.

(a) When a merger becomes effective:

(1) the surviving business organization continues or comes into existence;

(2) each constituent business organization that merges into the surviving business organization ceases to exist as a separate entity;

(3) all property owned by each constituent business organization that ceases to exist vests in the surviving business organization;

(4) all debts, liabilities, and other obligations of each constituent business organization that ceases to exist continue as obligations of the surviving business organization;

(5) an action or proceeding pending by or against any constituent business organization that ceases to exist may be continued as if the merger had not occurred;

(6) except as prohibited by other law, all of the rights, privileges, immunities, powers, and purposes of each constituent business organization that ceases to exist vest in the surviving business organization;

(7) except as otherwise agreed, if a constituent business organization is a limited partnership that ceases to exist, the merger does not dissolve the limited partnership for the purpose of [Article] 8;

(8) if the surviving business organization is created by the merger:

(A) if it is a limited partnership, the certificate of limited partnership becomes effective; or

(B) if it is a business organization other than a limited partnership, the organizational document that creates the business organization becomes effective; and

(9) if the surviving business organization preexists the merger, any amendments provided for in the plan of merger for the organizational document that created the business organization become effective.

(b) A surviving business organization that is a foreign entity consents to the jurisdiction of the courts of this State to enforce any obligation owed by the a constituent business organization that ceases to exist, if before the merger the constituent business organization was subject to suit in this State on that obligation. A surviving business organization that is a foreign entity and not authorized to transact business in this State appoints the [Secretary of State] as its agent for service of process for the purposes of enforcing an obligation under this subsection. Service on the [Secretary of State] under this subsection is made in the same manner and with the same consequences as stated in Section 117(c) and (d).

SECTION 1110. RESTRICTIONS ON NON–UNANIMOUS APPROVAL OF CONVERSIONS AND MERGERS. A partnership agreement that provides for the approval of a conversion or merger with the consent of less than all the partners is ineffective against a partner who:

(1) will have owner's liability for the obligations of the converted or surviving organization; and

(2) did not assent to the provision of the partnership agreement.

SECTION 1111. LIABILITY OF GENERAL PARTNERS AFTER CONVERSION OR MERGER.

(a) A conversion or merger under this article does not discharge any liability under Sections 404 and 607 of a person who was a general partner or dissociated as a general partner in a converting or constituent business organization, but:

(1) the provisions of this [Act] pertaining to the collection or discharge of that liability continue to apply to that liability;

(2) for the purposes of applying those provisions, the converted or surviving business organization is deemed to be the converting or constituent business organization; and

(3) if a person is required to pay any amount under this subsection:

(A) the person has a right of contribution from each other person who was a general partner when the obligation was incurred and who has not been released from that obligation under Section 607; and

(B) the contribution due from each of those persons is in proportion to the allocation of limited partnership losses in effect for those persons.

(b) In addition to any other liability provided by law:

(1) a person who immediately before a conversion or merger became effective was a general partner in a converting or constituent business organization and had owner's liability for that business organization's obligations is personally liable for each obligation of the converted or surviving business organization arising from a transaction with a third party after the conversion or merger becomes effective, if at the time the third party enters into the transaction the third party:

(A) does not have notice of the conversion or merger; and

(B) reasonably believes that the converted or surviving business is the converting or constituent business organization and that the person is a general partner in the converting or constituent business organization; .

(2) a person who was dissociated as a general partner from a converting or constituent business organization before the conversion or merger became effective is personally liable for each obligation of the converted or surviving business organization arising from a transaction with a third party after the conversion or merger becomes effective, if:

(A) immediately before the conversion or merger became effective the converting or surviving business organization was a limited partnership whose certificate of limited partnership included a statement under Section 404(b); and

407

(B) at the time the third party enters into the transaction less than two years have passed since the person dissociated as a general partner and the third party:

(i) does not have notice of the dissociation;

(ii) does not have notice of the conversion or merger; and

(iii) reasonably believes that the converted or surviving business organization is the converting or constituent business organization and that the person is a general partner in the converting or constituent business organization.

SECTION 1112. POWER OF GENERAL PARTNERS AND PERSONS DISSOCIATED AS GENERAL PARTNERS TO BIND AFTER CONVERSION OR MERGER.

(a) An act of a person who immediately before a conversion or merger became effective was a general partner in a converting or constituent business organization binds the converted or surviving business organization after the conversion or merger becomes effective, if:

(1) before the conversion or merger became effective, the act would have bound the converting or constituent business organization under Section 404; and

(2) at the time the third party enters into the transaction the third party:

(A) does not have notice of the conversion or merger; and

(B) reasonably believes that the converted or surviving business is the converting or constituent business organization and that the person is a general partner in the converting or constituent business organization.

(b) An act of a person who before a conversion or merger became effective was dissociated as a general partner from a converting or constituent business organization binds the converted or surviving business organization after the conversion or merger becomes effective, if:

(1) before the conversion or merger became effective the act would have bound the converting or constituent entity under Section 404 if the person had been a general partner; and

(2) at the time the third party enters into the transaction less than two years have passed since the person dissociated as a general partner and the third party:

(A) does not have notice of the dissociation;

(B) does not have notice of the conversion or merger; and

(C) reasonably believes that the converted or surviving business is the converting or constituent business organization and that the person is a general partner in the converting or constituent business organization.

(c) If a person having knowledge of the conversion or merger causes a converted or surviving business organization to incur an obligation under subsection (a) or (b), the person is liable:

(1) to the converted or surviving business organization for any damage caused to the business organization arising from the obligation; and

(2) if another person is liable for the obligation, to that other person for any damage caused to that other person arising from that liability.

SECTION 1113. [ARTICLE] NOT EXCLUSIVE. This [article] does not preclude an entity from being converted or merged under other law.

[ARTICLE] 12
MISCELLANEOUS PROVISIONS

SECTION 1201. UNIFORMITY OF APPLICATION AND CON-STRUCTION. In applying and construing this Uniform Act, consideration must be given to the need to promote uniformity of the law with respect to its subject matter among States that enact it.

SECTION 1202. SEVERABILITY CLAUSE. If any provision of this [Act] or its application to any person or circumstance is held invalid, the invalidity does not affect other provisions or applications of this [Act] which can be given effect without the invalid provision or application, and to this end the provisions of this [Act] are severable.

SECTION 1203. EFFECTIVE DATE. This [Act] takes effect January 1, 20___.

SECTION 1204. REPEALS. Except as otherwise provided in Section 1205 effective January 1, 20___, the following acts and parts of acts are repealed: [the State Limited Partnership Act as amended and in effect immediately before the effective date of this [Act]].

SECTION 1205. APPLICABILITY.

(a) Before January 1, 20___, this [Act] governs only:

(1) a limited partnership formed on or after the effective date of this [Act]; and

(2) a limited partnership formed before the effective date of this [Act], that elects, as provided by subsection (d), to be governed by this [Act].

(b) Except as otherwise provided in subsection (c), beginning January 1, 20___, this [Act] governs all limited partnerships.

(c) Each of the following provisions of [the State Limited Partnership Act as amended and in effect immediately before the effective date of this [Act]] continue to apply after January 1, 20___, to a limited partnership formed before the effective date of this [Act], except as the partners otherwise elect in the manner provided in the partnership agreement or by law for amending the partnership agreement:

(1) [To be determined]

(2)

(d) Before January 1, 20___, a limited partnership formed before the effective date of this [Act] voluntarily may elect, in the manner provided in its partnership agreement or by law for amending the partnership agreement, to be governed by this [Act]. If a limited partnership formed before the effective date of this [Act] makes that election, the provisions of this [Act] relating to the liability of the limited partnership's partners to third parties apply:

(1) before January 1, 20___, to:

(A) a third party who had not done business with the limited partnership within one year before the limited partnership's election to be governed by this [Act]; and

(B) a third party who had done business with the limited partnership within one year before the limited partnership's election to be governed by this [Act], only if the third party knows or has received a notification of the partnership's election to be governed by this [Act]; and

(2) after January 1, 20___, to all third parties.

SECTION 1206. SAVINGS CLAUSE. This [Act] does not affect an action or proceeding commenced or right accrued before this [Act] takes effect.

TEXAS LIMITED LIABILITY PARTNERSHIP ACT

[TEXAS REVISED PARTNERSHIP ACT, TEX.CIV.STATS. ART. 6132b]

Section 1.01. General Definitions

In this Act: . . .

(11) "Partnership" means an entity created as described by Section 2.02(a). The term includes a registered limited liability partnership formed under Section 3.08 or under the Texas Uniform Partnership Act . . . and its subsequent amendments. . . .

Section 3.08. Liability in and Registration of Registered Limited Liability Partnership

(a) LIABILITY OF PARTNER. (1) Except as provided in Subsection (a)(2), a partner in a registered limited liability partnership is not individually liable, directly or indirectly, by contribution, indemnity, or otherwise, for debts and obligations of the partnership incurred while the partnership is a registered limited liability partnership.

(2) A partner in a registered limited liability partnership is not individually liable, directly or indirectly, by contribution, indemnity, or otherwise, for debts and obligations of the partnership arising from errors, omissions, negligence, incompetence, or malfeasance committed while the partnership is a registered limited liability partnership and in the course of the partnership business by another partner or a representative of the partnership not working under the supervision or direction of the first partner unless the first partner:

(A) was directly involved in the specific activity in which the errors, omissions, negligence, incompetence, or malfeasance were committed by the other partner or representative; or

(B) had notice or knowledge of the errors, omissions, negligence, incompetence, or malfeasance by the other partner or representative at the time of occurrence and then failed to take reasonable steps to prevent or cure the errors, omissions, negligence, incompetence, or malfeasance.

(3) Subsections (a)(1) and (a)(2) do not affect:

(A) the liability of a partnership to pay its debts and obligations out of partnership property;

(B) the liability of a partner, if any, imposed by law or contract independently of the partner's status as a partner, or

(C) the manner in which service of citation or other civil process may be served in an action against a partnership.

(4) In this subsection, "representative" includes an agent, servant, or employee of a registered limited liability partnership.

(5) In the case of a registered limited liability partnership, Subsection (a) prevails over the other parts of this Act regarding the liability of partners, their chargeability for the debts and obligations of the partnership, and their obligations regarding contributions and indemnity.

(b) REGISTRATION. (1) In addition to complying with Subsections (c) and (d)(1), to become a registered limited liability partnership, a partnership must file with the secretary of state an application stating:

(A) the name of the partnership;

(B) the federal tax identification number of the partnership;

(C) the street address of the partnership's principal office in this state and outside this state, as applicable;

(D) the number of partners at the date of application; and

(E) in brief, the partnership's business.

(2) The application must be executed by a majority-in-interest of the partners or by one or more partners authorized by a majority-in-interest of the partners.

(3) Two copies of the application must be filed, accompanied by a fee of $100 for each partner.

(4) A partnership is registered as a registered limited liability partnership on filing a completed initial or renewal application, in duplicate with the required fee, or on a later date specified in the application. A registration is not affected by later changes in the partners of the partnership.

(5) An initial application filed under this subsection and registered by the secretary of state expires one year after the date of registration or later effective date unless earlier withdrawn or revoked or unless renewed in accordance with Subdivision (7).

(6) A registration may be withdrawn by filing in duplicate with the secretary of state a written withdrawal notice executed by a majority-in-interest of the partners or by one or more partners authorized by a majority-in-interest of the partners. A withdrawal notice must include the name of the partnership, the federal tax identification number of the partnership, the date of registration of the partnership's last application under this section, and a current street address of the partnership's principal office in this state and outside this state, if applicable. A withdrawal notice terminates the status of the partnership as a registered limited liability partnership as of the date of filing the notice or a later date specified in the notice, but not later than the expiration date under Subdivision (5).

(7) An effective registration may be renewed before its expiration by filing in duplicate with the secretary of state an application containing current information of the kind required in an initial application and the

most recent date of registration of the partnership. The renewal application must be accompanied by a fee of $200 for each partner on the date of renewal. A renewal application filed under this section continues an effective registration for one year after the date the effective registration would otherwise expire. . . .

(c) NAME. A registered limited liability partnership's name must contain the words "registered limited liability partnership" or the abbreviation "L.L.P." as the last words or letters of its name.

(d) INSURANCE OR FINANCIAL RESPONSIBILITY. (1) A registered limited liability partnership must:

(A) carry at least $100,000 of liability insurance of a kind that is designed to cover the kinds of errors, omissions, negligence, incompetence, or malfeasance for which liability is limited by Subsection (a)(2); or

(B) provide $100,000 of funds specifically designated and segregated for the satisfaction of judgments against the partnership based on the kinds of errors, omissions, negligence, incompetence, or malfeasance for which liability is limited by Subsection (a)(2) by:

(i) deposit in trust or in bank escrow of cash, bank certificates of deposit, or United States Treasury obligations; or

(ii) a bank letter of credit or insurance company bond.

(2) If the registered limited liability partnership is in compliance with Subdivision (1), the requirements of this subsection shall not be admissible or in any way be made known to the jury in determining an issue of liability for or extent of the debt or obligation or damages in question.

(3) If compliance with Subdivision (1) is disputed:

(A) compliance must be determined separately from the trial or proceeding to determine the partnership debt or obligation in question, its amount, or partner liability for the debt or obligation; and

(B) the burden of proof of compliance is on the person claiming limitation of liability under Subsection (a)(2).

(e) LIMITED PARTNERSHIP. A limited partnership may become a registered limited liability partnership by complying with applicable provisions of the Texas Revised Limited Partnership Act and its subsequent amendments.

**[TEXAS REVISED LIMITED PARTNERSHIP ACT,
TEX.CIV.STATS. ART. 6132a–1]**

Section 2.14.   Limited Partnership as Registered Limited Liability Partnership

(a) A limited partnership is a registered limited liability partnership as well as a limited partnership if it:

(1) registers as a registered limited liability partnership as provided by Section 3.08(b), Texas Revised Partnership Act, as permitted by its partnership agreement or, if its partnership agreement does not include provisions for becoming a registered limited liability partnership, with the consent of partners required to amend its partnership agreement;

(2) complies with Section 3.08(d), Texas Revised Partnership Act; and

(3) has as the last words or letters of its name the words "Limited Partnership" or the abbreviation "Ltd." followed by the words "registered limited liability partnership" or the abbreviation "L.L.P."

(b) In applying Section 3.08(b), Texas Revised Partnership Act, to a limited partnership:

(1) an application to become a registered limited liability partnership or to withdraw a registration must be executed by at least one general partner; and

(2) all other references to partners mean general partners only.

(c) If a limited partnership is a registered limited liability partnership, Section 3.08(a), Texas Revised Partnership Act, applies to its general partners and to any of its limited partners who, under other provisions of this Act, are liable for the debts or obligations of the limited partnership.

DELAWARE LIMITED LIABILITY COMPANY ACT
DEL.CODE ANN. TITLE 6, CHAPTER 18

SUBCHAPTER I. GENERAL PROVISIONS

SUBCHAPTER II. FORMATION; CERTIFICATE OF FORMATION

SUBCHAPTER III. MEMBERS

* Omitted.

* Omitted.

SUBCHAPTER I. GENERAL PROVISIONS

§ 18–101. Definitions.

As used in this chapter unless the context otherwise requires:

(1) "Bankruptcy" means an event that causes a person to cease to be a member as provided in § 18–304 of this title.

(2) "Certificate of formation" means the certificate referred to in § 18–201 of this title, and the certificate as amended.

(3) "Contribution" means any cash, property, services rendered or a promissory note or other obligation to contribute cash or property or to perform services, which a person contributes to a limited liability company in his capacity as a member.

(4) "Foreign limited liability company" means a limited liability company formed under the laws of any state or under the laws of any foreign country or other foreign jurisdiction and denominated as such under the laws of such state or foreign country or other foreign jurisdiction.

(5) "Knowledge" means a person's actual knowledge of a fact, rather than the person's constructive knowledge of the fact.

(6) "Limited liability company" and "domestic limited liability company" means a limited liability company formed under the laws of the State of Delaware and having 1 or more members.

(7) "Limited liability company agreement" means any agreement, written or oral, of the member or members as to the affairs of a limited liability company and the conduct of its business. A limited liability company agreement of a limited liability company having only one member shall not be unenforceable by reason of there being only one person who is a party to the limited liability company agreement. A written limited liability company agreement or another written agreement or writing:

a. May provide that a person shall be admitted as a member of a limited liability company, or shall become an assignee of a limited liability company interest or other rights or powers of a member to the extent assigned, and shall become bound by the limited liability company agreement:

1. If such person (or a representative authorized by such person orally, in writing or by other action such as payment for a limited liability company interest) executes the limited liability company agreement or any other writing evidencing the intent of such person to become a member or assignee; or

2. Without such execution, if such person (or a representative authorized by such person orally, in writing or by other action such as payment for a limited liability company interest) complies with the conditions for becoming a member or assignee as set forth in the limited liability company agreement or any other writing; and

b. Shall not be unenforceable by reason of its not having been signed by a person being admitted as a member or becoming an assignee as provided in subparagraph a. of this paragraph, or by reason of its having been signed by a representative as provided in this chapter.

(8) "Limited liability company interest" means a member's share of the profits and losses of a limited liability company and a member's right to receive distributions of the limited liability company's assets.

(9) "Liquidating trustee" means a person carrying out the winding up of a limited liability company.

(10) "Manager" means a person who is named as a manager of a limited liability company in, or designated as a manager of a limited liability company pursuant to, a limited liability company agreement or similar instrument under which the limited liability company is formed.

(11) "Member" means a person who has been admitted to a limited liability company as a member as provided in § 18–301 of this title or, in the case of a foreign limited liability company, in accordance

with the laws of the state or foreign country or other foreign jurisdiction under which the foreign limited liability company is organized.

(12) "Person" means a natural person, partnership (whether general or limited and whether domestic or foreign), limited liability company, foreign limited liability company, trust, estate, association, corporation, custodian, nominee or any other individual or entity in its own or any representative capacity.

(13) "Personal representative" means, as to a natural person, the executor, administrator, guardian, conservator or other legal representative thereof and, as to a person other than a natural person, the legal representative or successor thereof.

(14) "State" means the District of Columbia or the Commonwealth of Puerto Rico or any state, territory, possession or other jurisdiction of the United States other than the State of Delaware.

§ 18–102. Name Set Forth in Certificate

The name of each limited liability company as set forth in its certificate of formation:

(1) Shall contain the words "Limited Liability Company" or the abbreviation "L.L.C." or the designation LLC;

(2) May contain the name of a member or manager;

(3) Must be such as to distinguish it upon the records in the office of the Secretary of State from the name of any corporation, limited partnership, business trust, registered limited liability partnership or limited liability company reserved, registered, formed or organized under the laws of the State of Delaware or qualified to do business or registered as a foreign corporation, foreign limited partnership or foreign limited liability company in the State of Delaware; provided however, that a limited liability company may register under any name which is not such as to distinguish it upon the records in the office of the Secretary of State from the name of any domestic or foreign corporation, limited partnership, business trust, registered limited liability partnership or limited liability company reserved, registered, formed or organized under the laws of the State of Delaware with the written consent of the other corporation, limited partnership, business trust, registered limited liability partnership or limited liability company, which written consent shall be filed with the Secretary of State; and

(4) May contain the following words: "Company," "Association," "Club," "Foundation," "Fund," "Institute," "Society," "Union," "Syndicate," "Limited" or "Trust" (or abbreviations of like import).

§ 18–104. Registered Office; Registered Agent

(a) Each limited liability company shall have and maintain in the State of Delaware:

(1) A registered office, which may but need not be a place of its business in the State of Delaware; and

(2) A registered agent for service of process on the limited liability company, which agent may be either an individual resident of the State of Delaware whose business office is identical with the limited liability company's registered office, or a domestic corporation, or a domestic limited partnership, or a domestic limited liability company, or a domestic business trust, or a foreign corporation, or a foreign limited partnership, or a foreign limited liability company authorized to do business in the State of Delaware having a business office identical with such registered office, which is generally open during normal business hours to accept service of process and otherwise perform the functions of a registered agent, or the limited liability company itself. . . .

§ 18–105. Service of Process on Domestic Limited Liability Companies

(a) Service of legal process upon any domestic limited liability company shall be made by delivering a copy personally to any manager of the limited liability company in the State of Delaware or the registered agent of the limited liability company in the State of Delaware, or by leaving it at the dwelling house or usual place of abode in the State of Delaware of any such manager or registered agent (if the registered agent be an individual), or at the registered office or other place of business of the limited liability company in the State of Delaware. If the registered agent be a corporation, service of process upon it as such may be made by serving, in the State of Delaware, a copy thereof on the president, vice-president, secretary, assistant secretary or any director of the corporate registered agent. Service by copy left at the dwelling house or usual place of abode of a manager or registered agent, or at the registered office or other place of business of the limited liability company in the State of Delaware, to be effective, must be delivered thereat at least 6 days before the return date of the process, and in the presence of an adult person, and the officer serving the process shall distinctly state the manner of service in his return thereto. Process returnable forthwith must be delivered personally to the manager or registered agent.

(b) In case the officer whose duty it is to serve legal process cannot by due diligence serve the process in any manner provided for by subsection (a) of this section, it shall be lawful to serve the process against the limited liability company upon the Secretary of State, and such service shall be as effectual for all intents and purposes as if made in any of the ways provided for in subsection (a) of this section. In the event that service is effected through the Secretary of State in accordance with this subsection, the Secretary of State shall forthwith notify the limited liability company by letter, certified mail, return receipt requested, directed to the limited liability company at its address as it appears on the records relating to such limited liability company on file with the Secretary of State or, if no such address appears, at its last registered office. Such letter shall enclose a copy of the process and any other papers served on the Secretary of State pursuant to this subsection. It shall be the duty of the plaintiff in the event of such service to serve process and any other papers in duplicate, to notify the Secretary of State that service is being effected pursuant to this subsection, and to pay the Secretary of State the sum of $50 for the use of the State of Delaware, which sum shall be taxed as part of the costs in the proceeding if the plaintiff shall prevail therein. The Secretary of State shall maintain an alphabetical record of any such service setting forth the name of the plaintiff and defendant, the title, docket number and nature of the proceeding in which process has been served upon him, the fact that service has been effected pursuant to this subsection, the return date thereof, and the day and hour when the service was made. The Secretary of State shall not be required to retain such information for a period longer than 5 years from his receipt of the service of process.

§ 18–106. Nature of Business Permitted; Powers

(a) A limited liability company may carry on any lawful business, purpose or activity, whether or not for profit, with the exception of the business of granting policies of insurance, or assuming insurance risks or banking as defined in § 126 of Title 8.

(b) A limited liability company shall possess and may exercise all the powers and privileges granted by this chapter or by any other law or by its limited liability company agreement, together with any powers incidental thereto, including such powers and privileges as are necessary or convenient to the conduct, promotion or attainment of the business, purposes or activities of the limited liability company.

§ 18–107. Business Transactions of Member or Manager With the Limited Liability Company

Except as provided in a limited liability company agreement, a member or manager may lend money to, borrow money from, act as a surety, guarantor or endorser for, guarantee or assume 1 or more obligations of, provide collateral for, and transact other business with, a limited liability company and, subject to other applicable law, has the same rights and obligations with respect to any such matter as a person who is not a member or manager.

§ 18–108. Indemnification

Subject to such standards and restrictions, if any, as are set forth in its limited liability company agreement, a limited liability company may, and shall have the power to, indemnify and hold harmless any member or manager or other person from and against any and all claims and demands whatsoever.

421

§ 18–109. Service of Process on Managers and Liquidating Trustees

(a) A manager or a liquidating trustee of a limited liability company may be served with process in the manner prescribed in this section in all civil actions or proceedings brought in the State of Delaware involving or relating to the business of the limited liability company or a violation by the manager or the liquidating trustee of a duty to the limited liability company, or any member of the limited liability company, whether or not the manager or the liquidating trustee is a manager or a liquidating trustee at the time suit is commenced. A manager's or a liquidating trustee's serving as such constitutes such person's consent to the appointment of the registered agent of the limited liability company (or, if there is none, the Secretary of State) as such person's agent upon whom service of process may be made as provided in this section. Such service as a manager or a liquidating trustee shall signify the consent of such manager or liquidating trustee that any process when so served shall be of the same legal force and validity as if served upon such manager or liquidating trustee within the State of Delaware and such appointment of the registered agent (or, if there is none, the Secretary of State) shall be irrevocable. As used in this subsection (a) and in subsection (b) and (c) of this § 18–109, the term "manager" refers (i) to a person who is a manager as defined in § 18–101(10) of this chapter and (ii) to a person who is a member of a limited liability company and who, although not a manager as defined in § 18–101(10) of this chapter, participates materially in the management of the limited liability company, *provided, however,* that the power to elect or otherwise select or to participate in the election or selection of a person to be a manager as defined in § 18–101(10) of this chapter shall not, by itself, constitute participation in the management of the limited liability company.

(b) Service of process shall be effected by serving the registered agent (or, if there is none, the Secretary of State) with 1 copy of such process in the manner provided by law for service of writs of summons. In the event service is made under this subsection upon the Secretary of State, the plaintiff shall pay to the Secretary of State the sum of $50 for the use of the State of Delaware, which sum shall be taxed as part of the costs of the proceeding if the plaintiff shall prevail therein. In addition, the Prothonotary or the Register in Chancery of the court in which the civil action or proceeding is pending shall, within 7 days of such service, deposit in the United States mails, by registered mail, postage prepaid, true and attested copies of the process, together with a statement that service is being made pursuant to this section, addressed to such manager or liquidating trustee at the registered office of the limited liability company and at his address last known to the party desiring to make such service.

(c) In any action in which any such manager or liquidating trustee has been served with process as hereinabove provided, the time in which a defendant shall be required to appear and file a responsive pleading shall be computed from the date of mailing by the Prothonotary or the Register in Chancery as provided in subsection (b) of this section; however, the court in which such action has been commenced may order such continuance or continuances as may be necessary to afford such manager or liquidating trustee reasonable opportunity to defend the action.

(d) In a written limited liability company agreement or other writing, a manager or member may consent to be subject to the nonexclusive jurisdiction of the courts of, or arbitration in, a specified jurisdiction, or the exclusive jurisdiction of the courts of the State of Delaware, or the exclusivity of arbitration in a specified jurisdiction or the State of Delaware, and to be served with legal process in the manner prescribed in such limited liability company agreement or other writing.

(e) Nothing herein contained limits or affects the right to serve process in any other manner now or hereafter provided by law. This section is an extension of and not a limitation upon the right otherwise existing of service of legal process upon nonresidents.

(f) The Court of Chancery and the Superior Court may make all necessary rules respecting the form of process, the manner of issuance and return thereof and such other rules which may be necessary to implement this section and are not inconsistent with this section.

§ 18–110. Contested Matters Relating to Managers; Contested Votes

(a) Upon application of any member or manager, the Court of Chancery may hear and determine the validity of any admission, election, appointment, removal or resignation of a manager of a limited liability company, and the right of any person to become or continue to be a manager of a limited liability company, and, in case the right to serve as a manager is claimed by more than 1 person, may determine the person or persons entitled to serve as managers; and to that end make such order or decree in any such case as may be just and proper, with power to enforce the production of any books, papers and records of the limited liability company relating to the issue. In any such application the limited liability company shall be named as a party and service of copies of the application upon the registered agent of the limited liability company shall be deemed to be service upon the limited liability company and upon the person or persons whose right to serve as a manager is contested and upon the person or persons, if any, claiming to be a manager or claiming the right to be a manager; and the registered agent shall forward immediately a copy of the application to the limited liability company and to the person or persons whose right to serve as a manager is contested and to the person or persons, if any, claiming to be a manager or the right to be a manager, in a postpaid, sealed, registered letter addressed to such limited liability company and such person or persons at their post-office addresses last known to the registered agent or furnished to the registered agent by the applicant member or manager. The Court may make such order respecting further or other notice of such application as it deems proper under [the] circumstances.

(b) Upon application of any member or manager, the Court of Chancery may hear and determine the result of any vote of members or managers upon matters as to which the members or managers of the limited liability company, or any class or group of members or managers, have the right to vote pursuant to the limited liability company agreement or other agreement or this chapter (other than the admission, election, appointment, removal or resignation of managers). In any such application, the limited liability company shall be named as a party and service of the application upon the registered agent of the limited liability company shall be deemed to be service upon the limited liability company, and no other party need be joined in order for the Court to adjudicate the result of the vote. The Court may make such order respecting further or other notice of such application as it deems proper under [the] circumstances.

(c) Nothing herein contained limits or affects the right to serve process in any other manner now or hereafter provided by law. This section is an extension of and not a limitation upon the right otherwise existing of service of legal process upon nonresidents.

§ 18–111. Interpretation and Enforcement of Limited Liability Company Agreement

Any action to interpret, apply or enforce the provisions of a limited liability company agreement, or the duties, obligations or liabilities of a limited liability company to the members or managers of the limited liability company, or the duties, obligations or liabilities among members or managers and of members or managers to the limited liability company, or the rights or powers of, or restrictions on, the limited liability company, members or managers, may be brought in the Court of Chancery.

SUBCHAPTER II. FORMATION; CERTIFICATE OF FORMATION

§ 18–201. Certificate of Formation

(a) In order to form a limited liability company, 1 or more authorized persons must execute a certificate of formation. The certificate of formation shall be filed in the office of the Secretary of State and set forth:

(1) The name of the limited liability company;

(2) The address of the registered office and the name and address of the registered agent for service of process required to be maintained by § 18–104 of this title; and

(3) Any other matters the members determine to include therein.

(b) A limited liability company is formed at the time of the filing of the initial certificate of formation in the office of the Secretary of State or at any later date or time specified in the certificate of formation if, in either case, there has been substantial compliance with the requirements of this section. A limited liability company formed under this chapter shall be a separate legal entity, the existence of which as a separate legal entity shall continue until cancellation of the limited liability company's certificate of formation.

(c) The filing of the certificate of formation in the office of the Secretary of State shall make it unnecessary to file any other documents under Chapter 31 of this title.

(d) A limited liability company agreement may be entered into either before, after or at the time of the filing of a certificate of formation and, whether entered into before, after or at the time of such filing, may be made effective as of the formation of the limited liability company or at such other time or date as provided in the limited liability company agreement.

§ 18–202. Amendment to Certificate of Formation

(a) A certificate of formation is amended by filing a certificate of amendment thereto in the office of the Secretary of State. The certificate of amendment shall set forth:

(1) The name of the limited liability company; and

(2) The amendment to the certificate of formation.

(b) A manager or, if there is no manager, then any member who becomes aware that any statement in a certificate of formation was false when made, or that any matter described has changed making the certificate of formation false in any material respect, shall promptly amend the certificate of formation.

(c) A certificate of formation may be amended at any time for any other proper purpose.

(d) Unless otherwise provided in this chapter or unless a later effective date or time (which shall be a date or time certain) is provided for in the certificate of amendment, a certificate of amendment shall be effective at the time of its filing with the Secretary of State.

§ 18–203. Cancellation of Certificate

A certificate of formation shall be cancelled upon the dissolution and the completion of winding up of a limited liability company, or as provided in § 18–104(d) or § 18–1108 [cancellation of certificate of formation for failure to pay taxes] of this chapter, or upon the filing of a certificate of merger or consolidation if the limited liability company is not the surviving or resulting entity in a merger or consolidation, or upon the conversion of a domestic limited liability company approved in accordance with § 18–216 of this title. A certificate of cancellation shall be filed in the office of the Secretary of State to accomplish the cancellation of a certificate of formation upon the dissolution and the completion of winding up of a limited liability company or upon the conversion of a domestic limited liability company approved in accordance with § 18–216 of this title and shall set forth:

(1) The name of the limited liability company;

(2) The date of filing of its certificate of formation;

(3) The reason for filing the certificate of cancellation;

(4) The future effective date or time (which shall be a date or time certain) of cancellation if it is not to be effective upon the filing of the certificate;

(5) In the case of the conversion of a domestic limited liability company, the name of the entity to which the domestic limited liability company has been converted; and

(6) Any other information the person filing the certificate of cancellation determines.

§ 18–204. Execution

(a) Each certificate required by this subchapter to be filed in the office of the Secretary of State shall be executed by 1 or more authorized persons.

(b) Unless otherwise provided in a limited liability company agreement, any person may sign any certificate or amendment thereof or enter into a limited liability company agreement or amendment thereof by an agent, including an attorney-in-fact. An authorization, including a power of attorney, to sign any certificate or amendment thereof or to enter into a limited liability company agreement or amendment thereof need not be in writing, need not be sworn to, verified or acknowledged, and need not be filed in the office of the Secretary of State, but if in writing, must be retained by the limited liability company.

(c) The execution of a certificate by an authorized person constitutes an oath or affirmation, under the penalties of perjury in the third degree, that, to the best of the authorized person's knowledge and belief, the facts stated therein are true.

§ 18–205. Execution, Amendment or Cancellation by Judicial Order

(a) If a person required to execute a certificate required by this subchapter fails or refuses to do so, any other person who is adversely affected by the failure or refusal may petition the Court of Chancery to direct the execution of the certificate. If the Court finds that the execution of the certificate is proper and that any person so designated has failed or refused to execute the certificate, it shall order the Secretary of State to record an appropriate certificate.

(b) If a person required to execute a limited liability company agreement or amendment thereof fails or refuses to do so, any other person who is adversely affected by the failure or refusal may petition the Court of Chancery to direct the execution of the limited liability company agreement or amendment thereof. If the Court finds that the limited liability company agreement or amendment thereof should be executed and that any person required to execute the limited liability company agreement or amendment thereof has failed or refused to do so, it shall enter an order granting appropriate relief.

§ 18–206. Filing

(a) The original signed copy of the certificate of formation and of any certificates of amendment, correction, amendment of a certificate of merger or consolidation, termination of a merger or consolidation or cancellation (or of any judicial decree of amendment or cancellation), and of any certificate of merger or consolidation, any restated certificate, certificate of conversion to limited liability company, any certificate of transfer, any certificate of transfer and continuance, any certificate of limited liability company domestication, and of any certificate of revival shall be delivered to the Secretary of State. A person who executes a certificate as an agent or fiduciary need not exhibit evidence of his authority as a prerequisite to filing. Any signature on any certificate authorized to be filed with the Secretary of State under any provision of this chapter may be a facsimile, a conformed signature or an electronically transmitted signature. Unless the Secretary of State finds that any certificate does not conform to law, upon receipt of all filing fees required by law he shall:

(1) Certify that the certificate of formation, the certificate of amendment, the certificate of correction, the certificate of amendment or a certificate of merger or consolidation, the certificate of termination of a merger or consolidation, the certificate of cancellation (or of any judicial decree of amendment or cancellation), the certificate of merger or consolidation, the restated certificate, the certificate of conversion to limited liability company, the certificate of transfer, the certificate of transfer and continuance, the certificate of limited liability company domestication or the certificate of revival has been filed in his office by endorsing upon the original certificate the word "Filed", and the date and hour of the filing. This endorsement is conclusive of the date and time of its filing in the absence of actual fraud;

(2) File and index the endorsed certificate; and

(3) Prepare and return to the person who filed it or his representative a copy of the original signed instrument, similarly endorsed, and shall certify such copy as a true copy of the original signed instrument.

(b) Upon the filing of a certificate of amendment (or judicial decree of amendment) or restated certificate in the office of the Secretary of State, or upon the future effective date or time of a certificate of amendment (or judicial decree thereof) or restated certificate, as provided for therein, the certificate of formation shall be amended or restated as set forth therein. Upon the filing of a certificate of cancellation (or a judicial decree thereof), or a certificate of merger or consolidation which acts as a certificate of cancellation, or a certificate of transfer, or upon the future effective date or time of a certificate of cancellation (or a judicial decree thereof) or of a certificate of merger or consolidation which acts as a certificate of cancellation, or a certificate of transfer, as provided for therein, or as specified in § 18–104(d) of this title, the certificate of formation is cancelled. Upon the filing of a certificate of limited liability company domestication, or upon the future effective date or time of a certificate of limited liability company domestication, the entity filing the certificate of limited liability company domestication is domesticated as a limited liability company with the effect provided in § 18–212 of this title.　Upon the filing of a certificate of conversion to limited liability company, or upon the future effective date or time of a certificate of conversion to limited liability company, the entity filing the certificate of conversion to limited liability company is converted to a limited liability company with the effect provided in § 18–214 of this chapter.　Upon the filing of a certificate of amendment of a certificate of merger or consolidation, the certificate of merger or consolidation identified in the certificate of amendment of a certificate of merger or consolidation is amended.　Upon the filing of a certificate of termination of a merger or consolidation, the certificate of merger or consolidation identified in the certificate of termination of a merger or consolidation is terminated. . . . Upon the filing of a certificate of transfer and continuance, or upon the future effective date or time of a certificate of transfer and continuance, as provided for therein, the limited liability company filing the certificate of transfer and continuance shall continue to exist as a limited liability company of the State of Delaware with the effect provided in Section 18–213 of this title.

§ 18–207.　Notice

The fact that a certificate of formation is on file in the office of the Secretary of State is notice that the entity formed in connection with the filing of the certificate of formation is a limited liability company formed under the laws of the State of Delaware and is notice of all other facts set forth therein which are required to be set forth in a certificate of formation by § 18–201(a)(1) and (2) of this title and which are permitted to be set forth in a certificate of formation by § 18–215(b) of this chapter.

§ 18–209.　Merger and Consolidation

(a) As used in this section, "other business entity" means a corporation, or a business trust or association, a real estate investment trust, a common-law trust, or any other unincorporated business, including a partnership (whether general (including a registered limited liability partnership) or limited (including a registered limited liability partnership)), and a foreign limited liability company, but excluding a domestic limited liability company.

(b) Pursuant to an agreement of merger or consolidation, 1 or more domestic limited liability companies may merge or consolidate with or into 1 or more domestic limited liability companies or 1 or more other business entities formed or organized under the laws of the State of Delaware or any other state or the United States or any foreign country or other foreign jurisdiction, or any combination thereof, with such domestic limited liability companies or other business entity as the agreement shall provide being the surviving or resulting domestic limited liability companies or other business entity. Unless otherwise provided in the limited liability company agreement, a merger or consolidation shall be approved by each domestic limited liability company which is to merge or consolidate by the members or, if there is more than one class or group of members, then by each class or group of members, in either case, by members who own more than 50 percent of the then current percentage or other interest in the profits of the domestic limited liability company owned by all of the members or by the members in each class or group, as appropriate. In connection with a merger or consolidation hereunder, rights or securities of, or interests in, a domestic limited liability company or other business entity which is a constituent party to the merger or consolidation may be exchanged for or converted into cash, property, rights or securities of, or interests in, the surviving or resulting domestic limited liability company or other business entity or, in addition to or in lieu thereof, may be exchanged for or converted into cash, property, rights or securities of, or interests in, a domestic limited liability company or other business entity which is not the surviving or resulting limited liability company or other business entity in the merger or consolidation. Notwithstanding prior approval, an agreement of merger or consolidation may be terminated or amended pursuant to a provision for such termination or amendment contained in the agreement of merger or consolidation.

(c) If a domestic limited liability company is merging or consolidating under this section, the domestic limited liability company or other business entity surviving or resulting in or from the merger or consolidation shall file a certificate of merger or consolidation executed by one or more persons on behalf of the domestic limited liability company when it is the surviving or resulting entity in the office of the Secretary of State. The certificate of merger or consolidation shall state:

(1) The name and jurisdiction of formation or organization of each of the domestic limited liability companies and other business entities which is to merge or consolidate;

(2) That an agreement of merger or consolidation has been approved and executed by each of the domestic limited liability companies and other business entities which is to merge or consolidate;

(3) The name of the surviving or resulting domestic limited liability company or other business entity;

(4) The future effective date or time (which shall be a date or time certain) of the merger or consolidation if it is not to be effective upon the filing of the certificate of merger or consolidation;

(5) That the agreement of merger or consolidation is on file at a place of business of the surviving or resulting domestic limited liability company or other business entity, and shall state the address thereof;

(6) That a copy of the agreement of merger or consolidation will be furnished by the surviving or resulting domestic limited liability company or other business entity, on request and without cost, to any member of any domestic limited liability company or any person

holding an interest in any other business entity which is to merge or consolidate; and

(7) If the surviving or resulting entity is not a domestic limited liability company, or a corporation or limited partnership organized under the laws of the State of Delaware, or a business trust organized under Chapter 38 of Title 12, a statement that such surviving or resulting other business entity agrees that it may be served with process in the State of Delaware in any action, suit or proceeding for the enforcement of any obligation of any domestic limited liability company which is to merge or consolidate, irrevocably appointing the Secretary of State as its agent to accept service of process in any such action, suit or proceeding and specifying the address to which a copy of such process shall be mailed to it by the Secretary of State. In the event of service hereunder upon the Secretary of State, the procedures set forth in § 18–911(c) of this title shall be applicable, except that the plaintiff in any such action, suit or proceeding shall furnish the Secretary of State with the address specified in the certificate of merger or consolidation provided for in this section and any other address which the plaintiff may elect to furnish, together with copies of such process as required by the Secretary of State, and the Secretary of State shall notify such surviving or resulting other business entity at all such addresses furnished by the plaintiff in accordance with the procedures set forth in § 18–911(c) of this title.

(d) Unless a future effective date or time is provided in a certificate of merger or consolidation, in which event a merger or consolidation shall be effective at any such future effective date or time, a merger or consolidation shall be effective upon the filing in the office of the Secretary of State of a certificate of merger or consolidation. . . .

(e) A certificate of merger or consolidation shall act as a certificate of cancellation for a domestic limited liability company which is not the surviving or resulting entity in the merger or consolidation. Whenever this section requires the filing of a certificate of merger or consolidation, such requirement shall be deemed satisfied by the filing of an agreement of merger or consolidation containing the information required by this section to be set forth in the certificate of merger or consolidation.

(f) An agreement of merger or consolidation approved in accordance with subsection (b) of this section may:

(1) Effect any amendment to the limited liability company agreement; or

(2) Effect the adoption of a new limited liability company agreement . . . for a limited liability company if it is the surviving or resulting limited liability company in the merger or consolidation.

Any amendment to a limited liability company agreement or adoption of a new limited liability company agreement made pursuant to the foregoing sentence shall be effective at the effective time or date of the merger or consolidation. The provisions of this subsection shall not be construed to limit the accomplishment of a merger or of any of the matters referred to herein by any other means provided for in a limited liability company agreement or other agreement or as otherwise permitted by law, including that the limited liability company agreement of any constituent limited liability company to the merger or consolidation (including a limited liability company formed for the purpose of consummating a merger or consolidation) shall be the limited liability company agreement of the surviving or resulting limited liability company.

(g) When any merger or consolidation shall have become effective under this section, for all purposes of the laws of the State of Delaware, all of the rights, privileges and powers of each of the domestic limited liability companies and other business entities that have merged or consolidated, and all property, real, personal and mixed, and all debts due to any of said domestic limited liability companies and other business entities, as well as all other things and causes of action belonging to each of such domestic limited liability companies and other business entities, shall be vested in the surviving or resulting domestic limited liability company or other business entity, and shall thereafter be the property of the surviving or resulting domestic limited liability company or other business entity as they were of each of the domestic limited liability companies and other business entities that have merged or consolidated, and the title to any real property vested by deed or otherwise, under the laws of the State of Delaware, in any of such domestic limited liability companies and other business entities, shall not revert or be in any way impaired by reason of this chapter; but all rights of creditors and all liens upon any property of any of said domestic limited liability companies and other business entities shall be preserved unimpaired, and all debts, liabilities and duties of each of the said domestic limited liability companies and other business entities that have merged or consolidated shall thenceforth attach to the surviving or resulting domestic limited liability company or other business entity, and may be enforced against it to the same extent as if said debts, liabilities and duties had been incurred or contracted by it. Unless otherwise agreed, a merger or consolidation of a domestic limited liability company, including a domestic limited liability company which is not the surviving or resulting entity in the merger or consolidation, shall not require such domestic limited liability company to wind up its affairs under § 18–803 of this title or pay its liabilities and distribute its assets under § 18–804 of this title.

§ 18–210. Contractual Appraisal Rights

A limited liability company agreement or an agreement of merger or consolidation may provide that contractual appraisal rights with respect to a limited liability company shall be available for any class or group of members or limited liability company interests in connection with any amendment of a limited liability company agreement, any merger or consolidation in which the limited liability company is a constituent party to the merger or consolidation, or the sale of all or substantially all of the limited liability company's assets. The Court of Chancery shall have jurisdiction to hear and determine any matter relating to any such appraisal rights.

§ 18–211. Certificate of Correction

(a) Whenever any certificate authorized to be filed with the office of the Secretary of State under any provision of this chapter has been so filed and is an inaccurate record of the action therein referred to, or was defectively or erroneously executed, such certificate may be corrected by filing with the office of the Secretary of State a certificate of correction of such certificate. The certificate of correction shall specify the inaccuracy or defect to be corrected, shall set forth the portion of the certificate in corrected form and shall be executed and filed as required by this chapter. The certificate of correction shall be effective as of the date the original certificate was filed, except as to those persons who are substantially and adversely affected by the correction, and as to those persons the certificate of correction shall be effective from the filing date.

(b) In lieu of filing a certificate of correction, a certificate may be corrected by filing with the Secretary of State a corrected certificate which shall be executed and filed as if the corrected certificate were the certificate being corrected, and a fee equal to the fee payable to the Secretary of State if the certificate being corrected were then being filed shall be paid and collected by the Secretary of State for the use of the State of Delaware in connection with the filing of the corrected certificate. The corrected certificate shall be specifically designated as such in its heading, shall specify the inaccuracy or defect to be corrected, and shall set forth the entire certificate in corrected form. A certificate corrected in accordance with this section shall be effective as of the date the original certificate was filed, except as to those persons who are substantially and adversely affected by the correction and as to those persons the certificate as corrected shall be effective from the filing date.

§ 18–212. Domestication of Non–United States Entities

(a) As used in this section, "non-United States entity" means a foreign limited liability company (other than one formed under the laws of a state) or a corporation, a business trust or association, a real estate investment trust, a common-law trust or any other unincorporated business, including a partnership (whether general (including a registered limited liability partnership) or limited (including a registered limited liability limited partnership)) formed, incorporated, created or that otherwise came into being under the laws of any foreign country or other foreign jurisdiction (other than any state).

(b) Any non-United States entity may become domesticated as a limited liability company in the State of Delaware by complying with subsection (g) of this section and filing in the office of the Secretary of State in accordance with § 18–206 of this title:

(1) A certificate of limited liability company domestication that has been executed by 1 or more authorized persons in accordance with § 18-204 of this title; and

(2) A certificate of formation that complies with § 18-201 of this title and has been executed by 1 or more authorized persons in accordance with § 18-204 of this title.

(c) The certificate of limited liability company domestication shall state:

(1) The date on which and jurisdiction where the non-United States entity was first formed, incorporated, created or otherwise came into being;

(2) The name of the non-United States entity immediately prior to the filing of the certificate of limited liability company domestication;

(3) The name of the limited liability company as set forth in the certificate of formation filed in accordance with subsection (b) of this section;

(4) The future effective date or time (which shall be a date or time certain) of the domestication as a limited liability company if it is not to be effective upon the filing of the certificate of limited liability company domestication and the certificate of formation; and

(5) The jurisdiction that constituted the seat, siege social, or principal place of business or central administration of the non-United States entity, or any other equivalent thereto under applicable law, immediately prior to the filing of the certificate of limited liability company domestication.

(d) Upon the filing in the office of the Secretary of State of the certificate of limited liability company domestication and the certificate of formation or upon the future effective date or time of the certificate of limited liability company domestication and the certificate of formation, the non-United States entity shall be domesticated as a limited liability company in the State of Delaware and the limited liability company shall thereafter be subject to all of the provisions of this chapter, except that notwithstanding § 18-201 of this title, the existence of the limited liability company shall be deemed to have commenced on the date the non-United States entity commenced its existence in the jurisdiction in which the non-United States entity was first formed, incorporated, created or otherwise came into being.

(e) The domestication of any non-United States entity as a limited liability company in the State of Delaware shall not be deemed to affect any obligations or liabilities of the non-United States entity incurred prior to its domestication as a limited liability company in the State of Delaware, or the personal liability of any person therefor.

(f) The filing of a certificate of limited liability company domestication shall not affect the choice of law applicable to the non-United States entity, except that from the effective date or time of the domestication, the law of the State of Delaware, including the provisions of this chapter, shall apply to the non-United States entity to the same extent as if the non-United States entity had been formed as a limited liability company on that date.

(g) Prior to filing a certificate of limited liability company domestication with the Office of the Secretary of State, the domestication shall be approved in the manner provided for by the document, instrument, agreement or other writing, as the case may be, governing the internal affairs of the non-United States entity and the conduct of its business or by applicable non-Delaware law, as appropriate, and a limited liability company agreement shall be approved by the same authorization required to approve the domestication.

(h) When any domestication shall have become effective under this section, for all purposes of the laws of the State of Delaware, all of the rights, privileges and powers of the non-United States entity that has been domesticated, and all property, real, personal and mixed, and all debts due to such non-United States entity, as well as all other things and causes of action belonging to such non-United States entity, shall be vested in the domestic limited liability company and shall thereafter be the property of the domestic limited liability company as they were of the non-United States entity immediately prior to its domestication, and the title to any real property vested by deed or otherwise in such non-United States entity shall not revert or be in any way impaired by reason of this chapter, but all rights of creditors and all liens upon any property of such non-United States entity shall be preserved unimpaired, and all debts, liabilities and duties of the non-United States entity that has been domesticated shall thenceforth attach to the domestic limited liability company and may be enforced against it to the same extent as if said debts, liabilities and duties had been incurred or contracted by the domestic limited liability company.

(i) When a non-United States entity has become domesticated as a limited liability company pursuant to this section, the limited liability company shall, for all purposes of the laws of the State of Delaware, be deemed to be the same entity as the domesticating non-United States entity. Unless otherwise agreed, or as required under applicable non-Delaware law, the domesticating non-United States entity shall not be required to wind up its affairs or pay its liabilities and distribute its assets, and the domestication shall not be deemed to constitute a dissolution of such non-United States entity and shall constitute a continuation of the existence of the domesticating non-United States entity in the form of a domestic limited liability company. If, following domestication, a non-United States entity that has become domesticated as a limited liability company continues its existence in the foreign country or other foreign jurisdiction in which it was existing immediately prior to domestication, the limited liability company and such non-United States entity shall, for all purposes of the laws of the State of Delaware, constitute a single entity formed, incorporated, created or otherwise having come into being, as applicable, and existing under the laws of the State of Delaware and the laws of such foreign country or other foreign jurisdiction.

§ 18–213. Transfer or Continuance of Domestic Limited Liability Companies

(a) Upon compliance with the provisions of this section, any limited liability company may transfer to or domesticate in any jurisdiction, other than any state, that permits the transfer to or domestication in such jurisdiction of a limited liability company and, in connection therewith, may elect to continue its existence as a limited liability company in the State of Delaware.

(b) Unless otherwise provided in a limited liability company agreement, a transfer or domestication or continuance described in subsection (a) of this section shall be approved in writing by all of the managers and all of the members. If all of the managers and all of the members of the limited liability company or such other vote as may be stated in a limited liability company agreement shall approve the transfer or domestication described in subsection (a) of this section, a certificate of transfer if the limited liability company's existence as a limited liability company of the State of Delaware is to cease, or a certificate of transfer and continuance if the limited liability company's existence as a limited liability company in the State of Delaware is to continue, executed in accordance with § 18–204 of this title, shall be filed in the Office of the Secretary of State in accordance with § 18–206 of this title. The certificate of transfer or the certificate of transfer and continuance shall state:

(1) The name of the limited liability company and, if it has been changed, the name under which its certificate of formation was originally filed;

(2) The date of the filing of its original certificate of formation with the Secretary of State;

(3) The jurisdiction to which the limited liability company shall be transferred or in which it shall be domesticated;

(4) The future effective date or time (which shall be a date or time certain) of the transfer or domestication to the jurisdiction specified in subsection (b)(3) of this section if it is not to be effective upon the filing of the certificate of transfer or the certificate of transfer and continuance;

(5) That the transfer or domestication or continuance of the limited liability company has been approved in accordance with the provisions of this section;

(6) In the case of a certificate of transfer, (i) that the existence of the limited liability company as a limited liability company of the State of Delaware shall cease when the certificate of transfer becomes effective, and (ii) the agreement of the limited liability company that it may be served with process in the State of Delaware in any action, suit or proceeding for enforcement of any obligation of the limited liability company arising while it was a limited liability company of the State of Delaware, and that it irrevocably appoints the Secretary of State as its

agent to accept service of process in any such action, suit or proceeding;

(7) The address to which a copy of the process referred to in subsection (b)(6) of this section shall be mailed to it by the Secretary of State. In the event of service hereunder upon the Secretary of State, the procedures set forth in § 18–911(c) of this title shall be applicable, except that the plaintiff in any such action, suit or proceeding shall furnish the Secretary of State with the address specified in this subsection and any other address that the plaintiff may elect to furnish, together with copies of such process as required by the Secretary of State, and the Secretary of State shall notify the limited liability company that has transferred or domesticated out of the State of Delaware at all such addresses furnished by the plaintiff in accordance with the procedures set forth in § 18–911(c) of this title; and

(8) In the case of a certificate of transfer and continuance, that the limited liability company will continue to exist as a limited liability company of the State of Delaware after the certificate of transfer and continuance becomes effective.

(c) Upon the filing in the Office of the Secretary of State of the certificate of transfer or upon the future effective date or time of the certificate of transfer and payment to the Secretary of State of all fees prescribed in this chapter, the Secretary of State shall certify that the limited liability company has filed all documents and paid all fees required by this chapter, and thereupon the limited liability company shall cease to exist as a limited liability company of the State of Delaware. Such certificate of the Secretary of State shall be *prima facie* evidence of the transfer or domestication by such limited liability company out of the State of Delaware.

(d) The transfer or domestication of a limited liability company out of the State of Delaware in accordance with this section and the resulting cessation of its existence as a limited liability company of the State of Delaware pursuant to a certificate of transfer shall not be deemed to affect any obligations or liabilities of the limited liability company incurred prior to such transfer or domestication or the personal liability of any person incurred prior to such transfer or domestication, nor shall it be deemed to affect the choice of law applicable to the limited liability company with respect to matters arising prior to such transfer or domestication.

(e) If a limited liability company files a certificate of transfer and continuance, after the time the certificate of transfer and continuance becomes effective, the limited liability company shall continue to exist as a limited liability company of the State of Delaware, and the laws of the State of Delaware, including the provisions of this chapter, shall apply to the limited liability company, to the same extent as prior to such time. So long as a limited liability company continues to exist as a limited liability company of the State of Delaware following the filing of a certificate of transfer and continuance, the continuing domestic limited liability company and the entity formed, incorporated, created or that otherwise came into being as a consequence of the transfer of the limited liability company to, or its domestication in, a foreign country or other foreign jurisdiction shall, for all purposes of the laws of the State of Delaware, constitute a single entity formed, incorporated, created or otherwise having come into being, as applicable, and existing under the laws of the State of Delaware and the laws of such foreign country or other foreign jurisdiction.

§ 18–214. Conversion of Certain Entities to a Limited Liability Company

(a) As used in this section, the term "other entity" means a corporation, business trust or association, a real estate investment trust, a common-law trust or any other unincorporated business, including a partnership (whether general (including a registered limited liability partnership) or limited (including a registered limited liability limited partnership)) or a foreign limited liability company.

(b) Any other entity may convert to a domestic limited liability company by complying with subsection (h) of this section and filing in the office of the Secretary of State in accordance with § 18–206 of this title:

(1) A certificate of conversion to limited liability company that has been executed by 1 or more authorized persons in accordance with § 18–204 of this title; and

(2) A certificate of formation that complies with § 18–201 of this title and has been executed by 1 or more authorized persons in accordance with § 18–204 of this title.

(c) The certificate of conversion to limited liability company shall state:

(1) The date on which and jurisdiction where the other entity was first created, incorporated, formed or otherwise came into being and, if it has changed, its jurisdiction immediately prior to its conversion to a domestic limited liability company;

(2) The name of the other entity immediately prior to the filing of the certificate of conversion to limited liability company;

(3) The name of the limited liability company as set forth in its certificate of formation filed in accordance with subsection (b) of this section; and

(4) The future effective date or time (which shall be a date or time certain) of the conversion to a limited liability company if it is not to be effective upon the filing of the certificate of conversion to limited liability company and the certificate of formation.

(d) Upon the filing in the office of the Secretary of State of the certificate of conversion to limited liability company and the certificate of formation or upon the future effective date or time of the certificate of conversion to limited liability company and the certificate of formation, the other entity shall be converted into a domestic limited liability company and the limited liability company shall thereafter be subject to all of the

437

provisions of this chapter, except that notwithstanding § 18–201 of this title, the existence of the limited liability company shall be deemed to have commenced on the date the other entity commenced its existence in the jurisdiction in which the other entity was first created, formed, incorporated or otherwise came into being.

(e) The conversion of any other entity into a domestic limited liability company shall not be deemed to affect any obligations or liabilities of the other entity incurred prior to its conversion to a domestic limited liability company or the personal liability of any person incurred prior to such conversion.

(f) When any conversion shall have become effective under this section, for all purposes of the laws of the State of Delaware, all of the rights, privileges and powers of the other entity that has converted, and all property, real, personal and mixed, and all debts due to such other entity, as well as all other things and causes of action belonging to such other entity, shall be vested in the domestic limited liability company and shall thereafter be the property of the domestic limited liability company as they were of the other entity that has converted, and the title to any real property vested by deed or otherwise in such other entity shall not revert or be in any way impaired by reason of this chapter, but all rights of creditors and all liens upon any property of such other entity shall be preserved unimpaired, and all debts, liabilities and duties of the other entity that has converted shall thenceforth attach to the domestic limited liability company and may be enforced against it to the same extent as if said debts, liabilities and duties had been incurred or contracted by it.

(g) Unless otherwise agreed, or as required under applicable non-Delaware law, the converting other entity shall not be required to wind up its affairs or pay its liabilities and distribute its assets, and the conversion shall not be deemed to constitute a dissolution of such other entity and shall constitute a continuation of the existence of the converting other entity in the form of a domestic limited liability company. When an other entity has been converted to a limited liability company pursuant to this section, the limited liability company shall, for all purposes of the laws of the State of Delaware, be deemed to be the same entity as the converting other entity.

(h) Prior to filing a certificate of conversion to limited liability company with the office of the Secretary of State, the conversion shall be approved in the manner provided for by the document, instrument, agreement or other writing, as the case may be, governing the internal affairs of the other entity and the conduct of its business or by applicable law, as appropriate and a limited liability company agreement shall be approved by the same authorization required to approve the conversion.

(i) The provisions of this section shall not be construed to limit the accomplishment of a change in the law governing, or the domicile of, an other entity to the State of Delaware by any other means provided for in a limited liability company agreement or other agreement or as otherwise permitted by law, including by the amendment of a limited liability company agreement or other agreement.

§ 18–215. Series of Members, Managers or Limited Liability Company Interests

(a) A limited liability company agreement may establish or provide for the establishment of designated series of members, managers or limited liability company interests having separate rights, powers or duties with respect to specified property or obligations of the limited liability company or profits and losses associated with specified property or obligations, and, to the extent provided in the limited liability company agreement, any such series may have a separate business purpose or investment objective.

(b) Notwithstanding anything to the contrary set forth in this chapter or under other applicable law, in the event that a limited liability company agreement creates 1 or more series, and if separate and distinct records are maintained for any such series and the assets associated with any such series are held and accounted for separately from the other assets of the limited liability company, or any other series thereof, and if the limited liability company agreement so provides, and notice of the limitation on liabilities of a series as referenced in this subsection is set forth in the certificate of formation of the limited liability company, then the debts, liabilities and obligations incurred, contracted for or otherwise existing with respect to a particular series shall be enforceable against the assets of such series only, and not against the assets of the limited liability company generally or any other series thereof, and, unless otherwise provided in the limited liability company agreement, none of the debts, liabilities, obligations and expenses incurred, contracted for or otherwise existing with respect to the limited liability company generally or any other series thereof shall be enforceable against the assets of such series. The fact that a certificate of formation that contains the foregoing notice of the limitation on liabilities of a series is on file in the office of the Secretary of State shall constitute notice of such limitation on liabilities of a series.

(c) Notwithstanding § 18–303(a) of this title, under a limited liability company agreement or under another agreement, a member or manager may agree to be obligated personally for any or all of the debts, obligations and liabilities of one or more series.

(d) A limited liability company agreement may provide for classes or groups of members or managers associated with a series having such relative rights, powers and duties as the limited liability company agreement may provide, and may make provision for the future creation in the manner provided in the limited liability company agreement of additional classes or groups of members or managers associated with the series having such relative rights, powers and duties as may from time to time be established, including rights, powers and duties senior to existing classes and groups of members or managers associated with the series. A limited liability company agreement may provide for the taking of an action, including the amendment of the limited liability company agreement, without the vote or approval of any member or manager or class or group of members or managers, including an action to create under the provisions of the limited liability company agreement a class or group of [a] series of limited liability company interests that was not previously outstanding. A limited liability company agreement may provide that any member or class or group of members associated with a series shall have no voting rights.

(e) A limited liability company agreement may grant to all or certain identified members or managers or a specified class or group of the members or managers associated with a series the right to vote separately or with all or any class or group of the members or managers associated with the series, on any matter. Voting by members or managers associated with a series may be on a per capita, number, financial interest, class, group or any other basis.

(f) Unless otherwise provided in a limited liability company agreement, the management of a series shall be vested in the members associated with such series in proportion to the then current percentage or other interest of members in the profits of the series owned by all of the members associated with such series, the decision of members owning more than 50 percent of the said percentage or other interest in the profits controlling; provided, however, that if a limited liability company agreement provides for the management of the series, in whole or in part, by a manager, the management of the series, to the extent so provided, shall be vested in the manager who shall be chosen in the manner provided in the limited liability company agreement. The manager of the series shall also hold the offices and have the responsibilities accorded to the manager as set forth in a limited liability company agreement. A series may have more than 1 manager. Subject to § 18-602 of this title, a manager shall cease to be a manager with respect to a series as provided in a limited liability company agreement. Except as otherwise provided in a limited liability company agreement, any event under this chapter or in a limited liability company agreement that causes a manager to cease to be a manager with respect to a series shall not, in itself, cause such manager to cease to be a manager of the limited liability company or with respect to any other series thereof.

(g) Notwithstanding § 18-606 of this title, but subject to subsections (h) and (k) of this section, and unless otherwise provided in a limited liability company agreement, at the time a member associated with a series that has been established in accordance with subsection (b) of this section becomes entitled to receive a distribution with respect to such series, the member has the status of, and is entitled to all remedies available to, a creditor of the series, with respect to the distribution. A limited liability company agreement may provide for the establishment of a record date with respect to allocations and distributions with respect to a series.

(h) Notwithstanding § 18-607(a) of this title, a limited liability company may make a distribution with respect to a series that has been established in accordance with subsection (b) of this section; provided, that a limited liability company shall not make a distribution with respect to a series that has been established in accordance with subsection (b) of this section to a member to the extent that at the time of the distribution, after giving effect to the distribution, all liabilities of such series, other than liabilities to members on account of their limited liability company interests with respect to such series and liabilities for which the recourse of creditors is limited to specified property of such series, exceed the fair value of the assets associated with such series, except that the fair value of property of the series that is subject to a liability for which the recourse of creditors is limited shall be included in the assets associated with such series only to the extent that the fair value of that property exceeds that liability. A member who receives a distribution in violation of this subsection, and who knew at the time of the distribution that the distribution violated this subsection, shall be liable to a series for the amount of the distribution. A member who receives a distribution in violation of this subsection, and who did not know at the time of the distribution that the distribution violated this subsection, shall not be liable for the amount of the distribution. Subject to § 18–607(c) of this title, which shall apply to any distribution made with respect to a series under this subsection, this subsection shall not affect any obligation or liability of a member under an agreement or other applicable law for the amount of a distribution.

(i) Unless otherwise provided in the limited liability company agreement, a member shall cease to be associated with a series and to have the power to exercise any rights or powers of a member with respect to such series upon the assignment of all of the member's limited liability company interest with respect to such series. Except as otherwise provided in a limited liability company agreement, any event under this chapter or a limited liability company agreement that causes a member to cease to be associated with a series shall not, in itself, cause such member to cease to be associated with any other series or terminate the continued membership of a member in the limited liability company or cause the termination of the series, regardless of whether such member was the last remaining member associated with such series.

(j) Subject to § 18–801 of this title, except to the extent otherwise provided in the limited liability company agreement, a series may be terminated and its affairs wound up without causing the dissolution of the limited liability company. The termination of a series established in accordance with subsection (b) of this section shall not affect the limitation on liabilities of such series provided by subsection (b) of this section. A series is terminated and its affairs shall be wound up upon the dissolution of the limited liability company under § 18–801 of this title or otherwise upon the first to occur of the following:

(1) At the time specified in the limited liability company agreement;

(2) Upon the happening of events specified in the limited liability company agreement;

(3) Unless otherwise provided in the limited liability company agreement, upon the written consent of the members of the limited liability company associated with such series or, if there is more than

441

one class or group of members associated with such series, then by each class or group of members associated with such series, in either case, by members associated with such series who own more than two-thirds of the then-current percentage or other interest in the profits of the series of the limited liability company owned by all of the members associated with such series or by the members in each class or group of such series, as appropriate;

(4) At any time there are no members associated with the series, provided that, unless otherwise provided in the limited liability company agreement, the series is not terminated and is not required to be wound up if, within 90 days or such other period as is provided for in the limited liability company agreement after the occurrence of the event that terminated the continued membership of the last remaining member associated with the series, the personal representative of the last member associated with the series agrees in writing to continue the business of the series and to the admission of a personal representative of such member or its nominee or designee to the limited liability company as a member associated with the series, effective as of the occurrence of the event that terminated the continued membership of the last remaining member associated with the series; or

(5) The termination of such series under subsection (*l*) of this section.

(k) Notwithstanding § 18–803(a) of this title, unless otherwise provided in the limited liability company agreement, a manager associated with a series who has not wrongfully terminated the series or, if none, the members associated with the series or a person approved by the members associated with the series or, if there is more than 1 class or group of members associated with the series, then by each class or group of members associated with the series, in either case, by members who own more than 50 percent of the then current percentage or other interest in the profits of the series owned by all of the members associated with the series or by the members in each class or group associated with the series, as appropriate, may wind up the affairs of the series; but, if the series has been established in accordance with subsection (b) of this section, the Court of Chancery, upon cause shown, may wind up the affairs of the series upon application of any member associated with the series, the member's personal representative or assignee, and in connection therewith, may appoint a liquidating trustee. The persons winding up the affairs of a series may, in the name of the limited liability company and for and on behalf of the limited liability company and such series, take all actions with respect to the series as are permitted under § 18–803(b) of this title. The persons winding up the affairs of a series shall provide for the claims and obligations of the series as provided in § 18–804(b) of this title and distribute the assets of the series as provided in § 18–804(a) of this title. Actions taken in accordance with this subsection shall not affect the liability of members and shall not impose liability on a liquidating trustee.

(*l*) On application by or for a member or manager associated with a series established in accordance with subsection (b) of this section, the Court of Chancery may decree termination of such series whenever it is not reasonably practicable to carry on the business of the series in conformity with a limited liability company agreement.

(m) If a foreign limited liability company that is registering to do business in the State of Delaware in accordance with § 18–902 of this title is governed by a limited liability company agreement that establishes or provides for the establishment of designated series of members, managers or limited liability company interests having separate rights, powers or duties with respect to specified property or obligations of the foreign limited liability company or profits and losses associated with specified property or obligations, that fact shall be so stated on the application for registration as a foreign limited liability company. In addition, the foreign limited liability company shall state on such application whether the debts, liabilities and obligations incurred, contracted for or otherwise existing with respect to a particular series, if any, shall be enforceable against the assets of such series only, and not against the assets of the foreign limited liability company generally or any other series thereof, and, unless otherwise provided in the limited liability company agreement, none of the debts, liabilities, obligations and expenses incurred, contracted for or otherwise existing with respect to the foreign limited liability company generally or any other series thereof shall be enforceable against the assets of such series.

§ 18–216. Approval of Conversion of a Limited Liability Company

A domestic limited liability company may convert to a corporation, business trust or association, a real estate investment trust, a common-law trust, a general partnership (including a registered limited liability partnership) or a limited partnership (including a registered limited liability limited partnership), organized, formed or created under the laws of the State of Delaware, upon the authorization of such conversion in accordance with this section. If the limited liability company agreement specifies the manner of authorizing a conversion of the limited liability company, the conversion shall be authorized as specified in the limited liability company agreement. If the limited liability company agreement does not specify the manner of authorizing a conversion of the limited liability company and does not prohibit a conversion of the limited liability company, the conversion shall be authorized in the same manner as is specified in the limited liability company agreement for authorizing a merger or consolidation that involves the limited liability company as a constituent party to the merger or consolidation. If the limited liability company agreement does not specify the manner of authorizing a conversion of the limited liability company or a merger or consolidation that involves the limited liability company as a constituent party and does not prohibit a conversion of the limited liability company, the conversion shall be authorized by the approval by the members or, if there is more than 1 class or group of members, then by each class or group of members, in either case, by members who

443

own more than 50 percent of the then current percentage or other interest in the profits of the domestic limited liability company owned by all of the members or by the members in each class or group, as appropriate.

SUBCHAPTER III. MEMBERS

§ 18–301. Admission of Members

(a) In connection with the formation of a limited liability company, a person is admitted as a member of the limited liability company upon the later to occur of:

(1) The formation of the limited liability company; or

(2) The time provided in and upon compliance with the limited liability company agreement or, if the limited liability company agreement does not so provide, when the person's admission is reflected in the records of the limited liability company.

(b) After the formation of a limited liability company, a person is admitted as a member of the limited liability company:

(1) In the case of a person who is not an assignee of a limited liability company interest, including a person acquiring a limited liability company interest directly from the limited liability company and a person to be admitted as a member of the limited liability company without acquiring a limited liability company interest in the limited liability company, at the time provided in and upon compliance with the limited liability company agreement or, if the limited liability company agreement does not so provide, upon the consent of all members and when the person's admission is reflected in the records of the limited liability company;

(2) In the case of an assignee of a limited liability company interest, as provided in § 18–704(a) of this title and at the time provided in and upon compliance with the limited liability company agreement or, if the limited liability company agreement does not so provide, when any such person's permitted admission is reflected in the records of the limited liability company; or

(3) Unless otherwise provided in an agreement of merger or consolidation, in the case of a person acquiring a limited liability company interest in a surviving or resulting limited liability company pursuant to a merger or consolidation approved in accordance with Section 18–209(b) of this chapter, at the time provided in and upon compliance with the limited liability company agreement of the surviving or resulting limited liability company.

(c) In connection with the domestication of a non-United States entity (as defined in § 18–212 of this title) as a limited liability company in the State of Delaware in accordance with § 18–212 of this title or the conversion of an other entity (as defined in § 18–214 of this title) to a domestic limited liability company in accordance with § 18–214 of this title, a person is admitted as a member of the limited liability company at the time provided in and upon compliance with the limited liability company agreement.

(d) A person may be admitted to a limited liability company as a member of the limited liability company and may receive a limited liability company interest in the limited liability company without making a contribution or being obligated to make a contribution to the limited liability company. Unless otherwise provided in a limited liability company agreement, a person may be admitted to a limited liability company as a member of the limited liability company without acquiring a limited liability company interest in the limited liability company. Unless otherwise provided in a limited liability company agreement, a person may be admitted as the sole member of a limited liability company without making a contribution or being obligated to make a contribution to the limited liability company or without acquiring a limited liability company interest in the limited liability company.

§ 18–302. Classes and Voting

(a) A limited liability company agreement may provide for classes or groups of members having such relative rights, powers and duties as the limited liability company agreement may provide, and may make provision for the future creation in the manner provided in the limited liability company agreement of additional classes or groups of members having such relative rights, powers and duties as may from time to time be established, including rights, powers and duties senior to existing classes and groups of members. A limited liability company agreement may provide for the taking of an action, including the amendment of the limited liability company agreement, without the vote or approval of any member or class or group of members, including an action to create under the provisions of the limited liability company agreement a class or group of limited liability company interests that was not previously outstanding. A limited liability company agreement may provide that any member or class or group of members shall have no voting rights.

(b) A limited liability company agreement may grant to all or certain identified members or a specified class or group of the members the right to vote separately or with all or any class or group of the members or managers, on any matter. Voting by members may be on a per capita, number, financial interest, class, group or any other basis.

(c) A limited liability company agreement may set forth provisions relating to notice of the time, place or purpose of any meeting at which any matter is to be voted on by any members, waiver of any such notice, action by consent without a meeting, the establishment of a record date, quorum requirements, voting in person or by proxy, or any other matter with respect to the exercise of any such right to vote.

(d) Unless otherwise provided in a limited liability company agreement, on any matter that is to be voted on by members, the members may take such action without a meeting, without prior notice and without a vote, if a consent or consents in writing, setting forth the action so taken, shall be signed by the members having not not less than the minimum number of votes that would be necessary to authorize or take such action at a meeting at which all interests in the limited liability company entitled to vote thereon were present and voted. Unless otherwise provided in a limited liability company agreement, on any matter that is to be voted on by members, the members may vote in person or by proxy.

§ 18–303. Liability to 3rd Parties

(a) Except as otherwise provided by this chapter, the debts, obligations and liabilities of a limited liability company, whether arising in contract, tort or otherwise, shall be solely the debts, obligations and liabilities of the limited liability company, and no member or manager of a limited liability company shall be obligated personally for any such debt, obligation or liability of the limited liability company solely by reason of being a member or acting as a manager of the limited liability company.

(b) Notwithstanding the provisions of Section 18–303(a) of this chapter, under a limited liability company agreement or under another agreement, a member or manager may agree to be obligated personally for any or all of the debts, obligations and liabilities of the limited liability company.

§ 18–304. Events of Bankruptcy

A person ceases to be a member of a limited liability company upon the happening of any of the following events:

(1) Unless otherwise provided in a limited liability company agreement, or with the written consent of all members, a member:

a. Makes an assignment for the benefit of creditors;

b. Files a voluntary petition in bankruptcy;

c. Is adjudged a bankrupt or insolvent, or has entered against him an order for relief, in any bankruptcy or insolvency proceeding;

d. Files a petition or answer seeking for himself any reorganization, arrangement, composition, readjustment, liquidation, dissolution or similar relief under any statute, law or regulation;

e. Files an answer or other pleading admitting or failing to contest the material allegations of a petition filed against him in any proceeding of this nature;

f. Seeks, consents to or acquiesces in the appointment of a trustee, receiver or liquidator of the member or of all or any substantial part of his properties; or

(2) Unless otherwise provided in a limited liability company agreement, or with the written consent of all members, 120 days after the commencement of any proceeding against the member seeking reorganization, arrangement, composition, readjustment, liquidation, dissolu-

tion or similar relief under any statute, law or regulation, if the proceeding has not been dismissed, or if within 90 days after the appointment without his consent or acquiescence of a trustee, receiver or liquidator of the member or of all or any substantial part of his properties, the appointment is not vacated or stayed, or within 90 days after the expiration of any such stay, the appointment is not vacated

§ 18–305. Access to and Confidentiality of Information; Records

(a) Each member of a limited liability company has the right, subject to such reasonable standards (including standards governing what information and documents are to be furnished at what time and location and at whose expense) as may be set forth in a limited liability company agreement or otherwise established by the manager or, if there is no manager, then by the members, to obtain from the limited liability company from time to time upon reasonable demand for any purpose reasonably related to the member's interest as a member of the limited liability company:

(1) True and full information regarding the status of the business and financial condition of the limited liability company;

(2) Promptly after becoming available, a copy of the limited liability company's federal, state and local income tax returns for each year;

(3) A current list of the name and last known business, residence or mailing address of each member and manager;

(4) A copy of any written limited liability company agreement and certificate of formation and all amendments thereto, together with executed copies of any written powers of attorney pursuant to which the limited liability company agreement and any certificate and all amendments thereto have been executed;

(5) True and full information regarding the amount of cash and a description and statement of the agreed value of any other property or services contributed by each member and which each member has agreed to contribute in the future, and the date on which each became a member; and

(6) Other information regarding the affairs of the limited liability company as is just and reasonable.

(b) Each manager shall have the right to examine all of the information described in subsection (a) of this section for a purpose reasonably related to his position as a manager.

(c) The manager of a limited liability company shall have the right to keep confidential from the members, for such period of time as the manager deems reasonable, any information which the manager reasonably believes to be in the nature of trade secrets or other information the disclosure of which the manager in good faith believes is not in the best interest of the limited liability company or could damage the limited liability company or its business or which the limited liability company is required by law or by agreement with a 3rd party to keep confidential.

(d) A limited liability company may maintain its records in other than a written form if such form is capable of conversion into written form within a reasonable time.

(e) Any demand by a member under this section shall be in writing and shall state the purpose of such demand.

(f) Any action to enforce any right arising under this section shall be brought in the Court of Chancery. If the limited liability company refuses to permit a member to obtain or a manager to examine the information described in subsection (a)(3) of this section or does not reply to the demand that has been made within 5 business days after the demand has been made, the demanding member or manager may apply to the Court of Chancery for an order to compel such disclosure. The Court of Chancery is hereby vested with exclusive jurisdiction to determine whether or not the person seeking such information is entitled to the information sought. The Court of Chancery may summarily order the limited liability company to permit the demanding member to obtain or manager to examine the information described in subsection (a)(3) of this section and to make copies or abstracts therefrom; or the Court of Chancery may summarily order the limited liability company to furnish to the demanding member or manager the information described in subsection (a)(3) of this section on the condition that the demanding member or manager first pay to the limited liability company the reasonable cost of obtaining and furnishing such information and on such other conditions as the Court of Chancery deems appropriate. When a demanding member seeks to obtain or a manager seeks to examine the information described in subsection (a)(3) of this section, the demanding member or manager shall first establish (1) that the demanding member or manager has complied with the provisions of this section respecting the form and manner of making demand for obtaining or examining of such information, and (2) that the information the demanding member or manager seeks is reasonably related to the member's interest as a member or the manager's position as a manager, as the case may be. The Court of Chancery may, in its discretion, prescribe any limitations or conditions with reference to the obtaining or examining of information, or award such other or further relief as the Court of Chancery may deem just and proper. The Court of Chancery may order books, documents and records, pertinent extracts therefrom, or duly authenticated copies thereof, to be brought within the State of Delaware and kept in the State of Delaware upon such terms and conditions as the order may prescribe.

§ 18–306. Remedies for Breach of Limited Liability Company Agreement by Member

A limited liability company agreement may provide that:

(1) A member who fails to perform in accordance with, or to comply with the terms and conditions of, the limited liability company agreement shall be subject to specified penalties or specified consequences; and

(2) At the time or upon the happening of events specified in the limited liability company agreement, a member shall be subject to specified penalties or specified consequences.

SUBCHAPTER IV. MANAGERS

§ 18–401. Admission of Managers

A person may be named or designated as a manager of the limited liability company as provided in § 18–101(10) of this title.

§ 18–402. Management of Limited Liability Company

Unless otherwise provided in a limited liability company agreement, the management of a limited liability company shall be vested in its members in proportion to the then current percentage or other interest of members in the profits of the limited liability company owned by all of the members, the decision of members owning more than 50 percent of the said percentage or other interest in the profits controlling; provided however, that if a limited liability company agreement provides for the management, in whole or in part, of a limited liability company by a manager, the management of the limited liability company, to the extent so provided, shall be vested in the manager who shall be chosen in the manner provided in the limited liability company agreement. The manager shall also hold the offices and have the responsibilities accorded to the manager by or in the manner provided in a limited liability company agreement. Subject to § 18–602 of this title, a manager shall cease to be a manager as provided in a limited liability company agreement. A limited liability company may have more than 1 manager. Unless otherwise provided in a limited liability company agreement, each member and manager has the authority to bind the limited liability company.

§ 18–403. Contributions by a Manager

A manager of a limited liability company may make contributions to the limited liability company and share in the profits and losses of, and in distributions from, the limited liability company as a member. A person who is both a manager and a member has the rights and powers, and is subject to the restrictions and liabilities, of a manager and, except as provided in a limited liability company agreement, also has the rights and powers, and is subject to the restrictions and liabilities, of a member to the extent of his participation in the limited liability company as a member.

§ 18–404. Classes and Voting

(a) A limited liability company agreement may provide for classes or groups of managers having such relative rights, powers and duties as the limited liability company agreement may provide, and may make provision for the future creation in the manner provided in the limited liability company agreement of additional classes or groups of managers having such relative rights, powers and duties as may from time to time be

449

established, including rights, powers and duties senior to existing classes and groups of managers. A limited liability company agreement may provide for the taking of an action, including the amendment of the limited liability company agreement, without the vote or approval of any manager or class or group of managers, including an action to create under the provisions of the limited liability company agreement a class or group of limited liability company interests that was not previously outstanding.

(b) A limited liability company agreement may grant to all or certain identified managers or a specified class or group of the managers the right to vote, separately or with all or any class or group of managers or members, on any matter. Voting by managers may be on a per capita, number, financial interest, class, group or any other basis.

(c) A limited liability company agreement may set forth provisions relating to notice of the time, place or purpose of any meeting at which any matter is to be voted on by any manager or class or group of managers, waiver of any such notice, action by consent without a meeting, the establishment of a record date, quorum requirements, voting in person or by proxy, or any other matter with respect to the exercise of any such right to vote.

(d) Unless otherwise provided in a limited liability company agreement, on any matter that is to be voted on by managers, the managers may take such action without a meeting, without prior notice and without a vote, if a consent or consents in writing, setting forth the action so taken, shall be signed by the managers having not less than the minimum number of votes that would be necessary to authorize or take such action at a meeting. Unless otherwise provided in a limited liability company agreement, on any matter that is to be voted on by managers, the managers may vote in person or by proxy.

§ 18–405. Remedies for Breach of Limited Liability Company Agreement by Manager

A limited liability company agreement may provide that:

(1) A manager who fails to perform in accordance with, or to comply with the terms and conditions of, the limited liability company agreement shall be subject to specified penalties or specified consequences; and

(2) At the time or upon the happening of events specified in the limited liability company agreement, a manager shall be subject to specified penalties or specified consequences.

§ 18–406. Reliance on Reports and Information by Member or Manager

A member or manager of a limited liability company shall be fully protected in relying in good faith upon the records of the limited liability company and upon such information, opinions, reports or statements presented to the limited liability company by any of its other managers, members, officers, employees or committees of the limited liability company, or by any other person, as to matters the member or manager reasonably believes are within such other person's professional or expert competence and who has been selected with reasonable care by or on behalf of the limited liability company, including information, opinions, reports or statements as to the value and amount of the assets, liabilities, profits or losses of the limited liability company or any other facts pertinent to the existence and amount of assets from which distributions to members might properly be paid.

§ 18–407. Delegation of Rights and Powers to Manage

Unless otherwise provided in the limited liability company agreement, a member or manager of limited liability company has the power and authority to delegate to one or more other persons the member's or manager's, as the case may be, rights and powers to manage and control the business and affairs of the limited liability company, including to delegate to agents, officers and employees of a member or manager [of] the limited liability company, and to delegate by a management agreement or another agreement with, or otherwise to, other persons. Unless otherwise provided in the limited liability company agreement, such delegation by a member or manager of a limited liability company shall not cause the member or manager to cease to be a member or manager, as the case may be, of the limited liability company.

SUBCHAPTER V.   FINANCE

§ 18–501. Form of Contribution

The contribution of a member to a limited liability company may be in cash, property or services rendered, or a promissory note or other obligation to contribute cash or property or to perform services.

§ 18–502. Liability for Contribution

(a) Except as provided in a limited liability company agreement, a member is obligated to a limited liability company to perform any promise to contribute cash or property or to perform services, even if he is unable to perform because of death, disability or any other reason. If a member does not make the required contribution of property or services, he is obligated at the option of the limited liability company to contribute cash equal to that portion of the agreed value (as stated in the records of the limited liability company) of the contribution that has not been made. The foregoing option shall be in addition to, and not in lieu of, any other rights, including the right to specific performance, that the limited liability company may have against such member under the limited liability company agreement or applicable law.

(b) Unless otherwise provided in a limited liability company agreement, the obligation of a member to make a contribution or return money or other property paid or distributed in violation of this chapter may be compromised only by consent of all the members. Notwithstanding the compromise, a creditor of a limited liability company who extends credit, after the entering into of a limited liability company agreement or an amendment thereto which, in either case, reflects the obligation, and before the amendment thereof to reflect the compromise, may enforce the original obligation to the extent that, in extending credit, the creditor reasonably relied on the obligation of a member to make a contribution or return. A conditional obligation of a member to make a contribution or return money or other property to a limited liability company may not be enforced unless the conditions of the obligation have been satisfied or waived as to or by such member. Conditional obligations include contributions payable upon a discretionary call of a limited liability company prior to the time the call occurs.

(c) A limited liability company agreement may provide that the interest of any member who fails to make any contribution that he is obligated to make shall be subject to specified penalties for, or specified consequences of, such failure. Such penalty or consequence may take the form of reducing or eliminating the defaulting member's proportionate interest in a limited liability company, subordinating his limited liability company interest to that of nondefaulting members, a forced sale of his limited liability company interest, forfeiture of his limited liability company interest, the lending by other members of the amount necessary to meet his commitment, a fixing of the value of his limited liability company interest by appraisal or by formula and redemption or sale of his limited liability company interest at such value, or other penalty or consequence.

§ 18–503. Allocation of Profits and Losses

The profits and losses of a limited liability company shall be allocated among the members, and among classes or groups of members, in the manner provided in a limited liability company agreement. If the limited liability company agreement does not so provide, profits and losses shall be allocated on the basis of the agreed value (as stated in the records of the limited liability company) of the contributions made by each member to the extent they have been received by the limited liability company and have not been returned.

§ 18–504. Allocation of Distributions

Distributions of cash or other assets of a limited liability company shall be allocated among the members, and among classes or groups of members, in the manner provided in a limited liability company agreement. If the limited liability company agreement does not so provide, distributions shall be made on the basis of the agreed value (as stated in the records of the limited liability company) of the contributions made by each member to the extent they have been received by the limited liability company and have not been returned.

SUBCHAPTER VI. DISTRIBUTIONS AND RESIGNATION

§ 18–601. Interim Distributions

Except as provided in this subchapter, to the extent and at the times or upon the happening of the events specified in a limited liability company agreement, a member is entitled to receive from a limited liability company distributions before his resignation from the limited liability company and before the dissolution and winding up thereof.

§ 18–602. Resignation of Manager

A manager may resign as a manager of a limited liability company at the time or upon the happening of events specified in a limited liability company agreement and in accordance with the limited liability company agreement. A limited liability company agreement may provide that a manager shall not have the right to resign as a manager of a limited liability company. Notwithstanding that a limited liability company agreement provides that a manager does not have the right to resign as a manager of a limited liability company, a manager may resign as a manager of a limited liability company at any time by giving written notice to the members and other managers. If the resignation of a manager violates a limited liability company agreement, in addition to any remedies otherwise available under applicable law, a limited liability company may recover from the resigning manager damages for breach of the limited liability company agreement and offset the damages against the amount otherwise distributable to the resigning manager.

§ 18–603. Resignation of Member

A member may resign from a limited liability company only at the time or upon the happening of events specified in a limited liability company agreement and in accordance with the limited liability company agreement. Notwithstanding anything to the contrary under applicable law, unless a limited liability company agreement provides otherwise, a member may not resign from a limited liability company prior to the dissolution and winding up of the limited liability company. Notwithstanding anything to the contrary under applicable law, a limited liability company agreement may provide that a limited liability company interest may not be assigned prior to the dissolution and winding up of the limited liability company....

§ 18–604. Distribution Upon Resignation

Except as provided in this subchapter, upon resignation any resigning member is entitled to receive any distribution to which such member is entitled under a limited liability company agreement and, if not otherwise provided in a limited liability company agreement, such member is entitled to receive, within a reasonable time after resignation, the fair value of such member's limited liability company interest as of the date of resignation

453

based upon such member's right to share in distributions from the limited liability company.

§ 18–605. Distribution in Kind

Except as provided in a limited liability company agreement, a member, regardless of the nature of his contribution, has no right to demand and receive any distribution from a limited liability company in any form other than cash. Except as provided in a limited liability company agreement, a member may not be compelled to accept a distribution of any asset in kind from a limited liability company to the extent that the percentage of the asset distributed to him exceeds a percentage of that asset which is equal to the percentage in which he shares in distributions from the limited liability company. Except as provided in the limited liability company agreement, a member may be compelled to accept a distribution of any asset in kind from a limited liability company to the extent that the percentage of the asset distributed to him is equal to a percentage of that asset which is equal to the percentage in which he shares in distributions from the limited liability company.

§ 18–606. Right to Distribution

Subject to §§ 18–607 and 18–804 of this title, and unless otherwise provided in a limited liability company agreement, at the time a member becomes entitled to receive a distribution, he has the status of, and is entitled to all remedies available to, a creditor of a limited liability company with respect to the distribution. A limited liability company agreement may provide for the establishment of a record date with respect to allocations and distributions by a limited liability company.

§ 18–607. Limitations on Distribution

(a) A limited liability company shall not make a distribution to a member to the extent that at the time of the distribution, after giving effect to the distribution, all liabilities of the limited liability company, other than liabilities to members on account of their limited liability company interests and liabilities for which the recourse of creditors is limited to specified property of the limited liability company, exceed the fair value of the assets of the limited liability company, except that the fair value of property that is subject to a liability for which the recourse of creditors is limited shall be included in the assets of the limited liability company only to the extent that the fair value of that property exceeds that liability.

(b) A member who receives a distribution in violation of subsection (a) of this section, and who knew at the time of the distribution that the distribution violated subsection (a) of this section, shall be liable to a limited liability company for the amount of the distribution. A member who receives a distribution in violation of subsection (a) of this section, and who did not know at the time of the distribution that the distribution violated subsection (a) of this section, shall not be liable for the amount of the distribution. Subject to subsection (c) of this section, this subsection shall not affect any obligation or liability of a member under agreement or other applicable law for the amount of a distribution.

(c) Unless otherwise agreed, a member who receives a distribution from a limited liability company shall have no liability under this chapter or other applicable law for the amount of the distribution after the expiration of 3 years from the date of the distribution unless an action to recover the distribution from such member is commenced prior to the expiration of the said 3–year period and an adjudication of liability against such member is made in the said action.

SUBCHAPTER VII. ASSIGNMENT OF LIMITED LIABILITY COMPANY INTERESTS

§ 18–701. Nature of Limited Liability Company Interest

A limited liability company interest is personal property. A member has no interest in specific limited liability company property.

§ 18–702. Assignment of Limited Liability Company Interest

(a) A limited liability company interest is assignable in whole or in part except as provided in a limited liability company agreement. The assignee of a member's limited liability company interest shall have no right to participate in the management of the business and affairs of a limited liability company except as provided in a limited liability company agreement and upon:

(1) The approval of all of the members of the limited liability company other than the member assigning his limited liability company interest; or

(2) Compliance with any procedure provided for in the limited liability company agreement.

(b) Unless otherwise provided in a limited liability company agreement:

(1) An assignment of a limited liability company interest does not entitle the assignee to become or to exercise any rights or powers of a member;

(2) An assignment of a limited liability company interest entitles the assignee to share in such profits and losses, to receive such distribution or distributions, and to receive such allocation of income, gain, loss, deduction, or credit or similar item to which the assignor was entitled, to the extent assigned; and

(3) A member ceases to be a member and to have the power to exercise any rights or powers of a member upon assignment of all of his limited liability company interest. Unless otherwise provided in a limited liability company agreement, the pledge of, or granting of a security interest, lien or other encumbrance in or against, any or all of the limited liability company interest of a member shall not cause the

455

member to cease to be a member or to have the power to exercise any rights or powers of a member.

(c) A limited liability company agreement may provide that a member's interest in a limited liability company may be evidenced by a certificate of limited liability company interest issued by the limited liability company.

(d) Unless otherwise provided in a limited liability company agreement and except to the extent assumed by agreement, until an assignee of a limited liability company interest becomes a member, the assignee shall have no liability as a member solely as a result of the assignment.

(e) Unless otherwise provided in the limited liability company agreement, a limited liability company may acquire, by purchase, redemption or otherwise, any limited liability company interest or other interest of a member or manager in the limited liability company. Unless otherwise provided in the limited liability company agreement, any such interest so acquired by the limited liability company shall be deemed canceled.

§ 18–703. Rights of Judgment Creditor

On application to a court of competent jurisdiction by any judgment creditor of a member, the court may charge the limited liability company interest of the member with payment of the unsatisfied amount of the judgment with interest. To the extent so charged, the judgment creditor has only the rights of an assignee of the limited liability company interest. This chapter does not deprive any member of the benefit of any exemption laws applicable to his limited liability company interest.

§ 18–704. Right of Assignee to Become Member

(a) An assignee of a limited liability company interest may become a member as provided in a limited liability company agreement and upon:

(1) The approval of all of the members of the limited liability company other than the member assigning his limited liability company interest; or

(2) Compliance with any procedure provided for in the limited liability company agreement.

(b) An assignee who has become a member has, to the extent assigned, the rights and powers, and is subject to the restrictions and liabilities, of a member under a limited liability company agreement and this chapter. Notwithstanding the foregoing, unless otherwise provided in a limited liability company agreement, an assignee who becomes a member is liable for the obligations of his assignor to make contributions as provided in § 18–502 of this title, but shall not be liable for the obligations of his assignor under subchapter VI of this chapter. However, the assignee is not obligated for liabilities, including the obligations of his assignor to make contributions as provided in § 18–502 of this title, unknown to the assignee at the time he became a member and which could not be ascertained from a limited liability company agreement.

(c) Whether or not an assignee of a limited liability company interest becomes a member, the assignor is not released from his liability to a limited liability company under subchapters V and VI of this chapter.

§ 18–705. Powers of Estate of Deceased or Incompetent Member

If a member who is an individual dies or a court of competent jurisdiction adjudges him to be incompetent to manage his person or his property, the member's personal representative may exercise all of the member's rights for the purpose of settling his estate or administering his property, including any power under a limited liability company agreement of an assignee to become a member. If a member is a corporation, trust or other entity and is dissolved or terminated, the powers of that member may be exercised by its personal representative.

SUBCHAPTER VIII. DISSOLUTION

§ 18–801. Dissolution

(a) A limited liability company is dissolved and its affairs shall be wound up upon the first to occur of the following:

(1) At the time specified in a limited liability company agreement, but if no such time is set forth in the limited liability company agreement, then the limited liability company shall have a perpetual existence;

(2) Upon the happening of events specified in a limited liability company agreement;

(3) Unless otherwise provided in the limited liability company agreement, upon the affirmative vote or written consent of the members of the limited liability company or, if there is more than one class or group of members, then by each class or group of members, in either case, by members who own more than two-thirds of the then-current percentage or other interest in the profits of the limited liability company owned by all of the members or by the members in each class or group, as appropriate;

(4) At any time there are no members; provided that the limited liability company is not dissolved and is not required to be wound up if, (i) unless otherwise provided in a limited liability company agreement, within 90 days or such other period as is provided for in the limited liability company agreement after the occurrence of the event that terminated the continued membership of the last remaining member, the personal representative of the last remaining member agrees in writing to continue the limited liability company and to the admission of the personal representative of such member or its nominee or designee to the limited liability company as a member, effective as of the occurrence of the event that terminated the continued membership of the last remaining member; provided that a limited liability company agreement may provide that the personal representative of the last

remaining member shall be obligated to agree in writing to continue the limited liability company and to the admission of the personal representative of such member or its nominee or designee to the limited liability company as a member, effective as of the occurrence of the event that terminated the continued membership of the last remaining member, or, (ii) a member is admitted to the limited liability company in the manner provided for in the limited liability company agreement, effective as of the occurrence of the event that terminated the continued membership of the last remaining member, within 90 days or such other period as is provided for in the limited liability company agreement after the occurrence of the event that terminated the continued membership of the last remaining member, pursuant to a provision of the limited liability company agreement that specifically provides for the admission of a member to the limited liability company after there is no longer a remaining member of the limited liability company.

(5) The entry of a decree of judicial dissolution under § 18–802 of this title.

(b) Unless otherwise provided in a limited liability company agreement, the death, retirement, resignation, expulsion, bankruptcy or dissolution of any member or the occurrence of any other event that terminates the continued membership of any member shall not cause the limited liability company to be dissolved or its affairs to be wound up, and upon the occurrence of any such event, the limited liability company shall be continued without dissolution.

§ 18–802. Judicial Dissolution

On application by or for a member or manager the Court of Chancery may decree dissolution of a limited liability company whenever it is not reasonably practicable to carry on the business in conformity with a limited liability company agreement.

§ 18–803. Winding Up

(a) Unless otherwise provided in a limited liability company agreement, a manager who has not wrongfully dissolved a limited liability company or, if none, the members or a person approved by the members or, if there is more than 1 class or group of members, then by each class or group of members, in either case, by members who own more than 50 percent of the then current percentage or other interest in the profits of the limited liability company owned by all of the members or by the members in each class or group, as appropriate, may wind up the limited liability company's affairs; but the Court of Chancery, upon cause shown, may wind up the limited liability company's affairs upon application of any member or manager, his personal representative or assignee, and in connection therewith, may appoint a liquidating trustee.

(b) Upon dissolution of a limited liability company and until the filing of a certificate of cancellation as provided in § 18–203 of this title, the persons winding up the limited liability company's affairs may, in the name of, and for and on behalf of, the limited liability company, prosecute and defend suits, whether civil, criminal or administrative, gradually settle and close the limited liability company's business, dispose of and convey the limited liability company's property, discharge or make reasonable provision for the limited liability company's liabilities, and distribute to the members any remaining assets of the limited liability company, all without affecting the liability of members and managers and without imposing liability on a liquidating trustee.

§ 18–804. Distribution of Assets

(a) Upon the winding up of a limited liability company, the assets shall be distributed as follows:

(1) To creditors, including members and managers who are creditors, to the extent otherwise permitted by law, in satisfaction of liabilities of the limited liability company (whether by payment or the making of reasonable provision for payment thereof) other than liabilities for which reasonable provision for payment has been made and liabilities for distributions to members and former members under § 18–601 or § 18–604 of this title;

(2) Unless otherwise provided in a limited liability company agreement, to members and former members in satisfaction of liabilities for distributions under § 18–601 or § 18–604 of this title; and

(3) Unless otherwise provided in a limited liability company agreement, to members first for the return of their contributions and second respecting their limited liability company interests, in the proportions in which the members share in distributions.

(b) A limited liability company which has dissolved (i) shall pay or make reasonable provision to pay all claims and obligations, including all contingent, conditional or unmatured contractual claims, known to the limited liability company, (ii) shall make such provision as will be reasonably likely to be sufficient to provide compensation for any claim against the limited liability company which is the subject of a pending action, suit or proceeding to which the limited liability company is a party and (iii) shall make such provision as will be reasonably likely to be sufficient to provide compensation for claims that have not been made known to the limited liability company or that have not arisen but that, based on facts known to the limited liability company, are likely to arise or to become known to the limited liability company within 10 years after the date of dissolution. If there are sufficient assets, such claims and obligations shall be paid in full and any such provision for payment made shall be made in full. If there are insufficient assets, such claims and obligations shall be paid or provided for according to their priority and, among claims of equal priority, ratably to the extent of assets available therefor. Unless otherwise provided in the limited liability company agreement, any remaining assets shall be distributed as provided in this chapter. Any liquidating trustee winding up a limited liability company's affairs who has complied with this section shall not be personally liable to the claimants of the dissolved limited liability company by reason of such person's actions in winding up the limited liability company.

(c) A member who receives a distribution in violation of subsection (a) of this section, and who knew at the time of the distribution that the distribution violated subsection (a) of this section, shall be liable to the limited liability company for the amount of the distribution. A member who receives a distribution in violation of subsection (a) of this section, and who did not know at the time of the distribution that the distribution violated subsection (a) of this section, shall not be liable for the amount of the distribution. Subject to subsection (d) of this section, this subsection shall not affect any obligation or liability of a member under an agreement or other applicable law for the amount of a distribution.

(d) Unless otherwise agreed, a member who receives a distribution from a limited liability company to which this section applies shall have no liability under this chapter or other applicable law for the amount of the distribution after the expiration of 3 years from the date of the distribution unless an action to recover the distribution from such member is commenced prior to the expiration of the said 3–year period and an adjudication of liability against such member is made in the said action.

(e) Section 18–607 of this title shall not apply to a distribution to which this section applies.

SUBCHAPTER IX. FOREIGN LIMITED LIABILITY COMPANIES

§ 18–901. Law Governing

(a) Subject to the Constitution of the State of Delaware:

(1) The laws of the state, territory, possession, or other jurisdiction or country under which a foreign limited liability company is organized govern its organization and internal affairs and the liability of its members and managers; and

(2) A foreign limited liability company may not be denied registration by reason of any difference between those laws and the laws of the State of Delaware.

(b) A foreign limited liability company shall be subject to § 18–106 of this title.

§ 18–902. Registration Required; Application

(a) Before doing business in the State of Delaware, a foreign limited liability company shall register with the Secretary of State. . . .

SUBCHAPTER X. DERIVATIVE ACTIONS

§ 18–1001. Right to Bring Action

A member or an assignee of a limited liability company interest may bring an action in the Court of Chancery in the right of a limited liability company to recover a judgment in its favor if managers or members with authority to do so have refused to bring the action or if an effort to cause those managers or members to bring the action is not likely to succeed.

§ 18–1002. Proper Plaintiff

In a derivative action, the plaintiff must be a member or an assignee of a limited liability company interest at the time of bringing the action and:

(1) At the time of the transaction of which he complains; or

(2) His status as a member or an assignee of a limited liability company interest had devolved upon him by operation of law or pursuant to the terms of a limited liability company agreement from a person who was a member or an assignee of a limited liability company interest at the time of the transaction.

§ 18–1003. Complaint

In a derivative action, the complaint shall set forth with particularity the effort, if any, of the plaintiff to secure initiation of the action by a manager or member or the reasons for not making the effort.

§ 18–1004. Expenses

If a derivative action is successful, in whole or in part, as a result of a judgment, compromise or settlement of any such action, the court may award the plaintiff reasonable expenses, including reasonable attorney's fees, from any recovery in any such action or from a limited liability company.

SUBCHAPTER XI. MISCELLANEOUS

§ 18–1101. Construction and Application of Chapter and Limited Liability Company Agreement

(a) The rule that statutes in derogation of the common law are to be strictly construed shall have no application to this chapter.

(b) It is the policy of this chapter to give the maximum effect to the principle of freedom of contract and to the enforceability of limited liability company agreements.

(c) To the extent that, at law or in equity, a member or manager or other person has duties (including fiduciary duties) and liabilities relating thereto to a limited liability company or to another member or manager:

(1) Any such member or manager or other person acting under a limited liability company agreement shall not be liable to the limited liability company or to any such other member or manager for the member's or manager's or other person's good faith reliance on the provisions of the limited liability company agreement; and

461

(2) The member's or manager's or other person's duties and liabilities may be expanded or restricted by provisions in a limited liability company agreement.

(d) Unless the context otherwise requires, as used herein, the singular shall include the plural and the plural may refer to only the singular. The use of any gender shall be applicable to all genders. The captions contained herein are for purposes of convenience only and shall not control or affect the construction of this chapter.

§ 18–1102. Short Title

This chapter may be cited as the "Delaware Limited Liability Company Act."

§ 18–1104. Cases Not Provided for in This Chapter

In any case not provided for in this chapter, the rules of law and equity, including the law merchant, shall govern.

§ 18–1106. Reserved Power of State of Delaware to Alter or Repeal Chapter

All provisions of this chapter may be altered from time to time or repealed and all rights of members and managers are subject to this reservation. Unless expressly stated to the contrary in this chapter, all amendments of this chapter shall apply to limited liability companies and members and managers whether or not existing as such at the time of the enactment of any such amendment.

§ 18–1107. Taxation of Limited Liability Companies

(a) For purposes of any tax imposed by the State of Delaware or any instrumentality, agency or political subdivision of the State of Delaware, a limited liability company formed under this chapter or qualified to do business in the State of Delaware as a foreign limited liability company shall be classified as a partnership unless classified otherwise for federal income tax purposes, in which case the limited liability company shall be classified in the same manner as it is classified for federal income tax purposes. . . .

UNIFORM LIMITED LIABILITY COMPANY ACT (1996)

TABLE OF CONTENTS

Prefatory Note *

Sec.

* Omitted.

[ARTICLE] 1

GENERAL PROVISIONS

Sec.
101. Definitions.
102. Knowledge and Notice.
103. Effect of Operating Agreement; Nonwaivable Provisions.
104. Supplemental Principles of Law.
105. Name.
106. Reserved Name.
107. Registered Name.
108. Designated Office and Agent for Service of Process.
109. Change of Designated Office or Agent for Service of Process.
110. Resignation of Agent for Service of Process.
111. Service of Process.
112. Nature of Business and Powers.

Section 101.   Definitions.

In this [Act]:

(1) "Articles of organization" means initial, amended, and re-stated articles of organization and articles of merger. In the case of a

foreign limited liability company, the term includes all records serving a similar function required to be filed in the office of the [Secretary of State] or other official having custody of company records in the State or country under whose law it is organized.

(2) "At-will company" means a limited liability company other than a term company.

(3) "Business" includes every trade, occupation, profession, and other lawful purpose, whether or not carried on for profit.

(4) "Debtor in bankruptcy" means a person who is the subject of an order for relief under Title 11 of the United States Code or a comparable order under a successor statute of general application or a comparable order under federal, state, or foreign law governing insolvency.

(5) "Distribution" means a transfer of money, property, or other benefit from a limited liability company to a member in the member's capacity as a member or to a transferee of the member's distributional interest.

(6) "Distributional interest" means all of a member's interest in distributions by the limited liability company.

(7) "Entity" means a person other than an individual.

(8) "Foreign limited liability company" means an unincorporated entity organized under laws other than the laws of this State which afford limited liability to its owners comparable to the liability under Section 303 and is not required to obtain a certificate of authority to transact business under any law of this State other than this [Act].

(9) "Limited liability company" means a limited liability company organized under this [Act].

(10) "Manager" means a person, whether or not a member of a manager-managed company, who is vested with authority under Section 301.

(11) "Manager-managed company" means a limited liability company which is so designated in its articles of organization.

(12) "Member-managed company" means a limited liability company other than a manager-managed company.

(13) "Operating agreement" means the agreement under Section 103 concerning the relations among the members, managers, and limited liability company. The term includes amendments to the agreement.

(14) "Person" means an individual, corporation, business trust, estate, trust, partnership, limited liability company, association, joint venture, government, governmental subdivision, agency, or instrumentality, or any other legal or commercial entity.

(15) "Principal office" means the office, whether or not in this State, where the principal executive office of a domestic or foreign limited liability company is located.

(16) "Record" means information that is inscribed on a tangible medium or that is stored in an electronic or other medium and is retrievable in perceivable form.

(17) "Sign" means to identify a record by means of a signature, mark, or other symbol, with intent to authenticate it.

(18) "State" means a State of the United States, the District of Columbia, the Commonwealth of Puerto Rico, or any territory or insular possession subject to the jurisdiction of the United States.

(19) "Term company" means a limited liability company in which its members have agreed to remain members until the expiration of a term specified in the articles of organization.

(20) "Transfer" includes an assignment, conveyance, deed, bill of sale, lease, mortgage, security interest, encumbrance, and gift.

Comment:

Uniform Limited Liability Company Act ("ULLCA") definitions, like the rest of the Act, are a blend of terms and concepts derived from the Uniform Partnership Act ("UPA"), the Uniform Partnership Act (1994) ("UPA 1994", also previously known as the Revised Uniform Partnership Act or "RUPA"), the Revised Uniform Limited Partnership Act ("RULPA"), the Uniform Commercial Code ("UCC"), and the Model Business Corporation Act ("MBCA"), or their revisions from time to time; some are tailored specially for this Act.

"Business." A limited liability company may be organized to engage in an activity either for or not for profit. The extent to which contributions to a nonprofit company may be deductible for Federal income tax purposes is determined by federal law. Other state law determines the extent of exemptions from state and local income and property taxes.

"Debtor in bankruptcy." The filing of a voluntary petition operates immediately as an "order for relief." See Sections 601(7)(i) and 602(b)(2)(iii).

"Distribution." This term includes all sources of a member's distributions including the member's capital contributions, undistributed profits, and residual interest in the assets of the company after all claims, including those of third parties and debts to members, have been paid.

"Distributional interest." The term does not include a member's broader rights to participate in the management of the company. See Comments to Article 5.

"Foreign limited liability company." The term is not restricted to companies formed in the United States.

467

"Manager." The rules of agency apply to limited liability companies. Therefore, managers may designate agents with whatever titles, qualifications, and responsibilities they desire. For example, managers may designate an agent as "President."

"Manager-managed company." The term includes only a company designated as such in the articles of organization. In a manager-managed company agency authority is vested exclusively in one or more managers and not in the members. See Sections 101(10) (manager), 203(a)(6) (articles designation), and 301(b) (agency authority of members and managers).

"Member-managed limited liability company." The term includes every company not designated as "manager-managed" under Section 203(a)(6) in its articles of organization.

"Operating agreement." This agreement may be oral. Members may agree upon the extent to which their relationships are to be governed by writings.

"Principal office." The address of the principal office must be set forth in the annual report required under Section 211(a)(3).

"Record." This Act is the first Uniform Act promulgated with a definition of this term. The definition brings this Act in conformity with the present state of technology and accommodates prospective future technology in the communication and storage of information other than by human memory. Modern methods of communicating and storing information employed in commercial practices are no longer confined to physical documents.

The term includes any writing. A record need not be permanent or indestructible, but an oral or other unwritten communication must be stored or preserved on some medium to qualify as a record. Information that has not been retained other than through human memory does not qualify as a record. A record may be signed or may be created without the knowledge or intent of a particular person. Other law must be consulted to determine admissibility in evidence, the applicability of statute of frauds, and other questions regarding the use of records. Under Section 206(a), electronic filings may be permitted and even encouraged.

Section 102. Knowledge and Notice.

(a) A person knows a fact if the person has actual knowledge of it.

(b) A person has notice of a fact if the person:

    (1) knows the fact;

    (2) has received a notification of the fact; or

    (3) has reason to know the fact exists from all of the facts known to the person at the time in question.

(c) A person notifies or gives a notification of a fact to another by taking steps reasonably required to inform the other person in ordinary course, whether or not the other person knows the fact.

(d) A person receives a notification when the notification:

(1) comes to the person's attention; or

(2) is duly delivered at the person's place of business or at any other place held out by the person as a place for receiving communications.

(e) An entity knows, has notice, or receives a notification of a fact for purposes of a particular transaction when the individual conducting the transaction for the entity knows, has notice, or receives a notification of the fact, or in any event when the fact would have been brought to the individual's attention had the entity exercised reasonable diligence. An entity exercises reasonable diligence if it maintains reasonable routines for communicating significant information to the individual conducting the transaction for the entity and there is reasonable compliance with the routines. Reasonable diligence does not require an individual acting for the entity to communicate information unless the communication is part of the individual's regular duties or the individual has reason to know of the transaction and that the transaction would be materially affected by the information.

Comment:

Knowledge requires cognitive awareness of a fact, whereas notice is based on a lesser degree of awareness. The Act imposes constructive knowledge under limited circumstances. See Comments to Sections 301(c), 703, and 704.

Section 103. Effect of Operating Agreement; Nonwaivable Provisions.

(a) Except as otherwise provided in subsection (b), all members of a limited liability company may enter into an operating agreement, which need not be in writing, to regulate the affairs of the company and the conduct of its business, and to govern relations among the members, managers, and company. To the extent the operating agreement does not otherwise provide, this [Act] governs relations among the members, managers, and company.

(b) The operating agreement may not:

(1) unreasonably restrict a right to information or access to records under Section 408;

(2) eliminate the duty of loyalty under Section 409(b) or 603(b)(3), but the agreement may:

(i) identify specific types or categories of activities that do not violate the duty of loyalty, if not manifestly unreasonable; and

469

(ii) specify the number or percentage of members or disinterested managers that may authorize or ratify, after full disclosure of all material facts, a specific act or transaction that otherwise would violate the duty of loyalty;

(3) unreasonably reduce the duty of care under Section 409(c) or 603(b)(3);

(4) eliminate the obligation of good faith and fair dealing under Section 409(d), but the operating agreement may determine the standards by which the performance of the obligation is to be measured, if the standards are not manifestly unreasonable;

(5) vary the right to expel a member in an event specified in Section 601(6);

(6) vary the requirement to wind up the limited liability company's business in a case specified in Section 801(3); or

(7) restrict rights of a person, other than a manager, member, and transferee of a member's distributional interest, under this [Act].

Comment:

The operating agreement is the essential contract that governs the affairs of a limited liability company. Since it is binding on all members, amendments must be approved by all members unless otherwise provided in the agreement. Although many agreements will be in writing, the agreement and any amendments may be oral or may be in the form of a record. Course of dealing, course of performance and usage of trade are relevant to determine the meaning of the agreement unless the agreement provides that all amendments must be in writing.

This section makes clear that the only matters an operating agreement may not control are specified in subsection (b). Accordingly, an operating agreement may modify or eliminate any rule specified in any section of this Act except matters specified in subsection (b). To the extent not otherwise mentioned in subsection (b), every section of this Act is simply a default rule, regardless of whether the language of the section appears to be otherwise mandatory. This approach eliminates the necessity of repeating the phrase "unless otherwise agreed" in each section and its commentary.

Under subsection (b)(1), an operating agreement may not unreasonably restrict the right to information or access to any records under Section 408. This does not create an independent obligation beyond Section 408 to maintain any specific records. Under subsections (b)(2) to (4), an irreducible core of fiduciary responsibilities survive any contrary provision in the operating agreement. Subsection (b)(2)(i) authorizes an operating agreement to modify, but not eliminate, the three specific duties of loyalty set forth in Section 409(b)(1) to (3) provided the modification itself is not manifestly unreasonable, a question of fact. Subsection (b)(2)(ii) preserves the common law right of the members to authorize future or ratify past violations of the duty of loyalty provided there has been a full disclosure of all material facts. The authorization or ratification must be unanimous unless otherwise provided in an operating agreement, because the authorization or ratification itself constitutes an amendment to the agreement. The authorization or ratification of specific past or future conduct may sanction conduct that would have been manifestly unreasonable under subsection (b)(2)(i).

Section 104. Supplemental Principles of Law.

(a) Unless displaced by particular provisions of this [Act], the principles of law and equity supplement this [Act].

(b) If an obligation to pay interest arises under this [Act] and the rate is not specified, the rate is that specified in [applicable statute].

Comment:

Supplementary principles include, but are not limited to, the law of agency, estoppel, law merchant, and all other principles listed in UCC Section 1–103, including the law relative to the capacity to contract, fraud, misrepresentation, duress, coercion, mistake, bankruptcy, and other validating and invalidating clauses. Other principles such as those mentioned in UCC Section 1–205 (Course of Dealing and Usage of Trade) apply as well as course of performance. As with UPA 1994 Section 104, upon which this provision is based, no substantive change from either the UPA or the UCC is intended. Section 104(b) establishes the applicable rate of interest in the absence of an agreement among the members.

Section 105. Name.

(a) The name of a limited liability company must contain "limited liability company" or "limited company" or the abbreviation "L.L.C.", "LLC", "L.C.", or "LC". "Limited" may be abbreviated as "Ltd.", and "company" may be abbreviated as "Co.".

(b) Except as authorized by subsections (c) and (d), the name of a limited liability company must be distinguishable upon the records of the [Secretary of State] from:

(1) the name of any corporation, limited partnership, or company incorporated, organized or authorized to transact business, in this State;

(2) a name reserved or registered under Section 106 or 107;

(3) a fictitious name approved under Section 1005 for a foreign company authorized to transact business in this State because its real name is unavailable.

(c) A limited liability company may apply to the [Secretary of State] for authorization to use a name that is not distinguishable upon the records of the [Secretary of State] from one or more of the names described in

471

subsection (b). The [Secretary of State] shall authorize use of the name applied for if:

   (1) the present user, registrant, or owner of a reserved name consents to the use in a record and submits an undertaking in form satisfactory to the [Secretary of State] to change the name to a name that is distinguishable upon the records of the [Secretary of State] from the name applied for; or

   (2) the applicant delivers to the [Secretary of State] a certified copy of the final judgment of a court of competent jurisdiction establishing the applicant's right to use the name applied for in this State.

(d) A limited liability company may use the name, including a fictitious name, of another domestic or foreign company which is used in this State if the other company is organized or authorized to transact business in this State and the company proposing to use the name has:

   (1) merged with the other company;

   (2) been formed by reorganization with the other company; or

   (3) acquired substantially all of the assets, including the name, of the other company.

Section 106. Reserved Name.

(a) A person may reserve the exclusive use of the name of a limited liability company, including a fictitious name for a foreign company whose name is not available, by delivering an application to the [Secretary of State] for filing. The application must set forth the name and address of the applicant and the name proposed to be reserved. If the [Secretary of State] finds that the name applied for is available, it must be reserved for the applicant's exclusive use for a nonrenewable 120–day period.

(b) The owner of a name reserved for a limited liability company may transfer the reservation to another person by delivering to the [Secretary of State] a signed notice of the transfer which states the name and address of the transferee.

Comment:

   A foreign limited liability company that is not presently authorized to transact business in the State may reserve a fictitious name for a nonrenewable 120–day period. When its actual name is available, a company will generally register that name under Section 107 because the registration is valid for a year and may be extended indefinitely.

Section 107. Registered Name.

(a) A foreign limited liability company may register its name subject to the requirements of Section 1005, if the name is distinguishable upon the records of the [Secretary of State] from names that are not available under Section 105(b).

(b) A foreign limited liability company registers its name, or its name with any addition required by Section 1005, by delivering to the [Secretary of State] for filing an application:

(1) setting forth its name, or its name with any addition required by Section 1005, the State or country and date of its organization, and a brief description of the nature of the business in which it is engaged; and

(2) accompanied by a certificate of existence, or a record of similar import, from the State or country of organization.

(c) A foreign limited liability company whose registration is effective may renew it for successive years by delivering for filing in the office of the [Secretary of State] a renewal application complying with subsection (b) between October 1 and December 31 of the preceding year. The renewal application renews the registration for the following calendar year.

(d) A foreign limited liability company whose registration is effective may qualify as a foreign company under its name or consent in writing to the use of its name by a limited liability company later organized under this [Act] or by another foreign company later authorized to transact business in this State. The registered name terminates when the limited liability company is organized or the foreign company qualifies or consents to the qualification of another foreign company under the registered name.

Section 108. Designated Office and Agent for Service of Process.

(a) A limited liability company and a foreign limited liability company authorized to do business in this State shall designate and continuously maintain in this State:

(1) an office, which need not be a place of its business in this State; and

(2) an agent and street address of the agent for service of process on the company.

(b) An agent must be an individual resident of this State, a domestic corporation, another limited liability company, or a foreign corporation or foreign company authorized to do business in this State.

Comment:

Limited liability companies organized under Section 202 or authorized to transact business under Section 1004 are required to designate and continuously maintain an office in the State. Although the designated office need not be a place of business, it most often will be the only place of business of the company. The company must also designate an agent for service of process within the State and the agent's street address. The agent's address need not be the same as the company's designated office address. The initial office and agent designations must be set forth in the articles of organization, including the address of the designated office. See Section 203(a)(2) to (3). The current office and agent designations must be set forth in the company's annual report. See Section 211(a)(2). See also Section 109 (procedure for changing the office or agent designations), Section 110 (procedure for an agent to resign), and Section 111(b) (the filing officer is the service agent for the company if it fails to maintain its own service agent).

Section 109. Change of Designated Office or Agent for Service of Process.

A limited liability company may change its designated office or agent for service of process by delivering to the [Secretary of State] for filing a statement of change which sets forth:

(1) the name of the company;

(2) the street address of its current designated office;

(3) if the current designated office is to be changed, the street address of the new designated office;

(4) the name and address of its current agent for service of process; and

(5) if the current agent for service of process or street address of that agent is to be changed, the new address or the name and street address of the new agent for service of process.

Section 110. Resignation of Agent for Service of Process.

(a) An agent for service of process of a limited liability company may resign by delivering to the [Secretary of State] for filing a record of the statement of resignation.

(b) After filing a statement of resignation, the [Secretary of State] shall mail a copy to the designated office and another copy to the limited liability company at its principal office.

(c) An agency is terminated on the 31st day after the statement is filed in the office of the [Secretary of State].

Section 111. Service of Process.

(a) An agent for service of process appointed by a limited liability company or a foreign limited liability company is an agent of the company for service of any process, notice, or demand required or permitted by law to be served upon the company.

(b) If a limited liability company or foreign limited liability company fails to appoint or maintain an agent for service of process in this State or the agent for service of process cannot with reasonable diligence be found at the agent's address, the [Secretary of State] is an agent of the company upon whom process, notice, or demand may be served.

(c) Service of any process, notice, or demand on the [Secretary of State] may be made by delivering to and leaving with the [Secretary of State], the [Assistant Secretary of State], or clerk having charge of the limited liability company department of the [Secretary of State's] office duplicate copies of the process, notice, or demand. If the process, notice, or demand is served on the [Secretary of State], the [Secretary of State] shall forward one of the copies by registered or certified mail, return receipt requested, to the company at its designated office. Service is effected under this subsection at the earliest of:

(1) the date the company receives the process, notice, or demand;

(2) the date shown on the return receipt, if signed on behalf of the company; or

(3) five days after its deposit in the mail, if mailed postpaid and correctly addressed.

(d) The [Secretary of State] shall keep a record of all processes, notices, and demands served pursuant to this section and record the time of and the action taken regarding the service.

(e) This section does not affect the right to serve process, notice, or demand in any manner otherwise provided by law.

Comment:

Service of process on a limited liability company and a foreign company authorized to transact business in the State must be made on the company's agent for service of process whose name and address should be on file with the filing office. If for any reason a company fails to appoint or maintain an agent for service of process or the agent cannot be found with reasonable diligence at the agent's address, the filing officer will be deemed the proper agent.

Section 112. Nature of Business and Powers.

(a) A limited liability company may be organized under this [Act] for any lawful purpose, subject to any law of this State governing or regulating business.

(b) Unless its articles of organization provide otherwise, a limited liability company has the same powers as an individual to do all things necessary or convenient to carry on its business or affairs, including power to:

(1) sue and be sued, and defend in its name;

(2) purchase, receive, lease, or otherwise acquire, and own, hold, improve, use, and otherwise deal with real or personal property, or any legal or equitable interest in property, wherever located;

(3) sell, convey, mortgage, grant a security interest in, lease, exchange, and otherwise encumber or dispose of all or any part of its property;

(4) purchase, receive, subscribe for, or otherwise acquire, own, hold, vote, use, sell, mortgage, lend, grant a security interest in, or otherwise dispose of and deal in and with, shares or other interests in or obligations of any other entity;

(5) make contracts and guarantees, incur liabilities, borrow money, issue its notes, bonds, and other obligations, which may be convertible into or include the option to purchase other securities of the limited liability company, and secure any of its obligations by a mortgage on or a security interest in any of its property, franchises, or income;

(6) lend money, invest and reinvest its funds, and receive and hold real and personal property as security for repayment;

(7) be a promoter, partner, member, associate, or manager of any partnership, joint venture, trust, or other entity;

(8) conduct its business, locate offices, and exercise the powers granted by this [Act] within or without this State;

(9) elect managers and appoint officers, employees, and agents of the limited liability company, define their duties, fix their compensation, and lend them money and credit;

(10) pay pensions and establish pension plans, pension trusts, profit sharing plans, bonus plans, option plans, and benefit or incentive plans for any or all of its current or former members, managers, officers, employees, and agents;

(11) make donations for the public welfare or for charitable, scientific, or educational purposes; and

(12) make payments or donations, or do any other act, not inconsistent with law, that furthers the business of the limited liability company.

Comment:

A limited liability company may be organized for any lawful purpose unless the State has specifically prohibited a company from engaging in a specific activity. For example, many States require that certain regulated industries, such as banking and insurance, be conducted only by organizations that meet the special requirements. Also, many States impose restrictions on activities in which a limited liability company may engage. For example, the practice of certain professionals is often subject to special conditions.

A limited liability company has the power to engage in and perform important and necessary acts related to its operation and function. A company's power to enter into a transaction is distinguishable from the authority of an agent to enter into the transaction. See Section 301 (agency rules).

[ARTICLE] 2

ORGANIZATION

Section 201.   Limited Liability Company as Legal Entity.

A limited liability company is a legal entity distinct from its members.

Comment:

A limited liability company is legally distinct from its members who are not normally liable for the debts, obligations, and liabilities of the company. See Section 303. Accordingly, members are not proper parties to suits against the company unless an object of the proceeding is to enforce members' rights against the company or to enforce their liability to the company.

Section 202.   Organization.

(a) One or more persons may organize a limited liability company, consisting of one or more members, by delivering articles of organization to the office of the [Secretary of State] for filing.

(b) Unless a delayed effective date is specified, the existence of a limited liability company begins when the articles of organization are filed.

(c) The filing of the articles of organization by the [Secretary of State] is conclusive proof that the organizers satisfied all conditions precedent to the creation of a limited liability company.

Comment:

Any person may organize a limited liability company by performing the ministerial act of signing and filing the articles of organization. The person need not be a member. As a matter of flexibility, a company may be organized and operated with only one member to enable sole proprietors to obtain the benefit of a liability shield. The effect of organizing or operating a company with one member on the Federal tax classification of the company is determined by federal law.

The existence of a company begins when the articles are filed. Therefore, the filing of the articles of organization is conclusive as to the existence of the limited liability shield for persons who enter into transactions on behalf of the company. Until the articles are filed, a firm is not organized under this Act and is not a "limited liability company" as defined in Section 101(9). In that case, the parties' relationships are not governed by this Act unless they have expressed a

477

contractual intent to be bound by the provisions of the Act. Third parties would also not be governed by the provisions of this Act unless they have expressed a contractual intent to extend a limited liability shield to the members of the would-be limited liability company.

Section 203. Articles of Organization.

(a) Articles of organization of a limited liability company must set forth:

(1) the name of the company;

(2) the address of the initial designated office;

(3) the name and street address of the initial agent for service of process;

(4) the name and address of each organizer;

(5) whether the company is to be a term company and, if so, the term specified;

(6) whether the company is to be manager-managed, and, if so, the name and address of each initial manager; and

(7) whether one or more of the members of the company are to be liable for its debts and obligations under Section 303(c).

(b) Articles of organization of a limited liability company may set forth:

(1) provisions permitted to be set forth in an operating agreement; or

(2) other matters not inconsistent with law.

(c) Articles of organization of a limited liability company may not vary the nonwaivable provisions of Section 103(b). As to all other matters, if any provision of an operating agreement is inconsistent with the articles of organization:

(1) the operating agreement controls as to managers, members, and members' transferees; and

(2) the articles of organization control as to persons, other than managers, members and their transferees, who reasonably rely on the articles to their detriment.

Comment:

The articles serve primarily a notice function and generally do not reflect the substantive agreement of the members regarding the business affairs of the company. Those matters are generally reserved for an operating agreement which may be unwritten. Under Section 203(b), the articles may contain provisions permitted to be set forth in an operating agreement. Where the articles and operating agreement conflict, the operating agreement controls as to members but the articles control as to third parties. The articles may also contain any other matter not inconsistent with law. The most important is a

Section 301(c) limitation on the authority of a member or manager to transfer interests in the company's real property.

A company will be at-will unless it is designated as a term company and the duration of its term is specified in its articles under Section 203(a)(5). The duration of a term company may be specified in any manner which sets forth a specific and final date for the dissolution of the company. For example, the period specified may be in the form of "50 years from the date of filing of the articles" or "the period ending on January 1, 2020." Mere specification of a particular undertaking of an uncertain business duration is not sufficient unless the particular undertaking is within a longer fixed period. An example of this type of designation would include "2020 or until the building is completed, whichever occurs first." When the specified period is incorrectly specified, the company will be an at-will company. Notwithstanding the correct specification of a term in the articles, a company will be an at-will company among the members under Section 203(c)(1) if an operating agreement so provides. A term company that continues after the expiration of its term specified in its articles will also be an at-will company.

A term company possesses several important default rule characteristics that differentiate it dramatically from an at-will company. An operating agreement may alter any of these rules. Any dissociation of an at-will member dissolves a member-managed company unless a specified percentage of the remaining members agree to continue the business of the company. Before the expiration of its term, only specified dissociation events (excluding voluntary withdrawal) of a term member will dissolve a member-managed company unless a specified percentage of the remaining members agree to continue the business of the company. See Comments to Sections 601 and 801(b)(3). Also, even if the dissociation of an at-will member does not result in a dissolution of a member-managed company, the dissociated member is entitled to have the company purchase that member's interest for its fair value. Unless the company earlier dissolves, a term member must generally await the expiration of the agreed term to withdraw the fair value of the interest. See Comments to Section 701(a).

A company will be member-managed unless it is designated as manager-managed under Section 203(a)(6). Absent further designation in the articles, a company will be a member-managed at-will company. The designation of a limited liability company as either member- or manager-managed is important because it defines who are agents and have the apparent authority to bind the company under Section 301 and determines whether the dissociation of members who are not managers will threaten dissolution of the company. In a member-managed company, the members have the agency authority to bind the company. In a manager-managed company only the managers have that authority. The effect of the agency structure of a company on the Federal tax classification of the company is determined by federal law. The agency designation relates only to agency and does not preclude members of a manager-managed company from participating in the actual management of company business. See Comments to Section 404(b).

In a member-managed company, the dissociation of any member will cause the company to dissolve unless a specified percentage of the remaining members agree to continue the business of the company. In a manager-managed company, only the dissociation of any member who is also a manager threatens dissolution of the company. Only where there are no members who are also managers will the dissociation of members who are not managers threaten dissolution of a manager-managed company. See Comments to Section 801.

Section 204. Amendment or Restatement of Articles of Organization.

(a) Articles of organization of a limited liability company may be amended at any time by delivering articles of amendment to the [Secretary of State] for filing. The articles of amendment must set forth the:

(1) name of the limited liability company;

(2) date of filing of the articles of organization; and

(3) amendment to the articles.

(b) A limited liability company may restate its articles of organization at any time. Restated articles of organization must be signed and filed in the same manner as articles of amendment. Restated articles of organization must be designated as such in the heading and state in the heading or in an introductory paragraph the limited liability company's present name and, if it has been changed, all of its former names and the date of the filing of its initial articles of organization.

Comment:

An amendment to the articles requires the consent of all the members unless an operating agreement provides for a lesser number. See Section 404(c)(3).

Section 205. Signing of Records.

(a) Except as otherwise provided in this [Act], a record to be filed by or on behalf of a limited liability company in the office of the [Secretary of State] must be signed in the name of the company by a:

(1) manager of a manager-managed company;

(2) member of a member-managed company;

(3) person organizing the company, if the company has not been formed; or

(4) fiduciary, if the company is in the hands of a receiver, trustee, or other court-appointed fiduciary.

(b) A record signed under subsection (a) must state adjacent to the signature the name and capacity of the signer.

(c) Any person may sign a record to be filed under subsection (a) by an attorney-in-fact. Powers of attorney relating to the signing of records to be filed under subsection (a) by an attorney-in-fact need not be filed in the office of the [Secretary of State] as evidence of authority by the person filing but must be retained by the company.

Comment:

Both a writing and a record may be signed. An electronic record is signed when a person adds a name to the record with the intention to authenticate the record. See Sections 101(16) ("record" definition) and 101(17) ("signed" definition).

Other provisions of this Act also provide for the filing of records with the filing office but do not require signing by the persons specified in clauses (1) to (3). Those specific sections prevail.

Section 206. Filing in Office of [Secretary of State].

(a) Articles of organization or any other record authorized to be filed under this [Act] must be in a medium permitted by the [Secretary of State] and must be delivered to the office of the [Secretary of State]. Unless the [Secretary of State] determines that a record fails to comply as to form with the filing requirements of this [Act], and if all filing fees have been paid, the [Secretary of State] shall file the record and send a receipt for the record and the fees to the limited liability company or its representative.

(b) Upon request and payment of a fee, the [Secretary of State] shall send to the requester a certified copy of the requested record.

(c) Except as otherwise provided in subsection (d) and Section 207(c), a record accepted for filing by the [Secretary of State] is effective:

(1) at the time of filing on the date it is filed, as evidenced by the [Secretary of State's] date and time endorsement on the original record; or

(2) at the time specified in the record as its effective time on the date it is filed.

(d) A record may specify a delayed effective time and date, and if it does so the record becomes effective at the time and date specified. If a delayed effective date but no time is specified, the record is effective at the close of business on that date. If a delayed effective date is later than the 90th day after the record is filed, the record is effective on the 90th day.

Comment:

The definition and use of the term "record" permits filings with the filing office under this Act to conform to technological advances that have been adopted by the filing office. However, since Section 206(a) provides that the filing "must be in a medium permitted by the

[Secretary of State]'', the Act simply conforms to filing changes as they are adopted.

Section 207.   Correcting Filed Record.

(a) A limited liability company or foreign limited liability company may correct a record filed by the [Secretary of State] if the record contains a false or erroneous statement or was defectively signed.

(b) A record is corrected:

    (1) by preparing articles of correction that:

        (i) describe the record, including its filing date, or attach a copy of it to the articles of correction;

        (ii) specify the incorrect statement and the reason it is incorrect or the manner in which the signing was defective; and

        (iii) correct the incorrect statement or defective signing; and

    (2) by delivering the corrected record to the [Secretary of State] for filing.

(c) Articles of correction are effective retroactively on the effective date of the record they correct except as to persons relying on the uncorrected record and adversely affected by the correction. As to those persons, articles of correction are effective when filed.

Section 208.   Certificate of Existence or Authorization.

(a) A person may request the [Secretary of State] to furnish a certificate of existence for a limited liability company or a certificate of authorization for a foreign limited liability company.

(b) A certificate of existence for a limited liability company must set forth:

    (1) the company's name;

    (2) that it is duly organized under the laws of this State, the date of organization, whether its duration is at-will or for a specified term, and, if the latter, the period specified;

    (3) if payment is reflected in the records of the [Secretary of State] and if nonpayment affects the existence of the company, that all fees, taxes, and penalties owed to this State have been paid;

    (4) whether its most recent annual report required by Section 211 has been filed with the [Secretary of State];

    (5) that articles of termination have not been filed; and

    (6) other facts of record in the office of the [Secretary of State] which may be requested by the applicant.

(c) A certificate of authorization for a foreign limited liability company must set forth:

    (1) the company's name used in this State;

(2) that it is authorized to transact business in this State;

(3) if payment is reflected in the records of the [Secretary of State] and if nonpayment affects the authorization of the company, that all fees, taxes, and penalties owed to this State have been paid;

(4) whether its most recent annual report required by Section 211 has been filed with the [Secretary of State];

(5) that a certificate of cancellation has not been filed; and

(6) other facts of record in the office of the [Secretary of State] which may be requested by the applicant.

(d) Subject to any qualification stated in the certificate, a certificate of existence or authorization issued by the [Secretary of State] may be relied upon as conclusive evidence that the domestic or foreign limited liability company is in existence or is authorized to transact business in this State.

Section 209. Liability for False Statement in Filed Record.

If a record authorized or required to be filed under this [Act] contains a false statement, one who suffers loss by reliance on the statement may recover damages for the loss from a person who signed the record or caused another to sign it on the person's behalf and knew the statement to be false at the time the record was signed.

Section 210. Filing by Judicial Act.

If a person required by Section 205 to sign any record fails or refuses to do so, any other person who is adversely affected by the failure or refusal may petition the [designate the appropriate court] to direct the signing of the record. If the court finds that it is proper for the record to be signed and that a person so designated has failed or refused to sign the record, it shall order the [Secretary of State] to sign and file an appropriate record.

Section 211. Annual Report for [Secretary of State].

(a) A limited liability company, and a foreign limited liability company authorized to transact business in this State, shall deliver to the [Secretary of State] for filing an annual report that sets forth:

(1) the name of the company and the State or country under whose law it is organized;

(2) the address of its designated office and the name and address of its agent for service of process in this State;

(3) the address of its principal office; and

(4) the names and business addresses of any managers.

(b) Information in an annual report must be current as of the date the annual report is signed on behalf of the limited liability company.

(c) The first annual report must be delivered to the [Secretary of State] between [January 1 and April 1] of the year following the calendar year in which a limited liability company was organized or a foreign company was authorized to transact business. Subsequent annual reports must be delivered to the [Secretary of State] between [January 1 and April 1] of the ensuing calendar years.

(d) If an annual report does not contain the information required in subsection (a), the [Secretary of State] shall promptly notify the reporting limited liability company or foreign limited liability company and return the report to it for correction. If the report is corrected to contain the information required in subsection (a) and delivered to the [Secretary of State] within 30 days after the effective date of the notice, it is timely filed.

Comment:

Failure to deliver the annual report within 60 days after its due date is a primary ground for administrative dissolution of the company under Section 809. See Comments to Sections 809 to 812.

[ARTICLE] 3

RELATIONS OF MEMBERS AND MANAGERS TO PERSONS DEALING WITH LIMITED LIABILITY COMPANY

Sec.
301.   Agency of Members and Managers.
302.   Limited Liability Company Liable for Member's or Manager's Actionable Conduct.
303.   Liability of Members and Managers.

Section 301.   Agency of Members and Managers.

(a) Subject to subsections (b) and (c):

(1) Each member is an agent of the limited liability company for the purpose of its business, and an act of a member, including the signing of an instrument in the company's name, for apparently carrying on in the ordinary course the company's business or business of the kind carried on by the company binds the company, unless the member had no authority to act for the company in the particular matter and the person with whom the member was dealing knew or had notice that the member lacked authority.

(2) An act of a member which is not apparently for carrying on in the ordinary course the company's business or business of the kind carried on by the company binds the company only if the act was authorized by the other members.

(b) Subject to subsection (c), in a manager-managed company:

(1) A member is not an agent of the company for the purpose of its business solely by reason of being a member. Each manager is an agent of the company for the purpose of its business, and an act of a manager, including the signing of an instrument in the company's name, for apparently carrying on in the ordinary course the company's

business or business of the kind carried on by the company binds the company, unless the manager had no authority to act for the company in the particular matter and the person with whom the manager was dealing knew or had notice that the manager lacked authority.

(2) An act of a manager which is not apparently for carrying on in the ordinary course the company's business or business of the kind carried on by the company binds the company only if the act was authorized under Section 404.

(c) Unless the articles of organization limit their authority, any member of a member-managed company or manager of a manager-managed company may sign and deliver any instrument transferring or affecting the company's interest in real property. The instrument is conclusive in favor of a person who gives value without knowledge of the lack of the authority of the person signing and delivering the instrument.

Comment:

Members of a member-managed and managers of manager-managed company, as agents of the firm, have the apparent authority to bind a company to third parties. Members of a manager-managed company are not as such agents of the firm and do not have the apparent authority, as members, to bind a company. Members and managers with apparent authority possess actual authority by implication unless the actual authority is restricted in an operating agreement. Apparent authority extends to acts for carrying on in the ordinary course the company's business and business of the kind carried on by the company. Acts beyond this scope bind the company only where supported by actual authority created before the act or ratified after the act.

Ordinarily, restrictions on authority in an operating agreement do not affect the apparent authority of members and managers to bind the company to third parties without notice of the restriction. However, the restriction may make a member or manager's conduct wrongful and create liability to the company for the breach. This rule is subject to three important exceptions. First, under Section 301(c), a limitation reflected in the articles of organization on the authority of any member or manager to sign and deliver an instrument affecting an interest in company real property is effective when filed, even to persons without knowledge of the agent's lack of authority. The effect of such a limitation on authority on the Federal tax classification of the company is determined by federal law. Secondly, under Section 703, a dissociated member's apparent authority terminates two years after dissociation, even to persons without knowledge of the dissociation. Thirdly, under Section 704, a dissociated member's apparent authority may be terminated earlier than the two years by filing a statement of dissociation. The statement is effective 90 days after filing, even to persons without knowledge of the filing. Together, these three provisions provide constructive knowledge to the world of the lack of apparent authority of an agent to bind the company.

Section 302. Limited Liability Company Liable for Member's or Manager's Actionable Conduct.

A limited liability company is liable for loss or injury caused to a person, or for a penalty incurred, as a result of a wrongful act or omission, or other actionable conduct, of a member or manager acting in the ordinary course of business of the company or with authority of the company.

Comment:

Since a member of a manager-managed company is not as such an agent, the acts of the member are not imputed to the company unless the member is acting under actual or apparent authority created by circumstances other than membership status.

Section 303. Liability of Members and Managers.

(a) Except as otherwise provided in subsection (c), the debts, obligations, and liabilities of a limited liability company, whether arising in contract, tort, or otherwise, are solely the debts, obligations, and liabilities of the company. A member or manager is not personally liable for a debt, obligation, or liability of the company solely by reason of being or acting as a member or manager.

(b) The failure of a limited liability company to observe the usual company formalities or requirements relating to the exercise of its company powers or management of its business is not a ground for imposing personal liability on the members or managers for liabilities of the company.

(c) All or specified members of a limited liability company are liable in their capacity as members for all or specified debts, obligations, or liabilities of the company if:

(1) a provision to that effect is contained in the articles of organization; and

(2) a member so liable has consented in writing to the adoption of the provision or to be bound by the provision.

Comment:

A member or manager, as an agent of the company, is not liable for the debts, obligations, and liabilities of the company simply because of the agency. A member or manager is responsible for acts or omissions to the extent those acts or omissions would be actionable in contract or tort against the member or manager if that person were acting in an individual capacity. Where a member or manager delegates or assigns the authority or duty to exercise appropriate company functions, the member or manager is ordinarily not personally liable for the acts or omissions of the officer, employee, or agent if the member or manager has complied with the duty of care set forth in Section 409(c).

Under Section 303(c), the usual liability shield may be waived, in whole or in part, provided the waiver is reflected in the articles of organization and the member has consented in writing to be bound by the waiver. The importance and unusual nature of the waiver consent requires that the consent be evidenced by a writing and not merely an unwritten record. See Comments to Section 205. The effect of a waiver on the Federal tax classification of the company is determined by federal law.

[ARTICLE] 4

RELATIONS OF MEMBERS TO EACH OTHER AND TO LIMITED LIABILITY COMPANY

Section 401. Form of Contribution.

A contribution of a member of a limited liability company may consist of tangible or intangible property or other benefit to the company, including money, promissory notes, services performed, or other agreements to contribute cash or property, or contracts for services to be performed.

Comment:

Unless otherwise provided in an operating agreement, admission of a member and the nature and valuation of a would-be member's contribution are matters requiring the consent of all of the other members. See Section 404(c)(7). An agreement to contribute to a company is controlled by the operating agreement and therefore may not be created or modified without amending that agreement through the unanimous consent of all the members, including the member to be bound by the new contribution terms. See 404(c)(1).

Section 402. Member's Liability for Contributions.

(a) A member's obligation to contribute money, property, or other benefit to, or to perform services for, a limited liability company is not excused by the member's death, disability, or other inability to perform personally. If a member does not make the required contribution of property or services, the member is obligated at the option of the company to contribute money equal to the value of that portion of the stated contribution which has not been made.

(b) A creditor of a limited liability company who extends credit or otherwise acts in reliance on an obligation described in subsection (a), and without notice of any compromise under Section 404(c)(5), may enforce the original obligation.

Comment:

An obligation need not be in writing to be enforceable. Given the informality of some companies, a writing requirement may frustrate reasonable expectations of members based on a clear oral agreement. Obligations may be compromised with the consent of all of the members under Section 404(c)(5), but the compromise is generally effective only among the consenting members. Company creditors are bound by the compromise only as provided in Section 402(b).

Section 403. Member's and Manager's Rights to Payments and Reimbursement.

(a) A limited liability company shall reimburse a member or manager for payments made and indemnify a member or manager for liabilities incurred by the member or manager in the ordinary course of the business of the company or for the preservation of its business or property.

(b) A limited liability company shall reimburse a member for an advance to the company beyond the amount of contribution the member agreed to make.

(c) A payment or advance made by a member which gives rise to an obligation of a limited liability company under subsection (a) or (b) constitutes a loan to the company upon which interest accrues from the date of the payment or advance.

(d) A member is not entitled to remuneration for services performed for a limited liability company, except for reasonable compensation for services rendered in winding up the business of the company.

Comment:

The presence of a liability shield will ordinarily prevent a member or manager from incurring personal liability on behalf of the company in the ordinary course of the company's business. Where a member of a member-managed or a manager of a manager-managed company incurs such liabilities, Section 403(a) provides that the company must indemnify the member or manager where that person acted in the ordinary course of the company's business or the preservation of its property. A member or manager is therefore entitled to indemnification only if the act was within the member or manager's actual authority. A member or manager is therefore not entitled to indemnification for conduct that violates the duty of care set forth in Section 409(c) or for tortious conduct against a third party. Since members of a manager-managed company do not possess the apparent authority to bind the company, it would be more unusual for such a member to incur a liability for indemnification in the ordinary course of the company's business.

Section 404. Management of Limited Liability Company.

(a) In a member-managed company:

(1) each member has equal rights in the management and conduct of the company's business; and

(2) except as otherwise provided in subsection (c), any matter relating to the business of the company may be decided by a majority of the members.

(b) In a manager-managed company:

(1) each manager has equal rights in the management and conduct of the company's business;

(2) except as otherwise provided in subsection (c), any matter relating to the business of the company may be exclusively decided by the manager or, if there is more than one manager, by a majority of the managers; and

(3) a manager:

(i) must be designated, appointed, elected, removed, or replaced by a vote, approval, or consent of a majority of the members; and

(ii) holds office until a successor has been elected and qualified, unless the manager sooner resigns or is removed.

(c) The only matters of a member or manager-managed company's business requiring the consent of all of the members are:

(1) the amendment of the operating agreement under Section 103;

(2) the authorization or ratification of acts or transactions under Section 103(b)(2)(ii) which would otherwise violate the duty of loyalty;

(3) an amendment to the articles of organization under Section 204;

(4) the compromise of an obligation to make a contribution under Section 402(b);

(5) the compromise, as among members, of an obligation of a member to make a contribution or return money or other property paid or distributed in violation of this [Act];

(6) the making of interim distributions under Section 405(a), including the redemption of an interest;

(7) the admission of a new member;

(8) the use of the company's property to redeem an interest subject to a charging order;

(9) the consent to dissolve the company under Section 801(b)(2);

(10) a waiver of the right to have the company's business wound up and the company terminated under Section 802(b);

(11) the consent of members to merge with another entity under Section 904(c)(1); and

(12) the sale, lease, exchange, or other disposal of all, or substantially all, of the company's property with or without goodwill.

(d) Action requiring the consent of members or managers under this [Act] may be taken without a meeting.

(e) A member or manager may appoint a proxy to vote or otherwise act for the member or manager by signing an appointment instrument, either personally or by the member's or manager's attorney-in-fact.

Comment:

In a member-managed company, each member has equal rights in the management and conduct of the company's business unless otherwise provided in an operating agreement. For example, an operating agreement may allocate voting rights based upon capital contributions rather than the subsection (a) per capita rule. Also, member disputes as to any matter relating to the company's business may be resolved by a majority of the members unless the matter relates to a matter specified either in subsection (c) (unanimous consent required) or in Section 801(b)(3)(i) (special consent required). Regardless of how the members allocate management rights, each member is an agent of the company with the apparent authority to bind the company in the ordinary course of its business. See Comments to Section 301(a). A member's right to participate in management terminates upon dissociation. See Section 603(b)(1).

In a manager-managed company, the members, unless also managers, have no rights in the management and conduct of the company's business unless otherwise provided in an operating agreement. If there is more than one manager, manager disputes as to any matter relating to the company's business may be resolved by a majority of the managers unless the matter relates to a matter specified either in subsection (c) (unanimous member consent required) or Section 801(b)(3)(i) (special consent required). Managers must be designated, appointed, or elected by a majority of the members. A manager need not be a member and is an agent of the company with the apparent authority to bind the company in the ordinary course of its business. See Sections 101(10) and 301(b).

To promote clarity and certainty, subsection (c) specifies those exclusive matters requiring the unanimous consent of the members, whether the company is member- or manager-managed. For example, interim distributions, including redemptions, may not be made without the unanimous consent of all the members. Unless otherwise agreed, all other company matters are to be determined under the majority of members or managers rules of subsections (a) and (b).

Section 405. Sharing of and Right to Distributions.

(a) Any distributions made by a limited liability company before its dissolution and winding up must be in equal shares.

(b) A member has no right to receive, and may not be required to accept, a distribution in kind.

(c) If a member becomes entitled to receive a distribution, the member has the status of, and is entitled to all remedies available to, a creditor of the limited liability company with respect to the distribution.

Comment:

Recognizing the informality of many limited liability companies, this section creates a simple default rule regarding interim distributions. Any interim distributions made must be in equal shares and approved by all members. See Section 404(c)(6). The rule assumes that: profits will be shared equally; some distributions will constitute a return of contributions that should be shared equally rather than a distribution of profits; and property contributors should have the right to veto any distribution that threatens their return of contributions on liquidation. In the simple case where the members make equal contributions of property or equal contributions of services, those assumptions avoid the necessity of maintaining a complex capital account or determining profits. Where some members contribute services and others property, the unanimous vote necessary to approve interim distributions protects against unwanted distributions of contributions to service contributors. Consistently, Section 408(a) does not require the company to maintain a separate account for each member, the Act does not contain a default rule for allocating profits and losses, and Section 806(b) requires that liquidating distributions to members be made in equal shares after the return of contributions not previously returned. See Comments to Section 806(b).

Section 405(c) governs distributions declared or made when the company was solvent. Section 406 governs distributions declared or made when the company is insolvent.

Section 406. Limitations on Distributions.

(a) A distribution may not be made if:

(1) the limited liability company would not be able to pay its debts as they become due in the ordinary course of business; or

(2) the company's total assets would be less than the sum of its total liabilities plus the amount that would be needed, if the company were to be dissolved, wound up, and terminated at the time of the

distribution, to satisfy the preferential rights upon dissolution, winding up, and termination of members whose preferential rights are superior to those receiving the distribution.

(b) A limited liability company may base a determination that a distribution is not prohibited under subsection (a) on financial statements prepared on the basis of accounting practices and principles that are reasonable in the circumstances or on a fair valuation or other method that is reasonable in the circumstances.

(c) Except as otherwise provided in subsection (e), the effect of a distribution under subsection (a) is measured:

(1) in the case of distribution by purchase, redemption, or other acquisition of a distributional interest in a limited liability company, as of the date money or other property is transferred or debt incurred by the company; and

(2) in all other cases, as of the date the:

(i) distribution is authorized if the payment occurs within 120 days after the date of authorization; or

(ii) payment is made if it occurs more than 120 days after the date of authorization.

(d) A limited liability company's indebtedness to a member incurred by reason of a distribution made in accordance with this section is at parity with the company's indebtedness to its general, unsecured creditors.

(e) Indebtedness of a limited liability company, including indebtedness issued in connection with or as part of a distribution, is not considered a liability for purposes of determinations under subsection (a) if its terms provide that payment of principal and interest are made only if and to the extent that payment of a distribution to members could then be made under this section. If the indebtedness is issued as a distribution, each payment of principal or interest on the indebtedness is treated as a distribution, the effect of which is measured on the date the payment is made.

Comment:

This section establishes the validity of company distributions, which in turn determines the potential liability of members and managers for improper distributions under Section 407. Distributions are improper if the company is insolvent under subsection (a) at the time the distribution is measured under subsection (c). In recognition of the informality of many limited liability companies, the solvency determination under subsection (b) may be made on the basis of a fair valuation or other method reasonable under the circumstances.

The application of the equity insolvency and balance sheet tests present special problems in the context of the purchase, redemption, or other acquisition of a company's distributional interests. Special rules establish the time of measurement of such transfers. Under Section

406(c)(1), the time for measuring the effect of a distribution to purchase a distributional interest is the date of payment. The company may make payment either by transferring property or incurring a debt to transfer property in the future. In the latter case, subsection (c)(1) establishes a clear rule that the legality of the distribution is tested when the debt is actually incurred, not later when the debt is actually paid. Under Section 406(e), indebtedness is not considered a liability for purposes of subsection (a) if the terms of the indebtedness itself provide that payments can be made only if and to the extent that a payment of a distribution could then be made under this section. The effect makes the holder of the indebtedness junior to all other creditors but senior to members in their capacity as members.

Section 407.   Liability for Unlawful Distributions.

(a) A member of a member-managed company or a member or manager of a manager-managed company who votes for or assents to a distribution made in violation of Section 406, the articles of organization, or the operating agreement is personally liable to the company for the amount of the distribution which exceeds the amount that could have been distributed without violating Section 406, the articles of organization, or the operating agreement if it is established that the member or manager did not perform the member's or manager's duties in compliance with Section 409.

(b) A member of a manager-managed company who knew a distribution was made in violation of Section 406, the articles of organization, or the operating agreement is personally liable to the company, but only to the extent that the distribution received by the member exceeded the amount that could have been properly paid under Section 406.

(c) A member or manager against whom an action is brought under this section may implead in the action all:

(1) other members or managers who voted for or assented to the distribution in violation of subsection (a) and may compel contribution from them; and

(2) members who received a distribution in violation of subsection (b) and may compel contribution from the member in the amount received in violation of subsection (b).

(d) A proceeding under this section is barred unless it is commenced within two years after the distribution.

Comment:

Whenever members or managers fail to meet the standards of conduct of Section 409 and vote for or assent to an unlawful distribution, they are personally liable to the company for the portion of the distribution that exceeds the maximum amount that could have been lawfully distributed. The recovery remedy under this section extends only to the company, not the company's creditors. Under subsection (a), members and managers are not liable for an unlawful distribution provided their vote in favor of the distribution satisfies the duty of care of Section 409(c).

Subsection (a) creates personal liability in favor of the company against members or managers who approve an unlawful distribution for the entire amount of a distribution that could not be lawfully distributed. Subsection (b) creates personal liability against only members who knowingly received the unlawful distribution, but only in the amount measured by the portion of the actual distribution received that was not lawfully made. Members who both vote for or assent to an unlawful distribution and receive a portion or all of the distribution will be liable, at the election of the company, under either but not both subsections.

A member or manager who is liable under subsection (a) may seek contribution under subsection (c)(1) from other members and managers who also voted for or assented to the same distribution and may also seek recoupment under subsection (c)(2) from members who received the distribution, but only if they accepted the payments knowing they were unlawful.

The two-year statute of limitations of subsection (d) is measured from the date of the distribution. The date of the distribution is determined under Section 406(c).

Section 408. Member's Right to Information.

(a) A limited liability company shall provide members and their agents and attorneys access to its records, if any, at the company's principal office or other reasonable locations specified in the operating agreement. The company shall provide former members and their agents and attorneys access for proper purposes to records pertaining to the period during which they were members. The right of access provides the opportunity to inspect and copy records during ordinary business hours. The company may impose a reasonable charge, limited to the costs of labor and material, for copies of records furnished.

(b) A limited liability company shall furnish to a member, and to the legal representative of a deceased member or member under legal disability:

(1) without demand, information concerning the company's business or affairs reasonably required for the proper exercise of the member's rights and performance of the member's duties under the operating agreement or this [Act]; and

(2) on demand, other information concerning the company's business or affairs, except to the extent the demand or the information demanded is unreasonable or otherwise improper under the circumstances.

(c) A member has the right upon written demand given to the limited liability company to obtain at the company's expense a copy of any written operating agreement.

Comment:

Recognizing the informality of many limited liability companies, subsection (a) does not require a company to maintain any records. In general, a company should maintain records necessary to enable members to determine their share of profits and losses and their rights on dissociation. If inadequate records are maintained to determine those and other critical rights, a member may maintain an action for an accounting under Section 410(a). Normally, a company will maintain at least records required by state or federal authorities regarding tax and other filings.

The obligation to furnish access includes the obligation to insure that all records, if any, are accessible in intelligible form. For example, a company that switches computer systems has an obligation either to convert the records from the old system or retain at least one computer capable of accessing the records from the old system.

The right to inspect and copy records maintained is not conditioned on a member or former member's purpose or motive. However, an abuse of the access and copy right may create a remedy in favor of the other members as a violation of the requesting member or former member's obligation of good faith and fair dealing. See Section 409(d).

Although a company is not required to maintain any records under subsection (a), it is nevertheless subject to a disclosure duty to furnish specified information under subsection (b)(1). A company must therefore furnish to members, without demand, information reasonably needed for members to exercise their rights and duties as members. A member's exercise of these duties justifies an unqualified right of access to the company's records. The member's right to company records may not be unreasonably restricted by the operating agreement. See Section 103(b)(1).

Section 409. General Standards of Member's and Manager's Conduct.

(a) The only fiduciary duties a member owes to a member-managed company and its other members are the duty of loyalty and the duty of care imposed by subsections (b) and (c).

(b) A member's duty of loyalty to a member-managed company and its other members is limited to the following:

(1) to account to the company and to hold as trustee for it any property, profit, or benefit derived by the member in the conduct or winding up of the company's business or derived from a use by the member of the company's property, including the appropriation of a company's opportunity;

(2) to refrain from dealing with the company in the conduct or winding up of the company's business as or on behalf of a party having an interest adverse to the company; and

495

(3) to refrain from competing with the company in the conduct of the company's business before the dissolution of the company.

(c) A member's duty of care to a member-managed company and its other members in the conduct of and winding up of the company's business is limited to refraining from engaging in grossly negligent or reckless conduct, intentional misconduct, or a knowing violation of law.

(d) A member shall discharge the duties to a member-managed company and its other members under this [Act] or under the operating agreement and exercise any rights consistently with the obligation of good faith and fair dealing.

(e) A member of a member-managed company does not violate a duty or obligation under this [Act] or under the operating agreement merely because the member's conduct furthers the member's own interest.

(f) A member of a member-managed company may lend money to and transact other business with the company. As to each loan or transaction, the rights and obligations of the member are the same as those of a person who is not a member, subject to other applicable law.

(g) This section applies to a person winding up the limited liability company's business as the personal or legal representative of the last surviving member as if the person were a member.

(h) In a manager-managed company:

(1) a member who is not also a manager owes no duties to the company or to the other members solely by reason of being a member;

(2) a manager is held to the same standards of conduct prescribed for members in subsections (b) through (f);

(3) a member who pursuant to the operating agreement exercises some or all of the rights of a manager in the management and conduct of the company's business is held to the standards of conduct in subsections (b) through (f) to the extent that the member exercises the managerial authority vested in a manager by this [Act]; and

(4) a manager is relieved of liability imposed by law for violation of the standards prescribed by subsections (b) through (f) to the extent of the managerial authority delegated to the members by the operating agreement.

Comment:

Under subsections (a), (c), and (h), members and managers, and their delegatees, owe to the company and to the other members and managers only the fiduciary duties of loyalty and care set forth in subsections (b) and (c) and the obligation of good faith and fair dealing set forth in subsection (d). An operating agreement may not waive or eliminate the duties or obligation, but may, if not manifestly unreasonable, identify activities and determine standards for measuring the performance of them. See Section 103(b)(2) to (4).

Upon a member's dissociation, the duty to account for personal profits under subsection (b)(1), the duty to refrain from acting as or representing adverse interests under subsection (b)(2), and the duty of care under subsection (c) are limited to those derived from matters arising or events occurring before the dissociation unless the member participates in winding up the company's business. Also, the duty not to compete terminates upon dissociation. See Section 603(b)(3) and (b)(2). However, a dissociated member is not free to use confidential company information after dissociation. For example, a dissociated member of a company may immediately compete with the company for new clients but must exercise care in completing on-going client transactions and must account to the company for any fees from the old clients on account of those transactions. Subsection (c) adopts a gross negligence standard for the duty of care, the standard actually used in most partnerships and corporations.

Subsection (b)(2) prohibits a member from acting adversely or representing an adverse party to the company. The rule is based on agency principles and seeks to avoid the conflict of opposing interests in the mind of the member agent whose duty is to act for the benefit of the principal company. As reflected in subsection (f), the rule does not prohibit the member from dealing with the company other than as an adversary. A member may generally deal with the company under subsection (f) when the transaction is approved by the company.

Subsection (e) makes clear that a member does not violate the obligation of good faith under subsection (d) merely because the member's conduct furthers that member's own interest. For example, a member's refusal to vote for an interim distribution because of negative tax implications to that member does not violate that member's obligation of good faith to the other members. Likewise, a member may vote against a proposal by the company to open a shopping center that would directly compete with another shopping center in which the member owns an interest.

Section 410. Actions by Members.

(a) A member may maintain an action against a limited liability company or another member for legal or equitable relief, with or without an accounting as to the company's business, to enforce:

(1) the member's rights under the operating agreement;

(2) the member's rights under this [Act]; and

(3) the rights and otherwise protect the interests of the member, including rights and interests arising independently of the member's relationship to the company.

(b) The accrual, and any time limited for the assertion, of a right of action for a remedy under this section is governed by other law. A right to an accounting upon a dissolution and winding up does not revive a claim barred by law.

Comment:

During the existence of the company, members have under this section access to the courts to resolve claims against the company and other members, leaving broad judicial discretion to fashion appropriate legal remedies. A member pursues only that member's claim against the company or another member under this section. Article 11 governs a member's derivative pursuit of a claim on behalf of the company.

A member may recover against the company and the other members under subsection (a)(3) for personal injuries or damage to the member's property caused by another member. One member's negligence is therefore not imputed to bar another member's action.

Section 411.   Continuation of Term Company After Expiration of Specified Term.

(a) If a term company is continued after the expiration of the specified term, the rights and duties of the members and managers remain the same as they were at the expiration of the term except to the extent inconsistent with rights and duties of members and managers of an at-will company.

(b) If the members in a member-managed company or the managers in a manager-managed company continue the business without any winding up of the business of the company, it continues as an at-will company.

Comment:

A term company will generally dissolve upon the expiration of its term unless either its articles are amended before the expiration of the original specified term to provide for an additional specified term or the members or managers simply continue the company as an at-will company under this section. Amendment of the articles specifying an additional term requires the unanimous consent of the members. See Section 404(c)(3). Therefore, any member has the right to block the amendment. Absent an amendment to the articles, a company may only be continued under subsection (b) as an at-will company. The decision to continue a term company as an at-will company does not require the unanimous consent of the members and is treated as an ordinary business matter with disputes resolved by a simple majority vote of either the members or managers. See Section 404. In that case, subsection (b) provides that the members' conduct amends or becomes part of an operating agreement to "continue" the company as an at-will company. The amendment to the operating agreement does not alter the rights of creditors who suffer detrimental reliance because the company does not liquidate after the expiration of its specified term. See Section 203(c)(2).

Preexisting operating-agreement provisions continue to control the relationship of the members under subsection (a) except to the extent inconsistent with the rights and duties of members of an at-will company with an operating agreement containing the same provisions.

However, the members could agree in advance that, if the company's business continues after the expiration of its specified term, the company continues as a company with a new specified term or that the provisions of its operating agreement survive the expiration of the specIfied term.

[ARTICLE] 5

TRANSFEREES AND CREDITORS OF MEMBER

Sec.
501.   Member's Distributional Interest.
502.   Transfer of Distributional Interest.
503.   Rights of Transferee.
504.   Rights of Creditor.

Section 501.   Member's Distributional Interest.

(a) A member is not a co-owner of, and has no transferable interest in, property of a limited liability company.

(b) A distributional interest in a limited liability company is personal property and, subject to Sections 502 and 503, may be transferred in whole or in part.

(c) An operating agreement may provide that a distributional interest may be evidenced by a certificate of the interest issued by the limited liability company and, subject to Section 503, may also provide for the transfer of any interest represented by the certificate.

Comment:

Members have no property interest in property owned by a limited liability company. A distributional interest is personal property and is defined under Section 101(6) as a member's interest in distributions only and does not include the member's broader rights to participate in management under Section 404 and to inspect company records under Section 408.

Under Section 405(a), distributions are allocated in equal shares unless otherwise provided in an operating agreement. Whenever it is desirable to allocate distributions in proportion to contributions rather than per capita, certification may be useful to reduce valuation issues. The effect of certification on the Federal tax classification of the company is determined by federal law.

Section 502.   Transfer of Distributional Interest.

A transfer of a distributional interest does not entitle the transferee to become or to exercise any rights of a member. A transfer entitles the transferee to receive, to the extent transferred, only the distributions to which the transferor would be entitled.

Comment:

Under Sections 501(b) and 502, the only interest a member may freely transfer is that member's distributional interest. A member's transfer of part, all, or substantially all of a distributional interest will threaten the dissolution of the company under Section 801(b)(3)(i) only if the transfer constitutes an event of dissociation. See Section 601(3). Member dissociation has defined dissolution consequences under Section 801(b)(3)(i) depending upon whether the company is an at-will or term company and whether it is member- or manager-managed. Only the transfer of all or substantially all of a member's distributional interest constitutes or may constitute a member dissociation. A transfer of less than substantially all of a member's distributional interest is not an event of dissociation. A member ceases to be a member upon the transfer of all that member's distributional interest and that transfer is also an event of dissociation under Section 601(3). Relating the event of dissociation to the member's transfer of all of the member's distributional interest avoids the need for the company to track potential future dissociation events associated with a member no longer financially interested in the company. Also, all the remaining members may expel a member upon the transfer of "substantially all" the member's distributional interest. The expulsion is an event of dissociation under Section 601(5)(ii).

Section 503.   Rights of Transferee.

(a) A transferee of a distributional interest may become a member of a limited liability company if and to the extent that the transferor gives the transferee the right in accordance with authority described in the operating agreement or all other members consent.

(b) A transferee who has become a member, to the extent transferred, has the rights and powers, and is subject to the restrictions and liabilities, of a member under the operating agreement of a limited liability company and this [Act]. A transferee who becomes a member also is liable for the transferor member's obligations to make contributions under Section 402 and for obligations under Section 407 to return unlawful distributions, but the transferee is not obligated for the transferor member's liabilities unknown to the transferee at the time the transferee becomes a member.

(c) Whether or not a transferee of a distributional interest becomes a member under subsection (a), the transferor is not released from liability to the limited liability company under the operating agreement or this [Act].

(d) A transferee who does not become a member is not entitled to participate in the management or conduct of the limited liability company's business, require access to information concerning the company's transactions, or inspect or copy any of the company's records.

(e) A transferee who does not become a member is entitled to:

(1) receive, in accordance with the transfer, distributions to which the transferor would otherwise be entitled;

500

(2) receive, upon dissolution and winding up of the limited liability company's business:

(i) in accordance with the transfer, the net amount otherwise distributable to the transferor;

(ii) a statement of account only from the date of the latest statement of account agreed to by all the members;

(3) seek under Section 801(5) a judicial determination that it is equitable to dissolve and wind up the company's business.

(f) A limited liability company need not give effect to a transfer until it has notice of the transfer.

Comment:

The only interest a member may freely transfer is the member's distributional interest. A transferee may acquire the remaining rights of a member only by being admitted as a member of the company by all of the remaining members. The effect of these default rules and any modifications on the Federal tax classification of the company is determined by federal law.

A transferee not admitted as a member is not entitled to participate in management, require access to information, or inspect or copy company records. The only rights of a transferee are to receive the distributions the transferor would otherwise be entitled, receive a limited statement of account, and seek a judicial dissolution under Section 801(b)(6).

Subsection (e) sets forth the rights of a transferee of an existing member. Although the rights of a dissociated member to participate in the future management of the company parallel the rights of a transferee, a dissociated member retains additional rights that accrued from that person's membership such as the right to enforce Article 7 purchase rights. See and compare Sections 603(b)(1) and 801(b)(5) and Comments.

Section 504. Rights of Creditor.

(a) On application by a judgment creditor of a member of a limited liability company or of a member's transferee, a court having jurisdiction may charge the distributional interest of the judgment debtor to satisfy the judgment. The court may appoint a receiver of the share of the distributions due or to become due to the judgment debtor and make all other orders, directions, accounts, and inquiries the judgment debtor might have made or which the circumstances may require to give effect to the charging order.

(b) A charging order constitutes a lien on the judgment debtor's distributional interest. The court may order a foreclosure of a lien on a distributional interest subject to the charging order at any time. A purchaser at the foreclosure sale has the rights of a transferee.

(c) At any time before foreclosure, a distributional interest in a limited liability company which is charged may be redeemed:

(1) by the judgment debtor;

(2) with property other than the company's property, by one or more of the other members; or

(3) with the company's property, but only if permitted by the operating agreement.

(d) This [Act] does not affect a member's right under exemption laws with respect to the member's distributional interest in a limited liability company.

(e) This section provides the exclusive remedy by which a judgment creditor of a member or a transferee may satisfy a judgment out of the judgment debtor's distributional interest in a limited liability company.

Comment:

A charging order is the only remedy by which a judgment creditor of a member or a member's transferee may reach the distributional interest of a member or member's transferee. Under Section 503(e), the distributional interest of a member or transferee is limited to the member's right to receive distributions from the company and to seek judicial liquidation of the company.

[ARTICLE] 6

MEMBER'S DISSOCIATION

Sec.
601. Events Causing Member's Dissociation.
602. Member's Power to Dissociate; Wrongful Dissociation.
603. Effect of Member's Dissociation.

Section 601. Events Causing Member's Dissociation.

A member is dissociated from a limited liability company upon the occurrence of any of the following events:

(1) the company's having notice of the member's express will to withdraw upon the date of notice or on a later date specified by the member;

(2) an event agreed to in the operating agreement as causing the member's dissociation;

(3) upon transfer of all of a member's distributional interest, other than a transfer for security purposes or a court order charging the member's distributional interest which has not been foreclosed;

(4) the member's expulsion pursuant to the operating agreement;

(5) the member's expulsion by unanimous vote of the other members if:

(i) it is unlawful to carry on the company's business with the member;

(ii) there has been a transfer of substantially all of the member's distributional interest, other than a transfer for security purposes or a court order charging the member's distributional interest which has not been foreclosed;

(iii) within 90 days after the company notifies a corporate member that it will be expelled because it has filed a certificate of dissolution or the equivalent, its charter has been revoked, or its right to conduct business has been suspended by the jurisdiction of its incorporation, the member fails to obtain a revocation of the certificate of dissolution or a reinstatement of its charter or its right to conduct business; or

(iv) a partnership or a limited liability company that is a member has been dissolved and its business is being wound up;

(6) on application by the company or another member, the member's expulsion by judicial determination because the member:

(i) engaged in wrongful conduct that adversely and materially affected the company's business;

(ii) willfully or persistently committed a material breach of the operating agreement or of a duty owed to the company or the other members under Section 409; or

(iii) engaged in conduct relating to the company's business which makes it not reasonably practicable to carry on the business with the member;

(7) the member's:

(i) becoming a debtor in bankruptcy;

(ii) executing an assignment for the benefit of creditors;

(iii) seeking, consenting to, or acquiescing in the appointment of a trustee, receiver, or liquidator of the member or of all or substantially all of the member's property; or

(iv) failing, within 90 days after the appointment, to have vacated or stayed the appointment of a trustee, receiver, or liquidator of the member or of all or substantially all of the member's property obtained without the member's consent or acquiescence, or failing within 90 days after the expiration of a stay to have the appointment vacated;

(8) in the case of a member who is an individual:

(i) the member's death;

(ii) the appointment of a guardian or general conservator for the member; or

(iii) a judicial determination that the member has otherwise become incapable of performing the member's duties under the operating agreement;

(9) in the case of a member that is a trust or is acting as a member by virtue of being a trustee of a trust, distribution of the trust's entire rights to receive distributions from the company, but not merely by reason of the substitution of a successor trustee;

(10) in the case of a member that is an estate or is acting as a member by virtue of being a personal representative of an estate, distribution of the estate's entire rights to receive distributions from the company, but not merely the substitution of a successor personal representative; or

(11) termination of the existence of a member if the member is not an individual, estate, or trust other than a business trust.

Comment:

The term "dissociation" refers to the change in the relationships among the dissociated member, the company and the other members caused by a member's ceasing to be associated in the carrying on of the company's business. Member dissociation for any reason from a member-managed at-will company will cause a dissolution of the company under Section 801(b)(3) unless a specified percentage of the remaining members agree to continue the business of the company. If the dissociation does not dissolve the company, the dissociated member's distributional interest must be immediately purchased by the company under Article 7. Member dissociation from a member-managed term company, but only for the reasons specified in paragraphs (7) to (11), will cause a dissolution of the company under Section 801(b)(3) unless a specified percentage of the remaining members agree to continue the business of the company. Member dissociations specified in paragraphs (1) to (6) do not threaten dissolution under Section 801(b)(3) of a member-managed term company. If the dissociation does not dissolve the company, it is not required to purchase the dissociated member's distributional interest until the expiration of the specified term that existed on the date of the member's dissociation. If an at-will company or a term company is manager-managed, only the dissociation of a member who is also a manager or, if there is none, any member specified above threatens dissolution. The effect on the Federal tax classification of the company creating a member-manager with a minimal interest in the company is determined by federal law.

A member may be expelled from the company under paragraph (5)(ii) by the unanimous vote of the other members upon a transfer of "substantially all" of the member's distributional interest other than for a transfer as security for a loan. A transfer of "all" of the member's distributional interest is an event of dissociation under paragraph (3).

Although a member is dissociated upon death, the effect of the dissociation where the company does not dissolve depends upon whether the company is at-will or term and whether manager-managed. Only the decedent's distributional interest transfers to the decedent's estate which does not acquire the decedent member's management rights. See Section 603(b)(1). Unless otherwise agreed, if the company was at-will, the estate's distributional interest must be purchased by the company at fair value determined at the date of death. However, if a term company, the estate and its transferees continue only as the owner of the distributional interest with no management rights until the expiration of the specified term that existed on the date of death. At the expiration of that term, the company must purchase the interest of a dissociated member if the company continues for an additional term by amending its articles or simply continues as an at-will company. See Sections 411 and 701(a)(2) and Comments. Before that time, the estate and its transferees have the right to make application for a judicial dissolution of the company under Section 801(b)(5) as successors in interest to a dissociated member. See Comments to Sections 801, 411, and 701. Where the members have allocated management rights on the basis of contributions rather than simply the number of members, a member's death will result in a transfer of management rights to the remaining members on a proportionate basis. This transfer of rights may be avoided by a provision in an operating agreement extending the Section 701(a)(1) at-will purchase right to a decedent member of a term company.

Section 602. Member's Power to Dissociate; Wrongful Dissociation.

(a) Unless otherwise provided in the operating agreement, a member has the power to dissociate from a limited liability company at any time, rightfully or wrongfully, by express will pursuant to Section 601(1).

(b) If the operating agreement has not eliminated a member's power to dissociate, the member's dissociation from a limited liability company is wrongful only if:

   (1) it is in breach of an express provision of the agreement; or

   (2) before the expiration of the specified term of a term company:

      (i) the member withdraws by express will;

      (ii) the member is expelled by judicial determination under Section 601(6);

      (iii) the member is dissociated by becoming a debtor in bankruptcy; or

      (iv) in the case of a member who is not an individual, trust other than a business trust, or estate, the member is expelled or otherwise dissociated because it willfully dissolved or terminated its existence.

505

(c) A member who wrongfully dissociates from a limited liability company is liable to the company and to the other members for damages caused by the dissociation. The liability is in addition to any other obligation of the member to the company or to the other members.

(d) If a limited liability company does not dissolve and wind up its business as a result of a member's wrongful dissociation under subsection (b), damages sustained by the company for the wrongful dissociation must be offset against distributions otherwise due the member after the dissociation.

Comment:

A member has the power to withdraw from both an at-will company and a term company although the effects of the withdrawal are remarkably different. See Comments to Section 601. At a minimum, the exercise of a power to withdraw enables members to terminate their continuing duties of loyalty and care. See Section 603(b)(2) to (3).

A member's power to withdraw by express will may be eliminated by an operating agreement. The effect of such a provision on the Federal tax classification of the company is determined by federal law. An operating agreement may eliminate a member's power to withdraw by express will to promote the business continuity of an at-will company by removing the threat of dissolution and to eliminate the member's right to force the company to purchase the member's distributional interest. See Sections 801(b)(3) and 701(a)(1). However, such a member retains the ability to seek a judicial dissolution of the company. See Section 801(b)(5).

If a member's power to withdraw by express will is not eliminated in an operating agreement, the withdrawal may nevertheless be made wrongful under subsection (b). All dissociations, including withdrawal by express will, may be made wrongful under subsection (b)(1) in both an at-will and term company by the inclusion of a provision in an operating agreement. Even where an operating agreement does not eliminate the power to withdraw by express will or make any dissociation wrongful, the dissociation of a member of a term company for the reasons specified under subsection (b)(2) is wrongful. The member is liable to the company and other members for damages caused by a wrongful dissociation under subsection (c) and, under subsection (d), the damages may be offset against all distributions otherwise due the member after the dissociation. Section 701(f) provides a similar rule permitting damages for wrongful dissociation to be offset against any company purchase of the member's distributional interest.

Section 603. Effect of Member's Dissociation.

506

(a) Upon a member's dissociation;

(1) in an at-will company, the company must cause the dissociated member's distributional interest to be purchased under [Article] 7; and

(2) in a term company:

(i) if the company dissolves and winds up its business on or before the expiration of its specified term, [Article] 8 applies to determine the dissociated member's rights to distributions; and

(ii) if the company does not dissolve and wind up its business on or before the expiration of its specified term, the company must cause the dissociated member's distributional interest to be purchased under [Article] 7 on the date of the expiration of the term specified at the time of the member's dissociation.

(b) Upon a member's dissociation from a limited liability company:

(1) the member's right to participate in the management and conduct of the company's business terminates, except as otherwise provided in Section 803, and the member ceases to be a member and is treated the same as a transferee of a member;

(2) the member's duty of loyalty under Section 409(b)(3) terminates; and

(3) the member's duty of loyalty under Section 409(b)(1) and (2) and duty of care under Section 409(c) continue only with regard to matters arising and events occurring before the member's dissociation, unless the member participates in winding up the company's business pursuant to Section 803.

Comment:

Dissociation from an at-will company that does not dissolve the company causes the dissociated member's distributional interest to be immediately purchased under Article 7. See Comments to Sections 602 and 603. Dissociation from a term company that does not dissolve the company does not cause the dissociated member's distributional interest to be purchased under Article 7 until the expiration of the specified term that existed on the date of dissociation.

Subsection (b)(1) provides that a dissociated member forfeits the right to participate in the future conduct of the company's business. Dissociation does not however forfeit that member's right to enforce the Article 7 rights that accrue by reason of the dissociation. Similarly, where dissociation occurs by death, the decedent member's successors in interest may enforce that member's Article 7 rights. See and compare Comments to Section 503(e).

Dissociation terminates the member's right to participate in management, including the member's actual authority to act for the company under Section 301, and begins the two-year period after which a member's apparent authority conclusively ends. See Comments to Section 703. Dissociation also terminates a member's continuing duties of loyalty and care, except with regard to continuing transactions, to the company and other members unless the member participates in winding up the company's business. See Comments to Section 409.

[ARTICLE] 7

MEMBER'S DISSOCIATION WHEN BUSINESS NOT WOUND UP

Sec.
701. Company Purchase of Distributional Interest.
702. Court Action to Determine Fair Value of Distributional Interest.
703. Dissociated Member's Power to Bind Limited Liability Company.
704. Statement of Dissociation.

Section 701. Company Purchase of Distributional Interest.

(a) A limited liability company shall purchase a distributional interest of a:

(1) member of an at-will company for its fair value determined as of the date of the member's dissociation if the member's dissociation does not result in a dissolution and winding up of the company's business under Section 801; or

(2) member of a term company for its fair value determined as of the date of the expiration of the specified term that existed on the date of the member's dissociation if the expiration of the specified term does not result in a dissolution and winding up of the company's business under Section 801.

(b) A limited liability company must deliver a purchase offer to the dissociated member whose distributional interest is entitled to be purchased not later than 30 days after the date determined under subsection (a). The purchase offer must be accompanied by:

(1) a statement of the company's assets and liabilities as of the date determined under subsection (a);

(2) the latest available balance sheet and income statement, if any; and

(3) an explanation of how the estimated amount of the payment was calculated.

(c) If the price and other terms of a purchase of a distributional interest are fixed or are to be determined by the operating agreement, the price and terms so fixed or determined govern the purchase unless the purchaser defaults. If a default occurs, the dissociated member is entitled to commence a proceeding to have the company dissolved under Section 801(4)(iv).

(d) If an agreement to purchase the distributional interest is not made within 120 days after the date determined under subsection (a), the dissociated member, within another 120 days, may commence a proceeding against the limited liability company to enforce the purchase. The company at its expense shall notify in writing all of the remaining members, and any other person the court directs, of the commencement of the proceeding. The jurisdiction of the court in which the proceeding is commenced under this subsection is plenary and exclusive.

(e) The court shall determine the fair value of the distributional interest in accordance with the standards set forth in Section 702 together with the terms for the purchase. Upon making these determinations, the court shall order the limited liability company to purchase or cause the purchase of the interest.

(f) Damages for wrongful dissociation under Section 602(b), and all other amounts owing, whether or not currently due, from the dissociated member to a limited liability company, must be offset against the purchase price.

Comment:

This section sets forth default rules regarding an otherwise mandatory company purchase of a distributional interest. Even though a dissociated member's rights to participate in the future management of the company are equivalent to those of a transferee of a member, the dissociation does not forfeit that member's right to enforce the Article 7 purchase right. Similarly, if the dissociation occurs by reason of death, the decedent member's successors in interest may enforce the Article 7 rights. See Comments to Sections 503(e) and 603(b)(1).

An at-will company must purchase a dissociated member's distributional interest under subsection (a)(1) when that member's dissociation does not result in a dissolution of the company. The purchase price is equal to the fair value of the interest determined as of the date of dissociation. Any damages for wrongful dissociation must be offset against the purchase price.

Dissociation from a term company does not require an immediate purchase of the member's interest but certain types of dissociation may cause the dissolution of the company. See Section 801(b)(3). A term company must only purchase the dissociated member's distributional interest under subsection (a)(2) on the expiration of the specified term that existed on the date of the member's dissociation. The purchase price is equal to the fair value of the interest determined as of the date of the expiration of that specified term. Any damages for wrongful dissociation must be offset against the purchase price.

The valuation dates differ between subsections (a)(1) and (a)(2) purchases. The former is valued on the date of member dissociation whereas the latter is valued on the date of the expiration of the specified term that existed on the date of dissociation. A subsection (a)(2) dissociated member therefore assumes the risk of loss between the date of dissociation and the expiration of the then stated specified

509

term. See Comments to Section 801 (dissociated member may file application to dissolve company under Section 801(b)(6)).

The default valuation standard is fair value. See Comments to Section 702. An operating agreement may fix a method or formula for determining the purchase price and the terms of payment. The purchase right may be modified. For example, an operating agreement may eliminate a member's power to withdraw from an at-will company which narrows the dissociation events contemplated under subsection (a)(1). See Comments to Section 602(a). However, a provision in an operating agreement providing for complete forfeiture of the purchase right may be unenforceable where the power to dissociate has not also been eliminated. See Section 104(a).

The company must deliver a purchase offer to the dissociated member within 30 days after the date determined under subsection (a). The offer must be accompanied by information designed to enable the dissociated member to evaluate the fairness of the offer. The subsection (b)(3) explanation of how the offer price was calculated need not be elaborate. For example, a mere statement of the basis of the calculation, such as "book value," may be sufficient.

The company and the dissociated member must reach an agreement on the purchase price and terms within 120 days after the date determined under subsection (a). Otherwise, the dissociated member may file suit within another 120 days to enforce the purchase under subsection (d). The court will then determine the fair value and terms of purchase under subsection (e). See Section 702. The member's lawsuit is not available under subsection (c) if the parties have previously agreed to price and terms in an operating agreement.

Section 702. Court Action to Determine Fair Value of Distributional Interest.

(a) In an action brought to determine the fair value of a distributional interest in a limited liability company, the court shall:

(1) determine the fair value of the interest, considering among other relevant evidence the going concern value of the company, any agreement among some or all of the members fixing the price or specifying a formula for determining value of distributional interests for any other purpose, the recommendations of any appraiser appointed by the court, and any legal constraints on the company's ability to purchase the interest;

(2) specify the terms of the purchase, including, if appropriate, terms for installment payments, subordination of the purchase obligation to the rights of the company's other creditors, security for a deferred purchase price, and a covenant not to compete or other restriction on a dissociated member; and

(3) require the dissociated member to deliver an assignment of the interest to the purchaser upon receipt of the purchase price or the first installment of the purchase price.

(b) After the dissociated member delivers the assignment, the dissociated member has no further claim against the company, its members, officers, or managers, if any, other than a claim to any unpaid balance of the purchase price and a claim under any agreement with the company or the remaining members that is not terminated by the court.

(c) If the purchase is not completed in accordance with the specified terms, the company is to be dissolved upon application under Section 801(b)(5)(iv). If a limited liability company is so dissolved, the dissociated member has the same rights and priorities in the company's assets as if the sale had not been ordered.

(d) If the court finds that a party to the proceeding acted arbitrarily, vexatiously, or not in good faith, it may award one or more other parties their reasonable expenses, including attorney's fees and the expenses of appraisers or other experts, incurred in the proceeding. The finding may be based on the company's failure to make an offer to pay or to comply with Section 701(b).

(e) Interest must be paid on the amount awarded from the date determined under Section 701(a) to the date of payment.

Comment:

The default valuation standard is fair value. Under this broad standard, a court is free to determine the fair value of a distributional interest on a fair market, liquidation, or any other method deemed appropriate under the circumstances. A fair market value standard is not used because it is too narrow, often inappropriate, and assumes a fact not contemplated by this section—a willing buyer and a willing seller.

The court has discretion under subsection (a)(2) to include in its order any conditions the court deems necessary to safeguard the interests of the company and the dissociated member or transferee. The discretion may be based on the financial and other needs of the parties.

If the purchase is not consummated or the purchaser defaults, the dissociated member or transferee may make application for dissolution of the company under subsection (c). The court may deny the petition for good cause but the proceeding affords the company an opportunity to be heard on the matter and avoid dissolution. See Comments to Section 801(b)(5).

The power of the court to award all costs and attorney's fees incurred in the suit under subsection (d) is an incentive for both parties to act in good faith. See Section 701(c).

Section 703. Dissociated Member's Power to Bind Limited Liability Company.

For two years after a member dissociates without the dissociation resulting in a dissolution and winding up of a limited liability company's business, the company, including a surviving company under [Article] 9, is bound by an act of the dissociated member which would have bound the company under Section 301 before dissociation only if at the time of entering into the transaction the other party:

(1) reasonably believed that the dissociated member was then a member;

(2) did not have notice of the member's dissociation; and

(3) is not deemed to have had notice under Section 704.

Comment:

A dissociated member of a member-managed company does not have actual authority to act for the company. See Section 603(b)(1). Under Section 301(a), a dissociated member of a member-managed company has apparent authority to bind the company in ordinary course transactions except as to persons who knew or had notice of the dissociation. This section modifies that rule by requiring the person to show reasonable reliance on the member's status as a member provided a Section 704 statement has not been filed within the previous 90 days. See also Section 804 (power to bind after dissolution).

Section 704. Statement of Dissociation.

(a) A dissociated member or a limited liability company may file in the office of the [Secretary of State] a statement of dissociation stating the name of the company and that the member is dissociated from the company.

(b) For the purposes of Sections 301 and 703, a person not a member is deemed to have notice of the dissociation 90 days after the statement of dissociation is filed.

[ARTICLE] 8

WINDING UP COMPANY'S BUSINESS

Section 801. Events Causing Dissolution and Winding Up of Company's Business.

A limited liability company is dissolved, and its business must be wound up, upon the occurrence of any of the following events:

(1) an event specified in the operating agreement;

(2) consent of the number or percentage of members specified in the operating agreement;

(3) an event that makes it unlawful for all or substantially all of the business of the company to be continued, but any cure of illegality within 90 days after notice to the company of the event is effective retroactively to the date of the event for purposes of this section;

(4) on application by a member or a dissociated member, upon entry of a judicial decree that:

(i) the economic purpose of the company is likely to be unreasonably frustrated;

(ii) another member has engaged in conduct relating to the company's business that makes it not reasonably practicable to carry on the company's business with that member;

(iii) it is not otherwise reasonably practicable to carry on the company's business in conformity with the articles of organization and the operating agreement;

(iv) the company failed to purchase the petitioner's distributional interest as required by Section 701; or

(v) the managers or members in control of the company have acted, are acting, or will act in a manner that is illegal, oppressive, fraudulent, or unfairly prejudicial to the petitioner; or

(5) on application by a transferee of a member's interest, a judicial determination that it is equitable to wind up the company's business:

(i) after the expiration of the specified term, if the company was for a specified term at the time the applicant became a transferee by member dissociation, transfer, or entry of a charging order that gave rise to the transfer; or

(ii) at any time, if the company was at will at the time the applicant became a transferee by member dissociation, transfer, or entry of a charging order that gave rise to the transfer.

513

Section 802. Limited Liability Company Continues After Dissolution.

(a) Subject to subsection (b), a limited liability company continues after dissolution only for the purpose of winding up its business.

(b) At any time after the dissolution of a limited liability company and before the winding up of its business is completed, the members, including a dissociated member whose dissociation caused the dissolution, may unanimously waive the right to have the company's business wound up and the company terminated. In that case:

(1) the limited liability company resumes carrying on its business as if dissolution had never occurred and any liability incurred by the company or a member after the dissolution and before the waiver is determined as if the dissolution had never occurred; and

(2) the rights of a third party accruing under Section 804(a) or arising out of conduct in reliance on the dissolution before the third party knew or received a notification of the waiver are not adversely affected.

Comment:

The liability shield continues in effect for the winding up period because the legal existence of the company continues under subsection (a). The company is terminated on the filing of articles of termination. See Section 805.

Section 803. Right to Wind Up Limited Liability Company's Business.

(a) After dissolution, a member who has not wrongfully dissociated may participate in winding up a limited liability company's business, but on application of any member, member's legal representative, or transferee, the [designate the appropriate court], for good cause shown, may order judicial supervision of the winding up.

(b) A legal representative of the last surviving member may wind up a limited liability company's business.

(c) A person winding up a limited liability company's business may preserve the company's business or property as a going concern for a reasonable time, prosecute and defend actions and proceedings, whether civil, criminal, or administrative, settle and close the company's business, dispose of and transfer the company's property, discharge the company's liabilities, distribute the assets of the company pursuant to Section 806, settle disputes by mediation or arbitration, and perform other necessary acts.

Section 804. Member's or Manager's Power and Liability as Agent After Dissolution.

(a) A limited liability company is bound by a member's or manager's act after dissolution that:

(1) is appropriate for winding up the company's business; or

(2) would have bound the company under Section 301 before dissolution, if the other party to the transaction did not have notice of the dissolution.

(b) A member or manager who, with knowledge of the dissolution, subjects a limited liability company to liability by an act that is not appropriate for winding up the company's business is liable to the company for any damage caused to the company arising from the liability.

Comment:

After dissolution, members and managers continue to have the authority to bind the company that they had prior to dissolution provided that the third party did not have notice of the dissolution. See Section 102(b) (notice defined). Otherwise, they have only the authority appropriate for winding up the company's business. See Section 703 (agency power of member after dissociation).

Section 805.   Articles of Termination.

(a) At any time after dissolution and winding up, a limited liability company may terminate its existence by filing with the [Secretary of State] articles of termination stating:

(1) the name of the company;

(2) the date of the dissolution; and

(3) that the company's business has been wound up and the legal existence of the company has been terminated.

(b) The existence of a limited liability company is terminated upon the filing of the articles of termination, or upon a later effective date, if specified in the articles of termination.

Comment:

The termination of legal existence also terminates the company's liability shield. See Comments to Section 802 (liability shield continues in effect during winding up). It also ends the company's responsibility to file an annual report. See Section 211.

Section 806.   Distribution of Assets in Winding Up Limited Liability Company's Business.

(a) In winding up a limited liability company's business, the assets of the company must be applied to discharge its obligations to creditors, including members who are creditors. Any surplus must be applied to pay in money the net amount distributable to members in accordance with their right to distributions under subsection (b).

(b) Each member is entitled to a distribution upon the winding up of the limited liability company's business consisting of a return of all contributions which have not previously been returned and a distribution of any remainder in equal shares.

Section 807. Known Claims Against Dissolved Limited Liability Company.

(a) A dissolved limited liability company may dispose of the known claims against it by following the procedure described in this section.

(b) A dissolved limited liability company shall notify its known claimants in writing of the dissolution. The notice must:

(1) specify the information required to be included in a claim;

(2) provide a mailing address where the claim is to be sent;

(3) state the deadline for receipt of the claim, which may not be less than 120 days after the date the written notice is received by the claimant; and

(4) state that the claim will be barred if not received by the deadline.

(c) A claim against a dissolved limited liability company is barred if the requirements of subsection (b) are met, and:

(1) the claim is not received by the specified deadline; or

(2) in the case of a claim that is timely received but rejected by the dissolved company, the claimant does not commence a proceeding to enforce the claim within 90 days after the receipt of the notice of the rejection.

(d) For purposes of this section, "claim" does not include a contingent liability or a claim based on an event occurring after the effective date of dissolution.

Comment:

A known claim will be barred when the company provides written notice to a claimant that a claim must be filed with the company no later than at least 120 days after receipt of the written notice and the claimant fails to file the claim. If the claim is timely received but is rejected by the company, the claim is nevertheless barred unless the claimant files suit to enforce the claim within 90 days after the receipt of the notice of rejection. A claim described in subsection (d) is not a "known" claim and is governed by Section 808. This section does not extend any other applicable statutes of limitation. See Section 104. Depending on the management of the company, members or managers must discharge or make provision for discharging all of the company's known liabilities before distributing the remaining assets to the members. See Sections 806(a), 406, and 407.

Section 808. Other Claims Against Dissolved Limited Liability Company.

(a) A dissolved limited liability company may publish notice of its dissolution and request persons having claims against the company to present them in accordance with the notice.

(b) The notice must:

(1) be published at least once in a newspaper of general circulation in the [county] in which the dissolved limited liability company's principal office is located or, if none in this State, in which its designated office is or was last located;

(2) describe the information required to be contained in a claim and provide a mailing address where the claim is to be sent; and

(3) state that a claim against the limited liability company is barred unless a proceeding to enforce the claim is commenced within five years after publication of the notice.

(c) If a dissolved limited liability company publishes a notice in accordance with subsection (b), the claim of each of the following claimants is barred unless the claimant commences a proceeding to enforce the claim against the dissolved company within five years after the publication date of the notice:

(1) a claimant who did not receive written notice under Section 807;

(2) a claimant whose claim was timely sent to the dissolved company but not acted on; and

(3) a claimant whose claim is contingent or based on an event occurring after the effective date of dissolution.

(d) A claim not barred under this section may be enforced:

(1) against the dissolved limited liability company, to the extent of its undistributed assets; or

(2) if the assets have been distributed in liquidation, against a member of the dissolved company to the extent of the member's proportionate share of the claim or the company's assets distributed to the member in liquidation, whichever is less, but a member's total liability for all claims under this section may not exceed the total amount of assets distributed to the member.

Comment:

An unknown claim will be barred when the company publishes notice requesting claimants to file claims with the company and stating that claims will be barred unless the claimant files suit to enforce the claim within five years after the date of publication. The procedure also bars known claims where the claimant either did not receive written notice described in Section 807 or received notice [and] mailed a claim, but the company did not act on the claim.

Depending on the management of the company, members or managers must discharge or make provision for discharging all of the company's known liabilities before distributing the remaining assets to the members. See Comment to Section 807. This section does not contemplate that a company will postpone member distributions until all unknown claims are barred under this section. In appropriate cases, the company may purchase insurance or set aside funds permitting a distribution of the remaining assets. Where winding up distributions have been made to members, subsection (d)(2) authorizes recovery against those members. However, a claimant's recovery against a member is limited to the lesser of the member's proportionate share of the claim or the amount received in the distribution. This section does not extend any other applicable statutes of limitation. See Section 104.

Section 809. Grounds for Administrative Dissolution.

The [Secretary of State] may commence a proceeding to dissolve a limited liability company administratively if the company does not:

(1) pay any fees, taxes, or penalties imposed by this [Act] or other law within 60 days after they are due; or

(2) deliver its annual report to the [Secretary of State] within 60 days after it is due.

Comment:

Administrative dissolution is an effective enforcement mechanism for a variety of statutory obligations under this Act and it avoids the more expensive judicial dissolution process. When applicable, administrative dissolution avoids wasteful attempts to compel compliance by a company abandoned by its members.

Section 810. Procedure for and Effect of Administrative Dissolution.

(a) If the [Secretary of State] determines that a ground exists for administratively dissolving a limited liability company, the [Secretary of State] shall enter a record of the determination and serve the company with a copy of the record.

(b) If the company does not correct each ground for dissolution or demonstrate to the reasonable satisfaction of the [Secretary of State] that each ground determined by the [Secretary of State] does not exist within 60 days after service of the notice, the [Secretary of State] shall administratively dissolve the company by signing a certification of the dissolution that recites the ground for dissolution and its effective date. The [Secretary of State] shall file the original of the certificate and serve the company with a copy of the certificate.

(c) A company administratively dissolved continues its existence but may carry on only business necessary to wind up and liquidate its business and affairs under Section 802 and to notify claimants under Sections 807 and 808.

(d) The administrative dissolution of a company does not terminate the authority of its agent for service of process.

Comment:

A company's failure to comply with a ground for administrative dissolution may simply occur because of oversight. Therefore, subsections (a) and (b) set forth a mandatory notice by the filing officer to the company of the ground for dissolution and a 60 day grace period for correcting the ground.

Section 811. Reinstatement Following Administrative Dissolution.

(a) A limited liability company administratively dissolved may apply to the [Secretary of State] for reinstatement within two years after the effective date of dissolution. The application must:

(1) recite the name of the company and the effective date of its administrative dissolution;

(2) state that the ground for dissolution either did not exist or have been eliminated;

(3) state that the company's name satisfies the requirements of Section 105; and

(4) contain a certificate from the [taxing authority] reciting that all taxes owed by the company have been paid.

(b) If the [Secretary of State] determines that the application contains the information required by subsection (a) and that the information is correct, the [Secretary of State] shall cancel the certificate of dissolution and prepare a certificate of reinstatement that recites this determination and the effective date of reinstatement, file the original of the certificate, and serve the company with a copy of the certificate.

(c) When reinstatement is effective, it relates back to and takes effect as of the effective date of the administrative dissolution and the company may resume its business as if the administrative dissolution had never occurred.

Section 812. Appeal From Denial of Reinstatement.

(a) If the [Secretary of State] denies a limited liability company's application for reinstatement following administrative dissolution, the [Secretary of State] shall serve the company with a record that explains the reason or reasons for denial.

(b) The company may appeal the denial of reinstatement to the [name appropriate] court within 30 days after service of the notice of denial is perfected. The company appeals by petitioning the court to set aside the dissolution and attaching to the petition copies of the [Secretary of State's] certificate of dissolution, the company's application for reinstatement, and the [Secretary of State's] notice of denial.

(c) The court may summarily order the [Secretary of State] to reinstate the dissolved company or may take other action the court considers appropriate.

(d) The court's final decision may be appealed as in other civil proceedings.

[ARTICLE] 9

CONVERSIONS AND MERGERS

Section 901.   Definitions.

In this [article]:

(1) "Corporation" means a corporation under [the State Corporation Act], a predecessor law, or comparable law of another jurisdiction.

(2) "General partner" means a partner in a partnership and a general partner in a limited partnership.

(3) "Limited partner" means a limited partner in a limited partnership.

(4) "Limited partnership" means a limited partnership created under [the State Limited Partnership Act], a predecessor law, or comparable law of another jurisdiction.

(5) "Partner" includes a general partner and a limited partner.

(6) "Partnership" means a general partnership under [the State Partnership Act], a predecessor law, or comparable law of another jurisdiction.

(7) "Partnership agreement" means an agreement among the partners concerning the partnership or limited partnership.

(8) "Shareholder" means a shareholder in a corporation.

Comment:

Section 907 makes clear that the provisions of Article 9 are not mandatory. Therefore, a partnership or a limited liability company may convert or merge in any other manner provided by law. However, if the requirements of Article 9 are followed, the conversion or merger is legally valid. Article 9 is not restricted to domestic business entities.

Section 902.   Conversion of Partnership or Limited Partnership to Limited Liability Company.

(a) A partnership or limited partnership may be converted to a limited liability company pursuant to this section.

(b) The terms and conditions of a conversion of a partnership or limited partnership to a limited liability company must be approved by all of the partners or by a number or percentage of the partners required for conversion in the partnership agreement.

(c) An agreement of conversion must set forth the terms and conditions of the conversion of the interests of partners of a partnership or of a limited partnership, as the case may be, into interests in the converted limited liability company or the cash or other consideration to be paid or delivered as a result of the conversion of the interests of the partners, or a combination thereof.

(d) After a conversion is approved under subsection (b), the partnership or limited partnership shall file articles of organization in the office of the [Secretary of State] which satisfy the requirements of Section 203 and contain:

(1) a statement that the partnership or limited partnership was converted to a limited liability company from a partnership or limited partnership, as the case may be;

(2) its former name;

(3) a statement of the number of votes cast by the partners entitled to vote for and against the conversion and, if the vote is less than unanimous, the number or percentage required to approve the conversion under subsection (b); and

(4) in the case of a limited partnership, a statement that the certificate of limited partnership is to be canceled as of the date the conversion took effect.

(e) In the case of a limited partnership, the filing of articles of organization under subsection (d) cancels its certificate of limited partnership as of the date the conversion took effect.

(f) A conversion takes effect when the articles of organization are filed in the office of the [Secretary of State] or at any later date specified in the articles of organization.

(g) A general partner who becomes a member of a limited liability company as a result of a conversion remains liable as a partner for an obligation incurred by the partnership or limited partnership before the conversion takes effect.

(h) A general partner's liability for all obligations of the limited liability company incurred after the conversion takes effect is that of a member of the company. A limited partner who becomes a member as a result of a conversion remains liable only to the extent the limited partner was liable for an obligation incurred by the limited partnership before the conversion takes effect.

Comment:

Subsection (b) makes clear that the terms and conditions of the conversion of a general or limited partnership to a limited liability company must be approved by all of the partners unless the partnership agreement specifies otherwise.

Section 903.   Effect of Conversion; Entity Unchanged.

(a) A partnership or limited partnership that has been converted pursuant to this [article] is for all purposes the same entity that existed before the conversion.

(b) When a conversion takes effect:

(1) all property owned by the converting partnership or limited partnership vests in the limited liability company;

(2) all debts, liabilities, and other obligations of the converting partnership or limited partnership continue as obligations of the limited liability company;

(3) an action or proceeding pending by or against the converting partnership or limited partnership may be continued as if the conversion had not occurred;

(4) except as prohibited by other law, all of the rights, privileges, immunities, powers, and purposes of the converting partnership or limited partnership vest in the limited liability company; and

(5) except as otherwise provided in the agreement of conversion under Section 902(c), all of the partners of the converting partnership continue as members of the limited liability company.

Comment:

A conversion is not a conveyance or transfer and does not give rise to claims of reverter or impairment of title based on a prohibited conveyance or transfer. Under subsection (b)(1), title to all partnership property, including real estate, vests in the limited liability company as a matter of law without reversion or impairment.

Section 904.   Merger of Entities.

(a) Pursuant to a plan of merger approved under subsection (c), a limited liability company may be merged with or into one or more limited liability companies, foreign limited liability companies, corporations, foreign corporations, partnerships, foreign partnerships, limited partnerships, foreign limited partnerships, or other domestic or foreign entities.

(b) A plan of merger must set forth:

(1) the name of each entity that is a party to the merger;

(2) the name of the surviving entity into which the other entities will merge;

(3) the type of organization of the surviving entity;

(4) the terms and conditions of the merger;

(5) the manner and basis for converting the interests of each party to the merger into interests or obligations of the surviving entity, or into money or other property in whole or in part; and

(6) the street address of the surviving entity's principal place of business.

(c) A plan of merger must be approved:

(1) in the case of a limited liability company that is a party to the merger, by all of the members or by a number or percentage of members specified in the operating agreement;

(2) in the case of a foreign limited liability company that is a party to the merger, by the vote required for approval of a merger by the law of the State or foreign jurisdiction in which the foreign limited liability company is organized;

(3) in the case of a partnership or domestic limited partnership that is a party to the merger, by the vote required for approval of a conversion under Section 902(b); and

(4) in the case of any other entities that are parties to the merger, by the vote required for approval of a merger by the law of this State or of the State or foreign jurisdiction in which the entity is organized and, in the absence of such a requirement, by all the owners of interests in the entity.

(d) After a plan of merger is approved and before the merger takes effect, the plan may be amended or abandoned as provided in the plan.

(e) The merger is effective upon the filing of the articles of merger with the [Secretary of State], or at such later date as the articles may provide.

Comment:

This section sets forth a "safe harbor" for cross-entity mergers of limited liability companies with both domestic and foreign: corporations, general and limited partnerships, and other limited liability companies. Subsection (c) makes clear that the terms and conditions of the plan of merger must be approved by all of the partners unless applicable state law specifies otherwise for the merger.

Section 905. Articles of Merger.

(a) After approval of the plan of merger under Section 904(c), unless the merger is abandoned under Section 904(d), articles of merger must be signed on behalf of each limited liability company and other entity that is a party to the merger and delivered to the [Secretary of State] for filing. The articles must set forth:

(1) the name and jurisdiction of formation or organization of each of the limited liability companies and other entities that are parties to the merger;

(2) for each limited liability company that is to merge, the date its articles of organization were filed with the [Secretary of State];

(3) that a plan of merger has been approved and signed by each limited liability company and other entity that is to merge;

(4) the name and address of the surviving limited liability company or other surviving entity;

(5) the effective date of the merger;

(6) if a limited liability company is the surviving entity, such changes in its articles of organization as are necessary by reason of the merger;

(7) if a party to a merger is a foreign limited liability company, the jurisdiction and date of filing of its initial articles of organization and the date when its application for authority was filed by the [Secretary of State] or, if an application has not been filed, a statement to that effect; and

(8) if the surviving entity is not a limited liability company, an agreement that the surviving entity may be served with process in this State and is subject to liability in any action or proceeding for the enforcement of any liability or obligation of any limited liability company previously subject to suit in this State which is to merge, and for the enforcement, as provided in this [Act], of the right of members of any limited liability company to receive payment for their interest against the surviving entity.

(b) If a foreign limited liability company is the surviving entity of a merger, it may not do business in this State until an application for that authority is filed with the [Secretary of State].

(c) The surviving limited liability company or other entity shall furnish a copy of the plan of merger, on request and without cost, to any member of any limited liability company or any person holding an interest in any other entity that is to merge.

(d) Articles of merger operate as an amendment to the limited liability company's articles of organization.

Section 906. Effect of Merger.

(a) When a merger takes effect:

(1) the separate existence of each limited liability company and other entity that is a party to the merger, other than the surviving entity, terminates;

(2) all property owned by each of the limited liability companies and other entities that are party to the merger vests in the surviving entity;

(3) all debts, liabilities, and other obligations of each limited liability company and other entity that is party to the merger become the obligations of the surviving entity;

(4) an action or proceeding pending by or against a limited liability company or other party to a merger may be continued as if the merger had not occurred or the surviving entity may be substituted as a party to the action or proceeding; and

(5) except as prohibited by other law, all the rights, privileges, immunities, powers, and purposes of every limited liability company and other entity that is a party to a merger vest in the surviving entity.

(b) The [Secretary of State] is an agent for service of process in an action or proceeding against the surviving foreign entity to enforce an obligation of any party to a merger if the surviving foreign entity fails to appoint or maintain an agent designated for service of process in this State or the agent for service of process cannot with reasonable diligence be found at the designated office. Upon receipt of process, the [Secretary of State] shall send a copy of the process by registered or certified mail, return receipt requested, to the surviving entity at the address set forth in the articles of merger. Service is effected under this subsection at the earliest of:

(1) the date the company receives the process, notice, or demand;

(2) the date shown on the return receipt, if signed on behalf of the company; or

(3) five days after its deposit in the mail, if mailed postpaid and correctly addressed.

(c) A member of the surviving limited liability company is liable for all obligations of a party to the merger for which the member was personally liable before the merger.

(d) Unless otherwise agreed, a merger of a limited liability company that is not the surviving entity in the merger does not require the limited liability company to wind up its business under this [Act] or pay its liabilities and distribute its assets pursuant to this [Act].

(e) Articles of merger serve as articles of dissolution for a limited liability company that is not the surviving entity in the merger.

Section 907. [Article] Not Exclusive.

This [article] does not preclude an entity from being converted or merged under other law.

[ARTICLE] 10

FOREIGN LIMITED LIABILITY COMPANIES

Sec.

Section 1001. Law Governing Foreign Limited Liability Companies.

(a) The laws of the State or other jurisdiction under which a foreign limited liability company is organized govern its organization and internal affairs and the liability of its managers, members, and their transferees.

(b) A foreign limited liability company may not be denied a certificate of authority by reason of any difference between the laws of another jurisdiction under which the foreign company is organized and the laws of this State.

(c) A certificate of authority does not authorize a foreign limited liability company to engage in any business or exercise any power that a limited liability company may not engage in or exercise in this State.

Comment:

The law where a foreign limited liability company is organized, rather than this Act, governs that company's internal affairs and the liability of its owners. Accordingly, any difference between the laws of the foreign jurisdiction and this Act will not constitute grounds for denial of a certificate of authority to transact business in this State. However, a foreign limited liability company transacting business in this State by virtue of a certificate of authority is limited to the business and powers that a limited liability company may lawfully pursue and exercise under Section 112.

Section 1002. Application for Certificate of Authority.

(a) A foreign limited liability company may apply for a certificate of authority to transact business in this State by delivering an application to the [Secretary of State] for filing. The application must set forth:

(1) the name of the foreign company or, if its name is unavailable for use in this State, a name that satisfies the requirements of Section 1005;

(2) the name of the State or country under whose law it is organized;

(3) the street address of its principal office;

(4) the address of its initial designated office in this State;

(5) the name and street address of its initial agent for service of process in this State;

(6) whether the duration of the company is for a specified term and, if so, the period specified;

(7) whether the company is manager-managed, and, if so, the name and address of each initial manager; and

(8) whether the members of the company are to be liable for its debts and obligations under a provision similar to Section 303(c).

(b) A foreign limited liability company shall deliver with the completed application a certificate of existence or a record of similar import authenticated by the secretary of state or other official having custody of company records in the State or country under whose law it is organized.

Comment:

As with articles of organization, the application must be signed and filed with the filing office. See Sections 105, 107 (name registration), 205, 206, 209 (liability for false statements), and 1005.

Section 1003. Activities Not Constituting Transacting Business.

(a) Activities of a foreign limited liability company that do not constitute transacting business in this State within the meaning of this [article] include:

(1) maintaining, defending, or settling an action or proceeding;

(2) holding meetings of its members or managers or carrying on any other activity concerning its internal affairs;

(3) maintaining bank accounts;

(4) maintaining offices or agencies for the transfer, exchange, and registration of the foreign company's own securities or maintaining trustees or depositories with respect to those securities;

(5) selling through independent contractors;

(6) soliciting or obtaining orders, whether by mail or through employees or agents or otherwise, if the orders require acceptance outside this State before they become contracts;

(7) creating or acquiring indebtedness, mortgages, or security interests in real or personal property;

(8) securing or collecting debts or enforcing mortgages or other security interests in property securing the debts, and holding, protecting, and maintaining property so acquired;

(9) conducting an isolated transaction that is completed within 30 days and is not one in the course of similar transactions of a like manner; and

(10) transacting business in interstate commerce.

(b) For purposes of this [article], the ownership in this State of income-producing real property or tangible personal property, other than property excluded under subsection (a), constitutes transacting business in this State.

(c) This section does not apply in determining the contacts or activities that may subject a foreign limited liability company to service of process, taxation, or regulation under any other law of this State.

Section 1004.   Issuance of Certificate of Authority.

Unless the [Secretary of State] determines that an application for a certificate of authority fails to comply as to form with the filing requirements of this [Act], the [Secretary of State], upon payment of all filing fees, shall file the application and send a receipt for it and the fees to the limited liability company or its representative.

Section 1005.   Name of Foreign Limited Liability Company.

(a) If the name of a foreign limited liability company does not satisfy the requirements of Section 105, the company, to obtain or maintain a certificate of authority to transact business in this State, must use a fictitious name to transact business in this State if its real name is unavailable and it delivers to the [Secretary of State] for filing a copy of the resolution of its managers, in the case of a manager-managed company, or of its members, in the case of a member-managed company, adopting the fictitious name.

(b) Except as authorized by subsections (c) and (d), the name, including a fictitious name to be used to transact business in this State, of a foreign limited liability company must be distinguishable upon the records of the [Secretary of State] from:

(1) the name of any corporation, limited partnership, or company incorporated, organized, or authorized to transact business in this State;

(2) a name reserved or registered under Section 106 or 107; and

(3) the fictitious name of another foreign limited liability company authorized to transact business in this State.

(c) A foreign limited liability company may apply to the [Secretary of State] for authority to use in this State a name that is not distinguishable upon the records of the [Secretary of State] from a name described in subsection (b).   The [Secretary of State] shall authorize use of the name applied for if:

(1) the present user, registrant, or owner of a reserved name consents to the use in a record and submits an undertaking in form satisfactory to the [Secretary of State] to change its name to a name that is distinguishable upon the records of the [Secretary of State] from the name of the foreign applying limited liability company; or

(2) the applicant delivers to the [Secretary of State] a certified copy of a final judgment of a court establishing the applicant's right to use the name applied for in this State.

(d) A foreign limited liability company may use in this State the name, including the fictitious name, of another domestic or foreign entity that is used in this State if the other entity is incorporated, organized, or authorized to transact business in this State and the foreign limited liability company:

(1) has merged with the other entity;

(2) has been formed by reorganization of the other entity; or

(3) has acquired all or substantially all of the assets, including the name, of the other entity.

(e) If a foreign limited liability company authorized to transact business in this State changes its name to one that does not satisfy the requirements of Section 105, it may not transact business in this State under the name as changed until it adopts a name satisfying the requirements of Section 105 and obtains an amended certificate of authority.

Section 1006.   Revocation of Certificate of Authority.

(a) A certificate of authority of a foreign limited liability company to transact business in this State may be revoked by the [Secretary of State] in the manner provided in subsection (b) if:

(1) the company fails to:

(i) pay any fees, taxes, and penalties owed to this State;

(ii) deliver its annual report required under Section 211 to the [Secretary of State] within 60 days after it is due;

(iii) appoint and maintain an agent for service of process as required by this [article]; or

(iv) file a statement of a change in the name or business address of the agent as required by this [article]; or

(2) a misrepresentation has been made of any material matter in any application, report, affidavit, or other record submitted by the company pursuant to this [article].

(b) The [Secretary of State] may not revoke a certificate of authority of a foreign limited liability company unless the [Secretary of State] sends the company notice of the revocation, at least 60 days before its effective date, by a record addressed to its agent for service of process in this State, or if the company fails to appoint and maintain a proper agent in this State, addressed to the office required to be maintained by Section 108.   The notice must specify the cause for the revocation of the certificate of authority.   The authority of the company to transact business in this State ceases on the effective date of the revocation unless the foreign limited liability company cures the failure before that date.

Section 1007.   Cancellation of Authority.

A foreign limited liability company may cancel its authority to transact business in this State by filing in the office of the [Secretary of State] a certificate of cancellation.   Cancellation does not terminate the authority of the [Secretary of State] to accept service of process on the company for [claims for relief] arising out of the transactions of business in this State.

Section 1008.   Effect of Failure to Obtain Certificate of Authority.

(a) A foreign limited liability company transacting business in this State may not maintain an action or proceeding in this State unless it has a certificate of authority to transact business in this State.

(b) The failure of a foreign limited liability company to have a certificate of authority to transact business in this State does not impair the validity of a contract or act of the company or prevent the foreign limited liability company from defending an action or proceeding in this State.

(c) Limitations on personal liability of managers, members, and their transferees are not waived solely by transacting business in this State without a certificate of authority.

(d) If a foreign limited liability company transacts business in this State without a certificate of authority, it appoints the [Secretary of State] as its agent for service of process for [claims for relief] arising out of the transaction of business in this State.

Section 1009.   Action by [Attorney General].

The [Attorney General] may maintain an action to restrain a foreign limited liability company from transacting business in this State in violation of this [article].

[ARTICLE] 11

DERIVATIVE ACTIONS

Sec.

Section 1101.   Right of Action.

A member of a limited liability company may maintain an action in the right of the company if the members or managers having authority to do so have refused to commence the action or an effort to cause those members or managers to commence the action is not likely to succeed.

Comment:

A member may bring an action on behalf of the company when the members or managers having the authority to pursue the company recovery refuse to do so or an effort to cause them to pursue the recovery is not likely to succeed. See Comments to Section 411(a) (personal action of member against company or another member).

Section 1102.   Proper Plaintiff.

In a derivative action for a limited liability company, the plaintiff must be a member of the company when the action is commenced; and:

(1) must have been a member at the time of the transaction of which the plaintiff complains; or

(2) the plaintiff's status as a member must have devolved upon the plaintiff by operation of law or pursuant to the terms of the operating agreement from a person who was a member at the time of the transaction.

Section 1103.   Pleading.

In a derivative action for a limited liability company, the complaint must set forth with particularity the effort of the plaintiff to secure initiation of the action by a member or manager or the reasons for not making the effort.

Comment:

There is no obligation of the company or its members or managers to respond to a member demand to bring an action to pursue a company recovery. However, if a company later decides to commence the demanded action or assume control of the derivative litigation, the member's right to commence or control the proceeding ordinarily ends.

Section 1104.   Expenses.

If a derivative action for a limited liability company is successful, in whole or in part, or if anything is received by the plaintiff as a result of a judgment, compromise, or settlement of an action or claim, the court may award the plaintiff reasonable expenses, including reasonable attorney's fees, and shall direct the plaintiff to remit to the limited liability company the remainder of the proceeds received.

[ARTICLE] 12

MISCELLANEOUS PROVISIONS

Section 1201.   Uniformity of Application and Construction.

This [Act] shall be applied and construed to effectuate its general purpose to make uniform the law with respect to the subject of this [Act] among States enacting it.

Section 1202.   Short Title.

This [Act] may be cited as the Uniform Limited Liability Company Act (1995).

531

Section 1203.   Severability Clause.

If any provision of this [Act] or its application to any person or circumstance is held invalid, the invalidity does not affect other provisions or applications of this [Act] which can be given effect without the invalid provision or application, and to this end the provisions of this [Act] are severable . . .

Section 1204.   Effective Date.

This [Act] takes effect [_____].

FORM OF LIMITED LIABILITY COMPANY OPERATING AGREEMENT*

BY

ROBERT R. KEATINGE

MASTER: MANAGER MANAGED [LONG FORM] Revised 4/98

[OPERATING/LIMITED LIABILITY COMPANY] AGREEMENT

OF

_____, LLC

A [   ] LIMITED LIABILITY COMPANY
EFFECTIVE AS OF _____, 1998

THE INTERESTS DESCRIBED AND REPRESENTED BY THIS OPERATING AGREEMENT HAVE NOT BEEN REGISTERED UNDER THE SECURITIES ACT OF 1933 (THE "ACT" OR ANY APPLICABLE STATE SECURITIES LAWS ("STATE ACTS") AND ARE RESTRICTED SECURITIES AS THAT TERM IS DEFINED IN RULE 144 UNDER THE ACT. THE SECURITIES MAY NOT BE OFFERED FOR SALE, SOLD, OR OTHERWISE TRANSFERRED EXCEPT PURSUANT TO AN EFFECTIVE REGISTRATION STATEMENT OR QUALIFICATION UNDER THE ACT AND APPLICABLE STATE ACTS OR PURSUANT TO AN EXEMPTION FROM REGISTRATION UNDER THE ACT AND APPLICABLE STATE ACTS, THE AVAILABILITY OF WHICH IS TO BE ESTABLISHED TO THE SATISFACTION OF THE COMPANY.

CAVEAT: YOU NEED TO ENSURE THAT THIS FORM IS AMENDED AS APPROPRIATE TO FIT YOUR PARTICULAR DEAL. READ EVERY PROVISION AND ENSURE THAT IT MAKES SENSE FOR THE CLIENT IN THE PARTICULAR DEAL. PLEASE REMEMBER THAT BECAUSE AN OPERATING AGREEMENT PROVIDES GREAT FLEXIBILITY, IT IS ESSENTIAL IN EVERY TRANSACTION TO OBTAIN TAX REVIEW (FOR BOTH INCOME TAX AND, PARTICULARLY IN THE FAMILY CONTEXT, TRANSFER TAX EFFECTS), AND SECURITIES LAW REVIEW

TABLE OF CONTENTS

ARTICLE 1. DEFINITIONS

* © Holland & Hart LLP 1998. Reproduced by permission.

ARTICLE 6.   RIGHTS AND OBLIGATIONS OF MEMBERS

ARTICLE 7.   MEETINGS OF MEMBERS

ARTICLE 8.   CONTRIBUTIONS TO THE COMPANY
AND CAPITAL ACCOUNTS

ARTICLE 9.   ALLOCATIONS, INCOME TAX, DISTRIBUTIONS,
ELECTIONS AND REPORTS

* Omitted.

ARTICLE 10. TRANSFERABILITY

ARTICLE 11. ADDITIONAL MEMBERS

ARTICLE 12. DISSOLUTION AND TERMINATION

ARTICLE 13. MISCELLANEOUS PROVISIONS

EXHIBIT 8.1   INITIAL CAPITAL CONTRIBUTIONS

EXHIBIT 8.2   ADDITIONAL CAPITAL CONTRIBUTIONS

THIS Agreement is made and entered into this ___ day of _____, 1998, by and between the Company and each of the Members whose signatures appear on the signature page hereof.

RECITALS:

The Members formed the Company to acquire, own, improve, manage, operate, and dispose of real property.

A.   Articles of Organization for _____ LLC were filed with the Secretary of State of _____ on _____, 1998.

B.   The parties agree as follows:

ARTICLE 1

DEFINITIONS

The following terms used in this Agreement shall have the following meanings (unless otherwise expressly provided herein):

1.1 "Act" shall mean the _____ Limited Liability Company Act [,as amended].

1.2 "Adjusted Capital Contributions" shall mean an amount equal to such Equity Owner's Capital Contributions, if any, pursuant to Section 8.1 and Section 8.2, less any distributions made to such Equity Owner pursuant to 9.4(c) **[CAVEAT: THIS DEFINITION IS TO BE USED WHEN ALTERNATIVE 2 IN SECTION 9.4 IS USED.]**

1.2a "Agreement" shall mean this [**Operating/Limited Liability Company**] Agreement as originally executed and as amended from time to time.

1.3 "Affiliate" means, with respect to any Person, (i) any Person directly or indirectly controlling, controlled by, or under common control with such Person, (ii) any Person owning or controlling ten percent (10%) or more of the outstanding voting interests of such Person, (iii) any officer, director, or general partner of such Person, or (iv) any Person who is an officer, director, general partner, trustee, or holder of ten percent (10%) or more of the voting interests of any Person described in clauses (i) through (iii) of this sentence. For purposes of this definition, the term "controls," "is controlled by," or "is under common control with" shall mean the possession, direct or indirect, of the power to direct or cause the direction of the management and policies of a Person, whether through the ownership of voting securities, by contract or otherwise.

1.4 "Articles of Organization" shall mean the Articles of Organization of _____ as filed with the Secretary of State of [   ] as the same may be amended from time to time

1.5 "Capital Account" as of any given date shall mean the Capital Contribution to the Company by an Equity Owner as adjusted up to the date in question pursuant to Article 8.

1.6 "Capital Contribution" shall mean any contribution to the capital of the Company in cash or property by [an] Equity Owner whenever made.

"Initial Capital Contribution" shall mean the initial contribution to the capital of the Company pursuant to this Agreement.

1.7 "Code" shall mean the Internal Revenue Code of 1986, as amended from time to time.

1.8 "Company" shall refer to _____ LLC.

1.9 "Deficit Capital Account" shall mean with respect to any Equity Owner, the deficit balance, if any, in such Equity Owner's Capital Account as of the end of the taxable year, after giving effect to the following adjustments:

537

credit to such Capital Account any amount which such Equity Owner is obligated to restore under Section 1.704–1(b)(2)(ii)(c) of the Treasury Regulations, as well as any addition thereto pursuant to the next to last sentence of Sections 1.704–2(g)(1) and (i)(5) of the Treasury Regulations, after taking into account thereunder any changes during such year in partnership minimum gain (as determined in accordance with Section 1.704–2(d) of the Treasury Regulations) and in the minimum gain attributable to any partner nonrecourse debt (as determined under Section 1.704–2(i)(3) of the Treasury Regulations); and

debit to such Capital Account the items described in Sections 1.704–1(b)(2)(ii)(d)(4), (5) and (6) of the Treasury Regulations.

This definition of Deficit Capital Account is intended to comply with the provisions of Treasury Regulations Sections 1.704–1(b)(2)(ii)(d) and 1.704–2, and will be interpreted consistently with those provisions.

1.10 "Depreciation" means, for each Fiscal Year, an amount equal to the depreciation, amortization, or other cost recovery deduction allowable with respect to an asset for such Fiscal Year, except that if the Gross Asset Value of an asset differs from its adjusted basis for federal income tax purposes at the beginning of such Fiscal Year, Depreciation shall be an amount which bears the same ratio to such beginning Gross Asset Value as the federal income tax depreciation, amortization, or other cost recovery deduction for such Fiscal Year bears to such beginning adjusted tax basis; provided, however, that if the adjusted basis for federal income tax purposes of an asset at the beginning of such Fiscal Year is zero, Depreciation shall be determined with reference to such beginning Gross Asset Value using any reasonable method selected by the Manager(s).

1.11 "Distributable Cash" means all cash, whether revenues or other funds received by the Company, less the sum of the following to the extent paid or set aside by the Company: (i) all principal and interest payments on indebtedness of the Company and all other sums paid to lenders; (ii) all cash expenditures incurred incident to the normal operation of the Company's business; and (iii) Reserves.

1.12 "Economic Interest" shall mean [an] Equity Owner's share of one or more of the Company's Profits, Losses and distributions of the Company's assets pursuant to this Agreement and the Act, but shall not include any right to participate in the management or affairs of the Company, including, the right to vote on, consent to or otherwise participate in any decision of the Members or Managers.

1.13 "Economic Interest Owner" shall mean the owner of an Economic Interest who is not a Member.

1.14 "Entity" shall mean any general partnership, limited partnership, limited liability company, corporation, joint venture, trust, business trust, cooperative or association or any foreign trust or foreign business organization.

1.15 "Equity Owner" shall mean an Economic Interest Owner or a Member.

1.16 "Fiscal Year" shall mean the Company's fiscal year, which shall be the calendar year.

1.17 "Gift" or "gift" shall have the meaning set forth in Section 10.1.

1.18 "Gifting Equity Owner" shall mean any Equity Owner who gifts, bequeaths or otherwise transfers for no consideration (by operation of law or otherwise, except with respect to bankruptcy) all or any part of its Ownership Interest.

1.19 "Gross Asset Value" means, with respect to any asset, the asset's adjusted basis for federal income tax purposes, except as follows:

(a) The initial Gross Asset Value of any asset contributed by a Equity Owner to the Company shall be the gross fair market value of such asset, as determined by the contributing Member and the Manager(s), provided that the initial Gross Asset Values of the assets contributed to the Company pursuant to Section 8.1 hereof shall be as set forth in Exhibit 8.1, and provided further that, if the contributing Member is a Manager, the determination of the fair market value of any other contributed asset shall require the consent of the other Members owning a Majority Interest (determined without regard to the Voting Interest of such contributing Member);

(b) The Gross Asset Values of all Company assets shall be adjusted to equal their respective gross fair market values, as reasonably determined by the Manager(s) as of the following times: (i) the acquisition of an additional interest by any new or existing Equity Owner in exchange for more than a *de minimis* contribution of property (including money); (ii) the distribution by the Company to a Equity Owner of more than a *de minimis* amount of property as consideration for an Ownership Interest; and (iii) the liquidation of the Company within the meaning of Regulations Section 1.704–1(b)(2)(ii)(g); provided, however, that adjustments pursuant to clauses (i) and (ii) above shall be made only if the Manager(s) reasonably determine(s) that such adjustments are necessary or appropriate to reflect the relative economic interests of the Equity Owners in the Company;

(c) The Gross Asset Value of any Company asset distributed to any Equity Owner shall be adjusted to equal the gross fair market value of such asset on the date of distribution as **[reasonably]** determined by the distributee and the Manager(s), provided that, if the distributee is a Manager, the determination of the fair market value of the distributed asset shall require the consent of the other Members owning a Majority Interest (determined without regard to the Voting Interest of the distributee Member); and

(d) The Gross Asset Values of Company assets shall be increased (or decreased) to reflect any adjustments to the adjusted basis of such assets pursuant to Code Section 734(b) or Code Section 743(b), but only to the extent that such adjustments are taken into account in determining Capital Accounts pursuant to Regulation Section 1.704–1(b)(2)(iv)(m) and Section 8.3 and subparagraph (d) under the definition of Profits and Losses; provided, however, that Gross Asset Values shall not be adjusted pursuant to this subparagraph (d) of this definition to the extent the Manager(s) **[reasonably]** determine(s) that an adjustment pursuant to subparagraph (b) of this definition is necessary or appropriate in connection with a transaction that would otherwise result in an adjustment pursuant to this subparagraph (d).

If the Gross Asset Value of an asset has been determined or adjusted pursuant to subparagraph (a), (b) or (d) of this definition, then such Gross Asset Value shall thereafter be adjusted by the Depreciation taken into account with respect to such asset for purposes of computing Profits and Losses.

1.20 "Majority Interest" shall mean one or more Voting Interests of Members which taken together exceed 50% of the aggregate of all Voting Interests.

1.21 "Manager" shall mean one or more managers. Specifically, "Manager" shall mean _____, or any other persons that succeed him in that capacity. References to the Manager in the singular or as him, her, it, itself, or other like references shall also, where the context so requires, be deemed to include the plural or the masculine or feminine reference, as the case may be.

1.22 "Member" shall mean each of the parties who executes a counterpart of this Agreement as a Member and each of the parties who may hereafter become Members. To the extent a Manager has purchased Membership Interests in the Company, such Manager will have all the rights of a Member with respect to such Membership Interests, and the term "Member" as used herein shall include a Manager to the extent such Manager has purchased such Membership Interests in the Company. If a Person is a Member immediately prior to the purchase or other acquisition by such Person of an Economic Interest, such Person shall have all the rights of a Member with respect to such purchased or otherwise acquired Ownership Interest, as the case may be.

1.23 "Membership Interest" shall mean a Member's entire interest in the Company including such Member's Economic Interest and such other rights and privileges that the Member may enjoy by being a Member.

1.24 "Profits" and "Losses" shall mean for each taxable year of the Company an amount equal to the Company's net taxable income or loss for such year as determined for federal income tax purposes (including separately stated items) in accordance with the accounting method and rules used by the Company and in accordance with Section 703 of the Code with the following adjustments:

    (a) Any items of income, gain, loss and deduction allocated to Equity Owners pursuant to Section 9.2, 9.3 or Section 9.13 shall not be taken into account in computing Profits or Losses;

(b) Any income of the Company that is exempt from federal income tax and not otherwise taken into account in computing Profits and Losses (pursuant to this definition) shall be added to such taxable income or loss;

(c) Any expenditure of the Company described in Section 705(a)(2)(B) of the Code and not otherwise taken into account in computing Profits and Losses (pursuant to this definition) shall be subtracted from such taxable income or loss;

(d) In the event the Gross Asset Value of any Company asset is adjusted pursuant to subparagraphs (b) or (c) of the definition of Gross Asset Value, the amount of such adjustment shall be taken into account as gain or loss from the disposition of such asset for purposes of computing Profits and Losses;

(e) Gain or loss resulting from any disposition of any Company asset with respect to which gain or loss is recognized for federal income tax purposes shall be computed with reference to the Gross Asset Value of the asset disposed of, notwithstanding that the adjusted tax basis of such asset differs from its Gross Asset Value;

(f) In lieu of the depreciation, amortization and other cost recovery deductions taken into account in computing such taxable income or loss, there shall be taken into account Depreciation for such Fiscal Year; and

(g) To the extent an adjustment to the adjusted tax basis of any Company asset pursuant to Section 734(b) or Section 743(b) of the Code is required pursuant to Section 1.704–1(b)(2)(iv)(m)(4) of the Treasury Regulations to be taken into account in determining Capital Accounts as a result of a distribution other than in liquidation of an Ownership Interest, the amount of such adjustment shall be treated as an item of gain (if the adjustment [increases] the basis of the asset) or loss (if the adjustment decreases the basis of the asset) from the disposition of the asset and shall be taken into account for purposes of computing Profits or Losses.

1.26 "Ownership Interest" shall mean:

(a) in the case of a Member, the Member's Membership Interest; and

(b) in the case of an Economic Interest Owner, the Economic Interest Owner's Economic Interest.

1.27 "Person" shall mean any individual or Entity, and the heirs, executors, administrators, legal representatives, successors, and assigns of such "Person" where the context so permits.

1.28 "Reserves" shall mean, with respect to any fiscal period, funds set aside or amounts allocated during such period to reserves which shall be maintained in amounts **[reasonably]** deemed sufficient by the Managers for working capital and to pay taxes, insurance, debt service or other costs

541

or expenses incident to the ownership or operation of the Company's business.

1.28a "Reorganization" shall mean the merger or conversion of the Company, or a sale or other disposition of assets of the Company, or sale or other disposition of Ownership Interests, or other transaction pursuant to which a Person or Persons acquire all or substantially all of the assets of, or Ownership Interests in, the Company in a single or series of related transactions, *provided, however,* that a Reorganization shall not include the merger or conversion of the Company into a general partnership which is not a limited liability partnership.

1.29 "Selling Equity Owner" shall mean any Equity Owner which sells, assigns, or otherwise transfers for consideration all or any portion of its Membership Interest or Economic Interest.

1.30 "Sharing Ratio" shall mean:

Equity Owners	**Sharing Ratio**

1.31 "Transferring Equity Owner" shall collectively mean a Selling Equity Owner and a Gifting Equity Owner.

1.32 "Treasury Regulations" shall include proposed, temporary and final regulations promulgated under the Code in effect as of the date of filing the Articles of Organization and the corresponding sections of any regulations subsequently issued that amend or supersede such regulations.

1.33 "Two-Thirds Interest" shall mean one or more Voting Interests of Members which taken together exceed 66.67% of the aggregate of all Voting Interests.

1.34 "Voting Interest" shall mean:

Members	**Voting Interest**

1.35 "Unrecovered Losses" shall have the meaning set forth in Section 9.1.

ARTICLE 2

FORMATION OF COMPANY

2.1 Formation. On _____, 19__, _____ organized a _____ Limited Liability Company by executing and delivering articles of organization to the _____ secretary of state in accordance with and pursuant to the Act.

2.2 Name. The name of the Company is _____ LLC.

2.3 Principal Place of Business. The principal place of business of the Company within the State of _____ shall be _____. The Company may locate its places of business and registered office at any other place or places as the Manager or Managers may from time to time deem advisable.

2.4 Registered Office and Registered Agent. The Company's initial registered office and the name of the registered agent at such address shall be as set forth in the Articles. The registered office and registered agent may be changed from time to time by filing the address of the new registered office and/or the name of the new registered agent with the _____ Secretary of State pursuant to the Act.

2.5 Term. The Company shall continue in existence until it termination in accordance with the provisions of this Agreement or the Act.

ARTICLE 3

BUSINESS OF COMPANY

3.1 Permitted Businesses. The business of the Company shall be:

[To acquire, improve, manage, operate and dispose of real property and to accomplish any lawful business whatsoever, or which shall at any time appear conducive to or expedient for the protection or benefit of the Company and its assets.]

To exercise all other powers necessary to or reasonably connected with the Company's business which may be legally exercised by limited liability companies under the [ ] Act.

To engage in all activities necessary, customary, convenient, or incident to any of the foregoing.

[CONSIDER NARROWING THE PURPOSE AND BE SURE TO MAKE THE PURPOSE CLAUSE CONSISTENT WITH ARTICLE 5]

ARTICLE 4

NAMES AND ADDRESSES OF EQUITY OWNERS

The names and addresses of the Members are as follows:

NAME	ADDRESS
_____	_____
_____	_____
_____	_____
_____	_____

The names and addresses of the Economic Interest Owners, if any, are as follows:

NAME	ADDRESS
_____	_____
_____	_____
_____	_____
_____	_____

ARTICLE 5

RIGHTS AND DUTIES OF MANAGERS

5.1 <u>Management</u>. The business and affairs of the Company shall be managed by its Managers. Except for situations in which the approval of the Members is expressly required by this Agreement or by non-waivable provisions of applicable law, the Managers shall have full and complete authority, power and discretion to manage and control the business, affairs and properties of the Company, to make all decisions regarding those matters and to perform any and all other acts or activities customary or incident to the management of the Company's business. At any time when there is more than one Manager, any one Manager may take any action permitted to be taken by the Managers, unless the approval of more than one of the Managers is expressly required pursuant to this Agreement or the Act. Unless authorized to do so by this Agreement or by a Manager or Managers of the Company, no attorney-in-fact, employee or other agent of the Company shall have any power or authority to bind the Company in any way, to pledge its credit or to render it liable pecuniarily for any purpose.

5.2 <u>Number, Tenure and Qualifications</u>. The Company shall initially have one Manager. The number of Managers of the Company shall be fixed from time to time by the affirmative vote of Members holding at least a Two–Thirds Interest, but in no instance shall there be less than one Manager. Each Manager shall hold office until such Manager resigns pursuant to Section 5.9 or is removed pursuant to Section 5.10. Managers shall be appointed by the affirmative vote of Members holding at least a Majority Interest. Managers need not be residents of the State of _____ or Members of the Company.

5.3 <u>Certain Powers of Manager</u>. Without limiting the generality of Section 5.1, the Managers shall have power and authority, on behalf of the Company:

(a) To acquire property from any Person as the Managers may determine. The fact that a Manager or [an] Equity Owner is directly or indirectly affiliated or connected with any such Person shall not prohibit the Managers from dealing with that Person;

(b) To borrow money for the Company from banks, other lending institutions, the Managers, Equity Owners, or Affiliates of the Managers or Equity Owners on such terms as the Managers deem appropriate, and in connection therewith, to hypothecate, encumber and grant security interests in the assets of the Company to secure repayment of the borrowed sums;

(c) To purchase liability and other insurance to protect the Company's property and business;

(d) To hold and own any Company real and/or personal properties in the name of the Company;

(e) To invest any Company funds (by way of example but not limitation) in time deposits, short-term governmental obligations, commercial paper or other investments;

(f) To execute on behalf of the Company all instruments and documents, including, without limitation, checks; drafts; notes and other negotiable instruments; mortgages or deeds of trust; security agreements; financing statements; documents providing for the acquisition, mortgage or disposition of the Company's property; assignments; bills of sale; leases; partnership agreements, operating (or limited liability company) agreements of other limited liability companies; and any other instruments or documents necessary, in the **[reasonable]** opinion of the Managers, to the conduct of the business of the Company;

(g) To employ accountants, legal counsel, managing agents or other experts to perform services for the Company and to compensate them from Company funds;

(h) To enter into any and all other agreements on behalf of the Company, with any other Person for any purpose, in such forms as the Managers may approve;

(i) To do and perform all other acts as may be necessary or appropriate to the conduct of the Company's business;

(j) To execute and file such all such other instruments, documents and certificates which may from time to time be required by the laws of the State of [_____] or any other jurisdiction in which the Company shall determine to do business, or any political subdivision or agency thereof, to effectuate, implement, continue and defend the valid existence of the Company; and

(k) To cause the Company to be a party to a Reorganization.

5.4 <u>Limitations on Authority</u>. Notwithstanding any other provision of this Agreement, the Manager(s) shall not cause or commit the Company to do any of the following without the express written consent of Members holding a **[Two–Thirds Interest]**:

(a) Sell or otherwise dispose all or substantially all or the assets of the Company or any Company assets, real or personal, other than in the ordinary course of business;

(b) Mortgage, pledge, or grant a security interest (collectively, "pledge") in any property of the Company to the extent that the secured indebtedness from such pledge would exceed $_____;

(c) Incur or refinance any indebtedness for money borrowed by the Company, whether secured or unsecured and including any indebtedness for money borrowed from a Member if, after such financing, the aggregate indebtedness of the Company would exceed $_____;

(d) Incur any liability or make any single expenditure or series of related expenditures in an amount exceeding $_____ **[If Using**

545

Budget, these should be tied to the Budget, e.g. . . . **may not exceed budget by _____% or Budget line item by _____%];**

(e) Construct any capital improvements, repairs, alterations or changes involving an amount in excess of $_____; **[If Using Budget, these should be tied to the Budget, e.g. . . . may not exceed budget by _____% or Budget line item by _____%];**

(f) Lend money to or guaranty or become surety for the obligations of any Person;

(g) Compromise or settle any claim against or inuring to the benefit of the Company involving an amount in controversy in excess of $_____; or

(h) Cause the Company to file for bankruptcy.

[CAVEAT—Sections 5.3 and 5.4 need to be carefully conformed and tailored so that they are consistent with each other and fit the specific deal]

5.5 <u>Liability for Certain Acts</u>. (a) The Manager does not, in any way, guarantee the return of the Equity Owners' Capital Contributions or a profit for the Equity Owners from the operations of the Company.

(b) The Managers shall not be liable to the Company or to any Member for any loss or damage sustained by the Company or any Member (or successor thereto), except to the extent, if any, that the loss or damage shall have been the result of **[negligence,] [gross negligence,]** fraud, deceit, or willful misconduct.

5.6 <u>Managers and Members Have No Exclusive Duty to Company</u>. The Managers and Members shall have no exclusive duty to act on behalf of the Company. Each Manager and Member may have other business interests and may engage in other activities in addition to those relating to the Company. Neither the Company nor any manager shall have any right, by virtue of this Agreement, to share or participate in any other investments or activities of any other Manager or Member. Neither the Manager nor any Equity Owner shall incur any liability to the Company or to any of the Equity Owners as a result of engaging in any other business or venture.

5.7 <u>Bank Accounts</u>. The Managers may from time to time open bank accounts in the name of the Company, and the Managers shall be the sole signatory thereon, unless the Managers determine otherwise.

5.8 <u>Indemnity of the Managers, Employees and Other Agents</u>. (a) The Company shall indemnify the Managers and make advances for expenses to the maximum extent permitted under the Act, except to the extent the claim for which indemnification is sought results from an act or omission for which the Manager may be held liable to the Company or a Member under Section 5.5(b). The Company shall indemnify its employees and other agents who are not Managers to the fullest extent permitted by law, **[provided that such indemnification in any given situation is approved by Members owning a Majority Interest].**

(b) Expenses (including legal fees and expenses) incurred by a Manager in defending any claim, demand, action, suit or proceeding subject to subsection (a) above shall be paid by the Company in advance of the final disposition of such claim, demand, action, suit or proceeding upon receipt of an undertaking (which need not be secured) by or on behalf of the Manager to repay such amount if it shall ultimately be finally determined by a court of competent jurisdiction and not subject to appeal, that the Manager is not entitled to be indemnified by the Company as authorized hereunder.

5.9 Resignation. Any Manager of the Company may resign at any time by giving written notice to the Members of the Company. The resignation of any Manager shall take effect upon receipt of notice thereof or at such later time as shall be specified in such notice; and, unless otherwise specified therein, the acceptance of such resignation shall not be necessary to make it effective. The resignation of a Manager who is also an Equity Owner shall not affect the Manager's rights as an Equity Owner.

5.10 Removal. At a meeting called expressly for that purpose, all or any lesser number of Managers may be removed at any time for **[gross negligence which had a material adverse effect on the Company or for embezzlement, or if the Manager is adjudicated incompetent by a Court of competent jurisdiction/OR an action or omission with respect to which the Manager may be liable to the Company or a Member pursuant to Section 5.5(b)]** [**by the affirmative vote of Members holding a Majority Interest determined without regard to any Voting Interest held by the Manager or an Affiliate of the Manager]. [A Manager may removed with or without cause at any time by Members holding a Two–Thirds Interest.]** The removal of a Manager who is also a Member shall not affect the Manager's rights as a Member and shall not constitute a withdrawal of a Member. **[NOTE: Consider the advisability of including an option in favor of the Company and/or the other members to purchase the Ownership Interest of a Manager (assuming the Manager has an Ownership Interest) in the event that the Manager is removed for cause pursuant to this Section 5.10. For example, if the manager commits fraud, the Company will presumably wish it has an option to buy out any Membership Interest owned by the offending Member].**

5.11 Vacancies. Any vacancy occurring for any reason in the number of Managers of the Company shall be filled by the affirmative vote of Members holding a Majority Interest (determined without regard to any Voting Interest owned by a Manager who was removed pursuant to Section 5.10 during the preceding 24–month period). Any Manager's position to be filled by reason of an increase in the number of Managers shall be filled by the affirmative vote of a Majority Interest.

5.12 [Compensation, Reimbursement, Organization Expenses.]

(a) [The compensation of the Managers shall be fixed from time to time by an affirmative vote of Members holding at least a Majority Interest, and no Manager shall be prevented from receiv-

ing such compensation by reason of the fact that he is also a Member of the Company.] [No Member shall be entitled to compensation from the Company for services rendered to the Company as such. Upon the submission of appropriate documentation each Member shall be reimbursed by the Company for reasonable out-of-pocket expenses incurred on behalf, or at the request of, the Company.]

(b) [The Company shall reimburse _____ and _____ for the legal expenses reasonably incurred by them in connection with the formation, organization and capitalization of the Company, including the legal fees incurred in connection with negotiating and drafting this Agreement and _____.]

(c) The Manager shall cause the Company to make an appropriate election to treat the expenses incurred by the Company in connection with the formation and organization of the Company to be amortized under the 60-month period beginning with the month in which the Company begins business to the extent that such expenses constitute "organizational expenses" of the Company within the meaning of Code Section 709(b)(2).

5.13 [Annual Operating Plan.] [The Members have approved the Company's construction budget. The Manager shall prepare for the approval of the Members each Fiscal Year (no later than thirty (30) days prior to the end of the then current Fiscal Year) a business plan ("Annual Operating Plan") for the next Fiscal Year, setting forth at a minimum the estimated receipts (including capital calls) and expenditures (capital, operating and other) of the Company in sufficient detail to provide an estimate of cash flow, capital proceeds and other financial requirements of the Company for such year. Any such Annual Operating Plan shall also include such other information or other matters necessary in order to inform the Members of the Company's business and to enable the Members to make an informed decision with respect to their approval of such Annual Operating Plan. The Members shall review the proposed Operating Plan and shall offer any revisions thereto within [30] days. After the final Operating Plan has been approved by the Members, the Manager shall implement the Annual Operating Plan and shall be authorized to make only the expenditures and incur only the obligations provided for therein (subject to Section 5.4(b)). Notwithstanding the foregoing, the Manager may make any expenditure or incur any obligation, whether or not such expenditure or obligation is provided for in an Annual Operating Plan, which is the legal obligation of the Company and not within the reasonable control of the Manager (e.g., real or personal property taxes). If the Members are not able to agree on an Annual Operating Plan for any year, each line item in the Annual Operating Plan for the prior year shall be increased by the percentage increase in the CPI Index from the first day for which the previous Annual Operating Plan was in effect to the first day for which the new Annual Operating Plan is to be in effect. As used herein, "CPI Index" shall mean the Consumer Price Index for All Items All Urban Consumers (DPI–U) (1982–84 = 100) for the United States, as published by the United States

Department of Labor's Bureau of Labor Statistics (the "Bureau"). Should the Bureau discontinue the publication of the above index, or publish the index less frequently, or alter the index in some other manner, then the Manager shall, from time to time, adopt a substitute index or substitute procedure which reasonably reflects and monitors consumer prices. and the resulting plan shall be the Annual Operating Plan for the current year]

[THIS PROVISION (I.E., THE OPERATING BUDGET) WILL NEED TO BE CONFORMED WITH SECTION 5.3 AND 5.4.]

5.14 <u>Right to Rely on the Manager(s)</u>. Any Person dealing with the Company may rely (without duty of further inquiry) upon a certificate signed by any Manager as to:

(a) The identity of any Manager or Equity Owner;

(b) The existence or nonexistence of any fact or facts which constitute a condition precedent to acts on behalf of the Company by any Manager or which are in any other manner germane to the affairs of the Company;

(c) The Persons who are authorized to execute and deliver any instrument or document of the Company; or

(d) Any act or failure to act by the Company or any other matter whatsoever involving the Company or any Equity Owner.

ARTICLE 6

RIGHTS AND OBLIGATIONS OF EQUITY OWNERS

6.1 <u>Limitation of Liability</u>. Except as provided by the non-waivable provisions of the Act and by this Agreement no Equity Owner shall be liable for an obligation of the Company solely by reason of being or acting as an Equity Owner.

6.2 <u>List of Equity Owners</u>. Upon written request of any Member, the Manager shall provide a list showing the names, addresses and Ownership Interests of all Equity Owners.

6.3 <u>Members Have No Agency Authority</u>. Except as expressly provided in this Agreement, the Members (in their capacity as Members) shall have no agency authority on behalf of the Company.

6.4 <u>Company Books</u>. In accordance with Section 9.9 herein, the Managers shall maintain and preserve, during the term of the Company, and for five (5) years **[thereafter] [after dissolution]**, all accounts, books, and other relevant Company documents. Upon reasonable request, each Member shall have the right, during ordinary business hours, to inspect and copy such Company documents at the requesting Member's expense.

6.5 <u>Priority and Return of Capital</u>. Except as may be expressly provided in Article 9, no Equity Owner shall have priority over any other Equity Owner, either as to the return of Capital Contributions or as to Profits, Losses or distributions; provided that this Section [6.5] shall not

549

apply to loans (as distinguished from Capital Contributions) which an Equity Owner has made to the Company.

ARTICLE 7

MEETINGS OF MEMBERS

[NOTE: *IN MOST STATES FORMAL MEMBERS MEETINGS ARE OPTIONAL*]

7.1 [No Required Meetings]. The Members may but shall not be required to hold any annual, periodic or other formal meetings. However, meetings of the Members, may be called by any Manager, **[who is also a Member,]** or by any Member or Members holding at least 10% of the Voting Interests.

7.2 Place of Meetings. The Member or Members calling the meeting may designate any place within the State of [   ] as the place of meeting for any meeting of the Members; and Members holding a Two–Thirds Interest may designate any place outside the State of _____ as the place of meeting for any meeting of the Members. If no designation is made, or if a special meeting be otherwise called, the place of meeting shall be the principal executive office of the Company in the State of [   ].

7.3 Notice of Meetings. Except as provided in Section [7.4], written notice stating the place, day and hour of the meeting and the purpose or purposes for which the meeting is called shall be delivered not less than ten nor more than fifty days before the date of the meeting, either personally or by mail, by or at the direction of the Member or Members calling the meeting, to each Member entitled to vote at such meeting.

7.4 Meeting of all Members. If all of the Members shall meet at any time and place, either within or outside of the State of [   ], and consent to the holding of a meeting at such time and place, such meeting shall be valid without call or notice, and at such meeting lawful action may be taken.

7.5 Record Date. For the purpose of determining Members entitled to notice of or to vote at any meeting of Members or any adjournment thereof, or Members entitled to receive payment of any distribution, or in order to make a determination of Members for any other purpose, the date on which notice of the meeting is mailed or the date on which the resolution declaring such distribution is adopted, as the case may be, shall be the record date for such determination of Members. When a determination of Members entitled to vote at any meeting of Members has been made as provided in this Section [7.5], such determination shall apply to any adjournment thereof.

7.6 Quorum. Members holding at least a Two–Thirds Interest, represented in person or by proxy, shall constitute a quorum at any meeting of Members. In the absence of a quorum at any such meeting, a majority of the Voting Interests so represented may adjourn the meeting from time to time for a period not to exceed 60 days without further notice. However, if the adjournment is for more than 60 days, or if after the adjournment a new record date is fixed for the adjourned meeting, a notice of the adjourned meeting shall be given to each Member of record entitled to vote at the meeting. At such adjourned meeting at which a quorum shall be present or represented, any business may be transacted which might have been transacted at the meeting as originally noticed. The Members present at a duly organized meeting may continue to transact business until adjournment, notwithstanding the withdrawal during such meeting of that number of Voting Interests whose absence would cause less than a quorum.

7.7 <u>Manner of Acting</u>. If a quorum is present, the affirmative vote of Members holding a Majority Interest shall be the act of the Members, unless the vote of a greater or lesser proportion or number is otherwise required by the Act, by the Articles of Organization, or by this Agreement. Unless otherwise expressly provided herein, Members who have an interest (economic or otherwise) in the outcome of any particular matter upon which the Members vote or consent may vote or consent upon any such matter and their Voting Interest, vote or consent, as the case may be, shall be counted in the determination of whether the requisite matter is approved by the Members.

7.8 <u>Proxies</u>. At all meetings of Members a Member who is qualified to vote may vote in person or by proxy executed in writing by the Member or by a duly authorized attorney-in-fact. Such proxy shall be filed with the Managers of the Company before or at the time of the meeting. No proxy shall be valid after eleven months from the date of its execution, unless otherwise provided in the proxy.

7.9 <u>Action by Members Without a Meeting</u>. Action required or permitted to be taken at a meeting of Members may be taken without a meeting if the action is evidenced by one or more written consents or approvals describing the action taken and signed by Members holding sufficient Voting Interests, as the case may be, to approve such action had such action been properly voted on at a duly called meeting of the Members. Action taken under this Section 7.10 is effective when Members with the requisite Interests or Voting Interests, as the case may be, have signed the consent or approval, unless the consent specifies a different effective date. The record date for determining Members entitled to take action without a meeting shall be the date the first Member signs a written consent.

7.10 <u>Waiver of Notice</u>. When any notice is required to be given to any Member, a waiver thereof in writing signed by the person entitled to such notice, whether before, at, or after the time stated therein, shall be equivalent to the giving of such notice.

ARTICLE 8

CONTRIBUTIONS TO THE COMPANY
AND CAPITAL ACCOUNTS

8.1 <u>Members' Capital Contributions</u>. Not later than _____, each Equity Owner shall contribute such amount as is set forth in Exhibit 8.1 hereto as its share of the Initial Capital Contribution.

8.2 <u>Additional Contributions</u>. [Each Equity Owner shall be required to make such additional Capital Contributions as shall be determined by the Manager from time to time to be necessary to meet the expenses of the Company, provided, however, that the maximum amount which an Equity Owner shall be required to contribute to the Company pursuant to this Section 8.2 (i.e., in addition to the amount contributed by such Equity Owner pursuant to Section 8.1) shall not exceed the amount set forth corresponding to such Equity Owner's name on Exhibit 8.2. Upon the making of any such determination, the Manager shall give written notice to each Equity Owner of the amount of required additional contribution, and each Equity Owner shall deliver to the Company its pro rata share thereof (in proportion to **[Sharing Ratios/other?]** of the Member on the date such notice is given) no later than 30 days following the date such notice is given. None of the terms, covenants, obligations or rights contained in this Section 8.2 is or shall be deemed to be for the benefit of any Person other than the Equity Owners and the Company, and no such third person shall under any circumstances have any right to compel any actions or payments by the Manager and/or the Equity Owners.]

OR

[Except as set forth in Section 8.1, no Equity Owner shall be required to make any Capital Contributions. To the extent unanimously approved by the Managers, from time to time, the Equity Owners may be permitted to make additional Capital Contributions if and to the extent they so desire, and if the Managers determine that such additional Capital Contributions are necessary or appropriate in connection with the conduct of the Company's business (including without limitation, expansion or diversification). In such event, the Equity Owners shall have the opportunity (but not the obligation) to participate in such additional Capital Contributions proportionate to **[their Sharing Ratios].**

8.3 <u>Capital Accounts</u>. (a) A separate Capital Account will be maintained for each Equity Owner. Each Equity Owner's Capital Account will be increased by (1) the amount of money contributed by such Equity Owner to the Company; (2) the fair market value of property contributed by such Equity Owner to the Company (net of liabilities secured by such contributed property that the Company is considered to assume or take subject to under Section 752 of the Code); (3) allocations to such Equity Owner of Profits; (4) any items in the nature of income and gain which are specially allocated to the Equity Owner pursuant to Sections 9.2 and 9.3; and (5) allocations to such Equity Owner of income described in Section 705(a)(1)(B) of the Code. Each Equity Owner's Capital Account will be decreased by (1) the amount of money distributed to such Equity Owner by the Company; (2) the fair market value of property distributed to such Equity Owner by the Company (net of liabilities secured by such distributed property that such Equity Owner is considered to assume or take subject to under Section 752 of the Code); (3) allocations to such Equity Owner of expenditures described in Section 705(a)(2)(B) of the Code; (4) any items in the nature of deduction and loss that are specially allocated to the Equity

Owner pursuant to Sections 9.2 and 9.3 and (5) allocations to such Equity Owner of Losses.

(b) In the event of a permitted sale or exchange of [an] Ownership Interest in the Company, the Capital Account of the transferor shall become the Capital Account of the transferee to the extent it relates to the transferred Ownership Interest in accordance with Section 1.704–1(b)(2)(iv) of the Treasury Regulations.

(c) The manner in which Capital Accounts are to be maintained pursuant to this Section 8.3 is intended to comply with the requirements of Section 704(b) of the Code and the Treasury Regulations promulgated thereunder. If in the opinion of the Company's accountants the manner in which Capital Accounts are to be maintained pursuant to the preceding provisions of this Section 8.3 should be modified in order to comply with Section 704(b) of the Code and the Treasury Regulations thereunder, then notwithstanding anything to the contrary contained in the preceding provisions of this Section 8.3, the method in which Capital Accounts are maintained shall be so modified; provided, however, that any change in the manner of maintaining Capital Accounts shall not materially alter the economic agreement between or among the Equity Owners.

(d) Upon liquidation of the Company, liquidating distributions will be made in accordance with the positive Capital Account balances of the Equity Owners, as determined after taking into account all Capital Account adjustments for the Company's taxable year during which the liquidation occurs. Liquidation proceeds will be paid in accordance with Section 12.3. The Company may offset damages for breach of this Agreement by an Equity Owner whose interest is liquidated (either upon the withdrawal of the Equity Owner or the liquidation of the Company) against the amount otherwise distributable to such Equity Owner. **[Subject to Section 8.1 and 8.2)],** no Equity Owner shall have any liability to restore all or any portion of a deficit balance in such Equity Owner's Capital Account.

8.4 Withdrawal or Reduction of Equity Owners' Contributions to Capital. [An] Equity Owner shall not receive out of the Company's property any part of its Capital Contribution until all liabilities of the Company, except liabilities to Equity Owners on account of their Capital Contributions, have been paid or there remains property of the Company sufficient to pay them

[An Equity Owner, irrespective of the nature of its Capital Contribution, has only the right to demand and receive cash in return for its Capital Contribution.].

8.5 Remedies for Non–Payment of Additional Capital Contributions. (a) Failure of any Equity Owner to make full and timely payment to the Company of any additional Capital Contribution properly assessed hereunder shall constitute a breach of this Agreement (and any such Equity Owner shall be hereinafter referred to as a "Defaulting Equity Owner"). Upon such a breach, the Managers shall promptly give notice (the "Default Notice") to all Equity Owners of: (a) the breach and (b) a Special Meeting to discuss the appropriate course of action. The Equity Owners who timely satisfied their obligation to make the required Additional Capital Contributions (the "Non–Defaulting Equity Owners") may, upon the affirmative vote of Non–Defaulting Equity Owners which are Members holding a majority of the Voting Interests owned by all Non–Defaulting Equity Owners which are Members pursue the following courses of action:

The Non–Defaulting Equity Owners, shall have an option, but no obligation, to loan to the Company within 60 days after the Default Notice is given (the "Loan Decision Period") the amount which the Defaulting Equity Owners have failed to contribute to the Company (proportionate to the ratio of the interest in Profits held by each respective Equity Owner electing to loan funds, divided by the interest in Profits Interests held by all Equity Owners electing to advance funds). The amount that is loaned by any Non–Defaulting Equity Owner shall, at the election of each such Equity Owner (exercised by written notice to the Defaulting Equity Owner and the Company at the time the loan is made), be treated in either of the following manners:

(1) The loan may be treated as a loan to the Company, bearing interest at a floating rate equal to five percentage points higher than the prime commercial lending rate in effect from time to time at the principal bank used by the Company for banking and borrowing purposes (the "default rate"), payable out of any funds paid by, or withheld by the Company from, the Defaulting Equity Owner to cure the breach, or at such other time as the Company and the lending Equity Owner(s) may agree. Payments shall be credited first to accrued interest. The promissory note or other loan documentation shall contain such other terms and conditions as mutually agreed by the Company and the lending Equity Owner(s).

(2) The loan may be treated as a loan to the Defaulting Equity Owner, followed by a contribution of the borrowed funds to the Company by the Defaulting Equity Owner curing the breach in whole or in part. Such a loan shall be payable on demand and bear interest at the default rate provided above. Until the Defaulting Equity Owner's debt to any Non–Defaulting Equity Owners, together with interest thereon, is paid in full, any funds or property which would otherwise be distributed to the Defaulting Equity Owner from time to time hereunder shall be paid to such Non–Defaulting Equity Owners, according to their respective shares of loans (which are treated as loans to the Defaulting Equity Owner). Any such payments shall be deemed to be distributions to the Defaulting Equity Owner by the Company followed by appropriate payments by the Defaulting Equity Owner to the respective Non–Defaulting Equity Owners. Payments shall be credited first to accrued interest. Payments to Non–Defaulting Equity Owners of loans by them pursuant to either Section 8.5(a)(1) or 8.5(a)(2) shall be made *pari passu*.

(b) If the Non–Defaulting Equity Owners do not make loans pursuant to Section 8.5(a) in an amount at least equal to the amount which the Defaulting Equity Owner failed to contribute (and the Defaulting Equity

Owner has not cured said breach prior to the expiration of the Loan Decision Period), then promptly upon the expiration of the Loan Decision Period, the Managers shall give notice (the "Default Purchase Option Notice" as more fully described below) to all of the Equity Owners. The Non–Defaulting Equity Owners shall have the option (but no obligation) for the 60–day period commencing upon date of the Default Purchase Option Notice to purchase all, but not less than all, of a Defaulting Equity Owner's Interest as provided in this Section 8.5(b). The option granted in this Section 8.5(b) (the "Default Purchase Option") shall be exercisable in the following manner and in accordance with the following terms:

(1) The Default Purchase Option Notice shall notify the Non-Defaulting Equity Owners that they have the opportunity to purchase all, but not less than all, of the Ownership Interest owned by the Defaulting Equity Owner ("Available Ownership Interest").

(2) A Non–Defaulting Equity Owner wishing to exercise the De-fault Purchase Option shall so notify (the "Exercise Notice") the Defaulting Equity Owner and the Company within 45 days after the date that the Default Purchase Option Notice is given.

(3) Each Non–Defaulting Equity Owner electing to exercise the Default Purchase Option (each an "Electing Equity Owner" and collec-tively the "Electing Equity Owners") shall be entitled to purchase a portion of the Available Ownership Interest proportionate to **[their Sharing Ratios]**.

(c) The closing for any purchase and sale of the Available Owner-ship Interest pursuant to Section 8.5(b) shall take place within 90 days after the date that the Default Purchase Option Notice is given. The specific time and place of closing shall be as agreed by the Electing Equity Owners and the Defaulting Member, provided that in the absence of agreement the closing shall take place at the Company's principal office.

(d) The price for the Defaulting Equity Owner's Ownership Inter-est (the "Default Buyout Price") shall be equal to **[fifty percent]** of the Defaulting Equity Owner's Capital Account balance as of the last day of the month preceding the month in which the Exercise Notice is given. For purposes of this Section [8.5(d)], the Company's indepen-dent certified public accountant shall determine the balance in the Defaulting Equity Owner's Capital Account (without regard to any optional adjustments which may, but are not required, to be made for any purpose, including any optional adjustments that may be made in order to reflect the fair market value of the Company's property), and such determination shall be final for purposes of this Agreement.

Upon any purchase of a Defaulting Equity Owner's Ownership Interest pursuant to this Section 8.5(b), the Default Buyout Price may be paid at closing in immediately available funds, or, in the sole discretion of each Electing Equity Owner, by delivering at closing a note issued by the Electing Member(s) as payment for the portion of

555

the Buyout Price attributable to the portion of the Ownership Interest to be purchased by the Electing Equity Owner. The note(s) issued as payment ... of the Default Buyout Price shall be negotiable promissory note(s) of the Company or of each of the Electing Equity Owner, as appropriate, bearing interest per annum at a floating rate one percentage point over the prime commercial lending rate in effect from time to time at the First Interstate Bank of Denver, N.A. or any successor thereof. Any such note(s) shall provide for payments of principal and interest in equal consecutive monthly installments over a period of not more than five years from the date of issuance of such note, commencing from the date of issuance of such note. Any such note(s) shall be prepayable without penalty, in whole or in part, with prepayments applied to the last installment or installments coming due. Such note(s) shall provide that if any installment of principal or interest is not paid when due or if suit is brought thereon, the maker will pay all costs of collection, including reasonable attorneys' fees.

After purchasing an Available Ownership Interest, each Electing Equity Owner shall make an additional Capital Contribution to the Company in an amount equal to the proportionate share of the Defaulted Capital Contribution attributable to the portion of the Available Ownership Interest purchased by the Electing Equity Owner.

ARTICLE 9

ALLOCATIONS, INCOME TAX, DISTRIBUTIONS, ELECTIONS AND REPORTS

9.1 Allocations of Profits and Losses from Operations. Except as provided in Sections 9.2 and 9.3, the Profits and Losses of the Company for each Fiscal Year will be allocated as follows:

[(a) **Losses shall be allocated among the Equity Owners in accordance with their relative Sharing Ratios.**

(b) **Profits shall be allocated as follows:**

(i) **First, to each Equity Owner which previously has been allocated Losses pursuant to Section 9.1(a) which have not been fully offset by allocations of Income pursuant to this Section 9.1(b)(i) ("Unrecovered Losses") until the total amount of Profits allocated to each such Equity Owner pursuant to this Section 9.1 (b)(i) is equal to the total amount of Losses which have been allocated to such Equity Owner pursuant to Section 9.1(a). Profits allocated pursuant to this Section 9.1(b)(i) shall be allocated to the Equity Owners in proportion to their respective Unrecovered Losses;**

(ii) **Second, to each Equity Owner an amount equal to the total amount distributed to such Equity Owner pursuant to Section 9.4(b) proportionate with the total amount** distributed to the Equity Owners pursuant to Section 9.4(b) [CAVEAT: THIS SECTION 9.1(b) SHOULD BE USED WHEN SECTION 9.4(b) IS USED];

(iii) Third, to the Equity Owners in proportion to their Sharing Ratios.]

9.2 <u>Special Allocations to Capital Accounts</u>. Notwithstanding Section 9.1 hereof:

(a) In the event any Equity Owner unexpectedly receives any adjustments, allocations, or distributions described in Sections 1.704–1(b)(2)(ii)(d)(4), (5), or (6) of the Treasury Regulations, which create or increase a Deficit Capital Account of such Equity Owner, then items of Company income and gain (consisting of a pro rata portion of each item of Company income, including gross income, and gain for such year and, if necessary, for subsequent years) shall be specially allocated to such Equity Owner in an amount and manner sufficient to eliminate, to the extent required by the Treasury Regulations, the Deficit Capital Account so created as quickly as possible. It is the intent that this Section 9.2(a) be interpreted to comply with the alternate test for economic effect set forth in Section 1.704–1(b)(2)(ii)(d) of the Treasury Regulations.

(b) The Losses allocated pursuant to Section 9.1 hereof shall not exceed the maximum amount of Losses that can be so allocated without causing any Member to have a Deficit Capital Account at the end of any Fiscal Year. In the event some but not all of the Members would have [a] Deficit Capital Account as a consequence of an allocation of Losses pursuant to Section 9.1 hereof, the limitation set forth in the preceding sentence shall be applied on a Member by Member basis so as to allocate the maximum permissible Losses to each Member under Section 1.704–1(b)(2)(ii)(d) of the Treasury Regulations. All Losses in excess of the limitation set forth in this Section 9.2(b) shall be allocated to the Members in proportion to their respective positive Capital Account balances, if any, and thereafter to the Members in accordance with their interests in the Company as determined by the Managers in their reasonable discretion. In the event any Equity Owner would have a Deficit Capital Account at the end of any Company taxable year which is in excess of the sum of any amount that such Equity Owner is obligated to restore to the Company under Section 1.704–1(b)(2)(ii)(c) of the Treasury Regulations and such Equity Owner's share of minimum gain as defined in Section 1.704–2(g)(1) of the Treasury Regulations (which is also treated as an obligation to restore in accordance with Section 1.704–1(b)(2)(ii)(d) of the Treasury Regulations), the Capital Account of such Equity Owner shall be specially credited with items of Company income (including gross income) and gain in the amount of such excess as quickly as possible.

(c) Notwithstanding any other provision of this Section 9.2, if there is a net decrease in the Company's minimum gain as defined in Treasury Regulation Section 1.704–2(d) during a taxable year of the Company, then . . . the Capital Accounts of each Equity Owner shall be allocated items of income (including gross income) and gain for such year (and if necessary

557

for subsequent years) equal to that Equity Owner's share of the net decrease in Company minimum gain. This Section 9.2(c) is intended to comply with the minimum gain chargeback requirement of Section 1.704–2 of the Treasury Regulations and shall be interpreted consistently therewith. If in any taxable year that the Company has a net decrease in the Company's minimum gain, if the minimum gain chargeback requirement would cause a distortion in the economic arrangement among the Equity Owners and it is not expected that the Company will have sufficient other income to correct that distortion, the Managers may in their discretion (and shall, if requested to do so by a Member) seek to have the Internal Revenue Service waive the minimum gain chargeback requirement in accordance with Treasury Regulation Section 1.704–2(f)(4).

(d) Notwithstanding any other provision of this Section 9.2 except Section 9.2(c), if there is a net decrease in Member Nonrecourse Debt Minimum Gain attributable to a Member Nonrecourse Debt during any Company Fiscal Year, each Member who has a share of the Member Nonrecourse Debt Minimum Gain attributable to such Member Nonrecourse Debt (determined in accordance with Regulation § 1.704–2(i)(5)) as of the beginning of the year shall be specially allocated items of Company income and gain for such year (and, if necessary, subsequent years) equal to such Member's share of the net decrease in Member Nonrecourse Debt Minimum Gain attributable to such Member Nonrecourse Debt. A Member's share of the net decrease in Member Nonrecourse Debt Minimum Gain shall be determined in accordance with Regulation § 1.704–2(i)(4); provided that a Member shall not be subject to this provision to the extent that an exception is provided by Regulation § 1.704–2(i)(4) and any Revenue Rulings issued with respect thereto. Any Member Nonrecourse Debt Minimum Gain allocated pursuant to this provision shall consist of first, gains recognized from the disposition of Company property subject to the Member Nonrecourse Debt, and, second, if necessary, a pro rata portion of the Company's other items of income or gain for that year. This Section 9.2(d) is intended to comply with the minimum gain chargeback requirement in Regulation § 1.704–2(i)(4) and shall be interpreted consistently therewith.

(e) Items of Company loss, deduction and expenditures described in Section 705(a)(2)(B) which are attributable to any nonrecourse debt of the Company and are characterized as partner (Member) nonrecourse deductions under Section 1.704–2(i) of the Treasury Regulations shall be allocated to the Equity Owners' Capital Accounts in accordance with said Section 1.704–2(i) of the Treasury Regulations.

(f) Beginning in the first taxable year in which there are allocations of "nonrecourse deductions" (as described in Section 1.704–2(b) of the Treasury Regulations), such deductions shall be allocated to the Equity Owners in the same manner as Loss is allocated for such period.

(g) To the extent an adjustment to the adjusted tax basis of any Company asset pursuant to Section 734(b) of the Code or Section 743(b) of the Code is required pursuant to Section 1.704–1(b)(2)(iv)(m)(2) of the

Treasury Regulations or Section 1.704–1(b)(2)(iv)(m)(4) of the Treasury Regulations to be taken into account in determining Capital Accounts as the result of a distribution to a Equity Owner in complete liquidation of its Ownership Interest, the amount of such adjustment to Capital Accounts shall be treated as an item of gain (if the adjustment increases the basis of the asset) or loss (if the adjustment decreases such basis) and such gain or loss shall be specially allocated to the Equity Owners in accordance with their interests in the Company in the event Section 1.704–1(b)(2)(iv)(m)(2) of the Treasury Regulations applies, or to the Equity Owner to whom such distribution was made in the event Section 1.704–1(b)(2)(iv)(m)(4) of the Treasury Regulations applies.

(h) Any income, gain, loss or deduction realized by the Company as a direct or indirect result of the issuance of an interest in the Company by the Company to an Equity Owner (the "Issuance Items") shall be allocated among the Equity Owners so that, to the extent possible, the net amount of such Issuance Items, together with all other allocations under this Agreement to each Equity Owner shall be equal to the net amount that would have been allocated to each such Equity Owner if the Issuance Items had not been realized.

(i) Any credit or charge to the Capital Accounts of the Equity Owners pursuant to Sections 9.2(a), 9.2(b), 9.2(c), 9.2(d), 9.2(e), 9.2(f) and (g) hereof shall be taken into account in computing subsequent allocations of Profits and Losses pursuant to Section 9.1, so that the net amount of any items charged or credited to Capital Accounts pursuant to Sections 9.1 and 9.2(a), 9.2(b), 9.2(c), 9.2(d), 9.2(e) 9.2(f) and 9.2(g) hereof and this Section 9.3 shall to the extent possible, be equal to the net amount that would have been allocated to the Capital Account of each Equity Owner pursuant to the provisions of this Article 9 if the special allocations required by Sections 9.2(a), 9.2(b), 9.2(c), 9.2(d), 9.2(e), 9.2(f) and 9.2(g) hereof had not occurred.

9.4 Distributions. Except as provided in Section 8.3(d), The Managers shall distribute Distributable Cash to the Equity Owners **[not less frequently than quarterly]** as follows:

(a) Alternative 1/For illustrative purposes only: [First, to the Equity Owners in accordance with their [Sharing Ratios]. All distributions which, when made, exceed the recipient Equity Owner's basis in that Equity Owner's Ownership Interest shall be considered advances or drawings against the Equity Owner's distributive share of Income. To the extent it is determined at the end of the Fiscal Year that the recipient Equity Owner has not been allocated Income that equals or exceeds the total of such advances or drawings for such year, such Equity Owner shall be obligated to recontribute any such advances or drawings to the Company. Notwithstanding the foregoing sentence, an Equity Owner will not be required to recontribute such advances or drawings to the extent that, on the last day of the Fiscal Year, such Equity Owner's basis in its Ownership Interest in the Company has increased from the time of such advance or drawing.]

559

[Alternative 2/for illustrative purposes only:

(a) First, to the Equity Owners in proportion to their Sharing Ratios no later than 10 days prior to the dates that federal estimated quarterly taxes are due for individuals an amount equal to positive remainder, if any, of: (x) the product of [40%] multiplied times the estimated Income allocable to such Equity Owner for the portion of the year ending on the last day of the most recent quarter, minus (y) the sum of all distributions made to the respective Equity Owners pursuant to this Section 9.4 (a) with respect to such Fiscal Year, plus the 40% of any Unrecovered Losses attributable to such Equity Owner as of the first day of the current Fiscal Year.

(b) Second, to the Equity Owners until they have received aggregate distributions under this Section 9.4(b) equal to the mathematical equivalent of interest at the rate of ten percent simple interest per annum on the balance from time to time of their respective Adjusted Capital Contributions.

(c) Third, to the Equity Owners proportionate with their Adjusted Capital Contributions until the amount of their respective Adjusted Capital Contributions equals zero.

(d) Fourth, to the Equity Owners in accordance with their Sharing Ratios.

All distributions which, when made, exceed the recipient Equity Owner's basis in that Equity Owner's Ownership Interest shall be considered advances or drawings against the Equity Owner's distributive share of Income. To the extent it is determined at the end of the Fiscal Year that the recipient Equity Owner has not been allocated Income that equals or exceeds the total of such advances or drawings for such year, such Equity Owner shall be obligated to recontribute any such advances or drawings to the Company. Notwithstanding the foregoing sentence, an Equity Owner will not be required to recontribute such advances or drawings to the extent that, on the last day of the Fiscal Year, such Equity Owner's basis in its Ownership Interest in the Company has increased from the time of such advance or drawing.]

CAVEAT: THE FOREGOING ARRANGEMENT WOULD NEED TO BE CAREFULLY EVALUATED (IN LIGHT OF THE PARTICULAR FACTS OF THE TRANSACTION) UNDER THE DISGUISED SALE RULES. (I.R.C. Section 707(a)(2)(B) and Treas. Reg. Section 1.707–4 and 1.707–5.

9.5 <u>Limitation Upon Distributions</u>. No distribution shall be declared and paid unless, after the distribution is made, the assets of the Company are in excess of all liabilities of the Company, except liabilities to Equity Owners on account of their contributions.

9.6 <u>Accounting Principles</u>. The profits and losses of the Company shall be determined in accordance with accounting principles applied on a consistent basis using the accrual **[CAVEAT: IN MOST CASES THE ACCRUAL METHOD IS REQUIRED]** method of accounting. It is intended that the Company will elect those accounting methods which provide the Company with the greatest tax benefits.

9.7 <u>Interest On and Return of Capital Contributions</u>. No Member shall be entitled to interest on its Capital Contribution or to return of its Capital Contribution, except as otherwise specifically provided for herein.

9.8 <u>Loans to Company</u>. Nothing in this Agreement shall prevent any Member from making secured or unsecured loans to the Company by agreement with the Company.

9.9 <u>Accounting Period</u>. The Company's accounting period shall be the calendar year.

9.10 <u>Records and Reports</u>. At the expense of the Company, the Manager shall maintain records and accounts of all operations and expenditures of the Company. At a minimum the Company shall keep at its principal place of business the following records:

(a) A current list of the full name and last known business, residence, or mailing address of each Equity Owner and Manager, both past and present;

(b) A copy of the Articles of Organization of the Company and all amendments thereto, together with executed copies of any powers of attorney pursuant to which any amendment has been executed;

(c) Copies of the Company's federal, state, and local income tax returns and reports, if any, for the four most recent years;

(d) Copies of the Company's currently effective written Agreement, copies of any writings permitted or required with respect to [an] Equity Owner's obligation to contribute cash, property or services, and copies of any financial statements of the Company for the three most recent years;

(e) Minutes of every annual, special ... and court-ordered meeting;

(f) Any written consents obtained from Members for actions taken by Members without a meeting.

9.11 <u>Returns and other Elections</u>. (a) The Manager shall cause the preparation and timely filing of all tax returns required to be filed by the Company pursuant to the Code and all other tax returns deemed necessary and required in each jurisdiction in which the Company does business. Copies of such returns, or pertinent information therefrom, shall be furnished to the Equity Owners within a reasonable time after the end of the Company's Fiscal Year.

(b) All elections permitted to be made by the Company under federal or state laws shall be made by the Manager in his sole discretion, provided that the Manager shall make any tax election requested by Members owning a Majority Interest.

9.12 <u>Tax Matters Partner</u>. The Manager, so long as the Manager is also a Member, is hereby designated the Tax Matters Partner ("TMP") as defined in Section 6231(a)(7) of the Code. The TMP and the other Members shall use their reasonable efforts to comply with the responsibilities outlined in Sections 6221 through 6233 of the Code (including any Treasury Regulations promulgated thereunder), and in doing so shall incur no liability to any other Member.

9.13 <u>Certain Allocations for Income Tax (But Not Book Capital Account) Purposes</u>. (a) In accordance with Section 704(c)(1)(A) of the Code and Section 1.704–1(b)(2)(i)(iv) of the Treasury Regulations, if a Member contributes property with [an] initial Gross Asset Value that differs from its adjusted basis at the time of contribution, income, gain, loss and deductions with respect to the property shall, solely for federal income tax purposes (and not for Capital Account purposes), be allocated among the Equity Owners so as to take account of any variation between the adjusted basis of such property to the Company and its Gross Asset Value at the time of contribution pursuant to the **[traditional method under Regulation Section 1.704–3(b)///// traditional method with curative allocations pursuant to Regulation Section 1.704–3(c)///// remedial allocation method under Regulation Section 1.704–3(d)—PICK ONE OF THE PRECEDING AFTER EVALUATING EACH METHOD AND CONSULTING WITH THE CLIENT].**

(b) Pursuant to Section 704(c)(1)(B) of the Code, if any contributed property is distributed by the Company other than to the contributing Equity Owner within seven years of being contributed, then, except as provided in Section 704(c)(2) of the Code, the contributing Equity Owner shall, <u>solely for federal income tax purposes</u> (and not for Capital Account purposes), be treated as recognizing gain or loss from the sale of such property in an amount equal to the gain or loss that would have been allocated to such Equity Owner under Section 704(c)(1)(A) of the Code if the property had been sold at its fair market value at the time of the distribution.

(c) In the case of any distribution by the Company to a Equity Owner, such Equity Owner shall, <u>solely for federal income tax purposes</u> (and not for Capital Account purposes), be treated as recognizing gain in an amount equal to the lesser of:

(i) the excess (if any) of (A) the fair market value of the property (other than money) received in the distribution over (B) the adjusted basis of such Equity Owner's Ownership Interest immediately before the distribution reduced (but not below zero) by the amount of money received in the distribution, or

(ii) the Net Precontribution Gain (as defined in Section 737(b) of the Code) of the Equity Owner. The Net Precontribution Gain means the net gain (if any) which would have been recognized by the distributee Equity Owner under Section 704(c)(1)(B) of the Code if all property which (1) had been contributed to the Company within seven years of the distribution, and (2) is held by the Company immediately before the distribution, had been distributed by the Company to another Equity Owner. If any portion of the property distributed consists of property which had been contributed by the distributee Equity Owner to the Company, then such property shall not be taken into account under this Section 9.2(h) and shall not be taken into account in determining the amount of the Net Precontribution Gain. If the property distributed consists of an interest in an Entity, the preceding sentence shall not apply to the extent that the value of such interest is attributable to the property contributed to such Entity after such interest had been contributed to the Company.

(d) All recapture of income tax deductions resulting from sale or disposition of Company property shall be allocated to the Equity Owners to whom the deduction that gave rise to such recapture was allocated hereunder to the extent that such Equity Owner is allocated any gain from the sale or other disposition of such property.

ARTICLE 10

TRANSFERABILITY

10.1 <u>General</u>. Except as otherwise specifically provided herein no Equity Owner shall have the right to:

(a) sell, assign, transfer, exchange or otherwise transfer for consideration, (collectively, "sell" or "sale"),

(b) gift, bequeath or otherwise transfer for no consideration whether or not by operation of law, except in the case of bankruptcy (collectively "gift")

all or any part of its Ownership Interest. Each Equity Owner hereby acknowledges the reasonableness of the restrictions on sale and gift of Ownership Interests imposed by this Agreement in view of the Company purposes and the relationship of the Equity Owners. Accordingly, the restrictions on sale and gift contained herein shall be specifically enforceable. In the event that any Equity Owner pledges or otherwise encumbers any of its Ownership Interest as security for repayment of a liability, any such pledge or hypothecation shall be made pursuant to a pledge or hypothecation agreement that requires the pledgee or secured party to be bound by all the terms and conditions of this Article 10, and the pledging Equity Owner shall provide notice of such pledge or encumbrance to the Managers.

10.2 <u>Right of First Refusal</u>. (a) A Selling Equity Owner which desires to sell all or any portion of its Ownership Interest in the Company to a third party purchaser **[other than a Member/including a Member]** shall obtain from such third party purchaser a bona fide written offer to purchase such interest, stating the terms and conditions upon which the purchase is to be made and the consideration offered therefor. The Selling Equity Owner shall give written notification to the remaining Members, by certified mail or personal delivery, of its intention to so transfer such interest, furnishing to the remaining Members a copy of the aforesaid written offer to purchase such interest.

(b) The remaining Members, and each of them shall, on a basis pro rata to their Voting Interests or on a basis pro rata to the Voting Interests of those remaining Members exercising their right of first refusal, have the right to exercise a right of first refusal to purchase all (but not less than all) of the interest proposed to be sold by the Selling Equity Owner upon the same terms and conditions as stated in the aforesaid written offer to purchase by giving written notification to the Selling Equity Owner, by certified mail or personal delivery, of their intention to do so within ten (10) days after receiving written notice from the Selling Equity Owner. The failure of all the remaining Members (or any one or more of them) to so notify the Selling Equity Owner of their desire to exercise this right of first refusal within said ten (10) day period shall result in the termination of the right of first refusal and the Selling Equity Owner shall be entitled to consummate the sale of its interest in the Company, or such portion of its interest, if any, with respect to which the right of first refusal has not been exercised, to such third party purchaser.

(c) In the event the remaining Members (or any one or more of the remaining Members) give written notice to the Selling Equity Owner of their desire to exercise this right of first refusal and to purchase all of the Selling Equity Owner's interest in the Company which the Selling Equity Owner desires to sell upon the same terms and conditions as are stated in the aforesaid written offer to purchase, the remaining Members shall have the right to designate the time, date and place of closing, provided that the date of closing shall be within thirty (30) days after receipt of written notification from the Selling Equity Owner of the third party offer to purchase.

(d) In the event of either a sale or gift of a Ownership Interest by [an] Equity Owner to a Person who is not already [a] Member, and as a condition to recognizing one or more of the effectiveness and binding nature of any one or more such sales or gifts (subject to Section 10.3, below), the remaining Members may require the Transferring Equity Owner and the proposed successor-in-interest to execute, acknowledge and deliver to the Managers such instruments of transfer, assignment and assumption and such other certificates, representations and documents, and to perform all such other acts which the Managers may deem necessary or desirable to:

(i) constitute such successor-in-interest as an Equity Owner;

(ii) confirm that the proposed successor-in-interest as an Economic Interest Owner, or to be admitted as a Member, has accepted, assumed and agreed to be subject and bound by all of the terms, obligations and conditions of this Agreement, as the same may have been further amended (whether such Person is to be admitted as a new Member or will merely be an Economic Interest Owner);

(iii) preserve the Company after the completion of such sale, transfer, assignment, or substitution under the laws of each jurisdiction in which the Company is qualified, organized or does business;

(iv) maintain the status of the Company as a partnership for federal tax purposes; and

(v) assure compliance with any applicable state and federal laws including securities laws and regulations.

(e) Any sale or gift of an Ownership Interest and admission of a Member in compliance with this Article 10 shall be deemed effective as of the last day of the calendar month in which the remaining Members' consent thereto was given, or, if no such consent was required pursuant to Section 10.2(e), then on such date that the donee or successor in interest complies with Section 10.2(d). The Transferring Equity Owner hereby indemnifies the Company and the remaining Members against any and all loss, damage, or expense (including, without limitation, tax liabilities or loss of tax benefits) arising directly or indirectly as a result of any transfer or purported transfer in violation of this Article 10.

[(f) [Subject to Section 10.3, a Gifting Equity Owner may gift all or any portion of its Ownership Interest (without regard to Section 10.2(a) and 10.2(b)), provided, however, that the donee or other successor-in-interest (collectively, "donee") complies with Section 10.2(d) and further provided that the donee is either the Gifting Equity Owner's spouse, former spouse, or lineal descendent (including adopted children). In the event of the gift of all or any portion of a Gifting Equity Owner's Ownership Interest to one or more donees who are under 25 years of age, one or more trusts shall be established to hold the gifted interest(s) for the benefit of such donee(s) until all of the donee(s) reach the age of at least 25 years.]

10.3 <u>Transferee Not Member in Absence of Consent.</u> (a) Notwithstanding anything contained herein to the contrary (including, without limitation, Section 10.2 hereof), if all of the remaining Members do not approve by unanimous written consent the proposed sale of the Transferring Equity Owner's Ownership Interest to a transferee which is not a Member immediately prior to the sale, then the proposed transferee shall have no right to participate in the management of the business and affairs of the Company or to become a Member. Such transferee shall be merely an Economic Interest Owner. No transfer of a Member's Membership Interest (including any transfer of the Economic Interest or any other transfer which has not been approved as provided herein) shall be effective unless and until written notice (including the name and address of the proposed, transferee and the date of such transfer) has been provided to the Company and the non-transferring Member(s). **[Notwithstanding anything to the contrary herein, any gift by a Member which is permitted under Section 10.2(f) and made in accordance with Section 10.2(d) shall automatically constitute the transferee as a Member.]**

(b) Upon and contemporaneously with any sale or gift of a Member's Membership Interest the Transferring Equity Owner shall cease to have any residual rights associated with the Ownership Interest transferred to the transferee.

[CONSIDER WHETHER TO INCLUDE A SHOTGUN BUY–SELL PROVISION, ESPECIALLY IF ITS A TWO MEMBER LLC AND THE MEMBERS ARE DEALING AT ARM'S LENGTH. THE PURCHASE PRICE IN A SHOTGUN BUY–SELL WILL GENERALLY NEED TO BE DETERMINED WITH REFERENCE TO THE AMOUNT EACH MEMBER WOULD RECEIVE IF ALL OF THE COMPANY'S ASSETS WERE SOLD TO AN UNRELATED PARTY AND THE LLC WERE LIQUIDATED. THIS IS BECAUSE IN MOST LLC's THE MEMBER'S RELATIVE CAPITAL ACCOUNTS WILL NOT NECESSARILY BE EQUAL TO THEIR PERCENTAGE INTEREST IN PROFITS AND LOSSES.]

ARTICLE 11

ADDITIONAL MEMBERS

From the date of the formation of the Company, any Person acceptable to the **[same Member or Members entitled to consent to the admission of a transferee as a Member]** may become a Member in this Company either by the issuance by the Company of Membership Interests for such consideration as the Members by their unanimous votes shall determine, or as a transferee of a Member's Membership Interest or any portion thereof, subject to the terms and conditions of this Agreement. No new Members shall be entitled to any retroactive allocation of losses, income or expense deductions incurred by the Company. In accordance with the provisions of Section 706(d) of the Code and the Treasury Regulations promulgated thereunder, the Manager or Manager(s) may, at his or their option, at the time a Member is admitted, close the Company books (as though the Company's tax year had ended) or make pro rata allocations of loss, income and expense deductions to a new Equity Owner for that portion of the Company's tax year in which [an] Equity Owner became an Equity Owner.

ARTICLE 12

DISSOLUTION AND TERMINATION

12.1 <u>Dissolution</u>. (a) The Company shall be dissolved only upon the occurrence of any of the following events:

(i) by the **[unanimous written agreement of all Members]/[the agreement of Members holding a Two–Thirds Interest/CAVEAT: IN A FAMILY LLC CAREFULLY CONSIDER THE POTENTIAL IMPACT OF SECTION 2704(a)]**, or

(ii) [upon the expiration of the term, if any, specified in Section 2.5 of this Agreement].

Notwithstanding anything to the contrary in the Act the Company shall not be dissolved upon the death, retirement, resignation, expulsion, bankruptcy or dissolution of an Equity Owner

(b) As soon as possible following the occurrence of any of the events specified in ... Section 12.1(a) effecting the dissolution of the Company, the appropriate representative of the Company shall execute a statement of intent to dissolve in such form as shall be prescribed by the [   ] Secretary of State and file same with the [   ] Secretary of State's office.

[IF THE LLC IS NOT A COLORADO LLC, THE RESIGNATION OF A MEMBER MAY NEED TO BE SPECIFICALLY ADDRESSED. IN COLORADO, THE DEFAULT RULE UNDER THE COLORADO LLC ACT IS THAT THE A RESIGNING MEMBER HAS NO RIGHT TO DEMAND THE LIQUIDATION OF HIS INTEREST BY THE LLC AND THAT AFTER RESIGNING HE BECOMES A MERE ECONOMIC INTEREST OWNER.]

12.2 <u>Effect of Filing of Dissolving Statement</u>. Upon the filing by the [   ] Secretary of State of a statement of intent to dissolve, the Company shall cease to carry on its business, except insofar as may be necessary for the winding up of its business, but its separate existence shall continue until a certificate of dissolution has been issued by the Secretary of State or until a decree dissolving the Company has been entered by a court of competent jurisdiction.

12.3 <u>Winding Up, Liquidation and Distribution of Assets</u>. (a) Upon dissolution, an accounting shall be made by the Company's **[independent accountants][Managers]** of the accounts of the Company and of the Company's assets, liabilities and operations, from the date of the last previous accounting until the date of dissolution. The Manager(s) shall immediately proceed to wind up the affairs of the Company.

(b) If the Company is dissolved and its affairs are to be wound up, the Manager(s) shall:

(i) Sell or otherwise liquidate all of the Company's assets as promptly as practicable (except to the extent the Manager(s) may determine to distribute in kind any assets to the Equity Owners),

(ii) Allocate any Profit or Loss resulting from such sales to the Equity Owners' Capital Accounts in accordance with Article 9 hereof,

(iii) Discharge all liabilities of the Company, including liabilities to Equity Owners who are also creditors, to the extent otherwise permitted by law, other than liabilities to Equity Owners for distributions and the return of capital, and establish such Reserves as may be reasonably necessary to provide for contingent liabilities of the Company (for purposes of determining the Capital Accounts of the Equity

567

Owners, the amounts of such Reserves shall be deemed to be an expense of the Company),

(iv) Distribute the remaining assets in the following order:

(A) If any assets of the Company are to be distributed in kind, the net fair market value of such assets as of the date of dissolution shall be determined by independent appraisal or by agreement of the Members. Such assets shall be deemed to have been sold as of the date of dissolution for their fair market value, and the Capital Accounts of the Equity Owners shall be adjusted pursuant to the provisions of Article 9 and Section 8.3 of this Agreement to reflect such deemed sale.

(B) The positive balance (if any) of each Equity Owner's Capital Account (as determined after taking into account all Capital Account adjustments for the Company's taxable year during which the liquidation occurs) shall be distributed to the Equity Owners, either in cash or in kind, as determined by the Manager(s), with any assets distributed in kind being valued for this purpose at their fair market value. Any such distributions to the Equity Owners in respect of their Capital Accounts shall be made in accordance with the time requirements set forth in Section 1.704–1(b)(2)(ii)(b)(2) of the Treasury Regulations.

[IN THE CONTEXT OF THE PARTICULAR DEAL, THINK ABOUT THE POSSIBLE NEED FOR DISTRIBUTIONS OF CERTAIN LLC ASSETS TO CERTAIN MEMBERS. FOR EXAMPLE, IN STRATEGIC VENTURES, IT IS OFTEN IMPORTANT TO CAREFULLY ADDRESS THE EXIT STRATEGY [AND WHO GETS WHAT IF THE LLC DISSOLVES, AND IF SO EXACTLY WHAT HAPPENS] IN THE ORIGINAL OPERATING AGREEMENT, IN WHICH CASE, THE ABILITY OF ONE OF THE MEMBERS TO RECEIVE OR HAVE THE OPTION TO RECEIVE (OR BY DISTRIBUTION OR PURCHASE) SPECIFIED ASSETS MAY BE IMPORTANT. IT ALSO, MAY BE ADVISABLE FOR THE OPERATING AGREEMENT TO REQUIRE THE LLC OR MEMBERS WHO RECEIVE INTELLECTUAL PROPERTY ASSETS FROM THE LLC TO LICENSE THOSE ASSETS TO THE OTHER MEMBERS. ALSO, REMEMBER TO CONFORM THIS PROVISION TO 8.4]

(c) Notwithstanding anything to the contrary in this Agreement, upon a liquidation within the meaning of Section 1.704–1(b)(2)(ii)(g) of the Treasury Regulations, if any Equity Owner has a Deficit Capital Account (after giving effect to all contributions, distributions, allocations and other Capital Account adjustments for all taxable years, including the year during which such liquidation occurs), such Equity Owner shall have no obligation to make any Capital Contribution, and the negative balance of such Member's Capital Account shall not be considered a debt owed by such Equity Owner to the Company or to any other Person for any purpose whatsoever.

(d) Upon completion of the winding up, liquidation and distribution of the assets, the Company shall be deemed terminated.

(e) The Manager(s) shall comply with any applicable requirements of applicable law pertaining to the winding up of the affairs of the Company and the final distribution of its assets.

12.4 Articles of Dissolution. When all debts, liabilities and obligations have been paid and discharged or adequate provisions have been made therefor and all of the remaining property and assets have been distributed to the Equity Owners, articles of dissolution shall be executed in duplicate and verified by the person signing the articles, which articles shall set forth the information required by the [   ] Act. Duplicate originals of such articles of dissolution shall be filed with the [   ] Secretary of State.

12.5 Certificate of Dissolution. Upon the issuance of the certificate of dissolution, the existence of the Company shall cease, except for the purpose of suits, other proceedings and appropriate action as provided in the [   ] Act. The Manager shall have authority to distribute any Company property discovered after dissolution, convey real estate and take such other action as may be necessary on behalf of and in the name of the Company.

12.6 Return of Contribution Nonrecourse to Other Equity Owners. Except as provided by law or as expressly provided in this Agreement, upon dissolution, each Equity Owner shall look solely to the assets of the Company for the return of its Capital Contribution. If the Company property remaining after the payment or discharge of the debts and liabilities of the Company is insufficient to return the cash contribution of one or more Equity Owners, such Equity Owners shall have no recourse against any other Equity Owner.

ARTICLE 13

MISCELLANEOUS PROVISIONS

13.1 Notices. Any notice, demand, or communication required or permitted to be given by any provision of this Agreement shall be deemed to have been sufficiently given or served for all purposes if delivered personally to the party or to an executive officer of the party to whom the same is directed or, if sent by registered or certified mail, postage and charges prepaid, addressed to the Equity Owner's and/or Company's address, as appropriate, which is set forth in this Agreement. Except as otherwise provided herein, any such notice shall be deemed to be given three business days after the date on which the same was deposited in a regularly maintained receptacle for the deposit of United States mail, addressed and sent as aforesaid.

13.2 Books of Account and Records. Proper and complete records and books of account shall be kept or shall be caused to be kept by the Managers in which shall be entered fully and accurately all transactions and other matters relating to the Company's business in such detail and completeness as is customary and usual for businesses of the type engaged in by the Company. Such books and records shall be maintained as provided in Section 9.9. The books and records shall be at all times be maintained at the principal executive office of the Company and shall be open to the reasonable inspection and examination of the Equity Owners or their duly authorized representatives during reasonable business hours.

13.3 Application of [   ] Law. This Agreement, and the application of interpretation hereof, shall be governed exclusively by its terms and by the laws of the State of [   ], and specifically the [   ] Act.

13.4 Waiver of Action for Partition. Each Equity Owner irrevocably waives during the term of the Company any right that it may have to maintain any action for partition with respect to the property of the Company.

13.5 Amendments. [**This Agreement may not be amended except by the unanimous written agreement of all of the Equity Owners.**]

OR

[**This Agreement may be amended only with the written agreement of Members holding a [Two–Thirds Interest]. No amendment which has been agreed to in accordance with the preceding sentence shall be effective to the extent that such amendment has a Material Adverse Affect upon one or more Equity Owners who did not agree in writing to such amendment. For purposes of the preceding sentence, "Material Adverse Effect" shall mean any modification of the relative rights to distributions by the Company (including allocations of Profits and Losses which are reflected in the Capital Accounts). Without limiting the generality of the foregoing: (i) an amendment which has a proportionate effect on all Equity Owners (or in the case of a redemption of Ownership Interests or issuance of additional Ownership Interests, an amendment which has a proportionate effect on all Equity Owners immediately after such redemption or issuance) with respect to their rights to distributions shall not be deemed to have a Material Adverse Affect on Equity Owners who do not agree in writing to such amendment.**

13.6 Execution of Additional Instruments. Each Equity Owner hereby agrees to execute such other and further statements of interest and holdings, designations, powers of attorney and other instruments necessary to comply with any laws, rules or regulations.

13.7 Construction. Whenever the singular number is used in this Agreement and when required by the context, the same shall include the plural and vice versa, and the masculine gender shall include the feminine and neuter genders and vice versa.

13.7a Effect of Inconsistencies with the Act. It is the express intention of the Equity Owners and the Company that this Agreement shall be the sole source of agreement among them, and, except to the extent a provision of this Agreement expressly incorporates federal income tax rules by reference to sections of the Code or Regulations or is expressly prohibited or ineffective under the Act, this Agreement shall govern, even when inconsistent with, or different than, the provisions of the Act or any other law or rule. In the event the Act is subsequently amended or interpreted in such a way to make any provision of this Agreement that was formerly invalid valid, such provision shall be considered to be valid from the effective date of such interpretation or amendment. The Members and the Company hereby agree that the duties and obligations imposed on the Members of the Company as such shall be those set forth in this Agreement, which is [intended] to govern the relationship among the Company and the Equity Owners, notwithstanding any provision of the Act or common law to the contrary.

13.8 _Headings and Pronouns_. The headings in this Agreement are inserted for convenience only and are in no way intended to describe, interpret, define, or limit the scope, extent or intent of this Agreement or any provision hereof. All pronouns and any variations thereof shall be deemed to refer to masculine, feminine, or neuter, singular or plural as the identity of the Person or Persons may require.

13.9 _Waivers_. The failure of any party to seek redress for violation of or to insist upon the strict performance of any covenant or condition of this Agreement shall not prevent a subsequent act, which would have originally constituted a violation, from having the effect of an original violation.

13.10 _Rights and Remedies Cumulative_. The rights and remedies provided by this Agreement are cumulative and the use of any one right or remedy by any party shall not preclude or waive the right to use any or all other remedies. Said rights and remedies are given in addition to any other rights the parties may have by law, statute, ordinance or otherwise.

13.11 _Severability_. If any provision of this Agreement or the application thereof to any person or circumstance shall be invalid, illegal or unenforceable to any extent, the remainder of this Agreement and the application there of shall not be affected and shall be enforceable to the fullest extent permitted by law. Without limiting the generality of the foregoing sentence, to the extent any provision of this Agreement is prohibited or ineffective under the Act or common law, this Agreement shall be considered amended to the smallest degree possible in order to make the Agreement effective under the Act or common law.

13.12 _Heirs, Successors and Assigns_. Each and all of the covenants, terms, provisions and agreements herein contained shall be binding upon and inure to the benefit of the parties hereto and, to the extent permitted by this Agreement, their respective heirs, legal representatives, successors and assigns.

13.13 _Creditors_. None of the provisions of this Agreement shall be for the benefit of or enforceable by any creditors of the Company.

13.14 <u>Counterparts</u>. This Agreement may be executed in counterparts, each of which shall be deemed an original but all of which shall constitute one and the same instrument.

13.15 <u>Rule Against Perpetuities</u>. The parties hereto intend that the Rule Against Perpetuities (and any similar rule of law) not be applicable to any provisions of this Agreement. However, notwithstanding anything to the contrary in this Agreement, if any provision in this Agreement would be invalid or unenforceable because of the Rule Against Perpetuities or any similar rule of law but for this Section 13.16, the parties hereto hereby agree that any future interest which is created pursuant to said provision shall cease if it is not vested within twenty-one years after the death of the survivor of the group composed of _____ (all who are currently Members) and their issue who are living on the date of this Agreement and their issue, if any, who are living on the effective date of this Agreement.

[13.15a <u>Power of Attorney</u>. (a) Each Equity Owner hereby irrevocably makes, constitutes and appoints the Managers thereof, with full power of substitution, so long as such Managers are acting in such a capacity (and any successor Manager thereof so long as such Manager is acting in such capacity), its true and lawful attorney, in such Equity Owner's name, place and stead (it is expressly understood and intended that the grant of such power of attorney is coupled with an interest) to make, execute, sign, acknowledge, swear and file with respect to the Company:

(i) all amendments of this Agreement adopted in accordance with the terms hereof;

(ii) all papers which the Managers deem necessary or desirable to effect the dissolution and termination of the Company;

(iii) all such other instruments, documents and certificates which may from time to time be required by the laws of the State of [_____] or any other jurisdiction in which the Company shall determine to do business, or any political subdivision or agency thereof, to effectuate, implement, continue and defend the valid existence of the Company; and

(iv) all instruments, documents and certificates which the Managers deem necessary or desirable in connection with a Reorganization which has been authorized in accordance with the terms of this Agreement.

[OTHER? E.G. IF YOUR AGREEMENT PROVIDES FOR A FORFEITURE OF EQUITY INTEREST IN THE EVENT OF CERTAIN EVENTS (E.G. TERMINATION OF EMPLOYMENT, BREACH OF THE AGREEMENT, ETC.), THEN YOU MAY WANT TO GIVE THE [MANAGERS POWER OF ATTORNEY] TO EFFECTUATE ANY FORFEITURE OF THE OWNERSHIP INTEREST OF THE LIKELY UNCOOPERATIVE DEPARTING EQUITY OWNER.]

(b) This power of attorney shall not be affected by and shall survive the bankruptcy, insolvency, death, incompetency, or dissolution of [an] Equity Owner and shall survive the delivery of any assignment by the

Equity Owner of the whole or any portion of its Ownership Interest. Each Equity Owner hereby releases each Manager from any liability or claim in connection with the exercise of the authority granted pursuant to this power of attorney and in connection with any other action taken by such Manager pursuant to which such Manager purports to act as the attorney-in-fact for one or more Equity Owners if the Manager believed in good faith that such action taken was consistent with the authority granted to it pursuant to this Section [13.15].

[13.16 Investment Representations. The undersigned Equity Owners, if any, understand (1) that the Ownership Interests evidenced by this Agreement have not been registered under the Securities Act of 1933, the _____ Securities Act or any other state securities laws (the "Securities Acts") because the Company is issuing these Ownership Interests in reliance upon the exemptions from the registration requirements of the Securities Acts providing for issuance of securities not involving a public offering, (2) that the Company has relied upon the fact that the Ownership Interests are to be held by each Equity Owner for investment, and (3) that exemption from registrations under the Securities Acts would not be available if the Ownership Interests were acquired by a Equity Owner with a view to distribution.

Accordingly, each Equity Owner hereby confirms to the Company that such Equity Owner is acquiring the Ownership Interests for such own Equity Owner's account, for investment and not with a view to the resale or distribution thereof. Each Equity Owner agrees not to transfer, sell or offer for sale any of portion of the Ownership Interests unless there is an effective registration or other qualification relating thereto under the Securities Act of 1933 and under any applicable state securities laws or unless the holder of Ownership Interests delivers to the Company an opinion of counsel, satisfactory to the Company, that such registration or other qualification under such Act and applicable state securities laws is not required in connection with such transfer, offer or sale. Each Equity Owner understands that the Company is under no obligation to register the Ownership Interests or to assist such Equity Owner in complying with any exemption from registration under the Securities Acts if such Equity Owner should at a later date, wish to dispose of the Ownership Interest. Furthermore, each Member realizes that the Ownership Interests are unlikely to qualify for disposition under Rule 144 of the Securities and Exchange Commission unless such Equity Owner is not an "affiliate" of the Company and the Ownership Interest has been beneficially owned and fully paid for by such Equity Owner for at least three years.

Each Equity Owner, prior to acquiring an Ownership Interest, has made an investigation of the Company and its business, and the Company has made available to each Equity Owner, all information with respect to the Company which such Equity Owner needs to make an informed decision to acquire the Ownership Interest. Each Equity Owner considers himself, herself or itself to be a person possessing

573

experience and sophistication as an investor which are adequate for the evaluation of the merits and risks of such Equity Owner's investment in the Ownership Interest.]—[**CONSULT A SECURITIES LAWYER WITH VIRTUALLY EVERY LLC YOU FORM. MEMBERSHIP INTERESTS ARE IN MOST CASES PROBABLY GOING TO BE "SECURITIES' UNDER THE FEDERAL AND STATE SECURITIES LAWS. IT IS PROBABLY NOT A GOOD IDEA TO INCLUDE THIS PROVISION UNLESS YOU CONCLUDE, AFTER CONSULTING A SECURITIES LAWYER, THAT THE MEMBERSHIP INTERESTS ARE SECURITIES AND THEREFORE THAT STEPS WILL HAVE TO BE TAKE TO COMPLY WITH THE SECURITIES LAWS. IF A SUBSCRIPTION AGREEMENT IS USED AND A PROVISION LIKE THE FOREGOING IS USED IN THE OPERATING AGREEMENT, MAKE SURE THAT THE SECURITIES LAWYER ON THE DEAL CONFORMS THIS PROVISION TO THE LANGUAGE IN THE SUBSCRIPTION AGREEMENT.]**

[13.17 Representations and Warranties.

(a) **In General.** As of the date hereof, each of the Equity Owners hereby makes each of the representations and warranties applicable to such Equity Owner as set forth in Section 13.17 hereof, and such warranties and representations shall survive the execution of this Agreement.

(b) **Representations and Warranties.** [Each Member/OR SPECIFY THE CORPORATE MEMBER IF LESS THAN ALL ARE CORPORATIONS OR PARTNERSHIPS OR LLCs] hereby represents and warrants that:

(i) **Due Incorporation or Formation; Authorization of Agreement.** Such Equity Owner is a corporation duly organized or a partnership or limited liability company duly formed, validly existing, and in good standing under the laws of the jurisdiction of its incorporation or formation and has the corporate, partnership or limited liability company power and authority to own its property and carry on its business as owned and carried on at the date hereof and as contemplated hereby. Such Equity Owner is duly licensed or qualified to do business and in good standing in each of the jurisdictions in which the failure to be so licensed or qualified would have a material adverse effect on its financial condition or its ability to perform its obligations hereunder. Such Equity Owner has the corporate, partnership or limited liability company power and authority to execute and deliver this Agreement and to perform its obligations hereunder and the execution, delivery, and performance of this Agreement has been duly authorized by all necessary corporate, partnership or limited liability company action. This Agreement constitutes the legal, valid, and binding obligation of such Equity Owner.

(ii) <u>No Conflict with Restrictions; No Default.</u> Neither the execution, delivery, and performance of this Agreement nor the consummation by such Equity Owner of the transactions contemplated hereby (1) will conflict with, violate, or result in a breach of any of the terms, conditions, or provisions of any law, regulation, order, writ, injunction, decree, determination, or award of any court, any governmental department, board, agency, or instrumentality, domestic or foreign, or any arbitrator, applicable to such Equity Owner or any of its Affiliates, (2) will conflict with, violate, result in a breach of, or constitute a default under any of the terms, conditions, or provisions of the articles of incorporation, bylaws, partnership agreement, limited liability company agreement or operating agreement of such Equity Owner or any of its Affiliates or of any material agreement or instrument to which such Equity Owner or any of its Affiliates is a party or by which such Equity Owner, or any of its Affiliates is or may be bound or to which any of its material properties or assets is subject, (3) will conflict with, violate, result in a breach of, constitute a default under (whether with notice or lapse of time or both), accelerate or permit the acceleration of the performance required by, give to others any material interests or rights, or require any consent, authorization, or approval under any indenture, mortgage, lease agreement, or instrument to which such Equity Owner or any of its Affiliates is a party or by which such Equity Owner or any of its Affiliates is or may be bound, or (4) will result in the creation or imposition of any lien upon any of the material properties or assets of such Equity Owner or any of its Affiliates.

(iii) <u>Government Authorizations.</u> Any registration, declaration, or filing with, or consent, approval, license, permit, or other authorization or order by, any government or regulatory authority, domestic or foreign, that is required in connection with the valid execution, delivery, acceptance, and performance by such Equity Owner under this Agreement or the consummation by such Equity Owner of any transaction contemplated hereby has been completed, made, or obtained on or before the effective date of this Agreement.

(iv) <u>Litigation.</u> There are no actions, suits, proceedings, or investigations pending or, to the knowledge of such Equity Owner or any of its Affiliates, threatened against or affecting such Equity Owner or any of its Affiliates or any of their properties, assets, or businesses in any court or before or by any governmental department, board, agency, or instrumentality, domestic or foreign, or any arbitrator which could, if adversely determined (or, in the case of an investigation could lead to any action, suit, or proceeding, which if adversely determined could) reasonably be expected to materially impair such Equity Owner's ability to perform its obligations under this Agreement or to have a material adverse effect on the consolidated financial condition of such member; and such Equity Owner or any of its Affiliates has not received any currently effective notice of any default, and such Equity Owner or any of its Affiliates is not in default, under any applicable order, writ, injunction, decree, permit, determination, or award of any court, any governmental department, board, agency, or instrumentality, domestic or foreign, or any arbitrator which could reasonably be expected to materially impair such Equity Owner's ability to perform its obligations under this Agreement or to have a material adverse effect on the consolidated financial condition of such Equity Owner.

(v) <u>Investment Company Act; Public Utility Holding Company Act.</u> Neither such Equity Owner nor any of its Affiliates is, nor will the Company as a result of such Equity Owner holding an Ownership Interest be, an "investment company" as defined in, or subject to regulation under, the Investment Company Act of 1940. Neither such Equity Owner nor any of its Affiliates is, nor will the Company as a result of such Equity Owner holding an Ownership Interest be, a "holding company," "an affiliate of a holding company," or a "subsidiary of a holding company," as defined in, or subject to regulation under, the Public Utility Holding Company Act of 1935.

(vi) <u>Subsidiary.</u> All of the outstanding capital stock or ownership interests in the capital and profits of such Equity Owner is owned, directly or indirectly, by [_____].

(vii) <u>Confidentiality.</u> Except as contemplated hereby or required by a court of competent authority, each Equity Owner shall keep confidential and shall not disclose to others and shall use its reasonable efforts to prevent its Affiliates and any of its, or its Affiliates', present or former employees, agents, and representatives from disclosing to others without the prior written consent of the Manager(s) any information which (1) pertains to this Agreement, any negotiations pertaining thereto, any of the transactions contemplated hereby, or the business of the Company, or (2) pertains to confidential or proprietary information of any Member or the Company or which any Equity Owner has labeled in writing as confidential or proprietary; provided that any Equity Owner may disclose to its Affiliates' employees, agents, and representatives any information made available to such Equity Owner. No Equity Owner shall use, and each Equity Owner shall use its best efforts to prevent any Affiliate of such Equity Owner from using, any information which (1) pertains to this Agreement, any negotiations pertaining hereto, any of the transactions contemplated hereby, or the business of the Company, or (2) pertains to the

confidential or proprietary information of any Equity Owner or the Company or which any Equity Owner has labeled in writing as confidential or proprietary, except in connection with the transactions contemplated hereby.]

CERTIFICATE

The undersigned hereby agree, acknowledge and certify that the foregoing Agreement, consisting of ⎯⎯ pages, excluding the Table of Contents and attached Exhibits, constitutes the Agreement of ⎯⎯⎯⎯ LLC adopted by the Equity Owners of the Company as of ⎯⎯⎯⎯.

, LLC

By:

MEMBERS:

EXHIBIT 8.1
initial capital contributions

Initial Member	Initial Capital Contribution	Initial Share of Total Capital

EXHIBIT 8.2
additional capital contributions

Member	Maximum Additional Capital Contribution

INTERNAL REVENUE CODE 26 U.S.C. § 7701 AND REGULATIONS THEREUNDER

IRC § 7701

Sec. 7701. (a) When used in this title, where not otherwise distinctly expressed or manifestly incompatible with the intent thereof—

(1) PERSON.—The term "person" shall be construed to mean and include an individual, a trust, estate, partnership, association, company or corporation.

(2) PARTNERSHIP AND PARTNER.—The term "partnership" includes a syndicate, group, pool, joint venture, or other unincorporated organization, through or by means of which any business, financial operation, or venture is carried on, and which is not, within the meaning of this title, a trust or estate or a corporation; and the term "partner" includes a member in such a syndicate, group, pool, joint venture, or organization.

(3) CORPORATION.—The term "corporation" includes associations, joint-stock companies, and insurance companies. . . .

––––––

REGULATIONS UNDER IRC § 7701

Regulation 301.7701-1. **Classification of organizations for federal tax purposes.**—(a) *Organizations for federal tax purposes*—

(1) *In general.* The Internal Revenue Code prescribes the classification of various organizations for federal tax purposes. Whether an organization is an entity separate from its owners for federal tax purposes is a matter of federal tax law and does not depend on whether the organization is recognized as an entity under local law.

(2) *Certain joint undertakings give rise to entities for federal tax purposes.* A joint venture or other contractual arrangement may create a separate entity for federal tax purposes if the participants carry on a trade, business, financial operation, or venture and divide the profits therefrom. For example, a separate entity exists for federal tax purposes if co-owners of an apartment building lease space and in addition provide services to the occupants either directly or through an agent. Nevertheless, a joint undertaking merely to share expenses does not create a separate entity for federal tax purposes. For example, if two or more persons jointly construct a ditch merely to drain surface water from their properties, they have not created a separate entity for federal tax purposes. Similarly, mere co-ownership of property that is maintained, kept in repair, and rented or leased does not constitute a separate entity for federal tax purposes. For example, if an individual owner, or tenants in common, of farm property lease it to

a farmer for a cash rental or a share of the crops, they do not necessarily create a separate entity for federal tax purposes. . . .

(4) *Single owner organizations.* Under Regulations 7701–2 and 7701–3, certain organizations that have a single owner can choose to be recognized or disregarded as entities separate from their owners.

(b) *Classification of organizations.* The classification of organizations that are recognized as separate entities is determined under Regulations 7701–2, 7701–3, and 7701–4. . . .

Regulation 301.7701–2. **Business entities; definitions.**—(a) *Business entities.* For purposes of this section and Regulation 7701–3, a *business entity* is any entity recognized for federal tax purposes (including an entity with a single owner that may be disregarded as an entity separate from its owner under Regulation 7701–3) that is not properly classified as a trust under Regulation 7701–4 or otherwise subject to special treatment under the Internal Revenue Code. A business entity with two or more members is classified for federal tax purposes as either a corporation or a partnership. A business entity with only one owner is classified as a corporation or is disregarded; if the entity is disregarded, its activities are treated in the same manner as a sole proprietorship, branch, or division of the owner.

(b) *Corporations.* For federal tax purposes, the term *corporation* means—

(1) A business entity organized under a Federal or State statute, or under a statute of a federally recognized Indian tribe, if the statute describes or refers to the entity as incorporated or as a corporation, body corporate, or body politic;

(2) An association (as determined under Regulation 7701–3);

(3) A business entity organized under a State statute, if the statute describes or refers to the entity as a joint-stock company or joint-stock association;

(4) An insurance company;

(5) A State-chartered business entity conducting banking activities, if any of its deposits are insured under the Federal Deposit Insurance Act, as amended, 12 U.S.C. 1811 et seq., or a similar federal statute;

(6) A business entity wholly owned by a State or any political subdivision thereof;

(7) A business entity that is taxable as a corporation under a provision of the Internal Revenue Code other than section 7701(a)(3); and

(8) *Certain foreign entities*—. . .

Regulation 7701–3. **Classification of certain business entities.**—(a) *In general.* A business entity that is not classified as a corporation under Regulations 7701–2(b)(1), (3), (4), (5), (6), (7), or (8) (an *eligible* *entity*) can elect its classification for federal tax purposes as provided in this section. An eligible entity with at least two members can elect to be classified as either an association (and thus a corporation under Regulation 7701–2(b)(2)) or a partnership, and an eligible entity with a single owner can elect to be classified as an association or to be disregarded as an entity separate from its owner. Paragraph (b) of this section provides a default classification for an eligible entity that does not make an election. Thus, elections are necessary only when an eligible entity chooses to be classified initially as other than the default classification or when an eligible entity chooses to change its classification. An entity whose classification is determined under the default classification retains that classification ... until the entity makes an election to change that classification....

(b) *Classification of eligible entities that do not file an election*—(1) *Domestic eligible entities.* Except as provided in paragraph (b)(3) of this section, unless the entity elects otherwise, a domestic eligible entity is—

(i) A partnership if it has two or more members; or

(ii) Disregarded as an entity separate from its owner if it has a single owner....

(3) *Existing eligible entities*—(i) *In general.* Unless the entity elects otherwise, an eligible entity in existence prior to the effective date of this section will have the same classification that the entity claimed under Regulations 7701–1 through 7701–3 as in effect on the date prior to the effective date of this section; except that if an eligible entity with a single owner claimed to be a partnership under those regulations, the entity will be disregarded as an entity separate from its owner under this paragraph (b)(3)(i)....

Regulation 301.7701–3T—**Classification of certain business entities (temporary)**.

(a) *In general.* A business entity that is not classified as corporation under Regulation 7701–2(b)(1), (3), (4), (5), (6), (7), or (8) (an eligible entity) can elect its classification for federal tax purposes as provided in this section. An eligible entity with at least two members can elect to be classified as either an association (and thus a corporation under Regulation 7701–2(b)(2)) or a partnership, and an eligible entity with a single owner can elect to be classified as an association or to be disregarded as an entity separate from its owner. Paragraph (b) of this section provides a default classification for an eligible entity that does not make an election. Thus, elections are necessary only when an eligible entity chooses to be classified initially as other than the default classification or when an eligible entity chooses to change its classification. An entity whose classification is determined under the default classification retains that classification ... until the entity makes an election to change that classification....

(c)(1)(iv) *Limitation.* If an eligible entity makes an election ... to change its classification (other than an election made by an existing entity to change its classification as of the effective date of this section), the entity cannot change its classification by election again during the sixty months succeeding the effective date of the election. However, the Commissioner may permit the entity to change its classification by election within the sixty months if more than fifty percent of the ownership interests in the entity as of the effective date of the subsequent election are owned by person that did not own any interests in the entity on the filing date or on the effective date of the entity's prior election. . . .

*

INDEX

References are to Pages.